WHAT FUTURE FOR AMERICA?

Written by the nation's leading scholars and historians, this report is the most searching look at violence in America ever taken—in short, it is a classic of its kind. Here is a stern reminder of our past and an invaluable, precautionary guide to our future. Here, too, is an eloquent warning to the leaders of this nation that blatant injustices cannot be left to fester, that government force is rarely a solution.

"Almost every major act of violence in our history, whether public or private, has antagonized one group at the same time that it satisfied another . . . The grievances and satisfactions of violence have so reinforced one another that we have become a rather bloody-minded people in both action and reaction. We are likely to remain so as long as so many of us think that violence is an ultimate solution to social problems."

—Ted Robert Gurr and
Hugh Davis Graham

STATEMENT ON THE STAFF STUDIES

The Commission was directed to "go as far as man's knowledge takes" it in searching for the causes of violence and the means of prevention. These studies are reports to the Commission by independent scholars and lawyers who have served as directors of our staff task forces and study teams; they are not reports by the Commission itself. Publication of any of the reports should not be taken to imply endorsement of their contents by the Commission, or by any member of the Commission's staff, including the Executive Director and other staff officers, not directly responsible for the preparation of the particular report. Both the credit and the responsibility for the reports lie in each case with the directors of the task forces and study teams. The Commission is making the reports available at this time as works of scholarship to be judged on their merits, so that the Commission as well as the public may have the benefit of both the reports and informed criticism and comment on their contents.

DR. MILTON S. EISENHOWER, *Chairman*

A NEW YORK TIMES BOOK

VIOLENCE IN AMERICA:
Historical and Comparative Perspectives

by
Hugh Davis Graham
and
Ted Robert Gurr

A Report Submitted to the National Commission on
the Causes and Prevention of Violence

Special Introduction by John Herbers of

The New York Times

BANTAM BOOKS
NEW YORK • TORONTO • LONDON

VIOLENCE IN AMERICA:
HISTORICAL AND COMPARATIVE PERSPECTIVES
A Bantam Book / published June 1969

Published simultaneously in the United States and Canada

Bantam Books are published by Bantam Books, Inc., a subsidiary
of Grosset & Dunlap, Inc. Its trade-mark, consisting of the words
"Bantam Books" and the portrayal of a bantam, is registered in the
United States Patent Office and in other countries. Marca Registrada.
Bantam Books, Inc., 271 Madison Avenue, New York, N.Y. 10016.

PRINTED IN THE UNITED STATES OF AMERICA

CONTENTS

v

FIGURES

viii

Task Force on Historical and Comparative Perspectives

Co-Directors

Hugh Davis Graham
Ted Robert Gurr

Secretaries

Carol Voit
Frances Adams

Commission Staff Officers

Lloyd N. Cutler, *Executive Director*
Thomas D. Barr, *Deputy Director*
James F. Short, Jr., Marvin E. Wolfgang,
Co-Directors of Research
James S. Campbell, *General Counsel*
William G. McDonald, *Administrative Office*
Ronald Wolk, *Special Assistant to the Chairman*

National Commission on the Causes and Prevention
of Violence

Dr. Milton S. Eisenhower, *Chairman*

SPECIAL INTRODUCTION

On September 26, 1872, three mounted bandits rode to the gate of the Kansas City fair, where a crowd of 10,000 had gathered. They shot at the ticket seller, hit a small girl in the leg by mistake and made off for the woods with less than $1,000. In reporting the incident, the Kansas City *Times* called the robbery "so diabolically daring and so utterly in contempt of fear that we are bound to admire it and revere its perpetrators." Two days later the *Times* was even more enthralled. "It was as though three bandits had come to us from storied Odenwald, with the halo of medieval chivalry upon their garments and shown us how the things were done that poets sing of. Nowhere else in the United States or in the civilized world, probably, could this thing have been done."

This incident, along with the comment of the *Times,* reported by Joe B. Frantz in Chapter 4 of this book, is one of the many pieces of evidence that show how deeply engrained in American life is the tradition, even the love, of violence. Yet it is likely that some of the descendants of the journalists who wrote so glowingly of an armed robbery in which a child was wounded, and perhaps of the bandits themselves, are among those Americans who now sit over cocktails in the evening and express shock and anger over the urban riots, the rise of crime in the streets and the student takeover of a college administration building. Nothing they learned in their schools, in their homes and among their associates prepared them for the view that the domestic violence the nation has witnessed in the 1960's is not an aberration of United States history or a sign of the disintegration of American institutions but the usual type of behavior displayed in this country when there is a large division of purpose or when some group is trying to cast off some great wrong.

Many writers of history, the schools and the disciplines of the overall society have denied or de-emphasized the role of violence from the Colonial period to the present. Of course, many students of history, and members of minorities who have been the long subject of violence, have had no illusions about this matter. As early as 1967 Rap Brown, the young Negro militant, said, "Violence is as American as cherry pie." But as Hugh Davis Graham and

Ted Robert Gurr said in a summary of this volume prepared for the press, "Americans have always been given to a kind of historical amnesia that masks much of their turbulent past. Probably all nations share this tendency to sweeten memories of their past through collective repression, but Americans have probably magnified this process of selective recollection, owing to our historic vision of ourselves as a latter-day chosen people, a New Jerusalem."

This 350,000-word work may not be sufficient to dispel the myth but it should make a beginning. Its purpose is to evaluate "the historical antecedents and foreign parallels of the contemporary American experience with violence." The authors did not find all the answers they set out to find. Because of the short time involved and the lack of information needed, some of the studies are crude and incomplete. An effort to measure the amount of violence in previous generations by an examination of old newspapers, for example, produced, as could be expected, only a bare indication of the agonies of the past. The 22 chapters do provide, however, the first comprehensive study of the problem of violence in America and its comparison to violence in other countries.

Before going into that, however, it may be well to examine briefly how the study came about. In a sense, it was a product of the turbulent political year of 1968. In that spring, it seemed to many that Armageddon was upon us. The Rev. Dr. Martin Luther King, Jr., was assassinated in Memphis on April 4. In the next few days, scores of cities across the country were beset by riots. In Washington, smoke from burning stores swirled over the Capitol and the White House, which were ringed by federal troops. On June 5, Senator Robert F. Kennedy was shot and killed in Los Angeles while campaigning for the Democratic presidential nomination. The nation was thrown into another period of grief and soul-searching.

There is a saying in Washington that when a President does not know what to do he can always appoint a commission to study the problem. President Johnson particularly seemed to have a proclivity for this, even though some of his commission and task forces did not turn out exactly as he wanted them to. In the summer of 1967, he had appointed the National Advisory Commission on Civil Disorders (the Kerner Commission) to investigate urban rioting, but was put out when the Commission warned that white racism was the chief cause of increasing racial polarization and failed to commend the Johnson administration on steps it had taken to help minorities. Nevertheless, as the nation mourned the loss of the leaders most identified with the poor and the black, President Johnson appointed the National Commission on the Causes and Prevention of Violence and named Dr. Milton S. Eisenhower, President Emeritus of the Johns Hopkins University as chairman. Its membership was even more diverse than the usual Johnson commission, ranging from the conservative Republican senator from Nebraska, Roman Hruska, to the civil libertarian Senator Phillip A. Hart, Democrat of Michigan, and including such non-political figures as Eric Hoffer, the longshoreman-philosopher, and Archbishop Terrence J. Cooke of New York.

It was believed by many in Washington that the Commission represented more a show of concern on the part of the White House than a means of finding a way out of the violence that was besetting the nation. But commissions have a way of taking their tasks seriously and once appointed seek to make what impact they can on the well-being of the society. President Johnson directed the Commission to "go as far as man's knowledge takes" in searching for the causes of violence and the means of prevention. The Commission took him seriously. But as Lloyd N. Cutler, the able Washington lawyer who was picked as executive director, said later, the task was much bigger than anyone had imagined. Man's knowledge in this area had not gone very far. The Commission could find no significant work on violence in America, much less any that would relate it to that in other countries. The scholars simply had not organized their work in that manner.

What was needed, then, was a pulling together of information and judgments that existed across a wide range of disciplines and the amassing of new information that would fill the voids. There wasn't much time in which to work. The life of the Commission, under the executive order of June 10, 1968, was one year (President Nixon later extended the time to December 10, 1969). Two young men previously mentioned, Ted Gurr, Assistant Professor of Politics at Princeton University, and Hugh Graham, Associate Professor of History at The Johns Hopkins University, were chosen to direct the task force on historical and comparative perspectives. They secured the services of scholars in the fields of anthropology, industrial relations, law, psychiatry, psychology, sociology, history and political science. It is their work that makes up the 22 chapters of this book plus the Conclusion prepared by Dr. Graham and Dr. Gurr.

This, of course, is only one of several aspects of the Commission's work. There have been several other studies made under the Commission's auspices, the most noted of which was the Walker Report on disturbances in Chicago during the Democratic National Convention of 1968. A judgment of the Commission's work must await its final report, now scheduled for the early fall of 1969. All the studies have been released to the public without comment as to their merits or demerits. Dr. Eisenhower wants it that way, believing the work should be judged on its merits, so that the Commission as well as the public may benefit from the criticisms and comment on the contents. But in one sense the Eisenhower Commission can be compared to the Kerner Commission. That Commission told the American people, in effect, "Look here, we are becoming two nations, one black one white, separate and unequal, and we might as well face up to it. It is largely the fault of the white majority, which sometimes consciously, sometimes unconsciously, stands in the way of the freedom and well-being of black Americans." What the Kerner Commission had to say was all the more remarkable because it was composed of middle-class, mostly white Americans whose constituencies were those bearing the blame. Little wonder that the report created a controversy in the political campaigns.

What we have here is a task force appointed by a Commission of even more middle-class white orientation saying under the official auspices of the Commission that Rap Brown was right about violence in America—that, in effect: "Look here, illegal, collective violence is so much a part of our culture, so much used by virtually all interest groups, including the government from time to time, that it has become reinforced in our society, and it is high time we faced up to this fact and quit fooling ourselves." This is bitter medicine, all the more so because it is such a gross violation of the American ideal. But the evidence is there.

As Charles Tilly, Professor of Sociology at the University of Toronto, points out in chapter 1, western civilization and various forms of collective violence have always been close partners. He surveys European history to show in considerable detail that this is so and says that the really strange thing is how quickly men forget. Americans go to England and view the stately old houses and formal gardens and have the feeling that there a non-violent civilization has flourished for centuries when in fact that countryside over centuries witnessed strife and bloodletting. When Lincoln Steffens visited London in 1910, a time remembered here for its stability, Tilly recalls, he found leading members of Parliament convinced that England was on the brink of revolution as a result of the angry strikes of that time. An important reason for the distortion of history, Tilly suggests, is that historians concentrate on political history as seen from the top—"the only protests which matter are those which produce some rearrangement of power."

In the succeeding chapters, the authors view the American scene, detailing and analyzing the use and acceptance of violence in the frontier tradition, the labor movement, the proliferation of vigilante organizations, the West, the South and among fragmented cultures that have flourished here and in American literature. There is a summary and analysis of racial violence and of the current "crime waves" in the cities, which may not be as unusual or as extensive as is generally believed. There are studies comparing the nature of civil strife and violence among various nations, the processes of rebellion, the alternative responses to violence and the effects of crowding people into urban settings. The authors acknowledge that some of the chapters are "in many respects incomplete and tentative." But they hope that the volume will be the beginning of more scholarship and study in this area.

What, then, can be the value of the volume itself? What the sponsors of it seem to be saying, without actually doing so, is that it can serve as the beginning point for a search for a new tradition, for new ways of gaining rights and power under our system without resorting to collective violence. It sheds considerable light on what has happened in the Negro rights movement in recent years. The non-violent technique used by Dr. King and his followers with considerable success over a period of years ultimately failed, it would seem, not so much because it could not produce results as because many leaders believed results could better be achieved by adopting the standard American technique of collective violence. White Americans, it was felt, better understand this than Dr. King's adaptation of passive resistance, and in a sense they were right. There are American businessmen today hiring black employees and working on urban coalitions who were moved mainly by the thought of having their property go up in smoke. And it has been the violence and talk of violence that has kept the black man's cause in the public eye.

Likewise on college campuses, the New Left students in their use of force to change the structure of the educational system are resorting to an old-fashioned American tradition, one that everybody understands. Readers of this volume should not find it surprising, novel or unexpected that the police in their response resort to brutality against the pink-cheeked protestors. This kind of brutality has been a part of American life since the first settlers arrived. All across the land violence is being used for one purpose or another without qualms of conscience, just as it always has been in America. It is more noticeable now because we are in a period of great turbulence and change.

But if we have learned anything from history it is that violence breeds violence and leads to deep and lasting hatreds. The American labor movement showed that. The authorities did not successfully put down the agitation by shooting and maiming the strikers. Nor did the violent elements within the unions gain anything for the workers by blowing up railroad trestles and mining the company store.

Instead, lasting bitterness and hostilities were created that exist to this day, long after labor gained its recognition through legal channels. The authors of the labor section in this volume make this clear, scorning the idea of the "creative character" of labor violence that some have embraced. Even the "constructive violence" that has served the national purpose has had harmful effects that Americans tend to forget, the authors of these chapters bring out. The American Revolution was not an exercise in the restrained use of force and violence. Both sides resorted to the most barbaric practices. In the Indian wars, the whites used not only their own atrocities but those of the Indians as well, including the bashing of children's skulls against tree trunks, and the red men on the reservations of South Dakota still remember this and hang themselves at an early age. The Civil War preserved the nation, but this volume shows that it created divisions that may never heal. For generations after it was over the nation suffered from its vemon.

This, to me, is the central lesson that comes through these pages from a diversity of intellectual disciplines. The Kerner Report unfortunately was widely interpreted by sensitive politicians as an invitation for self-flagellation, and as a result many put it out of mind, although many others read it in the spirit in which it was intended. The authors of this volume are not asking for self-condemnation, nor are they discrediting the belief that America is a land of special promise and potential. They are laying out the facts and it is the facts that cry for a search for a non-violent tradition—one that would preserve the mobility of American classes and groups and allow for changes, refors and political pressures without the use of violence. Perhaps there must be a new tradition before there can be a New Jerusalem.

JOHN HERBERS

June 6, 1969

PREFACE

From the earliest days of organization, the Chairman, Commissioners, and Executive Director of the National Commission on the Causes and Prevention of Violence recognized the importance of research in accomplishing the task of analyzing the many facets of violence in America. As a result of this recognition, the Commission has enjoyed the receptivity, encouragement, and cooperation of a large part of the scientific community in this country. Because of the assistance given in varying degrees by scores of scholars here and abroad, these Task Force reports represent some of the most elaborate work ever done on the major topics they cover.

The Commission was formed on June 10, 1968. By the end of the month, the Executive Director had gathered a small cadre of capable young lawyers from various Federal agencies and law firms around the country. That group was later augmented by partners borrowed from some of the Nation's major law firms who served without compensation. Such a professional group can be assembled more quickly than university faculty because the latter are not accustomed to quick institutional shifts after making firm commitments of teaching or research at a particular locus. Moreover, the legal profession has long had a major and traditional role in Federal agencies and commissions.

In early July a group of 50 persons from the academic disciplines of sociology, psychology, psychiatry, political science, history, law, and biology were called together on short notice to discuss for 2 days how best the Commission and its staff might proceed to analyze violence. The enthusiastic response of these scientists came at a moment when our Nation was still suffering from the tragedy of Senator Kennedy's assassination.

It was clear from that meeting that the scholars were prepared to join research analysis and action, interpretation, and policy. They were eager to present to the American people the best available data, to bring reason to bear where myth had prevailed. They cautioned against simplistic solutions, but urged application of what is known in the service of sane policies for the benefit of the entire society.

Shortly thereafter the position of Director of Research was created. We assumed the role as a joint undertaking, with common responsibilities. Our function was to enlist social and other scientists to join the staff, to write papers, act as advisers or consultants, and engage in new research. The decentralized structure of the staff, which at its peak numbered 100, required research coordination to reduce duplication and to fill in gaps among the original seven separate Task Forces. In general, the plan was for each Task Force to have a pair of directors one a social scientist, one a lawyer. In a number of instances, this formal structure bent before the necessities of available personnel but in almost every case the Task Force work program relied on both social scientists and lawyers for its successful completion In addition to our work with the seven original Task Forces, we provided consultation for the work of the eighth "Investigative" Task Force, formed originally to investigate the disorders at the Democratic and Republican National Conventions and the civil strife in Cleveland during the summer of 1968 and eventually expanded to study campus disorders at several colleges and universities.

Throughout September and October and in December of 1968 the Commission held about 30 days of public hearings related expressly to each of the Task Force areas. About 100 witnesses testified, including many scholars, Government officials, corporate executives as well as militants and activists of various persuasions. In addition to the hearings, the Commission and the staff met privately with scores of persons, including college presidents, religious and youth leaders, and experts in such areas as the media, victim compensation, and firearms. The staff participated actively in structuring and conducting those hearings and conferences and in the questioning of witnesses.

As Research Directors, we participated in structuring the strategy of design for each Task Force, but we listened more than directed. We have known the delicate details of some of the statistical problems and computer runs We have argued over philosophy and syntax; we have offered bibliographical and other resource materials, we have written portions of reports and copy edited others. In short, we know the enormous energy and devotion, the long hours and accelerated study that members of each Task Force have invested in their labors In retrospect we are amazed at the high caliber and quantity of the material produced, much of which truly represents the best in research and scholarship. About 150 separate papers and projects were involved in the work culminating in the Task Force reports. We feel less that we have orchestrated than that we have been members of the orchestra, and that together with the entire staff we have helped compose a repertoire of current knowledge about the enormously complex subject of this Commission.

That scholarly research is predominant in the work here presented is evident in the product. But we should like to emphasize that the roles which we occupied were not limited to scholarly inquiry. The Directors of Research were afforded an opportunity to participate in all Commission meetings. We engaged in discussions at the highest levels of decisionmaking, and had great freedom in the selection of scholars, in the control of research budgets, and in the direction and design of research. If this was not unique, it is at least an uncommon degree of prominence accorded research by a national commission.

There were three major levels to our research pursuit: (1) summarizing the state of our present knowledge and clarifying the lacunae where more or new research should be encouraged; (2) accelerating known ongoing research so as to make it available to the Task Forces; (3) undertaking new research projects within the limits of time and funds available. Coming from a university setting where the pace of research is more conducive to reflection and quiet hours analyzing data, we at first thought that completing much meaningful new research within a matter of months was most unlikely. But the need was matched by the talent and enthusiasm of the staff, and the Task Forces very early had begun enough new projects to launch a small university with a score of doctoral theses. It is well to remember also that in each volume here presented, the research reported is on full public display and thereby makes the staff more than usually accountable for their products.

One of the very rewarding aspects of these research undertakings has been the exeperience of minds trained in the law mingling and meshing, sometimes fiercely arguing, with other minds trained in behavioral science. The organizational structure and the substantive issues of each Task Force required members from both groups. Intuitive judgment and the logic of argument and organization blended, not always smoothly, with the methodology of science and statistical reasoning. Critical and analytical faculties were sharpened as theories confronted facts. The arrogance neither of ignorance nor of certainty could long endure the doubts and questions of interdisciplinary debate. Any sign of approaching the priestly pontification of scientism was quickly dispelled in the matrix of mutual criticism. Years required for the normal accumulation of experience were compressed into months of sharing ideas with others who had equally valid but differing perspectives. Because of this process, these volumes are much richer than they otherwise might have been.

Partly because of the freedom which the Commission gave to the Directors of Research and the Directors of each Task Force, and partly to retain the full integrity of the research work in publication, these reports of the Task Forces are in the posture of being submitted to and received by the Commission. These are volumes published under the authority of the Commission, but they do not necessarily represent the views or the conclusions of the Commission. The Commission is presently at work producing its own report, based in part on the materials presented to it by the Task Forces. Commission members have, of course, commented on earlier drafts of each Task Force, and have caused alterations by reason of the cogency of their remarks and insights. But the final responsibility for what is contained in these volumes rests fully and properly on the research staffs who labored on them.

In this connection, we should like to acknowledge the special leadership of the Chairman, Dr. Milton S. Eisenhower, in formulating and supporting the principle of research freedom and autonomy under which this work has been conducted.

We note, finally, that these volumes are in many respects incomplete and tentative. The urgency with which papers were prepared and then integrated into Task Force Reports rendered impossible the successive siftings of data and argument to which the typical academic article or volume is subjected. The reports have benefited greatly from the counsel of our colleagues on the Advisory Panel, and from much debate and revision from within the staff. It is our hope, that the total work effort of the Commission staff will be the source and subject of continued research by scholars in the several disciplines, as well as a useful resource for policymakers. We feel certain that public policy and the disciplines will benefit greatly from such further work.

* * *

To the Commission, and especially to its Chairman, for the opportunity they provided for complete research freedom, and to the staff for its prodigious and prolific work, we, who were intermediaries and servants to both, are most grateful.

James F. Short, Jr.   Marvin E. Wolfgang
                        Directors of Research

INTRODUCTION

By Hugh Davis Graham* and Ted Robert Gurr†

Many unique aspects of our society and politics have contributed to the individual and collective violence that troubles contemporary America, among them the psychological residues of slavery, the coexistence of mass consumption with pockets and strata of sullen poverty, the conflict among competing ethics that leaves many men without clear guides to social action. Other sources of violence in our national life are inheritances of our own past: a celebration of violence in good causes by our revolutionary progenitors, frontiersmen, and vigilantes; immigrant expectations of an earthly paradise only partly fulfilled; the unresolved tensions of rapid and unregulated urban and industrial growth. Yet many societies as well as our own have experienced violent disorder as a consequence of such conditions at different times in their national development, in some cases disintegrating in a welter of blood and shattered institutions, in others emerging as stronger and more satisfying communities. Examination of our development as a nation provides a sense of understanding of the historical genesis of our present situation. Comparison with the historical experience of other societies

* Hugh Davis Graham is associate professor of history and Assistant Director of the Institute of Southern History at the Johns Hopkins University. His publications include *Crisis in Print: Desegregation and the Press in Tennessee* (Nashville: Vanderbilt University Press, 1967); "The Storm Over Black Power," *Virginia Quarterly Review*, XLII (Fall 1967); an edited volume, *Huey Long* (Englewood Cliffs, N.J.: Prentice-Hall, 1969); and *Since 1954, the Supreme Court and the Schools* (New York: *New York Times* and Harper and Row, forthcoming).

† Ted Robert Gurr is assistant professor of politics, faculty associate of the Center of International Studies, and Associate Director of the Workshop in Comparative Politics at Princeton University. He is author of *Why Men Rebel* (Princeton University Press, 1969); *The Conditions of Civil Violence: First Tests of a Causal Model*, with Charles Ruttenberg (Princeton: Center of International Studies, 1967); *American Welfare*, with Alfred de Grazia (New York: New York University Press, 1961); and a number of articles.

helps identify the points at which our cultural experience differed from that of more—and less—orderly societies. Contemporary comparisons provide a mirror that can tell us, without favor or rancor, how far we have fallen from our self-anointed status as the most favored of nations. By these comparisons we also begin to identify some of the general conditions, processes, and outcomes of violence, and ultimately to anticipate the effects of what we do now and tomorrow on the creation, maintenance, and destruction of political community.

Men often are accused of being blinded by the immediacy of contemporary events to the lessons of history. A difficulty of American scholarship is that those lessons are only partly studied and partly understood. Historians interested in the differential inclinations of a people or of groups within a society to resort to violence face four basic obstacles. The first is a familiar one: insufficient or inadequate evidence. To be sure, evidence of violence per se is abundant, sure as newspaper accounts of civil commotion, though few of them have been closely examined. But many kinds of precise data that contemporary social scientists require—e.g., consistent and reliable crime statistics, participant profiles, public opinion surveys—are generally unavailable to historians. Others, such as the results of systematic content analysis of documents and evaluation of court records, are only occasionally used by American historians.

A second barrier to historical understanding has been the lack of a general theoretical framework with which to order our perceptions of the motives and attitudes that impel groups toward violence and the social conditions conducive to it. Until fairly recently, American historians have been inclined to regard economic motives as paramount, and to explain violence either sympathetically as the protest of the have-nots or unsympathetically as a by-product of the defense of privilege. Sociologists and political scientists have usually focused on the tension-generating characteristics of incompatible social values and maladaptive institutions that lead to violent conflict among groups. Some social scientists have employed psychological instruments of analysis, such as frustration-aggression and cognitive dissonance theories, attempting to take into account social and political as well as economic motives, psychological dispositions as well as class cleavages. The variety of theoretical approaches reflected in this volume by no means exhausts the repertory, nor are all of them consistent in their assumptions or conclusions. But all assume that civil commotion has many causes, not just one, and that those causes have to do with both the nature of man and his social circumstances.

Ironically, professional specialization itself has in some ways impeded our understanding of the role of violence in our past. As the grand sweep of the multivolume historical surveys of the 19th century have given way to the penetrating but narrow monographic studies of the 20th, the quantity of American historical knowledge had been accumulating, but at the expense of synthesis. While the historians have been specializing by era, or through a process of professional tunneling that creates long but narrow channels of inquiry—diplomatic, constitutional, labor history—other social scientists have largely eschewed the study of violence in America and have concentrated almost exclusively on the peaceful and institutional processes of our social and political life. "Violence" does not even rate an entry in the new *International Encyclopedia of the Social Sciences*. We are not suggesting that the students of man add yet another specialty to their atomized ranks. But more of them should become more acutely aware of the bellwether function of civil strife. It is worth examining not only in its own right but as evidence of the character and social processes of the times and societies from which it rises. As Charles Tilly observes in chapter 1, violence is normal in political life, and changes in its form tell us that something important is happening in the political system. Not only may a closer attentiveness to the dynamics of civil turmoil increase our understanding of political and social life; it may be a healthy corrective to our habit of looking at society from the top down.

A fourth impediment to understanding our violent past has been the powerful strain of optimistic parochialism that has variously equated the growth of the American nation with the New Jerusalem, Manifest Destiny, and inelectably progressive Darwinian evolution. Historians have been perhaps less guilty of this ethnocentrism than have been chambers of commerce, but even historians who have eschewed flag waving have tended to focus their research so exclusively on American behavior that they have been denied the insights of the comparative dimension. Yet so disturbing is today's civil commotion and its attendant widespread disillusionment that it invites a reaction against the comfortable old certitudes. Contemporary Americans, confronted as they are with overseas war and domestic turmoil, may be tempted to overcompensate for past patriotic excesses by equating the American experience instead with slavery and imperialism, Indian genocide, and Judge Lynch. Similarly, some contemporary European intellectuals, such as Jean-Paul Sartre, have come to regard "that super-European monstrosity, North America" as a bastard child or satanic mutation of degraded Europe.[1] Clearly, this era of discontent demands a more careful and sober analysis, both historical and comparative, of the dimensions, antecedents, and consequences of violence. The borrowing by historians of the insights and, to a lesser extent, the methods of the other social sciences has considerably enriched historical understanding in recent years. But American historians in their traditional intranational inquiries have generally reflected the powerful strain of parochialism and ethnocentrism that has suffused the national character. If the essence of social science is comparison, American historians and, to a lesser extent, behavioral scientists are only beginning systematically to explore the rich comparative dimension. This volume represents less a triumphal synthesis than, we hope, a promising step toward exploring that fruitful conjunction between the vertical dimension of historical inquiry and the horizontal dimension of comparative analysis.

The organization of this volume reflects the questions to be answered by historical and comparative inquiry. Few of these questions are answered in any definitive sense, but our contributors provide much evidence and partial answers for most of them. The first is a descriptive, historical question: What have been the patterns and extent of violence by private individuals and groups in the United States, and what, by comparison, have they been in Western Europe? The papers by Tilly and Richard Maxwell Brown in part I offer some general historical answers with special reference to collective violence. The appendix to part I reports a sample study of 150 years of violence as reported in the American press. Together these studies suggest two summary judgements: one, that group violence has been chronic and pervasive in the European and American past; and second, that both Europeans and Americans have a noteworthy capacity to forget or deny its commonality. The chapters of part V provide some of the meager information we have on historical trends in violent crime in the United States.

The second general question is an analytic one: What are the historical conditions that have contributed to different kinds of violence in the American past and present? The chapters in part II suggest the relevance of the immigrant experience, the frontier and vigilante traditions, and the portrayal of violence in American literature and folklore. Parts III through VI sketch the sources and character of specific kinds of protest and private violence: labor and working-class strife, racial conflict, individual aggression, and antiwar protest.

The third general question is the contemporary, descriptive one: How do group protest and violence in the United States compare with similar activities elsewhere in the world? Part VII provides some of the most systematic answers now available. These answers are sought not solely for the purpose of descriptive comparison but in an attempt to answer a fourth question: What are the general conditions of group violence? The quantitative comparisons in this part and the case studies in Part VII provide evidence that makes it possible to identify some of the general political and social circumstances and patterns of change that are likely to lead to violence.

The final question is: What are the processes of violence, and what are some alternatives to it? The chapters in Parts VIII and IX examine this question in some specific cases; it is a peripheral or central issue of many other chapters. Taken in its entirety, this report provides a wealth of examples of the conditions that give rise to violence and of the extent to which private violence, public force, concession, and nonviolent group responses to discontent can lead to the resolution of those conditions.

Another issue, the definitional one, must be dealt with as a prelude to description and analysis of violence. All of us —citizens, officials, and scholars—look at "violence" from perspectives colored by our beliefs and cultural experience. In common usage the term is pejorative. We use it as a label to categorize, and implicitly to condemn, acts of which we disapprove, whether or not all of them are violent or illegal. If we are sympathetic with the motives underlying collective violence, we are likely to call it "protest." When violence is used by public individuals, such as police and soldiers, we typically refer to it as "legitimate force" and as such praise it. There are emotion-laden words whose customary uses are as likely to contribute to acrimonious debate as to understanding: "violence," "force," "protest," "legality," "legitimacy." A clear understanding of the phenomena discussed in this report requires not that we abandon such terms or the perspectives that underlie them, but that we distinguish among them and say what we mean by them.

"Violence" is narrowly defined here as behavior designed to inflict physical injury to people or damage to property. Collectively, and individually, we may regard specific acts of violence as good, bad, or neutral, depending on who engages in it and against whom. "Force" is a more general concept: we define it here as the actual or threatened use of violence to compel others to do what they might not otherwise do. Force, like violence, can be judged good or bad. Sixty years ago most Americans condemned workers' resort to strikes and picketing to gain union recognition and wage increases, but praised the forceful efforts of employers and state militias to break the strikes. By these definitions, force and violence are closely linked concepts. Force necessarily involves the threat if not the actuality of violence; violence is forceful if it is used with the intent to change others' actions. "Protest" does not have necessary implications of force or violence. We mean by protest the expression of dissatisfaction with other people's actions. It can take individual or collective, verbal or physical, peaceful or violent forms. The forms of protest that most concern Americans are the collective and physical ones, but collective public protest does not by definition include the use of force or violence, nor do public protestors in contemporary America frequently use them.

"Legality" and "legitimacy" are words that we use to pass judgement on the desirability of violence, force, and protest, as well as other acts. The"legality" of acts is determined by formal procedures of community decision making. Acts are "legitimate," in the sense meant here, if members of a community regard them as desirable or justifiable. We have laws that proscribe most uses of violence by private citizens, others that permit law officers to use forceful violence to deter private violence, and still others that regulate various kinds of protest. But the judgement that an act is legal or illegal is a formal one, made and enforced by a small segment of the community. In the perfect social order all acts judged legal would be regarded as legitimate by the community, all illegal acts would be illegitimate. No such clear-cut distinction holds in the United States so far as violence, force, and protest are concerned, nor has it ever. Our nation was founded in a revolutionary war that was illegal but widely regarded as legitimate. It survived a civil war whose competing causes most Northerners and most Southerners thought both legal and legitimate. Americans deplored the assassination of President John F. Kennedy, yet years earlier many had applauded the abortive attempt on the life of Adolph Hitler. Hundreds of vigilante movements grace the pages of American history: most of them entailed violence by private individuals that was technically illegal but popularly regarded as legitimate. On the other hand, such institutions and practices as de jure racial segregation and civil rights demonstrations have been technically legal in various regions and eras, but have been widely regarded as illegitimate.

The complexity of the American conflict between legitimacy and legality of actions is apparent in an analysis of the demonstrations and riots that accompanied the 1968 Democratic National Convention.[2] Some of the demonstrations were technically legal, others were not, by fiat of municipal authority. In other American cities all might have been approved, in some all might have been ruled illegal. Most demonstrators regarded their actions as legitimate, whatever their legality or their violence. Many Chicagoans, and perhaps a majority of Americans, had directly opposing perceptions: they apparently regarded the demonstrations as illegitimate, whatever their legality and whether or not they were violent. Some police actions in response to the demonstrations were technically legal, some not. The police and—according to opinion polls—the majority of Americans thought the police action in its entirety was legitimate, the demonstrators obviously did not.

These distinctions are not merely an exercise in semantics. They are intended to demonstrate that Americans historically have not agreed, and do not now agree, on the propriety of different kinds of force, violence, and protest. One group's legitimate protest has been another group's illegal violence throughout our history. This report is not designed to persuade the reader about the rightness of the views of any of these groups in conflict. It does try to provide a sense of understanding of three critical contemporary issues: how some of our differences of opinion over goals and means came into being, what some consequences of our failures to resolve them have been for civil peace, and what we and other peoples have done in the past to overcome such devisive disagreements. We are a diverse nation, linked together most fundamentally by our common desires for ways of life both civil and satisfying. To attain them we must cooperate with one another, all of us, for violent antagonisms expressed violently destroy peace, and men, and ultimately community. One blunt sentiment of our rebellious forefathers, voiced by Benjamin Franklin, is as applicable to life in the United States today as it was nearly two centuries ago: "We shall all hang together, or assuredly we shall all hang separately."

References

1. Preface to Frantz Fanon, *The Wretched of the Earth*, (New York: Grove Press, 1963), p. 22.
2. See Daniel Walker, *Rights In Conflict*, a report submitted to the National Commission on the Causes and Prevention of Violence (Washington: The Commission, 1968).

ACKNOWLEDGMENTS

The editors want to thank the Commissioners and staff of the National Commission on the Causes and Prevention of Violence, first, for recognizing the importance of historical and comparative studies for public understanding of violence, second for their consistent support and counsel in the task of compiling this report. We are especially grateful to Profs. Morris Janowitz and Richard Wade of the University of Chicago, James Q. Wilson of Harvard, and Benjamin Quarles of Morgan State College, whose criticisms and suggestions as members of the Commission's Advisory Panel helped strengthen the final report—as did the guidance and advice of the Commission's Co-Directors of Research, Dr. James F. Short, Jr., and Dr. Marvin E. Wolfgang. Similarly, the initial strategic guidance of several colleagues not officially associated with the Commission greatly facilitated our task: Profs. David M. Potter, John Hope Franklin, Harry Eckstein, David Donald, Carl Degler, and Paul Bohannan.

Most of all we are indebted to our contributors, who promptly set aside their other obligations to communicate to the Commission and to Americans generally some of what has been learned in the last several generations of scholarship on violent conflict. They proved willing not only to summarize the knowledge of their special fields but to make available many new findings and interpretations, and to do so within severe time constraints. In addition to their contributions per se, the critical advice they provided one another and to us added immeasurably to the report. Of course, responsibility for the interpretations we have placed on their findings in the part introductions and conclusion is ours, not theirs.

Appreciation also is due to Prof. Sheldon Levy of Brandeis University for his permission to include in our report of a revised version of his statistical study by newspaper sample of the past 150 years of American violence, and to Prof. Michael Hudson of Brooklyn College for an unpublished background paper comparing the American incidence of violence with its frequency in other nations.

xxxiii

Some members of the Commission staff deserve special recognition: James Campbell for his sustained and infectious enthusiasm for our work, Ronald Wolk for his valiant efforts to make sense of our prose, and finally the Commission's administrative and clerical staff, under the energetic direction of William McDonald, especially Carol Voit, Susan Lipsitch, and Frances Adams. Lastly we are indebted to our wives, Ann Graham and Erika Gurr, for providing moral and clerical support far beyond the call of duty.

Hugh Davis Graham
Ted Robert Gurr
Codirectors, Task Force on Historical
and Comparative Perspectives on Violence in America

PART I

HISTORICAL OVERVIEW OF VIOLENCE IN EUROPE AND AMERICA

Preliminary to any analysis of the role of violence in America, whether historical or comparative, is the task of surveying its historical occurrence. Although our primary concern is with the American experience, we have prefaced our survey of American violence with an overview of patterns in Western Europe. Since America's cultural antecedents are predominantly European, and since Europe has shared with the United States the experience of modern industrial transformation, much of our subsequent historical and comparative analysis contrasts the American tradition of violence to that of Europe.

In Chapter 1, Charles Tilly confronts the traditional view that the fundamentally transforming processes of industrialization and urbanization in western society have evolved through a standard life cycle: "an early stage consisting of chaotic responses to the displacements and disruptions caused by the initial development of urban industry, a middle stage consisting of the growth of a militant and often violent working class, [and] a late stage consisting of the peaceful integration of that working class into economic and political life." According to this conventional model, collective violence should decline as the modern nation-state matures; collective violence becomes increasingly anachronistic and abnormal.

On the contrary, Tilly's political analysis in chapter 1 reveals a commonality of collective protest and violence that suggests that it has historically functioned as an integral part of the political process, and as such has been quite normal in most European societies. The American belief that it is abnormal, shared by many Europeans, is a consequence of selective historical recollection. Tilly's sociological and historical studies of collective violence in France, the most extensive and systematic such studies ever made, provide precise documentation of these assertions. They are substantiated by comparative evidence from other European nations.

The European evidence demonstrates that the growth of the nation-state and industrialization do not in the long run minimize collective violence but lead to changes in its form, and especially to its politicization. Preindustrial societies are characterized by such "primitive" collective violence as brawls and communal clashes, usually with diffuse and unpolitical objectives. As the scope and power of the European state expanded, "reactionary" disturbances began to supplant primitive violence: revolts against tax collectors and food riots pitted either communal groups or loosely organized common people against the representatives of government, in retaliation for their infringement on or failure to protect old life ways. The third form of collective violence, the "modern," has almost entirely supplanted reactionary violence in Europe, under the impetus of industrialization, urbanization, and the development of enduring economic and political associations. The demonstration and the violent strike are the clearest examples. They involve specialized associations with relatively well-defined objectives, organized for political or economic action. They are "modern" not only in their organizational complexity but because their participants are forward looking: they are striking for rights due them but not yet enjoyed.

The periods of transition from reactionary to modern collective violence are clearly discernible in the histories of most European nations. Industrialization and urbanization are linked with the transition, but only indirectly. In France, urbanization damped collective violence in the short run. As in the ghetto riots of the United States, it was the long-resident urban Frenchman who was most likely to have both the sense of grievance and the associational means on the basis of which he forcefully demanded his rights. Other parallels between the American and European experience can be drawn. The most consequential point, however, is that collective violence in modern societies cannot be understood without reference to political life. Throughout Western history there has been a close connection between the basic political process and the predominant forms of conflict. The form and extent of collective violence reflect political conditions, and by inversion, polit-

2

ical conditions influence and make possible the transformation of collective violence.

The forms, extent and transformations of American violence are described in chapter 2 by Richard Brown. But he correctly perceives that collective violence in America has been employed as a means to an end, and that a society that has successfully employed violence to attain such desirable goals as national independence, continental domain, manumission of slavery, domestic order, and international security, will be reluctant categorically to condemn the instrument of their achievement. Accordingly, he has subdivided violence into the broad categories of "negative" and "positive" violence. Brown defines as negative those forms of violence which seem in no direct way to be connected with any socially or historically constructive development—i.e., criminal, feud, lynch-mob, racially and ethnically prejudicial violence, urban rioting, free-lance multiple murder, and political assassination. "Positive" violence would include police coercion, the Revolutionary, Civil, and Indian wars, vigilantism, agrarian uprisings, and labor strife. The loose categorical labels are not meant to imply, of course, that either group possessed a monopoly on good and evil. Brown's extensive documentation constitutes a uniquely comprehensive bibliographical guide to the historical literature on American violence. Although his essay is primarily descriptive, he has prepared in chapter 5 a theoretical analysis of the American vigilante tradition.

Finally, Sheldon Levy offers as an appendix to part I a statistical analysis of the past 150 years of American violence by sampling from representative newspapers. Owing to the limitations of the sample, Levy's conclusions are cautious. His generalizations, however, largely substantiate Brown's more impressionistic judgment that while our contemporary period ranks high in violence, we have historically been a violence-prone people, and probably exceeded present levels of civic turmoil in the latter third of the 19th century. Levy's analysis constitutes a unique quantitative study against which we can test our traditional qualitative assessments.

3

Chapter 1

COLLECTIVE VIOLENCE IN EUROPEAN PERSPECTIVE

By Charles Tilly*

As comforting as it is for civilized people to think of barbarians as violent and of violence as barbarian, Western civilization and various forms of collective violence have always been close partners. We do not need a stifled universal instinct of aggression to account for outbreaks of violent conflicts in our past, or in our present. Nor need we go to the opposite extreme and search for pathological moments and sick men in order to explain collective acts of protest and destruction. Historically, collective violence has flowed regularly out of the central political processes of Western countries. Men seeking to seize, hold, or realign the levers of power have continually engaged in collective violence as part of their struggles. The oppressed have struck in the name of justice, the privileged in the name of order, those in between in the name of fear. Great shifts in the arrangements of power have ordinarily produced—and have often depended on—exceptional movements of collective violence.

Yet the basic forms of collective violence vary according to who is involved and what is at issue. They have changed

* Charles Tilly is professor of sociology at the University of Toronto and, in 1968-69, a fellow of the Center for Advanced Study in the Behavioral Sciences at Stanford. His principle publications, in addition to a dozen articles, are *The Vendée* (Cambridge, Mass.: Harvard University Press, 1964) and, with James Rule, *Measuring Political Upheaval* (Princeton University: Center of International Studies, 1965). The research behind this essay is an examination of the evolution of collective violence in European countries, especially France, under the impact of the urbanization and industrialization of the 19th and 20th centuries. The Social Science Research Council, the National Science Foundation, and the Canada Council have generously supported different aspects of the investigation. Throughout the essay use is made of unpublished reports concerning various countries, prepared as part of the investigation by Lynn Hollen Lees, Edward Shorter, Louise Tilly, and Sandra Winston. Appreciation is due Muhammad Fiaz, Abdul Qaiyum Lodhi, and Ann Shorter for assistance with some of the research reported here. The essay incorporates material from two unpublished papers: "Urbanization and Protest in Western Europe" (presented to the American Political Science Association, Sept. 1968) and "Collective Violence in Nineteenth Century French Cities" (a lecture delivered at Reed College in February 1968). A revised version of the latter is scheduled for publication in a volume edited by John Rothney. James David Barber, Lewis Coser, Ted Robert Gurr, Ulf Himmelstrand, Albert Hirschman, Richard Lowenthal, Serge Moscovici, Albert J. Reiss, Jr., Edward Shorter, and Louise Tilly gave vigorous, helpful criticism of earlier drafts of this paper.

profoundly in Western countries over the last few centuries, and those countries have built big cities and modern industries. For these reasons, the character of collective violence at a given time is one of the best signs we have of what is going on in a country's political life. The nature of violence and the nature of the society are intimately related.

Collective violence is normal. That does not mean it is intrinsically desirable, or inevitable. For century after century, the inhabitants of southern Italy endured malaria as a normal fact of life; today, American city dwellers endure smog and nerve-rending traffic as normal facts of life; few people hail malaria, smog, or traffic jams. Europeans of other centuries often destroyed children they could not provide for. Now infanticide has become rare. Few of us mourn its passing. But the fact that infanticide persisted so long in the face of persuasive teachings and fearsome penalties tells us something about the poverty and population pressure under which people once lived in Western countries. It also may help us understand some apparently barbaric practices of people outside the West today. In a similar way, both the persistence of the phenomenon of collective violence and the changes in its form within European countries over the last few centuries have something to teach us about their political life, and even about contemporary forms of protest.

OURS IS VIOLENT HISTORY

Long before our own time, Europeans were airing and settling their grievances in violent ways. "To the historian's eyes," said Marc Bloch, the great historian of feudal Europe, "the agrarian rebellion is as inseparable from the seigniorial regime as the strike from the great capitalist enterprise." [1] The chief moments at which ordinary people appeared unmistakably on the European historical scene before the industrial age were moments of revolt: the Jacquerie of 1358, which lent its name to many later peasant rebellions; Wat Tyler's popular rebellion of 1381; the German peasant wars of 1525, the astonishing provincial insurrection against Henry VIII in 1536 and 1537, which came to be known as the Pilgrimage of Grace; the bloody revolt of the Don Cossacks in the 1660's. Much of the time the peasant suffered in silence. Now and then he found his tongue, and his voice was violent.

Collective violence as a voice is the metaphor that occurs to almost all historians of popular movements before our own time. In their discussion of the English agricultural laborer, J. L. and Barbara Hammond summed it up for all their colleagues:

The feelings of this sinking class, the anger, dismay, and despair with which it watched the going out of all of warm comfort and light of life, scarcely stir the surface of history. The upper classes have told us what the poor ought to have thought of these vicissitudes; religion, philosophy, and political economy were ready with alleviations and explanations which seemed singularly helpful and convincing to the rich. The voice of the poor themselves does not come to our ears. This great population seems to resemble nature, and to bear all the storms that beat upon it with a strange silence and resignation. But just as nature has her own power of protest in some sudden upheaval, so this world of men and women—an underground world as we trace the distances that its voices have to travel to reach us—has a volcanic character of its own, and it is only by some volcanic surprise that it can speak the language of remonstrance or menace or prayer, or place on record its consciousness of wrong.[2]

And then the Hammonds proceed to read the rebellion of 1830 for signs of what was happening to the agrarian population of England.

Even with the growth of representative political institutions, ordinary people continued to state their demands through violence. The French historian of England, Elie Halévy, stated the matter clearly:

Throughout the eighteenth century England, the sole European country where the reigning dynasty had been set up as the result of a successful rebellion, had been the home of insurrection. There had been an outbreak of anti-Jewish rioting in 1753, when the Government had decided to grant the right of naturalization to the Jews domiciled in England. The Cabinet had yielded and repealed the statute. . . . In 1768 there were riots against the Government. The popular hero Wilkes triumphed in the end over the opposition of court and Cabinet. In 1780 an anti-Catholic riot broke out; during four entire days the centre of London was given up to pillage. A government without a police force was powerless either to prevent these outrages or repress them promptly. The right to riot or, as it was termed by the lawyers, "the right of resistance," was an integral part of the national traditions.[3]

That "right of resistance" was, in fact, a part of the English legal tradition upon which the American colonists insisted

6

in the very act of separating themselves from the mother country, and emphasized in their writings about the new state they were bringing into being.

Nor did collective violence fade out with the American Revolution, or the French Revolution, or the multiple revolutions of 1848, or the American Civil War. Western history since 1800 is violent history, full enough of revolutions, coups, and civil wars, but absolutely stuffed with conflict on a smaller scale.

The odd thing is how quickly we forget. When Lincoln Steffens visited London in 1910, he found distinguished Members of Parliament convinced that England was on the brink of revolution as a result of the angry strikes of the time. The strikes and the talk of revolution spread through Great Britain during the next few years. In prickly Ireland —still part of the United Kingdom, but barely—a real revolution was shaping up. Now we look back to England as a country that solved its internal problems peacefully.

During the American rail strike of 1911,

> In New Orleans railroad workers stole company records, switched or destroyed identification cards on freight cars, and cut the air hoses of as many as fifteen to twenty cars a day. Mobs of varying size constantly bombarded nonstrikers with stones and gunfire. . . . In Illinois periodic incursions damaged or destroyed company property. On one occasion, strike sympathizers in Carbondale turned loose a switch engine, which rammed into a freight train on the main line. . . . Turbulence and bloodshed led to a complete breakdown of civil government in sections of Mississippi. . . . For two successive nights hordes swarmed through the streets of Central City, Kentucky. They set upon men in railroad cars and fired at employees lodged in temporary sleeping quarters. . . . In the neighboring state of Tennessee the strike bred a rash of mobbings, stonings, gun battles, and killings.[4]

Following the sacred ritual of such conflicts, the governor of Mississippi declared martial law and blamed his State's troubles on "foreign agitators." Then it was the Americans' turn to speak of revolution. Only comfortable hindsight permits us to congratulate ourselves on our peaceful resolution of conflict.

Few Frenchmen recall that as recently as the end of 1947 revolutionary committees blew up trains and seized control of railroad stations, post offices, city halls, and other public buildings in a dozen major French cities, including Marseille, Grenoble, Nice, and St. Etienne. Then the papers proclaimed "revolution" in fear or jubilation. Now November and December of 1947 look like little more than an exceptional period of strike activity—so much so that French and American newspapers alike commonly treated the momentous but essentially nonviolent student protests of May 1968 as "the largest French movement of protest since the war." The collective memory machine has a tremendous capacity for destruction of the facts.

There are many reasons for historical forgetfulness, besides the simple desire to ignore unpleasant events. The record itself tends to cover the rebel's tracks. The most detailed and bulkiest historical records concerning collective violence come from the proceedings of courts, police departments, military units, or other agencies of government working to apprehend and punish their adversaries. The records therefore support the views of those who hold power. Protestors who escape arrest also escape history.

Yet the most important reason is probably that so long as historians concentrate on political history as seen from the top, the only protests which matter are those which produce some rearrangement of power. The Hammonds again make the essential point when discussing the rebellion of 1830:

> This chapter of social history has been overshadowed by the riots that followed the rejection of the Reform Bill. Everyone knows about the destruction of the Mansion House at Bristol, and the burning of Nottingham Castle; few know of the destruction of the hated workhouses at Selborne and Headley. The riots at Nottingham and Bristol were a prelude to victory; they were the wild shout of power. If the rising of 1830 had succeeded, and won back for the labourer his lost livelihood, the day when the Headley workhouse was thrown down would be remembered by the poor as the day of the taking of the Bastille. But this rebellion failed, and the men who led that last struggle for the labourer passed into the forgetfulness of death and exile.[5]

This selective memory even operates at an international scale. Modern Spain and modern France have acquired reputations as violent nations, while Sweden and England pass for countries of domestic tranquility. Such differences are hard to measure objectively. But if numbers of participants or casualties or damage done are the standards, then the actual differences are far smaller than the differences in reputation. One international estimate of "deaths from domestic group violence per million population"

8

from 1950 through 1962 rates Sweden and England at 0, Spain at 0.2, and France at 0.3, as compared with 2 for Greece, 10 for Ethiopia, 49 for South Korea, or 1,335 for Hungary.[6] Of course Spain and France acquired their disorderly reputations well before the 1950's. Yet during the very period of these statistics France experienced the great riots brought on by the Algerian war and the series of insurrections that brought down the Fourth Republic. Obviously the amount of bloodshed is not what matters most.

The day-by-day record of these countries over a longer period likewise reveals much more collective violence in Sweden or England than their peaceable reputations suggest. The large difference in notoriety most likely comes from the fact that in Spain and France the protestors sometimes succeeded in toppling the regime. There is a real difference, an important puzzle: How did the British political system survive protest and yet change in fundamental ways, while Spanish regimes snapped and crumbled? But the secret is by no means simply the contrast between anarchic peoples and law-abiding ones.

The record so far available suggests that the histories of collective violence as such in Western European countries over the modern period have had a good deal in common. There have been large differences in the ways the rulers of different states have responded to collective violence, or initiated it, and consequently in its impact on the structure of power. There have been fewer differences in the evolution of the basic forms and conditions of collective violence.

In these circumstances, it is tempting to turn away from reflections on national politics or national character toward ideas about the impact of industrialization. A number of theories proposed to account for various forms of protest in contemporary nations as well as in the Western historical experience suggest a standard cycle: a relatively integrated traditional society breaks up under the stress and movement of industrialization, the stress and movement stimulate a wide variety of violent reactions—at first chaotic, but gradually acquiring a measure of coherence. New means of control and ways of reintegrating the displaced segments of the population into orderly social life eventually develop, and finally a mature industrial society held together by widespread, generally pacific political participation emerges. In such a theory, the stimulus to collective violence comes largely from the anxieties men experience when established institutions fall apart.

Not only scholars hold such a theory. It is our principal folk theory of social change. It reappears almost every time ordinary Americans (and, for that matter, government commissions and well-informed journalists) discuss riots, or crime, or family disorganization. It encourages, for example, the general illusion that highly mobile people and recent migrants to the city have greater inclinations to rioting, crime, or family instability than the general population. It encourages the dubious notion that if poor nations only become rich fast enough they will also become politically stable. But the theory runs into trouble when it turns out that recent migrants are not more disorganized than the rest of the population, that murder is about as common (proportionately speaking) in the country as it is in the city, or that the world's wealthiest nations are quite capable of domestic turmoil.

POLITICS AND VIOLENCE

My own explorations of Western Europe, especially France, over the last few centuries suggest a more political interpretation of collective violence. Far from being mere side effects of urbanization, industrialization, and other large structural changes, violent protests seem to grow most directly from the struggle for established places in the structure of power. Even presumably nonpolitical forms of collective violence like the antitax revolt are normally directed against the authorities, accompanied by a critique of the authorities' failure to meet their responsibilities, and informed by a sense of justice denied to the participants in the protest. Furthermore, instead of constituting a sharp break from "normal" political life, violent protests tend to accompany, complement, and extend organized, peaceful attempts by the same people to accomplish their objectives.

Over the long run, the processes most regularly producing collective violence are those by which groups acquire or lose membership in the political community. The form and locus of collective violence therefore vary greatly depending on whether the major ongoing political change is a group's acquisition of the prerequisites of membership, its loss of those prerequisites, or a shift in the organization of the entire political system.

The impact of large structural changes such as urbanization, industrialization, and population growth, it seems to me, comes through their creation or destruction of groups contending for power and through their shaping of the available means of coercion. In the short run, the growth of large cities and rapid migration from rural to urban areas in Western Europe probably acted as a damper on violent protest, rather than a spur to it. That is so for two reasons:

(1) The process withdrew discontented men from communities in which they already had the means for collective action and placed them in communities where they had neither the collective identity nor the means necessary to strike together.

(2) It took considerable time and effort both for the individual migrant to assimilate to the large city, and thus to join the political strivings of his fellows, and for new forms of organization for collective action to grow up in the cities.

If so, the European experience resembles the American experience. In the United States, despite enduring myths to the contrary, poor, uprooted newcomers to big cities generally take a long time to get involved in anything—crime, delinquency, politics, associations, protest, rioting—requiring contacts and experiences outside a small world of friends and relatives. These things are at least as true of European cities.

In the long run, however, urbanization deeply shaped the conditions under which new groups fought for political membership, and urbanization's secondary effects in the countryside stirred a variety of protests. The move to the city helped transform the character of collective violence in at least three ways:

(1) It grouped men in larger homogenous blocs (especially via the factory and the working-class neighborhood) than ever before.

(2) It facilitated the formation of special-interest associations (notably the union and the party) incorporating many people and capable of informing, mobilizing, and deploying them relatively fast and efficiently.

(3) It massed the people posing the greatest threat to the authorities near the urban seats of power, and thus encouraged the authorities to adopt new strategies and tactics for controlling dissidence.

11

For the people who remained in the country, the rise of the cities meant increasingly insistent demands for crops and taxes to support the urban establishment, increasingly visible impact on individual farmers of tariff and pricing policies set in the cities, and increasingly efficient means of exacting obedience from the countryman. All of these, in their time, incited violent protests throughout Europe.

Of course, definitive evidence on such large and tangled questions is terribly hard to come by. Until very recent times few historians have taken the study of collective violence as such very seriously. As Antonio Gramsci, the Italian socialist philosopher-historian, put it:

> This is the custom of our time: instead of studying the origins of a collective event, and the reasons for its spread . . . they isolate the protagonist and limit themselves to doing a biography of pathology, too often concerning themselves with unascertained motives, or interpreting them in the wrong way; for a social elite the features of subordinate groups always display something barbaric and pathological.[7]

Since World War II, however, a considerable number of French and English historians, and a much smaller number of Americans, have begun to study and write history "from below"—actually trying to trace the experiences and actions of large numbers of ordinary men from their own point of view. This approach has had a special impact on the study of protests and rebellions. As a result, we are beginning to get a richer, rearranged picture of the political life of plain people in France and England (and, to a lesser extent, other European countries) over the last few centuries.

The new variety of evidence makes it possible to identify some major shifts in the predominant forms of collective violence in those countries over the modern period. Without too much difficulty we can place the forms of collective violence which have prevailed during that long period in three broad categories: primitive, reactionary, and modern.[8] The primitive varieties once predominated, until centralized states began dragging Europeans into political life on a larger than local scale. As Thorstein Veblen put it in his sardonic *Imperial Germany and the Industrial Revolution,*

12

. . . so soon as the king's dominions increased to such a size as to take him personally out of range of an effectual surveillance by neighborly sentiment . . . the crown would be able to use the loyalty of one neighborhood in enforcing exactions from another, and the royal power would then presently find no other obstacle to its continued growth than the limit placed upon it by the state of the industrial arts.[9]

In the process, the king's retinue produced the apparatus of the state, which then acquired momentum of its own. That transformation accelerated through much of Western Europe after 1600. Since then, the primitive forms of collective violence have dwindled very slowly, but very steadily. Now they occur only rarely, only at the margins of organized politics.

The reactionary forms, by contrast, burgeoned as the national state began to grow. That was far from coincidence; they most often developed as part of the resistance of various communal groups to incorporation into the national state and the national economy. But the state won the contest; in most countries of Western Europe the reactionary forms of collective violence peaked and then faded away in their turn during the 19th century. They gave way to modern forms of collective violence, characterized by larger scale, more complex organization, and bids for changes in the operation or control of the state apparatus, rather than resistance to its demands. Although during very recent years we have seen what might be signs of another large shift in the form and locus of collective violence, for in the last century the modern forms have pushed all others aside.

PRIMITIVE COLLECTIVE VIOLENCE

Primitive varieties of collective violence include the feud, the brawl among members of rival guilds or communes, and the mutual attacks of hostile religious groups. (Banditry, as E. J. Hobsbawm has said, stands at the edge of this category by virtue of its frequent direction against the existing distribution of power and wealth, and its frequent origin in the state's creation of outlaws as part of the attempt to extend legal authority to formerly ungoverned areas.) Primitive forms of collective violence share several features: small-scale, local scope, participation by members of communal groups as such, inexplicit and unpolitical objectives. Almost regardless of the questions at issue, for example, Frenchmen could count on a national political crisis to produce battles between Protestants and Catholics in Nimes and Albi. Attacks on the persons and properties of Jews accompanied 18th-century rebellions in England and 19th-century rebellions in France. The vendetta and the bandit raid, too, took on a degree of political significance in times of national crisis.

The *rixe de compagnonnages*—the battle royal between members of rival craft corporations—often left blood in the streets. In 1830, a characteristic *rixe* in Bordeaux involved 300 artisans; two were reported dead, many were wounded, and the local inns were left a shambles. In 1835, the newspaper *Le Constitutionnel* carried the following story from Châlons-sur-Saône:

> The *compagnons du Devoir,* called *Dévorans,* following an altercation on the previous day and a challenge by letter to fight the *compagnons de Liberté,* called *Gavots,* in the open country, attacked the mother house of the latter in the rue St. Antoine. Huge stones, big enough to kill an ox, were thrown through the windows.[10]

The very prevalence of such fracases gave the inhabitants of 19th-century French cities a wide acquaintance with collective violence. In London, likewise:

> It was usual for the boys of St. Anne's parish to fight those of St. Giles armed with sticks for "a week or two before the holidays." This fact survives, because in 1722 the captain of the boys of St. Giles, a chimney sweep aged twenty-one, was killed by another boy, aged sixteen. Earlier still, "prentice riots were serious and frequent disturbances to the peace of London."[11]

The prevalence of the *rixe* in Europe before modern times simply expressed the intense solidarity of each group of urban craftsmen, for (as has been said of German artisans) "Their group spirit turned against other groups and took an insult to an individual as an affront to the whole association."[12] Something like that solidarity lies close to the core of most of the primitive forms of collective violence.

This does not mean the fighting was always in rage and deadly earnest. Just as today's lumbermen or sailors on a weekend will now and then tear up a bar out of sheer boredom, frustration, or high spirits, the workmen of Berlin or Turin sometimes brawled for the fun of it. On such occa-

14

sions, the traditional enmities provided no more than the pretext. In the European city of the preindustrial age, funerals, feasts, and fairs provided public occasions out of which flowed collective violence offering diversion to the young as well as expressing deeply rooted communal rivalries.

Students, and even schoolboys, displayed some of the same violent propensities. At the Jesuit college of La Flèche, during the carnival days of 1646, the boys declared they had been dishonored by the public flogging of some of their number, and staged an armed mutiny. "The rebels . . . stood in the avenues, armed with swords, sticks, blackjacks, and stones, driving back the pupils who came out when the bell rang to get to the classrooms."[13] In England—

There was indiscipline and rebellion everywhere. At Winchester, in the late eighteenth century, the boys occupied the school for two days and hoisted the red flag. In 1818 two companies of troops with fixed bayonets had to be called in to suppress a rising of the pupils. At Rugby, the pupils set fire to their books and desks and withdrew to an island which had to be taken by assault by the army. There were similar incidents at Eton.[14]

Again, the intense solidarity of the students—a kind of brotherhood in league against their masters—facilitated their indignation and their common action.

A number of the other common primitive forms of collective violence had this curious combination of esprit de corps, recreation, and grim determination, a combination that the English somehow managed to transmute into the sporting spirit. The free-for-all among men from different towns (from which it is said, in fact, that various forms of football developed) has some of this character. So does the rag, charade, or charivari. Yet it would be quite wrong to consider the primitive varieties of collective violence as nothing but early versions of soccer. The deadly vendetta, the endemic banditry of the European highlands, the pervasive Sicilian scourge called Mafia, and the occasional millenarian movements that have racked southern Europe share many traits with the apparently trivial kinds of collective violence. What sets the primitive forms of violence off from the others is not a lack of seriousness, but their activation of local communal groups as such, and usually in opposition to other communal groups.

15

Reactionary disturbances are also usually small in scale, but they pit either communal groups or loosely organized members of the general population against representatives of those who hold power, and tend to include a critique of the way power is being wielded. The forcible occupation of fields and forests by the landless, the revolt against the tax collector, the anticonscription rebellion, the food riot, and the attack on machines were Western Europe's most frequent forms of reactionary collective violence. The somewhat risky term "reactionary" applies to these forms of collective violence because their participants were commonly reacting to some change that they regarded as depriving them of rights they had once enjoyed; they were backward looking. They were not, however, simple flights from reality. On the contrary, they had a close connection with routine, peaceful political life.

For ordinary Europeans of a few centuries ago, the most persistent political issues were the demands of the nation-state and of the national economy. And the food riot, as unlikely as it seems, illustrates the pressing nature of these demands very well. Seemingly born of hunger and doomed to futility, the food riot actually expressed the indignation of men and women who felt they were being deprived of their rights and who, by rioting, were often able to restore a semblance of those rights—if only temporarily.

The Western European food riot had a classic form: seizure of grain being stored or transported in a town, demonstrations (and sometimes bodily harm) directed against those presumed to be profiteering through the shipment or hoarding of grain, and sale of the grain at a publicly proclaimed just price, the proceeds going to the owner of the grain. Such food riots occurred throughout the 18th century in England, and during the first third of the 19th century. They were, indeed, one of the chief components of England's large agrarian rebellion of 1816. A. J. Peacock describes the beginning of one of the principal incidents of that rebellion:

A crowd had started assembling in the market place at about nine o'clock that morning. About an hour later some women came along who announced that their men were following them but had stopped along the Thetford road to collect sticks. Eventually fifty or more, all armed, and led by William Peverett, a labourer, marched into the square carrying white and red flags. Whillett, the butcher, who was amongst the crowd, told Peverett that the parish would let them have flour at 2s. 6d. if they would disperse, and asked for a deputation to go along with him to meet the magistrates. Helen Dyer, a married woman, had earlier told Willett that, although she could not read, she had a paper containing the crowd's demands, which she wanted shown to the magistrates. On it was written, "Bread or Blood in Brandon this day."[15]

Finally, after several days of milling, grumbling, stoning of windows, and pulling down of buildings, the magistrates—

> guaranteed the price of flour at 2s. 6d. per stone, with an advance of wages to 2s. per head for a fortnight, and unless the millers reduce their prices by that time, the officers of the parish will purchase their grain at the cheapest rate, and furnish the poor with provisions at prime cost.[16]

To modern eyes, the curious feature of this event is that the rioters did not loot, did not steal, but demanded to buy food at a price they could afford. Furthermore, it is clear that the crowd directed their anger at the authorities, expected them to act, and, indeed, bargained with them.

In fact, the food riot was an attempt to make the merchants and the municipal authorities meet their traditional responsibilities: holding grain within the town to meet local needs before permitting it to enter the national market, and assuring the town poor of a supply of grain at a price adjusted to the local level of wages. As great cities grew up in Western Europe during the 17th and 18th centuries, and national markets in grain developed to feed them, it became harder and less profitable for merchants and officials to give priority to local needs. And so men rioted to hold them to the bargain. The geography of the food riot (at least in France, where it has been best mapped) suggests as much: such riots occurred not in the areas of greatest famine and poverty, but in the hinterlands of big cities and grain-shipping ports.

The case of Italy points up the importance of the control (as opposed to the sheer quantity) of the food supply.[17] In England, the classic food riot virtually disappeared after 1830; in France, after 1848; in Italy, toward the end of the 19th century. The timing of that disappearance corresponds approximately to the pace of technical improve-

17

ments in the production and distribution of grain. It also follows the destruction of traditional controls over the grain trade, but at a significant distance.

The bad harvests of 1853, for example, brought food riots through much of Western Europe. In the Italian peninsula, the riots of that year were concentrated in the prosperous north—Piedmont, Parma, Tuscany—although shortage was at least equally acute in the silent south. The northern authorities had generally adopted policies favoring free trade in grains; in the southern Kingdom of the Two Sicilies, paternalism reigned.

In 1859, however, the new, progressive King Francesco of the Two Sicilies began to liberalize the grain trade. In 1860 he faced widespread food riots of the south. At the time of the October 1860 plebiscite on the unification of Italy there were rebellions in the south, to the theme "The old king fed us." The old king was Francesco's father, who had maintained the traditional controls.

All this may appear unduly complicated for anything so simple as a food riot. That is the point: these recurrent, apparently spontaneous events rested on and grew from the local structure of politics, and the crises of local politics were responses to pressures from the center. Far from being a momentary, rural, local reaction to misery, the food riot recorded the urbanization and centralization of European nation-states.

The food riot had companions. The anticonscription rebellion, the resistance to the tax collector, the violent occupation of fields and forests, the breaking of reapers or power looms all had many of the same characteristics. Although they often appear in clusters, each of the events was more or less local and self-contained. Instead of pitting one communal group against another, they stood a significant segment of the population against the local elite or the representatives of the central power. ("When the French peasant paints the devil," said Karl Marx in 1850, "he paints him in the guise of the tax collector.")[18] The organization of the formations taking part was rudimentary. It was essentially the organization of everyday life: users of a common market, artisans of the same shop, a single commune's draft-age boys, and so on. Because of this tie with everyday groupings, those who took part often included women, children, and old people. The participants were either resisting some new demand (taxes, conscription) laid on them by outsiders, protesting against what they viewed as a deprivation of their traditional rights (the prohibition of gleaning in fields and forests, the introduction of machinery), or both. All of them, in one way or another, amounted to action against the forcible integration of local groupings into the national economy and the national state. I believe—but this is a hunch for which little evidence is yet available—that all the reactionary forms of collective violence will turn out to have had an extraordinary appeal for just those segments of the European population whose political and economic identities these changes were dissolving. The large numbers of rural artisans whose livelihoods disappeared with the expansion of urban industry during the 19th century are the most important case, but agricultural day laborers and petty nobles faced some of the same problems.

The rural unrest of England during the early-19th century falls into this general pattern. In addition to recurrent food riots, the English countryside produced movements of protest in 1816, 1822, 1830, 1834-35, and 1843-44, with the 1830 rebellion covering much of southeastern England. During the events of 1830, the village rebels concentrated on three sorts of action: (1) levying a once-traditional contribution of beer or money on the local rich; (2) imposing a wage agreement on the employers of day laborers; (3) destroying new farm machinery, especially threshers. For those who resisted, the crowds reserved personal attacks, the tearing down of buildings, and the burning of hayricks. During one of the larger outbreaks, in Wiltshire—

The mob destroyed various threshing machines of Mr. Bennet's farms, and refused to disperse; at last, after a good deal of sharp language from Mr. Bennett, they threw stones at him. At the same time a troop of yeomanry from Hindon came up and received orders to fire blank cartridges above the heads of the mob. This only produced laughter; the yeomanry then began to charge; the mob took shelter in the plantations round Pyt House and stoned the yeomanry, who replied by a fierce onslaught, shooting one man dead on the spot, wounding six by cutting off fingers and opening skulls, and taking a great number of prisoners.[19]

As hopeless as this sort of popular agitation may seem, it actually had a measure of success. As E. J. Hobsbawm

19

states it, "the day-laborers succeeded to a large degree in destroying the machines and achieving wage raises and other improvements, and they held onto their gains for some years, mostly because the unexpected sight of their massive force . . . instilled a salutary fear in the rural gentry and farm owners."[20] Of course, this was only a delaying action; the reactionary forms of rural protest did not last much longer, mechanized farming did win out, and millions of agricultural workers eventually left the land. Nevertheless, in the context the actions of 1830 had a logic poorly conveyed by words like "riot" and "protest."

The same may be said of the handloom weavers, whose 19th-century rebellions stirred the countryside in most sections of Europe. What we loosely call Luddism took the form of a well-concerted avenging action. Ned Ludd, the mythical enemy of shearing frames and power looms, who in 1811 and 1812 issued threats and manifestoes from his retreat in Sherwood Forest, had much in common with Captain Swing, the equally mythical leader in whose name the agrarian rebels of 1830 wrote their warnings. Here is a Luddite letter:

We will never lay down Arms (till) The House of Commons passes an Act to put down all Machinery hurtful to Commonality, and repeal that to hang Frame Breakers. But we. We petition no more—that won't do—fighting must.
Signed by the General of the Army of Redressers
                Ned Ludd   *Clerk*
Redressers for ever Amen.[21]

The Army of Redressers, they called themselves. Their pseudonym epitomizes the defensive, indignant, focused, rule-bound character of their rebellion. "Luddism," says E. P. Thompson, "must be seen as arising at the crisis-point in the abrogation of paternalist legislation, and in the imposition of the political economy of laissez faire upon, and against the will and conscience of, the working people."[22] Far from reacting in aimless confusion, the Luddites, and most of the European machine breakers, knew what they were doing. While the food riot and machine breaking were quite distinct in form and content, they shared the same sort of crude rationality.

Much of the popular protest that took place during the Italian Risorgimento has this reactionary character. During the 1850's there were scattered strikes in the industrial centers and a few revolts of fairly modern variety in cities like Milan, Livorno, and Genoa. But most of the disturbances took the familiar form of the food riot, or consisted of *occupazioni delle terre*—mass squatting on lands formerly held in common as a means of demanding their distribution in compensation for lost rights in the commons. Even as Giribaldi marched up the peninsula on his way to unifying Italy, Sicilians were attacking tax collectors and occupying the commons. At times, villagers in the south shouted "Down with the Constitution," "Down with the Nation," "Long live the King"—a set of cries which recalls the much older motif of French tax rebellions, "Vive le roy et sans gabelle."

By this time a rather different (and, to us, more familiar) kind of collective violence had been taking shape in the cities of Italy, as it had been in most cities of Europe. There, political clubs, secret societies, and workers' organizations were organizing collective action through strikes, demonstrations, banquets, meetings, and military coups. The most economically advanced people of the countryside were also being drawn into these newer forms of action. Although the new political and economic forms were not intrinsically violent in themselves, they became increasingly important contexts for collective violence.

When and how fast this happened varied from country to country. But it happened almost everywhere. The numerous disturbances that occurred in France at the middle of the 19th century were mixed in character. The great bulk of them fit the standard reactionary models: tax rebellions, food riots, machine breaking, and so on. The 1848 Revolution notwithstanding, strikes, demonstrations, and revolutionary movements produced only a small share of the collective violence. The violent disturbances of the 1930's, by contrast, grew almost entirely out of organized strikes and demonstrations; with the important exception of the Resistance during the Second World War, the 1940's and 1950's brought little change in this respect. Between the 1840's and the 1940's, transformation of the character of collective violence took place. Even in the mid-19th century, a growing minority of disturbances involved more complex and durable organization, more explicit and far-reaching objectives, a forward-looking perspective.

After 1848, these very rapidly became the prevailing characteristics of collective violence.

In the process, solid citizens and national leaders developed an acute fear of the masses and organized a whole set of new means for maintaining public order. The elite feared the ordinary people of country and city alike, although they concentrated their efforts at crowd control in the cities where they themselves lived. This was true in England. Looking back from 1862, Benjamin Disraeli wrote:

> Then arose Luddite mobs, meal mobs, farm riots, riots everywhere; Captain Swing and his rickburners, Peterloo "massacres," Bristol conflagrations, and all the ugly sights and rumours which made young lads, thirty or forty years ago, believe (and not so wrongly) that "the masses were their natural enemies, and they might have to fight, any year, or any day, for the safety of their property and the honour of their sisters."[23]

Englishmen and other Europeans of the time developed a set of beliefs that is still widespread today, essentially equating the "working classes" with the "dangerous classes" and arguing that misery, crime, personal disorganization, and rebellion sprang from approximately the same causes and occurred in approximately the same segments of the population. The causes were the breakdown of traditional social arrangements and the demoralizing overpopulation of the great cities.

A unique essay contest run by King Maximilian of Bavaria in 1848 produced hundreds of fearful statements from middle-class Germans concerning the rise of overpopulation, mechanization, and immorality.[24] It matters little that many of the analyses (for example, those attributing the growth of the urban population to the increase in illegitimacy) were wildly mistaken. The fear was there. And in France:

> On bourgeois opinion of the time, we can take the work of Balzac as the most remarkable piece of evidence, above all because it bears the marks of these two facts: on the one hand, the blending of the working classes and the dangerous classes, the proletariat and the underworld misery and crime; on the other hand, the division between two categories of the population, that daily settlement of differences of which criminality is an expression, and that sporadic settlement of differences of which riots and revolution are the expression.[25]

22

In response, some Frenchmen, Germans, and Englishmen organized inquiries into poverty; others organized police forces.

For several centuries before this time, the central task of the European police had been control of the grain trade, markets, and, by extension, public assemblies. The notion of a professional organization devoted mainly to the detection and apprehension of criminals took hold in the 19th century. But before that professionalism developed, the European States were expanding and reorganizing their police forces very largely as a means of dealing with the new threats from "the masses." The new police began to replace both the army and those older repressive forces which had been fairly well matched to the primitive and reactionary forms of collective violence: the local militias, part-time constabularies, the personal employees of justices of the peace. Sir Robert Peel's organization of the London metropolitan police in 1829 (which immortalized him by transferring his nickname "Bobby" to the police officers themselves) had the well-recognized dual purpose of putting aside thugs and putting down rebellions. It is even clearer that the establishment of a nationwide provincial police by the Rural Police Act of 1839 "was precipitated by the Chartist disturbances of that year and, in particular, by the desire to relieve the military of a pressure which was in the highest degree inconvenient and injurious."[26]

European police forces of the period acquired great political importance, not only as agents of crowd control but also as the organizers of political espionage via networks of spies and informers. Their reorganization throughout Europe in the early-19th century marked a victory of the national over the local, a nationalization of repressive forces. As Allan Silver says, "The police penetration of civil society . . . lay not only in its narrow application to crime and violence. In a broader sense, it represented the penetration and continual presence of central political authority throughout daily life." [27] Although the new police forces by no means succeeded in eliminating collective or individual violence from everyday life, they did speed the decline of the older forms of protest. By matching more complex and specialized organization of repression to the

23

more complex and specialized organization of the newer forms of protest, they probably even earned some of their reputation for staving off revolution.

MODERN COLLECTIVE VIOLENCE

The modern varieties of political disturbance (to use another tendentious term) involve specialized associations with relatively well-defined objectives, organized for political or economic action. Such disturbances can easily reach a large scale. Even more clearly than in the case of reactionary collective violence, they have a tendency to develop from collective actions that offer a show of force but are not intrinsically violent. The demonstration and the violent strike are the two clearest examples, but the coup and most forms of guerrilla also qualify. These forms deserve to be called "modern" not only because of their organizational complexity but also because the participants commonly regard themselves as striking for rights due them, but not yet enjoyed. They are, that is, forward looking.

In England, the modern varieties of collective violence came into their own fairly early. Joseph Hamburger, whose general purpose is to refute the notion that England came close to revolution before the 1832 Reform Bill, nevertheless describes some good-sized disturbances in 1831:

There were also disturbances in London during the days immediately after the Lords' rejection of the Bill. They mainly occurred in connection with a procession that was organized, with Place's help, by two London Radicals, Bowyer and Powell. Organized by parishes people were to march to the palace and present an address in support of the Bill to the King. When it took place on October 12, 300,000 persons were said to have taken part. The Home Secretary informed the deputations that the King could not receive their petitions, but they could present them through County Members. Hume received some of them in St. James Square and later left them at the palace. The procession then marched past the palace as the demonstration of its size and resolution. It consisted of "shopkeepers and superior artisans"; nevertheless, during the day there were attacks on some Tory peers as well as the usual broken windows.[28]

The violence in this case obviously was minor, but the order and size of the demonstration impressive. Much more so than in the case of reactionary disturbances, the extent of

24

violence in this sort of event depends heavily on the reactions of the demonstrators' opponents.

During the widespread Chartist agitation of the following two decades the standard routine involved a fire-eating speech by a Chartist leader, followed by a procession through the streets, whose members spewed threats and displayed weapons. The threats, however, rarely came to anything except when the marchers confronted the Queen's soldiers. While once in a great while a member of the crowd fired at the troops, their usual tactic was to stone them:

At Preston, during the Plug-Plot disturbances, a mob which had belaboured the soldiers with stones stood its ground for a while when the order to fire was given and several of its members were struck, but the shooting of a ringleader, who had stepped out in front of the mob to encourage his followers to continue the assault, put a damper on the proceedings, and caused the crowd to disperse.[29]

The British army and police soon developed effective, and largely nonviolent, methods of crowd control.

Despite the development of effective policing, England still witnessed much collective violence later in the century. There was a wave of "riots" in London in 1866, another in 1886 and 1887; most of these events consisted of demonstrations that got out of hand. But the real resurgence of this form of violence came early in the 20th century, as the movements for temperance and (more importantly) for woman's suffrage began to mount demonstrations in the course of which the women showed unwonted determination:

. . . they smashed windows, fired pillar-boxes, slashed pictures, threw things at M.P.'s, and even burned down churches and houses; in reply they were treated with great roughness by policemen and worse by crowds. They were kicked and beaten; their hair was pulled and their clothes half-torn off; hatpins were pushed into them; they were knocked down and trampled upon.[30]

It was about this time that Lincoln Steffens heard English leaders talking about the possibility of revolution. For three different movements were swelling and coalescing in the years just before World War I: the demand for woman's suffrage, huge (and sometimes insurrectionary) strikes, and opposition to war. A famous leaflet of the time communicates some of what was happening:

> You are Workingmen's Sons.
> When we go on Strike to better Our lot which is the lot also of Your Fathers, Mothers, Brothers and Sisters, *You* are called upon by your Officers to *Murder Us*.
> Don't do it. . . .
> Don't you know that when you are out of the colours, and become a "Civy" again, that You, like Us, may be on strike, and You, like Us, be liable to be Murdered by other soldiers.
> Boys, Don't Do It.
> "Thou shalt not kill," says the Book.
> Don't forget that!
> It does not say, 'unless you have a uniform on.'
> No! *Murder is Murder*.
> Think things out and refuse any longer to Murder Your Kindred. Help Us to win back Britain for the British and the World for the Workers.[31]

Some of these movements (like the drive for woman's suffrage) succeeded; some (like the various demands of organized labor) met a mixture of success and failure; and some (like pacifism) failed utterly. England survived. But the essential point is that the characteristic forms of collective violence accompanying those movements differed fundamentally from those which had prevailed a century before.

The rise of the strike as a context for collective violence followed a similar rhythm. Although European states often reimposed one restriction or another, most of them legalized the strike sometime during the 19th century: England in 1824, Saxony in 1861, France in 1864, Belgium in 1866, Prussia in 1869, Austria in 1870, the Netherlands in 1872. That did not, however, make all subsequent strikes peaceful. Occasionally the violence began when the workers themselves attacked a factory, mine, or manager's home. Sometimes the workers demonstrated, and the demonstration turned violent. More often the violence grew from a confrontation between strikers assembled at a workplace and tropos, police, or strikebreakers sent in to thwart or control them.

In France, occasional strikes broke out in the biggest cities as early as the 16th century. In the first half of the 19th century, several rounds of strikes—notably those of Lyon in 1831 and 1834—bubbled up into bloodily repressed insurrections. But the first sets of strikes approach-

26

ing a national scale came at the end of the Second Empire, in 1869 and 1870. A major strike movement swept the textile and metalworking plants of Alsace in July 1870, with some 20,000 workers out in the vicinity of Mulhouse. Then:

Peaceful parades took possession of the streets. First the carpenters: the evening of 4 July, 400 to 500 men "walked through the city singing, in an orderly fashion." And for three days the processions continued across the city, in groups, men, women, children marching "in a fairly disciplined way."[32]

Then the demonstrations grew. In a number of towns the strikers kept the nonstrikers out by force. Eventually the troops came in, and the minor violence ended. Total: a few injuries, a little property damage, perhaps 70 arrests.

Not all strikes were so peaceful, however. During the same period, a number of mining strikes involved pitched battles between troops and demonstrators. In the course of a strike of 15,000 miners around St. Etienne in June 1869, the troops killed 13 and wounded another nine members of a crowd which attacked them; this encounter went down in history as "the massacre of La Ricamarie." At Aubin (Aveyron), later in the year, the troops shot 30 to 40 strikers trying to break into a metalworking plant, and managed to kill 14 of them on the spot. The point is not so much that people sometimes died in the course of these conflicts as that both the strikes involving trivial damage and those involving loss of life took essentially the same form.

The tremendous Paris Commune of 1871 broke the continuity of modern collective violence to some extent, for its organization greatly resembled that of earlier Parisian rebellions, and its leitmotifs—local control, communal autonomy, equalization of advantages—were contrary to the prevailing nationalization of political conflict and the formation of special-interest associations. But the break occurred as the Prussians marched through northern France, as the government fled, as the rest of the nation, in effect, seceded from Paris. The break was short. With Paris tamed and the National Government reinstalled, Frenchmen returned quickly to the modern forms of violent conflict.

Later on strikes grew in amplitude and frequency. As they spread, they became increasingly common contexts

27

for collective violence, even though a decreasing proportion of all strikes were violent. After 1890, a number of strikes took on an insurrectionary character, with both the doctrine and the practice of the general strike growing in importance. (It was at just this time that Georges Sorel, in his famous *Reflections on Violence,* placed the "myth of the general strike" at the center of revolutionary action.) And the character of strike activity continued to change as the structure of labor unions, the structure of industry, and the relations of labor management and government all evolved. France's peak years for strike activity—1906, 1919-20, 1936, 1947—have all been years of great social conflict in other regards as well. Each of those crises marked a new stage in the scale and sophistication of conflict.

THE TRANSITION TO MODERN
COLLECTIVE VIOLENCE

Unlike the food riot or the *occupazioni,* all this is terribly familiar stuff to the 20th-century reader. In it he can see the collective violence of his own era. The only reason for reviewing it is to notice the deep differences in character among the primitive, reactionary, and modern forms. They lend importance to the fact that so many Western countries shifted from one type to another rapidly and decisively.

The nature, timing, and causes of these shifts from one major type of collective violence to another are complicated, controversial, and variable from one country to another. They are just as complicated, controversial, and variable, in fact, as the political histories of European nations. The transformations of collective violence depended on transformations of nonviolent political life. Rather different political systems emerged in different corners of Europe: communist, socialist, liberal-democratic, corporatist. Each had a somewhat different experience with collective violence. Yet everywhere two things happened and profoundly affected the character of violent protest.

The first was the victory of the national state over rival powers in towns, provinces, and estates; politics was nationalized. The second was the proliferation and rise to political prominence of complex special-purpose associations like parties, firms, unions, clubs, and criminal syndi-

28

cates. The two trends generally reinforced each other. In some countries, however, the state gained power faster and earlier than the organizational changes occurred; Russia and France are cases in point. In others, the organizational revolution came much closer to the nationalization of politics; Germany and Italy fit that pattern. In either case, the times of overlap of the two trends produced the most dramatic changes in the character of collective violence.

Some of the contrast appears in crude tabulations of disturbances occurring in France during the three decades from 1830 to 1860 and three later decades between 1930 and 1960.[33] This fairly representative set of disturbances includes 1,393 events, involving 3,250 formations (distinct groups taking part in the collective violence). The distribution over time is as follows:

Period	Number of disturbances	Number of formations	Formations per disturbance	Estimated total of participants (in thousands)
1830-39	259	565	2.2	293
1840-49	292	736	2.5	511
1850-60	114	258	2.3	106
1930-39	333	808	2.4	737
1940-49	93	246	2.6	223
1950-60	302	637	2.1	664

The figures show that France by no means became a peaceable nation as urbanization and industrialization transformed her between 1830 and 1960. The two decades from 1850 to 1860 and from 1940 to 1950 produced the fewest disturbances; what actually happened is that during two extremely repressive regimes (following Louis Napoleon's 1851 coup and during the German occupation and Vichy government of the 1940's) there was almost no open large-scale violence. The large numbers for the 1930's include the huge sitdown strikes of 1936 and 1937. Even without them the depressed thirties would look like troubled times. So would the prosperous fifties. In boom and bust, Frenchmen continue to fight.

We can look at the distribution of formations taking part in the disturbances in the top table of Page 30. The figures show a decided decline in the participation of the ordinary, mixed crowd without any well-defined political or economic identity, and a compensating rise in the participation of crowds labeled as supporters of particular creeds and programs. We find no marked change in the involvement of repressive forces in collective violence, but see an important shift of the task of repression from military forces to police. "Natural" groups like users of the same market (who were typical participants in food riots,

Type of formation	1830-39	1840-49	1850-60	1930-39	1940-49	1950-60
Simple crowd.....	16.5	17.2	8.9	1.5	3.3	1.5
Ideological crowd, activists........	17.5	10.4	32.3	48.3	21.5	35.2
Military..........	20.5	16.2	15.2	3.0	8.5	1.9
Police............	10.9	16.9	24.5	24.6	26.4	31.8
Public officials.....	3.5	6.0	4.3	1.0	3.7	1.5
Occupational group	17.0	17.3	4.7	14.6	24.4	17.7
Users of same market, fields, woods or water..	2.5	4.4	1.9	.7	.0	.0
Others...........	11.7	11.7	8.2	6.3	12.2	10.5
Total	100.1	100.1	100.0	100.0	100.0	100.1

invasions of fields, and other small reactionary disturbances) disappeared completely over the 130-year span.

Altogether, the figures show the rise of specialization and organization in collective violence. Just as industry shifted its weight from the small shop to the large factory and population rushed from little town to big city, collective violence moved from the normal congregations of communal groups within which people used to live most of their lives toward the deliberate confrontations of special-purpose associations. Collective violence, like so many other features of social life, changed from a communal basis to an associational one.

As one consequence the average size of incidents went up. Here are some measures of magnitude for the 1,393 disturbances in the sample:

	1830-39	1840-49	1850-60	1930-39	1940-49	1950-60
Mean number participating	1,130	1,750	925	2,215	2,405	2,200
Mean man-days expended.	1,785	3,295	1,525	2,240	2,415	2,200
Man-days per participant..	1.6	1.9	1.6	1.0	1.0	1.0
Percent lasting more than 1 day...............	18	18	25	4	4	5
Mean killed and wounded.	25	22	30	19	34	23
Mean arrests.............	20	53	327	24	22	43

The figures describe the average disturbance, of course, not the total amount of violence in a decade. They show a distinct rise in the average number of people taking part in a disturbance, despite a strong tendency for disturbances to narrow down to a single day. As the burden of repression shifted from the army to the police, interestingly enough, the use of widespread arrests declined while the number of people hurt stayed about the same. Relative to the number of participants, that meant some decline in the average demonstrator's chance of being killed or wounded. The main message, once again, is that, although the predominant forms of collective violence changed in fundamental ways, collective violence persisted as France became an advanced industrial nation.

The 20th-century figures from France include almost no primitive violence. By the beginning of the century the primitive forms had been fading slowly through most of Western Europe for three centuries or more. In some countries, however, the transition from predominantly reactionary to predominantly modern forms of collective violence occurred with striking rapidity. In England, the reactionary forms were already well on their way to oblivion by the time of the last agrarian rising, in 1830, although they had prevailed 30 years before. In Germany, demonstrations and strikes seem to have established themselves as the usual settings for collective violence during the two decades after the Revolution of 1848.

The situation was a bit more complicated in Italy, because of the deep division between north and south. The transition to modern forms of collective violence appears to have been close to completion in the north at unification. By the time of Milan's infamous *fatti di Maggio* of 1898, in which at least two policemen and 80 demonstrators died, the newer organizational forms unquestionably dominated the scene. In the south, mixed forms of the food riot and tax rebellion still occurred at the end of the century. Within 10 years, however, even in rural areas the agricultural strike and the organized partisan meeting or demonstration had become the most regular sources of violence on the larger scale.

Spain, as usual, is the significant exception: while the country as a whole displays the long-run drift from primitive to reactionary to modern forms of collective violence, it also displays a marvelous array of regressions, mixtures, and hesitations. Surely, the country's erratic industrialization, uncertain, fluctuating unification, and exceptional military involvement in politics lie behind its differentiation from the rest of Western Europe in this respect. Spain, as Gerald Brenan says,

. . . is the land of the *patria chica*. Every village, every town is the centre of an intense social and political life. As in classical times, a man's allegiance is first of all to his native place, or to his family or social group in it, and only secondly to his country and government. In what one may call its normal condition Spain is a collection of small, mutually hostile, or indifferent republics held together in a loose federation. . . . Instead of a slow building-up of forces such as one sees in other European nations, there has been an alternation between the petty quarrels of tribal life and great upsurges of energy that come, economically speaking, from nowhere.[34]

Thus Spain becomes the exception that tests the rule. For the rule says the shift from predominantly reactionary to predominantly modern forms of collective violence accompanies the more-or-less durable victory of the national state and the national economy over the particularisms of the past. In Spain, that victory was not durable, and the forms of violence wavered.

The precise timing and extent of the shift from reactionary to modern forms of collective violence in these countries remains to be established. For France, it is fairly clear that the shift was barely started by 1840, but close to complete by 1860. Furthermore, France experienced great, and nearly simultaneous, outbreaks of both forms of collective violence in the years from 1846 through 1851. The well-known events we customarily lump together as the Revolution of 1848 and the less-known but enormous insurrection of 1851 stand out both for their magnitude and for their mixture of reactionary and modern disturbances, but they came in the company of such notable outbreaks as the widespread food riots of 1846-47, the Forty-Five Centime Revolt of 1848-49, and the unsuccessful coup of 1849.

If this account of the transition from reactionary to modern collective violence in Western Europe is correct, it has some intriguing features. First, the timing of the transition corresponds roughly to the timing of industrialization and urbanization—England early, Italy late, and so on. Furthermore, the most rapid phase of the transition seems to occur together with a great acceleration of industrial and urban growth, early in the process: England at the beginning of the century, France of the 1850's, Germany of the 1850's and 1870's, Italy of the 1890's.

Second, there is some connection between the timing of the transition and the overall level of collective violence in a country. Over the last 150 years, if we think in terms of the frequency and scale of disturbances rather than the turnover of regimes, we can probably place Spain ahead of France, France ahead of Italy, Italy ahead of Germany, and Germany ahead of England. France is in the wrong position, and the contrast much less than the differences in the countries' reputations for stability or instability, but there is some tendency for the latecomers (or noncomers) to experience greater violence. If we took into account challenges to national integration posed by such peoples as the Catalans, and differences in the apparatus of repression, the connection would very likely appear even closer.

The information we have on hand, then, suggests that the processes of urbanization and industrialization themselves transform the character of collective violence. But how? We have a conventional notion concerning the life cycle of protest during the course of industrialization and urbanization: an early stage consisting of chaotic responses to the displacements and disruptions caused by the initial development of urban industry, a middle stage consisting of the growth of a militant and often violent working class, a late stage consisting of the peaceful integration of that working class into economic and political life. This scheme has many faults, as we have seen. Certainly we must correct and expand it to take account both of other groups than industrial workers and of the connections between industrialization and urbanization concerning the character of collective violence we have already reviewed raises grave doubts whether the underlying process producing and transforming protest was one of disintegration followed by reintegration, and whether the earlier forms of protest were so chaotic as the scheme implies.

The experience of France challenges the plausible presumption that rapid urbanization produces disruptions of social life that in turn generate protest. There is, if anything, a negative correlation over time and space between the pace of urban growth and the intensity of collective violence. The extreme example is the contrast between the

33

1840's, with slow urban growth plus enormous violence, and the decade after 1851, with very fast growth and extensive peace. Cities like St. Etienne of Roubaix that received and formed large numbers of new industrial workers tended to remain quiet while centers of the old traditional crafts, like Lyon and Rouen, raged with rebellion. When we can identify the participants in political disturbances, they tend to grossly underrepresent newcomers to the city and draw especially from the "little pepole" most firmly integrated into the local political life of the city's working-class neighborhoods. The geography of the disturbances itself suggests as much. It was not the urban neighborhoods of extreme deprivation, crime, or vice, George Rudé reports, "not the newly settled towns or quarters that proved the most fertile breeding-ground for social and political protest, but the old areas of settlement with established customs, such as Westminster, the City of London, Old Paris, Rouen, or Lyon."[35] The information available points to a slow, collective process of organization and political education—what we may loosely call a development of class consciousness—within the city rather than a process of disruption leading directly to personal malaise and protest.

As a consequence of this process, the great new cities eventually became the principal settings of collective violence in France. Furthermore, collective violence moved to the city faster than the population did. Even at the beginning of the 19th century, the towns and cities of France produced a disproportionate share of the nation's collective violence. Yet tax rebellions, food riots, and movements against conscription did occur with fair regularity in France's small towns and villages. After these forms of disturbance disappeared, the countryside remained virtually silent for decades. When rural collective violence renewed, it was in the highly organized form of farmers' strikes and marches on Government buildings. This sequence of events was, to some extent, a result of urbanization.

Early in the 19th century, the expansion of cities incited frequent rural protests—obviously in the case of the food riot, more subtly in the case of other forms of collective violence. We have some reason to believe that groups of people who were still solidly established within rural com-

34

munities, but were losing their livelihoods through the concentration of property and the urbanization of industry, regularly spearheaded such protests. The most important group was probably the workers in cottage industry. Their numbers declined catastrophically as various industries—especially textiles—moved to the city during the first half of the century. Large numbers of them hung on in the countryside, doing what weaving, spinning, or forging they could, seeking out livings as handymen, day laborers, and farmhands, and railing against their fate. Within their communities they were able to act collectively against power looms, farm machines, tax collectors, and presumed profiteers.

Slowly before midcentury, rapidly thereafter, the increasing desperation of the French countryside and the expanding opportunities for work in the new industrial cities drew such men away from their rural communities into town. That move cut them off from the personal, day-to-day contacts that had given them the incentive and the means for collective action against their enemies. It rearranged their immediate interests, placed them in vast, unfamiliar communities, and gave them relatively weak and unreliable relations with those who shared common interests with them.

The initial fragmentation of the work force into small groups of diverse origins, the slow development of mutual awareness and confidence, the lack of organizational experience among the new workers, and the obstacles thrown up by employers and governments all combined to make the development of the means and the will for collective action a faltering, time-consuming process. Collective violence did not begin in earnest until the new industrial workers began forming or joining associations—trade unions, mutual-aid societies, political clubs, conspiratorial groups—devoted to the collective pursuit of their interests. In this sense, the short-run effect of the urbanization of the French labor force was actually to damp collective violence. Its long-run effect, however, was to promot new forms of collective action that frequently led to violent conflicts, and thus to change the form of collective violence itself.

This happened in part through the grouping together of large numbers of men sharing a common fate in factories,

35

urban working-class neighborhoods, and construction gangs. Something like the class-conscious proletariat of which Marx wrote began to form in the industrial cities. This new scale of congregation combined with new, pressing grievances, improving communication, the diffusion of new organizational models from Government and industry, and grudging concessions by the authorities to the right of association. The combination facilitated the formation of special-interest associations. At first workers experimented with cramped, antique, exclusive associations resembling (or even continuing) the old guilds; gradually they formed mutual-aid societies, labor exchanges, unions, and national and international federations.

The new associations further extended the scale and flexibility of communication among workers; they made it possible to inform, mobilize, and deploy large numbers of men fast and efficiently in strikes, demonstrations, and other common action. These potentially rebellious populations and their demanding associations proliferated in the big cities, in the shadows of regional and national capitals. They therefore posed a greater (or at least more visible) threat to the authorities than had their smalltown predecessors. The authorities responded to the threat by organizing police forces, crowd-control tactics, and commissions of inquiry. The associations, in their turn, achieved greater sophistication and control in their show of strength. The process took time—perhaps a generation for any particular group of workers. In that longer run the urbanization of the labor force produced a whole new style of collective violence.

The experience of the industrial workers has one more important lesson for us. In both reactionary and modern forms of collective violence, men commonly express their feeling that they have been unjustly denied their rights. Reactionary disturbances, however, center on rights once enjoyed but now threatened, while modern disturbances center on rights not yet enjoyed but now within reach. The reactionary forms are especially the work of groups of men who are losing their collective positions within the system of power, while the modern forms attract groups of men who are striving to acquire or enhance such positions. The reactionary forms, finally, challenge the basic claims of a national state and a national economy, while the modern forms rest on the assumption that the state and the economy have a durable existence—if not necessarily under present management. In modern disturbances, men contend over the control and organization of the State and the economy.

What links these features together historically? The coordinate construction of the nation-state and the national economy simultaneously weakened local systems of power, with the rights and positions which depended on them, and established new, much larger arenas in which to contend for power. In Western European countries, as locally based groups of men definitively lost their struggle against the claims of the central power, reactionary disturbances dwindled and modern disturbances swelled. The rapid transition from one to the other occurred where and when the central power was able to improve rapidly or expand its enforcement of its claims. Accelerating urbanization and industrialization facilitated such an expansion by providing superior means of communication and control to the agents of the central power, by drawing men more fully into national markets, and by spreading awareness of, and involvement in, national politics. In the process, special-purpose associations like parties and labor unions grew more and more important as the vehicles in the struggle for power, whether violent or nonviolent. Thus urbanization and industrialization affected the character and the incidence of collective violence profoundly, but indirectly.

THE LOGIC OF COLLECTIVE VIOLENCE

Before rushing to apply this analysis of European collective violence to current American experience, we should pause to notice how much of it is a historical analysis—helpful in sorting out the past and identifying the context of the present, but not in predicting the future. Categories like primitive, reactionary, and modern have more kinship with timebound terms like Renaissance, Liberalism, or Neolithic than with more timeless concepts like urban, clan, or wealth. I would not argue for a moment that forward-looking protests are necessarily larger in scale than backward-looking ones, although that has been the usual experience of Western countries for several centuries. For those were centuries of growth and centralization, in which

37

to look backward meant to look toward the smaller scale. As a general statement, the analysis is too one dimensional.

To take the problem out of time, we must deal with at least two dimensions. One is the organizational basis of routine political life. To simplify the problem, we might distinguish between politics based on small-scale, local, traditional groupings (communal politics) and politics based on large-scale organizations formed to serve one well-defined interest (associational politics). Then we could say that both the primitive and the reactionary forms of collective violence spring from communal bases, although under differing circumstances, while the modern forms of collective violence develop from an associational base. In the primitive and reactionary cases, the links among those who join together in collective action— whether violent or not—come from traditional, localized, inherited, slow-changing memberships. The rhythm of collective violence therefore follows the rhythm of con- gregation and dispersion of existing communal groups; market days, holidays, harvest days produce more than their share of violence. In the purely modern case, on the other hand, deliberately created formal organizations pro- vide the crucial links. The organizations help shape the aspirations and grievances of their members, define their enemies, determine the occasions on which they will assemble and the occasions on which they will confront their antagonists, and thus the occasions on which violence can occur. The communal/associational distinction is one of the hoariest in the study of social life, and it turns out to apply to such apparently antisocial behavior as violence.

We have to consider another dimension: the relationship of the groups involved to the existing structure of power. Again simplifying radically, we might imagine a division among groups unrepresented in the existing structure of power, groups in the process of acquiring positions in that structure, groups holding defined positions in that struc- ture, and groups in the process of losing defined positions. Then it would be accurate to say that, on the whole, primi- tive disturbances involve groups holding defined positions in a (certain kind of) structure of power, whereas reaction- ary disturbances involve groups losing such positions, and modern disturbances involve groups acquiring them.

Strictly speaking, these are not types of violence. The

38

distinctions do not apply to acts of violence, or even to the collective actions characteristically producing violence. They sort out groups of people into differing political situations. Their relevance to violence as such rests on a simple argument: a population's organization and political situation strongly affect its form of collective action, and the form of collective action stringently limits the possibilities of violence. Thus each type of group takes part in a significantly different variety of collective violence.

That clarification gives us the means of putting the two dimensions together. We discover that there are some other possible types not discussed so far:

	Relation to Structure of Power		
	Acquiring position	Maintaining position	Losing position
Organizational base: Communal...... Associational.....	(?) Modern	Primitive (?)	Reactionary (?)

It is not so hard to fill in two of the blanks. There are really two varieties of modern collective violence; a frenzied variety on the part of people like the suffragettes who are trying to storm the system, and a more controlled but massive show of strength by groups like parties already established in the system. Violent movements of protest like Poujadism, on the other hand, resemble those I have called reactionary except that they have an associational base. This suggests placing them in the lower right-hand corner: the characteristic collective violence of groups losing position in a system built on an associational basis.

As for acquiring position in a communal system, common sense says it cannot be done. But we might throw common sense aside and speculate that the millenarian, transcendental, and fanatical movements that rack backward areas from time to time provide men with the means of acquiring totally new identities through religious conversion. This would lead us to expect these other-worldly protests to turn into modern protests as the organizational basis shifts from communal to associational. Some features of millenarian movements in such European areas as Andalusia and southern Italy lend this speculation a snippet of plausibility, but it is still only a speculation.

We have filled in the boxes. The table now looks like this:

	Relation to Structure of Power		
	Acquiring position	Maintaining position	Losing position
Organizational basis: Communal....... Associational.....	Other worldly? Offensive	Primitive Interest-group	Reactionary Defensive

The boxes are not airtight. We can easily locate groups standing halfway between the communal and associational forms of organization, or just barely maintaining their political positions. Organized criminals come to mind as an example of the first; languishing protest parties as an example of the second. The point of the scheme is to suggest that groups' usual collective actions, and therefore their usual forms of collective violence, will also fall halfway between those of their neighbors in the table.

All this box filling would be no more than a scholastic exercise if it were not possible to draw some interesting hypotheses from the discussion. The first is that, regardless of their organizational basis, groups acquiring position are likely to define their problem as the achieving of rights due them on general ground but so far denied, groups losing position to define their problem as the retention of specific rights of which they are being deprived, and groups maintaining position to pay less attention to rights and justice. Second, the actions of those acquiring or losing position are likely to be more violent than those maintaining position. Third, a larger proportion of collective actions on a communal basis results in violence, because the associational form gives the group a surer control over its own actions, and thus permits shows of force without damage or bloodshed. While historically the shift from communal to associational bases for collective violence did not, by any means, stop the fighting, it did bring into being a number of alternative nonviolent mechanisms for the regulation of conflicts: the strike, the parliament, the political campaign.

So when does this line of reasoning lead us to expect that collective violence will be widespread? It suggests that over the very long run the transformation of a population, a movement, or a society from a communal to an associational basis of organization diminishes its overall level of

40

violence, but only over the very long run. If we were to consider external war as well as internal civil disorders, even that timid inference would look dubious. The scheme implies much more definitely that collective violence clusters in those historical moments when the structure of power itself is changing decisively—because there are many new contenders for power, because several old groups of power holders are losing their grips, or because the locus of power is shifting from community to nation, from nation to international bloc, or in some other drastic way. Violence flows from politics, and more precisely from political change.

The extent of violence depends on politics in the short run as well. Violence is not a solo performance, but an interaction. It is an interaction that political authorities everywhere seek to monopolize, control, or at least contain. Nowadays almost all collective violence on a significant scale involves the political authorities and their professional representatives: policemen, soldiers, and others. This happens, first, because the authorities make it their business to intervene and thus maintain their monopoly on the use of force; second, because so much collective violence begins with a direct (but not necessarily violent) challenge to the authorities themselves.

As odd as it may seem, the authorities have far greater control over the short-run extent and timing of collective violence, especially damage to persons rather than property, than their challengers do. This is true for several reasons. The authorities usually have the technological and organizational advantage in the effective use of force, which gives them a fairly great choice among tactics of prevention, containment, and retaliation. The limits of that discretion are more likely to be political and moral—Can we afford to show weakness? Could we fire on women and children?—than technical. If the criterion of success is simply the minimization of violence, repression often works. In recent European experience few countries have been freer of civil disorder than Spain, a normally turbulent nation, when it was under the tight dictatorships of Primo de Rivera and Franco. In the heydays of the German and Italian Facists, virtually the only violence to occur was at the hands of Government employees.

The authorities also have some choice of whether, and

with how much muscle, to answer political challenges and illegal actions that are not intrinsically violent: banned assemblies, threats of vengeance, wildcat strikes. A large proportion of the European disturbances we have been surveying turned violent at exactly the moment when the authorities intervened to stop an illegal but nonviolent action. This is typical of violent strikes and demonstrations. Furthermore, the great bulk of the killing and wounding in those same disturbances was done by troops or police rather than by insurgents or demonstrators. The demonstrators, on the other hand, did the bulk of the damage to property. If we sweep away the confusion brought on by words like "riot," "mob," or "violence," a little reflection will make it clear that this division of labor between maimers and smashers follows logically from the very nature of encounters between police and their antagonists.

All this means that over the short run the extent, location, and timing of collective violence depend heavily on the way the authorities and their agents handle the challenges offered to them. Over a longer run, however, the kinds of challenges they face and the strength of those challenges depend rather little on their tactics of crowd control and a great deal on the way the entire political system apportions power and responds to grievances.

Discussions of these matters easily drift into praise and blame, justification and condemnation, fixing of responsibility for violence. If, when, where, and by whom violence should be permitted are inescapably difficult questions of moral and political philosophy. My review of European historical experience has not resolved them. Its purpose was the more modest one of sketching social processes lying behind the actual occurrence of collective violence in Western countries as they have existed over the last century or so. Yet the fact that the analytic and historical questions bring us so close to political philosophy underlines my main conclusions: collective violence is part and parcel of the Western political process, and major changes in its character result from major changes in the political system.

If that is the case, very recent changes in the character and locus of violent protest bear careful watching. Through much of Europe, students have reached a level of activism and anger never before equaled; the French events of May

1968 were only the most spectacular episode of a long series. Separatist movements long though dead, ludicrous, or at least under control—Welsh, Scottish, Breton, Basque, Slovak, Flemish—have sprung up with energy. Demands for autonomy, cohesion, insulation from state control, which virtually disappeared from European political debate a half-century ago, now appear to be growing rapidly. Of course it is possible that the widespread emergence of autonomist themes in collective violence is a coincidence, a passing fancy, or simply my misreading of the character of the new movements. If none of these is the case, we might consider the possibility that they record a transfer of power away from the national State, perhaps in part because its own weight keeps it from dealing with the most burning aspirations of its own citizens, and in part because power is devolving to international blocs of states. Then we might be witnessing a transformation comparable in scope to the 19th-century shift from reactionary to modern forms of collective violence. These are speculations, but they, too, emphasize the political significance of violence.

I must leave it to the well-informed reader to apply this analysis of European experience to the civil disorders of contemporary America. Naturally, analogies immediately come to mind. Recent studies of ghetto riots have been producing a picture of the average rioter that much resembles what we know of many 19th-century urban disturbances: the predominance of young males, overrepresentation of longtime residents rather than recent migrants, the relative absence of criminals, and so on. But why search for easy analogies? The chief lesson of the European experience is not that riots are all the same. Far from it!

What we have seen, instead, is a close connection between the basic political process and the predominant forms of conflict, both violent and nonviolent. That makes it hard to accept a recent characterization of American ghetto riots as "mainly for fun and profit." [36] It raises doubts about attempts to reduce current student rebellions to one more expression of adolescent anxiety. It makes one wonder whether the recent revival of violent and nonviolent separatist movements in such different Western countries as Belgium, Canada, Spain, France, and Great Britain indicates some larger change in international politics. For the basic conclusion is simple and powerful. Collective violence belongs to political life, and changes in its form tells us that something important is happening to the political system itself.

References

1. Marc Bloch, *Les caractères originaux de l'histoire rurale française* (Paris: Colin, 1952), I, 175.
2. J. L. and Barbara Hammond, *The Village Labourer* (London: Longmans, 1969), pp. 241-242.
3. Elie Halévy (E. I. Watkin and D. A. Barker, tr.), *England in 1815* (New York: Barnes & Noble, 1961), p. 148.
4. Graham Adams, Jr., *Age of Industrial Violence, 1910-1915* (New York: Columbia University Press, 1966), pp. 132-136.
5. Hammond and Hammond, *op. cit.*, pp. 242-243.
6. Bruce M. Russett and others, *World Handbook of Political and Social Indicators* (New Haven: Yale University Press, 1965), pp. 99-100.
7. Antonio Gramsci, *Il Risorgimento* (Torino: Einaudi, 1950, 3d ed.), pp. 199-200.
8. I have borrowed the general logic of this distinction (if not the precise formulation or the exact wording) from E. J. Hobsbawm, *Primitive Rebels* (Manchester: Manchester University Press, 1959). It also underlies much of the argument of George Rudé, *The Crowd in History* (New York: Wiley, 1964). These are the two best general books on the subject of this essay.
9. Thorstein Veblen, *Imperial Germany and the Industrial Revolution* (Ann Arbor: University of Michigan Press, 1966; paperback edition), p. 50.
10. *Le Constitutionnel*, Nov. 19, 1835.
11. M. Dorothy George, *London Life in the Eighteenth Century* (New York: Harper & Row, 1964; Torchbook edition), p. 280.
12. Rudolf Stadelmann and Wolfram Fischer, *Die Bildungswelt des deutschen Handwerkers um 1800* (Berlin: Duncker & Humblot, 1955), p. 71.
13. Philippe Ariès, *Centuries of Childhood* (New York: Vintage Books, 1965), pp. 317-318.
14. *Ibid.*, pp. 318-319.
15. A. J. Peacock, *Bread or Blood* (London: Gollancz, 1965), p. 79.
16. *Ibid.*, p. 81.
17. Here and later in the essay I have relied especially on an unpublished paper by Louise Tilly, "Popular Protest in the Risorgimento: 1850-1860" (University of Toronto, 1967).
18. Karl Marx, "The Class Struggles in France, 1848-1850" in Marx and Engels, *Selected Works* (Moscow: Foreign Languages Publishing House, 1958), vol. I, p. 213.
19. Hammond and Hammond, *op. cit.*, pp. 261-262.
20. E. J. Hobsbawm, "Le agitazioni rurali in Inghilterra nel primo ottocento," *Studi Storici*, Vol. VIII (Apr.-June 1967), 278.
21. E. P. Thompson, *The Making of the English Working Class* (London: Gollancz, 1964), p. 530.
22. *Ibid.*, p. 543.
23. Disraeli, preface to *Alton Locke*, as quoted in Walter E. Houghton, *The Victorian Frame of Mind* (New Haven: Yale University Press, 1957), p. 57.
24. Edward Shorter, "Middle Class Anxiety in the German Revolution of 1848" (forthcoming in the *Journal of Social History*).
25. Louis Chevalier, *Classes laborieuses et classes dangereuses* (Paris: Plon, 1958), p. 469.
26. F. C. Mather, *Public Order in the Age of the Chartists* (Manchester: Manchester University Press, 1959), p. 128.
27. Alan Silver, "The Demand for Order in Civil Society: A Review of Some Themes in the History of Urban Crime, Police, and Riot," in David J. Bordua, ed., *The Police: Six Sociological Essays* (New York: Wiley, 1967), pp. 12-13.
28. Joseph Hamburger, *James Mill and the Art of Revolution* (New Haven: Yale University Press, 1963), p. 147.
29. Mather, *op. cit.*, p. 21.

30. G. D. H. Cole and Raymond Postgate, *The British Common People, 1746-1946* (London: University Paperback, 1961), p. 490.
31. *Ibid.*, pp. 453-454.
32. Fernand L'Huillier, *La lutte ouvrière à la fin du Second Empire* (Paris: Colin, 1957; "Cahiers des Annales," No. 12), p. 65.
33. Our sampling procedure consisted of reading through two national newspapers for each day of the 60 years and pulling out each reported event involving some violence (wounding, property damage, or seizure of persons or property over resistance) in which at least one participating formation had 50 members or more. As well as we can determine, a sample thus assembled overweights events in cities, and especially in Paris, but in a relatively constant fashion. The descriptions of the events coded come not only from the newspaper accounts but also from historical works and French archival material. The data presented here are preliminary and probably contain minor errors. None of the errors I have in mind, however, would substantially affect the conclusions drawn from the data in this essay.
34. Gerald Brenan, *The Spanish Labyrinth* (Cambridge: Cambridge University Press, 1967), p. ix.
35. George Rudé, "The Growth of Cities and Popular Revolt, 1850-1950, with Particular Reference to Paris" (unpublished draft, 1967), p. 26. I am grateful to Mr. Rudé for permission to quote the paper, of which a later version is to be published in 1969.
36. Edward C. Banfield, "Rioting Mainly for Fun and Profit," in James Q. Wilson, ed., *The Metropolitan Enigma* (Cambridge: Harvard University Press, 1968), pp. 283-308.

Chapter 2

HISTORICAL PATTERNS OF VIOLENCE IN AMERICA

*By Richard Maxwell Brown**

American violence, historically, seems to fall into two major divisions. The first is negative violence: violence that seems to be in no direct way connected with any socially or historically constructive development. Varieties of negative violence are criminal violence, feuds, lynching, the violence of prejudice (racial, ethnic, and religious violence), urban riots, freelance multiple murder, and assassination.

Negative violence by no means exhausts the range of American violence. There has been a vast amount

* Richard M. Brown is professor of history at the College of William and Mary. His publications include *The South Carolina Regulators* (Cambridge, Mass.: Harvard University Press, 1963). An earlier version of this paper was delivered as a lecture in the College of William and Mary's Marshall-Wythe Symposium, 1968. The author wishes to acknowledge the advice and encouragement of Dr. Warner Moss, director of the Marshall-Wythe Institute, College of William and Mary.

connected with some of the most important events of American history—events that are considered constructive, positive, and, indeed, among the noblest chapters in our national history. Thus the Revolutionary War—both in its origins and its progress—was shot through with domestic violence. The Civil War, by which the slave eventually gained his freedom and the union of the nation was assured, engendered vast waves of violence. The very land we occupy was gained over the centuries in a continuing war with the Indians. Vigilante violence was used to establish order and stability on the frontier. Agrarian uprisings occurred again and again to ease the plight of the farmer and yeoman. Labor violence was part and parcel of the industrial workers' struggle to gain recognition and a decent life. Police violence has always been invoked to protect society against the criminal and disorderly. Again and again violence has been used as a means to ends that have been widely accepted and applauded. Positive violence is a broad term that relates violence to the popular and constructive movements just mentioned.

NEGATIVE VIOLENCE

Criminal Violence

The salient facts, chronologically arranged, are: (1) Organized interstate gangs of criminals are an old story, going well back into the 18th century. (2) Before the Civil War, the most prevalent type of criminal activity—especially in frontier areas—was horse theft and the counterfeiting of the myriad number of private banknotes then in circulation. (3) After the Civil War a new era of crime began with the popularization of train robbery by the Reno brothers of Indiana and bank robbery by the James-Younger gang of Missouri. (4) The modern era of big-city organized crime with its police and political connections began to emerge in the early 20th century.

America has long been ambiguous about the criminal. Official condemnation of the outlaw has been matched by social adulation. The ambiguity is not restricted to America, for the British historian, E. J. Hobsbawn, has shown the existence in European history of the "social bandit." [1] By social bandit, Hobsbawn means largely what we have come to denote by the Robin Hood symbol, i.e., the outlaw whom society views as its hero rather than its enemy, an outlook which reflects widespread social alienation.

There have indeed been American social bandits. Jesse and Frank James gained a strong popular following in mid-America after the Civil War. To the many Southern sympathizers in Missouri the James brothers, who were former Confederate guerrillas, could do no wrong, and to many Grange-minded farmers the Jameses' repeated robberies of banks and railroads were no more than these unpopular economic institutions deserved.[2] Other social bandits have been Billy the Kid (idolized by the poor Mexican herdsmen and villagers of the Southwest),[3] Pretty Boy Floyd (onetime Public Enemy No. 1 of the 1930's who retained the admiration of the sharecroppers of eastern Oklahoma from which stock he sprang),[4] and John Dillinger, the premier bank robber of the depression era. Modeling himself on an earlier social bandit, Jesse James, John Dillinger by free-handed generosity cultivated the Robin Hood image while robbing a series of Midwestern banks.[5] The rural-small-town era of American crime came largely to an end with the demise of John Dillinger, Pretty Boy Floyd, Clyde Barrow and Bonnie Parker, and the other "public enemies" of the 1930's. With them the American tradition of the social bandit died.

While the tradition of the rural American social bandit was waxing and waning, urban crime was increasing in importance. The first urban criminal gangs arose in New York and other cities in the pre-Civil War decades, but these gangs were limited in significance and restricted to ethnic "slum" neighborhoods such as Five Points and the Bowery in New York City.[6] Murder, mayhem, and gang vendettas were a feature of the proliferation of these gangs. Meanwhile, in the early decades of the 20th century the present pattern of centralized, city-wide criminal operations under the control of a single "syndicate" or "organization" began to take shape in New York under Arnold Rothstein.[7] Converging with this trend was, apparently, the Mafia tradition of criminal organization which Sicilian immigrants seem to have brought into East Coast port cities in the decades around 1900.[8] During the 1920's and 1930's the two trends merged into the predominant pattern of centralized operations under Mafia control which the

47

Kefauver crime investigation highlighted in 1951.[9] Systematic killing to settle internal feuds and the use of investment capital (gained from illicit activities), threats, and extortion to infiltrate the world of legitimate business have been characteristic of contemporary urban organized crime.[10]

Feud Violence

One classic phase of negative American violence has been the family feud. This phenomenon has been generally associated with the "hillbilly" of the southern Appalachians, and, of the two great geographic locales of the family feud, one has surely been the Southern mountains. Less generally recognized has been the prevalence of the family feud in Texas and the Southwest at the same time that murderous feuds were splotching the Southern highlands with blood.

The family blood feud is virtually nonexistent in this country before the Civil War. The feud appears on the scene quite dramatically in the decades following the war. The era between the Civil War and World War I is the great era of the Southern mountain feud in Kentucky, West Virginia, and Virginia. This is the period that produced the Hatfield-McCoy feud (1873-88) of the Kentucky-West Virginia border,[11] the Martin-Tolliver (1884-87) and Hargis-Cockrell (1902-03) feuds of eastern Kentucky,[12] and the Allen family outburst at Hillsville in the Virginia Blue Ridge in 1912.[13]

The evidence is convincing that Southern mountain feuding was triggered by the animosities generated by the Civil War. The mountains were divided country where Confederate and Union sympathizers fought in rival armies and slew each other in marauding guerrilla bands. After the war old hatreds did not die out but, fueled anew by political partisanship and moonshine whisky in a region bedeviled by isolation, poverty, and minimal education, flamed up as never before. The formal law barely operated; its power was manipulated for selfish purposes by close knit political and family factions. Because regular law and order was such a frail reed, families and individuals came increasingly to depend upon their own strong arms. Each feuding family for the sake of self-defense developed its own clan leader: a man who best combined in the highest quotients the qualities of physical strength, bravery, wealth, and family leadership. Such men were "Devil Anse" Hatfield and Judge James Hargis. In the absence of an effective system of law and order, these men functioned as family "enforcers" around whom the feuding families rallied for protection.[14]

The great feuds of Texas and the Southwest were strikingly similar to those of the southern Appalachians, were about as well known in their own day, and had similar origins. As in the Appalachians, the main era of Texas feuds was between the Civil War and World War I. The Texas feuds took place principally in the central portion of the State which, like the Southern mountains, was a region of conflicting Civil War loyalties and mordant Reconstruction hatreds. The war-spawned turbulence of Central Texas was heightened by a combination of other factors: extremely rapid development of the cattle industry with its byproducts of frantic competition, rustling, and various disorders; the fact that the western margins of the Central Texas region were seared repeatedly by one of the cruelest of all American Indian wars, that of the Comanches and Kiowas with the white settlers; and, finally, by the ethnic hostility between antislavery, pro-Union German settlers and native Southern inhabitants. The result was a series of fatal feuds that were every bit as terrible as their Appalachian counterparts.[15] Not even the Hatfield-McCoy feud exceeded for length, casualties, and bitterness the great Sutton-Taylor feud (1869-99) of DeWitt and Gonzales Counties, Texas.[16] Among the major feuds of Central Texas were the Horrell-Higgins feud of Lampasas County (1876-77), the Jaybird-Woodpecker feud of Fort Bend County (1888-90), and the Stafford-Townsend-Reese-Hope feuds of Colorado County (1890 to 1906).[17]

In New Mexico Territory the family and factional feud was built into the political system.[18] New Mexico before World War I was probably the only American State where assassination became a routine political tactic.[19] The most deadly of all American feuds was fought in neighboring Arizona from 1886 to 1892. This was the "Pleasant Valley War" between the Graham and Tewksbury families, a conflict that was exacerbated by the Grahams being cattle men and the Tewksburys being sheep men. The bitter feud was fought, like the title phrase of Zane Grey's novel of the vendetta, "to the last man." Only with the lone survivor of the two families did it come to an end.[20]

Lynch-Mob Violence

Lynch law has been defined as "the practice or custom by which persons are punished for real or alleged crimes without due process of law." [21] The first organized movement of lynch law in America occurred in the South Carolina back country, 1767-69.[22] It appeared again in the Virginia Piedmont during the latter years of the Revolutionary War near the present city of Lynchburg. The Virginia movement was initiated by Colonel Charles Lynch (from whom lynch law gained its name) and was employed against Tory miscreants.[23] Well into the 19th century lynch law meant merely the infliction of corporal punishment—usually 39 or more lashes well laid on with hickory withes, whips, or any readily available frontier instrument. By the middle of the 19th century, lynch law had, however, come to be synonymous, mainly, with hanging or killing by illegal group action. Organized movements of lynch law are treated below under the heading of "Vigilante violence." By the term "lynch-mob" is meant an unorganized, spontaneous, ephemeral mob which comes together briefly to do its fatal work and then breaks up. The more regular vigilante (or "regulator") movements engaged in a systematic usurpation of the functions of law and order.

Lynch-mob violence (in contrast to vigilante violence) was often resorted to in trans-Appalachian frontier areas before the Civil War, but it became even more common after the Civil War. In the postwar period (down to World War I) lynch-mob violence was employed frequently in all sections of the country and against whites as well as blacks, but in this period it became preeminently the fate of Southern Negroes. From 1882 to 1903 the staggering total of 1,985 Negroes were killed by Southern lynch mobs.[24] Supposedly the lynch-mob hanging (or, too often, the ghastly penalty of burning alive) was saved for the Negro murderer or rapist, but the statistics show that Negroes were frequently lynched for lesser crimes or in cases where there was no offense at all or the mere suspicion of one.[25] Lynch-mob violence became an integral part of the post-Reconstruction system of white supremacy.[26]

Although predominant in the South, lynch-mob violence was far from being restricted to that section. In the West the ephemeral "necktie party" was often foregathered for the summary disposal of thief, rapist, rustler, murderer, or all-around desperado. Frenzied mobs similarly worked their will in the North and East where (as in the West) villainous white men were the usual victims.[27]

The Violence of Racial, Ethnic, and Religious Prejudice

Lynch-mob activity by no means exhausts the violence involving whites and blacks. Racial conflict between Caucasians and Negroes is one of the most persistent factors in American violence, extending far back into the 18th century. The first slave uprising occurred in New York City in 1712 and was put down with great ruthlessness. In 1739 there was the Stono Rebellion in South Carolina, and in 1741 New York City was again wracked with fears (apparently justified) of a slave conspiracy. The result was that New York white men went on an hysterical rampage in which scores of Negroes were burned, hanged, or expelled.[28] There were a host of plots or uprisings in the 19th century: among the largest were the abortive Gabriel Prosser (Richmond, 1800)[29] and Denmark Vesey (Charleston, 1822)[30] plots. Southside Virginia was in 1831 the scene of the greatest of all American slave rebellions: that of Nat Turner in Southampton County,[31] the subject of William Styron's recent controversial novel, *The Confessions of Nat Turner*.[32] Although there was much restiveness and runaway activity on the part of American slaves, rebellion was not a major response to the slave system. Even Nat Turner's rebellion was quickly suppressed and was of little consequence compared to the great maroon enclaves and republics which rebelling and runaway slaves established in South America and the Caribbean. The American slave more typically resisted the system by passive resistance, by running away, and by making countless small, unorganized attacks on individual families, masters, or overseers.[33]

With the end of slavery and its conjoined slave patrols and black codes, the white men of the South developed a special organization for dealing with the Negro: the Ku

Klux Klan. The latter has been one of the most consistent features in the last hundred years of American violence. There have been three Ku Klux Klans: the first Ku Klux Klan of Reconstruction times, the second Ku Klux Klan of the 1920's, and the third, current, Ku Klux Klans of the 1950's and 1960's. The first Ku Klux Klan was employed to intimidate the Radical Republicans of the Reconstruction Era and, by violence and threats, to force the freedman to accept the renewed rule of Southern whites.[34] The second Ku Klux Klan differed significantly from both its predecessor and successor. Although the second Ku Klux Klan was founded in Atlanta in 1915, its greatest growth and strength actually took place beyond the borders of the old Confederacy. During the early 1920's it became a truly national organization. For a time it enjoyed great strength in the Southwest, West, North, and East. The strongest State Klan was in Indiana, and such wholly un-Southern States as Oregon and Colorado felt its vigor. The second Ku Klux Klan surely belongs to the violent history of America, but, unlike either the first or the third Klans, the Negro was only a secondary target for it. Although denunciation of Catholics and Jews ranked 1-2 in the rhetoric of the second Klan, recent students of the movement have shown that Klan violence—whippings, torture, and murder— were directed less against Catholics, Jews, and Negroes than against ne'er-do-wells and the allegedly immoral of the very same background as the Klansmen: white, Anglo-Saxon, Protestant. The Klan thus attacked Americans of similar background and extraction who refused to conform to the Bible Belt morality that was the deepest passion of the Klan movement of the 1920's.[35] The Ku Klux Klan resurgence of the last 10 years has been largely restricted to the South; it is only too well known for acts of violence against the civil rights movement and desegregation.

Paralleling the Ku Klux Klan have been a host of other movements of racial, ethnic, and religious malice. Before the Civil War the northeastern United States was lacerated by convent burnings and anti-Catholic riots.[36] This "Protestant Crusade" eventually bred the political Know Nothing movement. Anti-Chinese agitation that often burst into violence became a familiar feature of California and the West as the 19th century wore on.[37] In 1891, 11 Italian immigrants were the victims of a murderous mob in New

52

Orleans.[38] The fear and loathing of Catholics (especially Irish and Italians) that often took a violent form was organized in the nonviolent but bigoted American Protective Association (APA) of 1887.[39] Labor clashes of the late-19th century and early-20th century were often in reality ethnic clashes with native old-stock Americans ranged on one side as owners, foremen, and skilled workers against growing numbers of unskilled immigrants—chiefly Jews, Slavs, Italians, and others from Southern and Eastern Europe.[40]

Urban Riots

A number of examples have already exposed urban riots as one of the most tenacious strands in the long history of American violence. The situation seems at its worst today with the country widely believed to be on the verge of some sort of urban apocalypse, but the fact is that our cities have been in a state of more or less continuous turmoil since the colonial period.[41] As early as the latter part of the 17th century the nuclei of the organized North End and South End "mobs" that dominated Boston in the 18th century had already formed. Maritime riots occurred in Boston during the middle-18th century and were general in the colonies in the 1760's.[42] Leading colonial cities of the Revolutionary Era—Charleston, New York, Boston, and Newport, Rhode Island—were all flayed by the Liberty Boy troubles which embodied an alliance of unskilled maritime workers, skilled artisans, and middle-class business and professional men in riotous dissent against toughening British colonial policy as exemplified by the Stamp Act and Townshend Acts.[43]

Economic and political conditions brought more urban turmoil in the post-Revolutionary period of the 1780's and 1790's, and by the mid-19th century, with industrial and urban expansion occurring by leaps and bounds, the cities of America found themselves in the grips of a new era of violence. The pattern of the urban immigrant slum as a matrix of poverty, vice, crime, and violence was set by Five Points in lower Manhattan before the Civil War.[44] Ulcerating slums along the lines of Five Points and severe ethnic and religious strife stemming from the confrontation between burgeoning immigrant groups and the native American element made the 1830's, 1840's, and 1850's a

53

period of sustained urban rioting, particularly in the great cities of the Northeast. It may have been the era of the greatest urban violence that America has ever experienced. During this period at least 35 major riots occurred in the four cities of Baltimore, Philadelphia, New York, and Boston. Baltimore had 12,[45] Philadelphia had 11,[46] New York had 8,[47] and Boston had 4.[48] (The violence also extended into the growing cities of the Midwest and the lower Mississippi Valley; Cincinnati had four major riots during this period.)[49] Among the most important types of riots were labor riots,[50] election riots,[51] antiabolitionist riots,[52] anti-Negro riots,[53] anti-Catholic riots,[54] and riots of various sorts involving the turbulent volunteer firemen's units.[55] Except for Civil War draft riots, the urban violence subsided in the 1860's and 1870's until the year of 1877 produced a tremendous nationwide railroad strike that began along the Baltimore Ohio Railroad and spread to the Far West. Pathological rioting blistered Baltimore and great stretches of Pittsburgh were left in smoking ruins.[56] (The similarity of what befell Baltimore and Pittsburgh in 1877 and Los Angeles, Chicago, Newark, Detroit, Washington, and other cities in 1965-68 is striking.) Many other cities suffered less seriously.

The forces of law and order responded strongly to the 19th-century urban violence. The modern urban police system was created in reaction to the riots of the 1830's, 1840's, and 1850's, and the present National Guard system was developed in response to the uprisings of 1877.[57] To deal with urban tumult vigilantism was also used frequently in the 19th century. The greatest of all American vigilante movements occurred in the newly settled (by Americans) but thoroughly urban and up-to-date San Francisco of 1856; other 19th-century urban vigilante movements occurred in Los Angeles, New Orleans, San Antonio, St. Louis, Cincinnati, Rochester, and Natchez.[58]

The modern era of the urban race riot was inaugurated around the turn of our present century. From 1900 to 1949 there were 33 major interracial disturbances in the United States. During this half century the peak period of violence was from 1915 to 1919 when 22 of the 33 disturbances occurred. (The 1915-19 period of racial disorder was thus comparable to the period from 1964 to the present.) Major riots occurred in Atlanta (1906), Springfield, Ill. (1908),

54

East St. Louis (1917), Chicago (1919), Harlem (1935 and 1943), and Detroit (1943). With the exception of the Harlem riots, whites emerged as the main aggressors in these riots and the bulk of the casualties befell Negroes.[59] Not until the summer of 1964 with the Harlem and Rochester riots and Los Angeles' Watts riot of 1965 did the pattern decisively reverse itself to the present mode of Negro initiative.[60] Since 1964 black rioting has concentrated on property destruction rather than the taking of white lives; this is a new pattern, although it was foreshadowed in the Harlem riots of 1935 and 1943, and as early as 1947, Ralph Ellison brilliantly caught the mood of the property-destruction riot in his novel, *Invisible Man*.[61]

Freelance Multiple Murder

By this term I refer to the murder of many persons by one or two individuals unconnected with any larger organization. (Thus the Chicago St. Valentine's Day massacre of 1929 and the Kansas City Union Station "massacre" of 1933 are both ruled out of consideration here as being the result of large-scale, organized, underworld criminal activity.) It was the summer of 1966 that made Americans wonder whether the freelance multiple murder was becoming the characteristic American crime, for in the space of a few weeks two shocking multiple murders occurred. First, in Chicago, Richard F. Speck murdered, one-by-one, eight student nurses.[62] Then, less than a month later, Charles Whitman ascended to the top of the tower of the University of Texas library in Austin and left tower and campus strewn with 13 dead or dying and 31 wounded as a result of his unerring marksmanship.[63] The utter horror of these two killing rampages attracted worldwide attention, but not a year goes by without the disclosure of one or more multiple murderers. Speck, the hapless product of a blighted personal background, saw himself as "Born to Raise Hell." Whitman came from an upright and respectable middle-class background that was allegedly, on closer examination, a veritable witches cauldron of tensions and hatreds.

Neither Speck nor Whitman was normal in the usual sense of the word, and the freelance multiple murderer is often a fit subject for the abnormal psychologist. (Recently it has been suggested that male killers such as Speck arise from a genetic deficiency involving a chromosomal variation.)[64] But some observers have wondered whether the anxieties and neuroses of contemporary life in America have not led to a rise in the abnormal behavior exemplified by multiple (or "mass") murder. Crime statistics are not sufficiently available to answer the question, but there have been many examples of freelance multiple murderers in American history. The annals of crime in the United States abound with them. Among the earliest were the brutal Harpe brothers, Micajah (Big Harpe) and Wiley (Little Harpe), who in 1798-99 accounted for anywhere from about 20 to 38 victims in the frontier States of Kentucky and Tennessee. Dashing babies' brains against tree trunks in sudden frenzies was a practice that they may have learned from Indians. Finally, in August 1798, a party of Kentucky settlers ended the career of Micajah. Wiley escaped but was captured, tried, and hanged in Mississippi in 1804. So feared and hated were the Harpes that following death the head of each was cut off and displayed as a trophy of triumphant pioneer justice.[65]

Numerous freelance multiple murderers crop up in the 19th century. Among them was the evil Bender family of southeastern Kansas. The Benders from 1871 to 1873 did away with at least 12 unwary travelers who had the bad judgment to choose the Bender roadside house for a meal or lodging. Eventually the Benders were detected but seem to have escaped into anonymity one jump ahead of a posse.[66] Another mass murderer was H. H. Holmes (the *alias* of Hermann Webster Mudgett) of Englewood, Ill. (near Chicago), who confessed to killing 27 people from about 1890 to 1894, many of whom he lured to their death in his bizarre castlelike house while they were attending the Chicago World's Fair in the summer of 1893.[67] While example after example can be named, such questions as the actual number of multiple murders and their relationship to social conditions still await the serious study of the historian.[68]

Political Assassination

Quantitatively, assassination does not bulk large in the history of American violence, but at the highest level of our political system—the Presidency—it has had a heavy impact. In a 100-year span (1865 to 1965) four Presidents (Lincoln, Garfield, McKinley, and Kennedy) fell to assassin's bullets, and others were the intended objects of assassination. One of the victims, Lincoln, was the target of an assassination conspiracy. The other three victims—Garfield, McKinley, and Kennedy—were the prey of free-lance assassins in varying states of mental instability. Charles Guiteau, the slayer of Garfield, was a disappointed officeseeker, but mental derangement seems to have been at the bottom of his action.[69] Both Leon Czolgosz, the killer of McKinley, and Lee Harvey Oswald, Kennedy's assassin, appear to have had strong ideological commitments. Czolgosz was an anarchist, and Oswald was a self-styled Marxist. Both, however, were independent operatives. Czolgosz was rejected by the organized anarchist movement of his day; nor was Oswald a member of the Communist organization in America or of any of the American Marxist splinter groups. Czolgosz seems to have been in the incipient stages of insanity.[70] Evidence amassed by the Warren Commission strongly suggests that Oswald was psychotic, but the Commission itself cautiously refrained from reaching that conclusion.[71]

Although the mortality rate of American Presidents in the last century has been a high one at the hands of assassins, some comfort can be taken in the fact that assassination has not become a part of the American political system as has happened elsewhere in the world, the Middle East, for example. None of the major political parties has resorted—even indirectly—to assassination. Notable, also, is the immunity which other high political officials—the Vice President, the Supreme Court Justices, Cabinet officers, and leading Senators[72] and Congressmen—have enjoyed from assassination.

Despite some prominent cases, assassinations at the State and local level have, on the whole, been few and far between with the exception of New Mexico Territory (discussed below). During the often chaotic Reconstruction period in the South there was once cause celebre: John W. Stephens, a native white Southerner and a rising Radical Republican politician of Caswell County, N. C., was in 1870 the victim of an assassination plot by a local faction of his Klan-oriented Conservative political opponents. Stephens' killers certainly wanted him out of the way be-

57

cause of his political effectiveness, but the killing itself seems to have been more the result of the terrorist impulse of the Ku Klux Klan movement than of any attempt to raise assassination to the level of a systematic political weapon.[73] Apparently similar to the assassination of Stephens was the killing, by "parties unknown," of John M. Clayton, Republican congressional candidate in Arkansas. Although defeated in the fall 1888 election, Clayton was contesting the result when he was killed in January 1889, while visiting Plummerville, Ark.[74]

One of the most famous political assassinations in American history took place at the State level, the fatal wounding of nationally prominent Senator Huey P. Long of Louisiana on September 8, 1935. Long's assassin seems (like the Presidential assassins) not to have been part of a political plot but to have been motivated by personal emotion and grievance, with political resentment of the "Kingfish" being distinctly secondary.[75] An earlier famous (but now forgotten) assassination of a leading State figure did stem from a context of a political conflict. This was the fatal wounding of the Governor-elect of Kentucky, William Goebel, at Frankfort on Janury 30, 1900.[76] Goebel was the charismatic leader of the Democratic Party in Kentucky who had been waging a hot battle against the Republicans and the railroad interests of his State. Goebel's assassination occurred during an infusion into Frankfort of thousands of anti-Goebel Republicans from the hotblooded mountain region of eastern Kentucky. Fatal feuds had often been linked with local political rivalries in the Kentucky mountains in previous decades (see the section above on "Feud Violence"), and it is not surprising that Goebel's assassins seem to have sprung from that background.[77]

Apparently the only place in America where assassination became an integral part of the political system was New Mexico Territory from the end of the Civil War down to about 1900. Many assassinations occurred, among the most prominent being that of Col. Albert J. Fountain, a leading Republican of southern New Mexico, in 1896.[78] Other leading New Mexican politicians narrowly missed being killed, and many New Mexicans were convinced that the two chieftains of the Republican and Democratic Parties, respectively, had been involved in assassination plots. Thomas B. Catron, the autocratic Republican boss, was thought by many to have been a party to one of the notable assassinations of the era; Catron himself seems to have been the target of an unsuccessful assassination attempt.[79] The recent biographer of Colonel Fountain has brought forth strong evidence to support his charge that Albert Bacon Fall, the incisive Democratic leader,[80] was guilty of leading complicity in the plot against Fountain.[81] The most important point is that virtually all political factions in New Mexico accepted and used assassination as a way of eliminating troublesome opponents.[82]

The frightening phenomenon of assassination in territorial New Mexico still awaits searching study by the historian. In the absence of such a study it is hard to say just why assassination became such a prominent political feature in New Mexico alone. The territory was indeed a violent one at the time; it was scarred by a savage Indian war (with the Apaches), numerous vigilante movements and lynch mobs, a host of criminal outlaws (Billy the Kid, Clay Allison, and others), and mordant local conflicts such as the Lincoln County war and the Maxwell Land Grant troubles. Such a high level of violence might well have had the effect of skewing the political system in the direction of assassination as a tactic, although this did not happen in neighboring Texas, which at the time was every bit as violent as New Mexico. Nor does the large Latin element of the population seem to have imputed a fatal measure of volatility to the political climate of New Mexico Territory, for native Anglo-American politicians such as Catron (from Missouri) and Fall (from Kentucky) were leaders in a political system that was characterized, often, by assassination.

A third explanation of political assassination in New Mexico is suggested by social scientists who have recently posited a "contagion phenomenon" in regard to "highly publicized and dramatic acts of deviant behavior" such as prison riots, bomb scares, slum uprisings, mass murder, and psychopathic sexual acts.[83] Beginning with the first assassination in New Mexico (that of the Territorial chief justice, John P. Slough, in 1867), it is possible that something like a "contagion phenomenon" set in to perpetuate assassination until it became a part of the political system itself. After 1900 the level of general turbulence in New Mexico life subsided. It may have been no coincidence that the politics of assassination faded, too. Students of the "contagion phenomenon" have seen it as a short-run phenomenon characterized by an accelerating pace followed by an abrupt end which might, in long-run terms, be analogous to New Mexico's experience.

The tragic history of assassination in New Mexico Territory may be an ill portent for our own era. It is conceivable that the wave of assassinations in recent years which cut down John F. Kennedy, Robert F. Kennedy, Martin Luther King, Jr., Medgar Evers, and Malcolm X is a contemporary example of the "contagion phenomenon." The danger is not to be found in the "contagion phenomenon" alone but in the grim possibility that, as happened in New Mexico, assassination might become a persistent feature of the public behavior of our people.

POSITIVE VIOLENCE

Police Violence

The law enforcement system in colonial America was quite simple, consisting mainly of sheriffs for the counties and constables for the cities and towns. With the tremendous expansion of population and territory in the 19th century, the system took on much greater complexity. Added to the county sheriffs and local constables were municipal police systems, State police (including such special and elite forces as the Rangers of Texas[84] and Arizona), and Federal marshals and Treasury agents. The most important development of the century was the development of the modern urban police system in the midcentury years from 1844 to 1877. The new system was a direct response to the great urban riots of the 1830's, 1840's, and 1850's. The antiquated watch-and-ward system (daytime constables and nighttime watchmen) was simply inadequate to cope with the large-scale rioting and increasing urban disorder. The reform in the police system came first in New York, Philadelphia, Boston, and other cities which had acute problems of criminal violence and rioting.[85] Thus the riot era of the 1830-50's produced the present urban police system. Perhaps the riots of the 1960's will similarly spur the "professionalization" of the police—a major reform that is being widely called for at the present.

Scarcely less important than the development of the urban police system was the creation of the National Guard to replace the obsolete State militia system that dated back to the 18th century. The rapid development of the National Guard system in the 1880's was largely a response to the great urban labor riots of 1877. The National Guard was established first and most rapidly in the leading industrial States of the North that were highly vulnerable to labor unrest: Massachusetts, Connecticut, New York, Pennsylvania, Ohio, and Illinois. By 1892, the system was complete throughout the Nation.[86] Officered primarily by business and professional men and sometimes the recipients of large subsidies from wealthy industrialists,[87] National Guard contingents were often called out to suppress labor violence from the late-19th century down to the time of World War II.

In the latter half of the 19th century there also grew up a sort of parapolice system with the founding of numerous private detective agencies (headed by the famed Pinkerton National Detective Agency) [88] and the burgeoning of thousands of local antihorsethief associations or detecting societies which often were authorized by State laws and invested with limited law enforcement powers.[89] After the Civil War, industrial corporations frequently set up their own police forces. Most notable in this category were the private coal and iron police which the State of Pennsylvania authorized to deal with labor unrest in mines and mills.[90] It was during the 19th century, as well, that the science of crime detection was inaugurated.[91]

Undue violence in the course of enforcing the law has long been a matter of concern. In an earlier generation the public worried about the employment of the "third degree" to obtain criminal confessions.[92] In our own time the concern is with "police brutality," chiefly against Negroes. Related to the use of violence by police in the prosecution of their regular duties has been the large measure of violence associated with the incarceration of the convicted in jails and prisons. For over a century and a half we have gone through bursts of prison reform only to have the system as a whole lapse back into (if indeed it ever really transcended) its normal characteristics of brutality and sadism. As time has passed many of the most well-meaning reforms (such as the early-19th-century system of solitary confinement) have proved to be ill conceived.[93] Even as our knowledge and expertise have increased, prison reform has foundered again and again on the rock of inadequate financial support from an uncaring society.

Revolutionary Violence

Our nation was conceived and born in violence—in the violence of the Sons of Liberty and the patriots of the American port cities of the 1760's and 1770's. Such an event was the Boston Massacre of 1770 in which five defiant Americans were killed. British officers and troops had been goaded by patriotic roughnecks into perpetrating the so-called massacre. The whole episode stemmed naturally from the century-long heritage of organized mob violence in Boston. The same thing was true of the Boston Tea Party wherein the anciently organized South End Mob of Boston was enlisted in the tea-dumping work. During the long years of resistance to British policy in the 1760's and 1770's the North End and South End Mobs under the leadership of Samuel Swift and Ebenezer MacKintosh had been more or less at the beck and call of Samuel Adams, the mastermind of patriot agitation, and the middle-class patriots who made up the "Loyal Nine." [94]

With the decision in 1774 to resist the British by military means, the second round of Revolutionary violence began. The main goal of Revolutionary violence in the transitional period from 1774 to 1777 was to intimidate the Tories who existed in fairly large numbers in the seaport cities and hinterland. The countrywide Continental Association of 1774 was drawn up to cause an interruption of all trade between the Colonies and the mother country, but a related purpose was to ferret out Tories, expose them to public contumely and intimidation, and bring them to heel or to silence.[95] Where exposure in the newspapers was not enough, strong-arm tactics were used against the Tories. The old American custom of tarring and feathering was mainly a product of the patriotic campaign to root out Toryism.[96]

Aside from the regular clash of the Continental and British armies, the third and final phase of Revolutionary violence was the guerrilla strife that occurred all the way from the Hudson to the Savannah. Wherever strong British occupying forces were to be found—as in New York City,

Philadelphia, and Charleston—in opposition to an American-dominated hinterland, the result was the polarization of the population and the outbreak of savage guerrilla strife, desperate hit-and-run forays, and the thrust and counter-thrust of pillage and mayhem. Thus the lower Hudson valley of New York was the theatre of rival bush-whacking parties of Whigs and Tories. The Hackensack Valley of North Jersey, opposite the British bastion on Manhattan Island, was a sort of no man's land across which bands of Whigs and Tories fought and ravaged.[97] South Jersey's bleak and trackless pine barrens furnished ideal cover for the "land pirates" of both Whig and Tory persuasion spewed up by the British and American competition for the allegiance of New Jersey and the Philadelphia area.[98]

South Carolina emerged as the great battlefield of the war after 1780. North Carolina and Georgia suffered at the same time from the scourge of guerrilla strife, but their casualties were light compared to the dreadful cut-and-thrust of the Whig and Tory forces in the Palmetto State where Andrew Pickens, Thomas Sumter, and Francis Marion led Whig partisan bands in their own particular sectors of the back country. Negro slaves were stolen back and forth, and baleful figures like the half-crazed Tory leader, Bloody Bill Cunningham, emerged from the shadows to wreak special brands of murder and massacre. Neither side showed the other any mercy. Prisoners were tortured and hanged.[99] Virginia felt the destruction of Benedict Arnold's vengeful campaign (1781) but experienced nothing like the suffering of South Carolina. Still it was characteristic of the rising passions of the time that strife among Whigs and Tories in Virginia's Piedmont, as noted earlier, gave rise to an early manifestation of lynch law.

Two things stand out about the Revolution. The first, of course, is that it was successful and immediately became enshrined in our tradition and history. The second is that the meanest and most squalid sort of violence was from the very beginning to the very last put to the service of Revolutionary ideals and objectives. The operational philosophy that the end justifies the means became the keynote of Revolutionary violence. Thus given sanctification by the Revolution, Americans have never been loathe to employ the most unremitting violence in the interest of any cause deemed to be a good one.

Civil War Violence

Violence was interwoven with the creation of the American nation. By the same token, it became the ineradicable handmaiden of its salvation in the era of Civil War and Reconstruction. The Civil War era was not only one of pervasive violence in its own right but had an almost incalculable effect on the following decades. The latter part of the 19th century was one of the most violent periods of American history—an era of Ku Kluxers, lynch mobs, White Caps, Bald Knobbers, night riders, feudists, and outlaws. The major part of this violence is traceable to the Civil War.

The years of prelude to the Civil War were years of mounting violence in both North and South. Feeling against the Fugitive Slave Law in the North gave rise to vigilance committees concerned with protecting runaway slaves and to increasingly fervent abolitionism. Below the Mason-Dixon Line abolitionists had long since ceased to exist in anything but the hallucinations of slaveholders and Southern nationalists. But from these delusions were formed vigilante movements to deal with the nonexistent abolitionists. Violence of the most tangible sort was far from absent. Bleeding Kansas was truly just that as marauding bands of slaveholder and antislaveholder sympathizers surged through the unhappy territory.

In the East, John Brown's raid on Harpers Ferry sent a tremor of fear through those who genuinely wished to forestall a bloody civil war. For the more sanguinary in the North, John Brown was an inspiration for holy war against slavery; to the warminded in the South the John Brown raid was seen as proof that the South could never rest easy in a Union that included free States and harbored abolitionists. The nation sensed that it was on the verge of a grand Armageddon.[100] The general nervousness came to a height in the South in the summer of 1860 as that section gloomily awaited the almost certain election of Lincoln. Forebodings never far from the surface suddenly blazed to the top in the Great Fear that swept across the South in the summer of 1860. From the Rio Grande to

the Atlantic were exposed plot after plot by secret abolitionists and unionists for the raising up of slaves in bloody
rebellion.[101] At this distance it seems that the fears of slave
uprisings were groundless, but portions of the South were
in the grips of a hysteria that was real enough. Vigilante
groups and self-styled committees of safety blazed up.[102]
The Great Fear of the South in the summer of 1860 seems
to have been as baseless in fact as the remarkably similar
Great Fear that swept the French peasantry in the first
year of the French Revolution.[103] Both Great Fear and
grande peur revealed the profound anxieties which lacerated the white Southerners and the French peasants in the
summers of 1860 and 1789, respectively.

In symbolic terms, the Great Fear on the eve of the
Civil War was altogether fitting as a prelude to the decade
and more of violence and mischief that would follow. The
struggle between the Northern and Southern armies still
stands as the most massive military bloodletting in American history, but almost forgotten is the irregular underwar
of violence and guerrilla strife that paralleled the regular
military action. In numerous localities throughout the
North, resistance to the military draft was continuous and
violent. The apogee of resistance to the draft occurred
with the massive riots of 1863 in New York City when
the city was given over to three days of virtually uncontrolled rioting.[104] Related troubles occurred throughout the
war years in southern Indiana, southern Illinois, and southern Iowa where widespread Copperhead feeling caused
large-scale disaffection, antidraft riots, and guerrilla fighting between Union soldiers and Union deserters and other
Copperhead sympathizers.[105] The guerrilla war that took
place along the Kansas-Missouri border has seldom been
equaled for unmitigated savagery. Jim Lane and his fearsome Kansas Jayhawkers traded brutal blows with the
Confederate guerrillas of Missouri headed by the band of
William Quantrell that included Frank and Jesse James
and the Younger boys.[106] Kentucky, too, was the scene of
frequent ambushes and affrays.[107]

The Confederate South was bedeviled by pockets of resistance to official policy. The mountain regions of north
Arkansas, north Alabama, and eastern Tennessee had important centers of Unionist sentiment that never became
reconciled to the war effort.[108] Even Mississippi contained

one county (Jones) that was perforated with disloyalty to the Confederate cause[109]—as did Alabama (Winston). The frontier areas of northern and central Texas were liberally dotted with Unionist sympathizers and antislavery Germans. At best the German-Americans never gave more than grudging support to the War and sometimes resorted to sabotage. The result was brutal retaliation by the "heelflies" (Confederate home guards) who were often quite careless of whom they injured.[110]

Perhaps no event in American history bred more violence than the Civil War. Racial strife and Ku Klux Klan activity became routine in the old Confederate states. Regulator troubles broke out in central Kentucky and the Blue Grass region. Outlaw and vigilante activity flamed in Texas, Kansas, and Missouri. Outbreaks of feuding scorched the southern Appalachians and Texas. As late as the closing years of the century white capping, bald knobbing, and night riding, while spurred by particular social and economic causes, remained as legacies of the violent emotions and methods fired by the Civil War.[111]

Indian Wars

Unquestionably the longest and most remorseless war in American history was the one between whites and Indians that began in Tidewater, Virginia, in 1607 and continued with only temporary truces for nearly 300 years down to the final massacre at Wounded Knee, South Dakota in 1890. The implacable hostility that came to rule white-Indian relations was by no means inevitable. The small Indian population that existed in the continental United States allowed plenty of room for the expansion of white settlement. The economic resources of the white settlers were such that the Indians could have been easily and fairly reimbursed for the land needed for occupation by the whites. In fact, a model of peaceful white-Indian relations was developed in 17th-century New England by John Eliot, Roger Williams, and other Puritan statesmen. The same was true in 18th-century Pennsylvania where William Penn's humane and equitable policy toward the Indians brought that colony decades of white-Indian amity.[112] Racial prejudice and greed in the mass of New England whites finally reaped the whirlwind in King Philip's War of 1675-76, which shattered the peaceful New England model.[113] Much later the same sort of thing happened in Pennsylvania in 1763 when Pontiac's Rebellion (preceded by increasing tensions) ended the era of amicable white-Indian relations in the Keystone colony.

Other Indian wars proliferated during the 17th and 18th centuries, nor did the pace of the conflict slacken in the 19th century. It is possible that no other factor has exercised a more brutalizing influence on the American character than the Indian wars. The struggles with the Indians have sometimes been represented as being "just" wars in the interest of promoting superior Western civilization at the expense of the crude stone-age culture of the Indians. The recent ethnohistorical approach to the interpretation of white-Indian relations has given us a more balanced understanding of the relative merits of white and Indian civilizations. The norms of Indian warfare were, however, at a more barbaric level than those of Western Europe. Among the Indians of Eastern America torture was an accepted and customary part of warmaking.[114] In their violent encounters with Indians, the white settlers brought themselves down to the barbaric level of Indian warfare. Scalping was adopted by white men,[115] and down to the very last battle at Wounded Knee lifting the hair of an Indian opponent was the usual practice among experienced white fighters. Broken treaties, unkept promises, and the slaughter of defenseless women and children all, along with the un-European atrocity of taking scalps, continued to characterize the white American's mode of dealing with the Indians. The effect on our national character has not been a healthy one; it has done much to shape our proclivity to violence.

Vigilante Violence

The first large-scale American vigilante movement (and probably the first of any size) occurred in the South Carolina back country in the late 1760's.[116] The phenomenon of vigilantism seems to be native to the American soil. The British Isles—especially Scotland and Ireland—were violent enough in the 17th and 18th centuries, but vigilantism was unknown in the British Isles; taking the law into one's own hands (the classic definition of vigilantism) was repugnant to ancient British legal tradition. Vigilantism arose as a response to a typical American problem: the absence of effective law and order in a frontier region. It was a problem that occurred again and again beyond the Appalachian Mountains. It stimulated the formation of hundreds of frontier vigilante movements.

The first phase of American vigilantism happened mainly before the Civil War and dealt largely with the threat of frontier horsethieves and counterfeiters. Virtually every State or territory west of the Appalachians possessed one or more well-organized, relentless vigilante movements. We have tended to think of the vigilante movement as being typical of the Western plains and mountains, but in actuality there was much vigilantism east of the Missouri and Mississippi Rivers. The main thrust of vigilantism was to reestablish in each newly settled frontier area the community structure of the old settled areas along with the values of property, law, and order. Vigilante movements were characteristically in the control of the frontier elite and represented their social values and preferences. This was true of the first vigilante movement in South Carolina, 1767-69 (who were known as "Regulators"—the original but now obsolete term for vigilantes) and it was also true of the greatest of all American vigilante movements, that of San Francisco in 1856. The San Francisco vigilance committee of 1856 was dominated lock, stock, and barrel by the leading merchants of the city who organized to stamp out alleged crime and political corruption.[117]

Although the typical vigilante movements were dominated by social conservatives who desired to establish order and stability in newly settled areas, there were disconcertingly numerous departures from the norm. Many vigilante movements led not to order but to increasing disorder and anarchy. In such cases vigilantism left things in a worse condition than had been true before. Frequently the strife between vigilantes and their opponents (exacerbated by individual, family, and political hatreds) became so bitter and untrammeled that order could be restored only by the Governor calling out the militia. Such was the case when the Bald Knobbers of the Missouri Ozarks rose in 1885-86 to curb the evils of theft, liquor, gambling, and prostitution in Taney and Christian Counties. Intervention by outside authorities was finally needed.[118]

The elite nature of 19th-century vigilantism is revealed

by the prominent men who belonged to vigilante movements. Included in a "Who's Who of American Vigilantism" would be U.S. Senators and Congressmen, Governors, judges, wealthy capitalists, generals, lawyers, and even clergymen. Even Presidents of the United States have not been immune to the vigilante infection. While serving in the Presidency, Andrew Jackson once approved the resort of Iowa pioneers to vigilante methods pending the clarification of their territorial status.[119] As a young cattle rancher in North Dakota, Theodore Roosevelt begged to be admitted to a vigilante band that was being formed to deal with rustlers and horsethieves. The cattlemen rebuffed the impetuous young Harvard blueblood but went on with their vigilante movement.[120] Today among educated men of standing vigilantism is viewed with disapproval, but it was not always so in the 19th century. In those days leading men were often prominent members of vigilante movements and proud of it.

America changed from the basically rural nation it had been in the antebellum era to an urban, industrial nation after the Civil War. The institution of vigilantism changed to match the altering character of the nation. From a generally narrow concern with the classic frontier problems of horsethieves and counterfeiters, vigilantism broadened its scope to include a variety of targets connected with the tensions of the new America: Catholics, Jews, Negroes, immigrants, laboring men and labor leaders, political radicals, advocates of civil liberties, and nonconformists in general. Neovigilantism flourished as a symptom of the growing pains of post-Civil War industrial America but utterly failed as a solution to the complex social problems of the era.[121]

The post-Civil War era also saw the climax of two movements with strong affinities to vigilantism. One was the antihorsethief association movement which had its greatest growth in the rural Midwest and Southwest after the Civil War, although its roots were to be found in the northeastern United States as early as the 1790's. The antihorsethief society pattern involved State charter of local associations which were often vested with constabulary power. By 1900 the antihorsethief association movement numbered hundreds of thousands of members in its belt of greatest strength, which stretched from the Great Lakes to the Rio Grande. Forming a flexible and inexpensive (the members shared costs whenever they arose) supplement to immobile, expensive, and inefficient local law enforcement, the antihorsethief association afforded the farmer insurance against the threat of horse and other types of theft. With the rapid development of the automobile around the time of World War I the antihorsethief association movement lost its *raison d'etre*.[122]

Quite different in character was the White Cap[123] movement. White Caps first appeared in southern Indiana in 1888,[124] but in short order the phenomenon had spread to the four corners of the nation. The White Cap movement copied the vigilante movements of the late-18th and early-19th centuries in its preference for flogging as a mode of punishment. White Capping varied greatly from locality to locality and region to region. In North Texas the White Caps were anti-Negro;[125] in South Texas they were anti-Mexican;[126] and in northern New Mexico the White Caps were a movement of poor Mexican herders and ranchers against land-enclosing rich Mexicans and Americans.[127]

In general, however, White Capping was most prevalent as a sort of spontaneous movement for the moral regulation of the poor whites and ne'er-do-wells of the rural American countryside. Thus drunken, shiftless, and wife-beating whites who often abused their families were typical targets of White Cap violence.[128] Loose women frequently became the victims of White Caps.[129] Vigilantism going back to the South Carolina Regulators of 1767-69 had often been concerned with the moral regulation of incorrigible whites, and hence White Capping was in part a throwback to the early era of frontier vigilantism. At the same time, White Capping seems to have been an important link between the first and second Ku Klux Klans. White Cap methods in regard to punishment and costume seem to have been influenced by the first Klan, while White Cap attacks on immoral and shiftless whites foreshadowed the main thrust of the second Klan of the 1920's. Chronologically, the White Cap movement formed a neat link between the first and second Klans. White Capping began in the 1880's about two decades after the first Klan, and by the turn of the century it had become such a generic term for local American violence that Booth Tarkington made White Cap violence the pivot of his popular novel, *The Gentleman from*

Indiana (1899).[130] At the time of World War I, White Capping was fading from view; shortly thereafter the second Ku Klux Klan rose to take its place.

Agrarian Uprisings

The tree of liberty from time immemorial in America has been nurtured by a series of movements in behalf of the ever-suffering farmer or yeoman. Often these movements—generally considered to be liberal in their political character—have been formed for the purposes of redressing the economic grievances of the farmer; at times they have been land reform movements. The dissident-farmer movements have been deemed among the most heroic of all American movements of political insurgence; they have been the especial favorites of historians who with love and sympathy have chronicled their ups and downs. There have been a host of these agrarian uprisings, and they have been equally prevalent in both the colonial and national periods of our history. The initial agrarian uprising was that behind Nathaniel Bacon in late-17th-century Virginia[131] followed by the New Jersey land rioters of the 18th century.[132] Similarly, in the 1760's were the Paxton Boys movement of Pennsylvania,[133] the North Carolina Regulators (not a vigilante movement but one for reform of local government),[134] and the New York antirent movement (which stretched on into the 19th century).[135] With the gaining of independence there appeared Shays' Rebellion in Massachusetts (1786-87),[136] the Whiskey Rebellion in western Pennsylvania (1794),[137] and Fries' Rebellion in eastern Pennsylvania (1798-99).[138] Farther west—in the Mississippi Valley before the Civil War—there appeared the Claim Clubs to defend the land occupancy of squatters.[139]

After the Civil War a plethora of economic problems for the farmer gave rise to the Grangers, the Greenbackers, the Farmers' Alliance (which originally began in central Texas as a quasi-vigilante movement),[140] and the Populist Party.[141] About the same time there appeared a land-reform movement in California against the monopoly land-holding of the Southern Pacific Railroad,[142] and in New Mexico there appeared the previously mentioned White Cap movement of poor Mexicans against the land-enclosing tactics of well-to-do Mexicans and Americans. Western

Kentucky and the Ohio-Mississippi Valley area, generally, were the scene of a tobacco farmers' cooperative movement in the early 1900's to end the control of the American Tobacco Co. and foreign companies over the marketing system.[143] Farmers became increasingly attracted to the Socialist Party, and the nonindustrial State of Oklahoma soon led the nation in Socialist Party members. Connected with the rise of socialism among Oklahoma farmers was the appearance there during World War I of the Working Class Union which developed into a pacifist, antidraft movement of sharecroppers and small farmers.[144] In the upper Great Plains there rose in North Dakota in 1915 the radical Non-partisan League which enacted many reforms in that State and inspired similar progressive farm movements in other States of the Northwest.[145] The Farm bloc emerged in Congress in the 1920's to promote legislation for easing the agricultural depression. When conditions worsened in the 1930's, the Farmers' Holiday Association was formed in the Midwest to lead farmer strikes and boycotts against the economic system.[146] In our own 1960's the National Farmers' Organization has adopted similar tactics.

The insurgent farmer movements have thus formed one of the longest and most enduring chronicles in the history of American reform but one that has been blighted again and again with violence. Nathaniel Bacon's movement became a full-fledged rebellion that resulted in the burning of Jamestown. The New Jersey land rioters used violence to press their claims against the Jersey land companies. The New York antirent movement frequently used force against the dominant landlords. The North Carolina Regulators rioted against the courthouse rings that ground them under the burden of heavy taxes and rapacious fees. The Paxton Boys of Pennsylvania followed their massacre of Indians with a march on Philadelphia. The followers of Daniel Shays in Massachusetts broke up court sessions in order to forestall land foreclosures. The farmers of Pennsylvania rose in rebellion against taxes on liquor and land in the Whiskey and Fries uprisings. The Western Claims Clubs (which, paradoxically, were sometimes dominated by land speculators pursuing their own interests) used intimidation to protect "squatters' rights." The land reform movement in California spawned a night-rider league in Tulare County, 1878-80, to resist railroad land agents. The tobacco farmer cooperative movement in Kentucky did not succeed in breaking monopoly domination of the marketing system until it utilized a "Night Rider" organization that raided several western Kentucky towns, destroyed tobacco warehouses, and abused noncooperating farmers. The New Mexican White Caps employed a reign of terror to fight the land-enclosure movement. The Working Class Union of Oklahoma spawned the Green Corn Rebellion; the "rebels" contemplated only a peaceful march on Washington but did arm themselves and committed a few acts of violence before being rooted out of the hills and breaks along the South Canadian River by sheriffs and posses. The Farmers' Holiday Association dumped milk cans, blocked roads, and roughed up opponents. Farmer grievances have been serious. Repeatedly farmers used higher law—the need to right insufferable wrongs, the very justification of the American Revolution—to justify the use of violence in uprising after uprising.

Labor Violence

The labor movement in American history has been bathed in the same sort of glorification that has annointed the agrarian uprisings. Most would agree that by raising the health and living standard of the working man the American labor movement has been a significant factor in advancing the social well-being of the nation. But the labor movement reveals the same mixture of glorious ends with inglorious means—violence—that has characterized the agrarian movement. (Ironically, the white "backlash" against black uprisings in the cities of today has been strongest in the rural countryside and the "blue collar" metropolitan wards, i.e., among the inheritors of the violent agrarian and labor movements.)

A rudimentary labor movement was to be found in the port cities of the colonial period. While there was no organization of laborers as such, sailors, longshoremen, and other workers of the maritime industry occasionally rioted—stirred up by impressment gangs and sporadic economic stringency.[147] The unskilled workers and skilled artisans who contributed the force to the violent Liberty Boy movement of the 1760's were made especially restless and turbulent by the economic depression that followed the end of the Great War for the Empire.[148]

It is with the coming of the Industrial Revolution to America in the 19th century that the labor movement really gets underway, particularly as a concomitant of the tremendous growth of American industry after the Civil War. Various labor organizations mushroomed: the Knights of Labor, American Railway Union, American Federation of Labor, Western Federation of Miners (WFM), and the Industrial Workers of the World (IWW). All made the strike a major weapon, and in case after case violence broke out in accompaniment of the strike. The blame was certainly not on the side of labor alone. The unyielding attitude of capitalists in regard to wages, hours, working conditions, and the desire to unionize led to the calling of strikes. Violent attempts of capital to suppress unions and break up strikes frequently incited the workers to violence. But laborers, too, were often more than ready to resort to violence, as many of the great upheavals after the Civil War indicate. The great railroad strike of 1877 triggered massive riots that in Pittsburgh reached the level of insurrection. About the same time the decade-long Molly Maguire [149] troubles in the hard coal field of eastern Pennsylvania came to a climax. The Molly Maguires were a secret organization of Irish miners who fought their employers with assassination and mayhem.[150] Such events as the Haymarket Riot in Chicago (1886),[151] the Homestead strike (1892),[152] the Coeur d'Alene, Idaho, silver mining troubles (1892ff), and the 1910 dynamiting of the Los Angeles *Times* building (by the McNamara brothers of the supposedly conservative American Federation of Labor)[153] led Louis Adamic correctly to label the late-19th-early-20th-century period as the era of dynamite in American labor relations.

The Western mining State of Colorado affords a paradigm of the dynamite era of labor violence. From 1884 to 1914, Colorado had its own "Thirty Years War" of strikes and violence which typified the economic, class, and ethnic tensions of the period.[154] Colorado's 30-year period of acute labor violence came to a climax with what may have been the most violent upheaval in American labor history: the coal miners' strike against the Colorado Fuel & Iron Co., 1913-14. During the first 5 weeks of the strike

74

(which took place in southern Colorado) there were 38 armed skirmishes in which 18 persons were killed. The final horror took place on April 20, 1914, at Ludlow, Colorado. A 15-hour battle between strikers and militiamen ended in the burning of the strikers' tent city during which 2 mothers and 11 children suffocated to death in the "Black Hole of Ludlow." Following this tragedy, maddened miners erupted in a 10-day rebellion which brought "anarchy and unrestrained class warfare" to a 250-mile area of southern Colorado before the entrance of Federal troops ended the violence.[155] The Ludlow conflict was in truth an actualization of the apocalyptic visions of class warfare of Jack London (in *The Iron Heel*)[156] and other writers of the period.

The last great spasm of violence in the history of American labor came in the 1930's with the sitdown strike movement which accompanied the successful drive to unionize the automobile and other great mass-production industries.

CONCLUSION

What is to be made of this survey of violence in American history? The first and most obvious conclusion is that there has been a huge amount of it. It is not merely that violence has been mixed with the negative features of our history such as criminal activity, lynch mobs, and family feuds. On the contrary, violence has formed a seamless web with some of the noblest and most constructive chapters of American history: the birth of the nation (Revolutionary violence), the freeing of the slaves and the preservation of the Union (Civil War violence), the occupation of the land (Indian wars), the stabilization of frontier society (vigilante violence), the elevation of the farmer and the laborer (agrarian and labor violence), and the preservation of law and order (police violence). The patriot, the humanitarian, the nationalist, the pioneer, the landholder, the farmer, and the laborer (and the capitalist) have used violence as the means to a higher end.

All too often unyielding and unsympathetic established political and economic power has incited violence by its refusal to heed and redress just grievances. Thus Governor Berkeley of Virginia ignored the pleas of Virginia planters and the result was Bacon's Rebellion. Thus the British government in 1774-76 remained adamant in the face of patriot pleas, and the result was the American Revolution. Thus the tobacco trust scoffed at the grievances of farmers, and the result was the Kentucky Night Rider movement. Thus American capitalists ground workers into the dust, and the result was the violent labor movement. The possessors of power and wealth have been prone to refuse to share their attributes until it has been too late. Arrogance is indeed a quality that comes to unchecked power more readily than sympathy and forbearance.

By the same token, one can argue that the aggrieved in American history have been too quick to revolt, too hastily violent. We have resorted so often to violence that we have long since become a "trigger happy" people. Violence is ostensibly rejected by us as a part of the American value system, but so great has been our involvement with both negative and positive violence over the long sweep of our history that violence has truly become a part of our unacknowledged (or underground) value structure.

Two major problems remain if we as Americans are ever to break our bondage to violence. One is the problem of self-knowledge: We must recognize that, despite our pious official disclaimers, we have always operated with a heavy dependence upon violence in even our highest and most idealistic endeavors. We must take stock of what we have done rather than what we have said. When that is done, the realization that we have been an incorrigibly violent people is overwhelming. We must realize that violence has not been the action only of the roughnecks and racists among us but has been the tactic of the most upright and respected of our people. Having gained this self-knowledge, the next problem becomes the ridding of violence, once and for all, from the real (but unacknowledged) American value system. Only then will we begin to solve our social, economic, and political problems by social, economic, and political means rather than evading them by resort to the dangerous and degrading use of violence.

References

1. Eric J. Hobsbawm, *Social Bandits and Primitive Rebels* (Glencoe, Ill.: The Free Press, 1959).
2. William A. Settle, Jr., *Jesse James Was His Name or Fact and Fiction Concerning the Careers of the Notorious James Brothers of Missouri* (Columbia, Mo.: University of Missouri Press, 1966).

3. For the enormous literature on Billy the Kid, see Ramon F. Adams, *A Fitting Death for Billy the Kid* (Norman, Okla.: University of Oklahoma Press, 1960).

4. Paul I. Wellman, *A Dynasty of Western Outlaws* (New York: Doubleday, 1961), ch. 12. This provocative book traces a Southwestern criminal dynasty from William C. Quantrill and the Jameses to Pretty Boy Floyd.

5. John Toland, *The Dillinger Days* (New York: Random House, 1963).

6. Herbert Asbury, *The Gangs of New York: An Informal History of the Underworld* (New York and London: Alfred A. Knopf, 1928). A significant study of the general level of urban criminal violence is the paper in this volume by Roger Lane, "Urbanization and Criminal Violence in the Nineteenth Century: Massachusetts as a Test Case."

7. Leo Katcher, *The Big Bankroll: The Life and Times of Arnold Rothstein* (New York: Harper, 1959).

8. Fred J. Cook, *The Secret Rulers: Criminal Syndicates and How They Control the U.S.* (New York: Duell, Sloan & Pearce, 1966).

9. Estes Kefauver, *Crime in America*, Sidney Shalett, ed. (Garden City, N.Y.: Doubleday, 1961).

10. *The Challenge of Crime in a Free Society: A Report of the President's Commission on Law Enforcement and Administration of Justice* (Washington, D.C.: U.S. Government Printing Office, 1967), pp. 187-200.

11. Virgil C. Jones, *The Hatfields and the McCoys* (Chapel Hill, N.C.: University of North Carolina Press, 1948).

12. Meriel D. Harris, "Two Famous Kentucky Feuds and Their Causes" (unpublished M.A. thesis, University of Kentucky, 1940).

13. Rufus L. Gardner, *The Courthouse Tragedy, Hillsville, Va.* (Mt. Airy, N.C.: Rufus L. Gardner, 1962).

14. On "Devil Anse" Hatfield, see Jones, *Hatfields and McCoys*, pp. 2-3 and *passim*. On Judge James Hargis, see Harris, "Two Famous Kentucky Feuds," pp. 100, 104, and *passim*.

15. The major feuds of Texas are related by C[harles] L. Sonnichsen in two outstanding books: *I'll Die before I'll Run: The Story of the Great Feuds of Texas* (revised edition; New York: Devin-Adair, 1961), and *Ten Texas Feuds* (Albuquerque, N.Mex.: University of New Mexico Press, 1957).

16. Sonnichsen, *I'll Die before I'll Run*, pp. 35-115.

17. *Ibid.*, pp. 125-149, 232-281, and 299-315.

18. One of the most spectacular of the family-factional feuds in New Mexico was the Lincoln County War, 1878 ff., from which Billy the Kid emerged to fame. See Maurice G. Fulton, *History of the Lincoln County War*, Robert N. Mullin, ed. (Tucson, Ariz.: University of Arizona Press, 1968).

19. See the section in this paper on "Political Assassination."

20. Earle R. Forrest, *Arizona's Dark and Bloody Ground* (Caldwell, Idaho: Caxton Printers, 1936). Zane Grey, *To the Last Man* (New York and London: Harper, 1922).

21. Mitford M. Mathews, ed., *A Dictionary of Americanisms on Historical Principals* (one-volume edition, Chicago: University of Chicago Press, 1956), p. 1010.

22. Brown, *South Carolina Regulators*, pp. 38-39 ff.

23. James E. Cutler, *Lynch-Law: An Investigation into the History of Lynching in the United States* (New York: Longmans, Green, 1905), pp. 24-31.

24. *Ibid.*, p. 177.

25. *Ibid.*

26. In addition to Cutler, *Lynch-Law*, see Walter White, *Rope & Faggot: A Biography of Judge Lynch* (New York and London: Alfred A. Knopf, 1929), and Arthur F. Raper, *The Tragedy of Lynching* (Chapel Hill, N.C.: University of North Carolina Press, 1938).

27. Cutler, *Lynch-Law*, pp. 180-181 and *passim*. A total of 3,337 Americans were lynched from 1882 to 1903. Of the victims, 1,169 were whites, 2,060 were Negroes, and 108 were of other races.

28. Winthrop D. Jordan, *White Over Black: American Attitudes Toward the Negro, 1550-1812* (Chapel Hill, N.C.: University of North Carolina Press, 1968), pp. 115-120. Jordan's massive study is essential for understanding the major cause of American racial violence; i.e., white prejudice against the Negro.

29. Herbert Aptheker, *American Negro Slave Revolts* (New York: Columbia University Press, 1943), pp. 219-227. Aptheker's book is the most complete treatment of the subject, although some scholars feel that he has

exaggerated the degree of violent rebellion by slaves. An able recent treatment is M[artin] D. DeB. Kilson, "Towards Freedom: An Analysis of Slave Revolts in the United States," *Phylon*, vol. XXV (1964), pp. 175-187.

30. *Ibid.*
31. William S. Drewry, *The Southampton Insurrection* (Washington, D.C.: Neale Co., 1900). See also Herbert Aptheker, *Nat Turner's Slave Rebellion* (New York: Humanities Press, 1966), which reprints Turner's own "confession," pp. 127-151.
32. William Styron, *The Confessions of Nat Turner* (New York: Random House, 1967). For a critique of Styron's novel, see John H. Clark, ed., *William Styron's Nat Turner: Ten Black Writers Respond* (Boston, Mass.: Beacon paperback, 1968).
33. Kenneth M. Stampp, *The Peculiar Institution: Slavery in the Ante-Bellum South* (New York: Alfred A. Knopf, 1956), ch. III. Two recent statements on what has become a very controversial subject are Eugene D. Genovese, "Rebelliousness and Docility in the Negro Slave: A Critique of the Elkins Thesis," *Civil War History*, vol. XIII (1967), pp. 293-314, and George M. Fredrickson and Christopher Lasch, "Resistance to Slavery," *ibid.*, pp. 315-329.
34. Stanley F. Horn, *Invisible Empire: The Story of the Ku Klux Klan, 1866-1871* (Boston, Mass.: Houghton Mifflin, 1939).
35. Two outstanding recent studies of the second Ku Klux Klan are David M. Chalmers, *Hooded Americanism: The First Century of the Ku Klux Klan, 1865-1965* (Garden City, N.Y.: Doubleday, 1965), and Charles C. Alexander, *The Ku Klux Klan in the Southwest* (Lexington, Ky.: University of Kentucky Press, 1965).
36. Ray A. Billington, *The Protestant Crusade, 1800-1860: A Study of the Origins of American Nativism* (New York: Macmillan, 1938).
37. See, for example, Robert E. Wynne, "Reaction to the Chinese in the Pacific Northwest and British Columbia: 1850 to 1910" (unpublished Ph. D. dissertation, University of Washington, 1964).
38. John E. Coxe, "The New Orleans Mafia Incident," *Louisiana Historical Quarterly*, vol. XX (1937), pp. 1067-1110, and John S. Kendall, "Who Killa De Chief," *ibid.*, vol. XXII (1939), pp. 492-530. The lynching of the Italians (which brought a threat of an Italo-American war) was the result of a vigilante action. Although there had been a recent criminal incident (the murder of the police chief) which to some seemed to justify vigilante action, the lynching was not merely a simple case of vigilante action. Ethnic prejudice against the Italians (who were allegedly members of a local Mafia organization) was crucial.
39. Donald L. Kinzer, *An Episode in Anti-Catholicism: The American Protective Association* (Seattle, Wash.: University of Washington Press, 1964).
40. See, for example, David Brody, *Steelworkers in America: The Nonunion Era* (Cambridge, Mass.: Harvard University Press, 1960).
41. Two important comparative studies of violence in 18th-century America and England are Lloyd I. Rudolph, "The Eighteenth Century Mob in America and Europe," *American Quarterly*, vol. XI (1959), pp. 447-469, and William Ander Smith, "Anglo-Colonial Society and the Mob, 1740-1775" (unpublished Ph. D. dissertation, Claremont Graduate School, 1965). Another important study is Pauline Maier, "Popular Uprisings and Civil Authority in Eighteenth-Century America," *William and Mary Quarterly*, 3d series (forthcoming).
42. Jesse Lemisch, "Jack Tar in the Streets: Merchant Seamen in the Politics of Revolutionary America," *William and Mary Quarterly*, 3d series, vol. XXV (1968), pp. 387-393.
43. See, for example, Richard Walsh, *Charleston's Sons of Liberty: A Study of the Artisans, 1763-1789* (Columbia, S.C.: University of South Carolina Press, 1959), pp. 3-55, and R. S. Longley, "Mob Activities in Revolutionary Massachusetts," *New England Quarterly*, vol. VI (1933), pp. 108-111.
44. Asbury, *The Gangs of New York*, pp. 1-45.
45. J[ohn] Thomas Scharf, *The Chronicles of Baltimore . . .* (Baltimore, Md.: Turnbull Bros., 1874), pp. 468-469, 476-479, 523, 528, 548-552, 555, 565, 570-574. The 12 riots were: (1) 1834—political riot, (2) 1835—bank riot, (3) 1847—firemen's riots, (4) 1848—election riot, (5) 1855—firemen's riot, (6) 1856—club riot, (7-8) 1856—two election riots, (9) 1857—labor riot, (10) 1858—anti-German riot, (11) 1858—election riot,

and (12) 1859—election riot. In addition, Baltimore had three riots in 1861-62; they arose from Civil War tensions. *Ibid.*, pp. 588-594 ff., 622-624, 627.

46. Ellis P. Oberholtzer, *Philadelphia: A History of the City* (4 vols., Philadelphia et al.: S. J. Clarke, 1912), vol. II, 283, 285-289, 291, 293-296. John Thomas Scharf and Thompson Westcott, *History of Philadelphia, 1609-1884* (3 vols., Philadelphia: L. H. Everts, 1884), vol. III, p. 2184. The 11 riots were: (1) 1834—anti-Negro riot, (2) 1834—election riot, (3) 1835—anti-Negro riot, (4) 1838—Penn Hall (antiabolitionist) riot, (5) 1838—anti-Negro riot, (6) 1840—antirailroad riot, (7) 1842—anti-Negro riot, (8) 1843—labor (weavers' strike) riot, (9) 1844—anti-Irish Catholic riot, May, (10) anti-Irish Catholic riot, July, (11) 1849—California House (election and anti-Negro) riot. Scharf and Westcott are the source for the 1840 antirailroad riot; Oberholtzer is the source for all the other riots. In addition, there were riots in 1828 (a weavers' riot involving Irish vs. anti-Irish conflict) and 1871 (anti-Negro riot). Oberholtzer, *Philadelphia*, vol. II, p. 291. Joseph Jackson, *Encyclopedia of Philadelphia* (4 vols., Harrisburg, Pa.: National Historical Association, 1931-33), vol. I, p. 87. Sam Bass Warner, Jr., *The Private City: Philadelphia in Three Periods of Its Growth* (Philadelphia, Pa.: University of Pennsylvania Press, 1968), pp. 125-157, interprets the Philadelphia riots of the 1830's and 1840's as exemplifying "the interaction of most of the important elements of the big-city era: industrialization, immigration, mixed patterns of settlement, changing styles of leadership, weakness of municipal institutions, and shifting orientations of politics."

47. J[oel] T. Headley, *The Great Riots of New York, 1712 to 1783 . . .* (New York: E. B. Trent, 1873), pp. 66-135. The eight riots were: (1) 1834—election riots, (2) 1834—antiabolitionist riots, (3) 1835—antiabolitionist riots, (4) 1835—labor (stone cutters') riot, (5) 1837—food (flour) riot, (6) 1849—Astor Place (theatrical factions) riots, (7) 1857—police (Mayor's police vs. Metropolitan police) riot, (8) 1857—Dead-Rabbits' riot (gang conflict). In addition to these riots and the great draft riots of 1863 there were two "Orange" riots (Irish Catholics vs. Irish Protestants) in 1870-71. On the Orange riots, see Headley, *Great Riots of New York*, ch. XXI.

48. Roger Lane, *Policing the City: Boston, 1822-1885* (Cambridge, Mass.: Harvard University Press, 1967), pp. 26-33. George A. Ketcham, "Municipal Police Reform: A Comparative Study of Law Enforcement in Cincinnati, Chicago, New Orleans, New York and St. Louis, 1844-1877" (unpublished Ph. D. Dissertation, University of Missouri, 1967), p. 54. The four riots were: (1) 1834—anti-Catholic (Charlestown convent burning) riot, (2) 1835—antiabolitionist ("Broadcloth Mob" assault on William Lloyd Garrison) riot, (3) 1837—Broad Street riot, (4) 1843—anti-Negro riot. Boston also had draft riots in 1861 and 1863. Lane, *Policing the City*, pp. 118-134.

49. Ketcham, "Municipal Police Reform," pp. 50, 53, 153. The four riots were: (1) 1836—pro-slavery riot in April, (2) 1836—pro-slavery riot in July, (3) 1842—bank riots, (4) 1853—Bedini (nativist vs. Catholic) riots.

50. Labor riots occurred in New York, 1835; Philadelphia, 1843; and Baltimore, 1857.

51. There were election riots in Baltimore in 1848, 1856 (2), 1858, and 1859, in Philadelphia, 1834, 1849, and in New York, 1834.

52. There were antiabolitionist riots in New York, 1834, 1835; Boston, 1835; Cincinnati, 1836; and Philadelphia, 1838.

53. Anti-Negro riots occurred in Philadelphia in 1834, 1835, 1838, 1842, and 1849, and in Boston in 1843. New York's great draft riots of 1863 featured much anti-Negro violence.

54. Anti-Catholic riots occurred in Philadelphia in 1844 (two) and in Boston in 1834. Anti-Catholic feeling was basic to Cincinnati's Bedini riot of 1853.

55. See, for example, Andrew H. Neilly, "The Violent Volunteers: A History of the Volunteer Fire Department of Philadelphia, 1736-1871" (unpublished Ph. D. dissertation, University of Pennsylvania, 1959).

56. On the events of 1877, see one of the most important works on the history of American violence: Robert V. Bruce, *1877: Year of Violence* (Indianapolis and New York: Bobbs-Merrill, 1959).

57. See the section below on "Police Violence."

58. See my paper in this volume on "The American Vigilante Tradition."

59. The basic work on race riots in the first half of the 20th-century is Allen D. Grimshaw, "A Study in Social Violence: Urban Race Riots in the United States" (unpublished Ph. D. dissertation, University of Pennsylvania, 1959). A seminal treatment is Arthur I. Waskow, *From Race Riot to Sit-In, 1919 and the 1960's: A Study in the Connections between Conflict and Violence* (Garden City, N.Y.: Doubleday, 1966). Two important case studies are Elliot M. Rudwick, *Race Riot at East St. Louis: July 2, 1917* (Carbondale, Ill.: Southern Illinois University Press, 1964), and Robert Shogan and Tom Craig, *The Detroit Race Riot: A Study in Violence* (Philadelphia and New York: Chilton Books, 1964) which covers the 1943 riot.

60. Of the enormous literature on riots since 1964, the most important work is the monumental *Report of the National Advisory Commission on Civil Disorders* (New York: Bantam Books paperback, 1968). A useful brief survey is Joseph Boskin, "A History of Urban Conflicts in the Twentieth Century" in Audrey Rawitscher, comp., *Riots in the City: An Addendum to the McCone Commission Report* (Los Angeles, Calif.: National Association of Social Workers, Los Angeles Area Chapter, [1967]), pp. 1-24. See also the paper in this volume by Elliot M. Rudwick and August Meier, "Black Violence in the Twentieth Century: A Study in Rhetoric and Retaliation."

61. Ralph Ellison, *Invisible Man* (New York: Random House, 1952), ch. 25.

62. Jack Altman and Marvin C. Ziporyn, *Born to Raise Hell* (New York: Grove Press, 1967).

63. *Time,* Aug. 12, 1966, p. 19 ff. This was, apparently, the greatest single-handed mass-murder in American history. The night before Whitman had killed his wife and his mother.

64. *New York Times,* Apr. 21, 1968, I, p. 1, c. 3-6 ff.

65. Otto A. Rothert, *The Outlaws of Cave-In-Rock* (Cleveland, Ohio: Arthur H. Clark, 1924), pp. 55-156, 241-266. See also Coates, *Outlaw Years.*

66. John T. James, *The Benders of Kansas* (Wichita, Kans.: Kan-Okla Publishing Co., 1913).

67. Colin Wilson and Patricia Pitman, *Encyclopedia of Murder* (New York: G. P. Putnam's Sons, 1962), pp. 286-289.

68. In this direction a pioneering treatment is the paper in this volume by Sheldon Hackney. Indispensable to any study of murder in American history is Thomas M. McDade, *The Annals of Murder: A Bibliography of Books and Pamphlets on American Murders from Colonial Times to 1900* (Norman, Okla.: University of Oklahoma Press [1961]), whose 1,126 bibliographical entries are heavily annotated. A relevant literary study is David B. Davis, *Homicide in American Fiction, 1798-1860: A Study in Social Values* (Ithaca, N.Y.: Cornell University Press, 1957).

69. Charles E. Rosenberg, *The Trial of the Assassin Guiteau* (Chicago: University of Chicago Press, 1968).

70. Walter Channing, "The Mental Status of Czolgosz, the Assassin of President McKinley," *American Journal of Insanity,* vol. XLIX (1902-03), pp. 233-278.

71. *Report of the Warren Commission on the Assassination of President Kennedy* (New York: Bantam Books paperback, 1964), pp. 350-399, 596-659.

72. Two notable exceptions are, of course, the late Senators Huey P. Long and Robert F. Kennedy.

73. Luther M. Carlton, "The Assassination of John Walter Stephens," Historical Society of Trinity College [Duke University], *Historical Papers,* 2d series (1898), pp. 1-12. Albion W. Tourgée incorporated Stephens' assassination into his best-selling novel, *A Fool's Errand* (New York: Fords, Howard & Hulbert, 1879).

74. Daniel W. Crofts, "The Blair Bill and the Elections Bill: The Congressional Aftermath to Reconstruction" (unpublished Ph. D. dissertation, Yale University, 1968), pp. 244-245.

75. T. Harry Williams, "Louisiana Mystery—An Essay Review," *Louisiana History,* vol. VI (1965), pp. 287-291. Hermann B. Deutsch, *The Huey Long Murder Case* (Garden City, N.Y.: Doubleday, 1963). David Zinman, *The Day Huey Long Was Shot* (New York: Ivan Obolensky, 1963), holds that Long was accidentally shot by a stray bullet from a bodyguard.

76. Goebel's election as Governor was vociferously contested by Republicans who claimed that their candidate had really been elected.
77. Thomas D. Clark, "The People, William Goebel, and the Kentucky Railroads," *Journal of Southern History*, vol. V (1939), pp. 34-48.
78. Fountain and his young son disappeared and were never found. Contemporaries—and later historians—felt that Fountain had been assassinated.
79. Howard R. Lamar, *The Far Southwest, 1846-1912: A Territorial History* (New Haven, Conn.: Yale University Press, 1966), pp. 192-195.
80. In the 1890's, Fall was still a Democrat. He did not switch to the Republican Party until after the turn of the century. Today Fall is chiefly remembered for his connection with the unsavory Teapot Dome oil reserve affair as Harding's Secretary of the Interior.
81. Arrel M. Gibson in *The Life and Death of Colonel Albert Jennings Fountain* (Norman, Okla.: University of Oklahoma Press [1965]) has branded Fall as the leading plotter against Fountain. See also the milder but excellent treatment by C[harles] L. Sonnichsen in *Tularosas: Last of the Frontier West* (New York: Devin-Adair, 1960).
82. Two leading authorities attest assassination as political weapon in territorial New Mexico: Lamar, *Far Southwest*, pp. 192-195, and Warren A. Beck, *New Mexico: A History of Four Centuries* (Norman, Okla.: University of Oklahoma Press [1962]), p. 173.
83. See statements by Joseph Satten, Amitai Etzioni, and other social scientists reported in the *New York Times*, June 9, 1968, vol. I, p. 64, c. 1-3.
84. Walter Prescott Webb, *The Texas Rangers* (Boston, Mass.: Houghton Mifflin, 1935).
85. George A. Ketcham, "Municipal Police Reform: A Comparative Study of Law Enforcement in Cincinnati, Chicago, New Orleans, New York, and St. Louis, 1844-1877" (unpublished Ph. D. dissertation, University of Missouri, 1967). Roger Lane, *Policing the City: Boston, 1822-1855* (Cambridge, Mass.: Harvard University Press, 1967).
86. Martha Derthick, *The National Guard in Politics* (Cambridge, Mass.: Harvard University Press, 1965), pp. 16-17.
87. *Ibid.*
88. James D. Horan, *The Pinkertons: The Detective Dynasty That Made History* (New York: Crown, 1968).
89. See, for example, Anthony S. Nicolosi, "The Rise and Fall of the New Jersey Vigilant Societies," *New Jersey History*, vol. LXXXVI (1968), pp. 29-32, and Hugh C. Gresham, *The Story of Major David McKee, Founder of the Anti-Horse Thief Association* (Cheney, Kans.: Hugh C. Gresham, 1937). See also my brief account of the AHTA movement in this volume in my paper, "The American Vigilante Tradition."
90. J[eremiah] P. Shalloo, *Private Police: With Special Reference to Pennsylvania* (Philadelphia: American Academy of Political and Social Science, 1933), pp. 58-134.
91. Jürgen Thorwald, *The Century of the Detective,* transl. Richard and Clara Winston (New York: Harcourt, Brace, 1965).
92. On the "third degree" problem, see the study by the Wickersham Commission: National Commission on Law Observance and Enforcement, *Report on Lawlessness in Law Enforcement* (Washington: U.S. Government Printing Office, 1931), pp. 13-261.
93. The huge literature on jails and prisons has been dominated by the work of criminologists, penologists, and sociologists; see, for example, Paul W. Tappan, *Crime, Justice and Correction* (New York: McGraw-Hill, 1960). Two older historical studies are Harry E. Barnes, *The Story of Punishment* (Boston: Stratford, 1930), and Blake McKelvey, *American Prisons* (Chicago: University of Chicago Press, 1936). An able recent work is W. David Lewis, *From Newgate to Dannemora: The Rise of the Penitentiary, 1796-1848* (Ithaca, N.Y.: Cornell University Press, 1965).
94. G. P. Anderson, "Ebenezer Mackintosh: Stamp Act Rioter and Patriot," Colonial Society of Massachusetts, *Publications*, vol. XXVI (1924-26), pp. 15-64. On the background of Boston mob violence, see Smith, "Anglo-Colonial Society and the Mob," pp. 88-89, 108, 118, 157-159, 180-199, 208-222.
95. See, for example, Ivor Noël Hume, *1775: Another Part of the Field* (New York: Alfred A. Knopf, 1966), pp. 32-34, 125-130, 284-288.

96. Cutler, *Lynch-Law*, p. 61 ff.
97. Adrian C. Leiby, *The Revolutionary War in the Hackensack Valley* (New Brunswick, N.J.: Rutgers University Press, 1962).
98. Miles R. Feinstein, "The Origins of the Pineys of New Jersey," (unpublished B. A. thesis, Rutgers University, 1963), pp. 56-73.
99. Edward B. McCrady, *The History of South Carolina in the Revolution, 1780-1783* (New York: Macmillan, 1902). See also Richard Maxwell Brown, "Back Country Violence (1760-85) and Its Significance for South Carolina History," in Robert M. Calhoon, ed., *Loyalists in the American Revolution: Central Participants or Marginal Victims?* (Holt, Rinehart & Winston, forthcoming).
100. See, for example, Francis Grierson, *Valley of the Shadows*, Bernard De Voto, ed. (New York: Harper Torchbooks paperback, 1966).
101. Allan Nevins, *The Emergence of Lincoln*, Vol. II, *Prologue to Civil War, 1859-1861* (New York: Charles Scribner's Sons, 1950), pp. 306-308.
102. See, for example, the hysteria which swept Texas in 1860 as described in Frank H. Smyrl, "Unionism, Abolitionism, and Vigilantism in Texas, 1856-1865" (unpublished M. A. thesis, University of Texas, 1961), pp. 49-74.
103. Crane Brinton, *A Decade of Revolution: 1789-1799* (New York: Harper Torchbooks paperback, 1963), pp. 35-37. The standard work on the subject is Georges Lefebvre, *La Grande Peur de 1789* (Paris: A. Colin, 1932).
104. James McCague, *The Second Rebellion: The Story of the New York City Draft Riots of 1863* (New York: Dial, 1968).
105. Frank L. Klement, *The Copperheads in the Middle West* (Chicago: University of Chicago Press, 1960).
106. Richard S. Brownless, *Gray Ghosts of the Confederacy: Guerrilla Warfare in the West, 1861-1865* (Baton Rouge, La.: Louisiana State University Press, 1958).
107. E[llis] Merton Coulter, *The Civil War and Readjustment in Kentucky* (Chapel Hill, N.C.: University of North Carolina Press, 1926).
108. Georgia Lee Tatum, *Disloyalty in the Confederacy* (Chapel Hill, N.C.: University of North Carolina Press, 1934), pp. 36-44, 54-72, 143-155.
109. This was Jones County. Tatum, *Disloyalty in the Confederacy*, pp. 97-98.
110. *Ibid.*, pp. 44-53. See also Smyrl, "Unionism, Abolitionism, and Vigilantism."
111. See the following sections of this paper on vigilante and agrarian violence.
112. Douglas E. Leach, *The Northern Colonial Frontier, 1607-1763* (New York et al.: Holt, Rinehart & Winston, [1966]). See also Alden T. Vaughan, *New England Frontier: Puritans and Indians, 1620-1675* (Boston and Toronto: Little, Brown [1965]).
113. Douglas E. Leach, *Flintlock and Tomahawk: New England in King Philip's War* (New York: W. W. Norton paperback, 1966).
114. Leach, *Northern Colonial Frontier*, pp. 12-13.
115. *Ibid.*, p. 112. William T. Hagan, *American Indians* (Chicago: University of Chicago Press, 1961), is a general history in which the major Indian wars are duly treated.
116. Brown, *South Carolina Regulators*. For a fuller treatment of vigilantism, see my paper in this volume on "The American Vigilante Tradition." Vigilantism is also treated in the paper in this volume by Joe B. Frantz, "The Frontier Tradition: An Invitation to Violence."
117. Richard Maxwell Brown, "Pivot of American Vigilantism: The San Francisco Vigilance Committee of 1856" in John A. Carroll, ed., *Reflections of Western Historians* (Tucson, Ariz.: University of Arizona Press, 1969).
118. Lucile Morris, *Bald Knobbers* (Caldwell, Idaho: Caxton Printers, 1939).
119. Eliphalet Price, "The Trial and Execution of Patrick O'Conner," *Palimpsest*, vol. I (1920), pp. 86-97.
120. Granville Stuart, *Forty Years on the Frontier*, Paul C. Phillips, ed., (2 vols., Cleveland, Ohio: Arthur H. Clark, 1925); vol. II, pp. 196-197.
121. A well selected collection of documents that includes material on neovigilantism is John W. Caughey, ed., *Their Majesties the Mob* (Chicago: University of Chicago Press, 1960).

122. See the section on the antihorsethief association movement in "The American Vigilante Tradition."

123. White Caps: "A voluntary group formed ostensibly for punishing offenders not adequately dealt with by law." Mathews, *A Dictionary of Americanisms*, p. 1865.

124. White Capping seems to have begun in Crawford County, Ind., in 1888. Within the year it spread to Ohio. *Biographical and Historical Souvenir for the Counties of Clark, Crawford, Harrison, Floyd, Jefferson, Jennings, Scott and Washington: Indiana* (Chicago: John M. Graham & Co., 1889), p. 35. *Ohio State Journal* (Columbus), Nov. 26, 29, Dec. 1, 3, 5-7, 10, 12, 21, 1888.

125. Samuel L. Evans, "Texas Agriculture, 1880-1930" (unpublished Ph. D. dissertation, University of Texas, 1960), pp. 320-321. *Texas Farm and Ranch* (Dallas), Oct. 1, 8, 1898.

126. Sheriff A. M. Avant, Atascosa County, Sept. 20, 1898, to Governor C. A. Culberson in Letters to Governor C. A. Culberson (manuscripts in Texas State Archives, Austin).

127. "The 'White Caps,' 1890-1893" (file of manuscripts and clippings in the L. Bradford Prince papers in the New Mexico State Records Center, Santa Fe). See especially the August 12, 1890, memorandum of Governor Prince to John W. Noble, U.S. Secretary of the Interior.

128. For example, Robert E. Cunningham, *Trial by Mob* (Stillwater, Okla.: Redlands Press, 1957), pp. 12-13.

129. For example, E[thelred] W. Crozier, *The White-Caps: A History of the Organization in Sevier County* (Knoxville, Tenn.: Beam, Warters & Gaut, 1899), pp. 10-11, 87 ff., 180 ff.

130. Booth Tarkington, *The Gentleman from Indiana* (New York: Doubleday & McClure, 1899).

131. Wilcomb E. Washburn, *The Governor and the Rebel: A History of Bacon's Rebellion in Virginia* (Chapel Hill, N.C.: University of North Carolina Press, 1957). Thomas J. Wertenbaker, *Torchbearer of the Revolution: The Story of Bacon's Rebellion and Its Leader* (Princeton, N.J.: Princeton University Press, 1940).

132. Gary S. Horowitz, "New Jersey Land Riots, 1745-1755" (unpublished Ph. D. dissertation, Ohio State University, 1966).

133. Brooke Hindle, "The March of the Paxton Boys," *William and Mary Quarterly*, 3d series, vol. III (1946), pp. 461-486.

134. John S. Bassett, "The Regulators of North Carolina (1765-1771)," American Historical Association, *Annual Report for the year 1894*, pp. 141-212. Marvin L. M. Kay, "The Institutional Background to the Regulation in Colonial North Carolina" (unpublished Ph. D. dissertation, University of Minnesota, 1962).

135. Irving Mark, *Agrarian Conflicts in Colonial New York, 1711-1775* (New York: Columbia University Press, 1940). David M. Ellis, *Landlords and Farmers in the Hudson-Mohawk Region, 1790-1850* (Ithaca, N.Y.: Cornell University Press, 1946). See also Sung Bok Kim, "The Manor of Cortlandt and Its Tenants: New York, 1697-1783" (unpublished Ph. D. dissertation, Michigan State University, 1966).

136. Marion L. Starkey, *A Little Rebellion* (New York: Alfred A. Knopf, 1955). Robert A. Feer, "Shays' Rebellion" (unpublished Ph. D. dissertation, Harvard University, 1958).

137. Leland D. Baldwin, *Whiskey Rebels* (Pittsburgh, Pa.: University of Press, 1939).

138. William W. H. Davis, *The Fries Rebellion, 1798-1799* . . . (Doylestown, Pa.: Doylestown Publishing Co., 1899).

139. Allan G. Bogue, "The Iowa Claim Clubs: Symbol and Substance," *Mississippi Valley Historical Review*, vol. XLV (1958), pp. 231-253.

140. Robert Lee Hunt, *A History of Farmer Movements in the Southwest: 1873-1925* (n.p., n.d.), pp. 28-29.

141. Although its interpretation has come under heavy attack in the last 15 years, the most complete account of the Populist movement remains John D. Hicks, *The Populist Revolt* (Minneapolis, Minn.: University of Minnesota Press, 1931).

142. James L. Brown, *The Mussel Slough Tragedy* (n.p., 1958), deals with the settlers' land league in the Hanford vicinity and its night riding activities which came to a climax in the Mussel Slough gun battle, an episode which Frank Norris used as the basis of his novel, *The Octopus: A Story of California* (New York: Doubleday, Page, 1901).

143. James O. Nall, *The Tobacco Night Riders of Kentucky and Tennessee, 1905-1909* (Louisville, Ky.: Standard Press, 1939). See also Robert Penn Warren's brilliant novel, *Night Rider* (Boston: Houghton Mifflin, 1939).
144. John Womack, Jr., "Oklahoma's Green Corn Rebellion" (unpublished A.B. thesis, Harvard College, 1959).
145. Robert L. Morlan, *Political Prairie Fire: The Nonpartisan League, 1915-1922* (Minneapolis, Minn.: University of Minnesota Press, 1955).
146. John L. Shover, *Cornbelt Rebellion: The Farmers' Holiday Association* (Urbana, Ill.: University of Illinois Press, 1965).
147. Lemisch, "Jack Tar in the Streets," pp. 381-400.
148. Smith, "Anglo-Colonial Society and the Mob," pp. 175-179.
149. "Molly Maguire" was an anti-British persona in Irish folklore whom the Irish miners of Pennsylvania adopted as a symbol of their resistance to the authority of the mine owners and bosses.
150. Wayne G. Broehl, Jr., *The Molly Maguires* (Cambridge, Mass.: Harvard University Press, 1964), is an outstanding study which treats in depth the sometimes present and usually overlooked European roots of American violence.
151. Henry David, *The History of the Haymarket Affair* (New York: Farrar & Rinehart, 1936).
152. Leon Wolff, *Lockout . . .* (New York: Harper & Row, 1965).
153. Louis Adamic, *Dynamite: The Story of Class Violence in America* (revised edition, New York: Viking, 1934), pp. 179-253. Another old but still useful work is Samuel Yellen, *American Labor Struggles* (New York: Harcourt, Brace, 1936). An excellent recent study is Graham Adams, Jr., *Age of Industrial Violence, 1910-1915: The Activities and Findings of the United States Commission on Industrial Relations* (New York: Columbia University Press, 1966). A searching study is the paper in this volume by Philip Taft and Philip Ross, "American Labor Violence: Its Causes, Character, and Outcome."
154. George S. McGovern, "The Colorado Coal Strike, 1913-1914" (unpublished Ph. D. dissertation, Northwestern University, 1953), pp. 81-111.
155. *Ibid.*, pp. 151-307.
156. Jack London, *The Iron Heel* (New York: Macmillan, 1907).

Appendix

A 150-YEAR STUDY OF POLITICAL VIOLENCE IN THE UNITED STATES

By Sheldon G. Levy*

Political violence in the United States is not new. Attacks on groups and upon individuals to change perceived wrongs have been recurrent throughout American history. But the general impression seems to be that the United

* Sheldon G. Levy is a visiting associate professor of psychology at the Lemberg Center for the Study of Violence at Brandeis University. He is co-director, Task Force on Assassination and Political Violence of the National Commission on the Causes and Prevention of Violence. Some of his publications include: "Multidimensional Content Analysis of Editorials," *Journalism Quarterly*, 1968; *Black Activism and White Response* (book with Eliot Luby and others—in preparation); and "The Psychology of the Politically Violent," Pacific Sociology Association, Seattle, Wash., 1969.

States is currently in one of its more violent periods, if not its most violent. Racial conflict, protests over the Vietnam war, student unrest on campuses, and spiraling crime rates are cited as the basis for the popular judgment that this period is, in fact, one of our most violent.

An attempt to obtain objective information about the historical levels of political violence in the United States is the basis for discussion in this appendix. The presentation will be brief. An expanded version may be found elsewhere.[1]

The data are based on quantitative analyses of the coding of politically violent events as obtained from a sample of newspapers. The fact that only newspapers were used and the material only represents a sample of the available data means that the results may not be fully generalizable. In addition, of course, great changes in the means and speed of communication, in the role of newspapers as a news medium, and in the population, size, and other varying characteristics of this country qualify the interpretations that may be made. Nevertheless, 6,000 issues were sampled, spanning the years 1819-1968, and each issue was completely read. All politically violent events that were found in the almost 100,000 pages were coded.

SAMPLING PROCEDURE

Two sources were used during the 150-year period. From 1819 through 1850, the *Washington National Intelligencer* was used as the source. Issues were selected by choosing randomly a date in the month and then picking all issues in that month that fell on exactly the same day of the week as the date that was selected. For the next month, a new date within the month was selected as the starting point.

From 1851 to 1968, the *New York Times* was used as the source. From 1851 through 1899, the sampling procedure was the same as that described above. After 1899, only two issues per month were selected. The issues to be read were determined by first picking a random date in the first week of the month and then selecting that issue as well as the issue that fell exactly 2 weeks later.

DEFINITION OF POLITICAL VIOLENCE

Politically violent events were defined as those involving an attack on an official or group of officials for any reason or an attack on an individual or group of individuals for political or social reasons. Thus, an attack on a Congressman would be considered a politically violent event even though the reason for the attack may have been purely personal. Labor violence was coded as well as incidents arising out of other economic, racial, religious, or political antagonisms. Labor strikes were coded if they occurred before such forms of bargaining were legal. Criminal acts including gang warfare were not coded unless the acts were committed against noncriminals for political reasons or upon officials. The Civil War also was not coded.

THE INDEX OF POLITICAL VIOLENCE

Measuring political violence can be done in any one of several ways. These range from the number of events alone, to the number of people who died. This study utilized three such indices. One was the number of events, another was the number of deaths, and a third was the number who were injured. These indices are not interchangeable so that judgments about the amount of political violence depend on the particular index that is used. Interpretations that are based on a composite evaluation of the indices obviously require a subjective weighting of them separately, unless, of course, each provides the same information. Results will be presented for all three of the indices.

In addition to the absolute values across time, two separate controls were utilized. The first was an adjustment of the indices based on newspaper size and the second was based on population.

The adjustment for population indicates that the most recent period of American history is as violent as any previous periods, perhaps slightly more so. However, the control for the size of the newspaper does not confirm this finding. On this basis, the most recent period is far less violent than many previous ones have been. In fact, the control for the number of pages indicates that the post-Civil War period had the greatest amount of political violence. This violence peaked around the year 1885.

There was then a rather constant decline until the end of the Second World War.

The population adjustment confirms this result except that the whole period from about 1835 to 1900 had peaks of political violence followed by decreases in the amount of violence.

Trends Across Time: Deaths. Another index of political violence that was used was the number of people who were killed in politically violent events.

In order to obtain greater stability of the results, the data were collapsed into five 30-year intervals. Table 1 presents the total number of deaths on the part of both the attackers and the targets for each of the 30 year periods. Because the few large events in which more than 50 individuals were killed greatly affects the results, two totals have been presented. One is for all events in which not more than 50 people were killed. The other total is for all events including the large ones. It should be noted that about four out of the five deaths reported were among the targets. These results are presented in Table 1.

RESULTS

Examination of Trends Across Time: Number of Events

Figure 2-1 presents the results of the newspaper analysis of politically violent events across time. The results are presented for 10-year periods. The frequencies after 1899 have been multiplied by 2.2 to adjust for the use of a sample of only two issues per month after that year.

Three curves are given. The first presents the actual frequencies, weighted by 2.2 from 1900. The second represents the ratio of the weighted frequencies to the population of the country in that period. Finally, the third represents the ratio of the weighted frequencies to the number of pages of newspaper that were examined for the period.

The results for the three curves are consistent. The absolute number of politically violent events has been rising throughout American history with the exception of three periods. One was in the decade prior to the turn of the century. The second was prior to and following the First World War. This was followed by a sharp rise during the

Depression period, but there was then another drop shortly before through shortly after the Second World War. On the basis of the absolute number of events that have occurred, the most recent years have witnessed the greatest amount of political violence in American history.

However, there has been a steady and rapid rise in both the population of the United States and the size of newspapers. The increase in population makes homogeneous interpretations more difficult, and the increased reporting that has occurred, influenced by the increased speed of communication, should result in a greater number of events being reported in the newspapers. Of course, transportation and communications improvements have resulted in a more homogeneous population than would have been expected based on considerations of numbers alone. In any event, it is quite important to adjust the actual frequencies by the size of the population and by the size of the newspaper. (The size of the newspaper is, of course, only a rough index of the increase in reporting. A more refined index would be the column-inches devoted to news.)

Table 2-1.—Weighted frequencies of deaths among attackers and targets for both individuals and groups

Interval	Individuals	50 or fewer	Row total	50+	Grand total
1819–1848	5	22	27	0	27
1849–1878	17	55	72	300	372
1879–1908	65.4	224.8	290.2	150	440.2
1909–1938	41.8	138.6	180.4	0	180.4
1939–1968	44	46.2	90.2	0	90.2

Several conclusions are apparent from table 2-1. The first is that for no category, i.e., individuals, 50 or fewer, and 50+, has the last 30 years been the most violent in the United States. In fact, even without adjustments for population and for the amount of reporting, the number of deaths is far below that which has occurred in several other periods. *If adjustment is made for population, the ratio of target deaths to total population is lower during the last 30 years than for any prior 30-year period since 1819, and this holds for all three size categories.* (Of course, since several periods had 0 deaths in the largest size category, the lowest ratio occurs in each period for which this is true.)

The pre- and post-Civil War periods appear to have been quite violent ones. However, the judgment of the pre-Civil War period is greatly influenced by a single reported event in the sample in which an estimated 300 deaths occurred. Were it not for this event, the post-Civil War period would be the predominantly violent one. This judgment is consistent with historical analyses, such as those by Brown and by Taft and Ross in this volume, that have examined the post-Reconstruction period and the early labor violence. The relatively lower internal political violence of the present period is repeatedly confirmed, when violence is indicated by the number of people killed.

Table 2-2.—*Weighted frequencies of injuries to both targets and attackers over time*

Interval	Individuals	50 or fewer	Total	50+	Grand total
1819-1848	2	40	42	300	342
1849-1878	13	59	72	375	457
1879-1908	38.4	335.2	373.6	150	523.6
1909-1938	33	453.6	486.6	7,315	7,801.6
1939-1968	19.8	825.4	845.2	5,665	6,510.2

Figure 2-2 graphically presents these results over time for political deaths. Adjustments have been made for population and for newspaper size. Further, the deaths have been divided into two categories. One is of all political deaths that were recorded except those cases in which more than 50 people were killed. The other includes the large events. For the adjustment for newspapers, the denominator consists of the number of pages that were examined during the 30-year interval. For the adjustment for population, the denominator is based on the number of people in the country for each year during the 30-year period. These population figures were then summed for each of the 30-year periods. The result is called the number of person-years.

It is apparent from the figure that in every case in which an adjustment has been made, the latest interval has had the smallest ratio. The only inconsistency between the results based on deaths and those based on total deaths results from the comparison of the Civil War era and the post-Reconstruction period. This point has been discussed previously.

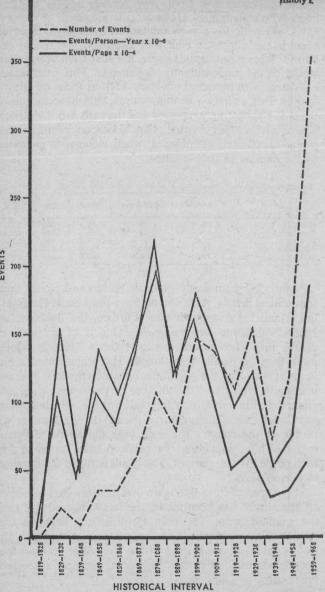

Figure 2-1.—Number of politically violent events, 10 year periods.

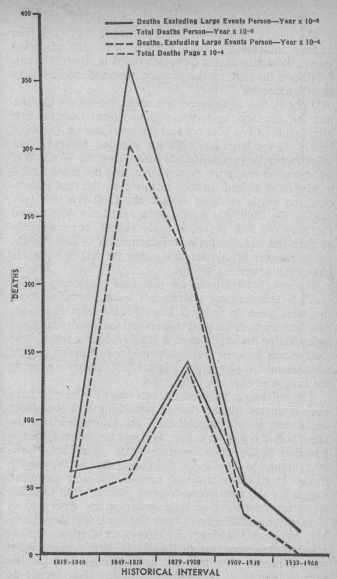

Legend:
——— Deaths Excluding Large Events Person—Year x 10⁻⁶
——— Total Deaths Person—Year x 10⁻⁶
- - - Deaths. Excluding Large Events Person—Year x 10⁻⁴
- - - Total Deaths Page x 10⁻⁴

Figure 2-2.—Deaths through time adjusted for population and news-papers size.

91

The results for injuries are presented in table 2-2. The findings indicate a pattern different than that discussed above: Whereas deaths have decreased in absolute numbers since the turn of the century, reported injuries have greatly increased.

If population adjustments are made, the results indicate that the last three periods are more violent than the first two, and the Civil War era and the latest one are the most violent. If the large incidents are included, however, and adjustments for population are made, then the World War I-Depression era is the most violent, and the latest period is next most violent. In fact, in this case, the post-Reconstruction era is the least violent, the Civil War era (excluding the Civil War itself) is the next least violent, and the pre-Civil War period is fairly violent, but much less so than the last two periods. Examination of just the absolute number of injuries shows that the last two periods have been extremely violent.

The results for injuries are presented graphically in figure 2-3. Denominator adjustments are the same as those that were given for figure 2. The chart indicates discrepancies between both the total injuries and the injuries obtained by excluding the largest events. It also indicates some slight discrepancy between the adjustment for population and the adjustment for newspaper pages when injuries excluding the largest events are considered.

The differences between the two totals for injuries have been discussed. In the case of population and newspaper adjustment for the smaller total, the injury ratio for the latest period is almost as high as it was for the post-Reconstruction period. The newspaper-page adjustment, however, results in a ratio for this period that is comparable in size to all other historical periods that were examined except for the post-Reconstruction period, when the ratio was more than twice as large as during any other period.

A major qualification of these findings is that there probably has been a tendency for injuries to be reported more often in the recent periods than in the 19th century, when violent events were reported in less detail, and for less serious injuries to be reported. Whether these trends do account for some or all the increase would require a much more detailed study than this.

MOTIVATION FOR VIOLENCE

The last section that will be analyzed will present the information on the reasons or motivation for the attacks over time. The data will be presented twice. First, the results for broad groups will be presented, and then the particular categories within the groups that contributed the most to the trend will be given. The advantage of this particular set of data is that it allows an objective collection to be matched against historical judgment. If the data do not accord well with history, the sample itself would be suspect, either because it was inadequate or because the newspaper sources were an insufficient basis upon which to make judgments about the history of violence in the United States.

The information that was collected accords well with prior historical analysis. Table 2-3 gives the numbers of events, weighted after 1899, in which different broad categories of motives were apparent.

Table 2-3.—Weighted frequencies of reasons for politically violent events over time

Interval	Personal gain	Action against authority	Foreign affairs protest	To change official leadership	Protests based on group antagonisms	Reaction of official groups	Total
1819–1848	6	0	0	0	16	0	22
1849–1878	27	11	0	0	60	2	100
1879–1908	89.7	18.4	0	3.2	178	12.4	301.7
1909–1938	50.6	77	6.6	6.6	191.4	33	365.2
1939–1968	61.6	123.2	39.6	2.2	235.4	4.4	466.4
Total	234.9	229.6	46.2	12	680.8	51.8	1,255.3

Several trends appear in the data. In the first column, "Personal gain" rises rapidly as a reason for attack and then, after the turn of the century, falls quite rapidly. This drop may well account for the smaller number of deaths in recent years. In contrast, column 2, "Action against authority," shows a sharp rise within the last two 30-year periods. "Foreign affairs protests," which are presented in column 3, appear to be a phenomenon almost unique to the contemporary United States. Almost all of the incidents

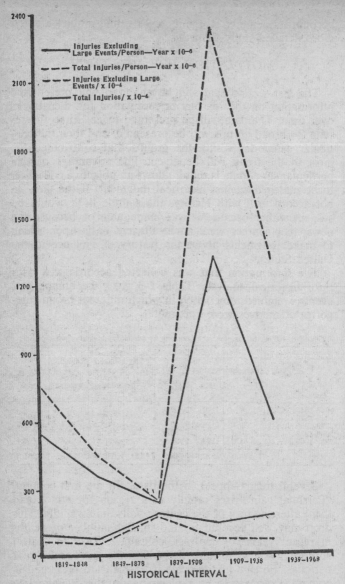

Figure 2-3.—Injuries through time adjusted for population and newspaper size.

94

appear in the last 30-year period and no events appear within the first three periods. It thus would appear that personal motivations for politically violent events have been replaced by more deep-seated controversies over the role of the Government.

Column 4 indicates that there have been very few attempts to change official leadership through politically violent events, which may be a positive sign that the elective procedures in this country are held to be appropriate ways for obtaining changes in the leadership.

Although table 3 indicates that there has been a steady increase in protests based on group antagonisms, the sharpest rise and the highest proportional ratios were in the 19th century. There is an exceptionally high point, relative to population, in the post-Reconstruction era.

Finally, a very important finding emerges when the political violence that is based on the reactions of official groups is considered. The result is a sharp decrease in the number of events that occurred because of the reaction of official groups. In fact, the last 30 years is almost as low as any previous period. The period in which this type of reaction was greatest was in the World War I and Depression era—the era of the Red scare and the bonus army —and, in fact, this period accounts for almost two-thirds of the incidents that were recorded.

The general impression is that protests currently are truly political—that is, they involve protests because of actions that authorities have taken or group antagonisms or, in the latest period, foreign affairs protests. Attempts to change official leadership have always been low. Official reactions as a basis for political violence only occurred frequently in the 1879-1938 period, and personal gain as a motivation, although fairly high, has been decreasing relative to population since the post-Reconstruction era.

To provide greater insight into the particular motives within the broad categories that have contributed to political violence, table 2-4 is presented. Table 2-4 shows some interesting changes within broad categories. For example, although there has been a decline in the general category of personal gain, there are counter-trends within subcategories. Personal revenge and political disagreements were the major reasons in the post-Recor-

Table 2-4.—Weighted frequencies of specific reasons for politically violent events over time

Interval	Personal gain				Action against authority				Foreign affairs protest		To change official leadership	Protests based on group antagonisms						Reaction of official groups
	1	2	3	4	5	6	15	16	23	25	31	40	41	42	43	44	45	50
1819–1848	1	.2	3.4	0	0	0	0	0	0	0	0	2.0	1.0	9.0	1.0	1.0	0	0
1849–1878	4.0	11.0	27.0		4.0	1.0	2.0	1.0	0	0	0	3.0	14.0	23.0	11.0	3.0	2.0	0
1879–1908	3.7	41.0	42.4	3.2		2.0	7.0	4.2	0	0	3.2	3.0	69.4	68.8	20.0	9.6	1.0	2.0
1909–1938	8.8	17.4	19.8	4.4	8.8	8.8	15.7	17.6	0	6.6	6.6	4.4	103.04	37.4	26.1	12.2	6.6	17.6
1939–1968	13.2	6.6	6.6	35.2	13.2	57.2	15.4	13.2	28.6	9.0	2.2	8.8	55.0	116.6	15.4	13.2	11.0	2.2

Code

1. Economic gain.
2. Personal revenge.
3. Political disagreement.
4. To gain political advantage.
5. To obtain a political goal.
6. Response to social conditions.

15. Protest police action.
16. Protest action of local officials.
23. Protest current involvement in war.
25. To protest Government action in foreign affairs.
31. To effect change in political personnel.
40. Religious antagonism.

41. Labor antagonism.
42. Racial antagonism.
43. Political antagonism.
44. Differences in social viewpoints.
45. Internal group antagonisms.
50. To maintain official authority by police.

struction era, whereas most of the incidents within the latest 30-year period have been to gain political advantage. In the "Action against authority" category, the changes result from the striking increase in the number of events that are a response to social conditions. Similarly, the increase in the "Foreign affairs" category arises from the contemporary protests over current involvement in the war.

The examination of the group antagonisms results is quite informative. There have been relatively few politically violent events owing to religious antagonisms. Similarly, relatively few incidents have been reported that deal with differences in social viewpoints or internal group antagonisms. Further, while there have been a greater number of events based on political antagonisms, this is not a major category, and the number has been decreasing.

Almost all of the events that have occurred because of group antagonisms have occurred either because of labor relations or racial animosity. The level for labor increases sharply in the post-Reconstruction era, reaches a peak during the World War I-Depression era, and then drops sharply in the most recent period. Relative to population in fact, the number of politically violent events based on labor antagonisms is less during this most recent period than for any but the pre-Civil War period. On the other hand, racial violence is highest in the latest period, although relative to population, it was highest in the post-Reconstruction era. In fact, there appears to have been a diversion from racial antagonisms to those of labor during the World War I-Depression period. During this period, if population is considered, the number of events prompted by racial antagonisms was lower than at any other period that has been studied.

GENERAL SUMMARY

This study has attempted to examine the levels and changes in the levels of violence in this country from the year 1819 to the present time. The study was based on a sampling of newspaper issues from two sources. The *Washington National Intelligencer* was used from 1819 to 1850. Then *The New York Times* became the source, and it was used from 1851 to the present. The study, therefore, commends itself because the data were obtained in a way that makes them representative of a long period of American history. However, several limitations must be placed on the interpretations of the material. The first is that the information was obtained from a sample. At no time in the 150-year period did the sample include more than an issue per week. Further, at no time did the sample include more than one newspaper. Consequently, there are time restrictions, geographical restrictions, and restrictions in reportorial and editorial viewpoints.

Further, the period of time studied saw vast changes within this country. Not only has the population increased greatly, but land area, industrialization, and a whole host of other conditions that inventive social scientists have labeled have changed. Perhaps the most important of the changes that affect interpretations of the material in this study has been the change in communications. It is quite reasonable to suppose that newspapers report more than they did previously, and do it sooner.

Consequently, the absolute figures that have been presented must be viewed carefully. Of course, the changes that have occurred generally lead to expectations of more internal violence. Thus, decreases in recent periods in the actual frequency would be even more noticeable if adjustments were made for the changes. However, increases are difficult to interpret. Some adjustment ought to be made so that the present period can be compared to previous ones. The primary adjustment that has been used is that for population. Basically, the question that is asked when population adjustments are made is, What are the chances that an individual will be killed or injured because of internal political violence? Of course, this answer would be greatly affected by other factors such as the amount of news reported in an issue of a paper. Consequently, the number of pages examined was taken as a general index of the amount of reporting. However, and this fact must be emphasized, not only have adjustments for other changes not been made, but the compound influence of these variables has also not been considered.

Allowing for the limitations of the sample considered above, this study leads to the following conclusions:

    1. The number of violent events has increased greatly in recent years. However, adjustments for both

newspaper size and population indicate that this period of history has not witnessed more internal political violence than previous periods.

2. The number of deaths as a result of political violence is far less in the most recent period than it has been in others. Part of the explanation may lie in the decrease in personal gain as a motivation for politically violent events.

3. The number of injuries as a result of political violence is quite large during the last 30-year period. However, absolutely and in proportion to population they are less numerous than those which occurred in the World War I-Depression period (1909-38). Allowance also should be made for the probability that modern newspaper reporting maximizes the number of injuries recorded. The best judgment must still be that the present period is no more violent than some previous ones have been.

4. The reasons for the political violence show important changes. Although there has been a decrease in the number of events inspired by desire for personal gain, the number of such events to gain political advantage is greatest within the current period. The present period has been the only one in which substantial protests over current involvement in war have occurred, and the number of these is quite large.

Group antagonisms have been the basis for many politically violent events. Labor and racial antagonisms have dominated the picture. The post-Reconstruction era and the present period have witnessed large amounts of racial strife. The period between these two (World War I-Depression) saw the height of labor violence.

Some reasons for politically violent events important in other nations have been almost completely absent in American history. Political violence to change official leadership has been rare. So has that based on religious antagonisms. Attempts by official authority to maintain control as a basis for an event has been quite low except for the period in which the greatest amount of labor violence occurred (1909-38). There were also a number of incidents reported in the 1879-1908 interval, but these constitute a very small portion of the number of events reported in that period (about 4 percent).

The picture, thus, is one of violence throughout American history, but not necessarily increasing amounts of it, with changing reasons for its occurrence, although racial violence has been consistently high for the 150-year period (except for the heyday of labor violence during the 1909-38 period). The problem of violence in America is not new. By its very persistence it is a more serious problem for our society than it would be were it new, for its roots run very deep.

Reference

1. Report of the Task Force on Assassination and Political Violence to the National Commission on the Causes and Prevention of Violence.

PART II

IMMIGRANT SOCIETIES AND THE FRONTIER TRADITION

In the introduction to his Pulitzer Prize-winning book on American immigrants, *The Uprooted,* Oscar Handlin writes: "Once I thought to write a history of the immigrants in America. Then I discovered that the immigrants *were* American history."[1] While technically correct, such a broad assertion tends to magnify both the uniqueness of the American experience and perhaps also the cultural impact of the latter-day mass of immigrants whose travail Handlin was recapturing. The vast overseas migration of the 17th, 18th, and 19th centuries was an international phenomenon of unprecedented magnitude, which in addition to the United States created immigrant societies in Canada, Latin America, South Africa, and Australasia. These emergent societies have shared the common experiences of frontier expansion and the necessities of dealing with native populations, relaxing or severing colonial bonds, and forging a cohesive and distinct if hybrid culture. A comparison of their similarities is necessary in order to balance the ethnocentricity that has characterized too much of American introspection.

But such a comparison, while properly emphasizing the degree to which the Statue of Liberty was not the only beacon tempting men to uproot themselves in search of a better life, also reveals important dissimilarities. Chief among them is the remarkable extent of ethnic diversity that has characterized the American experiment in cultural assimilation. Most other immigrant societies have tended to draw disproportionately from only a few favored ethnic stocks. The British have been predominant in Australia and New Zealand. Together with the French, they have dominated Canada; with the Dutch, South Africa. In a century of immigration, Argentina received 40 percent of its newcomers from Italy and another 27 percent from Spain. Italians and Spaniards, together with a large Portuguese contingent, constituted 76 percent of Brazil's immigration. Contrast this to the United States, which during the period

1820 to 1945 recruited the following ethnically diverse proportions: the British Isles, 33 percent; Germany, 16 percent; Austria-Hungary, 13 percent; Italy, 12 percent; Russia and Poland, 10 percent; Scandinavia, 6 percent; and in addition we of course received myriad smaller injections of ethnic pluralism.[2]

Indeed, it is probable that this very ethnic diversity and the protracted and diffuse nature of its infusion combined to limit its impact in America. John Higham, historian of American nativism, argues that we must exclude the founders of a society from the category of immigrant because as original settlers they (in the American case, the English —who in 1790 comprised approximately 60 percent of the white population) firmly extablished "the polity, the language, the pattern of work and settlement, and many of the mental habits to which the immigrants would have to adjust."[3] Given this preemption of the levers of power by the dominant Anglo-Americans, subsequent immigrant groups have been cast into fierce competition with one another in their collective quest for economic security and for acceptance as legitimate Americans. This scramble for material advantage and for status has produced violent confrontations, both between the newcomers and the often nativist Anglo-American establishment, and between the economically competing and status-conscious ethnic minorities themselves. The search for respectability has reinforced that exaggerated sense of "Americanism" which has been so deeply enshrined in the mythology of the revolutionary new nation. The stakes were high, and the quest was often explosive.

The American character, then, was forged through an extraordinary 300-year process of settlement during which the Indians were driven back, the English, Spanish, and French were driven off, the Africans were involuntarily driven over, the Mexicans involuntarily annexed, and the immigrant minorities were thrust irrevocably into a vibrant competition both with a raw physical environment and with one another. That Americans often resorted to violence under such trying circumstances is no surprise. But more important today is the question of the pervasiveness of the legacy of nativism, vigilantism, and ethnic aggression that was an inevitable byproduct of the interaction of immigrant and open continent. How deeply has the immigrant and frontier experience embedded a proclivity for violence in our national character, and how does a comparison with similar societies enlighten our experience?

In comparing in chapter 3 the cultural evolutions of the immigrant societies of Latin America, the United States, Canada, South Africa, and Australasia, Louis Hartz speaks of them as "fragment cultures" in which migrating European populations imposed their cultural values upon their new overseas societies. All have shared certain fundamental problems, such as the relationship with the mother country and with the native non-Western population, and all have experienced a tightening consensus through the shrinking of their social world. But crucial in determining their sharply varying forms of adjustment has been, first, the nature of their imported values—i.e., whether they were primarily feudal, as in the case of Spanish migrations, or liberal-enlightenments, as in the English. The second major determinant has been the mixture of the cultural fragmentation. In some a single fragment has been predominant, as in the case of the English in Australia and New Zealand or the Spanish in much of Latin America. In others, the fragmentation has been dual, as with the English and French in Canada and the English and Dutch in South Africa. In the latter case, both cultural fragments have inherited the values of bourgeois liberalism, whereas in Canada the two fragments have not only differed ethnically, but also their values have derived from conflicting traditions. Finally, there is the unprecedentedly fragmented United States, wherein the bourgeois-liberal ethnic, in combination with ethnic pluralism, has produced in the cult of "Americanism" a nationalistic impulse toward an iron conformity that has nurtured a particularly virulent strain of vigilantism.

While all of the fragment cultures created by the great international migration encountered frontier conditions which reacted upon the transplanted culture, in none was the admixture of imported values, frontier environment, and time so uniquely structured to maximize the impact of the frontier as in the United States. The essential ingredients were relatively modern liberal-capitalist values and a sufficient expanse of accessible and desirable land which would allow the frontier encounter to be repeated and prolonged.[4]

In Latin America, both the feudal values of Spain and Portugal and the difficult topography combined to blunt the frontier experience. Similarly, in Canada, the settlers of the Saint Lawrence River Valley carried prerevolutionary French cultural luggage, and the inhospitable Laurentian Shield deflected pioneers southward into the United States; when railroads opened the Canadian prairie provinces to British settlement in the late 19th century, the frontiersmen came directly from the more traditional east and the process of settlement was not nearly as prolonged as was the American experience. Siberia was settled by Czarist peasants. In Australia, pioneers pushed through the gaps in the Great Dividing Range only to discover the vast arid expanse of the outback. But in the United States an interminable stream of relatively propertyless individuals, armed with bourgeois-liberal values and a powerful acquisitive instinct, marched 3,000 miles to the Pacific in an epic migration lasting 2½ centuries.

The unique American character forged in the process, as Frederick Jackson Turner and his disciples have explained, was characterized by an intense individualism and an almost fanatical equalitarianism. This "new man" was democratic, optimistic, mobile, nationalistic, and hospitable to change. But he was also criminally wasteful, and at the core of his individualism was a materialistic philosophy which enshrined property rights and held them to be largely immune from governmental or public control. Hence, his equalitarianism was flawed by an inconsistency which held that such barriers to his acquisition as red Indians and Mexicans were exempt from the democratic embrace, and horse thieves were exempt from due process. In chapter 4, Joe B. Frantz recaptures through lively—and often deadly —anecdote the tone of a uniquely prolonged saga in which the pitting of man against nature and his fellowman constituted "an invitation to violence." Although the American frontier has been officially closed for over two-thirds of a century, its impact on our national character has been deep and abiding.

The deeply rooted tradition of vigilantism that was nurtured for so long by the American frontier experience has never comported well with the official commitment of the revolutionary young republic to a quest for "ordered liberty" through due process of law. Furthermore, this

American quest for ordered liberty has itself been an ambivalent one. Our dual commitment to liberty and equality—a commitment symbolized by the Declaration of Independence and the Constitution—has always embodied a fundamental conflict, for liberty and equality are often contradictory goals. Born in rebellion against traditionally constituted authority, the new Republic's noble task of constructing "a government of law, not men" has always been complicated by the unalterable reality that men must fashion, interpret, and enforce their laws.

That the origins of the venerable American vigilante tradition can be traced to the Revolutionary era is both symbolic and instructive. An authority on the South Carolina Regulators of 1767-96, Richard Brown observes in chapter 5 that the new spirit of populist vigilance, which was muted in our earlier environment of colonial deference, was logically nurtured by the democratic ethos of the Revolution. But because vigilantism constitutes at best extralegal enforcement of community mores, its proponents have perforce constructed a defensive rationale based upon the "higher law" doctrine of the rights of revolution, self-preservation, and sovereignty.

The American viligante tradition has been linked in the popular mind with the frontier, and it is true that the frontier's characteristic lack of effective agencies of law enforcement clearly invited and to a degree legitimized vigilante justice. Implicit in this view is the assumption that vigilantism should subside with the disappearance of the frontier. But Brown points out that as a flexible human institution, vigilantism was easily adapted to respond to the demands of an urban and industrial America. Symptomatic of this transition to a modern "neovigilantism" was the greatest of all vigilante movements: the San Francisco Vigilance Committee of 1856. Neovigilantism may be distinguished from the older frontier model not only by its urban environment but also, revealingly, by its victims. Whereas the old vigilantism sought to chastise mainly horse thieves, counterfeiters, outlaws, and bad men, the victims of neovigilantism have characteristically been ethnic, racial, and religious minorities, union organizers, and political radicals. Modern vigilance groups have frequently been supported by prestigious community leaders, often with the tacit support of the police. The tenacity of this American tradition, together with its institutional flexibility, suggest that its resurgence in our troubled times remains a distinct and sobering possibility.

Finally, students of national character rightly assume that a close scrutiny of the folk lore and creative literature of a culture will isolate certain fundamental themes and images that are far more revealing of its cultural values than are opinion polls or official rhetoric. If one pursues the theme of violence in the American folk and literary tradition, one will find it in abundance. Yet it is striking how America's historians, unlike her literary giants, have been so long insensitive to the white man's explosive encounter with Indian and African. The remarkably tenacious appeal of the Leather-stocking saga and the wild western surely reflect an abiding romantic fascination with our violence-prone frontier origins. Yet so rich is the lode of American literature that, like the Bible, one can "prove" almost any hypothesis by citing it. Are we a people peculiarly and morbidly fascinated by violence? In support of this contention, one might cite the savage humor and the bloodthirsty tall tale of frontier folklore, or the searing urban and industrial chaos and class animosity reflected in the utopian novels of Ignatius Donnelly and Jack London, the fascination with war of Stephen Crane, Ernest Hemingway, and John Dos Passos, and especially the racial agony mirrored in Mark Twain, Herman Melville, and Richard Wright. The trouble with citing these persistent themes as conclusive testimony to the sickness of American society has been, as Kenneth Lynn observes in chapter 6, that "they tend to extrapolate violent incidents in American writing out of their literary context, without regard to the curse-lifting effect of self-parody and other forms of humor, or to the ways in which fictional conventions and authorial prejudice affect representatives of reality, or to the dreams of peace which render ambivalent even the most violent of our writer's nightmares."

The unmatched ethnic diversity of American immigration and the protracted American encounter with the frontier larged a national character that mirrored that contradictions between the American creed and American practice that Gunnar Myrdal has labeled "the American Dilemma." That contemporary urban industrial America

106

continues to reflect ethnic animosities and a vigilante impulse is testimony to the persistent virulence of our ethnic pluralism and our frontier legacy.

References

1. Oscar Handlin, *The Uprooted* (New York: Grossett & Dunlap, 1951), p. 3.
2. These European figures of course omit original Indian inhabitants, African, Oriental, and Spanish-surname Americans. For an illuminating comparative discussion of immigration, see John Higham, "Immigration," in C. Vann Woodward (ed.), *The Comparative Approach to American History* (New York: Basic Books, 1968), pp. 91-105.
3. *Ibid.*, p. 93.
4. For a comparative analysis of frontier settlement, see Ray Allen Billington, "Frontiers," in C. Vann Wodward (ed.), *The Comparative Approach to American History*, pp. 75-90.

Chapter 3

A COMPARATIVE STUDY OF FRAGMENT CULTURES

By Louis Hartz*

The paradox of the fragment [1] cultures in respect to violence and legality is that they heighten consensus by shrinking the European social universe but at the same time discover new sources of conflict which Europe does not have. Some of these sources are inherent in the process of fragmentation itself, as with colonial revolution, but mainly they are to be found in the encounter of the fragment with new groups, Western and non-Western, as its history proceeds. In the end, to deal with these, the fragment is faced with the problem of transcending the new morality which it has established.

It is not hard to see how the migration of a group from Europe heightens social consensus. The group does not have to deal with other groups possessing different values. Thus the French Canadian corporate community does not have to deal with the Enlightenment, and the American

* Louis Hartz is professor of government at Harvard University. His publications include *The Liberal Tradition in America* (New York: Harcourt, Brace & World, 1955), and *The Founding of New Societies* (New York: Harcourt, Brace & World, 1964).

middle class does not have to deal with the institutions of the feudal order. Indeed the new intensity of shared values is matched precisely by an escape from Europe's social revolution and all of the violence it contains. The guillotine is missing in the fragment cultures. To be sure, there will be some disorder in the process of forging the new society and the shrunken consensus it contains, as with "frontier lawlessness" or ethnic strife, but these matters can be fairly well contained. It is in the nature of the migration culture that it leads to a new sense of social peace based upon a new sense of community. And when these emotions are fortified by the spirit of a new nationalism, as they almost always are, the moral world of the fragment is secured in an unusually powerful way.

Technically the violence involved in the colonial Revolution should have all of the transience of a frontier situation, since it is more or less an instrument for completing fragmentation. And indeeed in a liberal culture like that of the United States, or even in a case like India where a native liberal elite revolts, the Revolution has the effect of clarifying the situation. But this need not always be so, especially in the feudal cultures where the imperial order may itself represent a vital part of the domestic legitimacy system of the fragment. Latin America is a case in point. The national revolutions there, by abolishing a Spanish monarchy on which the spirit of authority depended, opened up a vacuum into which the military entered.

One would not suppose that the clash of one European settlement with another would have the same temporary character as the clash of migrants with a mother country, since this is a matter not of separation but of permanent connection. Moreover the very fact that each of the fragments is building its new and shrunken sense of community, fortified by nationalism, exacerbates the matter of the relationship. Indeed if we wish to measure what the fragment has avoided in the way of Europe's social revolution we can look at a country like Canada, where bourgeois and feudal cultures confront one another, but as "nations" rather than classes. This means, to be sure, a situation potentially much more explosive than the European, but this very fact drives from the outset toward some Federal solution which would be unthinkable within England or France themselves insofar as the relations of classes are concerned.

We are, of course, reminded here that in the inter-fragment confrontation the distance of the social values the fragments enshrine from one another is important. But we must not make too much of this. For the South African case shows us that where the fragments are really quite similar in social and national substance, Holland and England being parts of a North European cultural complex, extraneous factors such as race can enter into the relationship of the fragments and literally explode it.

Actually, for all of the tension between the English and the Dutch which resulted from the racial issue in South Africa, the underlying fact about the attitude of the fragment toward the non-European is that he is outside a consensus of values, European in character, which despite their limited social circumference all of the fragments share. And under these circumstances, a common European violence in relation to the non-European is almost inevitable. The aborigine, at whatever stage of culture, is the first to encounter it. Whether he is simply exterminated, or shoved off into reservations, or incorporated along Latin American lines into the fragment system, force becomes inevitable. Nor is this wholly a transient frontier matter, even in countries like Australia where the simple method of extermination was widely used. Aboriginal groups survive, creating issues of conscience and of policy alike. And of course in the Latin American situation, where the aboriginal elements become vital parts of the culture, their existence helps to define the very categories of social strife.

The same principle of violence holds even when the non-European is imported, as is the case with the African slave in all parts of the fragment world save Africa itself. Indeed the process of importation yields a major and peculiar form of violence in its own right, since there are the horrors involved in the voyage from Africa, a kind of "forced fragmentation" which matches, curiously, the more spontaneous movements on the part of the European population themselves. We must not forget, however, that the European fragment values themselves seek to absorb slavery into their own definitions of legitimacy, and this profoundly conditions the nature of the force associated with it. Feudal fragments such as those of Brazil instinctively seek to legitimize slavery along hierarchical lines, whereas bourgeois fragments like that of the United States oscillate between "property" and "personalty" as categories for the African. This oscillation, needless to say, has revolutionary implications, both for the European and the African in the United States, as the Civil War and its aftermath fully reveal.

The effort to "abolish" or "digest" the Indian and the African obviously has limits as a technique for cultural relatedness. It cannot easily be applied to the world at large which is descending on the fragments in the 20th century as it is upon all nations. Ironically, this experience brings the fragment into contact with the very revolutionary process it escaped at the time of migration, for the European revolution has been transferred, albeit in changed fashion, to large areas of the globe. That transfer is, to be sure, a phase of the European cultural fragmentation itself, which the new societies share, and there is a common theoretical bond here between the United States, India, and even Japan. But the differences are also immense, since the Enlightenment fragments of Europe in these instances usually work within the context of the most powerful traditionalisms. It is at this point, where 1789 returns, as it were, that the European settlement cultures face most vividly the challenge of transcending their perspectives. Whether they can meet this challenge, without descending into irrational violence at home and abroad, is still an open question. Perhaps a consolation is to be found in their record of Federal invention, not merely in two fragment cultures like the Canadian but within single fragment societies like the United States. Certainly, for the nations born of the drive of European groups to live separately, the fragment cultures have shown a remarkable concern with the institutional technique of "living together."

MIGRATION AND CONSENSUS

Let us look more closely at the process by which the fragments create a special sense of community out of their own contracted social substance. The fact that this process can override frontier disorders of a domestic kind is testimony to its force. But it will always be in contrast to the European social revolutions that the fragments escape, in contrast to their barricades and their civil wars, that the new spirit of consensus will be centrally measured. This is not merely a matter of escaping the old regime, or as in the feudal cases of French Canada and Latin America escaping the Enlightenment itself. Flight from the immediate enemy is, to be sure, a critical matter. But when the pilgrims leave, they leave not merely an opposing group; they leave a total historical process whose interactions generate constantly new results. Thus the integrity of the new fragment consensus is protected, by virtue of the same stroke of movement, from the enemies of the future as well as the past.

The threat of socialism illustrates this process almost everywhere. Since that subversive movement requires a mixture and a confrontation of both feudal and bourgeois elements, neither the feudal nor the bourgeois fragments can produce it; Marx is missing both in French and English Canada, despite the strain of the CCF, although he blossoms in France and England themselves where the fragments of North America interact on a class basis and keep the social revolution moving. This is a hidden source of unity within Canada as it is between Canada and the United States, for surely it would be a matter of concern throughout North America if any area within it produced something like a Bolshevik Revolution. The problem of Castro in a later and different context may give us a hint of this. To be sure, Western Europe does not itself produce many victorious revolutionary socialisms, but the Marxian force is a factor there, continuing the 1789 which most of the fragment cultures escaped. Historically, if the world of Boston and the world of Quebec are both to exist, even Harold Laski has to be excluded from their borders.

This is not to deny that labor violence can take place in the fragment cultures, as a Molly Maguire movement will show. But it is to deny that this violence will symbolize a major trend of proletarian revolution. Historically, the working class is typified by the AFL in the United States and English Canada and by Catholic syndicates in French Canada. Nor does the Australian case, where a series of major strikes in the 1890's led to the victory of the Labor Party, really disprove our point. For the fragment root of the culture of Australia was proletarian, even to some extent Chartist, so that socialism was an inherent outcome of its history—as, let us say, Jacksonian democracy was an inherent outcome of the bourgeois culture of the United States. In this sense the upheavals at the turn of the century

111

in Australia have something in common with Dorr's Rebellion in Rhode Island, manifestations in line with the fragment ethic, helping it forward, rather than challenging it in a subversive way. The Australian experience shows us that the process of European settlement can embrace more in the way of ideology than conservatism or liberalism, but it does not disprove the proposition that all settlements, in their own ideological terms, escape social revolution and go forward to a new experience of moral consensus.

That consensus is bound to be fortified by nationalism, because it is the only substitute the fragmented European has for the European national identity he has lost. How else can the migrant Puritan regain a sense of national wholeness than by calling the Puritan ethic itself the American way of life? This process varies in intensity from fragment to fragment depending on the clarity of the ideological substance, and the relationship to the European homeland. But it is to be found everywhere, even in English Canada where the ambiguities of the fragment identification are legendary. Of course, where it appears in extreme form, it produces itself a moral vigilantism which borders on the violent. "Americanism" in McCarthyite form or French Canadianism in Duplessis form can be terrifying things. But it is interesting that these are always "law and order" movements, and the label is not wholly meaningless. While there is a sad paradox in men being harried by movements boasting lawfulness, the fact is that such patriotic crusades do express, in pathological form, the normal spirit of legalism in the fragment world. That spirit rests on the new and contracted consensus arising out of migration. If an excess of national emotion sends militants off in the pursuit of subversive phantoms, then the legalism of the fragment has, in some sense, no right to complain. Here is a curious case of "law and order" against itself.

We must not overlook the role of fragment nationalism in containing the tensions implicit in new immigration, for by converting the fragment ethic into a source of national identity it permits the immigrant to "belong" simply by subscribing to it. To be sure, ethnic struggles are historic in the United States despite "Americanization." In other fragment cultures, where the blossoming of fragment nationalism has been inhibited, the "melting pot" has worked even less effectively. Indeed it might even be argued, insofar as strife is concerned, that in societies like English Canada or Latin America where ethnic separatism tends to persist, violence is itself minimized, since the homogenizing moral force which would hurl groups into contact with one another is limited. Canada is interesting on this count because there is a tendency for the newcomers of recent times, taking their cue from the Federal relationship of French and English, to rationalize explicitly the maintenance of their own identity. But after all of this has been said, and the complexities of the matter noted, it remains a fact that the conversion of the fragment ethic into a national code always contributes something to immigrant belonging. And the reason is that national membership is transmuted thereby from something inscrutable and unattainable into something doctrinal and embraceable. You cannot become an Englishman by subscribing to Magna Carta, but you can make at least some progress toward becoming an Australian by subscribing to the open egalitarianism of the national legend.

Politics betrays the new consensus, indeed rests upon it. When one says that the fragment cultures escape social revolution, one automatically says many things about their political systems. Their political struggles are usually not ideological, save in the sense that the national ideology is occasionally brought into play against subversives. It is illuminating to see how this principle works out in Australia, where even the socialism of the Labor Party relaxes into a pragmatism nourished by the general egalitarian consensus. What this often means, indeed, as once again the Australian experience illustrates, is a positive distrust of the intellectual, the ideologizer. This will be accentuated in fragment cultures of an intrinsically democratic type, for there the death of ideology coincides with an exaltation of the popular mind. In a relatively stratified bourgeois fragment such as the English Canadian there is a bit more place for the intellectual elite, and in the feudal fragments, leaving aside the habit of clerical leadership, there is a larger place as well. Given the torn fabric of Latin America, which was penetrated by French thought in the 18th century, we actually begin to get something like an "intelligentsia"—a phenomenon rare indeed in the new society.

All of this is merely to return us to the special spirit of legalism injected into the fragment world by the tighter

113

moral consensus which, as against Europe, it contains. Pragmatism is close to legalism, since it flourishes on the basis of a moral settlement which adjudication also requires. *Inter arma leges silent.* Nor does one need to concentrate on the courts alone here, for the spirit to which I am referring can have its incarnation in religion and in clerical establishments, also, as in the case both of French Canada and Latin America. What is at issue is a sense of the presence of objective norms nourished by the fact that the competition of norms has been narrowed and even eliminated through the process of flight from Europe. Surely it is clear enough that this emotion conquers the initial spirit of chaos in the new society, even in an instance like the American where the saloon and the badman are parts of the national legend. Of course the frontier outlaw in the United States is himself a kind of heroic individualist, far more in tune with the bourgeois ethos than a Bolshevik revolutionist, which is one of the reasons why the legend can nurture him. But even if we account him a deviant, his meaning lies in his transience. The roads are inevitably paved in the western town and the chamber of commerce takes over.

Indeed it is in the United States, with all of its Jesse James tradition, that the peculiar legalism of the fragment culture appears most vividly. The lucidity of the Puritan consensus creates the basis for nothing less than the remarkable power of judicial review of the Supreme Court, a power resting on the notion that there is enough moral agreement in the political world to permit the adjudication of even its largest questions. Surely nothing reveals more clearly the escape of the fragment from the revolutionary ideological turmoil of Europe than the presence of that power. The very notion of "sovereignty," that ally of all revolutionary enterprises, has to be missing where the higher law is so liberally applied. But if this is the case, if the Supreme Court is a projection of the fragment consensus, the question will always exist as to how far it can control that consensus when, for reasons of patriotism or cultural anxiety, the consensus gets out of hand. Can "law and order" really be protected against itself?

There will always be a question as to whether the colonial revolutions in the fragment world are not themselves "social revolutions," enactments of a peculiar 1789. But even though we face up to every social aspect of these upheavals, we have to insist that this is not the case. The colonial revolt is tied in with migration, the very process of social escape. And if the violence it engenders can cut in various directions, either the continuing turmoil of Latin America, for example, or the relative peace of the United States, it remains a fact that neither result can be understood apart from the exigencies of the imperial experience.

I have said that in the Latin American case the removal of the Spanish king through imperial revolt impaired the legitimacy structure of the fragment itself. Since efforts to produce New World monarchies failed, save in the case of Brazil where in fact it was a migrant Portuguese monarchy itself which served the purpose, the gap was soon filled by the legendary caudillo. There is no doubt that the feudal fragment has a peculiar vulnerability here, because of its authority needs. Of course these can be met inside the fragment itself, as they were for the most part in French Canada which was able, out of its own elite, to manufacture a fairly stable system, despite the reliance on Paris. However, it is worth noting that the French Canadian order was not put to the Latin American test on this count. French rule was abolished not by revolution but by external conquest, and the British supplied by their imperial authority much of the direction that they had destroyed on the French side. Nor, in terms of power itself, was the shift from the French to the British on this count as significant as might seem. The French Catholic ethos was in fact prenational, rationalizing authority per se, and it made an accommodation to the conquerors doctrinally possible. French Canada in this connection has not been forced to "stand on its own feet" as a feudal fragment as Latin America has.

Ideally, of course, even in the feudal case, colonial revolt should enhance the integrity of the fragment ethic by completing the escape from European enemies. It is merely a sign that there has not been a full social migration when imperial institutions serve domestic needs. In the case of the American Revolution we have an illustration of this fulfilling aspect of colonial revolt, and nothing brings out more vividly the contrast with Latin America than the issue of monarchy itself. By the time of the Revolution the British monarchy, for all of the reluctance of the colonists to break with it, had ceased to be a major factor in the legitimacy system of the American colonies. Due in part to imperial neglect, and in part to the growth of self-governing institutions, the American system was practically complete in its own terms. Paine celebrated American reality in *Common Sense*. That pamphlet was later translated in Latin America, but in a context of course entirely distinctive. Which reminds us, in addition to the differences in the monarchical question, of the differences in the whole doctrinal setting of revolution. In the United States the liberalism of revoluntionary doctrine carried forward the intrinsic liberalism of the culture, whereas in Latin America it contradicted not only the initial feudal ethos but also the drive of the creole revolutionary leaders themselves who remained elitist. It clarified the fragment spirit here, confused it there.

All of this, of course, is why the transition to republican government was easy in the United States, lacking further violence, Napoleonic coups, palace revolts. In the Latin American case the failure to develop domestic monarchs continued the legitimacy gap, but in the United States, had such an effort been successful, it would have impaired the evolving spirit of legitimacy itself. This, undoubtedly, despite all of the rumors at the time, is why no serious attempt at a "restoration" did take place. Certainly, under these circumstances, there was no need either for a military substitute for the monarchical figure, and once again despite rumors and a plot or two, this was why a caudillo dictatorship did not develop. The "critical period" of American history was, in fact, a period in which the American fragment was moving toward larger cultural stability, a wider articulation of its own original meaning. The Constitutional Convention of 1787 was a climax to this process, even if most of the men attending it seem to have been so worried that they did not understand the fact. The fundamental law these men forged, which could have gone the way of French or Latin American constitutions, has lasted down to the present day.

So here was a case, yearned for but never achieved in the theories of great social revolution, where violence was a "transitional" stage toward a purer legality. Surely in other fragment situations where the break with the mother country was not decisive there have been tensions and ambiguities which in the United States were resolved once and for all in the 18th century. Surely, too, as both Canada and Australia well illustrate, the persistence of the imperial connection qualifies and inhibits the full conversion of the fragment essence into a new nationalism, a new "way of life." In these terms one can repeat the proposition that the Latin American outcome is the "pathology" of the fragment revolutionary process, a situation traceable to the intrusion of extraneous imperial connections into the domestic heart of the fragment. And in these terms also one can say again that the process is to be associated not with the Jacobins of Europe but with the Mayflower voyage and the Pizarro trip.

FRAGMENT COMPETITION: FEDERALISM

The more one explores the nature of the fragment ethic and its expanding consensus, the more obvious it is that when fragments confront one another the possibilities are explosive. We are in fact dealing with emergent "nations," compounded out of the class substances of Europe, armed with nationalisms more sensitive than those of Europe because more ideological, more doctrinal. French Canada, put alongside the Protestantism of the English, is loaded with the latent dynamite of the holy war. When one adds to the situation the possibility of clashes over other issues, such as the racial issue of South Africa, one has a potential for struggle exceeding in significance any involved in the relationship to the mother country. No wonder that, in order to contain it, there has to be the most delicate kind of Federal diplomacy.

Nor must we assume that, as European class ethics confront one another, the rivalry of the European nationalisms themselves is entirely forgotten. Certainly the struggles that are possible over language are as intense as any in the interfragment relationship. To be sure, devotion to language can reflect attachment merely to a neutral carrier of culture, rather than to the nationalism of Europe, and it would be

117

a mistake to exaggerate its importance in European terms. All of the fragment languages vary from those of the mother countries, reflecting indeed the very simplifying processes by which the fragment itself becomes a distinctive nation. No one would seriously say that Afrikaans, the most dramatic of the linguistic variations, elicits the ardor of its support in South Africa because of the memory of Holland. But after this has been conceded, and the central importance of the fragment culture itself is stressed, the European sentiment cannot be wholly excluded. The fragment cultures, for all of their distinctive nationalist claims, have a manner of giving themselves away on this score, as, for example, when they always seem to prefer immigrants from the country of their own origin.

There can be little doubt that interfragment competition, in its own way, enhances the process by which the fragment converts its culture into nationalism. Without the English Canadian, would the French Canadian define his personality so vividly in nonbourgeois terms? To be sure, the normal nationalizing processes would be at work, as against France itself, and the articulation of the Canadian soul in terms of the rejection of Voltaire and Robespierre would go forward. But the challenge of British merchants in the 18th-century exacerbates, clearly, the conservative tendency which begins with the migration from France in the 17th. Nor does the peculiar "prenational" character of the feudal ethos to which I have referred in the French Canadian case, which in fact assists the reception of British authority, alter this fact. The submission to British monarchy as a formal authority affair is one thing, the preservation of French Canadian cultural integrity can be another. The two can exist within that ethos. But even here we must not overstate the case. There was resistance to the British, as with Papineau and the Rebellion of 1837. Nor does the fact that this resistance also took place in the English sector itself, as part of the drive for representative government, alter the point. What can be a democratic struggle in English Canada, as Papineau himself tends to reveal, can be a nationalist struggle in French.

Of course substantive alliances can be forged across the lines of the fragment, and these can betray numerous facets of the interfragment situation. In Canada the fact that French "reform" forces were interested in the preservation

118

of Catholic corporate culture made a link with the English radicals difficult, though the elites of seigneurial and clerical power often got together rather handily with the Family Compact forces of English conservatism. Indeed the latter relationship, understandable in light of the stratified nature of the English bourgeois fragment, was probably more solid than anything worked out between the fragments in South Africa after the conquest, even though there the cultural similarities were greater than in the Canadian case. The problem of the African instantly exploded the situation within the context of a common Protestant, North European background. And yet one cannot help noting that the gradual surrender of the English to the Dutch in the racial area, after the Boer War and into the present period, meant that that area itself could yield a substantive bond. Cultural surrender is always a possibility, though least likely in the case of the "first" fragment, i.e., the Dutch or the French, since the sense of fragment nationhood goes back farther in these cases.

Given the limits to the substantive synthesis of the fragments, federalism emerges automatically as a method for containing their relationship, a concession to the fact that we have left the class world of Europe and entered upon "international relations." This federalism, needless to say, must be distinguished from that in single fragment cultures such as the United States and Australia where size, settlement, and diversity of a different kind lead to decentralized structures. Federalism in the latter instances is far more "successful," since it is underwritten by the fragment consensus itself: when the consensus is impaired, as in the case of the South and the Civil War in the United States, it encounters troubles that approximate the interfragment type. But for all such troubles, there is no doubt that the efforts at authentic cultural federalism in the fragment world represent one of its greatest achievements. Where in general that world has narrowed the horizon of men, here is an instance in which it has broadened it also. Where the legalism of that world has tended to rest on the most explicit cultural agreements, here is a case where a legalism has arisen resting on the ethos of cultural diversity itself.

And yet is it really true to say that in the interfragment situation the moral consensus is fully missing? All of the fragments involved in Canada and South Africa are European. That is no minor matter, especially in societies which know also the North American Indian and the African. The truth is, the cultural federalism of the fragment experience, if it is not underwritten by the unity of a single fragment ethos, is underwritten by the common norms of the European experience. That may be why it is possible at all. When we move to the non-European, coming out of alien and simpler societies, violence begins to flourish on a grand scale.

THE IMPACT OF ABORIGINAL CULTURES

Technically it is not true to say that legalism breaks down completely when the non-European is involved, since in and through the treatment of the aborigine there are manifestations of fragment morality, as when the Spanish Catholic ethos protects the native or even the American bourgeois ethos speaks of an "Indian treaty." But given the threat of the stone age aborigine both to the explicit class morality of the fragment and to its implicit Europeanism, there are bound to be limits to the application of such norms. The fragment exterminates the aborigine, closes him off into separate areas, or absorbs him into its own social order on a certain level. And in all of these cases it uses force in full measure.

It vividly reveals the European edge of the moral conscience of the fragment that, when it comes to extermination, even fragments drenched in the Enlightenment ethic engage in the practice happily. Indeed, it is interesting to note that the brutal record established by the Australians in this respect coincided with a culture of the socially "radical" type. In Tasmania the aboriginal element was wiped out completely. Of course the Enlightenment morality, and above all its Puritan progenitor, has an exclusivity about it both in terms of the "democracy" and in terms of the "damned" which can lead to quite unexpected brutalities. The record here, in contrast to that of the feudal cultures, may have some of the distinctive quality it has in the realm of African slavery. Of course there is always the final pang of conscience in the Enlightenment cases, stemming from the retrospective inclusion of the aborigine into the Lockean community, which produces legislative results.

The method of isolating the aborigine is closely tied in with the violence of the "Indian war" itself, since as a result of that war he is driven off into separate territories. The social principle, moreover, is practically the same in both cases: protection of the morality of the fragment by a kind of Hebraic nonintercourse with the alien culture. When the idea is implemented by a conscious "reservation" policy, the culture of the European fragment has usually triumphed so fully in the land that the desperate fears which inspired the separatist drive in the first place are usually forgotten. Latin America represents, to be sure, a special problem here, because the presence of isolated Indian tribes, in the context of a culture which has incorporated the Indian, can involve a serious issue for the integrity of the State system itself. The Indian question in Mexico or Peru casts a curious light on fragment "separatism."

But we must not assume, of course, that the Latin American approach to the Indian was lacking in violence. Indeed the same type of extermination crusades which prevailed elsewhere are to be found in both the Spanish and the Portuguese cases where Indian tribes, as in Brazil or Chile, were unwilling to cooperate in terms of cultural incorporation. And incorporation itself was a violent process, involving a social upheaval for the Aztec and the Inca more drastic than anything to be found in the revolutions of Europe. Granted that there were reciprocities in these cultures on which the Iberians could rely, as in the systems of authority, religion, and production, still these were far from the social unities which linked all classes within the more advanced European order. Latin America, though feudal in substance, arises out of a great "social revolution," if we wish to use the term in this connection.

Of course, like all great enterprises of social renovation, this one was not wholly successful, remarkable as many of its achievements were. Nor was this entirely because certain aboriginal groups could not be absorbed into the Iberian system, or even because aboriginal practice, as in religion and elsewhere, persisted in sublimated form despite Europeanization and Christianization. It was also because the Indian groups that were absorbed, and hence made to serve as feudal substitutes, were left with racial scars that distributed the organic life of the Iberian order. If racial issues are more "social" in Latin America than elsewhere, it is probably true to say, without being deliberately paradoxical, that social issues are on the whole more racial. Certainly the tensions that arose historically on this score were very great, and in any assessment of the impairment of the feudal consensus in Latin America, they must be included in the record no less than the institutional ruptures arising from the breakdown of the imperial order. The Spaniards showed an absorptive genius here that the British did not—for whatever reason, feudal values, Iberian history, or the accidents of Indian culture—but they paid the price of a basic continuing problem for it. They have been denied the luxury of resolving the Indian problem by intermittent episodes of retrospective guilt.

One thing, in any case, is clear. Whether the European fragment destroys, isolates, or incorporates the aborigine, the record is vivid with bloodshed. Here is the ironic compensation it experiences for leaving its enemies in Europe behind, that it encounters even stranger antagonists abroad. The encounter brings out all of the hidden values it shared with others in the old country, its basic Europeanism, and doing so, unleashes a violent energy that transcends even that which produced the guillotines of the Old World. But insofar as the aboriginal victims of that violence are concerned, they are met by the fragment in the course of its travels, almost as a matter of happenstance. What of the non-European whom the fragment deliberately imports, the African slave?

SLAVERY AND ITS AFTERMATH

The African, of course, is open to all of the violence reserved for the non-European, but being imported as a slave, he will not in the nature of things, save possibly in South Africa, experience extermination or isolation. He will enter the fragment community on some incorporative basis, and this means that fragment legality will instantly encounter a problem with him. On the basis of the aboriginal experience in Latin America, one can predict the outcome here, an effort as in Brazil to bring the Negro like the Indian into the Iberian feudal system. But in the North American case, where the Indian has not been absorbed and where above all the Enlightenment norm prevails, the African produces a novel issue. It is one of the most complex issues in the entire pattern of fragment legality.

It is easy to forget the violence involved in the initial acquisition of the slave. In part, this is because the European is ordinarily not responsible for his capture, that work being done in Africa itself; there are no "Indian wars," save possibly again in South Africa, designed to obtain the slave. To be sure, the European enters the process at the point of migration from Africa, and he presides over what is probably the most brutal episode in the entire early process, the slave passage, but this is not easy to remember for another reason. Voyages in their nature are forgotten, since the children of the men who take them never relive the experience. In this sense, the fragmented African is like the fragmented European, the product of an act neither can recall, which reminds us of a most significant matter: that master and slave encountered each other in the Western Hemisphere when both were in the process of movement, both in the process of leaving an "old world" behind. True enough, the Mayflower voyage is celebrated, the passage of the slave repressed, but not all of the energy of all the patriotic societies in the Hemisphere have been able to intrude the initial European voyage into its active life. Who really cares about a trip from England to Plymouth, however "important," which not even the tourist agencies advertise?

Memory does begin, however, at the point of landing, for here the pattern of fragment life itself takes shape. And whether one views the matter from the standpoint of the European or the African, violence is at its heart. To be sure, because the experience of slavery was present in Africa itself, albeit in a manner quite different from that which came to prevail in the New World, there was a receptivity to it on the part of the African which did not exist, say, among Indian tribes like the Iroquois. It is a legendary fact that the African was imported in precisely those areas of the New World where the aboriginal population would not serve the labor purpose. But this does not alter the fact of force which pervaded the slave relationship. It was there, implicit or explicit, from the instant of purchase to the instant of death.

Of course, this is precisely where the morality of the fragments themselves appear, for the way in which a cul-

123

ture distributes the legitimate use of force is the clue to its ethical life. Feudal Iberia mitigated force theoretically in the slave relationship by feudalizing and Christianizing it, whatever the actual brutality of the system was. But the liberal spirit of the North Americans, being classless, actually precluded this. Human beings being equal; the slave must be somehow inhuman, a true object of property in the Lockean sense, and this produced a theoretical indifference to the force exerted against him. Of course slave codes existed limiting the power of the master, but they had a doctrinal incongruity in the liberal system which, ironically, they lacked in the feudal. And yet there was the inevitable other side of the coin. Accept the humanity of the slave in the liberal scheme, and you must instantly give him all of the rights accorded his master. He moves, without a theoretical moment of waiting, from bottom to top. That was the curiously revolutionary oscillation contained, insofar as the African was concerned, by the Declaration of Independence.

However complex the cause of the American Civil War, that oscillation was reflected in it. The radicalism of the liberal ethic, hidden beneath Supreme Court legalism in a fragment context, exploded in the bloodiest episode the fragment had seen. The Court could not prevent this, as its ultimate failure in the Dred Scott Case showed, for what was at stake was the meaning of the very consensus on which its power rested. And yet the clash here took place, for all of the activity of the Negro, mainly within the European population; the violence of the slave relationship, because it could not be digested by the fragment morality, was transferred to a struggle among the masters themselves. That struggle ended with the emancipation of the African, the termination of legalized force against him, but it did not bring him fully into the Lockean community. Despite the fixed and continuing radicalism of the liberal demand, and even despite Reconstruction Amendments which were written into the fundamental law itself, an ambiguous situation was the result.

That situation, however, was as unstable as the initial situation out of which the war had come. Given social change and the world impact in the 20th century, the radicalism of Jefferson would reassert itself, this time with the African himself as the most militant carrier of it. The violence of slavery, exploding within the European fragment in the 19th century, is turned by the Negro against the fragment in the 20th. However, the rioting in the streets was preceded by the desegregation decisions of the Supreme Court, which reminds us that the Negro is still working with the moral materials of the fragment establishment. To be sure, there is a Black Power, black separatist overtone to the Negro battle, which holds out the thought of a two-fragment federalism of the Canadian type or a kind of reverse bantustanism of the South African sort. But so far this has not crucially challenged the Jeffersonian base of the civil rights movement which binds the Negro to the European fragment itself, gives him allies within it and a weapon vastly more powerful than any he can find in another formula. In a fairly pure liberal fragment culture like the American, when you have the Declaration of Independence on your side you come close to having all that there is.

THE AMERICAN PARADOX

Certainly the most effective method for dealing with Negro violence in the United States is to bring the Negro finally fully into the Lockean world, to make him a complete part of consensus and legality. And yet this brings us to a paradox found everywhere in the fragment world, that while the most immediate resources for healing fragment wounds lie in the fragment ethic itself, the impact of a unifying globe requires also that that ethic be transcended. In the American case it has been proven that a blind Wilsonian pursuit of the Declaration of Independence is not the best method for handling world reality. On the other hand, insofar as the Negro is concerned, there is this consolation, which reminds us of the peculiar relationship a liberal fragment has to the forces at work on the international scene today. The American Lockean drive to include the Negro coincides with a world movement also designed to establish his equality, and it is even a fact that African nationalism has itself entered as an influence into the civil rights movement. To be sure, there is a difference between social revolution in Africa or Asia and final purification of an absolute liberal ethos derived from the Mayflower. The difference is at the heart of the matter. But

125

we are still dealing with types of "equality," and there ought to be possible an accommodation between them.

Surely when we look at the feudal fragments, with their traditionalized elitist instincts, we see the meaning of this point. The racial hierarchies of Latin America, granted that they are "feudalized," do not fall under the impact of an American civil rights impatience. Of course feudalism itself elicits a deep current of social change, and in this sense Latin America is closer than other fragment cultures to the "underdeveloped" world, as is French Canada. But it is the historic power of the fragment which resists this change. We must not forget that in the international sphere the feudal cultures of both North and South America have also been able to yield quite a considerable worship of Salazar, Franco, and even Hitler.

It will always be ironic that, as they confront the revolutionary world of the 20th century, the settlement cultures I have discussed here confront products of the European cultural fragmentation itself, sharing basic aspects of their own experience. Whether in Africa or China, it is the migration of European ideas which has disturbed the globe. But despite all the connections here, even that in the case of the American Negro, the "return to revolution" on the part of the fragments poses the most serious problems of understanding for them. Even the very Enlightenment ethos that most of them have can, in this context, be a special source of bitterness and violence. It is doubtful whether men fight more fiercely over the acceptance of the idea of "equality" than over the method of its application.

But one thing is certain. The world will never be reduced through violence by the settlement cultures to the limits of their own ethical outlook. To be sure, it is remarkable how "successful" violence was in this connection in the past, as with mother countries, Indians, Africans. Indeed, given this record, it is perhaps not surprising that the instinct of blind ferocity keeps asserting itself. But sooner or later all of the fragments will have to discover that if the Chinese cannot be deserted as Europe was deserted neither can they be eliminated like the Iroquois.

An intensified Federal outlook, greater than any generated within or among the fragments in the past, is inevitably needed. But if this takes place, what will the fragment have lost? It will have lost some of the cozy warmth of

its own shrunken consensus, some of the high righteous-
ness of its own sense of "law and order." Surely the world
offers compensations for this. What the fragment nations
have missed is the experience of cultural diversity, and
this is precisely what a Federal perspective on Africa and
Asia can yield. In our century the settlement cultures have
been entrapped by the world they tried to escape. But if
they have the courage to accept that world, they will discover a reward even greater than any they found in Kansas
or Quebec.

Reference

1. I use the term "fragment" here to describe societies arising from the
movement of European population, the principle being that the settlers
represent a part of the total culture of Europe. Theoretically, the cultural
fragmentation of Europe also includes narrower European imperial settlements and the carrying forward of European ideas by native groups as in
India or Japan. I shall refer occasionally here to the latter cases, but
mainly I shall be concerned with the fragment experience as it applies to
societies based significantly on European population, specifically the United
States, Latin America, Canada, South Africa, and Australia. For the general theoretical background I am using, see my discussion in chs. 1-3 of
The Founding of New Societies (New York: Harcourt, Brace & World,
1964).

Chapter 4

THE FRONTIER TRADITION:
AN INVITATION TO VIOLENCE

*By Joe B. Frantz**

On September 26, 1872, three mounted men rode up to
the gate of the Kansas City fair, which was enjoying a huge
crowd of perhaps 10,000 people. The bandits shot at the
ticket seller, hit a small girl in the leg, and made off for
the woods with something less than a thousand dollars. It
was highhanded, and it endangered the lives of a whole
host of holiday-minded people for comparatively little reward.

* Joe B. Frantz is professor of history at the University of Texas. He is
co-author, with Julian E. Choate, Jr., of *The American Cowboy* (Norman:
University of Oklahoma Press, 1955).

What makes the robbery and the violence notable is not the crime itself but the way it was reported in the Kansas City *Times* by one John N. Edwards. In his front-page story he branded the robbery "so diabolically daring and so utterly in contempt of fear that we are bound to admire it and revere its perpetrators."

Two days later the outlaws were being compared by the *Times* with the knights of King Arthur's Round Table:

It was as though three bandits had come to us from storied Odenwald, with the halo of medieval chivalry upon their garments and shown us how the things were done that poets sing of. Nowhere else in the United States or in the civilized world, probably, could this thing have been done.[1]

Quite likely this deed was perpetrated by the James brothers: Jesse and Frank, and a confederate. The details really do not matter. What pertains is the attitude of the innocent toward the uncertainly identified guilty. The act had been perpetrated by violent, lawless men. If the *Times* is any indication, a respectable section of the people approved of their action. No one, of course, thought to ask the little girl with the shattered leg how she felt about such courage. Nearly 17 months later, Edwards was quoted in the St. Louis *Dispatch* as preferring the Western highwayman to the Eastern, for "he has more qualities that attract admiration and win respect. . . . This come from locality . . . which breeds strong, hardy men—men who risk much, who have friends in high places, and who go riding over the land, taking all chances that come in the way." The purpose here is not to belabor one reasonably anonymous newspaperman of nearly a century ago, but merely to point up a fact—and a problem—of the American frontier.

The frontier placed a premium on independent action and individual reliance. The whole history of the American frontier is a narrative of taking what was there to be taken. The timid never gathered the riches, the polite nearly never. The men who first carved the wilderness into land claims and town lots were the men who moved in the face of dangers, gathering as they progressed. The emphasis naturally came to be placed on gathering and not on procedures. Great tales of gigantic attainments abound in this frontier story; equally adventurous tales of creative plundering mark the march from Jamestown to the Pacific. It was a period peopled by giants, towers of audacity with insatiable appetites. The heroes are not the men of moderate attitudes, not the town planners and commercial builders, not the farmers nor the ministers nor the teachers. The heroes of the period, handed along to us with all the luster of a golden baton, are the mighty runners from Mt. Olympus who ran without looking back, without concern about social values or anywhere they might be going except onward.

We revere these heroes because they were men of vast imagination and daring. We also have inherited their blindness and their excesses.

Just by being here, the frontier promised the spice of danger. And danger, to paraphrase Samuel Johnson, carries its own dignity. Danger therefore was the negotiable coin of the American frontier, and the man who captured his share of danger was a man of riches, beholden only to himself.

To live with danger means to be dependent to a considerable degree on one's own resources, and those resources in turn must be many and varied. Courage and self-reliance, while not exclusive with the frontiersman, take on an enlarged dimension because so many instances of their use can be recalled. Whereas the town neighbor or the corporate manager may need a type of moral courage that exceeds the physical in its wear and tear on the human soul, such downtown courage is hardly recountable and seldom even identifiable. But when the frontiersman has faced down an adversary, he usually has a fixed moment in his life when he can regale an audience or when others can recall admiringly his dauntlessness. Even a foolhardy adventure brings applause. To the human actor no reward is more desirable.

The fact that back East, which meant from ten miles behind the cutting edge of civilization all the way to the more sophisticated capitals of Europe, men were daily facing monumental problems of planning, and sometimes even of surviving, meant nothing to the frontiersman. Nothing in the frontiersman's way of life gave him any sympathy for the man who made his decisions on paper or in the vacuum of an office or stall. Decision was made on the spot, face to face. The questions were simple; the solutions, equally simple. Today that heritage of the frontier continues in more remote areas. The subtleties of law and order escape the isolated mountain man, for instance, whether he be in Wyoming or in eastern Kentucky. If a man does wrong, you chastise him. Chastisement can take any form that you think is necessary to hold him in line. One of the acceptable forms is murder, which means that lesser violence visited upon the offending person is even more acceptable. Such behavior has the advantage of being swift and certain, without the agony of deciding what is comparatively just and without the expense of trials and jails and sociologists and welfare workers.

Of course, one reason that this simplistic attitude toward settlement of problems prevailed on the frontier was a physical one of lack of jails. Where do you put a man when you possibly have no place to put yourself? To be neat and economical, you must put him away. This may mean tying him to a tree and leaving him to starve or be stung to death; if he has been real mean, you might like to wrap him in rawhide and then let the sun shrink the rawhide slowly around him until he is gradually strangled. Or you might find it more economical to find a convenient tree with a branch a sufficient height off the ground. The scarcity of jails then, either nonexistent or inadequate, often left the frontiersman with little choice, insofar as he was concerned, except to hang, lynch, or ignore the offender.[2]

What do you do with a man whose crime may not really warrant execution? Either you execute him anyway, stifling your doubts, or you let him go. If you let him go, as happened frequently, then you may have set a killer at large to roam. In Arkansas in the generation during which Judge Isaac C. Parker ran his notorious Federal court, more than 13,000 cases were docketed, of which 9,500 were either convicted by jury trial or entered pleas of guilty. During a 25-year period at Fort Smith, 344 persons were tried for offenses punishable by death, 174 were convicted, and 168 were sentenced to hang. Actually 88 of these were hanged, and six others died either in prison or while attempting to escape.

By current standards the hangings themselves would have been invitations to violence. One contemporary of the judge tells of the hanging of John Childers, a halfblood Cherokee Indian charged with killing a peddler for his

130

horse. A thunderstorm had come up, and a bolt of lightning struck nearby just as the death trap was sprung. "A moment later the ghastly work was done, the cloud had vanished and all that was mortal of John Childers hung limp and quivering," the reporter writes. "The entire proceeding, the grim service of the law . . . filled the spectators with awe."

Standing next to Judge Parker in local fame was George Maledon, a smallish Bavarian celebrated as "the prince of hangmen" for having executed more than 60 criminals and shooting two to death during 22 years prior to 1894. Twice he executed six men at one time and on three other occasions he hanged five together. People discussed his record with all the enthusiastic calm of a present-day discussion of Willie Mays' possibilities for overtaking the home-run record of Babe Ruth. As for Maledon, when he was once asked by a lady whether he had qualms of conscience, he replied in his soft way, "No, I have never hanged a man who came back to have the job done over." This same reporter describes Judge Parker as "gentle, kind, familiar and easily approached."[3]

The truth is, the lawman was as closely associated with violence as the outlaw. The greatest gunfighters frequently played both sides of the law, shooting equally well. Bill Hickok comes down as a great lawman in Kansas. He also shared a good many of the qualities of a mad dog. Hickok first came to public notoriety near Rock Creek, Nebr., where from behind a curtain in the Russell, Majors, and Waddell station he put a single rifle bullet through the heart of one David McCanles, who had come with a hired hand and his 12-year-old son to protest nonpayment of a debt. Hickok was acquitted on a plea of self-defense. For this dubious bit of law tending, Hickok became a national hero, although it took a half-dozen years for his notoriety to become nationwide. He filled in that time by doing creditable work for the Union Army, and pursuing a postwar career as a gambler in Missouri and Kansas. This stretch of social service was punctuated by a town square gun duel which left Hickok standing and his adversary forever departed.

In his long hair and deerskin suit, Hickok could have joined any police confrontation in Chicago or Berkeley a century later. Nonetheless he became a deputy U.S. marshal out of Fort Riley, and helped rescue 34 men besieged by redskins 50 miles south of Denver With this background he was elected sheriff of Ellis County, Kans., in August 1869. He killed only two men, which is not meant as an apologia, for he was credited with many more. His fame as a stanchion of the law brought him to Abilene as city marshal in the spring of 1871 Whereas his successor, the revered Tom Smith, had operated from the mayor's office, Hickok utilized the Alamo Saloon, where he could fill in his time playing poker and drinking the whiskey for which he also had a storied appetite. He ran a tight, two-fisted town, especially aimed at keeping undisciplined Texas cowboys in hand When 6 months later he killed Phil Coe, as well as (by mistake) his own policeman, he was soon sent packing by the town. Naturally enough, he left this life as the result of a shot in the back while playing poker in a Black Hills gambling joint.[4] This violent man is the hero who is supposed to have quelled violence on the frontier and to have brought the blessings of organized law and order to our Western civilization. But he was ever ready to kill, on either side of the law.

One writer, detailing the lives of the bad men of the West, has put together an appendix consisting of the bad men and another one of the peace officers. Among the bad men he lists are Judge Roy Bean, who dispensed the "Law West of the Pecos."[5] Hickok is also listed with the bad men. Ben Thompson shot up Kansas and almost crossed with Hickok, and wound up as a city marshal of Austin, Tex. Bill Longley was a deputy sheriff and one of the more notorious killers in the business. Doc Holliday was a lawman in both Kansas and Arizona under Wyatt Earp. And Arizona remains split to this day whether Earp belongs with the bad men or the good. Certainly the frontier story is replete with men of peace who were equally men of violence

Undoubtedly a lot of the violence spawned on the frontier emanated from the restlessness engendered by successive wars The American Revolution, the War of 1812, the Mexican War, and the Civil War all disgorged some men who had tasted action and could not return to the discipline of the settled world. Consequently they stayed on the frontier, where their training and penchant for direct action held some value. Undoubtedly this was more true of the survivors of Civil War action than of any of the other major wars. The men who fought in the Western areas of the Civil War, both North and South, enjoyed more than a little activity as guerrillas. But what does a guerrilla do when he has no more excuse for hit-and-run tactics? Either he settles down on a Missouri farm or he continues to hit and run against targets of his own devising. The most notorious of such men would have to be the James brothers, though their company is entirely too large. The Jameses could rob and kill almost with impunity if they selected their targets well. Since the James boys had been on the Southern side, they were cheered by their Southern fellows, embittered by the outcome of the war, who felt a bit of reflected glory in the harassment of the cold-blooded Yankees. Reputedly, Ben Thompson tried to get John Wesley Hardin to kill Wild Bill Hickok because Hickok shot only Southern boys. For once Hardin, the most prolific killer of them all, turned down an opportunity to notch his gun again. Had he shot the Yankee Hickok, he might have become a true Southern hero instead of just another killer —well, not just another killer—who needed to be put away. All across the West the antagonisms of the late conflict continued, and were justified really in the name of the war. It did not matter that you killed, so much as whom you killed.

Running parallel with this tendency for a strong individual to range himself actively on one side or the other of the law is the tendency throughout history of men and groups to take the law into their own hands, sometimes with reasonably lofty motives. As John Walton Caughey has written, "to gang up and discipline an alleged wrongdoer is an ancient and deep-seated impulse."[6] Whether such impulses run counter to a belief in the orderly pursuit of government is not debatable here. The fact is that throughout history societies, both frontier and long fixed, have moved through phases of private settlement of what should be public disputes. The operation of the Ku Klux Klan in a settled South with its centuries-old civilization is a case in point. Vigilantism is a disease or a manifestation of a society that feels a portion of its people are out of joint and must be put back in place whether the niceties of legal procedure are observed or not. That the end justifies the means is the authorizing cliché.

Not unmixed with vigilantism is frequently a fair share of racism, which has its own curious history on the American frontier. In some ways the frontier was the freest of places, in which a man was judged on the quality of his work and his possession of such abstractions as honesty, bravery, and shrewdness. The Chinese merchant, the Negro cowboy, the Indian rider—all were admired because of what they could do within the frontier community and not because of their pigmentation. On the other hand, the only good Indian was a dead Indian, "shines" could seldom rise above the worker level, and "coolies" were something to take pot-shots at without fear of retribution, either civic or con-science. Just as lynching a Negro in parts of the South was no crime, so shooting an Indian or beating an Oriental or a Mexican was equally acceptable. Like all societies, the frontier had its built-in contradictions.

In Kansas cowtowns, shooting Texas cowboys was a de-fensible act per se; popular agreement in that area was that although there might here and there be a decent cowboy, nonetheless most cowboys were sinister characters who were likely to ruin your daughter or your town. In other words, cowboys and Texans were in the same class as snakes—the garter snake can be a friendly reptile in your garden, but stomp him anyway in case he grows into a dangerous rattler.

But then, cowboys, whether Texan or Montanan, had a notoriously brazen unconcern toward nesters and grangers as Wyoming's Johnson County war will attest. How could the cattleman believe in legal law enforcement if, as one stockman put it, no jury of "Methodist, Grangers and Anti-Stock" would convict the most blatant cattle thief? A. S. Mercer, who felt that cattlemen were a menace to his Wyoming, nonetheless concluded that "as a matter of fact, less stealing and less lawlessness [occur] on the plains of the West than in any other part of the world."[7] Backing himself, Mercer quotes the Federal census report of 1890, which points out that the Northeastern states, "which are supposed to be most civilized," had 1,600 criminals to the million people while Wyoming ran 25 per cent less, or 1,200 to the million. However, the real cattleman dislike was for the sheepherder, who was lower than a nester, rustler, or even a cowboy who had married a squaw. As one Scotsman who emigrated opined, when he brought his

134

flock down from the hills in Scotland, people would exclaim, "here comes the noble shepherd and his flock." Out west, however, they said "here comes that damned sheepherder and his bunch of woolies!"[8]

Certainly the cowboy treatment of the sheepman showed something less than the normal extension of dignity due a fellowman. Cattlemen tried intimidation, and if that failed, they tried violence. If mere violence were not enough, next came murder, either for the sheepman or his flocks. As public sympathy was generally with the cattlemen, the sheepman had no recourse at law if his herder were killed or his sheep driven off the range. As a general rule, as in most vigilante situations, the cowboy always tried to outnumber his sheepherding adversary by five or ten to one, preferably all on horseback to the one herder on foot.

Nowhere was the sense of vigilante violence more noticeable than in the cattleman-sheepman feud. It was vigilantism, for the cowman looked on the sheepman's mere presence as immoral and illegal, an intrusion on his frontier life as he knew it. Along the upper reaches of Wyoming's Green River, for instance, a masked group, organized by the cattlemen, attacked four sheep camps simultaneously. The group blindfolded the herders, tied them to trees, and spent the remainder of the night clubbing to death 8,000 head of sheep. From wholesale dispatch of sheep to wholesale dispatch of men is really but a short, sanguine jump.

The Graham-Tewksbury quarrel furnishes another example. The Grahams and the Tewksburys had hated each other in Texas, and when both families moved to Arizona, the hatred moved in the wagons with them. Originally both Grahams and Tewksburys ran cattle, but in Arizona the Tewksburys turned to sheep after awhile. The usual charges of range violation, and the natural animosity for Tewksburys by Grahams, and vice versa, led to occasional potshotting that was looked upon by all but the participants as good clean fun.

Open conflict erupted when eight cowboys rode into the Tonto Basin of central Arizona, not really suspecting danger. But the Tewksbury brothers with five cronies were holed up in the basin, and in 10 seconds three cowboys were dead and two others wounded. Within a month, the cowboys had besieged the Tewksbury ranch headquarters, killing John Tewksbury. Retaliation followed retaliation. Within 5 years, all peaceable ranchers had been driven from the country, and 26 cattlemen and six sheepmen had been killed. None of this was considered murder, but simply an intermittent pitched battle to see who would prevail. And not at all incidentally, the Graham-Tewksbury feud provided the plot of one of Zane Grey's most widely accepted eye-popping novels, *To The Last Man,* read by youth and adult, western housewife and New York dentist alike.

The coming of barbed wire into the cattle country led to another outburst of vigilantism. Violence alone was insufficient against barbed wire because it was an inanimate object that did not directly pit man against man. Like the men it fenced in and fenced out, barbed wire was savage, unrefined, cruel, and hard. And in a sense, like the men whose ranges it controlled, it helped make the Great Plains finally fit for settlement.

As fence-cutting skirmishes broke out from Texas all the way north to Montana, people were killed, property destroyed, business crippled, and otherwise peaceful citizens alienated from one another. Men cut fences because their cattle were thirsty and their tanks were enclosed, or because they desired the good grass now out of bounds, or because the large ranching syndicates had fenced in whole counties. The XIT Ranch in Texas enclosed within wire grasslands approximately the size of the State of Connecticut. To fence in the XIT required 6,000 miles of single-strand wire. The Spur Ranch, also in Texas, erected a drift fence in 1884-85 that strung out for 57 miles, while an old Two Circle Bar cowboy told of seeing 10 wagonloads of barbed wire in the middle 1880's in transit from Colorado City, Tex., to the Matador Ranch. Again, men gunned down fence builders, violated enclosed land, and otherwise took the law into their own hands in resisting the coming of a new order. But legality eventually prevailed, and many men who had fought the new orderliness came to embrace it.

In effect, vigilantism was nothing more than lynching. Despite the fact that the South has been internationally damned for its lynching proclivities, it must share some of the tradition with other parts of the world, most notably with the frontier. Nowhere was lynch justice more swift, certain, or flourishing than on the frontier. Human life simply was not as valuable on the frontier as property. Taking a human life was almost as casual as our killing 50,000 people a year now by automobile murder. The fact that Colt's revolver and the repeating rifle were present and the courtroom was frequently absent undoubtedly aided such an attitude. Mitigating or extenuating circumstances for the transgressor were virtually unknown. Either he done it or he didn't.

Granville Stuart, the leading Montana vigilante, tells the story of a Billy Downs who was suspected of selling whiskey to Indians, stealing horses, and killing cattle. One July 4 the vigilantes ordered Downs and another man, an un-savory character known as California Ed, from Downs' house. Both men pleaded guilty to stealing horses from Indians, which was hardly a crime, but denied ever stealing from white men. On the other hand investigation showed their pen with 26 horses with white men's brands, none of the brands their own. A fresh bale of hides bore the brand of the Fergus Stock Co. The two men were carried out to a nearby grove and hanged.[9]

Cattle Kate, otherwise known as Ella Watson and mentioned in Owen Wister's *The Virginian,* and her companion Jim Averill were accused of branding mavericks. In the summer of 1889 they swung from a pine.[10]

In Las Vegas, N. Mex., the following warning was posted in 1880:

To murderers, confidence men, thieves:

The citizens of Las Vegas are tired of robbery, murder, and other crimes that have made this town a byword in every civilized community. They have resolved to put a stop to crime even if in obtaining that end they have to forget the law, and resort to a speedier justice than it will afford. All such characters are, there-fore, notified that they must either leave this town or conform themselves to the requirement of law, or they will be summarily dealt with. The flow of blood MUST and SHALL be stopped in this community, and good citizens of both the old and new towns have determined to stop it if they have to HANG by the strong arm of FORCE every violator of law in this country.

Vigilantes[11]

Not too far away, in Socorro, N. Mex., the vigilantes hanged a Mexican monte dealer because they were in-censed at his two employers, despite the fact that those

137

employers were paying the vigilantes $12 a day to keep their monte tables open.[12]

In effect, the Western frontier developed too swiftly for the courts of justice to keep up with the progression of people Therefore the six-gun or rope seemed superior to judicial procedure. In 1877, for instance, Texas alone had 5,000 men on its wanted list.[13] And Theodore Roosevelt pointed out, "the fact of such scoundrels being able to ply their trade with impunity for any length of time can only be understood if the absolute wildness of our land is taken into account." Roosevelt tells how in 1888 "notorious bullies and murderers have been taken out and hung, while the bands of horse thieves have been regularly hunted down and destroyed in pitched fights by parties of armed cowboys."[14] Small wonder that foppish Bat Masterson was once fined $8 for shooting a citizen through the lung. After all, the man had deserved it.

In Denver, according to one visitor from England, "murder is a comparatively slight offense," a sign of being fashionable.

Until two or three years ago, assassination—incidental not deliberate assassination—was a crime of every day . . . . Unless a ruffian is known to have killed half-a-dozen people, and to have got, as it were, murder on the brain, he is almost safe from trouble in these western plains. A notorious murderer lived near Central City; it was known that he had shot six or seven men; but no one thought of interfering with him on account of his crimes . . . .

The truth is that vigilantism, or "group action in lieu of regular justice," as Caughey calls it, reflects the thinking of a substantial body of local sentiment. The community sits in judgment. It condones because it believes. However, a vital difference exists between vigilantism of the frontier and the vigilantism of the latter 20th century. The pioneer was beyond the reach of regular justice; he had to fill the vacuum. Sometimes he filled it with grave concern for the decencies of human relations. More often he moved in a state of emotion, even as modern society would like to have done following the deaths of the two Kennedys, when the identities of the assassins were suspected.

In his penetrating study of vigilantism, Caughey points out the John Snyder-James Reed dispute arising out of the frustrations of the Donner party in 1846. A month behind schedule, nerves frayed, the members of the Donner party

138

were at each other's throats. When Snyder whipped Reed's team, Reed naturally objected. So Snyder brought his heavy whip down on Reed. To quote Caughey, "Reed drew his knife, Mrs. Reed rushed in between the two men and was struck by the whip, and then Reed, half-blinded in his own blood, plunged the knife into his antagonist. Immediately he was contrite as a man could be; he took the boards from his wagon to make the rude coffin in which Snyder was buried."[15]

What to do? The party was well beyond the reach of U.S. law, in the upper remoteness of Mexican territory, and totally out of touch with any legal jurisdiction. The members held a trial of some sort, Reed pled defense of his wife, and the evidence indicated unpremeditated and justifiable homicide. But his companions saw the action in another light, did not like to hang or shoot Reed, and so banished him empty-handed from the train. Undoubtedly it would have been a slow death sentence, except that his daughter slipped him a gun and ammunition in the night and he made it to California safely, later to participate in the rescue of what was left of that unfortunate party.

Caughey also mentions a rare acquittal. In this instance, in the Green River country of Wyoming, a man named Williams shot and killed a teamster who had repeatedly threatened his life. Williams offered to stand trial, but the group was not disposed to try him, believing that he had acted in self-defense. But when another man, apparently without provocation, killed one of his mates, a volunteer posse went after the malefactor, could not locate him, and brought Williams back to the Green River ferry to stand trial. Since it was the 4th of July, a festive crowd was on hand, court was convened, Williams challenged its jurisdiction, and an argument ensued which led to a riotous melee. The fact that it was the Fourth of July and that some of the Spirit of Independence was liquid undoubtedly contributed to the scuffle. The trial was not resumed, Williams felt that his presence was "wholly irrelevant" to the current circumstances, and he withdrew. The court was never adjourned, for it didn't seem necessary.

Far to the south, at the same time in Arizona, two young Arkansans quarreled, fought, and were pulled apart, whereupon one of them whipped out a knife and killed his assailant. The company promptly chose a judge and jury, found the knife-wielder guilty, and the next morning had the whole company vote on the verdict. A firing squad was chosen by lot, six men were given rifles with blank loads, and six had powder and ball. When they buried the man, they posted a brief statement over the grave of what had happened As Caughey concludes:

Months out of the trail, the emigrants certainly were beyond the reach of regular courts. There even was question what government had jurisdiction. If society was to do anything about crime on the trail, it would have to be through improvised group action. In their minds the forty-niners asserted this same justification—that they had left regular justice a couple of thousand miles behind and that it had to be the vigilante response or none at all. Other parts of the frontier could also assert that they were remote or cut off from established courts.[16]

The difficulty with frontier vigilantism is that it has no stopping place. Men accustomed to taking law into their hands continue to take law into their hands even after ːular judicial processes are constituted. They continue to take the law into their hands right into these days of the 1960's. They do not approve of a man or a situation, and they cannot wait for the regular processes to assist their realizations. They might not know a frontier if they saw one, and they certainly are not aware of the extension of the frontier spirit down to themselves. But they do know that they must get rid of the offending member or section of civilization. So they burn down a ghetto, they loot and pillage, they bury three civil rights workers beneath a dam, or they shoot a man in a caravan in Dallas or on a motel balcony in Memphis. True, to them the law and the other civilized processes may be available, but like the frontierman they cannot wait. But whereas some frontiersmen had an excuse, these people merely operate in a spirit which does violence even to the memory of the frontier.

So much of vigilantism of the frontier had no place at all in a legally constituted society. The vigilantes of San Francisco in the 1850's were operating after legal redress had been properly constituted. The Mexican, Juanita, "a very comely, quiet, gentle creature apparently, [who] behaved herself with a great deal of propriety," was visited in Downieville on the night of July 4, 1851, by a Joseph Cannon. When he literally fell through the door, Juanita sprang out of bed and stabbed the drunken intruder. She was seized, the cry went out that she had stabbed a popular citizen, a court was formed in the Downieville plaza, and a jury of 12 men was selected from the crowd that gathered.

Towards night they found the woman guilty and sentenced her to be hung at sundown . . . they gave her half an hour to get ready to die. She was finally taken down to the bridge, about four feet high from the bridge, and a rope put up over the crossbeam, with a noose attached to the end of it . . . this woman walked up the ladder, unsupported, and stood on the scantling, under the rope, with the hungriest, craziest, wildest mob standing around that ever I saw anywhere.

The woman adjusted the rope around her own neck, pulling out her braid of hair, and at the firing of a pistol, two men with hatchets, at each end, cut the rope which held the scantling, and down everything went, woman and all. The mob then turned upon Dr. Aiken, who was still a resident of that city, because he had tried to defend the woman; and they drove the gambler with whom the woman was living out of town, and also some other friends of the woman, showing from first to last the utter irresponsibility of mobs.

The hanging of the woman was murder. No jury in the world, on any principle of self-defense or protection of life and property, would ever have convicted the woman . . . there was considerable ill feeling toward Mexican gamblers and women generally, and there was no other way but to hang her. During the trial of the woman, ropes had to be brought into requisition to keep the mob back; they would once in a while make a rush for her, and the conductors of the prosecution would have to appeal to them, calling on them to remember their wives, mothers and daughters, to give this woman a fair trial; and in that way they were kept quiet until this woman was executed.[17]

The execution of Sheriff Henry Plummer in Montana ranks equally as a miscarriage of justice. Montana was sufficiently settled, as was Downieville, for men to have recourse to law. They did not choose to follow the slow process of judicial weighing of evidence but preferred to move with frontier dispatch. Undoubtedly Henry Plummer, sheriff at Lewiston, was the principal in a gang of road agents. Undoubtedly Plummer's agent had a hundred murders in their archives. How many assaults and robberies they had committed is impossible to determine. Certainly the vigilantes had provocation for forming. Certainly too the vigilantes had reason to believe that Plummer et al. were guilty beyond reasonable doubt. "Every good citizen in Alder Gulch" joined the vigilante organization, fearing that the Plummer gang might take alarm and disperse, not to be rounded up again.

141

Accordingly, four Virginia City vigilantes arrived at Bannack to order the immediate execution of Plummer and his confederates. Shortly Bannack had a branch organization of the Virginia City vigilantes. Off the Bannack vigilantes went, finding one of the confederates in a cabin and the other at a gaming table in a saloon. Plummer was found "at his cabin, in the act of washing his face . . . he was marched to a point, where . . . he joined Stinson and Ray, and thence the three were conducted under a formidable escort to the gallows." Plummer himself had erected the gallows the previous season.

Terrible must have been its appearance as it loomed up in the bright starlight, the only object visible to the gaze of the guilty men, on that long waste of ghastly snow. A negro boy came up to the gallows with rope before the arrival of the cavalcade. All the way, Ray and Stinson filled the air with curses. Plummer, on the contrary, first begged for his life, and, finding that unavailing, resorted to argument . . . .

"It is useless," said one of the Vigilantes, "for you to beg for your life; that affair is settled, and cannot be altered. You are to be hanged. You cannot feel harder about it than I do; but I cannot help it if I would."

Plummer asked for time to pray. "Certainly," replied the Vigilante, "but say your prayers up there," at the same time pointing to the crossbeam of the gallows-frame.

Regardless of whether they deserved to die, and the evidence indicates that they did, the three men had been executed without trial. They had been executed because the vigilantes of Virginia City had sent word to Bannack to seize them and execute them. To Montanans the presence of judicial procedures was not pertinent.[18]

Some excuse might be made for Montana being a truly crude frontier. Texas cannot hide behind such a claim. An independent republic in 1836, a State in 1845, by a comparison with the remainder of the western frontier it enjoyed a relatively sophisticated political society. And yet in the 1850's in Brownsville the Abbe' Domenech witnessed still another example of vigilante action. During a fandango a half-drunk North American killed a Mexican by stabbing him in the abdomen. As he fled for the sanctuary of Mexico across the river, the American was captured. On the next morning a trumpet summoned the people to pronounce sentence. A future sheriff took over, and without commentary called for "those who vote for his death step this way. Let the rest remain as they are." It was as casual as a New England town meeting voting an ordinance. The crowd shouted and to a man moved forward.

The action had been so precipitate that the gallows wasn't even ready, but a post was found outside a church. The future sheriff, inexperienced at this sort of thing, did not make a good gallows, so that the culprit was constrained to say to him, "Let me do it. You don't know your business." The prisoner seized the rope, tied the knot, and put it around his neck. After a short speech regarding the evilness of drunkenness, "which made a deep impression on the crowd," he hung from the post outside the church. Texas was a formal State in the United States of America, Brownsville was an old city that had gone through the war with Mexico, Texas had almost all the judicial procedures it has today, and the mob hanged a man for murder, even though the Mexican he had wounded did not actually die until the day after the hanging. A few years later a visitor to Texas was to observe: "in this lawless region men were seldom convicted of homicide, and never punished . . . if you want distinction in this country, kill somebody!"[19]

Kansas, of course, had been reasonably civilized since the latter 1850's. Perhaps some sympathy could be extracted for its problems with Texas cowhands, suddenly released from discipline like sailors in a foreign liberty port, but what do you do about a situation like the following?

The year is 1884. Caldwell, Kans., is undergoing a "moral spasm." Mayor Albert M. Colson and the council stand "for pure and simple good order." The town has a strong Women's Christian Temperance Union. Through the winter and spring of 1885 the movement for prohibition of liquor gathers strength, including the support of a Quaker-run newspaper, the Caldwell *Free Press*. Shortly after two whisky peddlers were arrested, the house of the *Free Press* editor burned to the ground. Then in November, 1885, the county attorney caused the arrest of a "blind tiger" operator. As he was being marched to the railroad depot, an armed mob besieged the two men escorting him in the baggage room of the train station. The new mayor, George Reilly, intervened and locked the prisoner in the city jail. But the mob reformed and turned the prisoner loose. The sheriff then arrested 18 Caldwellites.

Threats followed, one on top of the other. Finally on

December 8, at 1 o'clock in the morning, a group of men posing as law officers awakened one of the whisky peddlers and marched him off into the night. His body was found at dawn, "dangling stiffly from a crossbeam in the pelting sleet that prefaced the winter's first snow. A note protruding from one pocket—addressed 'To House Burners' and signed 'Vigilance Committee' "—advised the other peddler as well as six other whisky sellers to feel themselves warned. The mistress of the hanged man said she recognized two members of the lynching party, but when she was brought into court, she refused to confirm the identification, apparently having been threatened by the forces of law and order. As a grandson of the editor said years later, "Sentiment by the abiding element began to get so strong that someone had to be hung." The town leaders of Caldwell itself formed a 130-strong Law and Order League. Although some more deliberate citizens condemned such voluntary association, an assembly of perhaps 400 Caldwellites at the local opera house not only endorsed the Law and Order League's aim of enforcement of all laws in the statute books, but collected a private reward to help them in their work. These latter developments are a long generation removed from the frontier, but not from the frontier tradition.[20]

Forming a vigilance committee in Kansas carried no sinister implications within a community. Thus the editor of Topeka *Commonwealth* wrote routinely in the summer of 1875: "A vigilance committee has been organized at Dodge City, and it would not be surprising if some of the telegraph poles were found ornamented some of these days."[21]

Actually the idea of the vigilance committee goes back to puritan forefathers, whether it is their pointing out witches at Salem or their branding an "A" on a young girl's flesh. Back in 1830 in Illinois a mining rush wrapped around the unexciting metal of lead, ran the town of Galena, Illinois, into the usual welter of saloons, gambling halls, and disregard for law and order. Local citizens formed a vigilance committee. In effect the good moral people who violated the rights of the Mormons at Nauvoo were a self-constituted vigilance group. Iowa, never prominently associated with violence, had its own lead and land rush in the 1840's, and again the law-respecting farmers formed vigilance committees to rid Dubuque of its raffish lead-mining element and Keokuk of its "coarse and ferocious water men."

When in 1862 a gold strike along the Colorado River followed on the heels of a strike on the lower Gila, Tucson became a community cluttered with cut-throats. The moral people felt that these outlaws must surely have been spawned by the vigilance committees in San Francisco, who in ridding their town of a worthless element had sent it instead packing into the future Territory of Arizona.

Undoubtedly the most effective of the vigilance committees, insofar as numbers of hanged victims is concerned, belongs to the Black Hills of South Dakota during the middle and latter 1870's. Deadwood was wide open, which meant that it was wide open for riffraff and equally wide open for vigilantes. It was just a case of who could take over.

The truth is, every frontier State went through its period of lawlessness and its corresponding period of mobocracy designed to bring the lawless element under control. Further, the reformers did not cease imposing their personal ideas of reform with the coming of judicial processes. The truth is also that a century later, with or without our frontier background as justification, groups of citizens still make charges outside the law, and some even insist on enforcing those charges. A proper frontier tradition is great and effective, a true heritage for a people who must have heroes to point directions. But a frontier heritage misstated and misapplied is a disservice to the true cause of heritage and a negation of the freedom for which many frontiersmen gave their lives.

Invariably we return to a continuing, fundamental problem of race hatred. Nowadays it is dramatized as between black and white. Once it was between red and white. The hatred may not have been endemic, but the incursions of the white men on the Indian land drove the red man again and again to desperate, savage, and invariably futile war. The missionary loved the red man, from the days of the Spaniard clustered around the Texas and California missions down to the Quakers preaching brotherly love during the Indian massacres of President Grant's days. The fur trader also found the Indian a friend, and particularly found great comfort in the Indian woman. The Indian accepted both occupational groups.

But the one man who could neither assimilate the Indian nor be accepted by his red brother was the farmer. As the farmer moved westward, cutting back the forests, muddying up the streams, and beating back the game, the Indian's enmity toward him grew deadly. As for the frontiersmen, the Indian ranked somewhere below the dog. Certainly the Indian was well below the Negro slave, for the latter had function and utility. How do you handle an element for which there is no positive use? You exterminate it, especially if in your eyes it has murderous propensities. And so the inevitable, as virtually all the world knows, happened. The conflict between the two races, in the words of Ralph Gabriel, "like a forest fire, burned its way westward across the continent."[22] The noble savage was not noble at all in the sight of his adversary but a beast who bashed babies' heads up against trees and tore skin bit by bit from women's bodies. Each atrocity on either side evoked an equal retaliation. The list is long and painful, and no credit to either side.

From the standpoint of 20th century society, however, the white-Indian conflict for 300 years has important implications. For one thing, during the periodic lapses into peace which the young American nation enjoyed, these vacations from war did not by any means allow only for dull consolidation of the nation's politics and economics; instead they offered prime time for violent internal action. Almost always an Indian war was going on somewhere. On some wing of the frontier the white man was being menaced by the Indian, or he was menacing the Indian. He was running the Indian out of the woods, he was running him off the grasslands, he was running him across the desert and over the mountains to the west. With an insatiable earth hunger he was destroying the Indians' hunting grounds, until eventually he destroyed the game itself. This is not to discount those sincere Americans who had an interest in Indian culture and a desire for the two races to live side by side, but merely to point out that if any young man, full of the rising sap of the springtime of life, wanted to flex his muscles and pick a fight, he could find some Indian to fight against. The fact that the frontier also attracted the rootless and the drifters, and that these were often desperate men, added to the conflict and the inability to maintain peaceful Indian relations.

A mere listing of the battles with Indians would cover hundreds of pages in 6-point type. Take the Pequot War, King Philip's War, the French and Indian War, the Natchez War, the Fox War, Pontiac's Rebellion, Lord Dunmore's War, the problems of George Rogers Clark and at a later day William Henry Harrison, the Creek War, the Blackhawk War (which enlisted the attention of young frontiersman Abraham Lincoln), the Seminole War, all the raids by the Comanches and Apaches and Kiowas against the Texans and all the raids by the Texans against the Comanches, the Apaches, and the Kiowas, the Cheyenne-Arapaho War, the Sioux War, the Washita War, the Red River War, and the Ghost Dance Wars—these go on and on, seemingly without end. Where do you want to fight? When do you want to fight?

And if you get home from a war or a skirmish, you have instant hero status if you have halfway behaved yourself. There is a premium on killing Indians, a premium whose dividends continue through life. Men who came in after the end of Indian wars falsely delegated themselves as Indian fighters as they grew older and no one could prove them wrong. Often, criminal acts against other white men could be forgiven because a man had distinguished himself in combat against the Indians. Thus the retreating Indians constituted a kind of omnipresent safety valve for those people who liked to dance with danger, vitalize themselves with violence, and renew themselves with revenge.

Actually, although the only good Indian might be a dead one, there were two types of Indian. There were the peaceful ones, like California's 150,000 "Digger" Indians, a tranquil people who lived off the product of the land. There were also the warrior Indians, like the Sioux and the Apache. The white frontiersman generally looked on both with suspicion and distaste. California's miners murdered the Diggers as though they were endangered by them. On the other hand, murdering the warrior Indian was often a question of killing before you got killed, which simplified the problem. Skilled horsemen, these Indians, largely from the Great Plains, hit and ran with tactics that would have brought admiration from such mounted generals as Phil Sheridan, Jeb Stuart, or Erwin Rommel. Theirs was lightning warfare, and at full run they could loose twenty arrows while their longer-shooting foes were trying to reload. The wars themselves are reasonably straightforward, and could perhaps be condoned as inexorable conflicts. But the individual atrocities have no justification, even though at the time the perpetrators were often saluted as heroes. This latter statement holds true for both sides.

Nowhere has a lust for blood been more deeply etched than in the infamous Sand Creek massacre. Shortly after sundown on November 28, 1864, Col. J. M. Chivington and his men left Fort Lyon, Colo., to surround the followers of Chief Black Kettle. At dawn Chivington's militia charged through the camp of 500 peaceful Indians, despite Black Kettle's raising an American and then a white flag. Not just warriors were killed. Women and children were dragged out, shot, knifed, scalped, clubbed, mutilated, their brains knocked out, bosoms ripped open. Four hundred and fifty Indians in varying stages of insensate slaughter lay about the campground. There is no defense whatsoever for the action. It was bloodier than Chicago or Detroit or Harlem ever thought of being. Chivington and his cohorts were widely hailed as heroes by many of their fellow Americans.

Perfidy was not all on one side. During the summer of 1866, troops working on the Powder River road were constantly harassed by Indian attack. In a complete, efficient, and economical performance the Sioux killed every straggler, raided every wagon train bringing in supplies, and attacked every wood-cutting party. Finally in December, when a wood train was assaulted, Capt. W. J. Fetterman led a party to its relief. The Indians ambushed him, and left all 82 members of his party to rot on the field of battle. What Sitting Bull's detachment did to reckless and feckless Colonel George A. Custer at the Little Big Horn is known to everyone who ever looked at the Old Anheuser-Busch calendar or a Remington painting. Two hundred and sixty-five men were completely wiped out by 2,500 Sioux.[23]

Finally in the 1880's Geronimo, a "thin-lipped, square-cut, hard-eyed, savagely cruel hater of all white men" began his personal last frontier. In one 6-month period, Geronimo's raiders officially killed 85 soldiers, settlers, and reservation Indians in American territory, plus an uncounted number below the Mexican border. A superb strategist, Geronimo lost only six warriors during this period. Official United States decided that such activity could not be tolerated and sent 25 detachments under Gen. Nelson A. Miles after the ragged Apache. Desperate, Geronimo turned to needless terror, killing, among others, between 500 and 600 Sonorans during his campaign to escape capture. But time and space ran out on him, and he was caught and put aside.[24]

Of course, the classic account of racial arrogance, or disdain, belongs to Judge Roy Bean, who ranks with Billy the Kid as the most overrated, overblown character along the entire frontier. When a man was hauled before him for murdering a Chinese laborer along the Southern Pacific tracks building beyond the Pecos, Judge Bean freed the accused man, asserting that nowhere in his law book could he find a rule against killing a Chinese.

Sometimes it was not racial arrogance at all, but a simple antagonism to people with different outlooks. Thus Joseph Smith, Brigham Young, and other Mormons ran into the inflammatory and adamant opposition of local people, whether they lived in northeastern Ohio, Missouri, Illinois, or Utah. The Gentiles, believing presumably in all the Christian precepts, including love thy neighbor, did not love anyone whose faith was so far from theirs. It was difficult enough for a Campbellite on the frontier to accept a Baptist or one of John Knox's followers; Catholic and Jews were barely tolerable; the Mormon, a latecomer to the world of organized religion, was downright intolerable. His position was made less tenable by the fact that he tended to prosper, which induced Gentile grumbling that Mormons must be in league with the devil. And then one night at Carthage, Missouri, a properly organized area, a mob broke into the jail where Joseph Smith and his brother had been lodged for protection, and slaughtered the two Mormon leaders. Back east across the river, angry Gentiles served notice that the Mormons could leave or else.

Harassed even after they established their cooperative society in the midst of the individualistic West, the Mormons felt threatened as their first decade in the Territory of Utah came to a close. The result was another verse in that old chapter on retaliation. In September 1857, 140 emigrants were passing through southern Utah on their way to California. Although most were sincere, pious farmers

149

intent on a new life in California, there were a few hotspurs among the group. On September 7 the caravan was attacked by Indians, with seven white men killed. To relieve the ensuing siege, one Missourian in the party slipped out to seek assistance. A fanatical Mormon, perhaps mistaking his intention, killed him.

Fearful that his murder would bring Federal retaliation, the Mormon's neighbors hastened to cover the evidence. Accordingly, they sent word to the train that the Indians had been pacified and that the party could proceed across the territory. As the emigrants filed out of their siege site, they were shot down one by one. Altogether 120 persons were murdered, with 17 children only being spared. The years since have brought an understanding of the tensions under which the Mormons perpetrated this massacre at Mountain Meadows, but for purposes here the fact remains that feared violence was anticipated by preemptory violence.

The war with Mexico undoubtedly has some roots in racial arrogance on both sides. In fact, the whole severance of Texas from Mexico was brought about by men from the United States lately come to that vast area, and impatient with Mexican law and administration. Because the Mexicans felt that the Anglos represented a materialistic and restless culture, they were equally intolerant of their Anglo neighbors. To them, explaining the loss of Texas in the Texan revolution was no problem. After all, Texas had won only one battle during the entire altercation; it just happened to be the last one at San Jacinto. Mexico's army was experienced, and one Mexican soldier was certainly worth an indeterminate number of *yanqui* soldiers any day. War feeling in Mexico was as high and as bloodthirsty as it was in the States.

The ensuing overwhelming defeat of the Mexican forces and the wholesale dissection of Mexican territory into the giant maw of the North Americans only exacerbated distrust between the two nations. For the next 40 years Mexicans raided north of the Rio Grande. The Texans called them bandits. In pursuit of the Mexicans, Texans ranged south of the Rio Grande, where the Mexicans called them bandits. Both sides were right, and both were equally wrong. Again, as with the Indians, the killing of one race by another was perfectly justified back home. The Texas

Rangers, a law enforcement group, raided Mexicans along with Indians as natural enemies, and seldom gave any Mexican, whether a national of the United States or of Mexico, the benefit of the doubt.

Nor did the Rangers respect boundaries. In the best frontier tradition they pursued the enemy to his ultimate lair. There is the famous instance—famous at least to Texans—of Capt. L. H. McNelly, a 130-pound consumptive who was a living definition of deathless courage, chasing onto the Mexican side of the Rio Grande in the face of an overwhelming number of enemies, all pledged to his swift undoing. From the American bank of the river a sergeant in the U.S. Army sent Captain McNelly a note that the Secretary of War was ordering him back on the American side lest an international incident be provoked. McNelly's reply was terse and understandable, and must have caused some feeling when it was relayed to Washington. Simply and explicitly he told the Secretary of War to go to hell, this was his fight.

If during this essay it seems as if the frontier heritage is predominantly negative and directed toward violence, such a conclusion is misleading. The purpose here has been to examine a facet of the frontier heritage, that surface which not only condoned but actually encouraged the idea and practice of violence but which undoubtedly plays a role in shaping 20th-century American attitudes. The examination could go into as much detail as the danger, the frontier heritage established the idea of the individual's arming himself. This activity is almost unique with the United States frontier. Instead of a central armory to which men could go to gather their arms, each man bore his own. He thus had it always at the ready. When danger arose, he could get together with another man, and another and another, until an armed mob was on its way. It might be a mob in the best posse sense, or it might be an extra-legal group which felt that its private preserves and attitudes were threatened. But it was always a mob.

The prevalence of arms over the fireplace of every frontier cabin or stacked by the sod-house door endures in the defense which groups like the National Rifle Association membership carry on today against attempts to register arms and control the sale of guns and ammunition. A man had to have a gun, not solely for game to feed his family but because he had to be ready to defend. This heritage continues. As of this writing, it still prevails in most parts of the Nation. Almost no other country permits such widespread individual ownership, but the United States through its frontier experience has historical justification. In pioneer days a frontier boy came of age when his father presented him his own gun as surely as a town boy came of age by putting on long pants or his sister became a woman by putting up her hair. In many areas of the United States in A.D. 1969 a boy still becomes a man, usually on his birthday or at Christmas, when his father gives him a gun. A generally accepted age is twelve, although it may come even a half-dozen years sooner. The gun may be nothing more than a target weapon, but the boy is shown how to use it and how to take care of it, and he is a gun owner and user, probably for the next 60 years of his expected life on this earth. Whether he shoots sparrows out of the eaves of the house, quail and deer in season, or his fellowman with or without provocation remains for his personal history to unfold. The fact is that in his gun ownership he is following a tradition that goes back to John Smith and Jamestown and has persisted ever since.

And yet, as every schoolboy knows, the frontier has given us other traits which also mark us and often improve us. The frontier made us materialistic, because we needed things to survive. The frontier, by the very act of its being there for the taking and taming, gave us an optimistic belief in progress which again has marked the nation for greatness. The frontier fostered individualism as in no other region of the world. It gave us mobility; a man could move up and down the social, economic, and political scale without regard to what he had been before. The frontiersman could remold institutions to make them work. The frontiersman did not necessarily believe in individual freedom, except for himself, for he turned to his constituted government for every kind of help, particularly economic. The frontier also made him physically mobile long before the mechanics of transportation made such mobility easy. The frontier made him generous, even prodigal and extravagant, particularly where national resources were concerned. The frontier undoubtedly made the American nationalistic.

Thus we see a blending of a man's qualities that is both

152

good and bad. If the good could somehow be retained, while those qualities which have outlived their usefulness could be eschewed or dismissed forever, the human material which constitutes this nation could develop in the direction of an improved society. To argue which facets of the frontier experience have outlived their utility can be argued interminably, but certainly the wistful look backwards which Americans, informed and uninformed, cast toward the violence associated with the frontier has no place in a nation whose frontier has worn away. The time for everyone, from scenario writers to political breast beaters to economic and social individualists, to proclaim the virtues of the frontiersman and his reliance on simple solutions and direct action does not befit a nation whose problems are corporate, community, and complex.

References

1. William A. Settle Jr., *Jesse James Was His Name* (Columbia, Mo.: University of Missouri Press, 1966), pp. 44 ff.
2. William Ransom Hogan, *The Texas Republic* (Norman: University of Oklahoma Press, 1946), pp. 261 ff., relates several accounts of decisions engendered in early Texas by a lack of prison facilities.
3. Frank L. Van Eaton, *Hell on the Border* (Fort Smith, Ark.: Hell on the Border Publishing Co., 1953), pp. 72, 32 ff. Glenn Shirley, whose *Law West of Fort Smith* (New York: Henry Holt & Co., 1957) is the best book on Judge Parker, puts the figure at 160 men sentenced to die and 79 hanged, p. ix.
4. Kent Ladd Steckmesser, *The Western History in History Legend* (Norman: University of Oklahoma Press, 1965), pp. 106 ff.
5. George D. Hendricks, *The Bad Man of The West* (San Antonio: The Naylor Co., 1941), p. 272.
6. John Walton Caughey, *Their Majesties The Mob* (Chicago: University of Chicago Press, 1960), p. vii.
7. A. S. Mercer, *The Banditti of the Plains* (San Francisco: The Grabhorn Press, 1935), pp. 6-7.
8. Quoted in Charles Wayland Towne and Edward Norris Wentworth, *Shepherds' Empire* (Norman: University of Oklahoma Press, 1943), p. 256.
9. Granville Stuart, *Forty Years on The Frontier* (Cleveland: The Arthur H. Clark Co., 1925), vol. 11, p. 206.
10. Charles A. Guernsey, *Wyoming Cowboy Days* (New York: G. P. Putnam's Sons, 1936), p. 91.
11. Miguel Antonio Otero, *My Life on The Frontier 1864-1882* (New York: The Press of the Pioneers, 1935), pp. 205-206.
12. Jim McIntire, *Early Days in Texas; A Trip to Hell and Heaven* (Kansas City, Mo.: McIntire Publishing Co., 1902), pp. 142-143.
13. Carl Coke Rister, "Outlaws and Vigilantes of the Southern Plains, 1865-1885," *Mississippi Valley Historical Review*, XIX (1932-1933), pp. 537, 544-545.
14. "Sheriff's Work on a Ranch," *Century Magazine*, XXXVI, No. 1 (May-Oct., 1888), p. 40. "Ranch Life in the Far West," *Century Magazine*, XXXV, No. 4 (Feb. 1888), p. 505.
15. William Hepworth Dixon, *New American*, pp. 139-141, quoted in Carl Coke Rister, *Southern Plainsmen* (Norman: University of Oklahoma Press, 1938), pp. 192-193.
16. Caughey, *Their Majesties The Mob*, pp. 6-9.
17. David P. Barstow, Statement 1878, from the H. H. Bancroft Collection, University of California, Berkeley, quoted in Caughey, pp. 47-50.

18. Nathaniel Pitt Langford, *Vigilante Days and Ways* (Boston, 1890), vol.
    II, pp. 162-169, quoted in Caughey, pp. 80-85.
19. Albert D. Richardson, *Beyond The Mississippi*, p. 226, quoted in Rister,
    Southern Plainsmen, pp. 190-191.
20. Robert R. Dykstra, *The Cattle Towns* (New York: Alfred A. Knopf,
    1968), pp. 285-292.
21. Rister, *Southern Plainsmen*, pp. 196-197.
22. Ralph Henry Gabriel, *The Lure of The Frontier; A Story of Race Con-
    flict* (New Haven: Yale University Press, 1929), pp. 4-6.
23. Ray Allen Billington, *Westward Expansion* (New York: The Macmillan
    Co., 1960), pp. 653-672.
24. Joe B. Franz and Julian E. Choate Jr., *The American Cowboy* (Nor-
    man: University of Oklahoma Press, 1955), pp. 127-138.

Chapter 5

THE AMERICAN VIGILANTE
TRADITION

By Richard Maxwell Brown

The vigilante tradition, in the classic sense, refers to
organized, extralegal movements which take the law into
their own hands.* The first vigilante movement in American history occurred in 1767. From then until about 1900,
vigilante activity was an almost constant factor in American life. Far from being a phenomenon only of the far
western frontier, there was much vigilantism in the Eastern
half of the United States (Table 5-1). Although the first
vigilante movement occurred in Piedmont, S.C., in 1767-
69, most of the Atlantic Seaboard States were without
significant vigilante activity. But beyond the Appalachians
there were few states that did not have vigilante movements. There may have been as many as 500 movements,
but at the present only 326 are known.[1]

American vigilantism is indigenous. There were "regulators" in early-18th-century London who formed a short-
lived official supplement to London's regular system of law
enforcement,[2] but there was no connection between London's legal regulators and South Carolina's back country

* Grateful acknowledgment is made for research assistance on American
vigilantism provided by the American Council of Learned Societies, the New-
berry Library, the Huntington Library, the Rutgers Research Council, and the
Harvard University Center for the Study of the History of Liberty in America.

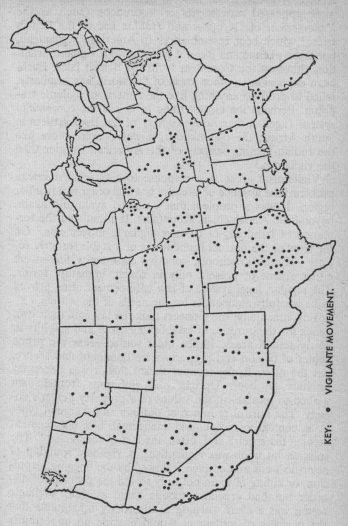

KEY: • VIGILANTE MOVEMENT.

Figure 5-1.—Vigilantism in the United States

"Regulators" of 1767 who constituted America's first vigilante movement. From time to time in European history there appeared movements or institutions (such as the *Vehmgericht* of Germany and *Halifax law* of the British Isles)[3] which bear resemblances to American vigilantism, but these phenomena did not give rise to a vigilante tradition either on the Continent or in the British Isles. European expansion in other areas of the world has, similarly, failed to produce anything like the American vigilante tradition. Perhaps the closest thing to it was the *commando* system (against marauding *kaffirs*) of the Boer settlers in South Africa; the *commandos,* however, were more like the Indian-fighting rangers of the American frontier than the vigilantes.[4]

Vigilantism arose as a response to a typical American problem: the absence of effective law and order in a frontier region. It was a problem that occurred again and again, beyond the Appalachian Mountains. It stimulated the formation of hundreds of frontier vigilante movements.[5] On the frontier the normal foundations of a stable, orderly society—churches, schools, cohesive community life—were either absent or present only in rough, immature forms. The regular, legal system of law enforcement often proved to be woefully inadequate for the needs of the settlers.

Fundamentally, the pioneers took the law into their own hands for the purpose of establishing order and stability in newly settled areas. In the older settled areas the prime values of person and property were dominant and secure, but the move to the frontier meant that it was necessary to start all over. Upright and ambitious frontiersmen wished to reestablish the values of a property holder's society. The hurtful presence of outlaws and marginal types in a context of weak and ineffectual law enforcement created the spectre and, often, the fact of social chaos. The solution hit upon was vigilantism. A vigilante roundup of ne'er-do-wells and outlaws followed by the flogging, expulsion, or killing of them not only solved the problem of disorder but had crucial symbolic value as well. Vigilante action was a clear warning to disorderly inhabitants that the newness of settlement would provide no opportunity for eroding the established values of civilization. Vigilantism was a violent sanctification of the deeply cherished values of life and property.

156

Table 5-1.—Leading Vigilante Movements[a]

1. 1767-69—South Carolina back country—R
2. 1816-17—Illinois (general)—R
3. 1820-30's—Indiana (general)—R
4. 1821-30—Illinois, Morgan and Scott Counties—R
5. 1830's—Georgia (northern)—S
6. 1830's—Mississippi (northern)—S
7. 1830-35—Alabama, Madison and Jackson Counties—S
8. 1835—Mississippi, Madison and Hinds Counties—R, O
9. 1835—Mississippi, Vicksburg—VC
10. 1839—Arkansas, Cane Hill, Washington County—O
11. 1840—Iowa, Bellevue—R
12. 1840-44—Texas, Sheby County—R
13. 1841—Illinois (northern)—R
14. 1842—Missouri, Benton and Hickory Counties—S
15. 1845—Kentucky, Christian and other Counties—R
16. 1846-49—Illinois (southern)—R
17. 1846-50—Kentucky, Paducah—R
18. 1849—California, San Francisco—R
19. 1849—California, San Francisco—O
20. 1851—California, San Francisco—VC
21. 1851-53—California, Sacramento—VC
22. 1851-53—California, Santa Cruz—VC
23. 1852-58—California, Los Angeles—VC
24. 1853-55—California, Jackson—V
25. 1856—California, San Francisco—VC
26. 1856—Texas, Orange and other Counties—R
27. 1857—Iowa, Iron Hill, Jackson County—VC
28. 1857—Iowa, Scott, Cedar and Clinton Counties—V
29. 1857-65—Texas, San Antonio—VC
30. 1858—Indiana, LaGrange and Noble Counties—R
31. 1859—Louisiana, Attakapas country—VC
32. 1859-61—Colorado, Denver—V
33. 1861-63, 1893-94—Texas, Coryell County—V
34. 1862-64, 1871—Idaho, Lewiston—VC
35. 1862-84—Montana (general)—V
36. 1863—California, Los Angeles—V
37. 1863-64—Montana, Bannack and Virginia City—V
38. 1863-98—Colorado and other States —Rocky Mountain Detective Association
39. 1864—Nevada, Aurora—O
40. 1864, 1874—Idaho, Payette Valley—C

41. 1864-66—Washington, Walla Walla—VC
42. 1864-68, 1872—Colorado, Pueblo—VC
43. 1864-85—Montana, Helena—VC
44. 1865—Idaho, Idaho City—VC
45. 1865-66—Mississippi (northeast)—R
46. 1866—Idaho, Boise—VC
47. 1866—Missouri, Greene County—R
48. 1866-71—Kentucky, Marion and other Counties—R
49. 1867—Missouri, Warrensburg and Johnson Counties—VC
50. 1867-68—Florida, Leon County—R
51. 1867-68—Indiana, Seymour—VC
52. 1868—Wyoming, Laramie—VC
53. 1868-69—Wyoming, Cheyenne and Laramie Counties—VC
54. 1868-70—Florida, Columbia County—R
55. 1868-70—Florida, Madison and other Counties—R
56. 1869-70—Georgia (southern)—R
57. 1870-71—Kansas, Butler County—V
58. 1871-82—New Mexico, Albuquerque—V
59. 1872—Louisiana, Atlanta, Montgomery and Winnfield—V
60. 1872-73—Louisiana, Vermillion Parish—V
61. 1872-86—Texas, Comanche County—V
62. 1875—Texas, Mason County—O
63. 1875-81—Nebraska, Sidney—V
64. 1876-77—California, Bakersfield—V
65. 1876-78—Texas, Shackelford County—VC
66. 1876-83—Texas, McDade, Bastrop County—V
67. 1877-78—South Dakota, Rapid City—V
68. 1877-79—South Dakota, northern Black Hills—V
69. 1880-82—New Mexico, Las Vegas—V
70. 1880-84—New Mexico, Socorro—V
71. 1880-96—Texas, San Saba County—O
72. 1882—Washington, Seattle—VC
73. 1883-84—Nebraska, Niobrara country—V
74. 1883-84—Florida, Sarasota—V
75. 1884—Montana (northern and eastern)—V
76. 1884—Ohio, Cincinnati—V
77. 1885-87—Missouri, Taney and Christian Counties—O
78. 1888—Oklahoma, Creek Nation—VC
79. 1891—Louisiana, New Orleans—V
80. 1892—Wyoming, Johnson County—R
81. 1892-97—Tennessee, Sevier County—O

[a] Large movements or increments of particular importance. Listed in chronological order. (Based upon Appendix.)

R—Regulators. S—Slickers. O—Other.
V—Vigilantes.
VC—Vigilance Committee.

Because the main thrust of vigilantism was to reestablish in each newly settled area the conservative values of life, property, and law and order, vigilante movements were usually led by the frontier elite. This was true of the greatest American vigilante movement—the San Francisco Vigilance Committee of 1856—which was dominated lock, stock, and barrel by the leading merchants of the city. Again and again it was the most eminent local community leaders who headed vigilante movements.

"Vigilance Committee" or "Committee of Vigilance" was the common name of the organization, but originally— and far into the 19th century—vigilantes were known by the now obsolete term of "regulators." Variant name for vigilante groups were "slickers," "stranglers," "committees of safety," and, in central Texas, simply, "mobs." (In this study "vigilante" will be used as a generic term to cover all phases of the general phenomenon of vigilantism.) The duration of vigilante movements varied greatly, but movements which lasted as long as a year were long lived. More commonly they finished their business in a period of months or weeks. Vigilante movements (as distinguished from ephemeral lynch mobs) are thus identifiable by the two main characteristics of (1) regular (though illegal) crganization and (2) existence for a definite (though possibly short) period of time.

COLONIAL ORIGINS:
THE SOUTH CAROLINA REGULATORS: 1767-69

The first American vigilante movement—the South Carolina Regulators, 1767-69—did not occur until 160 years after the first permanent English settlement at Jamestown. The reason for the late appearance of the phenomenon was the slow pace of frontier expansion. It was well into the 18th century before the settlement of the Piedmont began on a large scale, and at the time of the Revolution the settlement of the Piedmont was just coming to a close. Thus frontier expansion proceeded at a snail's pace in the colonial period, and it was possible to provide adequate systems of law enforcement for the slowly proliferating pioneer communities. The one exception to this pattern of orderly frontier expansion occurred in the South Carolina Piedmont in the 1760's.

Newly settled and recently devastated by the Cherokee Indian War, the disorder in the South Carolina back country of the 1760's was typical of later American frontier areas. During the Cherokee War so many habitations were burned, so many homes were broken up, and so many individuals were killed that the orphaned and homeless became a problem. Many drifted into outlaw bands formed by war veterans who were too restless or brutalized to settle down to peaceful pursuits. Outlaws, runaway slaves, and mulattoes formed their own communities where they enjoyed their booty. South Carolina way stations in an intercolonial network of horse thieves were established. "Crackers" and other frontier lower class people aided and abetted the outlaws. By 1766 and 1767 the back country was in the grip of a "crime wave," and the outlaws were almost supreme. They abducted young girls to be their paramours in the outlaw villages. They robbed and tortured plantation masters and raped their wives and daughters.

Lacking local courts and sheriffs to enforce law, respectable settlers of average or affluent means organized as "Regulators" in late 1767. A 2-year vigilante campaign was successful. Subscribing to articles to end the problem of crime and disorder, the Regulators attacked and broke up the outlaw gangs. The idle and immoral were rounded up by the Regulators, given trials, and flogged. If thought hopelessly incorrigible, the miscreants were driven from the area: those the Regulators deemed reclaimable were subjected to a system of forced labor on back-country plantations.

The South Carolina Regulator movement was constructive in that it did rid the back country of pervasive crime. Order and stability were at last established after many years of social chaos. But the Regulators were vindictive, and there was a streak of sadism in their punishments. The increasingly arbitrary, extreme, and brutal Regulators bred an opposition movement of "Moderators." Brought to a standstill by the equally violent Moderators and appeased by the Provincial government's provision for district courts and sheriffs, the Regulators disbanded in 1769.[6]

An American tradition had begun, for, as the pioneers moved across the Appalachian Mountains, the regulator-vigilante impulse followed the sweep of settlement toward the Pacific. The model for dealing with frontier disorder provided by the South Carolina Regulators was utilized over and over by American settlers.

Geographically, American vigilantism divides into Eastern and Western halves. Eastern and Western vigilantism are similarly distinct in regard to chronology. Eastern vigilantism mainly came to an end in the 1860's while Western vigilantism began in the 1850's. Eastern vigilantism was largely a feature of the first half of the 19th century and Western vigilantism of the second. Eastern vigilantism fell between the Appalachian Mountains [7] and the 96th meridian, while Western vigilantism stretched from the 96th meridian to the Pacific.[8] The humid Mississippi Valley, Great Lakes, and Gulf Coast regions furnished the main scenes of Eastern vigilantism; Western vigilantism took in the arid and semiarid Great Plains and the Rocky Mountains and the Pacific coast. Eastern vigilantism was a response, chiefly, to frontier horsethieves, counterfeiters, and ne'er-do-well white people. West of the 96th meridian the vigilantes were concerned largely with disorder in mining camps, cattle towns, and the open ranges.

In early-19th-century America, horsethieves and counterfeiters seemed to go together always, and when they did a vigilante movement was not far behind. The vulnerability of the settler to horse theft needs no comment, but counterfeiting as a frontier evil is a bit less familiar. The money problem made itself felt at the national level in the Age of Jackson in a number of famous issues such as the Bank War, but it was no less a problem in the backwoods and border country. Not only did the frontier suffer from a money shortage which counterfeiters as well as wildcat bankers tried to fill, but the frontier felt the lack of money especially in regard to the purchase of Federal public land. Added to the lively demand for cash at the land office was the chaotic condition of the paper money system. The lack of an effective system of Federal paper money and the plethora of private bank notes meant that never before or since in our history was counterfeiting easier.[9]

Counterfeiting and horse stealing were linked. Horsethieves commonly organized into gangs, stealing horses in one area and disposing of them hundreds of miles away—preferably across state lines.[10] For obvious reasons, counterfeiting operations were best carried on in the same way, and it was simple to combine the two occupations. The link between counterfeiting and horse theft had an effect on the geographical distribution of regulator and vigilante movements. The latter tended to be found in wilderness areas, close to State lines, or near Indian borders—all were places favored by horsethieves and counterfeiters.

From the 1790's well into the 19th century, vigilante activity was generally local in Kentucky, Tennessee, Indiana, and Illinois.[11] Thereafter there were four major peaks or waves of vigilantism. They occurred in the early 1830's, the early 1840's, the late 1850's, and the late 1860's. The first wave was from 1830 to 1835, and it took place mainly in the lower Southern States of Alabama and Mississippi where Captain Slick's bands operated against horsethieves and counterfeiters [12] and vigilantes attacked gamblers and the alleged Murrell conspiracy.[13] The second wave took place in the early 1840's and included the Bellevue vigilante war in Iowa,[14] the East Texas Regulator-Moderator conflict,[15] the Northern and Southern Illinois Regulators,[16] and the Slicker War of the Missouri Ozarks.[17] The vigilante wave of the early 1840's may have been a response to a shift in outlaw elements (caused by the 1830-35 vigilante campaign) from the Lower Mississippi River region of Alabama, Mississippi, Arkansas, and Louisiana to the Upper Mississippi area (northern Illinois, Eastern Iowa, and the Missouri Ozarks) and to the trans-Mississippi Southwest (East Texas).

The third peak of vigilantism was from 1857 to 1859 and featured the Iron Hills and other vigilante movements of Iowa,[18] the Northern Indiana Regulators,[19] the San Antonio [20] and New Orleans [21] vigilantes, and the *Comite's de Vigilance* of southwest Louisiana.[22] The movements of the late 1850's may have been inspired by the San Francisco Vigilance Committee of 1856 [23] which was well publicized throughout the nation. The fourth and final wave of vigilantism occurred in the immediate post-Civil War period (1866-71) with major movements erupting in Missouri,[24] Kentucky,[25] Indiana,[26] and Florida [27] as a reaction to postwar lawlessness.

Western Vigilantism

The nature of western natural resources determined the types of frontier disorder which gave rise to vigilantism.

Repeated strikes of precious and valuable metals in the Sierras and Rockies set off mining rushes that brought miners and others into raw new camps and towns by the thousands. In such places the law was often absent or ineffectual, with vigilantism the result. The other great natural resource of the West was the grassy rangeland of the Great Plains and mountain plateaus. The open-range system afforded an irresistible attraction to cattle- and horse-thieves who, in turn, invited vigilante retaliation.

Beginning with the first significant outbreak of vigilantism in the gold-rush metropolis of San Francisco in 1849 and continuing for 53 years down to 1902 there were at least 210 vigilante movements in the West. No vigilante movements in American history were better organized or more powerful than the San Francisco vigilance committees of 1851 and 1856. The San Francisco movements had an immense impact on American vigilantism in general and upon California vigilantism in particular. During the 1850's the San Francisco committees were copied all over the State in the new mining towns (Sacramento, Jackson, etc.) and in the old Spanish cities (Los Angeles, Monterey, etc.) Of California's 43 vigilante movements, 27 occurred in the 1850's.[28]

Montana was a most significant vigilante State. It had two of the most important movements in the history of the institution: the influential Bannack and Virginia City movement of 1863-65 (which gave the term "vigilante" to American English)[29] and the 1884 movement in northern and eastern Montana, which Granville Stuart led against horse and cattle thieves in a human roundup that claimed 35 victims and was the deadliest of all American vigilant movements.[30] In addition, Montana from the 1860's to the 1880's, was in the grips of a Territory-wide vigilante movement with headquarters, apparently, in the territorial capital, Helena.[31]

Texas had 52 vigilante movements—more than any other State. There were two important antebellum movements (Shelby County in East Texas, 1840-44; San Antonio, 1857 ff.), but the majority (at least 27) occurred in violence-torn central Texas in the post-Civil War period from 1865 to 1890.[32] There were dozens and dozens of vigilante movements in most of the other Western States; only Oregon and Utah did not have significant vigilante activity. Colorado's 16 movements were headed by the Denver vigilantes of 1859-61.[33] New Mexico had three potent vigilante movements in Albuquerque (1871-82),[34] Las Vegas (1880-82),[35] and Socorro (1880-84).[36] The Butler County vigilantes who enlisted almost 800 members and claimed eight victims formed the most notable of Kansas' 19 movements.[37] Wyoming vigilantism began with two lethal movements in the wild railroad boomtowns of Cheyenne and Laramie (1868-69) [38] and came to a climax with vigilantism's most famous failure, the cattlemen's Regulator movement which precipitated the Johnson County War of 1862.[39]

*　　*　　*

For purposes of analysis, the 116 Eastern vigilante movements and the 210 Western vigilante movements have been divided into the categories of large (L)—a large movement or one of particular significance; medium (M)—a movement of medium size or significance; and small (S)—a small movement or one for which there is insufficient information to otherwise categorize. All of the 326 American vigilante movements are listed alphabetically by state in appendix I. Table 5-2, which compares Eastern and Western vigilante movements, reveals that there were about twice as many vigilante movements in the West as in the East. (Here the figures probably undertstate the ubiquity of Eastern vigilantism; regulator activity was general in the early years of settlement in Kentucky, Tennessee, Indiana, and Illinois, but record of only a few of these movements has survived.) The ratio of large, medium, and small movements in the West was about 1:2:2; in the East it was approximately 1:1:1. Of the 729 known victims killed by vigilantes about 5/7 were claimed by Western vigilantes.

There were 81 large movements; they extended, chronologically, from 1767 to 1897. (See the listing in table 5-1.) Fifty-nine of the 81 large movements were clustered in the period from 1850 to 1889; 49 occurred in the midcentury decades from 1850 to 1879 when the nation was wracked by Civil War violence in the East and the tensions of rapid frontier settlement in the West. (See table 5-3b.) About 3/5 (190) of all vigilante movements took place after 1860, but, here again, it must be noted that the lack of specific information on many Kentucky, Tennessee, Indi-

Table 5-2.—Eastern and Western Vigilante Movements

Eastern Vigilantism

State	Large	Medium	Small	Total	Total Number of Killed Victims
Alabama	1	5	0	6	0
Arkansas	1	0	3	4	4
Florida	4	1	1	6	7
Georgia	2	1	1	4	6
Illinois	4	4	2	10	30
Indiana	3	2	6	11	15
Iowa	3	13	9	25	27
Kentucky	3	4	4	11	10
Louisiana	4	0	3	7	35
Minnesota	0	0	2	2	1
Mississippi	4	0	1	5	21
Missouri	4	1	7	12	21
Ohio	1	2	2	5	0
South Carolina	1	0	0	1	16
Tennessee	1	0	3	4	9
Virginia	0	2	0	2	0
Wisconsin	0	0	1	1	0
TOTAL*	36	35	45	116	202

Western Vigilantism

State	Large	Medium	Small	Total	Total Number of Killed Victims
Arizona	0	3	3	6	11
California	10	23	10	43	101
Colorado	3	4	9	16	23
Idaho	4	1	0	5	35
Kansas	1	5	13	19	18
Montana	4	2	0	6	101
Nebraska	2	8	6	16	20
Nevada	1	2	10	13	7
New Mexico	3	3	5	11	17
North Dakota	0	1	0	1	0
Oklahoma	1	1	2	4	2
South Dakota	2	1	1	4	10
Texas	9	15	28	52	140
Utah	0	1	1	2	0
Washington	2	1	3	6	11
Wyoming	3	2	2	7	31
TOTAL*	45	72	93	210	527
Plus Eastern States	36	35	45	116	202
GRAND TOTAL*	81	107	138	326	729

* Based upon App.

ana, and Illinois movements leads to an understatement of pre-1860 vigilante movements; 180 of the 190 movements were concentrated in the three decades from 1861 to 1890. (See table 5-3a.) By the same token, about 5/7 (511) of all the killed victims of vigilantism perished after 1860. (See table 5-6d.)

Behind the statistics lies the impact of vigilantism on the American consciousness. The original South Carolina Regulator movement of 1767-69 with its success in achieving order in the back country recommended itself to the pioneers who crossed the Appalachians and populated the Mississippi Valley. The regulator method, was, hence, applauded as a tool for establishing frontier social stability until, in the 1840's, three anarchic movements in southern

Table 5-3a.—All Movements by Chronological Periods[a]

Period	Number of Movements
1767-1849	65
1850-60	57
1861-90	180
1891-1910	10
Overlapped 2 Periods	14
TOTAL	326

[a] Based upon app. I.

Summary

Movements through 1860	122
Movements, 1861 and after	190
Overlapped the periods	14
TOTAL	326

Table 5-3b.—All Movements by Chronological Periods[a]

Period	Number of Movements
1767-1829	4
1830-39	6
1840-49	9
1850-59	13
1860-69	24
1870-79	12
1880-89	10
1890-1900	3
TOTAL	81

[a] Based upon app. I.

Summary

Movements through 1859	32
Movements, 1860 and after	49
TOTAL	81

Illinois, the Missouri Ozarks, and east Texas gave the institution an increasingly bad name. Soon thereafter, in 1851 and 1856, the restrained but deadly San Francisco vigilance committees restored to vigilantism an enormous prestige which it retained through the remainder of the century. Countless vigilante movements from coast to coast molded themselves upon the San Francisco vigilance committees. One of these was the vigilante movement of the gold camps of Bannack and Virginia City, Montana (1863-65), which in turn had something of the same effect on American attitudes as the earlier South Carolina and San Francisco movements. Thomas Dimsdale's classic book, *The Vigilantes of Montana* (1866), not only spread the fame of the Montana movement but was a veritable textbook on the vigilante method.

Significant vigilante activity did not always take the shape of a formally organized movement with officers, trials, etc. By the latter half of the 19th-century the ritual-like action of organizing a vigilante movement had been carried out so many times on so many frontiers that to many settlers it often seemed an unnecessary delay to swift lynch-law justice. A local consensus in favor of immediate vigilante action without any of the traditional formalities produced *instant vigilantism*. Instant vigilantism was more prevalent in the West than the East. Many of the "one-shot" vigilante actions in Western states were the result of the impulse for instant vigilantism. Thus instant vigilantism existed side by side with more formally organized vigilantism. Instant vigilantism meant that the public mind had long since been made receptive to vigilante action when general conditions or a particular crime seemed to warrant it. The ritual process of organization had been gone through so many times, the rationale of vigilantism was so well understood, and the course of action so obvious on the basis of past precedents that the settlers readily proceeded to the lynching.

Instant vigilantism seems to have occurred in all Western states but Oregon and Utah. Instant vigilantism was particularly effective in California. In the Golden State, regular vigilante action took 101 lives,[40] but the toll of instant vigilantism from 1851 to 1878 was almost as great in amounting to 79.[41] On a lesser scale the same things occurred in other Western states where time and again pre-cipitate lynchings were justified by vigilante tradition.

COMMUNITY RECONSTRUCTION AND VIGILANTISM

New settlers ordinarily desire new opportunities but not social innovation. Their main desire is to re-create the life they left behind them by reconstructing the communities from which they came. This is no great problem for entire communities that migrate en masse. There have been many examples of the latter. The Pilgrim settlers of Plymouth, Massachusetts, and the Mormon migrants to Great Salt Lake, Utah, are notable cases of "colonized" new communities.

More common have been the "cumulative" communities of inhabitants thrown together helter-skelter by the migration process.[42] The migrants to San Francisco, California, in 1849 and after furnish an example of the cumulative new community. The San Franciscans came from all over and were an immensely diverse lot. The only thing that united them, initially, was their desire to profit from the California Gold Rush.

Basic to the reconstruction of the community is the re-establishment of the old community structure and its values. To the extent that both are achieved, an orderly and stable new community life will be achieved. Although American frontiersmen of the 19th century came to their new localities from all points of the compass and were usually unknown and unrelated to each other, most came from essentially similar communities. The typical American community of the 18th and 19th centuries possessed a social structure of three levels:[43]

(1) The upper level consisted of the leading men and their families. Included were the well-to-do businessmen, the most eminent professional men, the affluent farmers and planters, and the prominent men of whatever occupation. This was the local elite, and in it were concentrated the community leaders.

(2) The middle level included the men of average means: farmers, craftsmen, tradesmen, and the less eminent lawyers, teachers, and other professionals. The in-

dustrious, honest middle level formed the core of the community. In this sector resided the legendary but real American yeoman.

(3) The lower level included the honest poor and also those who were either marginal to or alienated from the remainder of the community. In but not really *of* the community (and spurned by it) were the ne'er-do-well, shiftless poor whites. They constituted a true *lower people;* they were viewed with contempt and loathing by the members of the upper and middle levels who could not abide their slatternly way of life, their spiritless lack of ambition, their often immoral conduct, and their disorganized family life.[44]

The lower people were not outlaws but often tended to lawlessness and identified more with the outlaw element than the law-abiding members of the community. The outlaw element lived on the fringes of the community. In some cases they sprang from the lower people but were often men of good background who chose the outlaw life or drifted into it. They were alienated from the values of the community, although some occasionally joined respectable community life as reformed men.

A community has behavorial boundaries just as it has geographic boundaries. When a new community establishes its geographic boundaries it must also establish its behavioral boundaries. The latter represent the positive, mutual values of the community.[45] The values which supported the three-level community and the basis upon which it rested were the linked ideals of life and property. The American community of the 18th and 19th centuries was primarily a property-holder's community, and property was viewed as the very basis of life itself.

The vigilante leaders were drawn from the upper level of the community. The middle level supplied the rank-and-file. The lower people and outlaws represented the main threat to the reconstruction of the community and were the main targets of the vigilantes

In the cumulative new communities of frontier America, the lower people and outlaws met the representatives of the middle and upper levels in social conflict. The outlaws and lower people wished to burst their lower level bounds and "take over" the new communities. In sociological terms the outlaws and lower people constituted a "contraculture."[46] They rejected the respectable values of life and property and wished to upset the social structure in which the upper and middle level men were dominant. The lack of social bonds in the new settlements was their opportunity. On the other hand, the men of upper level background or aspirations were determined to reestablish the community structure in which they were dominant. In this they had the support of the middle level inhabitants, and with it they mounted vigilante campaigns to quell the insurgent outlaws and lower people.[47]

The danger of a takeover of newly settled areas by the alienated, outcast elements of society was a real threat. Whether or not the alleged Murrell conspiracy of the lower Mississippi Valley in the 1830's actually represented a concerted plot of white outlaws to raise a gigantic slave rebellion in the interest of an "underworld" dominion of the region, the phenomenon revealed the sensitivity of lawful society to large numbers, aggressiveness, and alienation of the outlaws of the region. In southern Illinois in the 1840's the "Flathead" element of horsethieves, counterfeiters, brigands, slave stealers, and Ohio River-bottom dwellers triggered a violent "Regulator" reaction.[48] In east Texas in the late 1830's a similar combine of horsethieves, counterfeiters, slave stealers, and "land pirates" incited a Regulator countermovement.[49] By 1841 a group of outlaw gangs had virtually taken over the Rock River counties of northern Illinois until challenged by a Regulator movement in that year.[50] Much earlier, in South Carolina in the middle 1760's a disorderly mixture of demoralized Indian war veterans, "straggling" refugee whites, "crackers," mulattoes, and outlaw horsethieves and counterfeiters well-nigh ruled the back country until honest men reacted in the Regulator movement.[51] West of the Mississippi and Missouri in the raw, new mining camps, cattle towns, railheads, and open ranges, the same threat emanated from the professional "bad men" and outlaw gangs, the "black leg" element, and the always troublesome "rustlers" and horsethieves. These and other challenges were thus met head on by the vigilantes.

The masonic lodge was often found in frontier communities, and the relationship between Freemasonry and vigilantism was frequently an intimate one. Typical was the situation in Bannack, Nevada City, and Virginia City,

Montana, rough, new mining camps in 1863-64. There the leading members of the potent vigilante movement of the winter of 1863-64 seem to have initially formed a bond as a result of their common membership in the masonic lodge.[52] The like happened elsewhere. The same impulse—desire to participate in the upper level dominance of the community—often caused the same person to join the masonic lodge (usually an elite local organization) and enlist in a vigilante movement. In Montana, Texas, and elsewhere, Freemasonry was often the shadowy background for the organization on a local vigilante movement.[53]

Sometimes the members of the upper level did not wait for an overt crime outbreak but formed a vigilante organization as a preventive measure and to cement the three-level community structure. Thus Thomas G. Wildman of Denver, Colo., wrote back East on September 8, 1859:

There is to be a Vigilance Committee organized in the town this evening. All of the leading men of the town has signed the Constitution, and its object is a good one. . . . It is thought that stabbing and drunkenness will be rampant here this winter, and we think that the rowdies and gamblers will be more careful when they find out that we are organized and that all the first men of the town are determined to punish crime.[54]

To the men of Butler County, Kansas, in 1870-71, vigilante action was the cornerstone of community construction. After killing eight men they justified their action by declaring, "it has become a question whether honest men of the country shall leave, or this gang." Invoking "self-preservation" as "the first law of nature," they asserted that "however much we deplore the further use of violence in order to secure life and property . . . we shall not hesitate to do justice to the guilty if it is necessary."[55]

James Hall described the challenge which outlaws and lower people presented in the early years of Midwest settlement:

We had whole settlements of counterfeiters, or horse thieves, with their sympathizers—where rogues could change names, or pass from house to house, so skillfully as to elude detection—and where if detected, the whole population were ready to rise to the rescue. There were other settlements of sturdy honest fellows, the regular backwoodsmen in which rogues were not tolerated. There was therefore a continual struggle between these parties—the honest people

170

trying to expel the others by the terrors of the law, and when that mode failed, forming *regulating* companies, and driving them out by force.[56]

An example of the problem was the bandit and "blackleg" community of the tamarack thickets and swamps of Noble County in northern Indiana. William Latta, William D. Hill, and George T. Ulmer were the pioneer founders and leaders of this illicit community which thrived for 25 years. The banditti and their blackleg allies were sworn to uphold each other. They robbed, murdered, stole, gambled, burned buildings, and made and sold counterfeit money. They exerted a pernicious influence on the sons and daughters of their respectable neighbors, leading hundreds of young men and women into lives of crime, debauchery, and prostitution.[57] Finally, in 1858, 2,000 Regulators rose and scattered the blacklegs and outlaws once and for all.

The loathing of upper level men for the lower element—the contraculture—of the frontier was stated with feeling by Thomas Dimsdale, who cried that "for the low, brutal, cruel, lazy, ignorant, insolent, sensual and blasphemous miscreants that infest the frontier we entertain but one sentiment—aversion—deep, strong, and unchangeable."[58] At times the deep aversion expressed itself in gruesome ways. Such an incident occurred in Rawlins, Wyoming, in 1881 where Dr. John E. Osborne (a future Governor of Wyoming) attended the hanging of the brutal Western outlaw, Big Nose George Parrott (or Parrotti). The next day Dr. Osborne "skinned 'Big Nose' George and cut away the top of the skull, in order to remove the brain. The skin was tanned and made into a medical instrument bag, razor strops, a pair of lady's shoes, and a tobacco pouch. The shoes were displayed in the Rawlins National Bank for years," and, in effect, constituted an upper level trophy in honor of the community values of life and property held by such men as Dr. Osborne.[59]

Vigilante Characteristics

Vigilante movements varied in size from the smallest of 12 to 15 members (the Pierre, South Dakota, vigilance committee) to the 6,000 to 8,000 who belonged to the San Francisco vigilance committee of 1856. (For the 10 largest movements, see table 5-5.) Of the 326 documented vigilante movements, information has survived on the number of members in 50 of them (see table 5-4). There were 13 movements of small size, ranging from 12 to 99 members. At the other extreme there were nine movements ranging from 700 to 8,000 members. Predominant were the 28 movements which ranged in size from 100 to 599 members. Thus the typical vigilante movement was one of from one hundred to several hundred members. Considering that the majority of American vigilante movements took place in new frontier localities of small population, the typical participation of from 100 to a few hundred members underscores the extent to which the community as a whole participated in them.

The characteristic vigilante movement was organized in command or military fashion and usually had a consti-

Table 5-4.—Vigilante Membership by Type of Movement[a]

Number of Members Per Movement	Movement			
	Large	Medium	Small	Total
12-99	4	5	4	13
100-199	3	4	–	7
200-299	6	2	–	8
300-399	2	1	–	3
400-499	5	0	–	5
500-599	4	1	–	5
600-699	0	–	–	0
700-799	2	–	–	2
800-899	0	–	–	0
900-999	2	–	–	2
1,000-4,999	3	–	–	3
5,000-8,000	2	–	–	2
Total	33	13	4	50

[a] Based upon App.

Table 5-5.—The 10 Largest Vigilante Movements[a]

Rank	Movement	Members
1.	San Francisco Vigilance Committee, 1856	6,000-8,000
2.	South Carolina Regulators, 1767-69	5,000-6,000
3.	Vigilance Committees of Attakapas country, Louisiana, 1859	4,000
4.	Northern Indiana Regulators, 1858	2,000
5.	Northern Illinois Regulators, 1841	1,000
6. (tie)	Idaho City (Idaho) Vigilance Committee, 1865	900
6. (tie)	Bald Knobbers of Christian and Taney Counties, Mo., 1885-87	900
8.	Butler County (Kans.) Vigilantes, 1879-71	798
9.	Denver (Colo.) Vigilantes, 1859-61	700[b]
10.	Slickers of Madison and Jackson Counties, Ala., 1830-35	500-600

[a] Based upon App.
[b] Actually 600-800 members, but ranked on basis of 700 members.

tution, articles, or a manifesto to which the members would subscribe. Outlaws or other malefactors taken up by vigilantes were given formal (though illegal) trials in which the accused had counsel or an opportunity to defend himself. An example of a vigilante trial is found in the northern Illinois Regulator movement of 1841. Two accused horse thieves and murderers were tried by 120 Regulators in the presence of a crowd of 500 or more. A leading Regulator served as judge. The defendants were given a chance to challenge objectionable men among the Regulators, and, as a result, the number of Regulators taking part in the trial was cut by nine men. Two lawyers were provided—one to represent the accused, and one to represent the "people." Witnesses were sworn, an arraignment was made, and the trial proceeded. In summation, the prosecuting attorney urged immediate execution of the prisoners. The crowd voted unanimously for the fatal sentence, and, after an hour allotted to the two men for prayer, they were put to death.[60] The accused were almost never acquitted, but the vigilantes' attention to the spirit of law and order caused them to provide, by their lights, a fair but speedy trial.

The punishments of whipping and expulsion were common in the early decades of vigilantism, but, as time passed, killing—usually by means of hanging—became the customary punishment. Through 1849 there are only 88 documented fatal victims of vigilante action (see table 5-6d). In the next decade 105 persons were killed by vigilantes, and it was at about this time—the 1850's—that the transition in the meaning of the term "lynching" from whipping to killing was occurring. The killing character of vigilantism, made firm in the 1850's, was accentuated during the remainder of the century; from 1860 to 1909 vigilantes took at least 511 lives (see table 5-6d.)

Of 326 known vigilante movements, 141 (43 percent) killed 729 victims. Of the movements by category (i.e., large, medium, or small), the large movements were, as might be expected, the most deadly, the medium movements less so, and the small movements hardly so at all. (See tables 5-6a, 5-6b, and 5-6c.) Of the 81 large movements, 59 (73 percent) took a total of 544 lives (76 percent of all vigilante killings) with an average of 9.2 lives per movement. Of the 107 medium movements, a substantial majority, 63 (59 percent) were fatal in effect; they took

Table 5-6a.—Number of Victims Killed by Type of Movement[a]

Number of Victims Killed	L Movements		M Movements		S Movements		All Movements	
	Number of Movements	Total Killed	Number of Movements	Total Killed	Number of Movements	Total Killed	Number of Movements	Total Killed
1	4	4	20	20	13	13	37	37
2	4	8	13	26	6	12	25	46
3	6	18	15	45	—	—	21	63
4	6	24	9	36	—	—	15	60
5	4	20	3	15	—	—	7	35
6	5	30	3	18	—	—	8	48
7	3	21	—	—	—	—	3	21
8	2	16	—	—	—	—	2	16
9	2	18	—	—	—	—	2	18
10	6	60	—	—	—	—	6	60
11-19	10	138	—	—	—	—	10	138
20-29	4	91	—	—	—	—	4	91
30-35	3	96	—	—	—	—	3	96
Total	59	544	63	160	19	25	141	729

[a] Based upon app.

Table 5-6b.—Average Number of Killed Victims Per Type of Movement[a]

Type of Movement	Number of Movements	Number of Killed Victims	Average Number Killed
L	59	544	9.2
M	63	160	2.5
S	19	25	1.3
All	141	729	5.2

[a] Based upon table 5-6a.

Table 5-6c.—Comparison of Movements With and Without Killed Victims[a]

Type of Movement	Movements With Killed Victims	Movements Without Killed Victims	Total Number of Movements
L	59	22	81
M	63	44	107
S	19	119	138
All	141	185	326

[a] Based upon app.

156 lives with an average of 2.5 per movement. There were 138 small vigilante movements in all; only 19 of these killed victims: 13 took single lives while six claimed double victims. Thus the overwhelming number of deaths attributed to vigilantism, 704 (or 97 percent of the total of 729) were exacted by 122 large and medium movements which, however, amounted to only 37 percent of all 326 vigilante movements. (See tables 5-6b and 5-6c.)

The tendency among the 141 vigilante movements taking lives was to stop after claiming four or fewer victims. (See table 5-6a.) Thus 98 movements (or 70 percent of the 141 movements) inflicted from one to four deaths. Only 17 of the 141 movements (12 percent) took more than 10 lives. The most lethal movement was that in Montana in 1884 led by Granville Stuart against the horse and cattle thieves of the eastern and northern part of the territory; its toll was 35 persons. (See table 5-6e.) [61]

Although the trend was for the large movements to kill the most victims (see table 5-6a), it was not always neces-

Table 5-6d.—*Number of Known Victims Killed by Chronological Periods*[a]

Period	Number of Killed Victims	Period	Number of Killed Victims
1760-69	16	1880-89	107
1770-79	0	1890-99	25
1780-89	0	1900-1909	1
1790-99	0		
1800-1809	0	Total	644
1810-19	0		
1820-29	3	Overlapped 2 or more periods	84[b]
1830-39	5		
1840-49	64	Year or decade unknown	1
1850-59	119		
1860-69	179		
1870-79	125	Grand Total	729

[a] Based upon app.

	Killed
[b] 1859-1860's	10
1860-1870's	10
1860-1890's	9
1870-1880's	30
1880-1890's	25
Total	84

Summary

Killed through 1859..207
Killed, 1860 and after...511
Killed in 1850-60's plus 1,
  year or decade unknown.......................................11

  Total...729

sary for a powerful movement to take a large number of lives. Often a vigilante movement could achieve its aims by taking only one or a few lives. The greatest of all vigilante movements (San Francisco, 1856) killed only four men. Two other significant movements—the northern Illinois Regulators of 1841 and the northern Indiana Regulators of 1858—executed only two men and one man, respectively. The fearful example of one or two hangings (fre-

Table 5-6e.—The 11 Deadliest Vigilante Movements[a]

Rank	Movement	Number of Victims Killed
1.	Vigilantes of Northern and Eastern Montana, 1884....	35
2.	Lewiston (Idaho) Vigilance Committee, 1862-64, 1871....................................	31
3.	Vigilantes of Bannack and Virginia City, Mont., 1863-65....................................	30
4.[b]	Montana's territory-wide vigilante movement, ca. 1862-84....................................	25
4.[b]	San Saba County (Tex.) Mob, 1880-1896..........	25
6.	Regulators and Committees of Safety of Madison and Hinds Counties (Miss.), 1835..................	21
7.	Southern Illinois Regulators, 1846-49..............	20
8.	Shackelford County (Tex.) Vigilance Committee, 1876-78....................................	19
9.	San Antonio (Tex.) Vigilance Committee, 1857-65.....	17
10.[b]	South Carolina Regulators, 1767-69..............	16
10.[b]	Cheyenne (city) and Laramie County (Wyo.) Vigilance Committee, 1868-69.....................	16

[a] Based upon app.
[b] Tie.

quently in conjunction with the expulsion of lesser culprits) was on many occasions enough to bring about the vigilante goals of community reconstruction and stability.

Vigilante leaders wished to reestablish the three-level community structure (in which they would be dominant) and the values of life and property that supported it. Specifically, they wished to check disorder and crime, but in some situations the threat of the latter was mild. In such cases their desire to use vigilantism underscored their basic, implicit goals of implanting community structure and values.

All this they wished to achieve as cheaply as possible. They were the typical frontier entrepreneurs. Their enterprize in commerce or land was often speculative, and they frequently skated on economic thin ice. The delicate balance of their own personal finances could be easily upset; hence, they had a lively awareness of the cost of public service and a yen to keep them down lest, as substantial taxpayers, their own circumstances suffer. No better resolution of the conflicting goals of public order and personal wealth could be found than vigilantism which provided a maximum of the former at minimum cost to the ambitious and well-to-do.

The typical vigilante leaders were ambitious young men from the old settled areas of the East. They wished to establish themselves in the upper level of the new community, a status they held or aspired to in the place of their origin. Two notable but representative examples of aggressive young vigilante leaders were William Tell Coleman and Wilbur Fisk Sanders.

Coleman was head of the San Francisco vigilance committee of 1856 and was 32 years old at the time. His father had been a Kentucky lawyer and legislator but died a bankrupt when the son was only 9 years old. The future vigilante, deprived of educational opportunity, spent his early years moving restlessly about the Midwest (Illinois, Missouri, and Wisconsin) in a fruitless quest to regain the upper level status of his father. Arriving overland in California in 1849 at the age of 25, Coleman embarked on a career which, by 1856, found him to be one of San Francisco's most successful importers.[62] His participation as a vigilante leader was, in effect, an action to cement his position in the upper level of the new city and to consolidate the three-level system there.

Wilbur Fisk Sanders was the courageous and incisive prosecuting attorney of the vigilantes at Virginia City, Montana, in 1864. Like Coleman, Sanders came from an upper level background but had not yet made firm his own position in that status. He was 29 years old when he served as a vigilante and had not long before accompanied his uncle, Sidney Edgerton (who had been appointed Territorial Chief Justice by Lincoln), from Ohio to Montana. Sanders' vigilante service did much to establish the three-level system in chaotic early Montana, and it was the beginning of one of the most spectacular careers in the Territory. Sanders went on to become one of the leading lawyers and top Republican politicians in Montana. He founded the Montana Bar Association and in 1889 was elected one of Montana's first two U.S. Senators.[63]

177

In frontier areas, law and order was often a tenuous thing. Outlaws—singly or in gangs—headed for the new areas and took every advantage they could of the social disorganization stemming from the newness of settlement and the weakness of the traditional institutions of state, society, and church.

Law enforcement was frequently inadequate. Throughout most of the 19th century (and not just on the frontier) it was pinned down to the immediate vicinity of county seat, town, or township.[64] Localities lacked the economic resources to support constables, policemen, and sheriffs in long journeys of pursuit after lawbreakers. A really large expenditure of funds for the pursuit, capture, jailing, trial, and conviction of culprits could easily bankrupt the typical frontier county or town.

There was also the handicap of poor transportation. The mobility of sheriffs and others was only as rapid and flexible as their horses afforded them. A fugitive, having gained any sort of lead, was difficult to catch. The development of the railroad was a help but was not without its disadvantages. The officer was bound to the fixed route of the railroad. There were large gaps, also, between the railroad lines—gaps into which the fugitives unerringly made. In the hinterland stretches unserved by the railroads, the authorities were forced to make their way over poor roads and disappearing trails.

Linked with inadequate law enforcement was an uneven judicial system. Through fear, friendliness, or corruption, juries often failed to convict the criminal.[65] Lack of jails (in the early days) or their flimsy condition made it nearly impossible to prevent those in custody from escaping.[66] The system presented numerous opportunities for manipulation by outlaws who could often command some measure of local support. Whenever possible outlaws would obtain false witnesses in their behalf, pack juries, bribe officials, and, in extreme cases, intimidate the entire system: judges, juries, and law enforcement officials.[67] Such deficiencies in the judicial system were the source of repeated complaints by frontiersmen. They made the familiar point that the American system of administering justice favored the accused rather than society. The guilty, then charged, utilized every loophole for the evasion of punishment. Compounding the problem was the genuinely heavy financial burden involved in maintaining an adequate "police establishment" and judicial system in a sparsely settled and economically underdeveloped frontier area.[68]

For many a frontiersman, vigilantism was the solution to these problems. W. N. Byers, and old Denver, Colorado, vigilante of 1860 reminisced:

We never hanged on circumstantial evidence. I have known a great many such executions, but I don't believe one of them was ever unjust. But when they were proved guilty, they were always hanged. There was no getting out it. *No, there were no appeals in those days; no writs of errors; no attorneys' fees; no pardon in six months. Punishment was swift, sure and certain.*[69]

THE IDEOLOGY OF VIGILANTISM

Vigilantism could never have become the powerful force in 19th-century America that it did become without having gripped the minds and emotions of Americans. This it did through a system of ideas and beliefs that emerged as the ideology of vigilantism. There were many elements in it.

1. The 19th-century doctrine of "Vigilance" suffused America in a way that had not been the case before nor since. To be vigilant in regard to all manner of things was an idea that increasingly commanded Americans as the decades passed. The doctrine of vigilance provided a powerful intellectual foundation for the burgeoning of vigilante movements, and, in turn, vigilante movements reinforced the doctrine of vigilance.

Vigilance committees were formed early for a host of things having nothing to do with the problem of frontier disorder. In 1813-14 the leading men of Richmond, Virginia, (headed by Chief Justice John Marshall) organized a Committee of Vigilance whose purpose was home-guard defense against a possible British attack during the War of 1812.[70] The attack never came, but the idea of vigilance did not die. In 1817 when Pensacola, Fla. (at that time still under Spanish rule but soon to become American), was threatened by a ship of Mexican filibusters, the citizens established a "Committee of Vigilance" for home defense which, however, like that of Richmond was never put to the test.[71] American settlers in Texas on the eve of the Texan Revolution founded Committees of Vigilance in Nacagdoches and other localities in 1835-36 by way of preparing for the looming hostilities with the Mexican mother country.[72]

The doctrine of vigilance had thus been utilized in regard to the early-19th-century crises of war and expansion; so, too, was it put to the service of sectional interests as the North and South moved toward confrontation in Civil War. Possibly the first "vigilance committee" involved in the sectional issue was that of the Ohio county of Meigs which lay across the Ohio River from western Virginia. In 1824 Meigs County men organized a vigilance committee to prevent Virginians from pursuing fugitive slaves into their locality.[73] As early as 1838, Philadelphia and New York had vigilance committees to aid fugitive slaves. In the 1850's Northern vigilance committees of this sort became increasingly common as they proliferated in response to the Fugitive Slave Act in Boston, Syracuse, Springfield, and smaller cities.[74] The South, conversely, fostered the founding of antiabolition vigilance committees as early as 1835 in Fairfax County, Va. Such committees spread through the South in the 1840's and 1850's.[75] By that time in Dixie abolitionists constituted an illusory threat at best. But the antiabolitionist vigilance committees probably helped increase the sectional solidarity of the South.

The doctrine of vigilance was not restricted to the great issues of war and sectional controversy but impinged upon the prosaic world of commerce. Thus, in a presage of the modern Better Business Bureau, the Merchant's Vigilance Association of New York City was organized in 1845 "to investigate and expose abuses in trade" and "to prevent frauds."[76] In time, the doctrine of vigilance merged with the earlier regulator tradition (that went back to the South Carolina back country) and the result, by the 1840's and 1850's was the "vigilance committee" dedicated to the eradication of frontier crime and turbulence.

2. The philosophy of vigilantism.—While the doctrine of vigilance was the background for the organizing of many vigilante movements, the vigilantes, knowing full well that their actions were illegal, felt obliged to legitimize their violence by fashioning a *philosophy of vigilantism*. The philosophy of vigilantism had three major components:

(a) *Self-preservation.*—By midcentury *self-righteous* vigilantes in as widely separated locales as Washington Territory, Montana, Missouri, and Louisiana were routinely invoking "self-preservation" or "self-protection" as the first principle of vigilantism. Thus the June 1, 1956, Vigilance Committee of Pierce County, Washington Territory, justified its existence by citing "self-preservation [as] the first law of society, & the basis upon which its structure is built."[77] The French Acadians of the *Louisiana Comités de Vigilance* were no less sure of their ground when on March 16, 1859, they declared, as a basis for taking the law into their own hands, that "self-protection is supreme."[78] The same note was struck by Thomas J. Dimsdale in his classic contemporary account when he stated that, for the honest Montana miners of Bannack and Alder Gulch (1863-64), the depredations of the "road agents" had narrowed the question down to "kill or be killed." Under the principle that "self-preservation is the first law of nature" the vigilantes "took the right side."[79] The very same language—"self-preservation is the first law of nature"—headed the resolutions of the Johnson County vigilance committee as it organized against post-Civil War horse thieves, murderers, and robbers in Warrensburg, Missouri, on February 28, 1867.[80]

(b) *Right of revolution.*—Vigilantes were well aware that their illegal action was, in effect, a blow at established authority. In order to deal with horsethieves and counterfeiters in Illinois in 1816-17 "the people," Governor Thomas Ford later wrote, "formed themselves into *revolutionary tribunals* . . . under the name of regulators."[81] Vigilante penmen cut right to the heart of the matter by unequivocally invoking the right of revolution. A Louisiana *Comités de Vigilance* proclamation of March 16, 1859, explicitly avowed its character as a "revolutionary movement."[82] The authorized historian of the *Comités,* Alexander Barde, cited the American Revolution as a justified popular insurrection and precedent for the movement he described. To condemn the vigilance committee in the context of intolerable conditions of lawlessness (analogous to the lack of justice that brought on the Revolution of 1776), said Barde, would be "to condemn our history" and to say "that if Nero governed us, we should submit to Nero."[83]

(c) *Popular sovereignty.*—Most vital to the philosophy

181

of vigilantism was the democratic ideal of popular sovereignty. An additional reason for the failure of vigilantism to appear before 1767 was the lack, up to that time, of a mature belief in democracy. The complete transition from deferential to democratic social values in America was a process that took from the time of the Revolution to the Age of Jackson. By the latter era (which coincided with the firm establishment of the vigilante tradition) the rule of the people was acknowledged by all but the most skeptical and reactionary.

"Popular sovereignty" was much more than a slogan used by the ambitious Stephen A. Douglas as a gimmick to solve the thorny problem of slavery in the territories; it represented a belief shared deeply by Americans of whatever political persuasion. The Regulators of the predominantly Republican counties of La Grange and Noble in northern Indiana saw no inconsistency (as they prepared for a lynch-law drive) in stating as the first of their Resolutions on January 9, 1858:

Whereas, We are believers in the *doctrine of popular sovereignty;* that the people of this country are the real sovereigns, and that whenever the laws, made by those to whom they have delegated their authority, are found inadequate to their protection, it is the right of the people to take the protection of their property into their own hands, and deal with these villains according to their just desserts. . . .[84]

The same idea was put a bit more pithily in 1902 when the following jingle was found pinned to the body of a man hanged by the vigilantes of Casper, Wyoming:

Process of law is a little slow
So this is the road you'll have to go.
Murderers and thieves, Beware!
PEOPLE'S VERDICT.[85]

"The *right of the people* to take care of themselves, if the law does not," said Professor Bigger of the local normal school to the Johnson County, Missouri, vigilantes in 1867, "is an indisputable right."[86] Hence, the 19th-century Americans the rule of the people was superior to all else—even the law. Vigilantism was but a case of the people exercising their sovereign power in the interest of self-preservation.

3. *The economic rationale of vigilantism.*—Although vigilantism rested on a bedrock democratic premise, the vigilante operation in practice was often not democratic. Ordinary men formed the rank and file of the vigilante organization, but, usually, its direction was firmly in the hands of the local elite. Local vigilante leaders were often the large local taxpayers. They had the customary desire to whittle down the tax rate and keep local expenses in check. From this point of view there was a persuasive economic rationale, for vigilante justice, was cheaper, as well as quicker and more certain, than regular justice. This was a theme that the vigilantes sounded time and again.

In 1858, northern Indiana regulators paraded under a banner that said, simply, *"No expense to the County."*[87] A *Denver Tribune* reporter probed opinion in Golden, Colo., in 1879 after a recent vigilante lynching and found that "on every side the popular verdict seemed to be that the hanging was not only well merited, but a positive gain to the county, saving it at least five or six thousand dollars."[88] The redoubtable vigilance committee of Las Vegas, New Mexico, was (like many others) dominated by the leading local merchants. One night in the early 1880's the vigilantes entered the local jail, took out all the inmates, and chased them out of town. The reason for the expulsion was to obtain economy in government as the inmates—"petty thieves, bunko men, and would-be bad men—were eating their heads off at the city's expense."[89] On September 3, 1887, the Mecker (Colorado) *Herald* praised a local vigilance committee and said, "We approve of this method of dealing with 'rustlers' as it is expeditious and saves the county the expense of prosecuting such cases."[90]

THE TWO MODELS OF VIGILANTISM

Two "models" of vigilante movements developed. One was the "good" or socially constructive model in which the vigilante movement dealt with a problem of disorder straightforwardly and then disbanded. The result was an increase in the social stability of the locality; the movement was, thus, socially constructive. The other model was the "bad" or socially destructive one in which a vigilante movement encountered such strong opposition that the result was an anarchic and socially destructive vigilante war.

Some movements, hence, behaved according to the ideal theory of vigilantism while others did not. Some were socially successful; others were not.

The Socially Constructive Model

The socially constructive movement occurred where the vigilantes represented a genuine community consensus. Here a decided majority of the people either participated in the movement or approved of it. Vigilantism of this sort simply mobilized the community and overwhelmed the unruly outlaws and lower people. The community was left in a more orderly and stable condition, and the social functions of vigilantism were served: the problem of community order was solved by the consolidation of the three-level social structure and the solidification of the supporting community values.

Although the methods used were often harsh and arbitrary, most vigilante movements—large and small—conformed to the socially constructive model. One of the best examples was the northern Illinois Regulator movement of 1841. The northern Illinois movement confronted a classic threat to community order: an agglomeration of outlaw gangs was nearing control of the area. With the regular government virtually powerless, the respectable leading men (the community upper level) took the law into their own hands with the help of the middle level farmers.

Since 1835 the situation in the Rock Valley of northern Illinois has gone from bad to worse. Several gangs of horse-thieves and counterfeiters found the Rock River country a convenient corridor for illicit operations in Wisconsin, Illinois, Iowa, and Missouri. The Driscoll and Brodie gangs had made Ogle and De Kalb Counties a virtual fief. The Oliver gang dominated Winnebago County. The Bliss-Dewey-West ring waxed strong in Lee County, while the Birch gang of horsethieves ranged in all quarters. By 1840 the desperadoes were numerous enough to control elections in Ogle County and similarly threaten other counties. One summer the outlaws even went so far as to burn down the newly constructed courthouse at Oregon, Illinois.

Finally, in April 1841, 15 "representative men" of Ogle County formed the first Regulator company. In no time at all the counties were dotted with Regulator squads, but the most vigorous were those of Ogle. The Regulators embodied the social, economic, and political prestige of Ogle County: John Phelps was the county's oldest and wealthiest settler and the founder of the county seat, Oregon. Peter Smith combined a bank presidency with the ownership of 1,600 acres of land. The farmers who made up the bulk of the movement were substantial property holders; they had taken up Government land claims ranging from 240 to 600 acres. These solid citizens brooked no opposition. They burned the Rockford *Star* to the ground soon after it published an anti-Regulator editorial. But on the whole, the local elite kept the movement well under control. Having accomplished their purpose in a campaign of whipping, hanging, and firing squads, the Regulator companies disbanded. Socially they left the Rock Valley in a better state than before they organized.[91]

The northern Illinois Regulator movement exhibited the major characteristics of the successful frontier vigilante movement. It was organized in a rational way. Mass participation of respectable men was the mode, but the movement was dominated, clearly, by the social and economic elite of the area. The Regulators were implacable in their war on the outlaws and unrelenting in the face of opposition. Although the Rockford *Star* opposed the Regulators, no anti-Regulator coalition, as a whole, developed. The outlaw gangs were isolated and broken up. The vigilante leaders desired the assurance of their position at the upper level of their communities but were not power mad. With the outlaw threat put down, peace and order reigned.

The Socially Destructive Model

In the socially destructive model, anarchy was the result of the vigilante movement. Because there was no community consensus behind the vigilante movement, strong opposition appeared, and civil conflict flared. In the socially constructive model, opposition to the vigilantes was narrowly restricted to outlaws and lower people who could gain no support from the remainder of the community. For the vigilantes to be stymied a broad antivigilante coalition was necessary. The formation of an antivigilante coalition almost inevitably condemned the community to a chaotic

185

internecine struggle between the vigilantes and their opponents.

Respectable men did not join the antivigilante coalition because of any great sympathy for the outlaws and lower people. They were impelled into opposition by things the vigilantes did or stood for. Sometimes two or three powerful local families would join the antivigilante movement. In some cases, these families had been carrying on a feud of sorts with leading vigilante families.[92] Sometimes a local political party or faction went into the antivigilante movement, because the vigilantes were dominated by the rival party or faction.[93] If the leading Democrats of a community, for example, were found among the vigilantes, the antivigilante coalition would probably attract the local Whigs. Political rivalries were often linked to vigilante strife, for in many instances vigilante leaders harbored political ambitions and were not above using the movement to promote their personal goals.[94] Economic rivalries among community leading men also were a factor in pro and con vigilante alignments; acute mercantile competition sometimes caused a leading storekeeper to go into the opposition if his rival was a vigilante.[95] Thus, personal, family, political, and economic antagonisms accounted for a readymade vigilante opposition in some communities.

At other times vigilante extremism drew into opposition decent men who otherwise probably would not have opposed them. The best of vigilante movements usually attracted a fringe of sadists and naturally violent types. Often these men had criminal tendencies and were glad to use the vigilante movement as an occasion for giving free reign to their unsavory passions. It was always a problem for vigilante leaders to keep these elements under control, and sometimes a movement was taken over or seriously skewed by these social misfits. Sadistic punishment and torture, arbitrary and unnecessary killings, and mob tyranny marked vigilante movements that had truly gone bad.[96] When this happened, many sound and conservative men felt they must oppose the vigilantes with whose original objectives they had probably felt no quarrel.

Examples of the socially destructive model did not occur as often as the constructive model, but when they did extremely violent conflicts tended to appear. Among the leading instances were the East Texas Regulators (versus the

Moderators), 1840-44; the Southwest Missouri Slickers (versus the Anti-Slickers), 1842-44; and the Southern Illinois Regulators (versus the Flatheads), 1846-50.[97] Sometimes an antivigilante coalition arose which, although unable to match vigilante strength, possessed the potential of calling in outside help and, hence, could define the limits of vigilante power. The antivigilante Law and Order faction in San Francisco, 1856, played this role. The vigilantes there would have liked to have hanged Judge David S. Terry but did not dare do so, for the Law and Order faction would have almost certainly obtained Federal action against the vigilantes.[98] Similarly, the Moderators in the South Carolina back country, 1769, were not strong enough to overturn Regulator domination, but they did check the movement and bring its excesses to an end.[99]

As the career of the socially destructive model proceeded, the moral standing of the vigilantes and the opposing coalition tended to be increasingly compromised. As the struggle became more violent, the respectable men of the antivigilante coalition put a higher premium on the violent talents of the outlaw element with which they otherwise had nothing in common. So, too, did the original vigilantes themselves recruit and acquire a criminal fringe which they put to mercenary use. With the community descending bloodily into chaos, wise and prudent men left if they could. The opposing movements tended to fall more and more into the control of the worst and most extreme of their adherents. About this time the desperate neutral residents would beseech State authorities for the intervention of the militia, and the "war" would subside fitfully in the presence of the state troops.[100]

The Regulator-Moderator war of east Texas (1840-44) was representative of the degenerate, socially destructive vigilante situation. The scene was the redland and piney wood country of east Texas in the days of the Lone Star Republic. The center of the conflict was in Shelby County. Fronting on the Sabine River where it formed the boundary between Louisiana and Texas, Shelby County lay in an old border area that had never been known for peace and calm. In 1840 the Regulator movement arose as a quite honest and straightforward attack on a ring of corrupt county officials who specialized in fraudulent land transactions. The rise of the Regulators was probably inevitable in any case, for the county had long wilted under a plague of counterfeiting, horse thievery, Negro stealing, and common murder and mayhem. However, the Regulators overplayed their hand, especially after their original leader, Charles W. Jackson, was killed and replaced by the nefarious adventurer, Watt Moorman. Bad elements infiltrated both the regulators and their opponents, the Moderators, but by comparison the latter seemed to become less obnoxious. Although some honorable and level-headed citizens like John W. Middleton stayed with the Regulators to the end, an attitude of wild vengefulness came to be more characteristic of the band. The early ne'er-do-well group among the Moderators dwindled. As more and more citizens were forced to take sides, many joined the Moderators in reaction to the sadism and vindictiveness of the swashbuckling Watt Moorman who affected a military uniform and blew great blasts on a hunting horn to summon his henchmen.

The original reasons for the founding of the Regulator movement were all but forgotten. The war became a thing in itself, a complexity of personal and family feuds that was consuming the area in blood lust. Several attempts to restore peace failed. Complete anarchy was the situation in 1844 when an all-out battle between two armies of several hundred men each was only forestalled by the dramatic intervention of Sam Houston and the militia. After 4 years, 18 men had been killed and many more wounded. A stream in the vicinity was called "Widow's Creek." The killing of so many leaders and the exhaustion of the survivors probably explain why the war was not revived after Sam Houston and the militia withdrew. Ex-Regulators and ex-Moderators warily fought side by side in separate companies in the Mexican War, but for 50 years east Texans were reluctant to discuss the episode lest old enmities be rekindled.[101]

VIGILANTISM AS A PARALLEL STRUCTURE

Vigilantism characteristically appeared in two types of situations: (1) where the regular system of law and order was absent or ineffective, and (2) where the regular system was functioning satisfactorily. The first case found vigilantism filling a void. The second case revealed vigilantism functioning as an extralegal structure of justice that paralleled the regular system.

Why did vigilantes desire to erect a parallel structure when the regular one was adequate? There were a number of reasons. By usurping the functions of regular law enforcement and justice or, at times, duplicating them—the cost of local government was greatly reduced. As taxpayers the vigilante leaders and the rank and file benefited from the reduction in public costs. Second, the process of community reconstruction through the re-creation of social structure and values could be carried on more dramatically by a vigilante movement than was possible through the regular functioning of the law. A vigilante hanging was a graphic warning to all potentially disruptive elements that community values and structure were to be upheld.

The sort of impression that vigilantes wanted to make was that received by young Malcolm Campbell who arrived in Cheyenne, Wyoming, in 1868 at the age of 28. No sooner had he arrived than there were four vigilante hangings. "So in rapid succession," he recalled, "came before my eyes instances which demonstrated the strength of law [as carried out by vigilantes], and the impotence of the criminal. Undoubtedly, these incidents went far in shaping my future life and in guiding my feet properly in those trails of danger where I was later to apprehend some of the most dangerous outlaws of the plains." [102] (Campbell later became a leading Wyoming sheriff.)

Finally, the vigilante movement sometimes existed for reasons that were essentially unrelated to the traditional problems of crime and disorder. The San Francisco vigilance committee of 1856 is one of the best examples of the vigilante movement as a parallel structure. The San Francisco vigilantes spoke of a crime problem, but examination of the evidence does not reveal a significant upsurge of crime in 1855-56. The regular authorities had San Francisco crime well under control. Fundamentally, the San Francisco vigilantes were concerned with local political and fiscal reform. They wished to capture control of the government from the dominant faction of Irish Catholic Democrats. The vigilantes actually left the routine enforcement of law to the regular police and intervened only in a few major cases. The parallel structure of the vigilante movement was utilized to organize a reform political party (the

People's Party) and to shatter the Irish Catholic Democratic faction by exiling some of its leading operatives.[103]

Sometimes the regular and parallel structures were intertwined. Law enforcement officials often connived with vigilantes. Here a sheriff or police chief was not taken by surprise when a vigilante force bent on a lynching converged upon his jail, for he had helped plan the whole affair. Appearances were preserved, usually, by a token resistance on the part of the law officer, but it was well known in the community that he had shared in the vigilante plot.[104]

Why would men violate their oaths and subvert their own functions as officers of the law? For some men the reason was that they were little more than hirelings of the local vigilante elite to whom they were beholden for office. Other officers were of higher social status but, as large landholders or businessmen themselves, they shared the vigilante desire to keep down governmental costs. Little interested in legal niceties, the vigilante-minded law officers were happy to have a nefarious bad man disposed of quickly, cheaply, and permanently by a lynching.

RELATED TO VIGILANTISM

The Antihorsethief Movement

American vigilantism has been paralleled by a number of related movements. Such movements as the three Ku Klux Klans, the White Caps, and the Night Riders have been illegal and violent. One legal, nonviolent movement existed side by side with vigilantism from the late 18th to the early 20th century. This was the antihorsethief movement. It is now almost forgotten, but hundreds of thousands of Americans from New England to the Rio Grande belonged to it.

The antihorsethief movement consisted of local societies, clubs, and associations of men—mainly farmers—who banded together to detect and pursue thieves, especially horsethieves. The antihorsethief societies were much like vigilante movements in respect to organization, objectives, and types of members. There was one crucial difference: they did not take the law into their own hands. Instead they restricted themselves to the detection and pursuit of culprits whom, after capture, they dutifully turned over to the local law enforcement officers. They eventually came to incorporate themselves under state law, and some states granted them constabulary powers.

The first antihorsethief societies arose spontaneously just after the Revolutionary fighting had ended.[105] The first such society was probably the Northampton Society for the Detection of Thieves and Robbers organized in Massachusetts in 1782. By 1800 similar groups had been founded up and down the Atlantic coast from Rhode Island to Delaware. The movement thrived in the northeastern United States as a legal supplement to regular law enforcement. It was vital and long lived in New Jersey—a typical state—where over 100 local societies were founded from 1788 to 1915. Official approval of the New Jersey societies were unstated until 1851, at which time the legislature explicitly approved organization of the societies; later it granted them the power of arrest. The societies flourished until the establishment of township police departments in the 1890's lessened the need for them. Inauguration of the state police in 1921 rendered them wholly unnecessary. Here and there they still exist but only as nostalgic social organizations.

The experience of New Jersey and the Northeast with the antihorsethief movement was duplicated in the Midwest and Southwest. The movement got underway in Indiana in 1852 with the legalization of regulator bands as antihorsethief societies. After the Civil War the movement grew rapidly and an interstate combine, the National Horse Thief Detective Association (with headquarters in Indiana) spread into Ohio and Illinois.[106] A similar development occurred across the Mississippi where a movement that began in northeast Missouri in the 1860's had, by the 1890's and later, became the farflung Antihorsethief Association with thousands of local chapters and over a hundred thousand members in Kansas, Oklahoma, Missouri, and Arkansas.[107]

Eventually the antihorsethief movement succumbed to the automobile. The latter supplanted the horse as the means of transportation which the members had joined together to protect. And the automobile immensely increased the range, mobility, and effectiveness of local law enforcement, thereby rendering obsolete the antihorsethief society as a supplemental crime-fighting agency.

191

A host of distinguished Americans—politicans, capitalists, lawyers, writers, and others—supported vigilantism by word or deed. Some of them were personally involved in vigilante movements; usually this was when they were younger men, but in later life they never repudiated their action.

As President of the United States, Andrew Jackson once advised Iowa settlers to punish a murderer by vigilante action,[108] and in his youthful ranching days Theodore Roosevelt sought—unsuccessfully—to join a vigilante movement.[109] William Tell Coleman, prominent capitalist and importer, was the great leader of the San Francisco vigilance committee of 1856. In addition to being a leading California capitalist (until he failed in 1886), Coleman was prominent in political circles. In 1865 he received 26 votes in the California Senate for the office of U.S. Senator, and in 1884 Charles A. Dana of the New York *Sun* boomed him for the Presidency of the United States.[110]

Leland Stanford, Sr., California Governor and one of the "Big Four" builders of the Southern and Central Pacific Railroads, was a member of the 1856 San Francisco vigilante movement as a young man of 32. A Republican, after serving as Governor from 1861 to 1863, Stanford also was in the U.S. Senate from 1885 to his death in 1893. In 1885 he founded Stanford University as a memorial to his son who died young.[111]

Many leading politicans took part in vigilante movements. Among them were Senator Francis M. Cockrell of Missouri. On February 28, 1867, at a public meeting in Warrensburg, Mo., Cockrell spoke strongly in favor of the organization of the Johnson County vigilantes. A lawyer, Cockrell had been a Confederate general. Ultimately he served Missouri as U.S. Senator from 1875 to 1905 and was on the Interstate Commerce Commisison from 1905 to 1910. In 1904 his name was placed in nomination (unsuccessfully) for President at the Democratic National Convention.[112]

Other prominent politicians who participated in Eastern vigilantism included Alexander Mouton of Louisiana. Mouton is an example of a man at the peak of state and national standing who chose to become a vigilante. One of the wealthiest sugar planters in Louisiana, Mouton had been trained in law at Georgetown College. After serving as U.S. Senator (1837-42) and Governor of Louisiana (1843-46), he became president in 1859 of the vigilance committee of Cote Gelée in Lafayette Parish, Louisiana.[113] Later, in 1872, Governor William Pitt Kellogg of Louisiana encouraged a deadly vigilante movement in Vermillion Parish which ultimately took 12 lives.[114] Much earlier and as a young man, Governor Augustus C. French took part in a Regulator movement in the early days of Edgar County, Illinois. A lawyer and a Democrat, French was a two-term Governor of Illinois from 1846 to 1853. He ended his career as a law professor at McKendree College in Illinois.[115]

A galaxy of Western "first citizens" participated in vigilante movements. Montana's leading pioneer and one of its most distinguished citizens of all time, Granville Stuart, was the main leader of the Montana vigilante movement of 1884. (The 1844 vigilantes disposed of 35 horse and cattle thieves and thus killed more victims than any other American vigilante movement; it was the movement that Theodore Roosevelt tried to join.) At the time he was one of the largest cattle ranchers in Montana as a member of Davis, Hauser & Stuart Co. Later he became state land agent; American minister to Uruguay and Paraguay, 1894-98; president of the Montana Historical Society, 1890-95; and Butte city librarian in 1904.[116]

William J. McConnell was one of Idaho's first two U.S. Senators (1890-91) and was Governor of Idaho, 1893-96. He was the author of a book for juveniles in which Idaho vigilantism of the 1860's (as well as his own role as a leading Payette Valley vigilante) was glorified. The book (in which Howard R. Driggs collaborated) was *Frontier Law: A Story of Vigilante Days* (1924). Conceiving the book essentially as a treatise on good citizenship for youth, McConnell had wished to dedicate the book to the Boy Scouts of America! Senator William E. Borah, of Idaho, one of the leading progressive statesmen of his generation, wrote a favorable introduction to McConnell's book.[117]

Two of the early governors of the State of Wyoming were participants in one of the famous episodes of Wyoming vigilantism: the lynching of the badman, Big Nose George Parrott, in Rawlins in 1881. Dr. John E. Osborne,

a leading Rawlins physician, was an enthusiastic participant in the event. Later, from 1893 to 1895, he was Governor of Wyoming.[118] The other distinguished vigilante was
Fennimore Chatterton, an eminent Wyoming lawyer, businessman, and promoter of irrigation projects. Chatterton
was Governor of Wyoming from 1903 to 1905.[119] Vigilantism in Wyoming—as in all states—was bipartisan: Osborne was a Democrat; Chatterton was a Republican.
Undoubtedly the weight of their approving participation
in the vigilante lynching of Parrott enhanced public acceptance of the act.

New Mexico likewise had two Governors with vigilante
backgrounds. Miguel Antonio Otero, son of a well-to-do
merchant (who was also an active vigilante in Kansas and
New Mexico—among many distinctions the senior Otero
was New Mexico territorial delegate to Congress and had
the honor of declining Abraham Lincoln's appointment of
him as American minister to Spain), took part in the Las
Vegas, New Mexico, vigilante movement of 1881-82 as a
young man of 22. At the time he was cashier of the San
Miguel National Bank. Becoming one of the most prominent New Mexicans of his generation, Otero was Governor
from 1897 to 1906. In politics he was a Republican and,
later, a Bull Moose Progressive.[120] New Mexico's other
vigilante Governor was George Curry who had been a
member of the Colfax County vigilance committee in 1885.
Later he became a Rough Rider protege of Theodore
Roosevelt and, partly upon the basis of that connection,
became a provincial Governor in the Philippine Islands and
Governor of New Mexico from 1907 to 1911. From 1911
to 1913 Curry served as one of New Mexico's first Congressmen.[121]

In Texas, James Buckner (Buck) Barry, like Granville
Stuart of Montana, was one of the famous pioneers of his
State. He participated in two Texas vigilante movements.
In 1860 he was a vigilante in a movement in Brazos and
surrounding counties, and after the Civil War he served
in a vigilante movement in turbulent Bosque County of
central Texas. Barry had been a Texas Ranger in 1845-46
and was a legendary Indian fighter. At one time a county
sheriff and treasurer, he served in the Texas Legislature in
1884-86 and was a leading member of the insurgent
Grange, Farmers' Alliance, and Populist movements in

Texas; he unsuccessfully ran for state treasurer on the Populist ticket in 1896.[122]

Frontier vigilantes were headed, thus, by the frontier elite—men who, in turn, gained the highest political positions in territory, state, and nation. Men who were actually vigilantes or had expressed strong approval of specific vigilante movements included two Presidents of the United States (Andrew Jackson, Theodore Roosevelt), five U.S. Senators, (Alexander Mouton, Louisiana; Francis M. Cockrell, Missouri; Leland Stanford, California; William J. McConnell, Idaho; Wilbur Fisk Sanders, Montana); eight Governors of states or territories (Alexander Mouton, Louisiana; Augustus C. French, Illinois; Leland Stanford, California; William J. McConnell, Idaho; Fennimore Chatterton and John E. Osborne, Wyoming; Miguel A. Otero and George Curry, New Mexico); one Congressman (George Curry); and one minister to a foreign country (Granville Stuart). At one time—in 1890—four ex-vigilantes served in the U.S. Senate; they were Francis M. Cockrell, Leland Stanford, William J. McConnell, and Wilbur Fisk Sanders.

Literary men were often outspoken in their support of vigilantism. Hubert Howe Bancroft, who wrote many volumes on Western history and who built his San Francisco publishing house into one of the leading businesses on the Pacific Coast, wrote a vigorous and highly favorable account of the San Francisco vigilance committees in his massive two-volume work, *Popular Tribunals* (1887).[123] Thomas J. Dimsdale, the Oxford-educated Montana superintendent of public instruction, wrote a popular and highly laudatory account of *The Vigilantes of Montana* in 1886[124] as did, later, Nathaniel Pitt Langford, the father of Yellowstone National Park.[125] Owen Wister, the socially prominent Harvard graduate and scion of an aristocratic Philadelphia family, in his immensely popular novel, *The Virginian* (1902),[126] strongly praised vigilantism and in so doing summed up the opinion of elite Americans. Andrew D. White, U.S. Minister to Germany, spoke for many when he maintained that "there are communities in which lynch law is better than any other."[127]

The 19th-century American elite walked a tightrope in regard to vigilantism. Most of them held conservative social and economic opinions and were not attracted by the revolutionary and democratic rationales of vigilantism. They carefully qualified their support of vigilantism. To them it was justified only in frontier areas where they saw it as being inevitable and necessary. This position was forcefully stated by Chief Justice Hosmer of Montana in an 1864 charge to a grand jury. Judge Hosmer praised vigilante organizations "which, in the absence of law, assumed the delicate and responsible office of purging society of all offenders against its peace, happiness and safety." Such organizations originated in "necessity," he said. "Their adaptation to the necessities of new settlements," he emphasized, "has obtained for them an approbation so universal, that they are the first measures resorted to, by well intentioned men, to free themselves of that vile class of adventurers which infest all unorganized communities for purposes of fraud, robbery and murder."[128]

As late as World War I, the American elite looked with favor upon the vigilante tradition. In 1918 a group of distinguished writers formed an organization to promote the war effort. Significantly, they chose to call themselves "the Vigilantes." Invoking the vigilante heritage, their pamphlet announced:

> There has been a disposition to associate the Vigilantes with those beloved rough-necks of the early California days, who established order in frontier towns and camps by methods distasteful to tender souls. We find no fault with this. In fact, we are rather proud of being linked up with the stern and vigorous pioneers who effectually squelched the anarchists and I. W. W. of their day.

The membership list of the Vigilantes was a "Who's Who" of the writers of the day. Among those who belonged were Hamlin Garland, Booth Tarkington, Ray Stannard Baker, Irvin S. Cobb, Edgar Lee Masters, Theodore Roosevelt, and many others.[129]

AN EVALUATION OF AMERICAN VIGILANTISM

In shortrun practical terms, the vigilante movement was a positive facet of the American experience. Many a new frontier community gained order and stability as the result of vigilantism which reconstructed the community structure and values of the old settled areas while dealing effectively with a problem of crime and disorder.

From a longer perspective, the negative aspects of vigilantism appear. Although the era of classic vigilantism came to an end in the 1890's, the tradition lived on. In fact, it was extended into areas of American life where it was wholly inappropriate. Thus arose the latter day phenomenon of neovigilantism.

Neovigilantism grew mainly after the Civil War and war largely a response to the problems of an emerging urban, industrial, racially and ethnically diverse America. The transition from the old to the new vigilantism was heralded by the San Francisco Vigilance Committee of 1856. The latter represented a blending of the methods of the old vigilantism with the victims of the new. Virtually all the features of neovigilantism were present in the San Francisco movement of 1856. Neovigilantism was to be frequently urban rather than rural, and that was the case in San Francisco. The old vigilantism had been directed mainly at horsethieves, counterfeiters, outlaws, bad men, and lower people. Neovigilantism found its chief victims among Catholics, Jews, immigrants, Negroes, laboring men and labor leaders, political radicals, and proponents of civil liberties. The actions and overtones of the San Francisco movement were strongly imbued with the passions and prejudices that came to feature the neovigilantism.

The San Franciscan vigilantes were ethnically biased; their ire focused on one group: the Irish.[130] The vigilantes were anti-Catholic; their hero and martyr was the anti-Romanist editor, James King of William, and most of their victims of 1856 were Catholics. Although their ranks included laborers and mechanics, there was a distinct class tinge to the 1856 movement: middle and upper class merchants were aligned against the lower class adherents of the San Francisco Democratic machine. Last but not least was a disregard for civil liberties. Angered by the arguments of John Nugent of the San Francisco *Herald* in favor of regular justice, the merchant vigilantes of '56 quickly organized an advertising boycott that transformed the *Herald* overnight from the strongest to the weakest of the city's major dailies.

Allegedly concerned with a crime problem, the San Francisco vigilantes of 1856 were in actuality motivated by a desire to seize control of the municipal government from the Democratic political machine that found the nucleus of its support among the lower class Irish Catholic workers of the city. Basic to the vigilante movement was the desire to establish a business-oriented local government which would reduce expenditures, deprive the Irish Catholic Democrats of access to municipal revenues, and lower taxes. To a considerable extent, the San Francisco vigilante episode of 1856 represented a struggle for power between two blocs of opposed religious, class, and ethnic characteristics. Thus, the vigilante leadership of upper and middle class, old American, Protestant merchants was aligned against a political faction based upon Irish Catholic lower class laborers. Such were the social and economic tensions that typically enlisted the violence of neovigilantism.

The protean character of neovigilantism precludes an extensive discussion of it at this time. Only significant tendencies may be noted. Negroes have been the targets of three distinct Ku Klux Klan movements over a 100-year period going back to 1867.[131] Catholics and Jews were singled out for verbal attack by the second Ku Klux Klan (of the 1920's), but the bulk of Klan violence in the 1920's seems to have been leveled against ne'er-do-well white Anglo-Saxon Protestants who did not measure up to the puritanical Klan moral standards[132] and was similar to the White Cap movement which violently regulated the immoral and shiftless from 1888 on into the 20th century.[133] Immigrants were repeatedly the victims of neovigilantism. One of the most spectacular instances was the lynching of 11 Sicilians in New Orleans in 1891.[134] Laboring men and labor union organizers (many of whom were immigrants) were frequently the subjects of vigilante violence when on strike or attempting to organize.[135]

Political radicals have often undergone vigilante harassment; one of the most striking examples was the arrest of thousands of Communists and radicals in the "Red raids" of January 1, 1920.[136] The raids were carried out under the color of law, but the whole action resembled nothing so much as a giant vigilante roundup. Proponents of civil liberties have at times fallen afoul of a quasi-vigilante spirit manifested in such waves of intolerance as the "McCarthyism" of the early 1950's. In contrast to the old vigilantism not even a pragmatic justification can be made for neovigilantism, whose efforts have been wholly pernicious. As an index of the tensions of America in an age of transition, neovigilantism is revealing, but as an attempt to apply vigilante methods to the solution of the complex social problems of urban, industrial, diverse America it has been a massive failure.

Neovigilantism is one phase of a larger American failing to which vigilantism has significantly contributed—the spirit of lawlessness. Americans have long felt that intolerable conditions justify defiance of law and its extension, revolution. In large part the spirit of American lawlessness (equal in importance to the spirit of lawfulness) goes back to the American Revolution where Americans learned a lesson that has never been forgotten: that it is sometimes good and proper to rebel and that rebellion succeeds.

Powerfully nurturing American lawlessness has been the vigilante tradition. A part of the historical heritage of hundreds of American communities from the Piedmont to the Pacific, vigilantism—like the American Revolution—has taught the lesson that defiance of law pays. The typical vigilante took the law into his own hands sincerely (but paradoxically) in the interest of law and order. He desired social stability and got it. But was it purchased at too high a cost?

Yes, said the principled opponents of vigilantism who hammered home a philosophy of antivigilantism that went as far back as the opposition to the original South Carolina movement of 1767-69. From the very beginning antivigilante theorists cogently argued that due process of law was a precious Anglo-American legacy, that true law and order meant observing the law's letter as well as its spirit, and, finally, that the only way to obtain real and lasting law and order was to pour all one's energies and substance into making the regular system work.

One trenchant opponent of the San Francisco Vigilance Committee of 1856 noted that "if the same energy which prompted the formation of the Committee and organized the armed force that assaulted the jail had been directed to strengthen the regular course of justice as public opinion can do it, there would have been no need for the [vigilante] outbreak." "The precedent is bad, the law of passion cannot be trusted, and the slow process of reform in the administration of justice is more safe to rely on than the action of any revolutionary committee, no matter how great may be the apparent necessity," he continued. "Better to endure the evil of escape of criminals than to inaugurate a

199

reign of terror which to-day may punish one guilty head, and tomorrow wreak its mistaken vengeance on many innocent lives," he concluded.[137]

Aside from the danger of vigilante action veering off into extremism, the critics of vigilantism were upset by its fundamentally subversive character. A southern Illinois opponent of the Regulator movement in Pope, Johnson, and Massac Counties, Richard S. Nelson, charged in 1847 that by attacking citizens and taking their property the Regulators had violated "those great principles of civil liberty" upon which the Illinois State constitution was based. Nelson also turned the vigilante justification of popular sovereignty against them by noting that in forcing elected county officials to leave the county or surrender their offices the Regulators had "made a direct attack upon the sovereignty of the people."[138] There is no doubt, however, that, for all the plausibility of Nelson's invocation of popular sovereignty against vigilantism, the appeal to popular sovereignty was made much more often by vigilantes than by their opponents.

Occasionally, vigilante opponents got at the sociological causes of the crime and turbulence which led to vigilantism. The Reverend William Anderson Scott was a courageous opponent of the powerful San Francisco vigilantes of 1856. In a sermon entitled "Education, and not Punishment, the True Remedy for the Wrong-Doings and Disorders of Society," Scott called for industrial education for the lower classes and for urban eleemosynary institutions as means of eradicating the root sources of crime. "You may depend upon it," he insisted, "the stream of blood will never be staid [sic] while men take the law into their own hands.[139]

Americans have for generations been ambiguous in their attitude to law. In one sense, Americans are a law-abiding people of exemplary character. But the many organized movements in our history which have openly flouted and ignored the law (Revolutionary Whigs, Northern abolitionists, Southern filibusters, regulators, vigilantes, Ku Klux Klansmen, White caps, lynch mobs, etcetra.) are an indication that lawlessness has been rife. In 1837, the young Abraham Lincoln delivered an address on "The Perpetuation of Our Political Institutions" and found that the chief threat came from "the increasing disregard for law which pervades the country—the growing disposition to substitute the wild and furious passions in lieu of the sober judgment of courts, and the worse than savage mobs for the executive ministers of justice."[140]

Basic to American lawlessness has been our proclivity to pick and choose the laws we would obey, respecting those which we approve and defying those with which we disagree.[141] Our arbitrary attitude toward law reflects a fundamental and deep-seated disrespect for law, or, to put it another way, reveals only a superficial allegiance to law. Perhaps the most important result of vigilantism has not been its social-stabilizing effect but the subtle way in which it persistently undermined our respect for law by its repeated insistence that there are times when we may choose to obey the law or not.

EPILOGUE

Vigilantism of the 1960's

The middle and late 1960's have produced a new upsurge of vigilantism. The following movements (to be listed chronologically and then analyzed) differ from classic vigilantism in the sense that, apparently, they have not yet taken the law into their own hands; they have restricted themselves to patrol activity and to assisting the police. In another sense, however, these movements are in the authentic vigilante tradition, for they are movements in which citizens join together for self-protection under conditions of disorder and lawlessness. Moreover, these movements have commonly been viewed as "vigilante" movements by their members, the police and the authorities, and by society at large.[142]

1964

1. May 1964 (through the summer of 1966 and perhaps later): The "Macabees," a neighborhood patrol organization is formed in the Crown Heights area, Brooklyn, New York. Nightly radio-car patrols are established for the purpose of spotting and reporting criminal actions. Predominantly Hasidic Jewish in its membership (but with some white Christians and Negroes) of 250, it was formed

after a mass meeting of 500 Jewish neighborhood leaders and led by Rabbi Samuel Shrage. The crime problem was mostly by teenage Negroes coming into Crown Heights from adjacent areas. By March 1966, the *New York Times* reported that crime had fallen in the Crown Heights area and that the Maccabees were patrolling at a reduced rate.[143] In June 1966, Rabbi Shrage was appointed assistant executive director of the Youth Board of New York City,[144] and since that time the Maccabees have dropped out of the news, suggesting that they are either inactive or no longer considered newsworthy.

2. December 1964: Apartment dwellers in the Delano Village complex of North Harlem, New York City, establish interracial anticrime foot patrols equipped with walkie-talkies. In one apartment building there had been 14 assaults on residents in one month.[145]

3. December 1964: Apartment dwellers in buildings on Manhattan's West Side in New York City in the vicinity of West End Avenue, Riverside Drive, and 103d Street form a patrol organization similar to the one in Delano Village. The problem is an increase in crime stemming from a recent rise in the price of heroin, many addicts resorting to robbery and burglary to support their expensive habit.[146]

4. December 1964: Twenty-four citizens of Port Chester, New York (near the Connecticut State line), form a "vigilante group" to deal with rowdy youngsters from Connecticut who came to Port Chester to take advantage of New York's law allowing 18-year-olds to drink. Patrol action was apparently contemplated by the "vigilante group."[147]

1965

5. March 1965: The Midland Beach Progressive Association, a civic organization of Staten Island, New York, forms a system of nightly unarmed radio-car patrols to protect Midland Beach women who have been the victims of recent assaults. The patrol cooperates with police.[148]

6. April 1965: On April 1, 100 Negroes in the Bedford-Stuyvesant area of Brooklyn, New York, establish automobile and foot patrols (the latter with big dogs) to prevent and discourage crime. Modeled on the Maccabees

of Crown Heights and cooperating with police, the organization was an outgrowth of a meeting of the Fulton Park Community Council.[149] Note that this was a Negro organization established to deal with a Negro crime problem.

7. May 1965 (through 1966 and perhaps later): Deacons for Defense and Justice, a Negro self-protection organization founded in Jonesboro and Bogalusa, Louisiana, in May 1965. An armed patrol-car system was set up to protect civil rights workers (some of whom were white) and Negro residents against violence and harassment by Ku Klux Klansmen, white rowdies, and the police. The tough, dynamic leader of the Deacons in violent, racially troubled Bogalusa was Charlie Sims, a non-middle-class Negro. Wholly successful in Jonesboro and Bogalusa, by May 1966, the Deacons claimed 7,000 members in Louisiana and 60 loosely federated chapters in Mississippi, Alabama, Florida, and the Carolinas, and were attempting to gain a foothold in Chicago.[150] The Deacons have not been mentioned lately, suggesting that they have become inactive or that their activities are no longer considered newsworthy.

1966

8. March 1966: A radio-car citizens' patrol of 15 members is established to prevent, discourage, and report crime in Bushwick, Brooklyn, New York. A recent robbery-killing and a rape precipitated the organization of the group which, however, had been in the planning stages for several months. Headed by a Lutheran minister, the Reverend Samuel L. Hoard, the group had the support of an organization of 12 Protestant and Catholic churches in the area. It was modeled on the Maccabees of Crown Heights and was cooperating with the police.[151]

1967

9. January 1967: The People's Civic Association of the East New York, Brownsville, and Flatbush areas of Brooklyn, launched a radio-equipped vigilante patrol of 350 members with five automobiles. Operating mainly around East 98th Street in order to spot and discourage criminal activity, it cooperated with the police.[152]

10. March 3, 1967: Thirty-five tenants (mostly wom-

en) form a "temporary vigilante committee" to patrol a large apartment building at 441 East 20th Street in Peter Cooper Village, Manhattan. The committee was an outgrowth of a mass meeting of building inhabitants called in response to a wave of rapings and muggings. Neither the police nor Metropolitan Life (the owner of the building) were able to supply adequate police protection. An irony in the situation was that New York Police Commissioner Howard R. Leary lived in an adjacent building.[153]

11. June 1967: A force of about 50 private security guards (called "vigilantes" by *Time*) armed with shotguns is formed in Houston, Texas by three drycleaning chains and six other businesses for the purpose of protecting their premises against robbery which had recently reached a crisis level. Another reason cited for the hiring of the vigilantes was Houston's extremely low police-citizenry ratio. Mayor Louie Welch gave the organization his approval.[154]

12. Summer of 1967 through 1968 and presumably still in existence: The North Ward Citizens' Committee of Newark, New Jersey, was organized to conduct nightly radio patrols for the dual purpose of spotting and discouraging criminal activity and repelling, should the need arise, an incursion of Negro rioters and looters from the adjacent Central Ward of Newark. Headed by its dynamic founder, Anthony Imperiale, the North Ward Citizens' Committee was an outgrowth of the racial confrontation in Newark stemming from the tremendous Negro riots of June 1967. The members of the committee are primarily Italians and thus reflect the ethnic composition of the North Ward.[155] The North Ward Citizens' Committee has been one of the most publicized vigilante organizations of the 1960's. Its founder, Anthony Imperiale was elected to the Newark city council in November 1968, largely upon the basis of popularity gained through his Committee leadership.

13. October 1967: Operation Interruption, an "armed police militia" was founded in Harlem (New York City) by the Reverend Oberia D. Dempsey, pastor of the Upper Park Avenue Baptist Church and the unofficial "mayor" of Harlem. A Negro organization of 2,600 members, of whom 200 armed and active members formed a core, it was formed to combat "criminalization" in Harlem stem-

ming from drug addiction and centering on 125th Street. The members maintained themselves in readiness to stop crimes, patrol areas, escort citizens, and work as informants for the city police, FBI, and the Federal Narcotics Bureau. Capt. William J. O'Rourke of the 25th Precinct police station, conceding the lack of an adequate number of police, worked closely with the Reverend Dempsey and Operation Interruption.[156] Note that this, too, was a Negro organization against Negro crime.

1968

14. June-July 1968: Self-proclaimed vigilantes of West Hollywood, Florida, consist of 12 businessmen who patrol nightly in prowl cars and are armed with shotguns. Their announced purpose was to protect their shops and stores against robbery, charging Sheriff Allen B. Michell of Broward County with negligence.[157]

15. July-September 1968: White vigilantes are said to be active in various areas of Cleveland, Ohio. They are mainly anti-Negro and are a response to Negro turbulence in the Hough section, a Negro "ghetto" area of Cleveland. The unsolved killings of two Negroes may have been the result of vigilante action.[158]

16. July-September 1968: "Night riders" in Irasburg, Vermont harass the Reverend David L. Johnson, a Negro accused of adultery with a white woman. The charge against Johnson was later dismissed in court.[159]

17. Summer of 1968: Fight Back, an anti-Negro organization in Warren, Michigan, is apparently similar in character to the North Ward Citizens' Committee of Newark.[160]

18. Summer of 1968: The Home Defense Association of Oakland, California, is an anti-Negro organization apparently similar in character to the North Ward Citizens' Committee of Newark.[161]

19. October 1968: Negroes form unarmed "vigilante units" in Pittsburgh, Pennsylvania, for nightly walking patrols in response, apparently, to crime and, especially, to Negro-white racial tensions. The Negroes had intended to have armed patrols but were discouraged from doing so by the Public Safety Director of Pittsburgh.[162]

20. December 1968: The *New York Times* reports the existence in New York City of various citizens' anticrime

operations, including private and volunteer guards in apartment-house lobbies, guards in public housing projects, and neighborhood block guards.[163]

1969

21. January 1969: The Community Patrol Corps in the Negro ghetto of Detroit, is an unarmed street patrol of 15-20 young Negro men in semimilitary dress. The patrol was formed for the dual purpose of curbing Negro criminality and white police brutality and was aided by a $50,000 grant from the New Detroit Committee, Detroit's local Urban Coalition group.[164]

(Related to the "vigilante" movements recounted above has been the Crime-Stop movement. Chicago's Police Superintendent, O. W. Wilson, originated Crime-Stop in that city in April 1964. The idea was for citizens to telephone in reports of crimes or suspicious activities to a special police number. In 1967 *Parade* reported that more than a million Chicagoans had pledged to cooperate with Crime-Stop and that the movement had spread to 111 cities [including Boston and Los Angeles] in 34 states.)[165]

The survey above indicates that there are three vigilante-prone segments of the population today: (1) Negro enclaves, South and North, which feel the need of self-protective organizations against white violence and harassment. The Deacons for Defense and Justice are the best example of a vigilante response in this situation. (2) White urban and suburban neighborhoods in the North which feel threatened by a possible incursion of Negro rioters and looters. The North Ward Citizens' Committee of Newark is the leading example of the vigilante response in this situation. (3) Urban neighborhoods beset by crime. The Maccabees of Crown Heights, Brooklyn, have served as the model for the vigilante response to this situation.

Both the white versus Negro and the Negro versus white vigilante-type organizations are heavily freighted with neo-vigilantism in that racial fear and animosity is a major motivating factor in the vigilante activity. The most typical vigilante organization thus far in the 1960's is, however, the pure anticrime combination exemplified by the Maccabees of Crown Heights, Brooklyn. Thus the typical vigilante organization arises in urban neighborhoods among residents who feel that there is a severe crime problem. The leadership of the organization—like the vigilantes of old—is indigenous, often consisting of neighborhood religious leaders (e.g., Rabbi Shrage of the Maccabees, the Reverend Hoard of the Bushwick, Brooklyn, movement of 1966, and the Reverend Dempsey of Operation Interruption in Harlem). Combination is a spontaneous act of the people but is often an outgrowth of an existing organization.

In contrast to the classic vigilantism of the 19th century, vigilantes of the 1960's do not take the law into their own hands nor do they kill.[166] Instead their main activity is patrol action in radio-equipped automobiles (linked to a central headquarters) for the purpose of spotting, reporting, and discouraging criminal acts. Characteristically these modern vigilantes cooperate with the police, although the latter have occasionally worried that the vigilantes would get out of hand. To a considerable extent the vigilantes of the 1960's resemble the antihorsethief societies (late 18th century to early 20th century) who restricted themselves to the pursuit and detention of malefactors and did not ordinarily take the law into their own hands.[167] Both the earlier antihorsethief societies and the current vigilantes supplemented but did not substitute for regular law enforcement.

The next stage—that of contemporary vigilantes taking the law into their own hands—may not come. That it may, however, was the recent warning of a spokesman for crime-ridden Harlem Negroes, Mr. Vincent S. Baker, chairman of the anticrime committee of the New York City branch of the NAACP. Invoking the vigilante tradition, Mr. Baker noted that "in towns of the Old West where there was no law, people paid gunslingers to protect them from the depredations of marauding outlaws." "There is an embryonic vigilante movement in this community," he declared. "It's cropping up all over. Tenant groups are arming themselves." Baker called for more police in Harlem and harsher penalties for criminals as a minimum program if the community was "to escape the reign of criminal terror without resorting to vigilantism." "Asserting that the Harlem situation was no better than Dodge City, Abilene, or other towns of the Old West," Mr. Baker attacked vigilantism as being "inherently undemocratic, antisocial and unsound," but contended "that it might be generated by a feeling of 'anarchy and complete helplessness against marauding hoodlums.' "[168]

Whether or not the crime rate is really rising or declining is currently being debated by experts, but in one way the question is beside the point. Most urban Americans, particularly in the largest cities, are firm in their belief that there is too much crime, that their persons or property are in danger, and that regular law enforcement is not coping with the problem. The same feelings in earlier times led Americans to resort to vigilantism.

References

1. It will probably be impossible to ever obtain a definitive count of American vigilante movements; many small movements undoubtedly left no traces in historical sources. The latter seems to have been especially true in the Old Northwest and Old Southwest in the first 20 or 30 years of the 19th century. The 326 movements, presently known, are listed in the appendix. For the number of movements per State, see table 5-2. Map 1 gives an idea of the geographical incidence of vigilantism.

2. [Charles Hitchin], *The Regulator* . . . (London: W. Boreham, 1718), and Christopher Hibbert, *The Road to Tyburn* . . . (Cleveland and New York: World Publishing Co., [1957]).

3. Hubert Howe Bancroft, *Popular Tribunals* (2 vols.; San Francisco: History Co., 1887), vol. I, pp. 2-6.

4. James G. Leyburn, *Frontier Folkways* (New Haven: Yale University Press, 1935), p. 219.

5. There have been, indeed, urban as well as rural vigilante movements. The greatest of all American vigilante movements—the San Francisco Vigilance Committee of 1856—was an urban one. Vigilantism has been by no means restricted to the frontier, although most typically it has been a frontier phenomenon.

6. Richard Maxwell Brown, *The South Carolina Regulators* (Cambridge: Harvard University Press, 1963).

7. Aside from the South Carolina Regulators there was little vigilante activity in the original 13 States of the Atlantic seaboard. The North Carolina Regulators (1768-71) did not constitute a vigilante movement, but, rather embodied a violent agrarian protest against corrupt and galling local officials and indifferent provincial authorities.

8. The 96th meridian coincides, approximately, with both physiographic and state boundaries. Physiographically it roughly separates the humid prairies of the East from the semiarid Great Plains of the West. The States of Minnesota, Iowa, Missouri, Arkansas, and Louisiana fall into the province of Eastern vigilantism. The States of North and South Dakota, Nebraska, Kansas, and Oklahoma mainly fall into the area of Western vigilantism. In Texas the 96th meridian separates east Texas from central and west Texas, hence east Texas vigilantism was a part of Eastern vigilantism, while central and west Texas vigilantism properly belongs to the Western variety. For the sake of convenience, however, all of Texas vigilantism (along with that of the Dakotas, Nebraska, Kansas, and Oklahoma) has been included under the heading of Western vigilantism in table 5-2.

9. Lynn Glaser, *Counterfeiting in America* . . . (New York: Clarkson N. Potter [1968]), ch. 5. On the relationship between counterfeiting and the frontier money shortage, see Ruth A. Gallaher, "Money in Pioneer Iowa, 1838-1865;" *Iowa Journal of History and Politics*, vol. XXXI (1934), pp. 42-45. The use of counterfeit money for public land purchases is revealed in *Counties of Warren, Benton, Jasper and Newton, Indiana: Historical and Biographical* (Chicago: F. A. Battey, 1883), p. 458.

10. See, for example, Randall Parrish, *Historic Illinois* . . . (Chicago: A. C. McClurg, 1906), pp. 405-406. Charles Edward Pancoast, *A Quaker Forty-Niner* . . . , Anna P. Hannum, ed. (Philadelphia: University of Pennsylvania Press, 1930), pp. 103-104.

11. William Faux, *Memorable Days in America* . . . [1823] (*Early Western Travels*, Reuben G. Thwaites, ed., vols. XI-XII; Cleveland: Arthur H. Clark, 1905), vol. XI, pp. 293-294. John L. McConnel, *Western Characters* (New York: Redfield, 1853), pp. 171-175. William N. Blane, *An Excursion through the United States and Canada during the Years 1822-23* (London: Baldwin, Cradock & Jay, 1824), pp. 233-235. Robert M Coates, *The Outlaw Years* . . . (New York: Macaulay [1930]). The leading American vigilante movements are listed in table 5-1.

12. James W. Bragg, "Captain Slick, Arbiter of Early Alabama Morals," *Alabama Review*, vol. XI (1958), pp. 125-134. Jack K. Williams, "Crime and Punishment in Alabama, 1819-1840," *ibid.*, vol. VI (1953), pp. 14-30.

13. *Ibid.*, p. 27. James E. Cutler, *Lynch-Law* (New York: Longmans, Green, 1905), p. 99. H. R. Howard, comp., *The History of Virgil A. Stewart* (New York: Harper, 1836), and Edwin A. Miles, "The Mississippi Slave Insurrection Scare of 1835," *Journal of Negro History*, vol. XLII (1957), pp. 58-60.

14. John E. Briggs, "Pioneer Gangsters," *Palimpsest*, vol. XXI (1940), pp. 73-90. John C. Parish, "White Beans for Hanging," *ibid.*, vol. I (1920), pp. 9-28. Harvey Reid, *Thomas Cox* (Iowa City: State Historical Society of Iowa, 1909), pp. 126, 154-155, 165-167. Jackson County Historical Society, *Annals of Jackson County, Iowa*, vol. II (1906), pp. 51-96.

15. [Charles] L. Sonnichsen, *Ten Texas Feuds* (Albuquerque: University of New Mexico Press, 1957), ch. 1. Lela R. Neill, "Episodes in the Early History of Shelby County" (unpublished M.A. thesis, Stephen F. Austin State College, 1950), pp. 77-153 and *passim*.

16. On the Northern Illinois Regulators, see Alice L. Brumbaugh, "The Regulator Movement in Illinois" (unpublished M.A. thesis, University of Illinois, 1927), pp. 3, 5-27, and William Cullen Bryant, *Letters of a Traveller* . . . (New York: George P. Putnam, 1850), pp. 55-68. Two of the most important sources on the Southern Illinois Regulators are Brumbaugh, "Regulator Movement," pp. 29-65, and James A. Rose, comp., Papers Relating to the Regulator and Flathead Trouble in Southern Illinois (bound typescript in Illinois State Historical Society, Springfield).

17. James H. Lay, *A Sketch of the History of Benton County, Missouri* (Hannibal, Mo.: Winchell & Ebert, 1876), pp. 46-61. Pancoast, *Quaker Forty-Niner*, pp. 101-121. J. W. Vincent, "The 'Slicker War' and Its Consequences," *Missouri Historical Review*, vol. VII (1912-13), pp. 138-145.

18. *The Iowan*, vol. VI (1958), pp. 4-11, 50-51. Jackson County Hist. Soc., *Annals*, vol. I (1905), pp. 29-34. *The History of Clinton County, Iowa* (Chicago: Western Historical Co., 1879), pp. 437 ff. Paul W. Black, "Lynchings in Iowa," *Iowa Journal of History and Politics*, vol. X (1912), pp. 151-209. Orville F. Graham, "The Vigilance Committees," *Palimpsest*, vol. VI (1925), pp. 359-370.

19. M. H. Mott, *History of the Regulators of Northern Indiana* (Indianapolis: Journal Co., 1859). Weston A. Goodspeed and Charles Blanchard, eds., *Counties of Whitley and Noble, Indiana: Historical and Biographical* (Chicago: F. A. Battey, 1882), pp. 33-37, 63-73.

20. Among many sources, see Dorothy K. Gibson, "Social Life in San Antonio, 1855-1860" (unpublished M.A. thesis, University of Texas, 1937), pp. 122-131.

21. George A. Ketcham, "Municipal Police Reform: A Comparative Study of Law Enforcement in Cincinnati, Chicago, New Orleans, New York and St. Louis, 1844-1877" (unpublished Ph.D. dissertation, University of Missouri, 1967), pp. 148-150.

22. Harry L. Griffin, "The Vigilance Committees of Attakapas Country; or Early Louisiana Justice," Mississippi Valley Historical Association, *Proceedings*, vol. VIII (1914-15), pp. 146-159. Alexander Barde, *History of the Committees of Vigilance in the Attakapas Country* [1861], transl. and ed., Henrietta G. Rogers (unpublished M.A. thesis, Louisiana State University, 1936).

23. The literature on this crucial organization is very large. The best and most complete account (although highly prejudiced in favor of the vigilantes) is the second volume of Bancroft's *Popular Tribunals*. See, also, Richard Maxwell Brown, "Pivot of American Vigilantism: The San Francisco Vigilance Committee of 1856," *Reflections of Western Historians*, John A. Carroll, ed. (Tucson: University of Arizona Press,

1969), pp. 105-119. The 1856 vigilance committee was preceded by that of 1851 which has been the subject of an outstanding scholarly study by Mary Floyd Williams, *History of the San Francisco Committee of Vigilance of 1851: A Study of Social Control on the California Frontier in the Days of the Gold Rush* (Berkeley: University of California Press, 1921). See, also, Bancroft, *Popular Tribunals*, vol. I, pp. 201-428. Among recent treatments, see George R. Stewart, *Committee of Vigilance: Revolution in San Francisco, 1851* (Boston: Houghton Mifflin, 1964).

24. *The History of Johnson County, Missouri* (Kansas City: Kansas City Historical Co., 1881), ch. 15. *History of Vernon County, Missouri* (St. Louis: Brown & Co., 1887), pp. 348-349. *History of Greene County, Missouri* (St. Louis: Western Historical Co., 1883), pp. 497-501.

25. Lewis and Richard H. Collins, *History of Kentucky* (2 vols.; Louisville: John Morton, 1924), vol. I, pp. 198-209. E. Merton Coulter, *The Civil War and Readjustment in Kentucky* (Chapel Hill: University of North Carolina Press, 1926), p. 359.

26. Wayne G. Broehl, *The Molly Maguires* (Cambridge: Harvard University Press, 1965), pp. 239-240, describes the Seymour, Indiana, vigilance committee of 1867-68.

27. Ralph L. Peek, "Lawlessness and the Restoration of Order in Florida" (unpublished Ph.D. dissertation, University of Florida, 1964), pp. 91, 105-108, 111, 125-126, 149-150, 216-220.

28. See, especially, Bancroft, *Popular Tribunals*, vol. I, pp. 441 ff., and the California listing in the appendix of this paper.

29. Thomas J. Dimsdale, *The Vigilantes of Montana . . .* (Virginia City, Mont.: Montana Post Press, 1866). Nathaniel Pitt Langford, *Vigilante Days and Ways . . .* (2 vols.; Boston, J. G. Cupples, 1890). Hoffman Birney, *Vigilantes* (Philadelphia: Penn Publishing Co., 1929).

30. Granville Stuart, *Forty Years on the Frontier*, Paul C. Phillips, ed. (2 vols.; Cleveland: Arthur H. Clark, 1925), vol. II, pp. 195-210. Michael A. Leeson, *History of Montana: 1739-1885* (Chicago: Warner, Beers & Co., 1885), pp. 315-316.

31. Montana Territory Vigilance Committee, *Notice!* (broadside, Helena, Mont., Sept. 19, 1865). Leeson, *History of Montana*, pp. 303-316.

32. Among the many vigilante movements of Central Texas (see the Texas listing in the appendix) were those of Bastrop County, 1874-83. (C[harles] L. Sonnichsen, *I'll Die before I'll Run* [New York: Devin-Adair, 1962], pp. 167-187), Shackelford County, 1876-1878 (*ibid.*, pp. 150-166), San Saba County, 1880-1896 (*ibid.*, pp. 206-231), and the German "Hoodoo" vigilantes of Mason County, 1875 (Sonnichsen, *Ten Texas Feuds*, p. 87 ff.). Ten counties with major vigilante activity were Bell, Comanche, Coryell, De Witt, Eastland, Gonzales, Hill, Llano, Montague, and Young. Virtually all of the many other Central Texas counties had vigilante activity of one sort or another in this troubled period. In addition to contemporary newspapers, Central Texas vigilantism can best be explored in dozens of county histories done as M.A. theses at the University of Texas. Some of these have been published; see, for example, Zelma Scott, *A History of Coryell County, Texas* (Austin: Texas State Historical Association, 1965), ch. V, and pp. 135, 143. Among the many unpublished M.A. theses, one of the best on vigilantism is Billy B[ob] Lightfoot, "The History of Comanche County, Texas, to 1920" (unpublished M.A. thesis, University of Texas, 1949).

33. Among many sources, see Jerome C. Smiley, *History of Denver . . .* (Denver: Denver Times/Times-Sun Publishing Co., 1901), pp. 338-350.

34. Albuquerque *Republican Review*, Feb. 18, 1871. *Santa Fe Weekly New Mexican*, Nov. 13, 22, 1879. Victor Westphal, "History of Albuquerque: 1870-1880" (unpublished M.A. thesis, University of New Mexico, 1947), pp. 34, 64-65. Bernice A. Rebord, "A Social History of Albuquerque: 1880-1885" (unpublished M.A. thesis, University of New Mexico, 1947), pp. 34, 64-65, and *passim*.

35. Miguel Antonio Otero, *My Life on the Frontier* (2 vols.; New York and Albuquerque: Press of the Pioneers and University of New Mexico Press, 1935-1939), vol. I, pp. 181-206; vol. II, pp. 2-3. *Santa Fe Daily New Mexican*, Mar. 12, 25-26, Apr. 13, 1881.

36. Erna B. Fergusson, *Murder & Mystery in New Mexico* (Albuquerque: Merle Armitage [1948]), pp. 15-32. Chester D. Potter, "Reminiscences of the Socorro Vigilantes," Paige W. Christiansen, ed., *New Mexico Historical Review*, vol. XL (1965), pp. 23-54.

37. On the Butler County vigilantes, see A. T. Andreas, *History of the State of Kansas* . . . (2 vols.; Chicago: A. T. Andreas, 1883), pp. 1431-1432, and Correspondence of Governor J. M. Harvey, File on County Affairs, 1869-1872 (MSS in Archives Department of Kansas State Historical Society, Topeka). Materials on Kansas vigilantism are also to be found in Nyle H. Miller and Joseph W. Snell, *Why the West Was Wild* . . . (Topeka: Kansas State Historical Society, 1963), and Genevieve Yost, "History of Lynching in Kansas," *Kansas Historical Quarterly*, vol. II (1933), pp. 182-219. See, also, Robert R. Dykstra, *The Cattle Towns* (New York: Alfred A. Knopf, 1968).

38. J. H. Triggs, *History of Cheyenne and Northern Wyoming* . . . (Omaha: Herald Steam and Book Job Printing House, 1876), pp. 14, 17-18, 21, 23-27. J. H. Triggs, *History and Directory of Laramie City* . . . (Laramie: Daily Sentinel, 1875), pp. 3-15.

39. The classic (but far from flawless) contemporary account by the anti-Regulator Asa Shinn Mercer was *The Banditti of the Plains* . . . (Cheyenne: privately printed, 1894). A very good recent study is Helena Huntington Smith, *The War on Powder River* (New York, London, and Toronto: McGraw-Hill, 1966). General treatments of Western vigilantism are found in Bancroft, *Popular Tribunals*, vol. I, pp. 593-743; Wayne Gard, *Frontier Justice* (Norman: University of Oklahoma Press, 1949), ch. 14; and Carl Coke Rister, "Outlaws and Vigilantes of the Southern Plains," *Mississippi Valley Historical Review*, vol. XIX (1933), pp. 537 ff.

40. See table 5-2.

41. The figure of 79 killings was gained from an analysis of Bancroft's narrative in *Popular Tribunals*, vol. I, pp. 515-576.

42. This distinction between "colonized" and "cumulative" new communities was formulated by Page Smith in *As a City upon the Hill: The Town in American History* (New York: Alfred A. Knopf, 1966), pp. 17-36.

43. The following sketch of the three-level American community structure is based upon my own research and recent studies of American society. Among the latter are Jackson Turner Main, *The Social Structure of Revolutionary America* (Princeton: Princeton University Press, 1965), and for the 19th century: Stephan Thernstrom, *Poverty and Progress: Social Mobility in a Nineteenth Century City* (Cambridge: Harvard University Press, 1964); Ray A. Billington, *America's Frontier Heritage* (New York, Chicago, and San Francisco: Holt, Rinehart & Winston, [1966]), ch. 5, "The Structure of Frontier Society"; and Merle Curti, *The Making of an American Community* (Stanford, Calif.: Stanford University Press, 1959), pp. 56-63, 78, 107-111 ff., 126, 417 ff., 448.

44. On the marginal "lower people" of the South (where they have been labeled "poor whites," "crackers," etc.), see Brown, *South Carolina Regulators*, pp. 27-29, and Shields McIlwaine, *The Southern Poor White from Lubberland to Tobacco Road* (Norman: University of Oklahoma Press, 1939), a literary study. For lower people in the North, see Bernard De Voto, *Mark Twain's America* (Boston: Little, Brown, 1932), pp. 54-58, and George F. Parker, *Iowa Pioneer Foundations* (2 vols.; Iowa City: State Historical Society of Iowa, 1940), vol. II, pp. 37-48.

45. Kai Erikson, *Wayward Puritans: A Study in the Sociology of Deviance* (New York: John Wiley & Sons, 1966), ch. 1.

46. J. Milton Yinger, "Contraculture and Subculture," *American Sociological Review*, vol. XXV (1960), p. 629, holds that a contraculture occurs "wherever the normative system of a group contains, as a primary element, a theme of conflict with the values of the total society. . . ." See, also, David M. Downes, *The Delinquent Solution: A Study in Subcultural Theory* (New York: Free Press [1966]), pp. 10-11.

47. See, for example, De Voto, *Mark Twain's America*, pp. 58-62, and Parker, *Iowa Pioneer Foundations*, vol. II, pp. 37-48, 247-265.

48. See Howard, *History of Virgil A. Stewart* and Miles, "Mississippi Slave Insurrection Scare" on the alleged Murrel plot. On the Flatheads, see Brumbaugh, "Regulator Movement," pp. 28-65; Rose, Papers Relating to Regulator and Flathead Trouble; Charles Neely, *Tales and Songs of Southern Illinois* (Menasha, Wis.: George Banta, 1938), pp. 7, 35, 41; and Norman W. Caldwell, "Shawneetown: A Chapter in the Indian History of Illinois," *Journal of the Illinois State Historical Society*, vol. XXXII (1939), pp. 199-200.

49. See note 101, below.

50. See note 91, below.
51. Brown, *South Carolina Regulators*, pp. 27-37.
52. Langford, *Vigilante Days*, vol. I, pp. 320-324. Howard A. Johnson, "Pioneer Law and Justice in Montana," Chicago Corral of the Westerners, *Brand Book*, vol. V (1948-49), p. 10.
53. About frontier masons in Texas, the late Walter Prescott Webb wrote, that "they believed in the law and aided in preserving order, often in ways best known to themselves." James D. Carter, *Masonry in Texas . . . to 1846* (Waco, Tex.: Committee on Masonic Education and Service for the Grand Lodge of Texas A.F. and A.M., 1955), p. xviii.
54. Thomas and Augustus Wildman, Letters, 1858-1865 (MSS in Western American Collection, Beinecke Rare Book and Manuscript Library, Yale University, New Haven).
55. *Cowley County Censor* (Winfield, Kans.), Jan. 7, 1871.
56. David Donald, ed., "The Autobiography of James Hall, Western Literary Pioneer," *Ohio State Archaeological and Historical Quarterly,* vol. LVI (1947), pp. 297-298.
57. Mott, *Regulators of Northern Indiana*, pp. 6-7, and *passim*.
58. Dimsdale, *Vigilantes of Montana*, p. 116.
59. Fred M. Mazzulla, "Undue Process of Law—Here and There," *Brand Book of the Denver Westerners,* vol. XX (1964), pp. 273-279. Dr. Osborne became Governor of Wyoming in 1893.
60. Brumbaugh, "Regulator Movement," pp. 18-20.
61. Although at present I know of only 729 vigilante killings, it is surely possible that American vigilantism took as many as a thousand lives and perhaps more. In general, the statistics in this paper are tentative. Future findings might alter some of the figures, but it is not very likely that the broad trends revealed by the statistics in this paper would be significantly changed.
62. On Coleman, see *Dictionary of American Biography, s.v.,* and James A. B. Scherer, *"The Lion of the Vigilantes: William T. Coleman and the Life of Old San Francisco"* (Indianapolis and New York: Bobbs-Merrill, 1939).
63. *Dictionary of American Biography, s.v.*
64. See, for example, Anthony S. Nicolosi, "The Rise and Fall of the New Jersey Vigilant Societies," *New Jersey History,* vol. LXXXVI (1968), pp. 29-32.
65. "Uses and Abuses of Lynch Law," *American Whig Review,* May 1850, p. 461. Pan Pancoast, *Quaker Forty-Niner,* pp. 103-104. Brumbaugh, "Regulator Movement," pp. 9-11.
66. Dwyn M. Mounger, "Lynching in Mississippi, 1830-1930" (unpublished M.A. thesis, Mississippi State University, 1961), p. 9.
67. Brumbaugh, "Regulator Movement," pp. 10-11.
68. James Stuart, *Three Years in North America* (2 vols.; Edinburgh: Robert Cadell, 1833), vol. II, pp. 212-213. Williams, "Crime and Punishment in Alabama," p. 26.
69. Smiley, *History of Denver,* p. 349. Emphasis mine.
70. "The Vigilance Committee: Richmond during the War of 1812," *Virginia Magazine of History and Biography,* vol. VII (1899-1900), pp. 225-241.
71. Harris G. Warren, "Pensacola and the Filibusters, 1816-1817," *Louisiana Historical Quarterly,* vol. XXI (1938), p. 816.
72. See, for example, Documents relating to the Committee of Vigilance and Safety of Nacogdoches, Texas, Jan. 3, 1835, to Dec. 5, 1837 (transcripts in University of Texas Archives, File Box B 15/40).
73. *Hardesty's Historical and Geographical Encyclopedia . . . of Meigs County, Ohio* (Chicago and Toledo: H. H. Hardesty & Co., 1883), pp. 273-275.
74. Wilbur H. Seibert, *The Underground Railroad from Slavery to Freedom* (New York: Macmillan, 1898), pp. 71 ff., 326 ff., 436-439. See, also, Larry Gara, *The Liberty Line: The Legend of the Underground Railroad* (Lexington: University of Kentucky Press [1961]), pp. 99, 104-109.
75. John Hope Franklin, *The Militant South* (Cambridge: Harvard University Press, 1956), pp. 87-90. Gara, *Liberty Line,* pp. 157-158.
76. *National Police Gazette,* Sept. 17, 1845, p. 5.
77. Pierce County, Washington Territory, Vigilance Committee, Draft of Compact, June 1, 1856 (MS in Western Americana Collection, Beinecke Rare Book and Manuscript Library, Yale University, New Haven).

78. Griffin, "Vigilance Committees of Attakapas," pp. 153-155.
79. Dimsdale, *Vigilantes of Montana*, p. 107.
80. *History of Johnson County*, pp. 372-373.
81. Thomas Ford, *A History of Illinois from Its Commencement as a State in 1818 to 1847* [1854], Milo M. Quaife, ed. (2 vols.; Chicago: R. R. Donnelly & Sons, 1945-46), vol. I, pp. 10-11.
82. Griffin, "Vigilance Committees of the Attakapas," pp. 153-155.
83. Barde, *History of the Committees*, pp. 26-27.
84. Mott, *Regulators of Northern Indiana*, pp. 15-18.
85. Alfred J. Mokler, *History of Natrona County, Wyoming 1888-1922* . . . (Chicago: R. R. Donnelly & Co., 1923).
86. *History of Johnson County*, pp. 372-373.
87. Mott, *Regulators of Northern Indiana*, p. 17.
88. *Denver Tribune*, Dec. 30, 1879, cited in John W. Cook, *Hands Up* . . . (2d ed.; Denver: W. F. Robinson, 1897), p. 103.
89. Otero, *My Life*, vol. II, pp. 2-3.
90. Pamphlet No. 342, Document No. 37 (typescript, State Historical Society of Colorado, Denver), pp. 118-119.
91. Brumbaugh, "Regulator Movement," pp. 3, 5-27. Bryant, *Letters of a Traveller*, pp. 55-68. Of the leading vigilante movements listed in table 5-1, all but the following seem to have been socially constructive: Madison and Hinds Counties movements, Mississippi, 1835 (no. 8); East Texas Regulators, Shelby County, 1840-1844 (no. 12); Southwest Missouri Slickers, Benton and Hickory Counties, 1842 (no. 14); Southern Illinois Regulators, 1846-1849 (no. 16); San Saba County, Texas, Mob, 1880-1896 (no. 71); Johnson County, Wyoming, cattlemen Regulators, 1892 (no. 80); and the Sevier County, Tennessee, White Caps, 1892-1897 (no. 81). The evidence is ambiguous about the following movements: Central Kentucky Regulators, Marion and other counties, 1866-1871 (no. 48); Northern Florida Regulators, Madison and other counties, 1868-1870 (no. 55); Los Angeles Vigilance Committee, 1852-1858 (no. 23); San Francisco Vigilance Committee, 1856 (no. 25); Socorro, New Mexico, Vigilantes, 1880-1884 (no. 70); and New Orleans vigilantes, 1891 (no. 79). Although the Los Angeles, San Francisco, Socorro, and New Orleans movements produced at least temporary stability, they did so by attacking Mexican, Irish, Mexican, and Italian ethnic groups, respectively, and, in the long run, may have exacerbated rather than reduced tensions.
92. For example, the Turk family (Slickers) *vs.* the Jones family (anti-Slickers) in Southwest Missouri. Lay, *History of Benton County*, pp. 46-61.
93. For example, in the Southwest Missouri Slicker conflict the Slickers were mostly Whigs, and the anti-Slickers were mostly Democrats. Pancoast, *Quaker Forty-Niner*, p. 104. In the Southern Illinois Regulator-Flathead struggle, the factor of local political rivalry was important. Parker B. Pillow, Elijah Smith, and Charles A. Shelby, Regulators and political "outs," were in conflict with a Flathead "in" faction led by Sheriff John W. Read. Report of Governor Augustus C. French, Jan. 11, 1847, and *Sangamo Journal*, Jan. 28, 1847—both in Rose, Papers Relating to Regulator and Flathead Trouble. See, also, Brumbaugh, "Regulator Movement," pp. 66, 69. Political factionalism also contributed to the Regulator-Moderator strife in Shelby County of East Texas where a political "in" faction of old pre-Texas Revolution settlers (Moderators) was opposed by a political "out" faction of post-Revolutionary newcomers (Regulators). Neill, "Shelby County" (unpublished M.A. thesis, Stephen F. Austin State College, 1950), pp. 75-77.
94. For example, in later years San Francisco's 1856 vigilance committee leader, William T. Coleman, criticized Charles Doane (the vigilantes' grand marshal) for running for sheriff on the People's Party ticket. Coleman felt that vigilante leaders such as Doane should not run for office. William T. Coleman, Vigilance Committee, 1856 (MS, ca. 1880, in Bancroft Library, University of California, Berkeley), p. 139.
95. In New Mexico's Lincoln County War of 1878-79, the McSween-Tunstall-Brewer mercantile faction organized (unsuccessfully) as Regulators against the dominant Murphy-Dolan mercantile faction. William A. Keleher, *Violence in Lincoln County: 1869-1881* (Albuquerque: University of New Mexico Press [1957]), pp. 152-154. Maurice Garland Fulton, *History of the Lincoln County War*, Robert N. Mullin, ed. (Tucson:

University of Arizona Press, 1968), pp. 137-142 ff.

96. In addition to the East Texas Regulators (see below), other movements which fell into sadism and extremism were, most notably, the Southern Illinois Regulators and the Southwest Missouri Slickers. There were other movements of this stripe; even in well controlled movements the elements of sadism and extremism often crept in in a minor way. The problem was inherent in vigilantism.

97. See also note 91 above.

98. See San Francisco *Daily Town Talk,* Aug. 8-9, 1856. Political factionalism was a factor in the 1856 San Francisco vigilante troubles. By and large, the vigilante leaders were composed of old Whigs and Know-Nothings who were in the process of becoming Republicans. The political "ins" who controlled San Francisco and whom the vigilantes attacked were the Irish Catholic Democrats led by David C. Broderick. The "Law and Order" antivigilante faction tended to draw its strength from the Southern oriented wing of the California Democratic Party. Unlike most San Francisco vigilante leaders, William T. Coleman was a Democrat, but as a native Kentuckian he maintained a lifelong devotion to the principles of Henry Clay, and, hence, had much in common with the many vigilante leaders who were also oriented to Henry Clay nationalism.

99. Brown, *South Carolina Regulators,* ch. 6. Down to about the 1850's opponents of regulators and vigilantes were often called Moderators.

100. For a contemporary paradigm of vigilante movements gone bad, see "Uses and Abuses of Lynch Law," pp. 462-463.

101. Sonnichsen, *Ten Texas Feuds,* ch. 1. Neill, "Shelby County," pp. 77-153, and *passim.*

102. Robert B. David, *Malcolm Campbell, Sheriff* (Casper, Wyo.: Wyoming-ana Inc. [1932]), pp. 18-21.

103. See Brown, "Pivot of American Vigilantism" and this paper, below.

104. Clear examples of local officials who collaborated with vigilantes include: (1) The sheriff in Omaha, Nebr., 1858. Bryan T. Parker, "Extra-Legal Law Enforcement on the Nebraska Frontier" (unpublished M.A. thesis, University of Nebraska, 1931), pp. 58-59. (2) The county attorney of Vernon County, Mo., 1867. *History of Vernon County,* pp. 348-349. (3) The sheriff of Platte County, Nebraska, 1867. A. T. Andreas, *History of the State of Nebraska . . .* (2 vols.; Chicago: Western Historical Co., 1882), vol. II, pp. 1265-1266. (4) The bailiff, deputy sheriff, and other officials of Brown and Erath Counties, Tex., 1872. *Report of the Adjutant-General of the State of Texas* (for 1872), pp. 22, 121-123. (5) The sheriff of Wilbarger County, Tex., 1882. Torrence B. Wilson, Jr., "A History of Wilbarger County, Texas" (unpublished M.A. thesis, University of Texas, 1938), p. 97. (6) The territorial governor and judges of Illinois who in 1816-17 "winked at and encouraged the proceedings of the regulators." Ford, *History of Illinois,* pp. 10-11. (7) Governor William Pitt Kellogg of Louisiana who in 1872 advised Vermillion Parish vigilantes to use their own judgment in dealing with a "horde of cattle thieves" with the result that they hanged 12. Houston (Texas) *Telegraph,* Oct. 3, 1872. (8) The Governor, Mayor, and Sheriff who (in one of the most flagrant instances of implicit official collaboration with vigilantes) were all in New Orleans in 1891 when vigilantes lynched 11 Italians and who did nothing whatsoever to prevent the action for which there had been ample advance warning. John E. Coxe, "The New Orleans Mafia Incident," *Louisiana Historical Quarterly,* vol. XX (1937), pp. 1067-1110. John S. Kendall, "Who Killa De Chief," *ibid.,* vol. XXII (1939), pp. 492-530.

105. On the Anti-Horse Thief movement in the Northeast and in New Jersey, see Nicolosi, "New Jersey Vigilant Societies," pp. 29-53.

106. On the National Horse Thief Detective Association of Indiana and neighboring States, see J. D. Thomas, "History and Origin of the National Horse Thief Detective Association" in *Journal of the National Horse Thief Detective Association,* 50th annual session (Union City, Ind., 1910), pp. 19-20, and Ted Gronert, *Sugar Creek Saga . . .* (Crawfordsville, Ind.: Wabash College, 1958), pp. 140, 256-257.

107. On the Anti-Horse Thief Association of the trans-Mississippi Midwest and Southwest, see Hugh C. Gresham, *The Story of Major David McKee, Founder of the Anti-Horse Thief Association* (pamphlet; Cheney, Kans.: Hugh C. Gresham, 1937), and, especially, the Association's newspaper, *A.H.T.A. Weekly News* (with variant titles) for 1902-43, on file in the Kansas State Historical Society, Topeka. The A.H.T.A.'s membership

was largest in Kansas with the Indian Territory (now part of the state of Oklahoma) also heavily represented. There were also substantial memberships in Oklahoma Territory, Missouri, and Arkansas. A number of other States had smaller memberships. Late in the history of the organization—long after it had passed its peak—Illinois had quite a large membership.

108. Eliphalet Price, "The Trial and Execution of Patrick O'Conner," *Palimpsest*, vol. I (1920), pp. 86-97.
109. Stuart, *Forty Years on the Frontier*, vol. II, pp. 196-197. Ray M. Mattison, "Roosevelt and the Stockmen's Association," *North Dakota History*, vol. XVII (1950), pp. 81-85.
110. *Dictionary of American Biography*, *s.v.* (on Coleman).
111. *Dictionary of American Biography*, *s.v.* On Stanford's vigilante membership, see Application of L. Stanford in Applications for Membership, San Francisco Committee of Viligance Papers, 1856 (MSS in Huntington Library, San Marino, Calif.).
112. *Dictionary of American Biography*, *s.v.* For Cockrell's participation in the vigilante movement, see *History of Johnson County*, pp. 372-373.
113. Barde, *History of the Committees*, pp. 43, 347, for Mouton's vigilante activity; *Dictionary of American Biography*, *s.v.*, for his life. Alexander Mouton's brother, General Alfred Mouton, a West Point graduate, was the drillmaster of the Attakapas vigilantes. Griffin, "Vigilance Committees of the Attakapas," p. 155.
114. Kellogg also served Louisiana in the U.S. Senate (1877-83) and House of Representatives (1883-85). On his public career, see *Dictionary of American Biography*, *s.v.* On his encouragement of vigilantism, see Houston (Tex.) *Telegraph*, Oct. 3, 1872.
115. *National Cyclopaedia of American Biography*, vol. XI, pp. 46-47. On the vigilante movement, see *The History of Edgar County, Illinois* . . . (Chicago: William LeBaron, Jr. & Co., 1879), pp. 332, 396-397, 590.
116. *Dictionary of American Biography, s.v.*
117. On McConnell, see *Who Was Who in America*, vol. I, p. 803. His book, *Frontier Law*, was published in 1924 in Yonkers, N.Y., and Chicago by the World Book Company.
118. Mazzula, "Undue Process of Law," pp. 273-279, describes Osborne's participation in the lynching which is also discussed, above, in this paper. On Osborne as Governor, see *Encyclopedia Americana* (1967), vol. XXIX, p. 580.
119. On Chatterton's public career, see *Who Was Who in America*, vol. III, p. 152, and *Encyclopedia Americana* (1967), vol. XXIX, p. 580. On his participation in the vigilante episode, see Mazzula, "Undue Process of Law," pp. 273-279.
120. Otero, *My Life*, vol. I, pp. 181-206; vol. II, pp. 1-3. *Who Was Who in America*, vol. II. *s.v.*
121. George Curry, *George Curry: 1861-1947: An Autobiography*, H. B. Henning, ed. (Albuquerque: University of New Mexico Press, 1958), pp. 50-52, and *passim*.
122. Diary of James Buckner Barry, 1855-1862 (MS in University of Texas Archives, file box B 13/167), James Buckner Barry, *A Texas Ranger and Frontiersman: The Days of Buck Barry in Texas, 1845-1906*, James K. Greer, ed. (Dallas: Southwest Press, 1932). William C. Pool, *Bosque Territory* . . . (Kyle, Texas: Chaparral Press [1964]), p. 65. James K. Greer, *Bois d'Arc to Barb'd Wire* . . . (Dallas: Dealey & Love [1936]), p. 392.
123. See John W. Caughey, *Hubert Howe Bancroft* (Berkeley and Los Angeles: University of California Press, 1946).
124. On Dimsdale, see pp. 5-8 of the edition of *The Vigilantes of Montana* (Helena, Mont.: State Publishing Co., 1940?), edited by A. J. Noyes.
125. Langford, *Vigilante Days*. On Langford, see *Dictionary of American Biography, s.v.*
126. *The Virginian* (New York: Macmillan, 1902), especially pp. 433-436. On Wister, see Fanny K. Wister, ed., *Owen Wister Out West* (Chicago: University of Chicago Press [1958]). Among the many lesser 19th-century and early 20th-century novelists who portrayed vigilantism favorably were James Weir, *Lonz Powers: or, the Regulators: A Romance of Kentucky* (Philadelphia: Lippincott, Grambo & Co., 1850), and Harris Dickson, *The House of Luck* (Boston: Small, Maynard & Co., [1916]). The enthusiastic reception of Walter Van Tilburg Clark's anti-vigilante *The Ox-Bow Incident* (New York: Random House, 1940)—the best novel

215

ever written on American vigilantism (upon which a classic film was based)—marked an important shift in public attitudes, from favoring to condemning vigilantism.

127. Quoted in Emerson Hough, *The Story of the Outlaw* . . . (New York: Outing Publishing Co., 1907), p. 399 ff.

128. *Charge of Chief Justice [H. L.] Hosmer, to the Grand Jury of the First Judicial District, M.T.,* delivered, December 5th, 1864 (broadside, Virginia City, Mont., 1864).

129. *The Vigilantes* (pamphlet; New York: The Vigilantes [1918]), pp. 5, 8-14. The pamphlet was probably written and compiled by the Vigilantes' managing editor, Charles J. Rosebault. The Vigilantes were aided by leading American capitalists who served as "underwriters" or associate members; among them were George F. Baker, Jr., Cleveland H. Dodge, Coleman Dupont, Jacob H. Schiff, Vincent Astor, Elbert H. Gary, Simon Guggenheim, Dwight Morrow, and George W. Perkins.

130. The following interpretation of the San Francisco vigilante movement of 1856 is based upon Brown, "Pivot of American Vigilantism."

131. On the first Ku Klux Klan, see Stanley F. Horn, *Invisible Empire* . . . (Boston: Houghton Mifflin, 1939). On the second K.K.K., see David M. Chalmers, *Hooded Americanism* (Garden City, N.Y.: Doubleday, 1965).

132. *Ibid.,* and two works by Charles C. Alexander, *The Ku Klux Klan in the Southwest* (Lexington: University of Kentucky Press, 1965), and *Crusade for Conformity: The Ku Klux Klan in Texas, 1920-1930* (Houston: Texas Gulf Coast Historical Association, 1962).

133. The White Cap movement is discussed in this volume in my paper, "Historical Patterns of Violence in America."

134. In one sense the mass lynching was a classic vigilante response to a crime problem (the Italians had apparently been Mafia members and seem to have been involved in the killing of the New Orleans chief of police), but the potent element of anti-Italian ethnic prejudice was crucial to the episode and typical of neovigilantism. See Coxe, "New Orleans Mafia Incident," and Kendall, "Who Killa De Chief."

135. For example, in 1917 in Tulsa, Okla., vigilantes attacked 17 I.W.W. members who were attempting to organize oil field workers. *The "Knights of Liberty" Mob and the I.W.W. Prisoners at Tulsa, Okla. (November 9, 1917)* (pamphlet; New York: National Civil Liberties Bureau, 1918). In this incident the police apparently connived with the vigilantes.

136. See William Preston, *Aliens and Dissenters* (Cambridge: Harvard University Press, 1963), which contains examples of neovigilante attacks upon workers, immigrants, and radicals. See also John W. Caughey, ed., *Their Majesties the Mob* (Chicago: University of Chicago Press [1960]), pp. 1-25, 100-205.

137. Editorial in the New York *National Democrat* quoted in Bancroft, *Popular Tribunals,* vol. II, pp. 554-555.

138. *Illinois State Register* (Springfield), Jan. 1, 1847 (transcript in Rose, Papers Relating to Regulator and Flathead Trouble).

139. William Anderson Scott, *A Discourse for the Times Delivered in Calvary Church, July 27, 1856* (pamphlet; San Francisco: N.p., 1856). On Scott, see Clifford M. Drury's aptly subtitled work, *William Anderson Scott: "No Ordinary Man"* (Glendale, Calif.: Arthur H. Clark, 1967).

140. John G. Nicolay and John Hay, eds., *Complete Works of Abraham Lincoln* (revised edition, 12 vols.; New York: Lamb Publishing Co. [1905]), vol. I, pp. 35-50. The quotations are from pp. 35 and 37. In his address Lincoln dwelled upon the ubiquity of "mob law" in the 1830's and specifically cited the Mississippi vigilante actions in 1835 in Madison and Hinds Counties and Vicksburg as well as a case of lynch law in St. Louis, Mo., *Ibid.,* pp. 38-39.

141. See, for example, James Truslow Adams, "Our Lawless Heritage," *Atlantic Monthly,* vol. XLII (1928), pp. 732-740.

142. The following list was gained from a survey of *The New York Times Index* and the two leading periodical indexes, *Readers' Guide to Periodical Literature* and *Social Sciences and Humanities Index* (formerly *International Index to Periodicals*), from 1961 to the present.

143. *U.S. News & World Report,* July 13, 1964, pp. 62-64. *New York Times,* May 27-July 28, 1964, *passim;* Mar. 11, 1966, p. 36, c. 3. The organization took its name from the Maccabees, a family of Jewish patriots who led a religious revolt in the reign of Antiochus IV, 175-164 B.C. *Web-*

ster's New Collegiate Dictionary (2d edition; Springfield, Mass.: G. & C. Merriam [1949]), p. 503.

144. *New York Times,* June 26, 1966, p. 75, c. 4.
145. *Ibid.,* Dec. 14, 1964, p. 1; c. 1, p. 19, c. 1-4; Dec. 15, 1964, p. 45, c. 5-7.
146. *Ibid.,* Dec. 14, 1964, p. 1, c. 1; p. 19, c. 1-4.
147. *Ibid.,* Dec. 10, 1964, p. 1, c. 1; p. 26, c. 3.
148. *Ibid.,* Mar. 30, 1965, p. 33, c. 3; Apr. 2, 1965, p. 37, c. 1.
149. *Ibid.,* Apr. 2, 1965, p. 37, c. 2-3; Apr. 14, 1965, p. 45, c. 4.
150. *New York Times,* May 24, 1965, p. 1, c. 4; Aug. 15, 1965, vol. VI, pp. 10-11 ff.; and *passim* in 1965 and 1966. *Newsweek,* Aug. 2, 1965, pp. 28-29; May 2, 1966, pp. 20-21. Floyd McKissick stated in 1965 that other Negro self-protection organizations similar to the Deacons had been founded in the South. Such an organization (which may or may not have been a chapter of the Deacons—the author used fictitious names in order to protect his Negro sources) is treated in Harold A. Nelson, "The Defenders: A Case Study of an Informal Police Organization," *Social Problems,* vol. XV (1967-68), pp. 127-147.
151. *New York Times,* Mar. 11, 1966, p. 36, c. 3.
152. *New York Post,* Jan. 17, 1967, p. 50, c. 1.
153. *New York Times,* Mar. 4, 1967, p. 56, c. 1-2.
154. *Time,* June 9, 1967, pp. 34-35.
155. *New York Times,* Apr. 27, 1968, p. 25, c. 2-3; June 24, 1968, p. 23, c. 1-7; Sept. 29, 1968, vol. VI, p. 30 ff.; Nov. 11, 1968, p. 23, c. 1.
156. *Ibid.,* Oct. 27, 1967, p. 33, c. 1-5.
157. *Daily Press* (Newport News-Hampton, Va.), July 11, 1968, p. 41, c. 1-3.
158. *New York Times,* Sept. 3, 1968, p. 40, c. 3-5.
159. *Ibid.,* Sept. 15, 1968, vol. I, p. 67, c. 1.
160. *Ibid.,* Sept. 29, 1968, vol. VI, p. 31.
161. *Ibid.*
162. *Ibid.,* Oct. 13, 1968, vol. I, p. 54, c. 3-6.
163. *Ibid.,* Dec. 11, 1968, p. 41, c. 7.
164. *Ibid.,* Jan. 8, 1969, p. 40, c. 6.
165. *Parade,* May 7, 1967, pp. 12-14. *The Challenge of Crime in a Free Society: A Report by the President's Commission on Law Enforcement and Administration of Justice* (Washington: U.S. Government Printing Office, 1967), p. 288.
166. In general, vigilantes of the 1960's have not killed. An exception may have occurred in Cleveland in July 1968. The *New York Times,* Sept. 3, 1968, p. 40, c. 4, reported that in July "two of the Negroes killed during the tension were miles away from where the gun battles [between police and Negro militants] occurred and in areas where white vigilantes are active."
167. See the section, above, in this paper entitled "Related to Vigilantism: The Anti-Horse Thief Movement."
168. *New York Times,* Jan. 8, 1969, p. 40, c. 1. See also *ibid.,* Feb. 21, 1969, p. 50, c. 2, where State Senator Basil A. Paterson of Harlem was reported, like Baker, to have warned a State legislative committee "that Harlem residents might organize vigilante groups unless law enforcement agencies took drastic steps to combat a crime wave said to be terrorizing the community."

Appendix

THE AMERICAN
VIGILANTE MOVEMENTS

Note: Being the product of several years of research, the following list attempts to be reasonably complete. It is probably beyond the power of one man to produce a definitive list of American vigilante movements. It is hoped, however, that few—if any—of the major movements have been omitted from the following list. Only movements which took the law into their own hands in an extralegal way are included. Movements whose purpose was not essentially the usurpation of law enforcement (e.g., the antislavery vigilance committees of the North before the Civil War, the North Carolina Regulators of the late colonial period) are omitted. This is a listing, then, of vigilante movements in the classic sense of the term.

Key to Symbols for Type of Movement

L—Large movement or one of particular importance.
M—Medium size movement or one of medium significance.
S—Small movement or one that cannot otherwise be categorized because of lack of adequate information.

Place and movement	Type	Dates	Number of victims killed	Number of members in movement
Alabama:				
Chambers and Randolph Counties—Slickers	M	1830's		
Cherokee County—Slickers	M	1830's		
Madison and Jackson Counties—Slickers	L	1830-35		500-600
Greensborough—Vigilance Committee	M	1830's		
Montgomery—Regulating Horn	M	ca. 1835		
Tuscaloosa—Vigilance Committee	M	1835		
Arizona:				
Holbrook—Vigilantes	S	1885		
Phoenix—Vigilantes, Law and Order Committee	M	1873, 1879	3	
Globe—Vigilantes	S	1882	1	
St. John—Vigilantes	S	1879	2	
Tombstone—Law & Order, Vigilantes	M	1881, 1884	1	
Tucson—Vigilantes	M	1873	4	

Place and movement	Type	Dates	Number of victims killed	Number of members in movement
Arkansas:				
Cane Hill, Washington—Committee of 36	L	1839	4	400
Carrollton and Carroll County— Regulators	S	1836		
Little Rock—Regulators	S	1835		
Randolph County—Regulators	S	1897		
California:				
Bakersfield—Vigilantes	L	1897-7	5	
Bodie—601	M	1881	1	200
Columbia—Vigilance Committee	M	1851-58	4	
Eureka—Vigilance Committee	M	1853	2	
Grass Valley—Vigilance Committee	M	1851-57	1	
Hanford—Vigilance Committee, Regulators	M	1880, 1884		
Jackson—Vigilantes	L	1853-55	10	
Los Angeles:				
Vigilance Committee	L	1852-58	8	
Vigilantes	L	1863	7	
Vigilance Committee	M	1870	1	500
Mariposa—Vigilance Committee	M	1854	2	
Marysville—Vigilance Committee	M	1851-58	3	
Modesto area—Regulators	M	1879		
Mokelumne Hill—Vigilance Committee	M	1852-56	1	
Monterey—Vigilance Committee	M	1851, 1856	5	
Mud Springs—Vigilantes	M	1851-53	4	
Natchez—Vigilance Committee	S	1851 ff.		
Natividad, Monterey County— Vigilance Committee	M	1854	1	
Nevada City—Vigilance Committee	S	1851	1	
Newton—Vigilantes	M	1851-52	1	
Ophir—Vigilance Committee	S	1851		
Sacramento—Vigilance Committee	L	1851-53	1	213
San Diego—Vigilantes	M	1852	2	
San Francisco:				
Regulators	L	1849		100
Law & Order	L	1849		400
Vigilance Committee	L	1851	4	500
Vigilance Committee	L	1856	4	6,000-8,000
San Jose—Vigilance Committee	M	1851-54	1	
San Juan—Vigilantes	M	1867, 1877	3	
San Louis Obispo—Vigilance Committee	M	1858	ca. 4	175
Santa Clara—Vigilance Committee	S	1851		
Santa Cruz:				
Vigilance Committee	L	1852-53	11	
Vigilantes	S	1877	2	
Shasta—Vigilance Committee	S	1851		
Sonora—Vigilance Committee	M	1851, 1854	3	
Stanislaus County—Regulators	S	1880's		
Stockton—Vigilance Committee	M	1851		
Truckee—601	M	1874		
Tulare County—Vigilance Committee	S	1873-74		
Visalia—Vigilance Committee	S	1865, 1872	1	
Watsonville—Vigilantes	M	1856, 1870	5	
Weaverville—Vigilance Committee	S	1852		
Willits—Vigilantes	M	1879	3	
Colorado:				
Alamosa—Vigilantes	S	Late 1870's– early 1880's	2	
Arkansas Valley (upper)—Vigilantes	S	1870's		
Canon City—Vigilantes	S	1888	1	
Del Norte—Vigilantes	S	Late 1870's– early 1880's	2	40

Place and movement	Type	Dates	Number of victims killed	Number of members in movement
Colorado—Continued				
Denver:				
Vigilantes....................	L	1859-61	6	600-800
Vigilantes....................	M	1868	1	90-100
Durango—Committee of Safety....	M	1881	1	300
Elbert County—Vigilantes.........	S	ca. 1899-1902		
Georgetown—Vigilantes...........	S	1877	1	
Golden—Vigilantes..............	M	1879	2	100-150
Leadville—Vigilantes.............	S	1879		
Meeker—Vigilance Committee	S	1887		
Ouray—Vigilantes................	S	1884	2	
Pueblo—Vigilantes...............	L	1864-68, 1872	3	
Silverton—Vigilance Committee....	M	1881	2	
Rocky Mountain Detective Association (headquarters in Denver with operations in Mountain and Great Plain States).................	L	1863-ca. 1898		
Florida:				
Columbia County—Regulators.....	L	1868-70		
Hernando County—Regulators.....	M	1870		
Leon County—Regulators.........	L	1867-68		
Madison, Suwanee, Taylor, and Hamilton Counties—Regulators..	L	1868-70		
Pine Level, De Soto County— Vigilantes....................	S	ca. 1900		
Sarasota—Vigilantes..............	L	1883-84	7	
Georgia:				
Andersonville Prison Camp— Regulators...................	M	1864	6	
Carroll County and Carrollton— Regulators...................	S	c. 1832		
Northern Georgia—Slickers........	L	1830's		
Southern Georgia—Regulators.....	L	1869-70		
Idaho:				
Boise—Vigilance Committee.......	L	1866	3	
Idaho City—Vigilance Committee..	L	1865		900
Lewiston—Vigilance Committee....	L	1862-64, 1871	30, 1	
Payette Valley—Vigilance Committee.....................	L	1864, 1874	1	40
Salmon River—Vigilance Committee	M	1862		
Illinois:				
Carlyle—Regulators.............	S	1882-23		
Clay County—Regulators........	M	Early 1820's	3	100-500
Edgar County—Vigilance Committee	S	1830's		
Gallatin County—Vigilantes.......	M	ca. 1842		
Grafton area, Jersey County— (Vigilantes).................	M	1866	5	
Morgan and Scott Counties— Regulators...................	L	1821-30	(?)	
Northern Illinois (Ogle, Winnebago, DeKalb, Lee, McHenry, and Boone Counties)—Regulators....	L	1841	2	ca. 1,000
Pope County—Regulators.........	M	1831		
Southern Illinois (Pope, Massac, and Johnson Counties)—Regulators..	L	1846-49	ca. 20	500
Illinois in general—Regulators.....	L	1816-17 ff.		
Indiana:				
Harrison and Crawford Counties— Regulators...................	S	1818		
Newton County—Rangers........	S	ca. 1858		
Northern Indiana (LaGrange & Noble Counties)—Regulators....	L	1858	1	2,000
Montgomery County—horsethief... detection society..............	M	ca. 1840's-60's		

Place and movement	Type	Dates	Number of victims killed	Number of members in movement
Indiana—Continued				
Noble County—Regulators........	S	1889		
Polk Township, Monroe County—				
Regulators.................	M	ca. 1850's	2	
Seymour—Vigilance Committee....	L	1867-68	12	
Vincennes—Regulators............	S	ca. 1820's		
Warren and Benton Counties—				
Vigilantes.................	S	1819		
White River (Bluffs area)—				
Regulators.................	S	1819		
Indiana in general...............	L	1820's-30's		
Iowa:				
Bellevue—Regulators.............	L	1840	ca. 6	
Benton County—Regulators.......	S	1848		
Burlington—Vigilantes............	S	1830's		
Cedar County:				
Vigilantes....................	S	1840-41		
Vigilantes....................	M	1857	3	
Comanche and DeWitt—Regulators	M	ea. 1840's-50's		
Dubuque—Miners' Court	M	1834	1	
Eldora—mutual protection society..	S	1857-58		
Emeline—Vigilantes.............	S	1857		
Fremont County—Vigilantes......	M	1866-69		
Hardin County—Vigilance society..	M	1884-85	2	
Iowa City—Vigilance Committee...	M	1844	1	
Iowa City—Committee of 100.....	M	1858	1	
Iron Hill, Jackson County—				
Vigilance Committee............	L	1857	2	300-400
Keokuk County—Vigilance Com-				
mittee.................	S	1857-58		
Linn County—Vigilantes..........	M	1840 ff.	1	
Linn Grove—Citizens Association				
(including Jones, Cedar, Linn,				
and Jackson Counties)..........	M	ca. 1838-39		
McGregor—Vigilantes............	S	1858		
Monroe County:				
Vigilance Committee...........	M	1886	1	60-300
Vigilance Committee............	M	1883	1	
Polk County—Rangers...........	S	1848		
Pottawattomie County—Vigilantes.	M	1853-65	4	
Scott, Cedar, and Clinton Counties—				
Vigilantes.................	L	1857	4	200
Story County—Protective Assoc....	M	Late 1860's		
Van Buren County—Vigilance				
Committee....................	S	1848		
Kansas:				
Atchison County—Vigilantes......	S	1877		
Butler County—Vigilantes........	L	1870-71	8	798
Cheyenne County—Vigilance				
Committee....................	S	1888		
Dodge City:				
Vigilantes....................	M	1873	4	30-40
Vigilance Committee............	S	1883		
Ellsworth—Vigilance Committee...	M	1873		
Hays City—Vigilance Committee...	S	1868		
Indianola—Vigilance Committee...	S	1862		
Labette County—Vigilance Com-				
mittee.................	S	1866		
Manhattan—Vigilantes............	S	Late 1860's		
Medicine Lodge—Vigilantes.......	S	1884		
Mound City—Vigilantes..........	S	Late 1860's		
Neosho—Vigilance Committee.....	M	ca. 1850-60's		
Rising Sun—Vigilantes...........	S	Late 1860's		
Sheridan—Vigilance Committee....	S	1868	1	
Sumner County—Vigilantes........	S	1876	2	
Topeka—Vigilantes...............	S	Late 1860's		
Wellington—Vigilantes...........	M	1874	3	
Wichita—secret police force.......	M	1874		40-50

Place and movement	Type	Dates	Number of victims killed	Number of members in movement
Kentucky:				
Christian, Muhlenberg, Todd, and Hopkins Counties—Regulators...	L	1845		
Green River and Little Barren River—Regulators..............	M	1790's		
Henderson County—Regulators....	M	ca. 1816-17		
Hopkins and Henderson Counties—Regulators.....................	S	1820-22		
Marion, Mercer, Madison, Boyle and Lincoln Counties—Regulators....	L	1866-71	10	
Muhlenberg County—Regulators....	S	ca. 1825-50		
Paducah—Regulators..............	L	1846-50		
Russellville—Regulators...........	S	1793		
Union County—Regulators........	S	1880-1881		30-40
Western Kentucky—Regulators.....	M	1798		
Kentucky in general—Regulators...	M	ca. 1810-30		
Louisiana:				
Abbeville—Regulators.............	S	1890's		
Atlanta, Montgomery, and Winnfield—Vigilantes.................	L	1872	11	
Attakapas—Vigilance Committee (Parishes of Lafayette, Calcasieu, St. Martin, Vermillion, and St. Landry).....................	L	1859	1	4000
Cameron—Regulators..............	S	1874		
New Orleans:				
Vigilance Committee.............	S	1858		
Vigilantes.....................	L	1891	11	61
Vermillion Parish—Vigilantes.....	L	1872-73	12	
Minnesota:				
Balsam Lake—people's court......	S	ca. 1870's	1	
Duluth—Vigilance Committee.....	S	1869		
Mississippi				
Madison and Hinds Counties—Regulators and Committees of Safety........................	L	1835	21	
Natchez—Vigilance Committee.....	S	1835		
Northern Mississippi—Slickers.....	L	1830's		
Northeast Mississippi—Regulators.	L	ca. 1865-66		
Vicksburg—Vigilance Committee...	L	1835		
Missouri:				
Benton and Hickory Counties—Slickers.....................	L	1842	3	
Camden County—Slickers.........	S	1836 ff.		
Christian and Taney Counties—Bald Knobbers................	L	1885-87	3	ca. 900
Clark County—Vigilantes.........	S	1840's-50's		
Greene County—Regulators.......	L	1866	3	280
Hickory County—Vigilance Committee.....................	M	Late 1860's	2	
Lees Summit—Vigilance Committee	S	Late 1860's		
Lincoln County—Slickers..........	S	1843-45		
St. Louis—Regulators............	S	1815		
Saline County—Honest Men's League........................	S	1866		
Vernon County—Marmaton League, Vigilance Committee.............	S	ca. 1866, 1867		
Warrensburg and Johnson County—Vigilance Committee............	L	1867	10	400
Montana:				
Bannack and Virginia City—Vigilantes.....................	L	1863-65	30	108
Helena—Vigilance Committee......	L	1864-85	10	
Miles City—Vigilantes............	M	1883	1	

Place and movement	Type	Dates	Number of victims killed	Number of members in movement
Montana—Continued				
Northern and Eastern Montana (Judith, Musselshell, and Missouri River areas)—Vigilantes	L	1884	35	
Sun River area—Rangers	M	ca. 1870-84		
Montana in general—Vigilantes	L	ca. 1862-84	25	
Nebraska:				
Cass County—Claim Club	M	1854-57	4	
Colfax County—Regulators	S	1863		25-40
Columbus—Vigilantes	S	1867	1	
Dixon County—People's Court	S	1870	1	
Fremont area—Regulators	M	1856 ff.		
Nebraska City—Anti-Jayhawk League	S	Early 1860's		
Nemaha County—Anti-Jayhawk Society River	S	1861		
Niobrara region (Brown, Holt, and neighboring counties)—Vigilantes	L	1883-84	6	250
Omaha—Vigilantes	M	1856-60	2	
Pawnee County—Regulators	M	1864	3	
Richardson County:				
Vigilantes	M	1858	1	200
Anti-Jayhawk Society	S	1861		
Sidney—Vigilantes	L	1875-81	2	400
Southeast Nebraska—Anti-Jayhawk Societies	M	1861-63		
Western Nebraska—Vigilantes	M	1875 ff.		
Nebraska (Eastern) in general—Claim Clubs	M	1850's		
Nevada:				
Aurora—Citizens Protection Committee	L	1864	4	350
Belmont—Vigilance Committee	S	1867, 1874		
Carson Valley and Genoa—Vigilance Committee	S	1855, 1860, 1875		
Cherry Creek—Vigilantes	S	(?)	1	
Egan Canyon (White Pine mine district)—Protection Society	S	1869		
Eureka—601	M	1873	2	
Hamilton—Vigilantes	S	(?)		
Hiko, Lincoln County—601	S	Late 1860's-early 1870's		
Pioche—Vigilantes	S	1871		
Treasure City—Vigilantes	S	(?)		
Truckee Valley—Vigilantes	S	1858		
Virginia City—601 and Vigilantes	M	1860's-81		
Winnemucca—Vigilance Committee	S	1877		
New Mexico:				
Albuquerque—Vigilantes	L	1871-82		
Colfax County—Vigilance Committee	S	1885		
Deming—Vigilantes	S	1883		
Farmington and San Juan River area—Vigilance Committee	M	1880-81		
Las Vegas—Vigilantes	L	1880-82	6	
Lincoln County—Regulators	M	1878		
Los Lunas—Vigilance Committee	S	1880's		
Raton—Vigilantes	M	1881-82	3	
Rincon—Vigilantes	S	1881		
San Miguel—Vigilantes	S	1882	1	
Socorro—Vigilantes	L	1880-84	6	
North Dakota:				
Little Missouri River area—Vigilantes	M	1884		

Place and movement	Type	Dates	Number of victims killed	Number of members in movement
Ohio:				
Ashland County—Black Canes.....	M	1825-33		
Cincinnati—Vigilantes...........	L	1884		
Cleveland—Vigilance Committee...	S	1860		
Logan—Regulators..............	M	1845		
Wood County—Regulators........	S	1837-38		
Oklahoma:				
Beaver County—Vigilance Committee......................	M	1887	2	
Choctaw County—Vigilantes......	S	1873		
Creek Nation—Vigilance Committee	L	1888		100
Okmulgee—Vigilance Committee...	S	ca. 1901		
South Carolina:				
Black Country (upper Coastal Plain and lower Piedmont area)— Regulators.....................	L	1767-69	16	ca. 5,000-6,000
South Dakota:				
Jerauld County—Vigilantes........	S	1882		
Northern Black Hills (Deadwood, Spearfish, Sturgis and vicinity)— Vigilantes....................	L	1877-79	5	
Pierre—Vigilance Committee......	M	1880	1	12-15
Rapid City and vicinity—Vigilantes	L	1877-78	4	
Tennessee:				
Knoxville vicinity—Regulators.....	S	ca. 1798		
Randolph and Covington—Regulators.....................	S	1830's		
Sevier County—White Caps.......	L	1892-97	9	
Stewart County—Regulators.......	S	1818		
Texas:				
Atascosa and Wilson Counties— Citizens Committee............	S	1875		
Bell County—Vigilance Committee.	M	1866, 1874		
Blanco County—Vigilance Committee......................	S	1870's-80's		
Blossom Prairie, Lamar County— Vigilance Committee............	S	1877		
Bosque County—Vigilantes........	M	1860, 1870	4	
Burnet County—Minute Men and Mob.........................	M	1869-1870's		
Callahan County—Vigilance Committee......................	S	1870's-80's		
Clarksville—Regulators...........	S	1830's-40's		
Comal County—Vigilance Committee......................	S	1870's-80's		
Comanche County—Vigilantes.....	L	1872-86	ca. 10	
Corpus Christi—Vigilance Committee......................	S	1860		
Corpus Christi area—Vigilantes....	S	1874-75		
Coryell County—Vigilantes........	L	1861-83, 1893-94	9	
Decatur—Vigilantes..............	S	1875		
Denton County—Minute Companies	S	1863, 1867		
DeWitt and Gonzales Counties— Vigilantes....................	M	1873		
Eastland County—Mob...........	S	1887		
El Paso—Vigilance Committee.....	S	1870's-80's		
Erath County—Mob.............	M	1872	3	37
Fort Griffin vicinity—Mob........	S	1850's		
Goliad—Vigilantes................	M	1858	6	
Hamilton County:				
Vigilantes....................	M	1860-62	2	
Mob.........................	M	1870's-80's	3	
Hardin County—Regulators.......	S	1850's		

Place and movement	Type	Dates	Number of victims killed	Number of members in movement
Texas—Continued				
Hays County—Vigilance Committee	S	1870's or 80's		
Hill County—Vigilantes	S	1873-78		
Llano County and Burnet County—Vigilance Committee	M	1870's		
McDade area, Bastrop County—Vigilantes	L	1876-83	13	ca. 200
McMullen County—Vigilance Committee	S	1860's-70's		
Madison County—Vigilance Committee	S	1867-68		
Mason County—Hoodoos (vigilantes)	L	1875 ff.		
Nueces River (lower) area—Minute Men	S	1875		
Montague County—Law and Order League	M	1872-75	1	
Navarro County—Vigilantes	M	1840's-50's		
Neuville—Vigilantes	M	1874-76	3	
Orange County (and surrounding Counties of Jefferson, Newton, and Jasper)—Regulators	L	1856	5	
Palo Pinto County—Vigilance Committee	S	1859		
Rockdale—Vigilantes	S	1875		
Rusk County—Vigilance Committee	S	1849		
San Antonio—Vigilance Committee	L	1857-65	ca. 17	
San Saba County—Mob	L	1880-96	ca. 25	
Scurry County—Mob	S	1899		
Shackelford County—Vigilance Committee	L	1876-78	19	ca. 70
Shelby County—Regulators	L	1840-44	10	
Springtown—Mob	M	1872	6	
Sulphur Springs—Vigilantes	S	1879		
Sarrant County—Regulators	S	1850's		
Trinity County—Law and Order League	M	ca. 1904		
Van Zandt County—Vigilantes	S	1876		
Wilbarger County—Vigilance Committee	M	1882	ca. 4	
Waco—antihorsethief association	S	1872		
Wrightsboro—Minute Company	S	1877		
Utah:				
Promontory—Vigilance Committee	S	1869		
Virginia:				
Norfolk—Vigilance committee	M	1834		
Richmond—Vigilance committee	M	1834		
Washington:				
New Dungeness—Vigilance Committee	S	1864		
Pierce County—Vigilance Committee	S	1856		
Pullman and Colfax—Vigilantes	M	1890's	ca. 3	
Seattle—Vigilance Committee	L	1882	3	500
Walla Walla—Vigilance Committee	L	1864-66	ca. 5	
Union Gap (then Yakima City)—Vigilantes	S	ca. 1885		
Wisconsin:				
Prairie du Chien—Regulators	S	1850's		
Wyoming:				
Bear River City—Vigilance Committee	M	1868	3	
Cambria—Vigilantes	S	1890's		
Casper—Vigilance Committee	S	1902	1	ca. 24

Place and movement	Type	Dates	Number of victims killed	Number of members in movement
Wyoming—Continued				
Cheyenne and Laramie County— Vigilantes	L	1868-69	16	ca. 200
Johnson County—Regulators	L	1892	2	50
Laramie—Vigilance Committee	L	1868	7	300-500
Rawlins—Vigilantes	M	1878, 1881	2	

Note: Inadvertently omitted from the above list was the Santa Barbara (Calif.) vigilante movement of 1857 which was L in type, killed 8 or more men, and had 150 members.

Chapter 6

VIOLENCE IN AMERICAN LITERATURE AND FOLK LORE

By Kenneth Lynn*

Recurring themes of violence in American literature and folk lore bear witness to the continuing violence of American life. The cruel practical jokes and bloodthirsty tall tales of frontier humorists tell us a good deal about what it was like to live on the cutting edge of a wilderness. The burning cities of Ignatius Donnelly's *Caesar's Column,* Jack London's *The Iron Heel,* and other social novels of the turn of the century reflect in their flames the revolutionary discontent of farmers and industrial workers in the 1890's. Mark Twain's *Pudd'nhead Wilson,* Melville's "Benito Cereno," and Richard Wright's *Native Son* measure the racial animosities with which black and white Americans have been struggling since the 17th century. The war novels of Stephen Crane, and of Hemingway and Dos Passos, register the central experience of life "in our time."

American literature and folk lore have great significance, therefore, for all those who are interested in the violent

* Kenneth Lynn is professor of American studies at the new Federal City College in Washington, D.C. Previously, from 1943 through 1968, he had studied American civilization and taught English literature at Harvard University. In the fall of 1969 Professor Lynn will join the department of history at the Johns Hopkins University. His publications include *The Dream of Success* (Boston: Little, Brown, 1960).

realities of our society. The trouble, however, with the way in which these materials have been used by historians, sociologists, anthropologists, and psychiatrists is that literature has been assumed to be nothing less (or more) than a mirror image of life. The effects of fictional conventions on representations of reality have been ignored, as have the needs of authors and audiences alike for the pleasures of hyperbolic exaggeration. Furthermore, by extrapolating violent incidents out of their literary contexts, social scientists have not taken into account either the mitigating dreams of peace which are threaded through the very bloodiest of our novels and stories, or the comic juxtapositions which take the curse off many of the most unpleasant episodes that the American imagination has ever recorded.

The false impressions created by social scientists have been reinforced by certain literary critics who have used their judgments of American literature as a basis for making larger judgments about American society. The errors of these critics have not proceeded out of any lack of literary subtlety, but rather out of their wish to be recognized as cultural messiahs. The messianic strain in modern literary criticism has been in any case very strong, embracing such diverse commentators as T. S. Eliot, Northrop Frye, F. R. Leavis, and Marshall McLuhan, but it has been particularly strong among commentators on American literature. From D. H. Lawrence in the 1920's to Leslie Fiedler in the 1960's the desire of literary critics to lead a revolution in American values has been continuing and powerful, and this desire has led them to insist that violence is the dominant theme of American literature, that American literature is more violent than other literatures, and that the violence of our literature has become more deadly with the passage of time. For the first stage in a revolution is to prove its necessity, and what better evidence could be offered as proof of the sickness of historic American values than the unique and obsessive concern of our literary artists with themes of blood and pain? To the messianic critics, the indictment of American books has opened the way to the conviction of American society.

The question of American literary violence thus needs reexamination. By looking closely at certain representative examples, from the humor of the Old Southwest to the tragic novels of our own time, we may be able to measure

227

more accurately than heretofore both the extent and the significance of violence in American literature and folk lore.

When we consider the humorists of the region between the Alleghenies and the Mississippi River, which in the 1830's and 1840's was known as the American Southwest, we are immediately struck by the theoretical possibility that the literature of violence in America has been written by losers—by citizens who have found their political, social, or cultural position threatened by the upward surge of another, and very different, group of Americans. For the Southwestern humorists were professional men—doctors, lawyers, and newspapermen, for the most part—who were allied on the local level with the big plantation owners and who supported on the national level the banker-oriented Whig party of Daniel Webster and Henry Clay; and what bound these writers together as a literary movement, what furnished the primary animus behind their violently aggressive humor, was their fear and hatred of Jacksonian democracy. Longstreet, Thompson, Kennedy, Noland, Pike, Cobb, Thorpe, Baldwin, Hooper: all the best known humorists of the Old Southwest were agreed that Andrew Jacksonism stood for a tyrannical nationalism which threatened to obliterate States' rights; for a revolutionary politics which by 1860 would democratize the constitution of every Southern state except South Carolina; and for a new spirit of economic competitiveness which everywhere enabled poor white entrepreneurs to challenge the financial supremacy of the bankers and the planters, even as Faulkner's Snopes clan would crawl out of the woodwork after the Civil War and take over the leadership of the biggest bank in Yoknapatawpha County.

Augustus Baldwin Longstreet's *Georgia Scenes* (1835) established the basic literary strategy of Southwestern humor, which was to define the difference between the emotionally controlled, impeccably mannered, and beautifully educated gentleman who sets the scene and tells the tale and the oafish frontiersmen who are the characters within the tale. By keeping his narrators outside and above the barbaric actions they described, Longstreet (and his successors) drove home the point that Southern gentlemen stood for law and order, whereas Jacksonian louts represented an all encompassing anarchy. However hot-tempered the author might be in private life (and Judge Longstreet was only one of many Southwestern humorists who had a notoriously bad temper); however much the hideously cruel, eyeball-popping fights they described gave vent to their own sadistic sense of fun; whatever the political satisfaction that they secretly derived from the spectacle of Jacksonians clawing and tearing at one another; the literary mask of the Southwestern humorists was that of a cool and collected personality whose thoughts and conduct were infallibly above reproach. Politically and socially, the humorists had a vested interest in maintaining that mask.

They also had a vested interest in enlarging upon the violence of backwoods bully boys, riverboat toughs, and other representatives of the new Democracy. Because the more inhuman his Jacksonian characters were made to appear, the severer the gentleman-narrator's judgment of them could become. No matter how much lipservice they paid to realism as a literary ideal, there was a built-in political temptation to exaggerate the truth which Whig humorists found impossible to resist. One and all, they wrote comic fantasies, which the historian of American violence will cite at his own risk.

Even those social scientists who are aware that the purported reality described by a story must always be understood as a projection of the story teller's mind generally distort the meaning of Southwestern humor by taking its violence out of context. Doubtless, as I have already suggested, the humorists' fascination with scenes of violence tells us a good deal about the frustrations and fears of the Southern Whig mind. Yet if we set out to calculate the total imaginative effect of, say, Longstreet's *Georgia Scenes,* we find that the "frame" devices which encapsulate the stories within a gentleman's viewpoint and the balanced, rational, Addisonian language of the gentleman-narrator's style remove a good deal of the horror from the stories. As in Henry Fielding's *Tom Jones,* a novel of which Judge Longstreet was very fond, violence becomes funny rather than frightening, sanative rather than maddening, when it is seen from a certain elevation, when it is understood by the audience to be a kind of mraionette show that is controlled by, but does not morally implicate, the master of ceremonies.

In the years after 1850, when relationships between the sections steadily deteriorated and the South gave way to a kind of collective paranoia, Southwestern humor finally lost its cool. Instead of speaking through the mask of a self-controlled gentleman, the humorist of the new era told his sadistic tale in the vernacular voice of the sadist himself. Whereas Judge Longstreet had been at pains to keep his distance, imaginatively speaking, from the clowns he wrote about, George Washington Harris gleefully identified himself with the prankster-hero of *Sut Lovingood's Yarns* (1867)—for in a world ringed by enemies, the only hope of survival which a paranoid imagination could summon up was to strike first, an ungentlemanly act of which Longstreet's narrator would have been manifestly incapable. Just as the Whig party disappeared after the mid-1850's, so did the literary persona who had incarnated Whiggery's conservative ideals. In his place there arose a grotesque child-hero who was the literary equivalent of the fire-eating, secessionist spirit which increasingly dominated Southern politics after 1855. The vernacular narration of young Sut Lovingood is not intended to remind us of the virtues of moderate behavior—indeed, just the reverse. For Sut's humor blocks intellectual awareness in order to release a tremendous burst of vindictive emotion; he is concerned not to instruct society, but to revenge himself upon it. A rebel without a cause, Sut tells us much about the rebels of the Lost Cause of 1861-1865.

Yet in the overall picture of Southwestern humor, *Sut Lovingood* is the exception, not the rule, a rare instance of the sadistic humor of the frontier being expressed in a manner unqualified by any kind of stylistic or formal restraint. For the most part, the humorists of the Old Southwest had a more ambivalent attitude toward violence. Clearly, they were fascinated by it, no matter what they said to the contrary. The way in which the narrators of their stories linger over the details of physical punishment indicates that there was a lurking hypocrisy in the law-and-order stance of the humorists. However, in dealing with Southwestern humor, the historian of the Whig mind must be as careful about leaping to exaggerated conclusions as the historian of Jacksonian reality. If the humorists were hypocrites to a degree, they were also sincere to a degree. If they secretly delighted in the human cockfights they pretended to deplore, they also were genuinely committed to a social standard of moderation in all things. This commitment was expressed in the literary qualities of their writing. In Southwestern humor, the style was, in a very real sense, the man

Another striking outburst of violent stories in American literature occurred in the social fiction of the turn of the century. Thus Ignatius Donnelly's widely read novel, *Caesar's Column* (1891) projects a dystopian vision of American society in 1988. At first glance, New York City is a smokeless, noiseless, dream city, with glass-roofed streets, glittering shops, and roof-garden restaurants. But beneath the surface, the narrator of the novel (a white visitor from Uganda) discovers that the city, like the nation at large, is engaged in a deadly social struggle between a ruling oligarchy, which maintains itself in power with a dirigible fleet armed with gas bombs, and a brutalized populace, made up for the most part of a sullen-tempered, urban proletariat, but also supported by a degraded peasantry. The story climaxes in a lurid account of the definitive breakdown of the social order, which occurs when the looting and burning of the city by a revolutionary organization called the Brotherhood of Destruction raged beyond the control of the oligarchy's troops. The number of corpses littering the streets finally becomes so great that an immense pyramid of dead bodies is stacked up and covered with cement, partly as a sanitary precaution and partly as a memorial to the violence. In the end, the entire city is put to the torch, and except for a small band of Christian socialists who escape to Africa, the entire population is consumed in the holocaust.

The apocalyptic fury of the novel relates very directly to the political hysteria of the 1880's and to the agricultural and industrial unrest of the 1890's—to the fears of an anarchist takeover, for example, that swept the nation after the Haymarket riot in Chicago in 1886, and to the bitter, bloody strikes at Homestead, Pennsylvania, and Pullman, Illinois, in the mid-1890's. The novel is also a startling prophecy of the events of the summer of 1967 in Newark and Detroit. Yet in the very act of calling attention to these resemblances between literature and life, we are also confronted with the important difference, which is that the novel is much more extreme than the reality. As in the case of the Southwestern humorists, Ignatius Donnelly was not a mere seismograph, passively recording social shocks, or even forecasting them; rather, he was a man who had

231

been driven to become a writer by the experience of political loss, and the apocalyptic darkness of his novelistic vision tells us more about Donnelly's state of mind than it does about American society, past or present.

A political reformer from Minnesota, Donnelly had been deeply upset in 1889 by the overtly corrupt practices of the legislature in his state. In addition to his commitment to good government, Donnelly was a Populist, who combined a concern for the deteriorating economic position of the Midwestern farmer with a political and moral concern that American life was coming to be dominated by its big cities. If the demographic trends of his time continued, Donnelly realized, they would reduce the importance of the farm vote and would spread the spirit of corruption that had so appalled him in the Minnesota legislature. In equating the spread of urbanism with the spread of corruption, and in envisioning damnation and destruction as the ultimate penalty of city life, Donnelly revealed himself, in the judgment of Richard Hofstadter, as a sadist and a nihilist. *Caesar's Column* is "a childish book," so Hofstadter has written, "but in the middle of the twentieth century it seems anything but laughable: it affords a frightening glimpse into the ugly potential of frustrated popular revolt."[1] Donnelly's novel is thus for Hofstadter a key to the provincial spirit of Midwesten America, a spirit ruled by suspicions of the East, distrust of intellectuals, and hatred of Jews, and given to raging fantasies of Babylonian destruction. The violence depicted in *Caesar's Column* may never have been matched by the social data of American history, but Hofstadter would contend that the sado-nihilism of the American hick is very much a part of the emotional actuality of our civilization, and that Donnelly's novel is expressive of a profoundly dangerous phenomenon.

Yet Donnelly's ambivalent view of the city—a place on the one hand of glittering amusements and technological marvels and on the other hand of social exploitation and spiritual degradation—is a view he shares with a vast number of American writers from all centuries of our history, all sections of the country, and all ranges of literary excellence from the least memorable to the most distinguished, the most intellectual, and the most cosmopolitan. The urban imagery summoned up by Hawthorne and Melville in the 1850's is characterized by starkly symbolic contrasts

232

of blazing light and sinister darkness, as is the imagery of *New York By Gaslight* and other trashy books of the period. E. P. Roe's bestselling novel, *Barrriers Burned Away* (1872), which depicts the great Chicago fire as a judgment upon a wicked city, is part of an incendiary tradition which not only includes Donnelly's mediocre novel, but Part IV of T. S. Eliot's *The Waste Land* (1922). Clearly, what Donnelly was expressing in his novel was a frustration which fed into a familiar American concern, at heart, a religious concern, with the question of whether honor, charity, and other traditional values of western civilization were capable of surviving in the modern city. That Donnelly gave a gloomy answer does not necessarily prove that his political frustration contained an "ugly potential" of violence. It is, indeed, more likely that the ending of his novel was a religious strategy that went back through Hawthorne and Melville to the Puritans. By issuing a jeremiad which warned of the terrible consequences of abandoning the Christian life, he hoped to bring an urban America back to the faith of its fathers.

Jack London's *The Iron Heel* (1905) also ends cataclysmically. Although the plot of the socialists to overthrow capitalism in America has been led by the dynamic Ernest Everhard (whose medium size, bulging muscles, and omnivorous reading habits recall Jack London himself), the awesome power of the ruling oligarchy—the so-called Iron Heel—is too much for the outnumbered revolutionaries. At the climax of the book, the slum classes —for whom Everhard and his fellow socialists feel nothing but contempt—go pillaging through the city. However, this act is the self-indulgent gesture of a degenerate, racially mongrelized mob which does nothing to benefit the military position of the gallant elitists of socialism. According to the novel's 27th-century editor, 300 years of blood letting were to pass before the Iron Heel is finally overthrown and the Brotherhood of Man established.

The question at once arises as to why London, after building up his hero as a superman, should have permitted him to be defeated, especially since he was an exponent of the same revolutionary cause as Everhard was. The answer has seemed unavoidable to some readers that London was interested in violence for violence's sake, even if it meant denying himself the pleasure of a socialistically happy ending. However, the confusion which London displayed in his ideological writings suggests another explanation for the ending of *The Iron Heel*. For these ideological writings reveal that London was as committed to a belief in the competitive ethic of American success as he was to socialism, and that he was hagridden by the conviction that the victory of socialist principles would lead to social rot, because it would terminate competition between individuals; consequently he found it imaginatively impossible to write a novel depicting the triumph of the socialist revolution. To portray Everhard and company in charge of a socialist America would have meant that London would have been forced to show his autobiographical hero presiding over a society characterized by declining production, degenerating racial stocks, and decaying institutions.

It is not surprising, therefore, that even though *The Iron Heel* is supposedly edited by a man living under the reign of the Brotherhood of Man in the 27th century, no description is given of how this socialist Utopia is organized or operated, no hint is offered as to the steps that have been taken to avoid social decay. Unable to portray a paradise that he knew in his heart was really a hell, London found it an easier imaginative task to concentrate on describing the defeat of the socialist revolution. To lament the defeat of socialism was infinitely easier than to pretend to rejoice in its triumph.

A third possible explanation for the ferocious violence of *The Iron Heel's* conclusion is that it reflected London's awareness of all the disappointments that American radicals had suffered in the course of his lifetime. The Greenback movement had gone nowhere, except to oblivion; the Supreme Court had reversed the Granger cases; the Populists had never become anything more than a regional movement; in the climactic election of 1896, Bryan had been badly beaten; and Eugene Debs had polled a disappointing number of votes in the presidential elections of 1900 and 1904. London's Socialist hopes were simply overwhelmed by his inability to forget the bitter lessons of recent American history: in the new era of Standard Oil trust and other big-business combinations, American radicals could scarcely be optimistic.

All three explanations of London's novel are equally compelling. Unquestionably, London was neurotically fascinated by tests of mental and physical endurance; long before his suicide, his mind was thronged with images of violent death. To literary critics interested in establishing the sickness of the American psyche, London's personal life simply reinforces their thesis that his novels and stories are obsessed by violence. Because it damages their thesis, these critics ignore the fact that violent endings offered London a means of resolving his contradictory ideological commitments to success and socialism—and that therefore the conclusion of *The Iron Heel* ought to be understood as a literary strategy which enabled a philosophically troubled writer to resolve his ambivalence and complete his books. Equally damaging to the interpretation of *The Iron Heel* as symptomatic of an author's (and a nation's) psychological illness is the fact that a socialist novelist who foresaw the continuing hegemony of capitalist combinations in America was simply being realistic. Can we really be sure that the ending London gave his novel represented anything else than his unwillingness to fool either himself or his readers about the changes of building a socialist Utopia in 20th-century America? The apocalyptic fury with which *The Iron Heel* concludes may well have been the sign of London's sanity as a social prophet, rather than of his psychological imbalance.

Writing about the experience of modern war begins in American literature with Stephen Crane in 1895. Our first modern conflict had ended 30 years before, but for a generation after the Civil War American writers had either ignored or romanticized that terrible struggle. The one exception was John W. DeForest's novel, *Miss Ravenel's Conversion from Secession to Loyalty* (1867), which had portrayed the fighting in grim and realistic detail. However, *Miss Ravenel* had been a failure, commercially speaking, and in the wake of its failure there arose a genre of writing called the intersectional romance, which typically told of a wounded Union Army officer being nursed back to health by a predictably beautiful Southern belle, whom he finally led to the altar. Even the literary reminiscences of soldiers who had served in the war told a good deal less than the whole truth. Thus the *Century* magazine's notable series of military recollections, "Battles and Leaders of the Civil War," represented only an officer's eye view of what had in fact been a democratic war won by a mass army. The

235

same fault afflicted Ambrose Bierce's otherwise superbly honest *Tales of Soldiers* (1891). Before Crane published *The Red Badge of Courage* (1895), only a very minor writer named Wilbur F. Hinman had recorded, in a comic novel entitled *Corporal Si Klegg and His "Pard"* (1887), how the violence made possible by modern military technology had affected the men in the ranks.

That Crane should have been impelled to measure the impact of the war on ordinary Americans was certainly not the result of his own experience of violence, for he was not even born until 1871, six years after the close of the war, and in the course of his middle-class New Jersey boyhood had never heard a shot fired in anger. What fascinated him about the Civil War was what also fascinated him about the submarginal world of the Bowery, which he had come to know during his salad days as a reporter on the New York *Herald*. Like the seamist of New York's slums, the most tragic war in our history represented American life *in extremis,* and such representations suited Crane's subversive frame of mind.

Political and social events of the early 1890's had revealed to Crane an enormous disparity between the official version of American life as conveyed by such popular authors of the day as James Whitcomb Riley and Thomas Bailey Aldrich, and the often brutal realities that were attendant upon the Nation's transformation into an urban and industrial civilization. The effect of this revelation on a young man who had already been engaged throughout his youth in a Tom Sawyerish rebellion against his middle-class upbringing was to turn him against all the optimistic beliefs in the pursuit of happiness, the inevitability of progress, etc., which most Americans cherished. Revolted by blandness and complacency, Crane went in search of misery and violence—in the lower depths of Manhattan; in sleazy bars down Mexico way, where he was nearly murdered one scary night; on the battlefields of Greece, where he served as a correspondent covering the Greco-Turkish War; and again as a war reporter in Cuba, where he differentiated himself from Richard Harding Davis and other correspondents by the risks he took, by the deliberate way he exposed himself to the fire of Spanish rifles.

In the world of his imagination, Crane craved the same experiences, and he often wrote of them before he had lived them. *Maggie. A Girl of the Streets* (1893), the story of an East Side girl whose descent into prostitution concludes with her descent into the East River, was largely worked out before Crane quit college and went to live in New York, just as *The Red Badge of Courage* was published before he saw Greece or Cuba. For his books were not *reportage;* they were works of art which endeavored to make the American novel relevant to a new generation of socially skeptical readers, as the works of Zola, Crane's literary idol, had done for the French novel. The restlessness, the guilt, and the itch to change things that impelled middle-class, urban Americans into the Progressive movement of 1901-17 were first manifested in the fiction of Stephen Crane in the mid-1890's. Paradoxically, a body of work dominated by a black humor and an ironic style, and by scenes of violence often culminating in horridly detailed descriptions of dead bodies, had a life-giving effect, a revitalizing effect on American art and politics. For his mordant skepticism about official American culture and all his efforts to flee—both spatially and spiritually—from the world he had been brought up in, Crane was really a middle-class spokesman. Unlike the Whig humorists of the 1830's or the Utopian novelists who were his contemporaries, Crane was not a loser in American life. He was, rather, an outsider, who had assumed his critical role by choice rather than necessity. Whereas Judge Longstreet and his fellow humorists had lamented a way of life, a scheme of values, that was irrevocably passing out of the national scene, and whereas Jack London and Ignatius Donnelly were lamenting an American civilization that would never come to be, Crane offered violent versions of a modern war we had already fought and would fight again, and of a city which has been the archetype of our collective life from his own time to the present. As with most outsiders in American life, including the runaway Tom Sawyer, rebellion was a halfway house for Stephen Crane and violence a means of ultimate accommodation.

The violence of Ernest Hemingway's early novels and stories are expressive, so we have been told, of a far more cruel, pointless, and degrading war experience than the Civil War that Stephen Crane conjured up out of talking with veterans and reading the *Century* magazine. Why this should be so is not entirely clear, inasmuch as the Civil

War was infinitely more costly to our soldiers and to our people. Indeed, the violence of Hemingway's fiction has become so famous as to obscure the fact that none of his stories, and none of the stories of Dos Passos or E. E. Cummings or any other American writer who served overseas in World War I, come anywhere near matching the butchery described in Erich Maria Remarque's *All Quiet on the Western Front*, Henri Barbusse's *Under Fire*, Guy Chapman's *A Passionate Prodigality*, and other European chronicles of the Great War. In only one way are the novels of the Americans more nightmarish than those of the European writers. Hemingway, Dos Passos, and company did not, and indeed could not, outrival the details of endless horror that four years in the trenches had etched in Guy Chapman's or Erich Remarque's memory. Yet Remarque and the other European writers also paid grateful tribute in their books to the psychological comforts of mass comradeship, whereas the heroes of Hemingway and Dos Passos are loners who feel lost in the midst of the crowd. They may find one other kindred spirit, generally Italian, or possibly a girl friend, generally British, but they know nothing of the group feeling that Remarque and the European writers were grateful to. A desolate sense of alienation is the special mark of the best American fiction to come out of World War I. In seeking to assess the meaning of the violence expressed by the "lost generation" writers, we must therefore reckon with the loneliness which accompanies it and which gives it its peculiarly devastating and memorable effect.

Perhaps the alienation may be explained by the very special role which our writers played in the war. For the striking fact is that unlike their literary equivalents in England, France, and Germany, the American writers were not soldiers but ambulance drivers or some other kind of auxiliary. Malcolm Cowley worked for military transport; Hemingway was with the Red Cross in Italy; Dos Passos and Cummings were with the Norton-Harjes ambulance unit, and so were Slater Brown, Harry Crosby, and other young men who would achieve some kind of literary distinction in the 1920's. They were in the war, but not of it; involved and yet not involved. They could not pay tribute to the comradeship of the trenches because they had never really experienced it, they had never really belonged.

But this is only a partial explanation of the loneliness recorded in their fiction. For it does not answer the question of why they became ambulance drivers in the first place. And here we come to the heart of the matter. For their enlistment as ambulance drivers was not so much a cause of their alienation as an expression of it. They were outside the mainstream of American life, already suspicious of what Hemingway would later call the "sacred words," before they ever landed in Europe. The war did not cause them to feel lonely, but rather confirmed and intensified a pre-existent feeling of not fitting in. When these future ambulance drivers had been high school and college students in the period of 1900-17, they had been disgusted by the discrepancy between the consistently idealistic theory and often grubby practice of America in the Progressive era. Ironically, the young men whose imaginations had been kindled by the violence of Stephen Crane in the 1890's had become the adult establishment twenty years later, and thus in turn became the target of a new generation of rebels —who also chose to express their dissent from the going values of society by means of violence. That the younger literati of 1917 sought out the war did not mean that they were patriotically responding, as millions of other young men in America were, to the high-flown rhetoric of Woodrow Wilson. Dos Passos, a political radical, went to Europe in order to witness the death throes of capitalism. Hemingway, who already knew that the woods of northern Michigan contained truths undreamed of in the suburban philosophy of his native Oak Park, Illinois, made his way to the front line at Fossalta di Piave because he knew that that line offered a great opportunity to a young writer who was seeking—as Stephen Crane had before him—for materials with which to rebuke his middle-class American heritage. When fragments of an Austrian mortar shell hit him in the legs, and he was hit twice more in the body by machinegun fire, he found his materials with a vengeance. Thereafter a wound was to become the central symbol of nearly all his work and the consequences of a wound his recurrent theme. In many ways a highly personal testament, Hemingway's work also captures, in hauntingly symbolic terms, the permanently scarring effects of World War I on American

239

society. In so doing, the violent expression of an outsider has become the means by which generations of modern Americans have understood themselves. Originating as a criticism of peacetime America, Hemingway's violence turned into an explanation of what 20th-century warfare has done to us as a people. Leslie Fiedler would have it that Hemingway's concern with violence signifies a pathological inability to deal with adult sexuality,[2] but this interpretation ignores the fact that violence has an intrinsic importance in our history, especially in this era of global wars—as Hemingway precociously understood from childhood onward.

The literature dealing with race relations is very different from all other expressions of violence in American writing. Even in Hemingway's most tragic stories, his protagonists make a separate peace which for a fleeting time is a genuine peace; the universe of pain inexorably closes down on them again, but the memories of happiness remain as a defense against despair and madness. However, with the notable exception of *The Adventures of Huckleberry Finn* (1884), in which Huck's memory of his life on the raft with Nigger Jim sustains him against all his sordid encounters with the slave-owning society on shore, the important American books on race are unredeemed by such recollections. The sanative qualities of Southwestern humor are also missing from this literature, as are the long-range hopes of social justice that arise out of the ashes of *The Iron Heel* and *Caesar's Column.* "Benito Cereno," Melville's brilliant short story of the early 1850's; Mark Twain's mordant novel, *Pudd'nhead Wilson* (1894); and Richard Wright's smashingly powerful *Native Son* (1940): these three representative works offer us no hope whatsoever for believing that the violence and the hatred, the fear and the guilt that separate black and white Americans from one another will ever end. As I have tried to indicate, the nihilism that has been imputed to works dealing with other aspects of American violence is highly debatable, as is the charge that the violence of American literature is sick, sick, sick, because it really stands for our alleged maladjustment to sex or some other cultural sickness. In the literature of racial violence, however, terms like "nihilism" and "sickness" seem very applicable, indeed.

What hope, for instance, does Melville offer us in telling

the story of "Benito Cereno"? The kindness and compassion of Don Benito are not sufficient to keep his black servant from putting a razor to his master's throat, and while Don Benito does manage to escape from violent death, he is unable to shake the shadow of his racial guilt. Haunted by the hatred that the revolt of his slaves has revealed, but powerless to expiate a crime that is far older than himself, Don Benito dies, the very image of the impotent white liberal, on the slopes of the aptly named Mount Agonia.

The tragic hopelessness of Melville's story becomes in *Pudd'nhead Wilson* one of the later Mark Twain's bitterest jokes. With his superior intelligence, *Pudd'nhead Wilson* is able to solve a bewildering racial crime: his exposure of the fact that the "Negro woman" who has murdered one of the leading white men of the town is in reality a man, Tom Driscoll, whose entire life has been a masquerade in white face, is a masterpiece of detective work. Even more impressive is Wilson's discovery that the masquerade was made possible by Tom Driscoll's light-skinned Negro mother, who switched a white baby and her own baby into one another's cradle, a deception made possible by the fact that both babies had the same white father. Yet finally, Pudd'nhead Wilson is a helpless man. His superior intelligence is powerless to overcome the accumulated racial crimes of American history. To be sure, his trial testimony sends the Negro masquerader to jail and thence to the auction block, where he is sold to a slave trader from "down the river." But if Wilson's testimony succeeds in condemning a black man, it does not succeed in freeing a white man. For the real Tom Driscoll, who has been a slave for 20 years, is not restored to freedom by being given back his identity. Thanks to what society has done to him, he can neither read nor write, nor speak anything but the dialect of the slave quarter; his walk, his attitudes, his gestures, his bearing, his laugh—all are the manners of a slave.

Mark Twain's awareness of the interwoven strands of sex and violence in the racial tragedy of American life is amplified in *Native Son* into a terrifying story of sexual temptation, murder, and legal revenge. The crippling fears of the white man that dominate Bigger Thomas's mind have their white counterparts in the hysterically anti-Negro editorials in the Chicago newspapers and the demonic racism of the police. Nowhere in this implacable novel does the author give us any grounds for belief in the possibility of genuine communication and mutual trust between the races.

It is, of course, possible that "Benito Cereno" has no other reference than to the darkness into which Melville's mind descended after 1851, *Pudd'nhead Wilson* no other reference than to the celebrated misanthropy of the later Mark Twain, *Native Son* no other reference than to Richard Wright's own tortured soul. Yet it is significant that these three extraordinarily gifted writers, two white, one black, agree so completely about the insolubility of American race hatred. Conceivable, their fictions reveal not only the tragic thoughts of three authors, but the tragic truth of American society as well.

References

1. Richard Hofstadter, *The Age of Reform* (New York: Vintage, 1955), p. 70.
2. Cf. *Love and Death in the American Novel* (New York, 1960), pp. 125, 175, 186, 304-309, 341, 350-352.

PART III

THE HISTORY OF WORKING-CLASS PROTEST AND VIOLENCE

A cursory glance at the histories of Western Europe and the United States during the past two centuries suggests that working-class demands for resolution of economic and related political grievances have been the most common and persistent source of turmoil, if not of revolution or civil war. This was true especially during England's industrial revolution. Many Americans, dismayed by the domestic tumult of recent years, admire wistfully both the quiet grace of the English countryside and the impressive political rituals that are the capstone of contemporary English civil peace. An historical corrective is provided by Professor Roberts, one of Britain's leading authorities on labor relations, in the first of the following two chapters. In the 18th and 19th century, the gentle English countryside was wracked by riotous mobs, arsonists, and machine breakers, its city streets echoed the cries of demonstrators for economic and political reform. The English body politic was afflicted by innumerable real and imagined conspiracies and insurrections, enmeshed in a web of spies and agents provocateurs employed by the state, and defended by armed garrisons and harsh penal codes administered harshly.

In the United States workers seldom made political demands, but the chronicles of conflict between them and their employers have been extraordinarily bloody, seemingly more so than those of any industrial nation in the world. Although many historical instances of labor violence in America have been examined in detail, the study by Profs. Philip Taft and Philip Ross, below, is the first to examine systematically the cumulative records of strike violence in America. The core of their study is an interpretative chronicle of violent strikes from the 1870's to the present. Labor violence was unquestionably pervasive and intense, occurring in every region, in almost every type of industry, and with great frequency in almost every decade from the 1870's to the 1930's. At one of its peaks, between

1902 and 1904, the loss of life reportedly exceeded that of recent ghetto riots in both absolute and relative terms.

The general causes of English tumult and insurrection in the late 18th and early 19th centuries were the tensions generated by unregulated industrialization. But the most striking characteristic of 19th century English society was not its civil disorder, which has afflicted all industrializing societies, but its avoidance of revolution or civil war and its ultimate resolution of the causes of tumult. In the United States the same tensions of rapid economic growth underlay labor conflict. The most common immediate causes of its violent manifestations were employers' denial of the right of labor to organize and their attempt to break strikes. Employers and unions were both guilty of violence. In the majority of cases, however, including the most bloody ones, overt violence was initiated by the armed guards hired by employers or by local law enforcement officers and deputized citizens acting in consort with employers.

The workers who participated directly in the English movements of protest and violence seldom benefited directly from them. Similarly, the outcome of labor violence in the United States very seldom favored the workers or the unions. Hundreds of workers were killed, thousands injured, tens of thousands jailed or forcibly expelled from their communities. The unions most involved in violent disputes usually lost their organizational effectiveness, and their leaders and organizers were constantly harassed. Despite this dismal record, violence in American labor disputes persisted for several generations.

Yet in contemporary England and the United States, expressions of workers' grievances have been muted. Most political demands of English workers are expressed through conventional party and union activities rather than by the riotous demonstrations of the 19th century. Strikes in the United States are no longer likely to be bloody affrays but tests of economic strength played out by labor and management following mutually accepted rules. The circumstances of the passing of violence seem even more dimly perceived than its origins. But it is evident that some patterns of events, some balance among increased economic well-being, coercion, accommodation, and regulation, led to the abatement of violent economic-based conflict in these two nations. We know, for example, that employers and governments often responded forcefully to worker protest, and that their responses sometimes minimized protest, sometimes exacerbated it. Concessions by either employers or governments were slow to come and, when they were made, were seldom in direct response to violence. The more specific questions concern the circumstances in which specific kinds of coercion were effective, the extent to which various kinds of protest were successful for those who made them, either in the short or the long run, and the merits of different kinds of accommodation for minimizing grievances and disruptive protest.

No final answers can be given to these questions, but persuasive evidence about a number of them are provided in these two chapters. Working-class protest and violence have largely been meliorated in the two countries studied here. The means by which this was accomplished may hold some general and specific lessons for the expression and resolution of contemporary discontents.

Chapter 7

ON THE ORIGINS AND RESOLUTION OF ENGLISH WORKING-CLASS PROTEST

By Ben C. Roberts*

THE ROLE OF THE MOB IN BRITISH POLITICS BEFORE 1760

Disorderly gatherings of discontented citizens have been a potent factor in the political history of every nation. Two thousand years ago the emperors of ancient Rome had cause to fear the influence of the mob upon the deliberations of the Senate.

In feudal England the peasants of Essex and Kent, an-

---
* Professor Roberts is head of the department of industrial relations at the London School of Economics. His major publications include *Trade Unions in a Free Society* (London: Hutchinson, for the Institute of Economic Affairs, 1959); *Unions in America, A British View* (Princeton: Industrial Relations Section, Princeton University, 1959); and *A Short History of the T.U.C.*, with John Lovell (London: Macmillan, 1968).

gered by high taxes and attempts to reestablish old feudal practices, and exasperated at the failure of the government to protect them from the pillage and exploitation of murderous bands, assembled and marched on London in 1381 to demand redress from their rulers. Stirred by the radical doctrines preached by a militant priest, they asked for a charter of freedom from the thraldom of villenage, lower taxes, and an end to the lawlessness of bands of demobilized soldiery wandering the countryside after fighting the King's wars. Little or nothing was immediately gained from the revolt, which was bloodily suppressed as were the other risings which occurred all over the country, except that the King and the Lords were made aware that unless popular feeling was assuaged turbulence would again break out.

During the next century the Wars of the Roses kept the country in a continuous state of civil conflict. The Black Death reduced the population and labor grew scarce. Serfdom collapsed and peasants were able to obtain land and rise to the status of yeoman farmers. When the Tudors came to power in 1485 they were able by firm government and social paternalism to create a stable society. The combination of severe punishment for vagrancy and the provision of charitable aid through the parishes, together with the economic security and opportunity which the system of apprenticeship gave to the more intelligent members of the working class, effectively curbed any disposition of the poor to seek the improvement of working conditions through revolt. The one factor that did provoke bitter hostility was the enclosure of common lands by powerful landowners seeking to increase their flocks of sheep to take advantage of the rapidly expanding demand for wool.

Between the death of Elizabeth I in 1603 and the death of Anne in 1714, England went through a major transformation. During the 17th century, modern English society and a modern state began to take shape. At the beginning of the period the economy was highly regulated by the King, who—

acted arbitrarily in matters affecting the stability of the country's economic life—raising or lowering the customs, granting industrial monopolies, controlling prices, prohibiting land enclosure. . . . At the end of the period economic policy was formulated by Parliament and *laissez faire* had succeeded regulation in most spheres.[1]

246

England, which under the Tudors had been a second-class power, was by the beginning of the 18th century the greatest world power. The boundaries of Great Britain extended to America, Asia, and Africa, and her merchants dominated world trade. The City of London had become the financial capital of the world. Newton and his fellow scientists were laying the foundations for scientific progress and with it the industrial revolution. The breaking down of the old securities and opening up of new opportunities to men of vision and vigor created turmoil and resentment as well as satisfying ambition by removing its shackles.

It was after the Civil War and the restoration of the Stuarts in 1660 that gatherings of unruly crowds of the poorer classes, called "the mobile"—or simply "the mob" —became a recurrent feature of city life. There was no single cause for the many riotous assemblies that occurred during this period. Poor harvests, high food prices, unemployment and low wages in the weaving trades caused by the competition of cheap imports of cloth, the hearth tax, customs and excise duties, all gave rise to these manifestations of popular discontent. Nor were the riots confined to the metropolis, though the London mob was the most notorious of all; the poor everywhere were prepared to follow its example.

There does not seem to have been any significant attempt by the mob in one area to concert its actions with the mob in another. Most of the riots were spontaneous, "excited by some local and temporary grievance,"[2] wrote the Webbs, who were unable to find any evidence of a concerted desire to overthrow those who were in authority. The fact was that a working-class movement had not yet come into existence. Where the discontents of the poor led to disorderly assemblies, "the rioting which ensued was animated by no common aim beyond that of immediate revenge upon the nearest personification of the people's enemies, a corn-dealer, an exciseman or an East Indian merchant."[3]

A factor of considerable importance in the growth of mob riots was the weakness of the central authorities. "Neither in London nor in rural England could the civil power unassisted be relied upon for the maintenance of public peace."[4] If order could not be maintained by a local constabulary it was necessary to call out the militia, but there was little disposition to deal with mobs in the ferocious way they had been suppressed in the times of the Tudors and the early Stuarts.

"The problem of the urban mob was one of the problems handed on by this age to its successors."[5] The elements of Tudor society had largely disappeared, but the techniques for protecting the poor from the vicissitudes of a market economy had not been developed. Nor had the political system developed to the stage where major issues of social discontent could be resolved through a democratic political process which was still in embryonic form.

UPSURGE OF POLITICAL AND RELIGIOUS PROTEST

In 1768 the London mob "whose presence is continually felt in the political history of the eighteenth century"[6] found a hero in John Wilkes. Member of Parliament for Aylesbury and a notorious roistering character. Wilkes had been a member of the Hell Fire Club, whose scandalous activities had shocked even the lax standards of 18th-century England. His cynical contempt for the King and the aristocrats who controlled the British Parliament, expressed in witty and obscene lampoons, appealed to the ribald tastes of the London mob. The arrest of Wilkes and his imprisonment for making an insulting attack upon the King and the leaders of the House of Commons and the House of Lords drew huge crowds to the jail where he was awaiting trial. The crowd, shouting "damn the King, damn the Government, damn the Justices," was cleared away from the outside of the prison walls by a volley from the rifles of a Scottish regiment. This "massacre" changed the temper of the mob and gave the Wilkes riots a political significance that had not previously been present. However much a scoundrel Wilkes might be, the mob was prepared to follow him against the entrenched authorities—King, Church, and the wealthy aristocrats who dominated a corrupt parliament.

For the next 10 years London and the South of England seemed to be "a Bedlam under the domination of a beggarly, idle and intoxicated mob without keepers, actuated solely by the word *Wilkes*."[7] The supporters of Wilkes were a motley crowd, but they were by no means all drunks, criminals, and prostitutes. As E. P. Thompson has pointed out, the London artisans had developed a dissenting tradition and were concerned with the political issues arising out of Wilkes' conflict with the authorities.[8] The most popular slogan of the crowds that assembled to support Wilkes was "Liberty." The liberty that was called for was both the political freedom to oppose the King and the ruling oligarchy and the license to attack and despoil the property of the rich and highborn. The Wilkes riots had about them both the character of the traditional mob out for entertainment and a protest movement against social injustice.

The Gordon Riots of 1780, which were a further manifestation of mob violence, were inspired by a revival of the deep suspicions of Catholic plots to seize power, suspicions that were kept alive by the annual celebration with bonfires and fireworks of the capture of Guy Fawkes in 1605, as he and his associates were about to blow up the Houses of Parliament. The Gordon Riots occurred after a large, well-ordered crowd had marched to the Houses of Parliament and presented a petition organized by the Protestant Association against Catholic toleration. When Parliament refused to debate the petition the crowd, urged on by the intemperate demagoguery of Lord George Gordon, ran amok to the cry of "no popery."

The first objects of attack were Catholic chapels and the homes of well-to-do Catholics, then the residences of the Lord Chief Justice and the Archbishop of York, who, it was believed, had Catholic sympathies. After venting its fury on Catholics the mob turned its attention to the prisons, from which it released the inmates. Finally an assault was launched on the Bank of England, the bastion of the power of the city and the heart of the capitalist system.

Up to the final stage of the riots the city authorities, who had not found the outbreak of rioting unwelcome, since it was directed at the much-disliked King and Parliament, refrained from intervention. This license given to the mob has been interpreted as actual connivance and political manipulation that ceased only when the rioters turned on those who had encouraged it.[9] As soon as the Bank came under attack, the Lord Mayor called out the army, which rapidly dispersed the crowds.

The London mob had in fact become an important factor in the battle for the control of Parliament and the reduction, if not elimination, of the political power of the King. In 1780 the people of London, despite their excesses, were under the protection of the libertarian Whigs, who saw them as a counterweight to the Tories and their ally on the Throne. Burke deplored the use of the military in subduing the riots, while Fox declared that he would "much rather be governed by a mob than by a standing army."[10]

This somewhat cynical and calculated "populism," encouraged by the Whigs, rapidly declined after the French Revolution, when the grim excesses of the "liberators" of the Bastille made painfully clear the dangers that lurked in stirring the people to seek reform through direct action.

The last great riot which occurred in the 18th century was in fact provoked by a dinner held in Birmingham by a group of middle-class reformers, many of whom were religious dissenters, to celebrate the fall of the Bastille. It was also encouraged by the Tories. The French Revolution had sharply divided political opinion in Britain. The established authorities and the lower orders were generally extremely hostile. Support for the revolution in the name of liberty came mainly from radical members of the middle class and from religious dissenters.

The fact that Birmingham was a stronghold of dissenting opinion made it the center of the agitation for the repeal of the Test and Corporation Acts, which excluded dissenters from public office. The repeal of the Test Acts was violently opposed by the Anglican clergy and the country gentry, who associated dissenters with atheistic, money-grubbing industrialists whose activities threatened to destroy the old order. The Birmingham riots of 1791 have been described as "an episode in which the country gentlemen called out the urban mob to draw the dissenting teeth of the aggressive and successful Birmingham bourgeoisie."[11] Evidence suggests that the Birmingham mob was skillfully led to well-chosen targets by small groups of rioters who had the support of local Tory magistrates and clergy, who were extremely reluctant to convict and condemn the rioters.

During the next few years the urban mob, recruited from the squalid, over-crowded, and decaying areas of the rapidly growing cities, was adroitly directed by the Tories against the doctrines of the French Revolution. The rioters were for Church and King, and their main targets were now the

250

English Jacobins and the supporters of Tom Paine. Paine's great pamphlet, *The Rights of Man,* had a phenomenal success and stimulated the establishment of reform societies and clubs. This success was due in part to the fact that the philosophy the pamphlet preached was in harmony with the development of a laissez faire market economy, the limitation of the power of the Church and King, and the development of the parliamentary system of government. In short, Paine's plea was for the establishment of a democratic system of government, and had a powerful appeal to dissenters of all kinds.

The activities of Paine and the organizers of the reform clubs greatly alarmed the authorities. Many authorities saw in the doctrines the seeds of an English revolution similar to the one they had at first welcomed in France, but which, they now saw, was leading to the growth of a chauvinistic nationalism that threatened to create a new menace to the peace of Europe.

This development of the French revolution convinced the British government that the Jacobin movement in Britain had to be firmly quashed. *The Rights of Man* was proclaimed a seditious libel and Paine, already in France, was outlawed. The outbreak of war between Britain and France in 1793 transformed the political situation. Only a year before, the British Prime Minister, Pitt, had confidently proclaimed that many years of peace could be expected. It was Pitt's belief that the French revolutionaries were internationalist in outlook, concerned to improve the prosperity of the great mass of the French people by encouraging production and trade. His own policy of peace with Europe, economic retrenchment and gradual reform had been based on this assessment of the consequences of the French revolution. Realization of his mistake was rapid and within a year Pitt was taking steps to ensure that Britain should not succumb to a resurgent and bellicose France.

In the atmosphere of war with France, Jacobinism was not to be tolerated. *The Rights of Man* was a threat to the national unity that was needed to win the war. Patriotism, always the most potent of appeals to man's social instincts, rapidly became the prime motivation of the mob. Effigies of Paine were burned all over Britain and the impulse towards liberty, equality, and fraternity was vigorously suppressed. Dissenting Ministers were clapped in jail for mildly suggesting that the King should be accountable to Parliament, printers for publishing libertarian pamphlets, and publicans for permitting radical societies to meet on their premises.

In spite of the repression of every manifestation of social organization against the established order, there were many outbreaks of unrest and disturbance directed against the loss of old rights and the degradation of life brought about by the advance of industrialism.[12] These clashes between workers and employers were conflicts between the two social classes that were emerging as politically the most important elements in the structure of British society.

LUDDITE DISTURBANCES AND THE STATUS OF WORKERS

The series of disturbances directed against new types of weaving and knitting machines which plagued England during the period from the American revolution to the collapse of Chartism in the early 1850's have been given the name Luddism. The origin of the name has been variously ascribed to a certain Ned Ludlam, a Leicestershire apprentice, who lost his temper on being ordered to square up his frames and beat the offending frame into pieces with a hammer; and to a "general" commanding the forces of Luddism calling himself "Ned Ludd" and living in Sherwood Forest, whence he issued orders and organized attacks on property.[13] Whatever the origin of the name, the essence of the Luddite disturbances was the smashing of machinery, particularly in Nottinghamshire, Yorkshire, Lancashire, and Cheshire. What alarmed the Government and property-owning classes, in addition to the destruction of property and the fear of revolution it engendered, was the suspicion, astutely fanned by innumerable Government spies, of a widespread and organized conspiracy, a belief which does not appear to be borne out by the facts.

It is true that attacks upon property and even persons, such as the murder of the manufacturer Horsfall in 1813 by three men who had been detailed to do it, showed evidence of some amount of organization; the stubborn unity of the workers and absolute refusal to inform baffled all those sent to quell the riots. The outbreaks seem to have been sporadic, arising as a response to intolerable circumstances and dying out when these circumstances improved. The alarm which they aroused, however, can be gauged by the fact that 12,000 soldiers were used for their suppression, a larger army than the 9,000 men who set sail with Wellesley in 1808 for Portugal. Pitt, the Prime Minister, abolished the old custom of billeting troops in people's homes, for fear that soldiers might become contaminated by Radicalism; he built barracks at strategic points to house them, and in addition created the Volunteers and the Yeomanry to deal with civil commotion at home. The Yeomanry, a mounted force drawn from the upper ranks of the agricultural classes, had little sympathy with the town dwellers and could be relied on for complete support of the Government in times of violence. By the end of the war with France in 1815, there were 163,000 men in 200 barracks up and down the country.

Yet all the evidence goes to prove that the outbreaks, far from being aimed at the overthrow of the Government, were inspired by sheer, unrelieved distress. General Maitland, commanding troops in the North, was certain that there was no elaborate organization. William Wilberforce, one of the committee appointed by the Commons to investigate the Luddite disturbances, complained in his diary that none of his colleagues would agree with him that "the disease was of a political nature." Despite careful searches, the large dumps of arms reported by spies were never found, and no connection was traced between the disaffected in one district and those in another. Part of the explanation for the belief in a widespread plot must consist in the existence of many other forms of protest and violence at the same time—secret attempts at combination among workers, secret political agitations, and also bands of marauders and robbers—who all became included in the popular mind in the group known as Luddites.

It must be emphasized, on the other hand, in justification of the near panic which at times gripped the property-owning classes, that the destruction of machinery caused by Luddite attacks was considerable, especially in the Midlands, where the most successful movement existed. Between March 1811 and February 1812, 1,000 machines were smashed, and by the time that a law had been passed in 1812 making machine breaking a capital offense the rioters had become so expert that "they could destroy a frame almost noiselessly in one minute; and protected by sentinels and the sympathy of their fellow workers, they seldom failed to escape detection."[14] Furthermore, later riots developed from attacks on machines to raids on firearm shops, and the famine price of food led to attacks on provision shops and grain dealers.

The hostility toward machinery stemmed from the disruption of the lives of the people brought about by technological change, and was intensified by a series of disastrous harvests. There was at the same time a ferment in political thought, precipitated by revolutions in America and France, which was driving political opinion to both revolutionary and conservative extremes, and a long war, accompanied by all the social, economic and chauvinistic changes which war invariably brings. The period of rapid development that occurred in England during the latter part of the 18th and the early part of the 19th centuries was unprecedented. In the space of less than a century, greater and more widespread changes took place than in the entire recorded history of the country. The remarkable increase in the size of the population which occurred during the 19th century had begun before the outbreak of the Napoleonic Wars; mid-18th-century England had a population of about 7 million people, mainly rural, whilst in 1815 the population was 13 million. This increase was accompanied by a still more rapid growth of urbanization. The development of small towns to large urban centers meant that numbers of rootless workers found themselves in bewildering circumstances, deprived of all the traditional background to orderly living. They were deprived, too, of the stabilizing influence of the parish and the local social order in which they had recognized their "place," without even the protection of a police force—not then in existence—and at the mercy of economic forces which overturned all the safeguards under which they and their forbears had lived and worked.

Still in force at this time was the old Elizabethan Statute of Artificers, under which conditions of employment were regulated and magistrates were empowered to fix wages. In practice this and other old statutes had fallen into disuse, and when workers looked to the State for protection, hoping for a Minimum Wages Act, for instance, what they encountered was an attitude which had been moulded on

Adam Smith's *Wealth of Nations*. It was expressed in the laissez faire doctrine, on the basis of which all attempts to interfere with freedom of contract between employers and workers were repudiated. Long before the formal repeal in 1813 of the clauses for the regulation of wages in the Elizabethan statute, and the abrogation in 1814 of the apprenticeship clauses, the workers had ceased to derive protection from this legislation. In addition, the Combination Acts of 1799, passed against combinations of workers and employers, were in practice enforced only against the former, while a Minimum Wage Bill was rejected in 1808, making it plain that workers could expect no help from the Government to alleviate the disastrous situation in which so many of them were placed.

The organization of the knitting and lace-making trades was based partly on the new factories and workshops which were organized around new machines and sources of power, but largely on the old domestic system which, however, had developed to the point at which production was still largely carried on in the homes of the workers but with machines owned by the employers. In the Midlands, the hosiers who used home workers began themselves to experience the pressure of competition, and reduced their payments to the knitters by means of arbitrary deductions or by making their payments in kind or by paying in credits on their own shops, at which they could charge what price they wished. The competition from which they suffered, but which pressed far harder on the workers, came from the use of the "wide frame," formerly used for the making of pantaloons, to produce a shoddy material which was then "cut up" to make inferior, unfashioned stockings. At one blow this practice made possible the use of partly trained labor by masters who took on more than the permitted number of apprentices, reduced the price of labor in the industry by this dilution, and produced a class of goods which spoiled the good name of the products of the area. It bore particularly hard on the small domestic producers in villages surrounding Nottingham, whose goods, being of the lower quality, were more subject to the resulting competition and who, because of their scattered locations, were unable to bargain as the stockingers in Nottingham, fortunate in their leaders, were at times able to do. When Luddite attacks occurred, it was against the wide frames and undercutting employers that their wrath was directed. Indeed, warnings which were issued to employers, and other papers to be found in the Home Office file marked "Disturbances," make it plain that by their attacks the Luddites hoped to obtain a series of concessions which they had long been seeking by negotiation, by petitions to Parliament, by the formation of the Nottingham "Union," and by strikes. In one document in the Home Office files they sought to establish their constitutional right so to act by stating that the Charter of the old Framework Knitters Company gave the men the right to break frames. The document declared that the Act making framebreaking a felony had been obtained in the "most fraudulent, interested, and electioneering manner" and was therefore null and void. It warned that the Luddites would destroy frames making "spurious" articles, for which the workmen were not paid "in the Current Coin of the Realm." In another of the papers their objects are set out in verses entitled, "General Ludd's Triumph":[15]

> The Guilty may fear but no vengeance he aims
>   At the honest man's life or Estate,
> His wrath is entirely confined to wide frames
>   And those that old prices abate.

The attacks on machinery which occurred in Lancashire and Cheshire from 1811 to 1813 and in Yorkshire from 1812 to 1813 were occasioned more by the distress into which unemployment, low wages, and high prices had brought the workers than by any hopes such as those entertained in the Midlands that corrections could be made in the industry. In the Northern counties workers had been replaced by larger machines, steam looms, gig mills, and shearing machines which put out of work large numbers of men formerly employed to undertake the same processes by hand. These were the machines against which their attacks were directed. The older machines, even when the men employed on them were paid starvation wages, were not the object of destruction. Attacks took place on the factories where the new machines were operating, taking the form of assaults, often by night, in which relatively large bodies of men were involved and against which the employers put up vigorous resistance. Evenutally there occurred the murder of one employer, the attempted murder of another, and attacks on the local officer commanding the troops, on militia, and on suspected informers. Once disorder had reached this level the character of the attacks altered. From the smashing of machines and collection of arms, which had been the avowed and actual policy of the Luddites, the assaults began to include an increased number of common robberies, a circumstance which was a great inducement to ordinary criminals to profit by the prevailing disorder. The efforts of the authorities, spurred by the frantic appeals of terrified householders, were redoubled. Troops were assisted by spies and informers, and after some instances of arrests the Luddites knew that their secrets were no longer safe; the strength of the movement began to wane. By the autumn of 1812 it was the opinion of the Treasury Solicitor that many of the robberies still being committed were the work of a gang who were sheltering under the name of Luddites. During January 1813, trials were held of those who had been arrested in the summer and autumn; after nearly half of those charged had been discharged for lack of evidence, 34 cases were tried. The sentences passed were heavy; 17 men were hanged and 8 transported. Great publicity was given to the trials, and the severity of the sentences struck terror into the Luddites. Much of the steam had in any case gone out of their movement because the harvest of 1812 had been a good one. Moreover, trade with Europe had improved enough to make good much of the loss suffered by the loss of American trade caused by the Orders in Council and ensuing war, and there had been an upward turn in employment. After the 1813 trials, Luddism in Yorkshire died down; it recurred in the Midlands, in 1814 and in 1816, and later, sporadically, for many years.

Reference has already been made to the economic distress which the workers suffered during these years, to the disruptions of employment brought about by technological forces and the exigencies of war, and to the food shortages caused by a series of disastrous harvests which occurred during this period. Prices rose considerably; taking 1790 as the base year, prices in 1817 were 87 percent above their prewar level. Throughout the period 1790 to 1810 prices rose faster than wages; in many cases wages even fell, and General Maitland, commanding the troops in the North, in 1812, estimated that in the previous year prices had risen and wages had fallen by almost one-third.

The employers themselves by no means universally benefited from the demand situation created by the wars; Napoleon's attempts to strangle trade with England, and the Orders in Council that aimed at a blockade of Europe, had imposed constraints on trade which were greatly exacerbated when the Americans, exasperated at claims to search their merchant ships, imposed a cessation of trade with Europe. In 1809 a diminution of £11 million took place in trade, and imports of cotton fell from £32 million to £5 million, causing untold hardship in Lancashire. Of 38 mills in Manchester, for instance, only six were working in 1809. In the same year there was a spectacular collapse of the trade with South America, which had been expected to replace trade lost elsewhere. Even after the end of the war in 1815, there was no respite from distress for the workers; in addition to the disruption to manufacture caused by the cessation of Government orders, unemployment was increased by the discharge of 300,000 soldiers and sailors. And the Government, which saw revolution in every shadow and had become accustomed to the military solution of such dangers, saw in the workers' expression of their distress a state of affairs to be dealt with by strict repression.

Why was it that such widespread distress and the repression of working class protest did not lead to revolution, as it had elsewhere? Most of the reforming ideas current then had a common origin with the ideas that inspired the French revolution. That they did not lead to the same conclusion was in great measure due to the different role played in events by the intellectuals and the bourgeoisie.

THE CREATING OF A RADICAL MOVEMENT

Instead of the growth of a revolutionary movement, there developed in Britain during the last decades of the 18th century and the early part of the 19th century, a movement for the radical reform of Parliament and the social system. The excesses of the French revolution and the decline into despotism, foretold by Burke in his *Reflections,* had convinced the English bourgeoisie that revolution would be fatal to their interests. Their support was given to promoting innumerable societies, presenting petitions to Parliament, and holding meetings to promote reforms. Out of this activity grew a habit of thought that political reform should proceed constitutionally rather than by the violent destruction of established modes and patterns of government. At the end of the 18th century there were on hand a number of tenacious leaders of thought ready to impel the movement of popular reform in the direction of peaceful political change.

Towards the end of the Napoleonic war the political activities of the middle class and working class alike were increasingly channeled into these streams of reform.

It was generally reported by the authorities, and the evidence of spies seems to confirm the fact, that petitions for peace and parliamentary reform, and the formation of Spencean Societies and Hampden Clubs, began to absorb the energies of the people. The political, radical movement, the work of Cartwright, Cobbett and Place, upon the one hand, and the more disjointed, ineffective revolutionary seditious movement, the work of agitators like Benbow, Thistlewood and the Watsons, on the other, which had been factors in many of the events of 1811-13, and had unnecessarily confused the spies and some of the authorities of those days, because they seemed to be, though in fact they were not, connected with Luddism, now replaced Luddism as the centre of interest.[16]

These interests were channelled by a number of organizations such as the Corresponding Societies and Hampden Clubs, the latter organized on much the same basis as the Methodists, with local groups and traveling orators or preachers. One of the most zealous of these was Maj. John Cartwright, indefatigable organizer of Hampden Clubs and of petitions, and a believer in constitutional reform and universal suffrage; in 1811, aged over 70, the major made a tour of the North and Midlands in order to start Hampden Clubs among workingmen there. In another direction, William Cobbett's *Register* and pamphlets had a tremendous influence on the currents of working-class and middle-class thought.

The tremendous expansion of the employed labor force between 1760 and 1820 had led to a growing awareness of a common working-class interest. The social protest which had centered on the displacement of the hand loom weaver and stocking frame knitter began to assume a broader significance. In every field of employment men were clearly in conflict with masters over rates of pay and conditions of employment. The market was now the dominant factor determining what a man might earn, but what a man had to spend on the necessities of life, his "cost of living," was regulated to benefit the farmer and landowner. The landed interests looked upon the growth of manufacturing industry as a threat to their economic welfare and traditional way of life. During the Napoleonic wars, corn growing had been expanded, but the end of this war brought a sudden and sharp fall in prices and a flood of imported grain. Parliament, which was dominated by landowners, acted quickly by passing a Corn Law in 1815 to protect rural income standards against a fall in price. This law prohibited the import of corn until the price on the home market reached 80 shillings a quarter.

The effect of the Corn Law was to raise the price of bread, the staple diet of most workers, thus reducing their ability to buy other commodities and increasing their hostility to the landed interests who controlled Parliament. The manufacturing employers, as well as their workers, were also in favor of the import of cheap foodstuffs, since they knew that they had much to gain from this policy. However, free trade, which would increase the employers' profits and give the workers cheap food, could only be obtained by withdrawing protection from the farmers. Free trade could not be achieved until Parliament had been reformed and rural interests subordinated to those of industry and the urban community.

In the period immediately after the end of the Napoleonic War, the workers were hard hit by unemployment, high food prices, and indirect taxation. They reacted to these adverse circumstances by demonstrations in favor of radical social and economic reforms. There were riots in the Midlands and elsewhere over decisions of employers to reduce wages and the high price of bread and other foods. In Nottinghamshire and Leicestershire, violent outbreaks of machine wrecking occurred which the authorities suppressed by arresting and executing a number of men. In the following year the frameknitters were on strike again in protest against the unsatisfactory prices they were paid for their products. An abortive attempt was made in Derbyshire to begin an armed revolt, but this was quickly crushed and the ringleaders executed.

The Government response to these outbreaks of unrest

was the same as it was during the Napoleonic Wars, namely, ruthless suppression. It suspended the Habeas Corpus Act, and passed an act which forbade all public meeting except those held under a license from a magistrate. Penalties for uttering or publishing seditious works were increased.

The Government was convinced by various incidents and the information it received from its spies that there was a serious threat of insurrection. Although an army of informers was being paid to keep a close eye on the activities of workingmen and radicals, Britain possessed no professional police force capable of evaluating the flood of dubious reports of plans for revolution. Law and order was precariously maintained by a system of law enforcement devised in the time of the Tudors. Outside London the Lord Lieutenant of each county was responsible, as the representative of the Crown, for ensuring that civil peace was kept. Under the Lord Lieutenant was a body of Justices of the Peace that administered the criminal law and was empowered to take other steps to prevent a breach of the peace. If necessary, a Justice of the Peace could issue warrants for arrest, enroll special constables, and summon the military. In most towns and villages there were volunteer constables and "trained bands" of citizens who could be called upon when required, but this private police system was unreliable and inefficient. The need for a professional police force was recognized by liberal reformers as the key to making the criminal law more humane. However, police were regarded by many liberal-minded men as well as diehards as an alien, continental device for maintaining a tyrannical form of government.[17] In the absence of a police force, mobs were given a good deal of latitude. Civil strife was kept within bounds by the savage punishments—including executions and deportation—that could be imposed by Justices of the Peace, and by calling out the army when the situation threatened to get completely out of hand.

The turning point in popular attitudes followed the "Peterloo Massacre." Terrified by a vast gathering that had assembled in St. Peter's Fields, Manchester, on August 16, 1819, to hear the celebrated orator, Hunt, speak about the Reform of Parliament, the local magistrate called out the military to disperse the crowd. A charge by mounted yeomanry followed by another by Hussars cleared the fields, but at the cost of 11 dead and several hundred injured.

The local authorities had demonstrated their determination to prevent large-scale gatherings that threatened to lead to attempts to overthrow the civil authorities, but the effect of the "Peterloo Massacre" proved very different from that which had been expected. The country was horrified at the brutality of the military in "breaking up" a completely peaceable gathering. The Government was not disposed to apologize for events at Manchester, or to draw back from their implications. It knew that there had been a good deal of drilling and marching in readiness for revolt by radical groups in the North, and shortly after the "Peterloo Massacre" it introduced Six Acts of Parliament, designed to prevent revolutionary gatherings and to deter any groups that might be plotting insurrection.

The Six Acts of 1819 gave to Justices of the Peace powers to close any meeting which they believed might be a threat to public order; to search any building for weapons and seditious literature and to confiscate them when found; to stop drilling or training in the use of firearms; and summarily to convict political offenders. Dominated by anti-Jacobin fears, the Government took particular exception to the flood of radical publications, which it was determined to suppress. It sought to do so by greatly increasing the penalties for publishing blasphemous and seditious libels and by extending the tax on newspapers to every type of periodical. The objective of the Government was to close down the radical journals of Cobbett, Carlile, and Wooler and to prevent the selling of reprints of Tom Paine's *Rights of Man* and *Age of Reason*. Since the tax put the radical journals beyond the pocket of the workers, their editors had to issue them unlawfully, without the tax stamp. During the next 15 years the "great unstamped" radical press became one of the most important factors in the struggle for political reform. Hundreds of editors, printers, and publishers were arrested and sent to prison for defying the law, but the Government was unable to stamp out this circulation of cheap, untaxed, radical publications. The stamp tax was reduced from 4 d. to 1 d. in 1836—four years after the Reform Act of 1832—but it was not until 1855 that it was finally agreed by the Government that an untaxed free press was not likely to subvert respect for authority or to encourage the lower classes of society to acts of rebellion.

The harsh repression of every manifestation of social protest effectively limited working-class organizations. Apart from one or two relatively isolated instances of conspiracy to organize an insurrection, which were swiftly and ruthlessly crushed, the next few years saw no attempt to organize political unrest. Although this quiescence owed a good deal to the manifest determination of the Government to put down any activity that threatened to lead to seditious utterances or public disorder, it was also due to an economic boom that brought an improvement in wages.

The punitive measures the Government used so fiercely failed to prevent the transformation of the radical movement from a series of sporadic insurrectionary protests against High Toryism into a powerful political force. Factors that particularly stimulated the growth of the radical movement were (1) the unpopularity of George IV and his discreditable efforts to rid himself of a wife whom he no longer wanted; (2) the development of trade unionism, and with it the uniting of work-class and middle-class Radicalism; (3) the growth of Tory reformism.

The working and middle classes found a common cause in the defense of Queen Caroline against the King and his ministers. The popular ferment aroused by this squalid matrimonial quarrel undermined the authority of the Government and doomed High Toryism to defeat from within by encouraging the growth of Tory radicalism.

THE LIBERATION OF THE UNIONS

The death of Queen Caroline in 1821, followed by buoyant economic conditions for some years, quieted the voice of radical protest. During this period Francis Place, with the support of a group of radical Members of Parliament, conducted a successful campaign to secure the repeal of the Combination Act of 1800. Place was able to persuade Parliament to sweep away the restrictions on trade unions mainly because its members were no longer afraid of revolutions. He was also able to convince members that the unions would not be able to influence the level of wages significantly.

Advantage was immediately taken of the rights granted

to workers to organize. The newly established unions quickly made demands for bargaining rights and improvements in pay which were followed by widespread strikes. This outbreak of industrial militancy led the Government to amend Place's Act in the following year, but it resisted calls to return to its previous policy of suppression. This more tolerant attitude was due in no small degree to the ascendancy in the Government of a group of liberal Tories. The death in 1822 of Lord Castlereagh, who had been the chief exponent of the Government's vigorous anti-Jacobin domestic policy, had opened the way to a major shift in Tory policy. Although he had saved Britain by organizing the defeat of Napoleon, Castlereagh had become a detested figure and his death by suicide was celebrated with popular rejoicing by crowds of workers throughout the country.

Sir Robert Peel was perhaps the most able and far sighted of the liberal Tories, and during the next few years he was able to bring about a revolution in the system of law enforcement. Appointed Home Secretary in 1822, Peel at once began to abolish the system of spies and agents provocateurs which had aroused such hatred and bitterness among workers and radical groups during the Napoleonic period. He abandoned the persecution of the radical press and greatly humanized the whole pattern of criminal justice. The death penalty was abolished for over a hundred offenses. But perhaps his most important achievement was the establishment in 1829 of the metropolitan police force. Until the creation of Peel's police force there was no force capable of dispersing a mob or controlling a demonstration other than the army. The new police were not provided with firearms, only with stout sticks. Peel's aim was that they should become respected rather than feared by the populace. It is difficult to overestimate the significance of a police force that relied not on the weapons of war to enforce its authority, but on winning popular support for its function.

The Reform Act 1832

The trend towards more liberal policies was suddenly checked in 1828 by the death of the liberal Tory Prime Minister, Canning, and the succession of Wellington, the victor at Waterloo, to the office. Wellington hated the idea of Parliamentary reform, but under the influence of Peel he was persuaded of the necessity to repeal the Test and Corporation Acts, which prohibited Dissenters from holding national or local government offices, and to pass a Catholic Emancipation Act which allowed Irish Catholics to take seats in the House of Commons. This decision led to the downfall of the Tory Government and opened the way for a Whig administration under Lord Grey, who was ready to introduce a reform bill.

With the prospect of Parliamentary reform now much closer, the reform movement began to gather momentum. Following the lead of Birmingham, political unions were formed in many towns to agitate for parliamentary reform. In 1831 these associations linked up to form a National Political Union, which became the spearhead of the campaign for a reform bill.

The campaign became a crusade which united all classes and groups in the greatest political movement that Britain had ever seen. "Down with the rotten boroughs" was a cry which rallied support from all quarters. In the majority of Parliamentary constituencies the ordinary Englishman had no vote and Government was an aristocratic privilege.

Every class that was hoping to exert influence over Parliament was enraged that more than half of the House of Commons owed their seats to individual peers and commoners. The borough owners, who for generations back had pulled the strings of ministerial favour and lived on the fat of patronage—they had their kinsmen and their servants—suddenly found themselves objects of universal execration, and the "borough property" which they had inherited or purchased was denounced as having been stolen from the nation. The cry against the "borough mongers" rose on every side. Capitalists, clerks, shopkeepers, besides that great majority of the inhabitants who were comprised under the two categories of workingmen and Dissenters, all were talking against "old corruption." The very ostlers and publicans entered into the spirit of the hour. Even country gentlemen who did not happen to have an "interest" in a borough, began to think that they would like to see a fairer proportion of country members in the House, honestly chosen by themselves and their farmers. The only class that remained solid for the old system was the Church clergy who were so conscious of their unpopularity that they believed Reform would lead to the destruction of the Establishment.[18]

As the campaign was beginning to gather speed a new factor excited political opinion. Charles X and his Government in France had illegally suspended the Constitution and had been overthrown by the Revolution of 1830. The

Belgians also revolted against the unification with Holland that had been imposed after the defeat of Napoleon. The effect of these uprisings and constitutional changes greatly influenced the general election that took place in Britain in 1831, bringing into the House a good many new Whig members who were ready to vote for a reform bill.

The French Revolution of 1830 was a victory for the French middle class and it suggested to the British middle classes that they too might get rid of aristocratic rule if they were determined to do so. Fear that the British middle class might follow the example of the French was a potent factor in persuading the leaders of both the Whigs and Tories that the time had arrived to make concessions peacefully, on pain of risking a revolution against the propertied and aristocratic classes. When the reform bill was introduced, it went further than even most Radicals expected by sweeping away all the "rotten boroughs."

The bill passed the House of Commons with a large majority, but the House of Lords was determined to keep the constitutional power of its members intact and threw the reform bill out. The populace was outraged by the peers and the bishops who had voted against the bill and the country teetered on the brink of civil war. In the north, workingmen prepared to oppose the Lords with arms if necessary. In the south, hay ricks were burned night after night. The national mood was turning to anger and the resentment that had produced the riots could easily have turned to more violent opposition to the established order. Recognizing the danger, Wellington lent his great support to the passing of the bill. The King, who hated the idea of reform, had rid himself of Grey, but Wellington's attempt to form a new government failed and the King had to summon Grey again and then accept the inevitability of reform. Had he not done so, the upsurge of radicalism might have welled over into a revolution that could have turned Britain into a republic.

The Reform Acts abolished the tied boroughs and substituted a popular election for the nomination of members by those who owned the "rotten boroughs." The right to vote was limited, however, to those who paid a £10 tax rate, and most workingmen were thereby excluded from the provisions of the bill.

The leaders of the working-class radical movement,

Cobbett and Place, decided, reluctantly, to support the bill, believing that once the principle of reform had been put into practice it could soon be extended to cover all urban workers and to achieve the secret ballot.

The importance of the reform bill and the campaign that had preceded its passing lay in the fact that it was a victory of the people over the peers. The "sovereignty of the people" was beginning to be made meaningful. The King and the aristocratic members of the House of Lords could no longer ignore the great majority of the people. They had been obliged to recognize that the price of survival was reform and with that the old order was over.

UNIONISM AND CHARTISM

The Reform Act of 1832 was a victory for the middle class, but to most workers it was little more than a fraud. The pressure from the working-class radical movement had been an important factor in convincing the Whigs of the importance of Parliamentary Reform. It had not been significant enough, however, to convince the Government that they should concede the right to vote to workingmen as well as to middle-class property owners. Not surprisingly the growing numbers of skilled workers turned their attention to forming trade unions to protect their interests. They saw trade unions as the means for reshaping society which had been denied them by the Reform Act.

The most remarkable development occurred with the founding by Robert Owen of the Grand National Consolidated Trades Union in 1834. The object of the leaders of the Grand National was to embrace all workers, irrespective of their trades, in one vast trade union which would be able to regenerate society by eventually taking over industry and running it cooperatively.

Robert Owen's scheme captured the imagination of workers everywhere and within a matter of 6 months the Grand National was said to have grown to half a million strong. Exhilarated by this remarkable development, many branches of the union spontaneously decided to call out their members on strike. They met with fierce resistance from the employers and in most cases they had to abandon the union as the price of returning to their employment. Some of the leaders of the Grand National wanted to coordinate strike activities so as to bring about a general strike which would overthrow all the employers at once. Owen was much opposed to this class war concept of trade unionism. He saw men and masters as having a common interest as producers and wished to see them solve their problems by cooperation rather than by conflict. Confused by this dispute about aims and tactics, the local leadership lost heart as opposition from employers and the Government mounted.

The rapid growth of the Grand National Consolidated stirred the fears of the propertied classes, who were determined to defend their interests by invoking the aid of the courts when possible. The establishment of a branch of the Grand National in the village of Tolpuddle in Dorsetshire brought the union into direct conflict with the heirs of the Tory despotism that had managed and controlled rural Britain for 300 years. The Government had encouraged the judiciary to deal with the unions energetically, and the Judge who tried six farm laborers of Tolpuddle for swearing an unlawful oath was not wanting in this respect. They were tried, found guilty, and sentenced to transportation for 7 years.

The dreadful punishment imposed on these six farm laborers who, in their innocence, had formed a union to seek better wages, was greeted by workers and liberal-minded men in all classes as an outrage. A massive protest was made, which at first had little effect, but eventually compelled the Government to bring back William Loveless and his friends and grant them a pardon.

The persecution of trade unionists by threatening them with transportation did not check union growth. Nor did the new poor law, passed in 1834, solve the problem of poverty and pauperism. The new industrial-based ruling class was opposed to the system of parish relief, which was administered in a relatively easygoing way. Henceforth, "out relief" would not be given to able-bodied males who, it was assumed, if out of work, were so for willful reasons. Relief was to be given only in workhouses, where the conditions were to be as "disagreeable as consistent with health." It was believed that unless the applicants for public assistance were harshly treated, workers would cease to work in preference for relief.

There was considerable resistance to the merciless administration of the new poor law and in the North the operation of the Act was held up for some years by the effective opposition of employers as well as workers. One effect of the new poor law was to underline the fact that workers had no vote; it provided a stimulus that helped to bring into being a national political agitation to achieve the rights that workers had been denied in 1832.

Chartism, as the new movement was called, grew out of the efforts of the Government to check the circulation of the unstamped radical periodicals. In 1836 a group of radical editors and supporters met together in London to consider how editors, printers, and publishers could be protected from persecution. Out of this gathering was established the *London Workingmen's Association for Benefitting, Politically, Socially and Morally the Useful Classes.* In 1837, the London Workingmen's Association presented a petition to the House of Commons asking for: (1) universal suffrage; (2) equal electoral districts; (3) annual Parliaments; (4) payment of members; (5) secret ballots; (6) no property qualifications. Having attracted tremendous support, William Lovett incorporated the six points of the Charter into a Parliamentary Bill.

The Charter aroused tremendous enthusiasm. A national petition in support of the Charter, signed by over one million citizens, was presented to the House of Commons. When the petition was rejected, the Chartists, meeting in convention, decided to call for a Sacred Month of general strike.

There were sharp divisions of opinion among the Chartist leaders on the tactics that should be followed. William Lovett and his friends believed they should rely on moral force. At the other extreme, George Harney and his followers believed that only armed insurrection could overcome the opposition from the established political parties. Between the two extremes were those whose advocacy vacillated and changed with the circumstances.

With the failure to persuade Parliament to accept the petition for the Charter, those in favor of armed revolt achieved an ascendancy. An attempt was made to capture Newport by a force of 4,000 Chartists. This was to be the signal for general insurrection, but the adventure came to an inglorious end. Some 30 soldiers, well hidden, put the Chartist army to flight. The leaders of the abortive revolt were arrested. Three of them were sentenced to death, later commuted to transportation, and most of the others were sent to jail.

The Chartist leaders, after a considerable degree of recrimination about the Newport fiasco and argument about future tactics, decided to establish a National Charter Association which was to be a strictly political organization. However, the leadership remained divided. Under the influence of Fergus O'Connor, a messianic but unstable Irishman, the Chartists aggressively demanded the immediate political emancipation of the working class. Other Chartist leaders had become convinced that the only way in which the workers would achieve the right to vote was by an alliance with the middle class. They proposed the establishment of a "Complete Suffrage Association" which would bring together traders, employers, and workers.

A second petition to Parliament, launched in 1842, secured over three million signatures. Again the House of Commons rejected it by an overwhelming majority. However, support came for the Chartists from the Free Trade Radicals who were seeking through the Anti-Corn Law League to end the protection enjoyed by the landed interests. When the price of wheat rose, and with it the price of bread, workers in Scotland, Lancashire, and the Midlands went on strike against the increase in the cost of living and were supported both by Chartists and the Anti-Corn Law League. This spontaneous development took the leadership of the Chartist Association by surprise. There was fear that the strike would get out of hand to become another insurrection which the authorities would ruthlessly crush. Fergus O'Connor, after wavering, supported the strike, then a week later came out in opposition to it. Without effective leadership, no clear strategy, and unwise tactics, the strike inevitably collapsed and with it the Chartists as an effective movement.

Under the wayward leadership of O'Connor, the movement lingered on, but many former active supporters turned their attention elsewhere. The Anti-Corn Law League, which was more effectively led and had a more practical goal, attracted a good deal of the popular support which had gone to Chartism. Following the repeal of the Corn Laws in 1846, working-class supporters again turned their attention to political reform, and support for the Chartists began to grow once more. Economic depression sharpened the edge of the demand for political rights and with the European revolutions of 1848 the Chartists' hopes of achieving a successful revolution were revived, but these were no more than romantic illusions that were swiftly dispelled by a Government that would not tolerate even O'Connor's comic-opera efforts to organize an insurrection. More serious attempts by a group of determined militants to turn the movement into a genuine revolutionary force were quickly frustrated by the police. The whole of the group was convicted and the main leaders sentenced to transportation for life, thus finally ending the threat of a popular revolution.

As has been pointed out, Chartism, like Luddism, was a movement of social protest against adverse economic conditions. Its rise and fall was almost as exact as a barometer.[19] The high waves of Chartism in 1839, 1842, and 1848 were closely linked to immediately preceding periods of trade depression. "In 1849 revival started and Chartism began to weaken; in 1850 prosperity was general and Chartism collapsed."[20]

It was not only the improvement in economic circumstances that lost Chartism its following. Workers were shifting their allegiance to other organizations. The trade unions were steadily growing and were gradually gaining acceptance as organizations that would bring succor to workers in times of economic distress due to unemployment, sickness, injury, and death. Most of the Trade Societies had stood aloof from the activities of the Chartist Movement, not wishing to embroil themselves in situations which might lead to their destruction. In 1845, the Trade Societies established a National Association of United Trades for the Protection of Labor, whose purpose was to strengthen the bargaining power of the unions. This organization betrayed in its constitution and activities evidence of Owen's influence, and it encouraged the establishment of Societies for the Redemption of Labor for the purposes of establishing cooperative workshops and consumer societies. However, its administration was from the first characterized by moderation. Its main objectives became the promotion of peaceful industrial relations through conciliation and arbitration.

The most important advance in trade union organization

was achieved in 1851, with the successful creation of the Amalgamated Society of Engineers out of several small societies. The significance of the establishment of the ASE lay in the fact that it represented a coming to terms with mid-Victorian capitalism. Its founders turned their backs on the revolutionary ideas of Robert Owen and Chartists. The men who founded the ASE were a group of young, skilled workers, who had been much influenced by religious nonconformity and the development of an affluent society. Their revolution, for that is what it was, "was a revolt in favor of prudence, respectability, financial stability and reasonableness and against pugnacity, imagination and any personal indulgence."[21] The growth of a national trade union movement after 1850 and the development of a leadership that embodied the recognized virtues of the Victorian middle class ended all danger of a workers' revolution.

The moralistic approach of the trade union leaders to social problems was strongly buttressed by the pervasive influence of religious education. Religious teaching and its social implications was at the core of every type of educational establishment, village dame schools, grammar and charity schools, factory and workhouse classes. The influence of Sunday schools assiduously conducted by chapels and churches throughout the country was enormous. One employer was moved to say of Sunday schools that they had brought about an extraordinary change in the children that he employed in his factory. It was as if they had been transformed from wolves and tigers into men.[22]

Another effect of the education offered in Sunday schools by the thousands of chapel-based religious groups was the experience of organization gained by their members. The broad Methodist movement had well-ordered arrangements, and its visiting preachers extolled the virtues of diligence, thrift, punctuality, temperance, and good will. In other small chapels up and down the country, nonconformists who had broken away from the main movement tried to organize their chapels on democratic lines and formed radical political views in the process. They also learned at the same time about constitutional procedure and the reconciliation of differing points of view. Nonconformism helped to change them into punctual, diligent factory workers; it also gave the working-class movement a tremendous moral strength. And because their religious beliefs led them into a faith that right would prevail if steadfastly upheld, they eschewed violent methods and strove to win respect and acceptance for their just demands.

The middle class provided an exemplar of a pattern of life to which the skilled worker could with reasonable expectation aspire. The artisan with his apprentice-acquired skill and membership in a friendly society, cooperative society, and trade union had a secure place in the structure of society that placed him only a step below the counting-house clerk, the shopkeeper, and the small factory employer.

The importance of the link between the working class and the middle class was held by James Mill to be one of the most important safeguards against violent revolution. He stated that—

The opinions of that class of people who are below the middle rank are formed and their minds are directed by that intelligent and virtuous rank who come most immediately in contact with them, who are in the constant habit of intimate communication with them, to whom they fly for advice and assistance in all their numerous difficulties, upon whom they feel an immediate and daily dependence, in health and in sickness, in infancy and old age; to whom their children look up as models for their honour to adopt.[23]

The desire to emulate the middle class was undoubtedly a factor in the remarkable growth of village savings clubs and of mutual credit, insurance, thrift, and friendly societies. The activities of these societies together with savings banks, building societies, and cooperatives provided workingmen with an opportunity to build up a modest sum of capital which could ensure freedom in days of distress from the degradation of the workhouse and the ultimate disgrace of a pauper's grave.

The Victorian workman learned readily the lesson which his masters were fain to teach him. He was as thrifty as they could desire; and in many respects his thrift both made him more tolerant than his fathers of the system under which he lived and led him to assimilate its ways of action and thought.[24]

The consumer cooperative movement was perhaps the most ingenious example of that combination of thrift, idealism, and commonsense that characterized the mid-19th century labor movement. The cooperative movement, which started in 1844 at Toad Lane, Rochdale, enlisted the energies and aspirations of workers who had regular jobs, and who while wanting to insure that the wages they earned were spent on unadulterated food at economical prices, also wanted to see the reform of society. Cooperation provided an alternative form of ownership to private capitalism, one which could be achieved without conflict. But as the Christian Socialists, who played a prominent part in developing the cooperative movement, pointed out, it embodied the fundamental characteristics of capitalist trading and manufacturing, providing a means of saving, and perhaps most important of all, offered working men an opportunity to participate in running an enterprise which had to accumulate capital and pay a dividend. In this respect it gave workers both an understanding of and a stake in capitalist society.

SUMMARY AND CONCLUSIONS

The period from 1783 to 1867 has been called an age of improvement.[25] There can be no doubt that during this time the most remarkable changes occurred in Britain. Perhaps the most astonishing of all was the change from a conflict-ridden society in which mob violence was matched by the savage brutality of hangings and transportation for life to a society in which conflict was regulated by rules adopted voluntarily. The principal factors responsible for transmuting the tradition of violent behavior on the part of both the poorer classes and the authorities into a pattern of orderly procedure for the settlement of social and political conflicts were economic growth, political reform, moral suasion, and institutional developments. It is difficult to assign an exact weight to each of these factors; however, they combined to influence decisively the course of events.

There can be no doubt that the tremendous growth of industrial employment and output in the midyears of the 19th century brought about a significant improvement in the standard of living of the urban working classes. What was perhaps even more important was that it created a climate of confidence and a readiness to seek change in an orderly way. The cult of progress, which was strongly manifested in the Great Exhibition of 1851, was shared by all groups. The leaders of the trade unions and the workers they represented had come to terms with society. Their aim was to secure the benefits that liberal capitalism had to offer rather than to seek its overthrow by violent revolution.

By the time of the death of Lord Palmerston in 1865, the unions had gained acceptance as legitimate organizations, although they continued to be denounced by employers as an unwarranted interference with their freedom to conduct their business affairs as they might choose, and by the courts, who found the activities of the unions in conflict with the basic tenets of a laissez-faire society. The decision by Disraeli in 1867 to seek to bring the two Englands of *Sybil* closer together, by extending the franchise to the urban worker, guaranteed that the position of the unions would be strengthened and the role of organized workers become politically more significant.

The reaction of both the main body of union leaders and the Government to the resort to violence by a group of Sheffield trade unionists, whose economic circumstances had been seriously injured by a depression in their trade, illustrated the extent to which the unions had become an established social institution. This type of coercion was swiftly and completely repudiated by the unions, and the Royal Commission set up by the Government exonerated them; it recommended changes in the law which would give the unions a secure legal position and permit them to develop their collective bargaining functions within a framework of reasonable constraints. Had the unions not been able to demonstrate effectively through their leaders that they repudiated violence, it is probable that the laws regulating union behavior would have been made as repressive as they were on the Continent.

There was continuously, throughout the 19th century, an interplay of constraint imposed by law and public concession to the notion of voluntary collective self-regulation. The fears of those who believed that the removal of legal restrictions on the rights of the unions to organize and to bargain collectively, including the right to strike, would lead to civil violence and revolutionary strife, were never realized. There were many demonstrations against major and minor grievances, but these always evaporated into the orderly procedures of collective bargaining or parliamentary action.

The emergence of a labor movement and its assimilation into the political structure of the state was a factor of major importance. This development directed protest into a channel where social grievances could be remedied by legislation passed by a Parliament in which the labor movement after 1874 was represented by its own members, and after 1900 by its own party.

The balance between the pressure for social change and the concession of those in authority to that force was constantly shifting, but was always kept within bounds by the desires of the leaders of the labor movement to retain their independence and the desires of those wielding the political authority to retain the democratic party system.

Throughout the 19th century all Governments insisted on the maintenance of law and order; the resort to violence was swiftly and effectively countered by firm action by the authorities. This sometimes harshly repressive policy provoked bitter cries of protest, but these were tempered by the knowledge that Governments could be changed and the power of the state used to ameliorate the conditions of the working classes.

By the 1840's it had become increasingly obvious to Tory radicals that laissez-faire, which was so wholeheartedly supported by manufacturers, merchants, and the financial and trading community, had appalling consequences for the weakest groups in society. The succession of factory and mines acts to protect women and children from the gross exploitation of their labor were the result of combined action between enlightened legislators and the working-class leaders. The Poor Law of 1834, which abolished outdoor relief and was administered with a deliberate inhumanity, was gradually tempered by enlightenment and was eventually swept away by the introduction of a state-administered system of social security. The wretched conditions of the overcrowded and unsanitary large towns were vastly improved by the work begun by Chadwick in the 1840's. Corrupt local government was swept away, the foundations of an effective public health service laid, and a public system of education created.

Over the second half of the 19th century the discontents of the working-class were met by piecemeal social reforms.

These were not secured without a struggle, since the opposition of the well-to-do classes was often considerable and was only overcome by sustained popular pressure and the skillful use of political influence and bargaining power.

It is difficult to estimate the exact effect that demonstrations, riots and the threat of large-scale public disorder had at various times in the 19th century. Luddism and Chartism clearly failed to achieve their immediate objectives, but they certainly contributed to the creation of a working-class community of interest and established in the public mind the significance of the goals that workers involved in these movements were seeking to achieve. The tactics of sabotage and threatened insurrection failed because they provoked extreme hostility and met superior force. Success came when organized labor had established its respectability and had created sufficient confidence and sympathy to evoke a positive response to its protests.

A remarkable aspect of the development of the British working-class movement during the 19th century, with its increasing emphasis on respectability and constitutional action, was the fact that London was for a long time the headquarters of the international revolutionary movement. During the 1840's a large number of political refugees from many European countries were living in London, actively engaged in fomenting revolution in their own countries. In 1840 the German Communist League was formed by exiles in London; in 1844 Engels settled in London; in 1847 Marx and Engels drafted the Communist Manifesto there; in 1864 the International Working Men's Association was formed with its headquarters in London; in 1867, Marx, known to most English working-class leaders more as an academic German exile than as a socialist leader, published the first volume of *Capital*. Yet despite all this frantic and often conspiratorial activity, contact with these exiled revolutionaries had at the time amazingly little influence on the thinking of the English workers. Participation by English leaders in the International Working Men's Association was mainly out of sympathy for downtrodden continental workers, and to discourage the importation of foreign blacklegs in times of strikes. Few English union leaders were ideologically involved, and as the revolutionary character of the continental sections of the movement became clear the British trade union leaders grew increasingly alienated and, as Marx said, "offered up the principle of Trade Unionism on the altar of middle class legitimisation."

The British trade union movement never had to face the kind of problems that confronted the labor movement in either 19th-century America or Europe. In the United States unions were repulsed by employers who were ready and able to take the law into their own hands. The revolutionary tradition was a fundamental fact of American history. The country had been created out of violence and was rent apart by a civil war less than 100 years later. Frontier wars continued until the end of the 19th century. In the frontier areas men had to make and enforce their own law at the end of a gun. On the eastern seaboard waves of immigrants who had relieved the pressures of discontent in Britain and Europe arrived in the United States to threaten the jobs of those who had arrived earlier. In the scramble for security and for riches that were often there for the taking, violence was inevitably always close at hand. It would have been so in any society in which these factors prevailed.

The contrast with the situation in Britain was startling. Britain was a long-settled country whose population was relatively stable. The roots of its working class struck deep and they were not easily disturbed. British employers were firmly established, and, aspiring to an aristocratic way of life with its acceptance of civic responsibilities, were much less ruthless than their American counterparts. British employers were prepared to take a more tolerant attitude towards the unions and their activities, since they often found the unions understood even if they did not share their views on major issues of economic and international policy. There was to be a much greater divergence of views at the end of the 19th century, once the working-class movement abandoned its liberal philosophy to embrace its own muted version of socialism.

A final point that is necessary to stress as of fundamental significance in the erosion of working-class violence in Britain in the 19th century is the fact that the working class was by no means homogeneous. Without going into the problem of the definition of class,[26] it can be said without question that wage earners, while sharing certain common interests, certainly did not share others. There were significant differences of economic interest between skilled and unskilled workers; rural and urban workers; between those workers who were able to impose a "closed shop" and those who were not; between newly arrived immigrants from Ireland and native-born Englishmen; between workers in the north and those in London and the south.

The common interest shared by all those who were excluded from the right to vote was diluted by the differences of interests among the groups that made up the whole. This conflict of interests was most clearly revealed in the Chartist agitations, when the skilled workers showed the utmost reluctance to hazard their organizations in active and wholehearted support of the Chartists' policies and programs of action. These dichotomies, real or imagined, again and again influenced the course of events and blurred the clean edges of social conflict. In this respect the firm but complex structural hierarchy of British social classes in the 19th century made for relatively peaceful relations among groups. Each group knew where it stood in relation to another group; its station gave it security and satisfaction as well as dissatisfaction. The members of any one group might well resent the social group at the top but they were prepared to accept the right of the next group above to protect its interests by organizing restrictions on entry. Although social mobility was limited, workers were prepared to accept this limitation so long as it was made tolerable by the steady improvement in their economic conditions, and by their integration, through their trade unions, into the structure of political democracy. By good fortune or intuitive understanding, the social groups in Britain in the 19th century managed to achieve a balance of relations that reduced violent conflict to low levels of intensity. When in the 1880's and 1890's and again in the periods immediately before and after the First World War, conflict between employers and workers threatened to become dangerously violent, the firmly established pattern of responsible behavior enabled both sides to moderate their actions and reach an accommodation of their differences even when these were at their most acute.

References

1. C. Hill, *The Century of Revolution* (London: Nelson, 1960), p. 9.
2. Sidney and Beatrice Webb, *English Local Government: Statutory Authorities for Special Purposes* (London: Longmans, Green, 1922).

3. Max Beloff, *Public Order and Popular Disturbances* (London: Oxford University Press, 1938).
4. Beloff, *op. cit.*, p. 152.
5. Beloff, *op. cit.*, p. 154.
6. E. P. Thompson, *The Making of the English Working Class* (London: Pelican Books, 1968).
7. George Rudé, *Wilkes and Liberty* (London: Oxford University Press, 1962).
8. Thompson, *op. cit.*
9. *Ibid.*, p. 78.
10. *Ibid.*, p. 78.
11. Richard B. Rose, "The Priestly Riots of 1791," *Past and Present*, 1960, p. 84.
12. See J. and B. Hammond, *The Skilled Labourer* (London: Longmans, Green, 1919).
13. F. O. Darvall, *Popular Disturbances and Public Order in Regency England* (London: Oxford University Press, 1934), pp. 1, 67.
14. W. L. Mathieson, *England in Transition* (London: Longmans, Green, 1920), p. 137.
15. Darvall, *op. cit.*, p. 171, quoting Home Office papers 42.119.
16. Darvall, *op. cit.*, p. 136.
17. "They have an admirable police at Paris, but they pay for it dear enough. I had rather half a dozen people's throats should be cut in Ratcliffe Highway every three or four years than be subject to domiciliary visits, spies and all the rest of Fouche's conspiracies." J. W. Ward, *Letters to Fry*, Dec. 27, 1811, quoted by R. J. White, *Waterloo to Peterloo* (London and Baltimore: Penguin Books, 1957).
18. G. M. Trevelyan, *British History in the Nineteenth Century and After, 1782-1919* (London: Longmans, Green, 1922).
19. S. D. H. Cole and Raymond Postgate, *The Common People, 1746-1945* (London: Methuen, 1946), p. 320.
20. *Ibid.*
21. *Ibid.*, p. 367.
22. Mathieson, *op. cit.*, p. 45.
23. James Mill, *On Government*, quoted by White, *op. cit.*, p. 38.
24. G. D. H. Cole, *A Short History of British Working-Class Movements 1789-1947* (London: Allen Unwin, 1948), p. 168.
25. A. Briggs, *The Age of Improvement* (London: Longmans, Green, 1959).
26. See the Preface to E. P. Thompson's *The Making of the English Working Class* (London: Gollancz, 1968).

Chapter 8

AMERICAN LABOR VIOLENCE:
ITS CAUSES, CHARACTER,
AND OUTCOME*

By Philip Taft and Philip Ross†

The United States has had the bloodiest and most violent labor history of any industrial nation in the world. Labor violence was not confined to certain industries, geographic areas, or specific groups in the labor force, although it has been more frequent in some industries than in others. There have been few sections and scarcely any industries in which violence has not erupted at some time, and even more serious confrontations have on occasion followed. Native and foreign workers, whites and blacks have at times sought to prevent strike replacements from taking their jobs, and at other times have themselves been the object of attack. With few exceptions, labor violence in the United States arose in specific situations, usually during a labor dispute. The precipitating causes have been attempts by pickets and sympathizers to prevent a plant on strike from being reopened with strikebreakers,[1] or attempts of company guards, police, or even by National Guardsmen to prevent such interference. At different times employers and workers have played the roles of aggressors and victims. Union violence was directed at limited objectives; the prevention of the entrance of strikebreakers or raw materials to a struck plant, or interference with finished products

* This research has been supported by a grant from the Ford Foundation.
† Philip Taft was a member of the economics department at Brown University from 1937 to 1968 and in 1968-69 was visiting professor at the State University of New York at Buffalo. He has contributed to scholarly journals, served on wage boards and State government commissions, and has written seven books and coauthored four others. Among them are *History of Labor in the United States, 1896-1932*, with Selig Perlman (New York: Macmillan, 1935); *Organized Labor in American History* (New York: Harper & Row, 1964); *Labor Politics American Style* (Cambridge: Harvard University Press, 1968); and two volumes on the American Federation of Labor.

Philip Ross is professor of industrial relations, State University of New York at Buffalo. He has served as a consultant to a number of Government and State agencies, including the National Labor Relations Board and the U.S. Departments of Commerce and Transportation. His publications include *The Government as a Source of Union Power* (Providence: Brown University Press, 1965) and *The Labor Law in Action: An Analysis of the Administrative Process* (Washington, D.C.: National Labor Relations Board, 1966), as well as numerous articles.

leaving the premises. While the number seriously injured and killed was high in some of the more serious encounters, labor violence rarely spilled over to other segments of the community.

Strikers, no matter how violent they might be, would virtually always seek to win the sympathy of the community to their side, and therefore attacks or even incitements against those not connected or aiding the employer would be carefully avoided. Such conduct was especially common in the organized strikes, those which were called and directed by a labor organization. Strike violence can therefore be differentiated from violence that is stimulated by general discontent and a feeling of injustice. Moreover, the unions were normally anxious to avoid violence and limit its impact because, simultaneously with the strike, the organization might also be operating under a contract and negotiating with other employers in an attempt to solve differences and promote common interests. Unions seek and must have at least the grudging cooperation of employers. No major labor organization in American history ever advocated violence as a policy, even though the labor organizations recognized that it might be a fact of industrial life.

Trade unions from the beginning of their existence stressed their desire for peaceful relations with employers. However, minority groups within the labor movement or without direct attachment to it advocated the use of violence against established institutions and also against leaders in government, industry, and society. The union leader might hope to avoid violence, but recognized that in the stress of a labor dispute it might be beyond the ability of the union to prevent clashes of varying seriousness. They might erupt spontaneously without plan or purpose in response to an incident on the picket line or provocation. Those who saw in violence a creative force regarded the problem differently; they had no objectives of immediate gain; they were not concerned with public opinion. They were revolutionaries for whom the radical transformation of the economic and social system was the only and all-consuming passion.

The most virulent form of industrial violence occurred in situations in which efforts were made to destroy a functioning union or to deny to a union recognition.

There is only a solitary example in American labor history of the advocacy of violence as a method of political and economic change. In the 1880's a branch of anarchism emerged that claimed a connection with organized and unorganized labor and advocated individual terror and revolution by force. The principle of "propaganda by the deed," first promulgated at the anarchist congress in Berne, Switzerland, in 1876, was based upon the assumption that peaceful appeals were inadequate to rouse the masses. This view could be interpreted as a call upon workers to create their own independent institutions, such as trade unions, mutual aid societies, and producer and consumer cooperatives. However, almost from the beginning this doctrine was interpreted to mean engaging in insurrectionary and putschist activities, and in terror directed against the individual.[2] Emphasis upon individual force gained added strength from the terroristic acts of members of the People's Will, an organization of Russian revolutionaries who carried out campaigns of violence against persons, culminating in the assassination of Czar Alexander II in 1881.[3]

Not all anarchists approved these tactics. Many thought that social problems could be solved only by addressing oneself to the removal of evils, by changing institutions and the minds of men. In addition, the reaction against acts of terror, the arrests and imprisonment of militants, weakened the movement by depriving it of some of its more vigorous and courageous elements. Nevertheless, the London congress of 1881, which established the International Working People's Association as the center for the national anarchist federations, came out in favor of "propaganda by the deed" as a creative method for carrying on warfare against capitalist society and its leaders.[4]

Social revolutionary views were not widely accepted in the United States during the 1880's, but the difference between the moderates and the militants, which divided the European movement, was also in evidence here. As early as 1875 education and defense organizations (Lehr und Wehr Vereine) were organized in Chicago, and they soon spread to other cities. Members met regularly and drilled with arms. It was the issue of using arms which was largely responsible for the split in the Socialist Labor Party in

1880, and the more militant social revolutionaries gradually approached the anarchist position on politics and violence.

An attempt to unite the scattered groups of social revolutionaries was made by the Chicago conference of 1881 and was unsuccessful. The meeting adopted a resolution recognizing "the armed organizations of workingmen who stand ready with the gun to resist encroachment upon their rights, and recommend the formation of like organizations in all States." [5] This was only a prelude to the convention held in Pittsburgh in 1883, dominated by Johann Most, a German-born revolutionary who had served prison terms in a number of countries. Most had come to the United States in December 1882, and transferred his journal, *Freiheit*, to New York. Through the spoken and written word he became the leader of the anarchists in the United States and the leading figure of the predominantly immigrant revolutionaries.

In typically Socialist fashion, the congress explained the causes of the evils afflicting modern society. Since all institutions are aligned against him, the worker has a right to arm himself for self-defense and offense. The congress noted that no ruling class ever surrendered its privileges and urged organization for planning and carrying out rebellion. Capitalists will not leave the field except by force. [6] These ideas had some influence among a limited number of workers, largely immigrants. Most himself did not favor trade unions, regarding them as compromising organizations, and even refused to support the 8-hour movement in the 1880's. Anarchists, however, were active in union organizations and some regarded them as the ideal type of workmen's societies. Albert Parsons, August Spies, and Samuel Fielden, all of them defendants in the Haymarket Trial, had close connections with a part of the Chicago labor movement.

The anarchists were not all of the same view, but many of them including Most not only advocated the formation of armed societies, but published materials on the making of explosives. *Revolutionary War Science (Revolutionäre Kriegswissenschaft)* is a treatise on the use of arms and the making of what we would call "Molotov cocktails." There is little evidence that these suggestions were ever taken seriously by many workers, and the anarchist movement's greatest influence in the United States was in the 1880's. Even at the height of their influence the anarchists had few supporters. Whatever violence took place in the United States cannot be traced to the thinking of Most or any of his coworkers. In fact, even then it was widely believed that the armed societies were engaging in playing a game, and that they represented little danger to the community. It is quite certain that violence in labor disputes was seldom inspired by the doctrine of "propaganda by the deed," whose self-defeating nature convinced many of its exponents of its fallacy. In this regard, experience was a more potent force than moral considerations. Governments reacted to these terrorist methods with savage repression. One of the few incidents of anarchist violence in the United States was an attack by Alexander Berkman on Henry Frick during the Homestead strike. The boomerang effect of this action was to transform the hated Frick into a folk hero when, though wounded, he fought off his attacker. The assassination of William McKinley by the anarchist Czolgosz is another example. Most did not repudiate the tactic, but laid down conditions for its use that were critical of Berkman's conduct.

In France, Italy, and Spain anarchist-inspired violence was savagely repressed, as were the few attempts in Germany and Austria.[7]

THE INDUSTRIAL WORKERS OF THE WORLD (1WW)

Unlike the other national federations such as the Knights of Labor, the American Federation of Labor, and the Congress of Industrial Organizations, the IWW advocated direct action and sabotage. These doctrines were never clearly defined, but did not include violence against isolated individuals. Pamphlets on sabotage by Andre Tridon, Walker C. Smith, and Elizabeth Gurley Flynn were published, but Haywood and the lawyers for the defense at the Federal trial for espionage in Chicago in 1918 denied that sabotage meant destruction of property. Instead Haywood claimed it meant slowing down on the job when the employer refused to make concessions.[8]

It is of some interest that IWW activity was virtually free of violence. The free-speech fight was a form of passive resistance in which members mounted soapboxes and filled the jails. The IWW did not conduct a large number of strikes, and aside from the one in McKee's Rock, Pa., a spontaneous strike which the IWW entered after it was called, the IWW strikes were peaceful.

The two bloodiest episodes in the life of the IWW were in Everett and Centralia, Wash., each connected with the attempt to organize lumber workers. The Everett confrontation started when the Lumber Workers Industrial Union No. 500 opened a hall in Everett in the spring of 1916, in an effort to recruit members. Street meetings were prevented and the sheriff deported the speakers and other members of the IWW to Seattle on a bus. It is of some interest to note that a speaker who advocated violence at a meeting at the IWW hall in Everett was later exposed as a private detective. For a time the deportations were stopped, but they were resumed in October 1916. An estimated 300 to 400 members were deported by the sheriff and vigilantes from Everett. On October 30, 1916, 41 IWW men left Seattle by boat. They were met by the sheriff and a posse, seized, and made to run the gauntlet between two rows of vigilantes who beat their prisoners with clubs.

On November 5, 1916, the IWW in Seattle chartered a boat, the *Verona,* and placed an additional 39 men on another vessel. The chartered boat set out for Everett. Having been informed of the attempt of the IWW to land peacefully, the sheriff and about 200 armed men met the chartered vessel at the dock. The sheriff sought to speak to the leaders. When none came forward and the passengers sought to land, a signal to fire into the disembarking men was given by the sheriff. Five members of the IWW and two vigilantes were killed, and 31 members of the IWW and 19 vigilantes were wounded by gunfire. The *Verona* and the other vessel carrying members of the IWW returned to Seattle without unloading at Everett. Almost 300 were arrested, and 74 were charged with first-degree murder. The acquittal of the first defendant led to the dismissal of the case against the others.[9]

Another tragedy occurred in Centralia, Wash., a lumber town of almost 20,000 inhabitants. Several times the IWW sought to open a hall in that community, but in 1916 the members were expelled by a citizens' committee, and 2 years later the IWW hall was wrecked during a Red Cross parade. With dogged persistence the IWW opened another hall. When threats were made to wreck it, the IWW issued a leaflet pleading for avoidance of raids upon it. During the Armistice Day parade in 1919, members of the IWW were barricaded in their hall and when the hall was attacked, opened fire. Three members of the American Legion were killed, and a fourth died from gunshot wounds inflicted by Wesley Everest, himself a war veteran. Everest was lynched that night by a citizen mob. Eleven members of the IWW were tried for murder. One was released, two were acquitted and seven were convicted of second degree murder. A labor jury from Seattle that had been attending the trial claimed that the men fired in self-defense and should have been acquitted.[10] It is not necessary to attempt to redetermine the verdict to recognize that the IWW in Everett and Centralia was the victim, and the violence was a response to attacks made upon its members for exercising their constitutional rights.

A number of States, beginning with Minnesota in 1917, passed criminal syndicalist laws that forbade the advocacy of force and violence as a means of social change. On the basis of the theory that the IWW advocated force and violence to bring about industrial changes, several hundred men were tried, and 31 men served in the penitentiary in Idaho, 52 in Washington, and 133 in California. These convictions were not based upon acts of violence committed by those tried.[11]

THE PRACTICE OF VIOLENCE
IN THE 1870's AND 1880's

Repudiation of theories did not eliminate the practice of violence from the American labor scene. The pervasiveness of violence in American labor disputes appears paradoxical because the great majority of American workers have never supported views or ideologies that justified the use of force as a means of reform or basic social change, nor have American workers normally engaged in the kind of political activity that calls for demonstrations or for physical confrontation with opponents. Through most of its history, organized labor in the United States has depended largely upon economic organizations—unions— for advancement through collective bargaining, and upon pressure politics and cooperation with the old parties for achieving its political aims Yet we are continually confronted with examples of violent confrontations between labor and management Does industrial violence reveal a common characteristic with basic causes and persistent patterns of behavior, or is it a series of incidents linked only by violence? Labor violence has appeared under many conditions, and only an examination of the events themselves can reveal their nature and meaning

1. The Strikes and Riots of 1877

The unexpected strikes and riots which swept over the United States in 1877 with almost cyclonic force began in Martinsburg, W. Va., after the Baltimore Ohio Railroad had announced its second wage cut in a relatively short period. The men left their trains and drove back those who sought to replace them. Governor Henry W. Mathews called upon President Rutherford B. Hayes for Federal assistance, and the latter, despite his reluctance, directed troops to be sent.[12] Federal troops had a calming influence on the rioters in Martinsburg, but 2 days later, on July 20, Governor John Lee Carroll of Maryland informed the President that an assemblage of rioters ". . . has taken possession of the Baltimore Ohio Railroad depot" in Baltimore, had set fire to it, and "driven off the firemen who attempted to extinguish the same, and it is impossible to disperse the rioters." Governor Carroll also asked for Federal aid.[13]

Order was restored immediately by Federal troops, but Governor Carroll then appealed for help in putting down a disturbance at Cumberland. Requests also were made for troops to be sent to Philadelphia, where the authorities feared outbreak of rioting. The most serious trouble spot, however, was Pittsburgh, where the attempt to introduce "double headers" was the cause of one of the more serious disturbances of the year. The changes might have been accepted if they had not followed cuts in pay and loss of jobs—both caused by declining business. Open resistance began, and when a company of militia sought to quell the disturbance it was forced to retreat before the mob and take refuge in a railroad roundhouse where it was under constant attack. A citizens' posse and Federal troops restored order.

Railroads in Pennsylvania, New York, and New Jersey suffered almost complete disruption. The Erie, New York Central, the Delaware Lackawanna Western, and the Canada Southern operating in Ohio, Pennsylvania, and New York States were struck on July 24, idling about 100,000 workers. Federal and State troops were used to suppress rioting, and sometimes the State police were themselves the cause of violence. After 13 persons were killed and 43 wounded in a clash between militia and citizens in Reading, Pa., for example, a coroner's jury blamed the troops for an unjustified assault upon peaceful citizens.

In Ohio the railroads were blocked, but the Governor's plea for Federal aid was not met. "In the end the State authorities, assisted by the National Guard and the citizens' committees succeeded in quelling the disturbances at Zanesville, Columbus, Toledo, and Cleveland, but it was nearly the middle of August before order had been completely restored." The strikes and rioting moved westward and Indiana and Illinois were affected. In the face of a threatened strike, the Governor of Indiana refused to appeal for Federal troops and the latters' duties were limited to protecting Federal property and enforcing orders of the Federal courts. Work on the railroads entering Chicago was suspended, and rioting broke out in the city. On the 26th of July a bloody skirmish between the police, National Guardsmen, and a mob resulted in the killing of 19 and the wounding of more than 100 persons. It started with resistance of a mob to the attempts of the police to clear the streets, and it ended when the police and militia charged the crowd.

During July all traffic was suspended in East St. Louis, and a large crowd took possession of the streets and dared the police and guardsmen to come out and fight. It was only when Federal troops responded to the pleas of a Federal court that peace was restored. At the same time, work in St. Louis was completely suspended.

In summary, a recent student tells us:

In 1877 the disorders swept through the major rail centers of the nation: Baltimore, Philadelphia, Pittsburgh, Buffalo, Cleveland, Toledo, Columbus, Cincinnati, Louisville, Indianapolis, Chicago, St. Louis, Kansas City, and Omaha, to name only the more important. Outside this central area there were brief flare-ups in New York City and Albany in the Northeast, in Little Rock, New Orleans, and Galveston in the South, and in San Francisco on the Pacific Slope. About two-thirds of the country's total rail mileage lay within the strike-affected area, and in those zones strikers halted most freight trains and delayed many passenger and mail trains.[14]

The *Report of the Committee to Investigate the Railroad Riots in July, 1877,* issued by the Pennsylvania Legislature, limits itself to events within that State. Nevertheless, it alludes to factors which were present in virtually every other community in which rioting took place. The report states that the riots

> . . . were the protests of laborers against the system by which his wages were arbitrarily fixed and lowered by his employer without consultation with him, and without his consent . . . . The immediate cause of the first strike . . . that at Pittsburgh, July 19th, was the order by the Pennsylvania Railroad Company to run "double headers" . . . . This order of itself, had there been no previous reductions of wages or dismissals of men on account of the depression in business, would probably have caused no strike, but following so soon after the second reduction . . . and the feeling of uneasiness and dissatisfaction existing among the laboring men of the country generally, caused by the want of labor and the low price thereof as compared with a few years previous, all together combined to set in motion this strike . . . Each strike was independent of those on other roads, each having a local cause particularly its own. As before stated, there was a sort of epidemic of strikes running through the laboring classes of the country, more particularly those in the employ of large corporations, caused by the great depression of business which followed the panic of 1873, by means whereof many men were thrown out of work, and the wages of those who get work were reduced.[15]

The riots of 1877 mirrored deeply felt grievances generated by several years of unemployment and wage cuts. All the rioting cannot be attributed to striking workmen and their sympathizers. Railroads, urban transportation systems, and trucking are among the industries that are almost completely exposed to attack during a labor dispute. They operate in the open, and it is difficult to prevent attacks by strikers and sympathizers upon working personnel and property. The strikes and riots of 1877 were, however, a violent protest against deteriorating conditions and the suffering and misery endured during a great depression. The widespread and ferocious reaction has no parallel in our history, but there are others of lesser magnitude that were important in shaping labor-management relations.[16]

There is no evidence that the riots of 1877 brought reforms in the handling of railroad disputes, which was the initial cause of the disturbances. They did demonstrate that the United States would not escape the trials and tribulations affecting other industrial nations, and that more attention must be given to the problems that industrial societies tend to generate. It was, however, more than a decade later that the first hesitant step was taken by the Federal Government to provide a method of adjusting labor disputes, a method that was never tried. Not until the Erdman Act of 1898 did the Federal Government provide a usable procedure for settling labor-management disputes on the railroads. An added provision guaranteeing railroad workers protection of the right to organize was declared unconstitutional by the U.S. Supreme Court when challenged by a carrier, *Adair v. United States,* 1908.

2. The Southwestern Railroad Strike

The railroads were the scene of another extensive strike in 1885-86, although it was comparatively a mild contest. The Southwestern strike was a two-stage affair. It began in March 1885 in the shops of the Missouri Pacific Railroad, when a demand by an assembly of the Knights of Labor for the restoration of a wage cut of the previous year was not met. Intervention of the Governors of Kansas and Missouri ended the walkout. The strike had the support of the citizens along the right of way, and no violence took place during the walkout. In the next year the Knights of Labor had another encounter with Jay Gould, who controlled the Southwestern roads, and another settlement was reached. However, the parties were not happy with the settlement, and in January of 1886 another strike was called by assemblies of the Knights of Labor. This time the company rejected compromises, and the sheriff of the area around Parsons, Kan., reported, on March 27, 1886, that efforts to move trains "were forcibly resisted. . . . Many agents had been 'killed' and disabled, and a serious wreck had occurred."[17] Four hundred troops were ordered to Parsons by the Governor. In Fort Worth, Tex., a train proceeding under guard encountered a switch open and men hiding besides the track. An exchange of fire resulted in the wounding of three policemen and a striker.[18] Troops were ordered to the scene of the trouble. On April 9, 1886, the sheriff of St. Clair County, Ill., where East St. Louis is located, reported: "There is shooting going on . . . between a force of deputies and the mob." Six men and a woman were killed, and it was later established that the deputies had fired rifle shots into a crowd and then escaped to St. Louis. The congressional committee investigating the strike noted "that in addition to the striking railroad men, a large and irresponsible mob had collected and were the most active in inciting violence. Some of the men had never been railroad employees; others, it is alleged, had long been black-listed by the railroads." The incident in which six men and a woman were killed started as a result of the determination of the Louisville Nashville Railroad to operate its trains out of East St. Louis, Ill. It fortified its determination by the employment of a large force of guards following the forcible efforts of strikers and sympathizers to close down railroad operations at this point. On April 9 an attempt to move a coal train encountered opposition from armed men. A posse directed the mob to disperse, and attempted to arrest a man.

The squad of deputies was then furiously assailed with stones, as is alleged by the deputies, several of them being struck. One of the deputies raised his rifle, fired, and a man was seen to fall. The showers of stones and pistol-shots from all directions began to rain upon the officers, who returned the fire with their guns and pistols, with deadly effect, into the crowd. The firing was kept up until the crossing was clear, the people fleeing panic-stricken and rushing into houses in every direction for protection and safety . . . .

Bloodshed was succeeded by incendiarism.

About 40 railroad cars were burned. At the request of the sheriff, a large force of State troops was sent to East St. Louis and they succeeded in restoring order.[19]

3. Other Strikes in 1886

Employers who refused to deal with the organizations of their workmen began to rely on local and State governments for assistance during labor disputes. Although the great majority of strikes were peaceful, whether they succeeded or failed to obtain their objectives, the possibility of violence tended to be smaller in contests in which union recognition was not an issue. Under such circumstances the employer was likely to regard the strike as a temporary rupture of relations between himself and his labor force. When recognition was in question, the employer might seek to demonstrate that the strikers could be replaced and that their cause was lost. For the workers, the issue was not only the demands for which they struck, but the possibility that they would be replaced by newly hired workmen. Employers were therefore anxious to have the support of additional police and State troops if possible. An obliging sheriff might, as in the Chicago stockyards strike of 1886, plead for the sending of troops, who upon their arrival would find the community peaceful and threats of disorder nonexistent.[20]

Strikes in 1886 were generally peaceful. The U.S. Commissioner of Labor reported that in that year 1,572 strikes took place involving 610,000 workers. Some employers, including powerful ones, were likely to refuse to deal with a labor organization representing their employees. Workers were not then any more than now inclined to give up their unions without a struggle. In the anthracite coal fields of Pennsylvania, the operators had decided to deny recognition to the union with which they had been dealing, and the miners reacted to this change by striking. Their peaceful conduct did not save the area from violence. A committee from the U.S. House of Representatives noted: "Throughout the Lehigh region there were no riots. . . . These men were not a mob. They obeyed the law. They simply declined to work for shriveled wages. . . . During the whole of the strike serious violence was incited by the company rather than the men."[21]

Nor was this an isolated instance of the use of force against workers on strike. When the textile workers of Fall River, Mass., went on strike in July 1875, the mayor called for troops. The strikers were boisterous, but peaceful, and the Massachusetts Adjutant General reported that the "evening and night" after the arrival of troops "was remarkably quiet, more so than usual." No reports of disorders were made, but the presence of the troops obviously cowed the strikers, who withdrew to their homes.[22]

This use of troops was not always unquestioned. General C. H. Grosvenor on March 19, 1875, submitted a resolution requesting the Governor to inform the House, "what, if any, public reason or necessity existed for the calling out, arming and sending to Nelsonville, the Ohio Independent Militia, on the 11 and 12 of June 1874." It was called out during a strike of coal miners. "The statute of Ohio provides for the organization of the independent militia, and the Governor is ex-officio commander-in-chief; but he has no power to call out the militia until an exigency has arisen which requires the presence of troops." Grosvenor denied the existence of riot or disorder:

> Was there insurrection or not? The Governor says there was not. Was there invasion? Nobody pretends it. Was there any resistance to the enforcement of law? There was not. If there was no riot or insurrection, if there was no invasion, if there was no resistance to civil authority, then the Governor of this State had no jurisdiction to call upon these companies, and his order was in violation of law, and without the authority of law.[23]

LABOR VIOLENCE IN THE 1890's

Not all violence was inspired by employers. While employer obduracy might lead to rejection of recognition, such conduct was in itself legally permissible. Had workers passively accepted such decisions, the level of violence in American labor disputes would have been reduced. Workers were, however, unwilling to watch their jobs forfeited to a local or imported strikebreaker. Employers could shut down their plants and attempt "to starve" their employees out of the union. Such a policy might have worked, but employers cognizant of their rights and costs frequently refused to follow such a self-denying tactic. As a consequence violence initiated from the labor side was also prevalent. In the 1890's violent outbreaks occurred in the North, South, and West, in small communities and metropolitan cities, testifying to the common attitudes of Americans in every part of the United States. While workers might react against the denial of what they regarded as their rights, the outcome of their violent behavior seldom changed the course of events. Serious violence erupted in several major strikes of the 1890's, the question of union recognition being a factor in all of them. As will be noted below, the Homestead strike, which was a defensive action in behalf of an existing and recognized union, and the Pullman strike, which was called in behalf of other workers denied recognition, also failed. Violence in the Coeur d'Alene copper area eventually led to the destruction of the Western Federation of Miners in that district. Violence was effective in the Illinois coalfields only because the community and the Governor of the State were hostile to the efforts of two coal producers to evade the terms of a contract acceptable to the great majority of producers in Illinois.

Although steel workers in Pennsylvania and copper miners in Idaho had different ethnic origins and worked under dissimilar conditions, each reacted with equal ferocity to the attempts of their employers to undermine their unions.

1. Homestead

In Homestead, Pa., the domineering head of the Carnegie Steel Co., Henry C. Frick, used a difference over wages and a contract expiration date as an excuse for breaking with the union. When the union called a strike against the demands of Frick, the latter was ready to bring in a bargeload of Pinkerton operatives to guard his plant from the harassment of union pickets. Frick's plan became known, and the guards were met by several hundred steelworkers. In the battle to land the guards from the barges, two Pinkertons and two strikers were killed. Another attempt to land also ended in failure. Eventually the Pinkertons were forced to surrender and some were severely mauled by strikers and sympathizers. At the plea of the sheriff, the Governor ordered 7,000 troops to Homestead. Leaders were arrested, but juries refused to convict.

While the violence was temporarily successful in holding off the landing attempted on July 4, it was unable to change the outcome of the contest between the union and Frick. Under the cover of the protection given to him by the National Guard, he was able to open his mills. Furnaces were lit on July 15, and the company announced that applications for work would be received until July 21. The following day a large force of nonunion men entered the plant. Ultimately the union was defeated, and according to a leading student of the steel industry of another generation, John A. Fitch, the union never recovered from its defeat in Homestead. The steel workers were fearful of Frick's attempt to break the union. The hiring of several hundred Pinkertons and their stealthy efforts to land convinced the strikers that a serious movement to destroy their organization was on the way, and the use of the hated Pinkertons sharpened their anger. An investigation by the

U.S. Senate noted: "Every man who testified, including the proprietors of the detective agencies, admitted that the workmen are strongly prejudiced against the so-called Pinkertons and their presence at a strike serves to unduly inflame the passions of the strikers."[24]

2. Coeur d'Alene

Organization of the metal miners in the Coeur d'Alene region in Idaho was followed by the mine operators' establishment of an association after the miner's union had successfully won a wage increase. A lockout was called several months after the miner's success, and every mine in the area was closed down. An offer of lower wages was rejected. The strikers were not passive. Strikebreakers were urged to leave or were forcibly expelled; court injunctions against violence were ignored. In July 1892 the situation deteriorated. A union miner was killed by guards, and it brought an attack by armed miners upon the barracks housing guards employed by the Frisco mill. It was dynamited, and one employee was killed and 20 wounded. An attack on the Gem mill followed and although five strikers were killed and more wounded, the mill surrendered. The guards gave up their weapons and were ordered out of the county. Armed with Winchesters, the armed strikers marched on Wardner, where they forced the Bunker Hill mine to discharge its nonunion contingent.

At the request of the Governor, who sent the entire National Guard, Federal troops were sent to restore order. The commanding general ordered all union men arrested and lodged in a hastily built stockade or bullpen. The commander of the State militia removed local officials sympathetic to the strikers and replaced them with others favorable to his orders. Trains were searched and suspects removed. Active union men were ordered dismissed from their jobs. The district was treated like a military zone, and companies were prohibited from employing union men. About 30 men were charged with conspiracy, and four were convicted, but subsequently released by the U.S. Supreme Court. Nevertheless, the miners were able to win recognition from all but the largest of the mining companies, which set the stage for a more spectacular encounter 7 years later.[25]

3. Use of Troops in Minor Disputes

The use of State troops against strikers was common in the 1890's. In some instances it was in response to violence or to attempts to prevent interference with strike-breakers or to the closing down of the properties. In 1894 the United Mine Workers of America called a national strike in the bituminous coal industry and the strike became the occasion for intervention of troops in many coal-mining communities. When miners in Athens County, Ohio, interfered with the movement of coal trains, the militia was sent into the area to restore order. The Kansas National Guard also saw service.[26] However, the tendency of local police officers to seek the aid of State troops during industrial disturbances did not always depend upon the existence of disorder. Sometimes it was precautionary and designed to overawe the strikers. Reporting the activity of the Illinois National Guard for 1893 and 1894, the Adjutant General noted that it "has performed more active service than during its entire prior existence." At two points, the troops found no disorder and withdrew after several days. In others, militiamen prevented interference with the movement of coal, and in a third group of places, soldiers and miners staged a series of armed encounters.[27]

The tendency to order troops into coal-mining areas during a strike was not limited to Illinois. During the strike of 1894, troops were moved into the southwestern area of Indiana and into Mahaska County, Iowa. Fourteen companies of militiamen were on duty from 8 to 20 days in the Indiana coalfields. No report of violence was made by the authorities, and the sending of troops was evidently based on rumor or on hope that the presence of troops would intimidate the strikers.[28]

4. The Pullman Strike

Railroad strikes have been among the more violent types of labor dispute. Normally, railroad workers are not more aggressive than other workers. However, railroads cover large open areas and their operations are always open to the rock thrower or the militant picket who may take it upon himself to discourage strikebreaking. A sympathy strike by the newly organized American Railway Union with the workers in the Pullman shops led to a widespread suspension of railroad service in 1894. What stands out in this bitter clash is the sympathy that the losing struggle generated among thousands of railroad workers. The refusal of the Pullman Co. to discuss the restoration of a wage cut with its employees was interpreted as an example of corporate arrogance. Like 1877, 1894 was a depression year, and many workers were without a job or income.

The strike started in May, and the American Railway Union, meeting in convention the following month, sought to bring about a settlement of the differences. When the American Railway Union imposed its boycott upon Pullman equipment, its action was challenged by the General Manager's Association, made up of the executives of the 24 railroads entering Chicago. Special guards were engaged, Federal marshals were appointed to keep the trains moving, and if an employee refused to handle Pullman equipment he was discharged. Attempts to operate with strikebreakers led to fearful resistance. Rioting was widespread, and at the request of the railroads and advice of Attorney General Richard Olney, Federal troops were sent to Chicago, over the protests of Governor John B. Altgeld. Every road west of Chicago felt the impact of the strike. Clashes between strikers and strikebreakers brought out Federal or State troops in Nebraska, Iowa, Colorado, Oklahoma, and California. Although the loss of life and property was not as serious as during the disturbances of 1877, the Pullman strike affected a wider area. An estimated 34 people were killed and undetermined millions of dollars were lost in the rioting connected with this conflict. President Grover Cleveland claimed "that within the states of North Dakota, Montana, Idaho, Colorado, Washington, Wyoming, California, and the territories of Utah and New Mexico it was impracticable to enforce federal law by the ordinary course of judicial procedure. For this reason, he revealed, military forces were being used."[29]

The immediate cause of the violence was the determination of the General Manager's Association to defeat the sympathy strike. When the boycott of Pullman cars was announced, the association declared that the employees of the railroads had no right to punish the carriers nor impose hardships upon the traveling public. The association declared "it to be the lawful right and duty of said railway companies to protect against said boycott, to resist the same in the interest of their existing contracts, and for the benefit of the traveling public, and that we will act unitedly to that end."[30] The extension of support by the union brought forth the support of the carriers for the Pullman Co. It is however, as has been noted, extremely difficult to avoid disorders in a strike in an industry whose operations are carried on over an open and extensive area. Any occurrence can attract hundreds and even thousands of people who because of sympathy or search for excitement or loot can expand a simple incident into a large-scale riot. The chief inciters to violence were not known, and the police and the officers of the railroads did not agree on whether union members or city toughs were the chief promoters of the turmoil.

The Federal Government hired marshals in numerous railroad centers to protect the property of the carriers. Attorney General Richard Olney stated that the extra funds expended for this purpose by the Federal Government amounted to at least $400,000.[31]

The responsibility for violence rests largely on the behavior of George Pullman. His attitude was similar to those held by many industrialists. He was unwilling to allow his workers the slightest influence upon the decisions of the company which greatly affected their welfare. Like other firms, the Pullman Co. was suffering losses of business as a result of the depression, and it may not have been able to meet the demands of its employees. It could, however, have conferred in good faith and explained its position instead of following a policy of peremptory rejection and dismissal of those who had asked for a reconsideration of a wage cut. Pullman's attitude, shared by many industrialists, tells us something about the cause of violence in labor disputes. Arrogant, intransigent, unwilling to meet with their employees, owners depended upon their own or the Government's power to suppress protest. Behind the powerful shield they could ignore the periodic outbreaks by their labor force; they knew that these seldom were strong enough to gain victory.

5. Streetcar Strike in Brooklyn, N.Y.

Homestead, the Coeur d'Alene, and Pullman are large markers in the record of industrial disputes. Violence also erupted in a number of less significant disputes. Local authorities were quick to call for help from the state in the face of labor disputes, and Governors frequently answered their summons. For example, in Brooklyn, New York, District Assembly No. 75 Knights of Labor and the Brooklyn City Railroad Co. had established collective-bargaining relations in 1886, and annually renewed the agreement. Negotiations broke down in 1895 and the company turned to strikebreakers. "Men came from all parts of the country and as a result the railroad companies were able entirely to reorganize their working staffs."[32] When the strikers sought to interfere with operations, 7,500 State troops were sent into the city at the request of the mayor. Cars began operating under military protection on January 22. Two soldiers rode on each car. In one encounter, shots were exchanged among strikers, strikebreakers, and troops; one man was killed and a number wounded.[33]

6. Coal Miners' Strike

Three separate incidents involving coal-mining violence illustrate the fragility of peaceful methods in this industry. In two of the three cases, the use of force did not end in failure, but there were exceptional circumstances in each. Much depended upon the attitude of the authorities and the sympathies of the public. Free miners in Tennessee were able to control changes in the system of working convict labor in the coal mines. Leasing of convicts for work in the mines was begun in 1865, and the competition of these men, who had no influence on their working conditions or pay, was a threat to the free miners. Other grievances also played a role. Payment of wages by scrip, absence of checkweighmen at the mines, and the use of yellow dog contracts were sources of protest. When the free miners went on strike in 1891 the companies introduced convict labor as replacements. On July 21, 1891, hundreds of armed miners demanded that convict workers leave the mining camps at Briceville and Coal Creek. State troops were ordered into the area, but the governor agreed to the discontinuance of convict labor in the mines.[34]

Violence was also a factor in the settling of the coal miners' strikes in Alabama in 1894. A month after the strike started, miners in Johns, Adger, and Sumpter were ordered to leave the company houses. The company "strategy in breaking the strike was to import Negro labor to work in the mines. During the strike's first week, 100 Negroes were brought from Kansas."[35] On May 7, 1894, a band of armed men invaded the Price mine at Horse Creek "blowing up boilers, burning supplies and destroying property." On July 16, in a gunfight at Slope, 5 miles from Birmingham, three Negro strikebreakers and a deputy were killed. Troops were ordered into the area by the governor and remained there until August 14, when the strike was settled.[36]

In 1897, the United Mine Workers of America tried again to establish itself as the bargaining agent for the bituminous coal miners. Despite the UMW low fortunes and virtual lack of resources, a national strike was called on July 4. Although unsuccessful in West Virginia, the union was able to establish bargaining rights in Indiana, Illinois, Ohio, and western Pennsylvania. The central competitive field agreement was developed, which aimed at a wage scale which would allow operators from all of the above regions to operate on the basis of rough equality. Not all operators were willing to go along with the arrangement. The Pana Coal Co., which had refused to accept the agreement, tried to operate with Negro strikebreakers. A report indicated that an additional carload was on the way, resulting in armed miners halting a train and removing the strikebreakers. No harm befell them; they were sent home. Governor John B. Tanner sent a company of National Guardsmen to Pana with instructions not to assist the company to operate its mines.

More serious was the outcome of the attempt of the Chicago-Virden Coal Co., Virden, Ill., to carry on operations with strikebreakers. On October 12, 1898, the company attempted to land a carload of strikebreakers. A report of the company's intention had reached the strikers, and many of them lined the sides of the tracks carrying loaded rifles. However, the train did not attempt to discharge its cargo at the railroad station, but moved ahead to a stockade. Shots had been exchanged between the miners and the occupants of the car, and when the car reached the stockade, guards firing rifles rushed out. In the exchange of fire 14 men, eight of them strikers, were killed and a number of others wounded. Governor Tanner denounced the company and sent National Guardsmen to Virden. They restored order, and prevented a group of strikebreakers from landing in the city the day after the riot.[37] The two recalcitrant companies eventually signed the central competitive agreement, but without the support of the Governor the outcome might have been different.

These coal strikes were exceptional in that the use of force did not fatally injure the union. As the full chronicle of labor disputes demonstrates, violence was rarely a successful union weapon, despite the fact that it was ordinarily a defensive measure employed against guards or strikebreakers who were attempting to destroy the effectiveness of a strike.

The importance of public opinion in supporting labor's side of a dispute has seldom won for unions the help or neutrality of public authorities in a context of labor violence. In the strike against convict labor, the Governor had and exercised his power to eliminate the cause of the strike. In the Illinois coal strike, the coal companies had broken ranks with other employers by refusing the terms of a negotiated agreement. Moreover, the violence was directed against armed outsiders who were brought into the community to replace local miners. But as the next section shows, in general, violence in labor disputes was likely to lead to repression by public force.

7. A Return to Coeur d'Alene

A completely different outcome followed the second act of the Coeur d'Alene story. In 1892, the union signed all of the companies except the Bunker Hill and Sullivan, which over the years remained a holdout. In the spring of 1899, Edward Boyce, president of the Western Federation of Miners, visited the area and began a campaign to bring that company into line.

In April 1899, a Northern Pacific train was seized at Burke, Idaho. At Gem, where the engineer was compelled to stop, dynamite was loaded on the train. Others joined the train at Wallace, and the engineer was then ordered to switch his train onto the tracks of the Oregon Northern Railroad and proceed to Wardner. Masked men got off the train, proceeded to the Bunker Hill and Sullivan mill and, after dispersing the guards, destroyed the mill, inflicting damages of about a quarter of a million dollars. Governor Frank Steunenberg, on learning of these events, requested Federal aid, the Idaho National Guard being on duty in the Philippines.

Federal troops were dispatched and the State auditor, Bartlet Sinclair, was directed by the Governor to take command. He jailed every member and sympathizer of the union that could be found. All were, in his opinion, morally guilty of the dynamiting. Makeshift jails were used until the prisoners had constructed a stockade where they were lodged. Local officials sympathetic to the miners were removed, and others friendly to the company replaced them. Sinclair was determined to root out the Western Federation of Miners. A permit system was instituted under which applicants for work were required to repudiate the union by agreeing that it was a criminal conspiracy. Protests to the Secretary of War by Samuel Gompers and others brought orders to the commanding Federal general not to meddle in union affairs. But Sinclair was in charge of that phase, and he was acting under the orders of Governor Steunenberg.

The secretary of the Burke local union was tried for conspiracy to murder and was convicted and sentenced to prison. Ten others were convicted of interfering with the U.S. mail. Most of the miners were kept in the bullpen until November 1899, but the military occupation of the district continued until April 1901, when a new State administration ended it. The miners' leaders imprisoned by the State were also pardoned, but the union never regained its vigor in the Coeur d'Alene area. The violence against the company boomeranged; it did not serve the union's interest.

In Coeur d'Alene the attack on the Bunker Hill and Sullivan mill was an attempt to compel a company to accept a union contract, but the aggressive invasion and destruction was one that no Governor could tolerate. Governor Steunenberg, who was to be killed by a bomb 8 years later, had little option except to act against those who seized a train and dynamited property. His prior background was

303

not on its face antilabor. He had had the support of the Western Federation of Miners in his campaign for the governorship, and he boasted that he was a member of the International Typographical Union. However, he might have been less severe and avoided arresting and imprisoning many innocent miners. The lesson that can be derived from the episodes in the Coeur d'Alene area is that violence is a risky tactic for those who need public tolerance if not public support in behalf of their demands, no matter how just or righteous their cause.[38]

THE 10 YEARS BETWEEN 1900 AND 1910

The first decade of the 20th century witnessed expansion of union membership, which increased opportunities for conflicts with employers. As in previous periods, strikes were on occasion marked by violence. The prospect of violence was heightened by rising employer resistance to union objectives. The signs of this new employer response consisted of the founding of many employer associations, the beginning of the open-shop campaign, and the use of Citizen Alliances as assault troops on union picket lines.

1. Pennsylvania Anthracite Coalfields

Violence in Illinois and in the Coeur d'Alene was carried out primarily by native or Americanized workers. Through the 1870's the Pennsylvania anthracite area was dominated by English-speaking workers: Americans, English, Scotch, Irish, and Welsh were the principal sources of labor.[39] By 1900, large numbers of Eastern and Southern Europeans had come into the area, and the English-speaking ratio in the population had dropped from 94 percent in 1880 to 52 percent in 1900.[40] With the destruction of the Knights of Labor and the Amalgamated Association of Anthracite Miners, no offset to the companies' power existed. Absence of checkweighmen, the existence of the company store, and the complete domination of the area by the coal companies were unrestrained evils. Nothing better demonstrates the abuse of power than an attack in 1897 upon miners who had struck against the high prices at the company store and were peacefully marching from Hazleton to Latimer. The sheriff and a force of deputies met the marchers on the road and ordered them to disperse. When they failed to obey instantly, the sheriff ordered his deputies to fire on the unresisting paraders. Eighteen were killed and 40 seriously wounded. Many of the killed and wounded were shot in the back. The sheriff and several deputies were tried for murder but were acquitted.[41]

In 1900, the United Mine Workers of America was able to challenge successfully the anthracite coal operators. Although the union had only about 7 percent of the miners in the area in the organization, it called a strike in September of 1900. There was only one serious clash between strikers and guards, which led to the death of a strikebreaker. Immediately 2,400 troops were sent into the area by the Governor. The strike was settled on terms not unfavorable to the union, and the single violent encounter played no role in the outcome.[42] Peace in the anthracite mines was brought about by political pressure but also by the skillful leadership of John Mitchell, the president of the United Mine Workers. Mitchell had always deplored the use of violent methods and constantly pleaded for negotiations as a peaceful means of settling labor disputes. He further recognized the importance of retaining public sentiment on the strikers' side, and he was determined to prevent the use of widespread prejudice against the Southern European immigrant worker to defeat them. This strike was, however, only a skirmish; the anthracite workers were to face a more serious trial 2 years later.

When negotiations between the operators and the union broke down in April 1902, it appeared that the strike would be more violent than the preceding one. A more aggressive spirit was evident among the men, and the companies appeared to be equally determined to scotch further progress of the union. Hundreds of commissions for iron and coal police to guard mining property were issued, and the companies decided to recruit strikebreakers and operate during the strike. An attack on a colliery at Old Forge on July 1 resulted in the killing of a striker; another was killed at Duryea the next day. Shootings and assaults became more common as the strike dragged on, and at the end of July the Governor ordered two regiments to Shenandoah, where the town was literally taken over by rioters. In this community a merchant suspected of supplying ammunition to deputies was beaten to death, and deputies and strikebreakers were assaulted. On August 18, troops were sent to Carbon County after a coal and iron policeman killed a striker. Trestles and bridges were dynamited and non-strikers assaulted. The Governor, in September, sent troops into the three anthracite counties. Violence did not abate. On September 28, a striker was killed, and later in the day, 700 strikers assaulted and wrecked the Mount Carmel office of the Lehigh Valley Coal Co. and seized the roads leading to the colliery. In a summary of violence at the end of September, the *New York Tribune* claimed that in the disturbances arising out of the strike, 14 had been killed, 16 shot from ambush, 42 others severely injured, and 67 aggravated assaults had occurred; 1 house and 4 bridges were dynamited, 16 houses, 10 buildings, 3 washrooms around mines, and 3 stockades were burned; 6 trains were wrecked and there were 9 attempted wrecks, 7 trains attacked, and students in 14 schools went on strike against teachers whose fathers or brothers were working during the strike.[43]

Despite the extent of violence, it is doubtful whether it had any decisive effect on the outcome of the strike. In insisting that the strikers were prevented from working because of union intimidation, the operators claimed that the mines would be opened and fully manned if adequate protection were granted. The Governor of Pennsylvania sent the entire National Guard of the State into the anthracite area, but their presence did not increase the output of coal. This demonstration that the tieup was not the result of coercion but of the determination of the miners to bargain through a union ended the impasse.

What made the union victory possible was the conciliatory attitude of Mitchell. Firm on essentials, he was ready to compromise on details. Careful not to antagonize public opinion, he emphasized the justice of the miners' cause, the right of men to bargain collectively over the terms of employment. Although considerable violence developed during the second anthracite strike, none of it had the spectacular features of some of the battles in the Rocky Mountain area (see below). Mitchell and his subordinates always pleaded for peaceful behavior, and while the advice was often honored in the breach, neither he nor any other leaders could be attacked for advocating destruction of property or assaults upon persons which, had they done so, would have given employers a powerful argument with which to sway public sentiment.

2. The Colorado Labor War

The use of force to settle differences was more common in the Western mining camps at the turn of the century than in Eastern manufacturing or even mining communities. In the West there was a tendency for violence to erupt on a larger scale. In 1894 Colorado's Governor, David M. Waite, ordered the dispersal of an army of company-employed deputies in a mining-labor dispute. Only the intervention of the troops prevented a battle between strikers and deputies.

Later, in 1901, after a successful walkout, the union miners deported a group of strikebreakers who had taken their jobs during the strike. The tendency for each side to resort to force to settle differences led to a gradual escalation of the level of violence, which reached a point where the Western Federation of Miners faced the combined power of the Mine Operator's Association, aided by the State government and a private employer's group, the militant Citizen's Alliance. It was an unequal struggle in which men were killed and maimed; union miners imprisoned in the bullpen; union halls, newspapers, and cooperatives sacked; and many strikers deported. There is no episode in American labor history in which violence was as systematically used by employers as in the Colorado labor war of 1903 and 1904. The miners fought back with a ferocity born of desperation, but their use of rifles and dynamite did not prevent their utter defeat.

The war opened in 1903. It started with a peaceful withdrawal from work in the Colorado City mill of the United States Reduction Refining Co., after demands for a wage increase and union recognition had been rejected. The strike quickly spread to the other mines and mills in the area. Although no reports of lawlessness had been made, the Governor sent in several companies of militia at the request of the sheriff. Although settlement was made, with the assistance of the Governor, the manager of the United States Reduction Refining Co. refused to accept its terms. District No. 1 of the Western Federation of Miners on August 3, 1903, called strikes in mines shipping ore to the refineries of the United States Reduction Refining Co. This was denounced by the Colorado Mine Owners Association as an "arbitrary and unjustifiable action" which "mars the annals of organized labor, and we denounce it as an outrage against both the employer and the employee."[44]

The association announced that it was determined to operate without the cooperation of the federation and, in response to a plea from the operators, State troops were sent to Teller County, where Cripple Creek was located, on September 3, 1904. At the same time a strike for shorter hours was going on in Telluride, and troops were sent into that area, although no reports of trouble were published. Active union men were arrested through September, lodged in a bullpen for several days, and then released. The militia officers took umbrage at an editorial in the *Victor Record,* and arrested its staff, who were held for 24 hours in the bullpen before they were released.[45]

The first significant violence attributed to the strikers was the blowing up of the Vindicator mine in Teller County, in which two were killed. Martial law was declared in Teller County and the military informed the editor of the *Victor Herald* that editorial comments would be censored. When the union secured a writ of habeas corpus directing the military to bring an arrested miner before a State court, the Governor suspended the writ "on the ground of military necessity."[46] Deportations of strikers were begun, and temporarily halted by an order from a State court. The military obeyd this court order. When 16 men were killed by the fall of a cage at the Independence mine at Victor, bitter feeling increased. Violation of safety rules was blamed by the union for the accident.

By February 2, 1904, conditions in Teller County were sufficiently close to normal for the Governor to withdraw troops. The mining companies then put into effect a "rustling-card" system that required applicants for employment in mines and smelters to obtain a card authorizing them to seek work. Each time a person changed jobs he had to procure a new card, which gave the mining companies an opportunity to blacklist all who did not meet their standards. The strike dragged on, and on June 6, 1904, while nonunion miners were returning from work, a charge of dynamite exploded under the Independence railroad station, killing 13 and seriously wounding 16. After the explosion, the Citizen's Alliance went into action. County and city officials sympathetic to the union were forced to resign, and a roundup of union members and sympathizers started. They were placed in a bullpen, and many of them were later deported to Kansas and New Mexico. The commander of the militia, General Sherman Bell, set up a commission to decide the fate of the prisoners held in the bullpen. A person's attitude towards the Western Federation of Miners determined whether he would be released or deported. On July 26, 1904, the Governor ended military rule and left the field to the Citizen's Alliance. During its tenure, since June 8, the commission examined 1,569 men, recommending 238 for deportation and 42 for trial in the criminal courts; the rest were released from the bullpen.[47] Gradually, normal conditions were restored, but the union continued its nominal strike until December 1907, when it was called off.[48]

Simultaneously with the Cripple Creek strike, the union was directing another in the San Juan area of Telluride County, Colo. The same scenario was played here. Troops were sent into the area soon after the calling of the strike in September 1903. Censorship, deportations, and arrests accompanied the troops. The union fought a losing battle, and the Telluride Miner's Association announced it would never employ members of the Western Federation of Miners. When the resistance of the strikers was broken, the Governor withdrew the State troops, but by that time the Citizen's Alliance could itself handle deportations and assaults.[49]

The effect of this organized violence upon the miner's organization is summarized by Sheriff Edward Bell of Teller County, and a leader in the campaign against that union. After the assaults and deportations had broken the back of the resistance, the sheriff announced:

The danger is all past. There are less than 100 of the radical miners left in the Cripple Creek district. The rest have been deported, or have left the district because they were unable to gain employment. They can never get work again. The mine owners have adopted a card system by which no miner can gain admittance to a mine unless he has a card showing that he does not belong to a union.[50]

The miners were no easy victims. They resisted as well as they could, but they faced the overwhelming power of the mine operators aided by the business community, the Governor, and the courts.[51]

3. A Collection of Strikes: Two Teamster, Two Seamen, and One Sawmill Workers' Strike

In 1901 a citywide teamsters strike took place in San Francisco that had the backing of the waterfront unions. The dispute started over demands for exclusive employment of union members at one of the companies, and eventually involved all the draying employees in the city. An attempt to replace the strikes was made, and trucks and nonunion drivers were mercilessly assaulted. A number of business groups pleaded with the Governor for State troops, but he refused to grant the requests. The violence continued to the end of a strike in which five persons were killed and assult victims were said to exceed 300. Notwithstanding the violence, the strike ended in a compromise favoring the employers.[52]

The Chicago teamsters' strike was one of the more violent of the decade. Although it lacked the dramatic confrontations typical of the Western mining camps, the strikers' constant clashes with strikebreakers, guards, and police resulted in a number of deaths, hundreds of injuries, and the arrest of 1,108 persons. The teamsters' strike started on April 6, 1905, as a sympathetic walkout in defense of a small union of clothing cutters. It lasted 106 days and involved 4,500 out of the more than 38,000 union teamsters in Chicago. During the strike, 1,763 special policemen were added to the Chicago police department. The sheriff of Cook County employed 913 extra deputies, and an additional 4,157 unpaid deputies were recruited for strike duty, largely from the business community. The police department reported that 14 deaths and 31 injuries were caused by firearms; there were 202 other casualties. The police brought 930 cases against strikers, and 178 against nonunion men who had been arrested. Constant demands were made upon the Governor for State troops, and the President of the United States was asked to send Federal aid. Both requests were rejected. Strikebreakers were brought from other cities, and professional strike guards and police rode the wagons delivering goods to boycotted firms. The entire business community was united against the union, and hundreds of thousands of dollars were raised to fight the walkout. In the end, the union was forced to surrender without attaining any of its demands.

It was a serious loss which had repercussions within the teamster's union as well as the Chicago labor movement.[53]

After dealing with the International Seamen's Union for a number of years, the Lake Carriers' Association, a group of ship operators, decided to end its union relationships. In 1908, it inaugurated a welfare plan, a continuous discharge book containing a record of the holder's performance aboard ship, and a program of benefits for those killed in service. The agreement with the union was not signed and active union men were denied employment. When the 1909 session opened, the union called a strike. It lasted for the next 3 years, and encounters between pickets and strikebreakers and guards took place in most of the Great Lakes ports. Five pickets were reported to have been killed, and many injured on both sides.[54]

In the May 1906 strike of the Sailor's Union of the Pacific, two men working on the vessel *Fearless* were killed in Gray's Harbor, Wash., by strikers led by the union agent, William Gohl, who was subsequently convicted and sentenced to prison. A crew working in Portland, Oreg., on a struck vessel was assaulted by a gang led by the union agent. During the same year, a strike of sawmill workers in Humboldt, Calif., resulted in a number of clashes between strikers and workers, in which two were killed and many injured.[55]

4. Minor Disputes: Seven Streetcar Strikes

Many disputes in this period took place which failed to attract national attention because of the fewer numbers of employees involved and the smaller economic importance of the firms. The significance of these minor strikes lies not only in their demonstrations of the ease with which violence arose in the industrial arena, but in the dispersion of violence in virtually every part of the country. No region or industry can claim a monopoly on violent confrontation, although labor disputes in some industries were more susceptible to the exercise of force.

Strikes in municipal transportation services were often accompanied by riots and general disorder.[56] Attempts to replace strikers by operating with new employees could easily lead to rioting, because surface cars often passed through neighborhoods which strongly supported the strikers. Disturbances on open streets could also be joined by sympathizers and even uninvolved seekers of excitement. During the 1901 transit strike in Albany, N.Y., the sheriff asked for troops. They remained in the city between May 14 and 18, and the Adjutant General reported "three persons were shot . . . who were guarding a car, they having been assailed by a mob that had quickly gathered. . . ."

The following year the Governor of Rhode Island sent troops to Pawtucket to help escort vehicles through jeering crowds. Troops arrived on June 11, 1902, and aided deputy sheriffs who had fired at missile-throwing crowds. "Martial law was declared on June 13 and the troops began to clear streets of all crowds, and forced the closing of doors and windows on the streets on which cars were operated."[57] The same year the Governor of Louisiana ordered troops to New Orleans to help put down the rioting connected with the streetcar strike. The troops remained in the city for a month.[58]

During the 1903 strike of streetcar men in Waterbury, Conn., troops were sent by the Governor to "aid the civil authorities in suppressing whatever disorder might occur on account of the strike trouble."[59] Troops left on February 4, 1903, and when the streetcars resumed operations without the protective shield of the troops, trouble again started. On March 8, 1903, a special policeman on a streetcar was killed by a revolver shot. Eight strikers and a boy were arrested and tried for murder; they were acquitted.[60]

A successful effort to break the union of transit workers in San Francisco brought with it considerable violence. Strikebreakers opened fire on pickets, and "some twenty men were wounded, five it was said, mortally." The head of the surface lines explained: "We are going to establish the open shop on the California street line." At the same time, the company was anxious to retain the older employees. "But we will deal with them individually only," he explained.[61]

The issue in dispute on the Philadelphia transit lines was the continued existence of the local of the Amalgamated Association of Street Railway Employees, with which the Philadelphia Rapid Transit Co. had an agreement. The union had been recognized in 1909 as a result of pressure by local politicians who wished to avoid a controversy in the midst of a municipal campaign for public offices. However, the company encouraged the establishing of the Keystone Carmen, a company-dominated union, and at the same time discharged 173 members of the regular labor organization. When no bargaining agreement was reached, the union called a strike, and the company countered by importing strikebreakers and guards under the direction of James Farley, a notorious street fighter and supplier of armed guards during strikes. In the first days of the strike, the police and private guards were helpless against mobs who roamed the streets wrecking cars and smashing windows; the company claimed 298 cars had been destroyed, and more than 2,000 windows broken. Much of the violence during the Philadelphia dispute was caused by traveling pickets and their sympathizers. The guards were, however, inured to violence and engaged in it themselves. In Philadelphia on March 8 "a band of 'strikebreakers,' men furnished by private detective agencies . . . for temporary use, took a car down the crowded thoroughfare at high speed shooting into the crowds on the sidewalk and wounding several persons."[62] Eventually the strike was settled with the abandonment of the legitimate union and the establishment of a company-dominated organization.[63]

A strike in Columbus, Ohio, in 1910 was also caused by the unwillingness of a rapid transit company to deal with a union established in that year. Intervention by the State board of arbitration resulted in a temporary agreement, but it was ended by a union charge of bad faith after the company discharged a number of union men. Many members of the police force refused to ride on the streetcars and protect strikebreakers. The "first few days of the strike was attended with riots from the downtown streets in which men were pulled from cars and beaten, cars stoned, trolley ropes and wires cut."[64] The company imported 450 trained guards and strikebreakers from Cleveland, and the strike "settled down to guerrilla warfare. Cars have been stoned and dynamited in all parts of the city; attempts have been made to blow up car houses where non-union members are quartered and the public intimidated from riding by systematic picketing and boycotting."[65] At the request of the local authorities, troops were sent into the city on July 28, 1910. "While enroute to Columbus, a sympathizer of the lawless conditions in Columbus deliberately wrecked the first section of the Fourth Infantry train."[66] A number of men were injured. The violence subsided after the arrival of troops, and service was resumed.

5. Three Strikes in the Clothing Industry

Two strikes in this period surrounded by considerable violence ended with the recognition of the unions involved. In New York City the International Ladies' Garment Workers' Union was able to win collective-bargaining rights in the New York market after two strikes, each in a different branch of the industry. On November 22, 1909, almost 20,000 workers in the dress and waist industry, the large majority of whom were young women, went out on strike. The walkout lasted until February 15, 1910. During the strike, 771 pickets were arrested, of whom 19 were given jail terms in the workhouse and 248 fined. The pickets, on the other hand, complained that they were victims of repeated assaults by the police and hired sluggers of the employers. The union charges were supported by a number of social workers who joined in union complaints to the mayor. The settlement of the strike was followed by the cloak-maker's walkout, involving more than 50,000 workers. In this strike both sides engaged in considerable violence. The employers engaged dozens of private guards, and the union countered by hiring its own strong-arm men. During one encounter a private detective engaged by one of the employers was killed; several union members were tried for the offense but were acquitted.[67] This strike was successful and marked the beginning of permanent collective bargaining in the ladies' garment industry in New York. Pressures to reach an agreement came from sources outside the industry, including the Jewish community, which found the internecine struggle between Jewish employers and employees highly distasteful.

A much more violent encounter was the strike of the men's clothing workers in Chicago during the same year. Beginning on September 22, 1910, as a protest against a cut in rates paid for the stitching of seams, the strike spread and eventually involved virtually all of the 40,000 workers employed in the Chicago market. The United Garment Workers of America, the union with jurisdiction in the trade, took over direction of the walkout, but the industry was unwilling to deal with a labor organization. Police were active in breaking picket lines, and considerable violence ensued. On December 4, the first picket was killed, and another 11 days later. A private detective escorting strike-breakers was killed in the first days of January, and before the strike ended four others were killed. The strike lasted 133 days, during which 874 arrests were made, mostly of union pickets or their sympathizers. It succeeded in gaining union recognition from Hart, Schaffner & Marx, one of the leading firms in the Chicago market, recognition which was later expanded to the entire industry. The Hart, Schaffner & Marx decision to accept collective bargaining in large part arose from one partner's strong personal dis-taste of the violence generated in this dispute.[68]

6. Three Pennsylvania Strikes

These strikes in Pennsylvania, in 1909-10, were all spon-taneous, unorganized walkouts. A reduction in pay was the cause of the strike of steel workers in the plant of the Pressed Steel Car Co. of McKee's Rock, Pa., in July of 1909. In August the IWW entered the leaderless strike and sent its general organizer, William Trautman, to aid the strikers. Trautman had been active in the Brewery Work-er's Union before the launching of the IWW and he was an experienced labor organizer. The strikers, mostly German, Polish, and Hungarian immigrants, were not concerned with the philosophy of the IWW as much as assistance in conducting a walkout. After the strike was called the Pennsylvania constabulary arrived, and killed a striker dur-ing August. Soon thereafter a deputy sheriff was murdered by a group of pickets when he refused to leave a streetcar as directed. By the end of the strike, 11 strikers and 2 deputies had been killed. A committee from the U.S. House of Representatives heard testimony that men were forcibly kept in stockades, and in the cars in which they arrived—

there was an armed guard at each end of the car, and [passengers were] not allowed to leave the train, and when they got in the camp they were forced to work there by the deputies of the car companies, the car companies being authorized by the sheriff to appoint whatever deputies they choose. [Men were] forced to work there at the point of a gun by men armed with blackjacks.[69]

The experience in the Westmoreland County coal area was somewhat different. Although the coal miners were

315

unaffiliated with a union, the United Mine Workers of America was anxious to bring these workers into its ranks. As soon as the strike began, trouble arose with police officers. "Conflicts between peace officers and the strikers," noted a congressional committee:

were numerous during the strike; in fact, were a matter of daily occurrence. Most of the police officers were deputy sheriffs or constables and many of both classes came from other counties and other states. The coal companies hired them and boarded them. . . . The deputies and constables paraded the highways and in many cases, it is claimed, treated the strikers with undue severity. They were armed with pistols and clubs or blackjacks and many of them were mounted. Many strikers were attacked by the deputies or constables on the road and when parties of strikers were met, the mounted officers often dispersed them by beating them or riding them down . . . . Many strikers were severely beaten by the deputies and constables, even when they were not near the mines or mine villages.[70]

The committee observed that the deputies and constables were not well disciplined and that they acted with needless brutality. Six strikers and sympathizers were killed, and two strikebreakers and a deputy sheriff also perished.

The third unorganized strike, at the steel mill of the Bethlehem Steel Co. at South Bethlehem, Pa., followed the dismissal of a committee protesting the discharge of a machinist for evading Sunday work. It was, at first, an unorganized walkout, but the metal and building trades organized a majority of those who had left their jobs. On February 26, 1910, the State constabulary arrived, and on their way to the office of the company, the constabulary "assaulted a number of people standing peaceably on the street . . . and they shot down an innocent man . . . who was standing in the Majestic Hotel when one of the troopers rode up to the pavement at the hotel door and fired two shots into the barroom." To pleas for recognition of the union, President Charles M. Schwab said: "It must be understood that under no circumstances will we deal with men on strike or a body of men representing organized labor."[71] All three of the strikes failed.

7. Special Police

In Pennsylvania, every railroad in 1865 and every colliery, iron furnace, or rolling mill in 1866 was granted by statute liberty to employ as many policemen as it saw fit, from such persons as would obey its behests, and they were clothed with all authority of Pennsylvania, were paid such wages and armed with such weapons as the corporation determined—usually revolvers, sometimes Winchester rifles or both—and they were commissioned by the governor.[72]

Appointments under the Coal and Iron Police Act were made without difficulty. Corporations would file requests, and as a rule no investigation of the need for such appointments or restrictions on the behavior of those selected were made. In 1871 a fee of $1 was charged for each commission issued. From then until 1931, when the coal and iron police were abolished, the mining companies of Pennsylvania were able to utilize police under their own control in labor disputes. "There was no investigation, no regulation, no supervision, no responsibility undertaken by the State, which had literally created 'islands' of police power which was free to float as the employers saw fit."[73] The Pennsylvania system was not duplicated elsewhere. In its stead, in other States sheriffs, and other local officials were authorized to appoint persons paid by the employer for strike and other private police duty.

On numerous occasions mercenaries were guilty of serious assaults upon the person and rights of strikers, and their provocative behavior was frequently an incitement to violence and disorder. Their presence, when added to the special deputies and company policemen and guards, increased substantially the possibility of sanguinary confrontations in strike areas.[74] Furthermore, the availability of private police figured in many events which have been ignored in American labor history. These would include the expulsion of organizers from a county, the forceful denial to union organizers of the opportunity to speak in company towns, and the physical coercion of individual employees because of their union affiliation or sympathies.

8. Use of Troops Under Peaceful Conditions

As we have seen, outbreaks of labor violence frequently required the intervention of State troops, whose activities in restoring order usually resulted in defeating the strike. This lesson was not lost to some employers who, with the connivance of local public officials, secured military aid in situations where violence was absent or insignificant.

During the general strike of silk workers in Paterson, N.J., in 1902, it was claimed that the mills faced an attack by a mob. At the request of the sheriff, troops were sent to the city on June 19. They found no disorder, and left after 9 days.[75]

A more flagrant instance of misrepresentation took place in the Goldfield, Nev., dispute between the Industrial Workers of the World (IWW) and the craft unions. Trouble started when the IWW announced that members of the carpenter's union would have to join the IWW by March 7 "or be thrown off the job and run out of town. The carpenters did not submit their applications, but did carry guns to work on the morning of March 7. The IWW in the face of this armed opposition was to call off all the helpers from the jobs where A.F. of L. men were employed."[76] Tension increased, and at the request of the Governor, President Theodore Roosevelt sent Federal troops to Goldfield. The President also appointed a commission to investigate the disturbance. It said:

The action of the mine operators warrants the belief that they had determined upon a reduction in wages and the refusal of employment to members of the Western Federation of Miners, but that they feared to take this course of action unless they had the protection of Federal troops and that they accordingly laid a plan to secure such troops and then put their program into effect."[77] The commission found no basis for the statement that "there was a complete collapse of civil authority here." [78]
[On the] question of deportation, the evidence sustains at the very maximum probably 25 cases in the last two years. Last March an acute labor dispute existed, lasting some weeks, in which the city was practically an armed camp . . . the best evidence indicates the number with arms is no greater than commonly found in mining camps. Representatives of trades in American Federation of Labor here all agree that practically no members of their crafts have felt any occasion to carry arms since the acute conditions of last March. Our investigation so far has completely failed to sustain the general and sweeping allegations in the governor calling for troops, and the impression as to conditions here given in that call is misleading and without warrant.[79]

The same course of events took place in two other widely separate cases. In a strike at the National Fireproofing plant at Raritan, N. J., troops were sent during a strike in November 1908. Although no violent incident or threats had been made, the sheriff asked the Governor to send troops. His request was met, but they stayed only a few days. It may be that the sheriff feared that violence would follow, since the strikers were mostly Poles, Hungarians, and other Southern Europeans.[80] At almost the same time, State troops were summoned to a tunnel job in McCloud, Calif. The sheriff had informed the Governor that strikers had taken over the "powder house, undoubtedly for use as bombs or like service." The sheriff claimed the strikers threatened to kill anyone who went to work. Troops were sent and they helped the sheriff arrest the leaders of the strike. When this was accomplished, the troops left.[81]

9. Campaigns of Violence by Unions

Despite explicit repudiation of force as an accepted tactic, a number of unions pursued systematic campaigns against opponents. These campaigns were directed against workers who refused to join a given labor organization, against employers, or both. One such campaign was carried on by the Western Federation of Miners against mine managers, company agents, and public officials. Harry Orchard, a member of the federation, confessed to the commission of many crimes, including the murder of Governor Frank Steunenberg of Idaho on December 30, 1905, at the alleged orders of the chief union officers.

The outstanding example of a campaign of force is the one conducted by the International Association of Bridge Structural Iron Workers in the first decade of the century against some employers. When the National Erectors' Association decided in 1906 that it would no longer continue its agreement with the union, the latter turned to terror and dynamite. In the first few years of the open-shop fight, about 100 nonunion ironworkers and company guards were assaulted, three guards being killed. Between 1906 and 1911, about 100 structures were damaged or destroyed by charges of explosives.[82] Luke Grant, who studied this episode for the Commission of Industrial Relations, concluded "that the dynamite campaign was ineffective as far as it was directed against the National Erectors' Association and that it weakened the influence of the organization with some independent employers." Others believed that the campaign kept the small contractors in line.[83] Moreover, Grant was convinced that the dynamiting campaign did the union a great deal of harm. "It stirred the public mind as few labor wars have done."[84] The "main reason for the resort to dynamite is found in the uncompromising attitude of the open-shop employers. The American Bridge Co. offered to compromise in the early stages of the fight and the union representatives rejected the terms of the compromise." After that the attitude of the employers was unyielding. Every effort on the union side to bring about a conference, after it realized the mistake that had been made, proved unavailing.

Without a conference, no settlement of the strike was possible. For the union it meant either unconditional surrender or a fight to the finish. There was no middle course open while the employers refused to confer. . . . When the hopelessness of the situation became apparent to the union officials, resort was made to the destruction of property. Diplomacy was out of the question, so dynamite was tried. It proved to be a colossal blunder, as was the rejection of the peace terms offered in the beginning of the fight.[85]

Elements within the Molders' Union also carried on aggressive attacks against employees, guards, and members of the National Founders Association in 1904. The union and the association had negotiated past agreements, but differences over apprentice ratios, piecework, and efficiency resulted in a break in relations in 1904. A series of strikes took place throughout the country and lasted from 1904 to 1907. The employers operated across picket lines nearly everywhere and the union response was predictable. According to the National Founders Association, violence occurred in Utica, Cincinnati, Philadelphia, Glassport, Pa., Trenton, Milwaukee, Columbus, Chicago, Buffalo, Kansas City, St. Paul, Minneapolis, Iola, Kansas, Detroit, Seattle, Rutland, Paterson, and Meadville, Pa.[86] In these series of episodes, 400 affidavits of alleged union violence were obtained, 34 injunctions restraining violence were issued by state courts, and 32 contempt convictions of these orders were obtained. The most serious trouble took place in Milwaukee, where there were 22 contempt citations and 5 separate assault incidents. Two strikebreakers were killed in the course of the dispute.

INDUSTRIAL VIOLENCE 1911-16

These 6 years rank among the most violent in American history, except for the Civil War. Although the origins of violent encounters were not different from those in the past, they frequently attained a virulence seldom equaled in industrial warfare in any nation. This was as true of many small disputes as it was of the major confrontations in Michigan copper and the West Virginia and Colorado coalfields.

1. The Illinois Central Shopmen's Strike

This strike differed from others in which serious violence took place in that union recognition was not the cause of the conflict. Single crafts had been recognized by this carrier for a number of years, but the carrier refused to negotiate a common contract with the system federation, a central body of several crafts. Following the establishment of the Railway Employees Department, the Illinois Central Railroad was requested, in June 1911, to deal jointly instead of singly with the Machinists', Steam Fitters', Railway Clerks', Blacksmiths', Boilermakers', and Sheet Metal Workers' Unions. The carrier refused, and a strike was called on the entire line of the Illinois Central. The railroad decided to replace the strikers. Violence was reported all along the right of way of the carrier. In Mississippi, one of the more important areas served by the Illinois Central, violence erupted at a number of points. When a train carrying strikebreakers arrived at McComb on October 3, 1911, it was met by about 250 armed men who opened fire on the new arrivals. Ten men were killed, cars were burned, and strikebreakers were afterward removed from the strike zone by militia called in by the Governor. Demonstrations against those working were also carried on. On January 17, 1912, five Negro laborers employed as helpers at McComb were fired upon while returning from work; three were killed, the others wounded. Strikebreakers were temporarily escorted out of the strike zone.[87] The shops at Water Valley, Miss., were attacked and the Governor ordered troops to that community on October 6, 1911. Serious violence was reported in New Orleans and a company guard was killed at Athens, Tex., and a guard and strikebreaker at the Illinois Central roundhouse at Houston, Tex. In Clinton, Ill., Carl Person, a leader of the strike, killed a strikebreaker who had brutally assaulted him. Person was tried for murder and acquitted on the ground of self-defense.[88] Despite the strike's formal continuance until June 28, 1915, it was in effect lost within several months after its start.

2. Five IWW Strikes

Despite its temporary advocacy of direct action and sabotage, the strikes of the IWW were not particularly violent. In 1912-13, the IWW led two textile strikes in the East, and an affiliate, the Brotherhood of Timber Workers, operating in Louisiana, struck for improved wages and in working conditions in the Louisiana timber area. An exchange of gunfire between pickets and guards before the Gallaway Lumber Co. at Grabow, La., resulted in the killing of three union men and a company guard. A score of others were wounded. Several companies of troops were sent into the area and remained 3 days. A clash between strikers and strikebreakers at Merryville, on November 14, brought State troops into the area. The trouble ceased with their arrival, and the business community was anxious that the troops remain. More than 1,000 men were on strike, and "the people in the area were mostly in sympathy with the strike."[89] It was, however, insufficient to help the strikers win. Several of the leaders were indicted for murder, but they were later acquitted.

The textile strike in Lawrence, Mass., including more than 25,000 workers, was the most important IWW-led strike and made a deep impression on contemporary observers.[90] Refusal of employers to offset the loss of wages that followed the reduction of hours required for women workers by a recently enacted law was the cause of the walkout on January 11, 1912. As the workers belonged to no union, they invited the general organizer of the IWW, Joseph Ettor, to aid them. He succeeded in having specific demands formulated and presented to each employer of the strikers. Troops were sent into the city, and their number was increased as the strike continued. At the same time, the Governor of Massachusetts sought to have the State board of arbitration settle the dispute. The strikers were willing, but the American Woolen Co., the largest employer, refused to participate. A number of clashes between pickets and the militia took place, and in one a woman was killed. The strike continued until March 12, and was ended by the offer of a wage increase. Although the strike was a victory for the textile workers, the IWW was unable to gain a permanent foothold in Lawrence or in the textile industry. While arrests are not necessarily a measure of strike violence, it is interesting that in Lawrence during the strike, more than 350 arrests were made. Several were sentenced to 2 years in prison; 24 to 1 year; and 22 were fined.

The third strike of the IWW, one which was almost equal to Lawrence in the public attention it attracted, took place in the silk mills of Paterson, N.J. The IWW capitalized on dissatisfaction which other organizations were unable to use to their advantage. A strike called against one of the large mills on February, 1, 1913, was later expanded to embrace all the silk mills and dye works. Mass arrests of pickets began quietly, early in the walkout, and the attorney for the IWW claimed that innocent strikers had been arrested. Many private detectives were employed by the firms on strike, and on April 18, a bystander was killed when between 16 and 20 shots were fired at pickets. There was considerable violence, much of it due to the behavior of the private guards and detectives hired by employers. The strike ended without victory after 22 weeks. During its course, 2,338 had been arrested, 300 held for the grand jury, and more than 100 sentenced to prison.[91]

While the IWW strikes in the East represented forays into geographical areas where the union had few members, the strike in the Wheatland, Calif., hop fields took place in the union's natural habitat. The workers in this strike were typical of the IWW membership. The strike began on August 13, 1913, as a spontaneous protest against the miserable conditions at the Durst brothers' ranch, where several thousand pickers had assembled awaiting the beginning of the season. Through extensive advertising, several thousand pickers had been attracted to the ranch in search of employment. Even by the standards prevailing in migrant-worker camps, living conditions were very bad there. Inadequate toilet facilities, charges for drinking water, absence of housing for many hundreds, and the low sanitary state of the campsite caused sufficient dissatisfaction that the migrants elected a negotiating committee. Richard Ford and Herman Suhr, members of the IWW, were on the committee. Demands for improvements in sanitation and an increase in the price of picking were made, and the committee, headed by Ford and Suhr, met with one of the Durst brothers. Durst flicked his glove across Ford's face and rejected the demands. The resident constable then tried to arrest Ford. When a warrant was insisted upon, the constable left and returned with the district attorney of the county and several deputy sheriffs. An attempt to arrest Ford led to an argument which ended in general shooting. The district attorney, a deputy sheriff, and two hop pickers were killed. The next day the militia arrived, but quiet had already been restored.[92] Ford and Suhr and two others were tried for murder, and the first two were convicted and sentenced to prison. The affair ended without improvements, although it stimulated a legislative investigation.

The IWW leadership of the spontaneous strike on the Mesabi iron range in Minnesota was by invitation, in that many of the strikers had been brought into the area in 1906 to replace predecessors who were then on strike against the same employers. Ten years later, in June 1916, the miners were sufficiently dissatisfied to go on strike. Early in July, a group of deputy sheriffs invaded a boardinghouse and tried to arrest one of the strikers. A fight started; a deputy and a passerby were killed and a striker wounded by gunfire. In the meantime, the U.S. Steel Corp., the major employer, would make no concessions nor meet with a strike committee. Eventually the strikers returned to work, having gained nothing. Three leaders of the walkout and several strikers were arrested and charged with murder. The IWW leaders were released and left the range, and several of the strikers were convicted and given prison terms.

Although IWW strikes were not unusually violent, the reputation of the IWW made its members an easy target for repressive action by the authorities, but the harsh treatment accorded to strikers was unrelated to the organization to which they belonged. Prof. Henry F. Grady, commenting on the killing of two pickets in the 1916 San Francisco longshoremen's strike, said that "neither of these murders were provoked. When the gunmen were brought to trial, Chamber of Commerce lawyers were there to defend them. The labor man sees no essential difference between the violence he may use to protect his right to work and the conditions which he claims fair, and the violence of an armed guard who is paid to oppose him."[93] The strike was the result of the violation of contract by the longshoremen's union. The action was denounced by U.S. Secretary of Labor William B. Wilson. The strike had serious repercussions for it served as a pretext for the launching of the open-shop campaign in San Francisco. In the defense of acts of terror against pickets, the open-shop forces claimed that 38 nonunion men had been assaulted and only six union men had suffered similar experiences.[94]

3. The Application of Public Force in Coal Disputes

(a) Strikes in which militia intervened.—The appearance of State troops in a community during a labor dispute was generally, although not always, the result of threats of overt violence. In nearly all cases troops acted as a screen behind which it was easier to operate a struck plant. Furthermore, the presence of troops was likely to overawe if not intimidate strikers and their sympathizers. In 1911 State troops were ordered to Jacksonville, Fla., to prevent violence. They remained in the city from October 30 to November 21.[95] During 1912 and 1913, the militia in New York was asked to intervene in three labor disputes. In April 1912, several companies were sent to Oneida, N.Y., during a textile strike in that city. They remained there for 13 days. In the following year, the troops were sent to Auburn while a textile strike was going on. In requesting troops, the local authorities claimed that "great disorder in the city and some shooting by the disorderly element . . . necessitated the calling out of troops. After their arrival, order was promptly restored."[96]

During a strike for union recognition, which the management of the Buffalo, N.Y., streetcar company refused to grant, strikebreakers and guards were brought to the city. Widespread rioting accompanied the protests against these imports. Troops were dispatched at the order of a county judge under a statute which made the county liable for the costs of bringing and maintaining the troops.[97]

In a strike in 1912 at the Consolidated Mining Co. in Ely, Nev., strikebreakers were imported and picketing violence developed.[98] Two men were killed and two were wounded. Soon thereafter, Governor Taskie L. Odie declared martial law in the Robinson mining district, and directed the Nevada State Police superintendent to use his entire force to restore order. No further violence followed.

A strike of unorganized steelworkers for a wage increase started at the East Youngstown, Ohio, plant of the Youngstown Sheet Tube Co. on January 5, 1916. Three days later a group of pickets was ordered to get off company property. They began to throw rocks at the guards who were herding them off the company property. The guards fired into the crowd, killing two and wounding 23 others. The riot spread, and arson and looting followed. A hastily organized posse restored order, and the militia arrived on January 6. The strike ended with a compromise wage settlement.[99]

The attempt of the transit company in Indianapolis, Ind., to operate its streetcars during a strike with out-of-town strikebreakers led to a riot on November 2, 1913, in which a strikebreaker was killed.[100] The Governor ordered 2,000 State troops into the city and their "mobilization caused a cessation of rioting and destruction of life and property and the Guardsmen were not actually used to quell the riots."[101] Both sides agreed to arbitration.

(b) Local police action.—Many violent incidents occurred in disputes in which the militia was not called. Clashes involving police officers or private guards were frequently destructive of life and property. During a parade of several hundred strikers on April 4, 1913, from Harmon, N.Y., to Mamaroneck, the police ordered the parade to disperse because they had no permit. A scuffle followed in which a marcher was killed and a guard seriously hurt.[102] In a textile strike at Ipswich, Mass., the local police sought to disperse a picket line at a struck textile plant. When the strikers resisted, the police fired into the crowd, killing one woman striker and wounding seven others.[103] When the unorganized workers in Rankin, Pa., in the plant of the American Steel & Wire Co. went on strike and set up a picket line, a group of deputy sheriffs fired into the picket line, killing one and wounding a number of others. The strike lasted 5 days, and the men returned on the company's terms.[104] In the strike of the Empire Steel Co. at Mount Hope, N.J., an attack by armed strikers upon guards sworn in as deputy sheriffs led to the wounding of six of the guards, who left soon thereafter.[105]

In most of the reported cases, guards rather than strikers were likely to be the aggressors. During a strike at the Metuchen, N.J., plant of the American Agricultural Co., a body of strikers met an incoming train to discover if any strikebreakers had arrived. When someone announced "No scabs had come," a number of guards ran toward the men and fired several rounds into their midst. Five were killed and many wounded. According to the "attending physicians, all the strikers' wounds were on the backs or legs which seems to indicate the deputies were on the aggressive." Twenty-two of the guards were arrested and nine subsequently convicted for manslaughter.[106]

A similar role was played by company guards during the strike of oil refinery workers in June 1915 at Bayonne, N.J. The strike began with the still cleaners employed by the Standard Oil Co. of New Jersey, and spread to employees of the Vacuum Oil Co. and the Tidewater Oil Co. On June 21, 1915, trouble started in front of the Standard Oil plant, and "guards were accused of 'sniping' from behind piles of lumber at different times."[107] Before the battle ended, six had been killed and a number wounded. After the shooting, Sheriff E. F. Kincaid intervened and announced he did not "like the methods of wealth in employing gunmen and toughs to shoot defenseless men and women, any more than I like the methods of strikers destroying property."[108] The sheriff arrested 129 guards, 10 of whom were held for the grand jury. He denounced the leaders of the strike, struck and arrested one of the volunteer organizers, and received assurance of a wage increase from the company.[109]

The sheriff's settlement was effective only for 1 year. On October 10, 1916, another spontaneous strike began at the plant of the Standard Oil Co. On the same day, four policemen and two strikebreakers were wounded by gunfire. The next day an angry mob of strikers surrounded the police station. On October 12, police and deputy sheriffs swept the Constable hill section where many of the strikers lived. Many were clubbed, shot, or herded into their homes; the police wrecked saloons in the strikers' neighborhood which remained open against orders to close. Four persons died from wounds. The strikers remained out for 2 weeks, and returned without the wage increase, the main demand of the strike.[110]

Violence was not limited to the eastern part of the country, although it appears to have been concentrated in that region during this period. However, among other bloody affairs, two pickets during a lead miners' strike in Flat River, Mo., were shot by deputy sheriffs.

4. Three Major Labor Wars

(a) *The Michigan copper strike.*—The strike in the Michigan copper district followed the refusal of the operators to confer with committees of the Western Federation of Miners; they would not even acknowledge a letter. As a result a strike was called on June 22, 1913. Clashes began almost simultaneously with the strike, and at the request of the sheriff of Houghton County, troops were sent by the Governor. Over 1,700 imported and local special deputy sheriffs were also appointed. By the middle of July two strikers were killed. A much greater tragedy took place at the Christmas party given to strikers' children in Calumet. Hundreds of children and parents attended, and when the hall was filled, an unknown voice yelled "fire." Panic broke out causing the loss of 72 lives, mostly children. Because Charles H. Moyer, the president of the Western Federation of Miners, rejected an offer of $25,000 for relief of the stricken families, offered by the Citizen's Alliance, he was assaulted and dragged through the streets of Hancock, where he was staying. Moyer was brought before James McNaughton, the president of Calumet & Hecla Copper Co., who slapped Moyer's face and threatened to have him hanged if he returned to the Michigan copper district. Moyer returned and was not molested. The strike, however, was not going well. The companies made a number of concessions and promised not to discriminate against strikers if they had not been guilty of lawlessness. The strike ended without union recognition.[111]

(b) *West Virginia.*—The West Virginia and Colorado coal strikers were fought with an unrelenting fury that shocked the conscience of the country. Since 1897 the United Mine Workers of America had held contracts for the majority of bituminous coal miners, but union efforts to organize the expanding West Virginia mines failed a number of times after the beginning of the central competitive field agreement in 1898. Conscious that the failure to organize West Virginia constituted a serious threat to the union-held fields, the union sought greater recognition in the Paint Creek district, and a wage increase. Rejection by the operators led to a strike on April 20, 1912. Later the miners in the Cabin Creek district joined the walkout.

Guards provided by the Baldwin-Felts detective agency entered the area in large numbers and began evicting strikers from company-owned houses. On June 5, the first miner was killed, and nine guards were indicted for murder. Miners and Baldwin-Felts guards fought a pitched battle at Mucklow, on July 26, in which 12 men, mostly guards, were killed. The Governor sent several companies of militia into the strike area, and arrests of strikers began. The military force was withdrawn at the end of 30 days, but with an increase in violence, it was reimposed on October 12. A military court was established which tried and sentenced strikers. Complaints by miners against the behavior of company guards led to the appointment of a citizens' commission by the Governor. It reported that company guards had been guilty of "denials of the right of peaceable assembly, free speech, many and grievous assaults on unarmed miners, and that their main purpose was to overawe the miners and their adherents, and if necessary beat and cudgel them into submission."[112] The commission also charged that the miners were not entirely innocent and it held that their efforts to bring the West Virginia area under union control was an important cause of the troubles.

The mines were reopened in September with the assistance of imported workmen. Sporadic violence continued, with the tent colonies housing the dispossessed miners as a target. On February 7, 1913, an armored Chesapeake Ohio train, the "Bull Moose Special," attacked the tent colony in Holly Grove and poured more than 200 shots into the village. Quinn Morton, the general manager of the Imperial Co. who was in charge of the train, was accused of saying: "We will go back and give them another round." When testifying before a committee of the U.S. Senate, Morton was asked if he, "a cultured gentleman, approves the use of a machine gun on a populous village." In retaliation, an armed contingent of miners moved towards Mucklow, and fought a battle with guards in which 12 miners and 4 guards were killed. Martial law was then declared for the third time. The U.S. Senate committee criticized the denial of the rights of the miners, but it held the union was not blameless for the tragedy in the coalfields. A new Governor was elected in 1912, and in April

1913 he proposed a compromise, which the union hesitantly accepted. A few concessions were made, but the union was not recognized and soon dispersed.

(c) *War in Colorado.*—The Colorado coal industry was virtually nonunion. A number of efforts to establish collective-bargaining relations had been made, but all failed. In 1913 the United Mine Workers of America tried again, and Frank J. Hayes, vice president of the union, came to Colorado and enlisted the aid of Governor Elias Ammons towards obtaining a conference with the mine operators. The Governor tried and failed. Further efforts to gain a conference were made by the union, and when they did not succeed a strike was called on September 25, 1913. An estimated 8,000 to 10,000 miners left their jobs, and they and their families left their company-owned houses for the tent colonies which the union rented. In the meantime the companies had been preparing for the strike. "Spies, camp marshals and armed guards infested the mining camps and the city of Trinidad. In Huerfano County alone, 326 men, many imported from other states, had been commissioned as deputy sheriffs."[113]

Before the strike, a union organizer had been shot by a detective employed by the Colorado Fuel Iron Co. A marshal employed by the same company was killed on September 24. On October 7, 1913, after an exchange of shots between strikers and guards, the latter attacked the tent colony at Ludlow and killed a miner. On October 17, a party of mine guards attacked the tent colony at Forbes, killing a miner and wounding a young boy. Three strikers were shot and killed and one was wounded at Walsenberg several days later when a group of guards fired into a striker's meeting. On the following day, a battle was fought between armed miners and a contingent of guards at Berwind Canyon, which ended with the killing of a guard. Another battle between strikers and guards was fought there without reported casualties. An armored train, the "death special," was outfitted and while on the way to Ludlow, it was shot up by armed miners who killed the engineer. The train was forced back. On October 27 strikers attacked a building sheltering guards at Forbes Junction.

While the fighting was going on, Governor Ammons was trying to bring about a settlement. Failing in the attempt, he sent the entire National Guard to the strike zone.

Their arrival was not opposed by the strikers, who felt that troops would behave better than company guards. The Governor, while directing that protection be accorded to property and those who wished to work, advised against the use of troops in assisting in the importation of strike-breakers. More than 2,000 guns of strikers were turned in at the request of the commanding general. Others were, however, kept in reserve. Great pressures were exercised on the Governor for stronger measures against the strikers and he capitulated by allowing Gen. John C. Chase, the head of the militia, to carry out a policy of repression.

Chase had been the commander in the metalliferous miners' strike in 1903-04, and his union animosity was well known. Militiamen began harassing strikers, many of whom were arrested and detained for long periods of time. At the request of the State federation of labor, the Governor appointed an investigating committee, which found that militia men had abused strikers and their wives and daughters. It reported that many of the guards had been allowed to join the National Guard, replacing regular members who were anxious to return to their homes and occupations. These men hated the strikers, and were not averse to assaulting and even killing them. The committee requested the removal of Chase as partial to the mine owners, and charged that many militiamen were guards on the payroll of the mine owners, and that the entire contingent had shown consistent bias in favor of the employers.

During February and March of 1914 there were few clashes, but it was believed that the presence of a congressional investigating committee in the State had a moderating influence on behavior. Most of the Guard was accordingly withdrawn, but a troop of 35 men was left at Ludlow and Berwind Canyon. This was a tough group, made up mostly of company guards and professional adventurers, whose commander was a Lt. K. E. Linderfelt, whose animosity to the strikers was well known. On April 20 the Ludlow tent colony was attacked by the soldiers under Linderfelt and five men and a boy were killed by rifle and machinegun fire. The militiamen then fired the tents, and 11 children and two women were smothered. The tents were stripped of all portable things of value. Hundreds of women were driven from this colony of 1,200 people to seek shelter in the ranches and homes of the area. Three prisoners, including Louis Tikas, the Greek leader of the strike, were shot by the troops, ostensibly while trying to escape. The militiamen had one fatality.

Two days later, the Colorado labor movement notified President Woodrow Wilson that it had called on the workers of the State to arm themselves and to "organize the men in your communities in companies of volunteers to protect the workers of Colorado." The call was signed by the heads of the State federation of labor and the miners' union. A "military camp of strikers was established. . . . Inflamed by what they considered the wanton slaughter of their women, children and comrades, the miners attacked mine after mine, driving off or killing the guards and setting fire to the buildings."[114] In one action, 200 armed strikers left their base near Trinidad and attacked the mining camp at Forbes. Burning buildings, they poured deadly fire into the camp, killing nine guards and one strikebreaker; the strikers lost one man. Twenty-four hours later, Federal troops arrived, and the fighting ended. "During the ten days of fighting, at least fifty persons had lost their lives, including twenty-one killed at Ludlow."[115] The Ludlow war ended with a total of 74 dead.

Despite the bloodshed, no recognition of the union was granted. Efforts of President Wilson to achieve permanent peace were in vain. A large number of miners, including John R. Lawson, the head of the miner's union in Colorado, were indicted. The latter was convicted of murder, but the verdict was overturned by the Colorado Supreme Court. The Ludlow war, one of the more tragic episodes in labor's history, failed to dissolve the adamantine opposition to unionism, which had become a fixed and immovable article of faith among many of the great industries of the United States.[116]

VIOLENCE IN LABOR DISPUTES DURING AND AFTER WORLD WAR I (1917-22)

Strike statistics, which were published by the Commissioner of Labor beginning with the year 1881, ceased to appear in 1905, and were resumed by the U.S. Bureau of Labor Statistics in 1915. The number of strikes between 1917 and 1922 was high compared with the following decade. The influence of wartime demand for labor, the dislocations which accompany wartime economic activity, the sharp rise in union membership, and reduced unemployment all exercised an influence on the potential for labor violence. Strikes tended to be shorter during wartime, but with the ending of hostilities the country experienced severe tension in the labor market. Several factors accounted for heightened labor discontent. Union membership rose sharply between 1916 and 1920, from 2,772,000 to 4,881,000. Considerable dissatisfaction existed as a result of rises in the cost of living during wartime and the general malaise that war normally generates. Many employers who had accepted union organization as a wartime necessity or as a result of government fiat were now anxious to rid themselves of labor organizations. This is evident from the power of the campaign by antiunion employers who espoused the American Plan of Employment, a program designed to support employers opposing the presence of unions in industry. The large accretion of union members also brought demands for changes in union policy and for the use of more aggressive tactics in labor disputes.

1. Lynching of Frank Little

Despite the growth of strikes, the levels of violence during World War I were low, and the violence was mainly directed against strikers. In Butte, Mont., during the 1917 copper strike, the room of Frank Little, a member of the general executive board of the IWW, was invaded by a group of masked men. He was seized and hanged on a trestle. The strike itself had been called for improvement in the terms of employment and for the abolition of the "rustling card," a notice allowing the holder to seek employment in the mines which aided in the enforcement of a blacklist against union members. The Governor requested troops, and Federal soldiers arrived in Butte on September 10, 1917. The troops remained until December 18, 1917, and were returned to Butte on February 7, 1919, during a strike against a wage reduction led by the IWW. They departed 10 days later. The third appearance of Federal troops was during the miner's strike of April 1920. They remained in the city until January 1921.[117]

333

2. The Arizona Deportations

During World War I, strikes in most of the Arizona copper mines were called by the Industrial Workers of the World, or the International Union of Mine, Mill & Smelter Workers, an affiliate of the American Federation of Labor. A common response of employers was to deport the strike leaders and their followers. On July 10, for example, a Loyalty League, which had been organized by businessmen and mining officials in Jerome, deported 76 "offensive radicals."[118]

The Jerome deportation was carried on by only a small number of businessmen. However, virtually the entire business and mining employer community participated in the deportations of 1,284 men from Bisbee, Ariz., on July 12, 1917. Great discontent with wages and working conditions existed in the Arizona copper county during 1917 and 1918. In addition, the IWW and Mine & Smelter Workers were competing for members among the miners. The latter had originally organized a large number of workers in the Warren district, of which Bisbee was the most important community. It had, however, lost its place to Metal Mine Workers Industrial Union No. 800, an IWW affiliate. A set of demands was drawn up and presented to the companies in the area. They refused to confer with the IWW committee and a strike was called for June 26.[119]

A large proportion of the miners in the Bisbee area responded to the strike call. Testimony showed that there was no violence. In fact, some witnesses claimed that petty crime had diminished because the IWW had told the bootleggers not to carry on their activities during the strike. Nevertheless, a Loyalty League was organized, and several mine managers suggested that the strikers and their sympathizers be deported from the city. The cooperation of Sheriff Harry Wheeler was obtained. On the morning of July 12 the streets of Bisbee were filled with men wearing white handkerchiefs on their sleeves. They had been deputized by Sheriff Wheeler. Men on the street were stopped and their business ascertained. Those unable to give satisfactory explanations were seized and taken to the local ball park which served as the assembly point for "undesirables." Homes of known strikers and sympathizers, including some lawyers, tradesmen, business men, and property owners, were visited and many were taken into custody. A deputy seeking to arrest a member of the IWW was killed, and his assailant slain by a fellow deputy. This was the only violent incident in the rounding up of 1,284 men.

After 2 hours in the ball park under a hot Arizona sun, the prisoners were compelled to march between two lines of armed men and to board a cattle train which the railroad provided. According to Fred W. Brown, a voluntary organizer of the American Federation of Labor, the tracks along the first stop of the train were "lined with gunmen" who had left Bisbee and had overtaken the train. Mounted guns stood on both sides of the track and no one was allowed to leave. The train arrived in Columbus, stayed for an hour, and left for Hermanes, where the men were dumped. On the morning of July 14, a company of U.S. soldiers arrived and brought the deportees back to Columbus, where they were provided with food and shelter by the U.S. Government. After 8 days, they were allowed to leave. A majority stayed until September; food was cut off on September 12.

During the deportation, no messages were allowed to leave Bisbee. The sheriff then established a screening committee, a "kangaroo court," before which the deportees and others seeking to enter Bisbee had to appear. Many of those who came to seek work or reclaim their clothes and other personal possessions were forced to leave the community, even when they owned property. The President's Mediation Commission, during its inquiry in Arizona, was told by Sheriff Wheeler that he had heard from a chambermaid and others that there was "a plan on foot when they [the strikers] go down in the mines to get their clothing . . . that they were to block those tunnels and keep the men down at work in the mines. I am told these things; I cannot swear to them."[120] U.S. Secretary of Labor William B. Wilson, who was chairman of the commission, made his feelings known by asking:

And on the strength of rumors of that kind you directed the picking up of twelve hundred people here, some only for a brief period and some, as we are informed, here for a long time, and under the authority to use whatever power is necessary you undertook to use that power not only within your own bailiwick, but outside your own bailiwick . . . where you had no authority and where you were not authorized or directed to use power.[121]

In a message to the Legislature, Governor George P. Hunt denounced the—

mob of nearly two thousand men directed by county authorities . . . [who] under cover of darkness, calmly, premeditatedly, deliberately, swooped down at dawn upon the homes of unsuspecting, unoffending miners who committed no violence, nay more who had threatened no violence but who had every lawful reason to feel secure as citizens under the guarantees vouchsafed by the Constitution of the United States of America.[122]

Sheriff Wheeler and 21 leading businessmen were indicted for violating the rights of the deportees by a Federal grand jury. The indictment was invalidated by the U.S. circuit court, and the decision was upheld in *United States v. Wheeler*. An indictment by the State for illegal kidnaping was obtained against 224 leading businessmen, Sheriff Wheeler, and many deputies and police officers. One case was tried, and the verdict of acquittal after several weeks of trial led to the dismissal of the charges against the other defendants. President Wilson and the President's Mediation Commission sharply criticized the conduct of the mob guilty of the deportation.[123]

3. The Steel and Coal Strikes

Changes in attitudes were noticeable with the coming of peace. During the war the Government sought to prevent protracted labor disputes, because they inevitably lowered output. Once the war was over, the restraints of the Government in the name of patriotism were no longer effective. Moreover, a large amount of discontent among workers led to an increase in wildcat as well as in authorized strikes. Workers in some industries were trying to fortify bargaining rights that they had gained as a result of Government pressure. Unions had carried on more vigorous organizing drives than before the war, and American Federation of Labor affiliates had sponsored a joint campaign for organizing the open-shop steel industry. The organization campaign was successful in enlisting the support of most steelworkers, but a barrier was posed by the refusal of the U.S. Steel Corp. and the smaller companies in the industry to deal with unions. Elbert Gray, on behalf of his own company and the industry, refused to meet with a committee of union officers claiming to represent employees of his company. Neither the pleas of the President of the United States nor clergymen nor any other force would induce him to recede from his position. Reluctantly a strike was called by the cooperating unions, and it turned out to be one of the more bloody of the period. Meetings were suppressed in many steel communities, union organizers and officers harassed, and behind the protection of police and hired guards the companies reopened their plants and were able to compel the unions to surrender without gaining any concessions. Violence was widespread in steel communities such as Gary, Ind., and State and Federal troops were brought in to restore order. In other towns, troops were not required. Twenty people were killed during the strike, and many more injured.

Coal was the center of some of the bloodiest labor disputes after World War I. The disputes centered around the efforts of the United Mine Workers of America to organize the nonunion counties of McDowell, Mingo, and Logan Counties in West Virginia. In September 1919, armed union miners were set to invade Logan County, but turned back at the request of the Governor and district officers of the union in order to preserve peace. A strike for union recognition was called in Mattewan, Mingo County, in May 1920, and in an argument over evictions of miners from company houses, shooting between Baldwin-Felts guards and Sheriff Sid Hatfield left 10 dead, seven of them guards. The strike spread to McDowell County, which was soon caught up in the developing violence. Troops were sent in by the State, and after the killing of six in a battle between miners and deputies, Federal troops arrived. Federal troops were withdrawn, to be replaced by large numbers of deputies.

In the first months of 1921 it appeared that peace had been restored, but by May each side was arming for renewed warfare. Hundreds of armed miners were determined to march again into Logan County and the sheriff was prepared to prevent their entry. Union officers at first convinced the miners to withdraw and go home, but a report that miners had been ambushed and killed led the miners to re-form their ranks. Several thousand armed miners began a march on Logan County, and the Governor called for Federal aid. President Warren Harding ordered the miners to disperse and sent 2,100 Federal troops to enforce his order. Six hundred miners surrendered to the U.S. Army, and after being disarmed, were released. The arrival of Federal troops ended the miner's war. Several hundred were indicted in State courts for sedition and conspiracy, but juries refused to convict. In all, at least 21 people lost their lives. A Senate committee found that both sides were guilty of acts of violence. The conduct of the union was found "absolutely indefensible. Men have been killed, property had been destroyed, telephone wires cut, trains commandeered and misused, and a march of some thousands of men organized and policies carried out which bordered close on insurrection."[124] The committee criticized the system of "paying sheriffs out of funds contributed by the operators," and the prevention of union members from coming into the area. "There is complete industrial autocracy in this country."[125]

4. The Use of Troops in Labor Disputes

Before World War I armed soldiers were usually employed once labor disputes became seriously disruptive; in the war and postwar period troops often were sent to trouble spots as a precautionary measure. The diversified circumstances in which troops were employed can be examined by viewing the experience of several major industries. For unrecorded reasons, the Governor of Colorado sent troops into two coal communities during 1921 and 1922.[126] Earlier, in 1919 and 1920, the Governor of Alabama had sent the militia into the coal areas during labor troubles; they were there in November 1919 and September 1920.[127]

After the breakdown of an interstate conference with the United Mine Workers in summer of 1922, the coal operators informed the President of the United States that, given adequate protection, they could operate their mines despite a prospective strike. Thereupon the President appealed to the Governors of 28 States to provide adequate policing so that the mines would start producing.

The Governor of Pennsylvania sent more than 1,100 state troops to the strike fields of Western Pennsylvania for guard duty. The Governor of Colorado sent troops to the coal fields of that state. The Governor of Kentucky did likewise. Troops patrolled the highways. They broke up union meetings. They refused to permit

338

miners to stop in the streets and roads to talk to each other. The Governor of Indiana sent 800 troops into Clay and other counties to afford protection while coal was being produced.[128]

The National Guard was also on duty in New Mexico and Utah and at a number of points in other States. The War Department dispatched Federal troops at the request of the Governors to the following States: West Virginia, Pennsylvania, Tennessee, Wyoming, Utah, New Mexico, Oklahoma, Kansas, and Washington.[129]

The bloodiest encounter during the coal strike occurred near Herrin, Ill. One of the operators, the Southern Illinois Coal Co., was allowed to uncover dirt from the overlay on condition that no coal would be shipped. The company had dealt with the union, as did all the operators in the Illinois District No. 12, United Mine Workers of America. The miners employed left their jobs, as did all others in the district, when the union issued a strike call. Later during the strike the company broke relations with the union and began mining coal. The workers whom it had imported were supposed to be members of the Shovelmen's Union. When John L. Lewis was asked about the organization, he replied that it was an "outlaw" organization, meaning it was unaffiliated. William J. Lester, head of the company, in addition to carrying on mining, had imported a number of guards. Three miners who approached the mining operation, presumably for a conference, were killed. Miners in the neighboring town armed themselves, and in the latter part of June sprayed the mining area with gunfire and stormed the stockade. Those who surrendered were beaten and shot to death, including Lester. Twenty-one, three of them strikers, died in this attempt to create a nonunion enclave in District No. 12, which had been completely unionized since 1898.[130]

Apart from Herrin, in which troops were not used, there was little violence associated with the coal strike. This lack of violence was due essentially to the success of miners in shutting down operations completely and the fact that reopening of the mines took place under the protection of State and Federal troops. The inability of the coal operators to resume production despite military protection compelled them to resume bargaining with the United Mine Workers, which led to an agreement.

339

5. Railroad Disputes

A strike on the Missouri & North Arkansas Railroad had begun early in 1921, more than a year before the National Shopmen's strike, and lasted into 1923. On January 16, 1923, a mob congregated at Harrison, Ark., and strikers and their sympathizers were brought before a self-appointed committee of 12. The home of E. C. McGregor, an active strike leader and a member of the Machinist's Union, was invaded. McGregor was seized and lynched. Strikers were driven from their homes and ordered not to return or face death. A legislative committee, investigating the lynching found,

> The testimony in bulk disclosed the undisputed fact that on Monday, January 16, 1923, the citizens along the railroad arose en masse and took the situation in hand. . . . That in carrying out this movement they took charge of persons and entered into private homes without due process of law, and without legal authority, and that in many instances men were ordered or advised to leave, with the single purpose to break the existing strike on the Missouri and North Arkansas Railroad and to guarantee the operations of its trains. We find that the situation in Harrison was in charge of a large body of armed men.[131]

The Shopmen's Unions had greatly expanded as a result of favorable treatment they received from the Government. The return of the railroads to private management after the war led to the establishment of the Railway Labor Board, which authorized several general wage cuts. Rank-and-file pressures forced the unions, against the wishes of some of their leaders, to call a national strike on July 1, 1922, in which 400,000 men participated. The National Guard was sent to a number of points, although there were no reports of violence or intimidation. In Missouri the entire Guard was mobilized, and units were sent "to Franklin, Moberly, Macon, Poplar Bluff, and Chaffee, these being prominent railroad centers."[132] Since no violence was reported, it can only be assumed that the troops were used as either a precautionary device or as an attempt to overawe the strikers. The Kentucky Guard was sent to two localities and soldiers of the Illinois militia were called out at three points in connection with the railroad strike. Three other States—Kansas, Texas, and Idaho—sent troops to two railroad centers within each State. In addition, the entire National Guard of California was mobilized for service in the railroad strike of 1922 "in readiness for possible trouble . . . but were not placed on active duty."[133]

The shopmen's strike did not force the carriers to suspend operations. The operating crafts were not asked to respect the picket line and worked throughout the strike. As a result, the spectacular assaults of the strikes in 1877 and 1894 were absent. Nevertheless, there was a large amount of serious violence during this walkout. In the application for a restraining order, the United States charged that 20 persons had been killed in a number of incidents stretching across the entire country. On July 9, a Negro strikebreaker was killed in Birmingham, Ala. In Arkansas a striker was killed, and two others wounded on August 2. A strikebreaker was killed in Atlanta on August 5. In Illinois a strikebreaker was killed at Joliet and another at Centralia on August 4. Three days later the chief special agent of the Elgin, Joliet & Eastern Railroad was killed and the sheriff was wounded. A Negro strikebreaker was killed at Samesett, Ky., on August 21, and a railroad watchman in Kansas City on July 28. Three shopmen in Cleveland were killed on August 10, and another was stabbed to death in Toledo on July 27. Another fatality connected with the shopmen's strike took place at Willard, Ohio, on July 10. Two Negro strikebreakers employed in the Illinois Central shops were killed near Memphis on July 26. Two others were killed at Hulbert on August 11, and one near Memphis on August 17. A Negro strikebreaker lost his life near Dallas, Tex., on July 15, and in Virginia two more died in connection with the strike, one on the Seaboard Airline near Portsmouth and another at Harrisonburg.[134]

The Government claimed that assaults with deadly weapons upon strikebreakers had taken place in 27 States and that sabotage had been practiced against railroad structures or the right-of-way in 20 States. Specifically, these included the dynamiting of bridges, the wrecking of trains, the derailment of others, the throwing of bombs. These episodes resulted principally in damage to property; a derailment in Worcester, Mass. was an exception, leading to the death of two persons and injury to 30 others.[135]

In a digest of reports from Federal attorneys and marshals, 60 out of 81 Federal districts reported—

increasing trouble and violence until September 1, 1922, and thereafter a decided decrease. Intimidation and picketing practically ceased after the month of September, even in those districts in which the strike was continued . . . seventy-two out of 81 districts reported aggravated acts of intimidation practiced by strikers and sympathizers against all who either remained on the job or sought work.[136]

The acts of intimidation ranged from the use of profanity to—

threats of death and violence not only against the workman but against his wife and children . . . bombing, painting with yellow paint, and the writing of inflammatory words upon the workman's house. The secondary boycott, which forced merchants not to sell to workmen; kidnapping and abductions, followed by tar and feathers or whipping and beatings, which resulted in bleeding backs and broken bones; robberies; forcible withdrawal from work and even from the cities; bombing of roundhouses and trains and throwing of bombs near workmen; firing bridges and the homes of workmen; sending of letters and circulars containing threats, abusive and insulting language; picketing, which included clubbings and beatings whenever there was no officer present . . . terrorism by mobs; persuasion under threat of violence; the nightly shootings by large crowds of men with high-powered rifles into railroad shops in which men were working; forcible entrance into the railroad shops, whereupon they destroyed and damaged engines and railroad property, and dragging the women out, beat them and sent away with instructions never to return.[137]

According to the same reports, there were "at least 13 murders, numerous attempts at murder, numerous shots with deadly weapons, and several deaths due to wrecks which were traceable to the strikers. The number of personal attacks were in the thousands."[138]

The Attorney General stated that there were over 2,000 arrests made in connection with the strike, and punishment ranged from costs to fines of $2,000, and imprisonment from 1 day to 2 years. The majority of fines in the Federal courts were $50, and the average imprisonment was for 30 days.

Very incomplete reports were received relative to State and local prosecutions, but so far over 150 arrests are reported, with fines ranging from costs to $5,000, and imprisonment ranging from one day to seven years; and the major cases involving arson, murder, wreckings and bombings have not been tried. Over 500 convictions in the State Federal courts have been reported.[139]

The Federal Government has appointed 3,259 special deputy marshals; the largest number, 571, in Texas, and the fewest, 2, in Illinois.[140]

The widespread violence did not change the outcome. The leaders were dubious about the success of the strike, and they went along because of pressure from the rank and file. Violence began almost at once because the carriers decided, at the beginning, upon replacing the strikers. The strikers reacted with savage violence in many places, but their acts were unable to reverse the defeat which they faced. The strike failed everywhere. Among the major contributing causes were the unremitting hostility of the Federal Government, which secured sweeping injunctions based upon the Sherman Anti-Trust Act, and the decision of the operating brotherhoods to cross picket lines and run the trains. Before it had ended, 19 persons had been killed, almost all of them strikebreakers, guards, or special railroad watchmen.[141]

6. Soldiers and Local Disputes

Federal troops were sent to Denver, Colo., during the street railway strike of 1920.[142] The Denver streetcar strike was the result of the failure of the city to continue the increase in wages ordered by the War Labor Board. When the Board ordered higher wages to meet the rising cost of living, it suggested that the Public Service Commission allow for a fare increase from 5 to 6 cents. In May 1919, Dewey C. Bailey was elected mayor on a platform that he would rescind the fare increase. When the fare was reduced, the company cut wages. A strike was called, and after 4 days the repeal of the 6-cent fare and the wage cut were rescinded. This was only a temporary pause. In July 1920 the level of the fare and wages were again in dispute, and when the company refused to recede from its plan to reduce wages, the men voted by 887 to 10 to go out on strike. The strike started on August 1, and by August 3 "Black Jack" Jerome led his contingent of guards and strikebreakers into Denver and announced he would break the strike. Some violence had taken place on August 5 and 6, but the most serious event took place on August 7. Streetcars were wrecked, and a large crowd congregated around the carbarn. Firing began from inside the barn, and before the clash had ended, 7 persons had been killed, 4 of them unconnected with the strike, and 81 had been injured, 21 of whom were strikebreakers. Federal troops were brought into the city, and rioting ceased. Use of strikebreakers ceased on September 1. The union lost its bargaining rights.[143]

State troops were continually used during the early 1920's. The Governor of Kansas sent troops to Crawford County in December 1921. In the same month militia were sent by the Governor of Minnesota to South St. Paul, where a strike at the Armour Meat Packing plant was in progress. Strikers were cleared from streets adjacent to the plant. Strikes in the cotton mills in Concord, N.C., led the Governor to send troops, presumably because of threats made by pickets. A strike of paper workers in Vermont led the Governor to send troops to Bellows Falls and Wilder during July 1921.[144] The Chief of the Militia Bureau observed:

Emergency duty in the strike area is the most disagreeable feature of National Guard service. Not only does such duty require a man in the ranks to use arms when necessary, perhaps against his own friends and fellow-workmen, but such duty also imposes actual hardship on the Guardsmen, both in the matter of long absences from his business and in the violence which he is frequently called upon to overcome.[145]

THE PERIOD BETWEEN 1923 AND 1932

Union membership sharply declined between 1920 and 1923, from the high point of 4,881,000 in 1920 to 3,622,000 in 1923. Union activity similarly declined. Even more consequential than the decline in membership was the loss of elan and confidence that overcame the labor organizations as a result of repeated lost strikes. In effect, the removal of Government protection made many of the wartime's gains temporary, and numerous employers reverted to a nonunion status. Although membership did not fluctuate sharply through the rest of the decade, the failure to make substantial gains in a generally prosperous period reflected a low level of organizing capacity, which was in turn a sign of loss of confidence.

The number of strikes dropped sharply, and while they varied from year to year, the number in 1928 was below those of any year of record since 1884. The years from 1920 through 1932 reveal the same experience, a moderate number of strikes. One result was a lowering of the level of industrial violence, although it erupted in the Chicago building trades as a result of the efforts of the business community to compel the building trades to accept an arbitration award of Judge Kenesaw M. Landis. The award followed an agreement between the Chicago building trades unions and the building trades contractor associations to allow Judge Landis to settle their differences over wages. Judge Landis' award was rejected by the unions on the ground that he had exceeded the powers under which he acted as an arbitrator. Employers denied the charge, and, with the support of the entire business community, decided to ignore the union's protests. When the contractors began to operate with new recruits, they found many of them assaulted and equipment and jobs damaged or dynamited. Two watchmen at one of the jobs were killed, and many others, workmen and pickets, were injured. The fight over the Landis award lasted from 1923 to 1926, when the industry returned to its former relationships.[146] It is difficult to determine the role of force in this sequence of changes. Many contractors found the award unworkable because it made bidding more difficult, and they welcomed participation in wage-setting and work rules enforcement.

The low strike level elsewhere in the country reduced the possibilities for violent confrontations, although the Governors of Indiana, North Carolina, and Rhode Island each sent State troops to the scenes of strikes.[147] In none of the three cases was violence reported. As usual, continuous strife took place in the bituminous coal industry. In Colorado, the Industrial Workers of the World notified the State industrial commission that a strike would be called in 30 days unless the operators made concessions. Thereupon the city council of Walsenberg ordered all members of the IWW out of town, and a mob led by the mayor wrecked the IWW headquarters. The companies refused concessions and a strike was called on October 18, 1927. During the strike a new constabulary was established, and on November 21 the constables, against the wishes of the Rocky Mountain Fuel Co., appeared before the Columbine, owned by the latter company, and ordered the cessation of picketing. When the pickets refused, and some rocks were thrown at the constables, they emptied their guns at the pickets, killing six and wounding a number of others.[148] During a parade of strikers to a meeting with the Industrial Commission, on January 12, 1928, the lines were ordered to disperse. Shooting began, and a boy and a striker were killed.

This strike attracted nationwide attention but it was much less significant than the efforts of the bituminous coal miners to maintain their union in the coal fields of Pennsylvania, West Virginia, and Ohio. Investigating the reported abuses, a U.S. Senate committee noted:

Everywhere your committee made an investigation in the Pittsburgh district we found coal and iron police and deputy sheriffs visible in great numbers. In the Pittsburgh district your committee understands there are employed at the present time between 500 and 600 coal and iron police and deputy sheriffs. They are all very large men; most of them weighing from 200 to 250 pounds. They are all heavily armed and carry clubs usually designated as a "black jack."

Everywhere your committee visited they found victims of the coal and iron police who had been beaten up and were still carrying the scars on their faces and heads from the rough treatment they had received.[149]

There were also a number of textile strikes in the South, which attracted more than ordinary attention because of the resistance to the unions shown by the industry. In 1927, troops were sent to Hendersonville, N.C., during a textile strike because of the reported threats of violence.[150] Strike leaders were kidnaped and run out of town during a strike at Elizabethtown, Tenn., in April 1929. After a short organizing campaign, the National Textile Workers Union called a strike on August 1, 1929, at the Loray mill of Manville-Jenckes Co., in Gastonia, N.C. About 1,800 workers joined the strike. Although no violence had taken place, Governor Max Gardner sent troops into the area on August 4; they were withdrawn on August 20.

An attempt to organize the employees of the Marion Manufacturing Co., Marion, N.C., led to a strike of 1,000 hosiery workers on July 11, 1929. Workers employed at the Clinchfield mills joined the strikers after 1 month. As a result of sporadic clashes, Governor Max Gardner sent the militia to the area on August 11. The troops arrested 148 strikers, charging them with rioting. On September 11 the strike was called off, and the men returned to work, but as a result of a dispute over work payment, the night shift went on strike on October 2. The strikers remained before the mill gates seeking to notify the day shift that a strike had been called. Without warning deputies fired into the line of pickets, killing 6 and wounding 24. The militia, which had been withdrawn, was sent back to Marion. The sheriff, 12 deputies, and 2 mill officials were arrested and charged with homicide. Eight were tried and acquitted, although all the dead and wounded had been shot in the back.[151] In 3 months in which the two strikes had taken place—July through early October—7 strikers had been killed, 24 were wounded by gunfire, and about 150 were arrested, charged with rioting.[152]

In addition to the above, constant violence accompanied labor disputes in Kentucky's Harlan and Bell Counties in 1931 and 1932. In February 1931, several thousand mine workers went out on strike in Bell County. In April, Jerse Pace, a deputy, wounded William Burnett, who returned the fire and killed Pace. On May 5 a battle between miners and deputies at Evarts resulted in the death of Jim Daniels, a deputy sheriff, two other deputies and a miner. In Harlan County on May 7, 325 guards armed with machineguns were sent to the mine areas. On August 30, Deputy Sheriff Ed Rose killed Calo Hyatt, a 19-year-old miner, and wounded his father. Two striking miners, Joe Moore and Julius Baldwin, were killed by Deputy Sheriff Lee Fleenor. In Knox County on February 11, 1932, Harry Simms, an organizer, was killed by Deputy Sheriff Artie Miller. During this period attorneys from the American Civil Liberties Union, Arthur Garfield Hayes and Dudley Field Malone, were prevented from entering Bell County.[153]

Many strikes during this period involved agricultural workers. Imperial Valley was the scene of an extensive strike in 1930 under the auspices of the Agricultural Workers Industrial Union, a Communist-dominated organization. Sixteen participants were indicted for criminal syndicalism, of whom six Mexicans were convicted; the others were paroled. Organization drives in California by the Cannery & Agricultural Workers Industrial Union in 1933 met with some success. A union demand for 35 cents an hour was the major strike issue. Violence occurred during disorders in El Centro on January 9, 1933, but was suppressed. In October 1930, cottonpickers in the San Joaquin Valley went on strike for a pay increase from 60 cents to $1 for 100 pounds of cotton picked. Acts of violence were carried out against strikers. At Pixley two strikers were killed and 12 injured on October 10. Another striker was killed at Arvin. A trial followed, which lasted 16 weeks and resulted in the conviction of 14 men for criminal syndicalism. In the onion fields of Hardin County, Ohio, in June 1934, 800 workers went on strike. Okey O'Dell led in forming the Agricultural Workers Union, AFL. Shortly thereafter he was abducted and beaten, and ordered not to return to the area. The strike was lost. On September 7, 1934, 67 persons were arrested, but the grand jury would not indict.[154]

THE NEW DEAL

Between 1933 and 1937 the labor movement underwent profound changes internally as well as in its relations to employers. For the first time in peacetime history, union organizations had the attention and approval of the Federal Government. Influenced by the labor legislation of the first years of the Roosevelt administration, unions began to expand, and by 1937 more members were enrolled in unions than at any time in history. The increases in union membership were reflected in a doubling of strikes between 1932 and 1933, and another doubling from 2,172 in 1936 to 4,740 in 1937. Almost half of the strikes in 1937 were for union recognition.

State troops were frequently employed during 1933. The Governor of Minnesota sent soldiers to restore order in a strike of packinghouse workers in Austin, and the Guard was used during a walkout in Amoskeag and Manchester, N.H. The Guard was also directed to Bath, Langley, and Clearwater, S.C., to handle a textile workers' strike. In Barre and Graniteville, Vt., during a dispute involving granite workers, and at Salah and Yakima, Wash., during a strike of orchard workers, troops were used because of threats made.[155]

1. Coal Again

The increase in strikes increased the number of occasions for clashes between workers, strikebreakers, and the police. Violence occurred in the coal areas in a number of States where organization was progressing rapidly, with the most serious episodes occurring in the captive mine districts of Pennsylvania and in Kentucky, where resistance to new unionizing drives was carried on by deputies on the payroll of the mine companies.[156]

The bloody character of coal labor disputes brought out the National Guard in Indiana, New Mexico, and Utah, as well as in Ohio, where the death of a miner at Sullivan was responsible for the presence of State troops. The prime reason for calling up the Guard appeared to have been actual or threatened clashes between strikers and their replacements.[157] In Fayette County, Pa., where the captive mines were located, the companies refused to recognize the United Mine Workers of America. After a dozen pickets had been injured, Governor Gifford Pinchot ordered State troops into the area. A temporary agreement was reached, but the companies tried to operate as soon as the agreement broke down. Attempts of pickets to prevent the movement of strikebreakers towards the mine led to firing in which 17 pickets and a deputy were wounded. With the aid of President Roosevelt, an agreement to hold an election was reached and the violence ceased.[158]

The most sanguinary episodes took place in Kentucky, where coal operators in Harlan and Bell Counties continued aggressive resistance to unionization that they had used in the past. Neither changes in public or worker sentiment, nor Government suasion could soften their determination to keep their operations on a nonunion basis. Soon after the enactment of the National Industrial Recovery Act, the United Mine Workers sought to organize the miners employed by the U.S. Coal & Coke Co., a subsidiary of the U.S. Steel Corp. at Lynch, a mining community in the eastern part of Harlan County. The union succeeded in establishing a local in June 1933. After a time an open meeting was held in Cumberland, and two members of the Lynch police force stood in front of the hall and noted who was present at the meeting from their town. Subsequently, men were discharged, and in July and August 1933, the police department of Lynch purchased tear gas, 41 rifles, 21 revolvers, and 500 cartridges. A company union was also formed. Under this pressure, organizing was suspended.[159]

In December 1934 the Mine Workers resumed its campaign, and its organizers were harried by company police who justified their surveillance by the claim that the town was private property and strangers could be watched and forced to leave town. Union organizers were not allowed to enter Lynch by the sheriff and his deputies, and organizers were subjected to "rough shadowing," a procedure under which "a man is under surveillance in such a manner that not only he knows he is being followed but anyone he meets becomes aware of it. The value of such a device to discourage contact with union organizers by workers in a mine or plant is obvious."[160] After the signing of the agreement between the U.S. Steel Corp. and the Steel Workers Organizing Committee in 1937, the harassing of organizers ceased in Lynch. Other methods were adopted in other parts of Harlan County. Evidence was adduced showing how the Harlan County Coal Operators Association learned through its spies of the trip planned by Lawrence Dyer, organizer of the United Mine Workers of America. As Dyer's car was passing beneath a clump of bushes, a volley of shots from the top of the cliff wounded two of the car's occupants. Later, Dyer's home in Pineville, Bell County, was dynamited.

When the contract between the Harlan County Coal Operators Association and the United Mine Workers of America expired, in April 1934, armed deputies and company guards were in full command. Peaceful meetings of the miners were suppressed, union miners were severely beaten, and organizers driven out of town. After the enactment of the National Labor Relations Act in 1935, renewed efforts to organize were undertaken by the United Mine Workers, which had contracts with three coal companies in Harlan County. During July and August 1935, the Kentucky National Guard was in Harlan keeping order at the direction of Governor Ruby Lafoon. During its stay, union organizers were not molested. However, the sheriff successfully sought an injunction against bringing the National Guard into Harlan County. It was set aside by the Kentucky Supreme Court, on the ground that the sheriff "did not have a property right in the preservation of law and order," and that a judge could not prohibit the National Guard from entering the county. In September 1935, miners in 13 camps went on strike. A union member was kidnapped and compelled to leave the county. The union was not at this time successful in organizing, and abandoned its efforts temporarily.[161]

When a new organizing drive was launched in 1937, the sheriff increased the number of deputy sheriffs to 163, only 3 of whom were paid from public funds. At first no violence was used against union organizers.[162] They were not, however, able to obtain lodgings at some hotels, and in one instance tear-gas bombs were thrown into the place where organizers were staying. On February 8, 1937, as a group of organizers were driving through the countryside, they were fired upon from a car and one of the occupants was wounded. The driver of the organizer's car accelerated his speed and managed to escape into a garage. "Fearful of their safety and concerned over the wound [received by one of their number], the organizers . . . boarded a bus which took them out of the county." [163] The incident had been witnessed by three small boys who related what they had seen to Lloyd Clouse. After being warned to keep quiet, Clouse was shot and killed on April 24, 1937, by a deputy. Marshall Musick, a union organizer who had lived in Evarts for 14 years, was forced to leave town because he feared he would be killed after he had been warned and shot at several times. After Musick had left, his son was killed by a volley fired through the window of his house.[164]

On November 27, 1937, the National Labor Relations Board found the Clover Fork Co. guilty of discriminating against members of the United Mine Workers of America, and found the Harlan County Coal Operators Association guilty of coercion and restraint of workers in the "mines of Harlan County in the exercise of their right to self-organization." [165] Reinstatement of 60 miners improperly dismissed was ordered. The decision was upheld by the Circuit Court of Appeals for the Sixth Circuit.

As a result of this decision, the other coal companies of Harlan County, which had not abandoned the unyielding attitude toward the union, settled their disputes with the union. On August 19, 1938, the Harlan County Coal Operator's Association signed an agreement with the United Mine Workers extending the terms of the Southern Appalachian contract to the Harlan County Coal Operators Association.[166]

Peace was finally established in the Kentucky coal mines.

While violence in labor disputes usually arises out of differences between employers and employees, interunion differences can also be a cause of serious collisions. One

351

of the more violent disputes took place in the Illinois mining area, where an independent union, the Progressive Mine Workers of America, was organized in 1932, after differences over a contract with the United Mine Workers of America. When the Progressives sought to gain control over the entire mining area of the State, they encountered resistance from those loyal to the old union. In Taylorville, Governor Henry Horner was forced to send the National Guard to put down the rioting and restore order. Each faction controlled part of the mining territory, and the efforts of one to invade the domain of the other were forcibly resisted. The struggle, which started in 1932 and continued to 1937, cost an estimated 24 lives and countless dollars for legal fees and relief.[167]

2. Violence and the Use of Troops in 1934

The increase in demands for recognition brought about by a rapidly growing union membership led to violence on many picket lines. In 1934, State troops were called out in connection with the national textile strike during September. The major reason for the violence and the use of troops appears to have been the determination of employers not to deal with the union. This was the basic impediment to a peaceful settlement in the national textile strike, the San Francisco longshoremen's strike, and the Minneapolis textile and the Kohler strikes of that year, which were the centers of the most serious violence.

In Toledo, Ohio, the newly organized United Automobile Workers sought recognition from the Electric Auto-Lite Co., the Bingham Tool & Stamping Co., and the Logan Gear Co. The demands of the union were rejected, and a strike began on May 23. Assaults upon nonstrikers brought a contingent of National Guardsmen into the city. In a clash between troops and strikers on May 25, 2 pickets were killed and 25 were injured. A wage increase and limited recognition ended the walkout.[168] Strikers were also killed in the coal mines around Empire and Leeds, Ala., and in Pike County, Ky.; in a walkout at a steel plant in Latrobe, Pa.; in a strike of ore miners around Birmingham, Ala.; and during a longshore strike in Galveston, Tex.

The Kohler Co. strike at Kohler, Wis., also concerned union organization. Kohler Village was established by the

Kohler family at the end of the 1890's, and the company pursued a paternalistic policy. Higher than prevailing wage rates were paid, and workers were encouraged to save and purchase homes. A union reared its head after the enactment of the National Industrial Recovery Act, and in July 1934 it sought recognition. It was refused by the company. A strike followed on July 16, and the company employed a force of deputies to protect its properties. Simultaneously, the company announced it would not bargain with nonemployees, which meant outside union representatives. No untoward incidents took place until July 27, when strikers and guards clashed before the American Club in which the deputies were housed. Troops were sent by the Governor. One striker and a strike sympathizer were killed, and 35 others required hospital treatment.[169]

3. The Minneapolis Teamster's Strike

During 1933, the teamsters established Local 574 in Minneapolis. A strike of coal drivers led to a compromise settlement. This victory encouraged the expansion of unionization to the cartage companies. When a demand for increased wages and improved working conditions was rejected by cartage employers, a strike was called on May 15, 1934; about 5,000 truck drivers, helpers, and platform and inside men were involved. Rioting began immediately, a riot on May 21 resulting in injuries to a score of strikers. The next day a battle among pickets, police, and special deputies led to the killing of a businessman acting as a special policeman. A number of others were seriously injured. A truce was called, but when no agreement followed a second strike was called. The employers still refused to recognize the union, and the walkout continued. At the end of July, National Guardsmen were sent into the city by Governor Floyd Olson. Another striker was killed on August 2. The Governor would not allow the movement of trucks except for those in interstate commerce or carrying necessities. In the end a compromise settlement was reached, influenced by the suggestions of Federal mediators. It was the basis of a tremendous expansion of the union into many parts of the Middle West.

4. General Strike in Cotton Textiles

The 1934 strike that involved the largest number of workers took place in the cotton textile industry after the convention of the United Textile Workers of America had demanded a general wage increase and other improvements in working conditions. When all proposals for meetings were rejected by the industry, a strike was called on August 31, 1934. The workers in Alabama commenced their walkout earlier, on July 15, and an estimated 20,000 in 28 mills were reported on strike. In Alabama, the president of the Decatur local was shot and two of his aides were beaten. The National Guard was sent to Chambers and Lee Counties. In Georgia, complaints of roving pickets were made at the beginning of the strike. Clashes between pickets and strike guards led the Governor to proclaim martial law, and to set up an internment camp. In a fight between strikers and guards at Trion, 2 were killed and 24 wounded. In North Carolina, a number of pickets and strikebreakers were wounded, and the Governor sent troops to the strike zone. The troops were directed to "afford protection to those citizens who wanted to work and were being denied that privilege. . . . This policy extended to the protection of strikers and other citizens whose action and conduct was within their legal rights; this thought with reference to picketing." [170]

In South Carolina, troops were ordered to Greer, Lyman, and Greensville. In the latter town, a deputy sheriff had killed a striker; but the worst riot took place at Honea Path, where six were killed. Similar conditions in the North brought out the National Guard in a number of centers in Maine, Massachusetts, Rhode Island, and Connecticut. In Saylesville, R.I., 3 were shot and killed, 8 wounded, and 132 injured on September 12. The following day another picket was wounded and a number of others were wounded in a later scuffle when troops charged pickets. Throughout the strike, 5,000 State troops were active in New England, and an estimated 2,000 strikers were interned in Georgia. The strike cost 15 lives, and an unestimated number of wounded by gunfire and other means.[171] The textile strike was completely lost.

5. The Pacific Longshore Strike

Unions in the Pacific coast seafaring and longshore industry, which had been largely eliminated in the 1920's, were reestablished in 1933. Negotiations between unions and their employers did not move on an even keel. At best, the shipowners and stevedore companies accorded the labor groups grudging recognition and waited for an opportunity to eliminate the unions. In the spring of 1934 no agreement could be reached with the Pacific coast longshoremen, who were then affiliated with the International Longshoremen's Association. At the same time, the seagoing unions made demands for recognition. The demands of both groups were rejected by the employers and the longshoremen and seamen struck, respectively, on May 9 and May 16, 1934. After several plans for ending the walkout had failed, a movement for reopening the San Francisco port was undertaken by the Industrial Association. On July 3, trucking operations were begun, and several trucks loaded with cargo were taken through the picket lines. On the following day the Belt Line Railway, a State-owned line, was attacked by strikers and sympathizers. Governor Frank Merriam then sent the National Guard into the city to restore order. On July 6 the worst riot of the strike, and the encounter that was to bring on a local general walkout, took place. Two pickets were killed and many injured. The San Francisco Labor Council sponsored the general strike, which lasted from July 15 to July 19 and was called off after employer concessions resulted in full recognition of the Longshoremen & Sailor's Union, and union control of hiring halls.

Several other Pacific coast ports did not escape from rioting. In Seattle, Mayor Charles L. Smith led the police, against the wishes of the chief of police, in opposing the attempts of pickets to disrupt work by strikebreakers. On July 7 a policeman was killed, and on the 11th four pickets were seriously wounded. The Portland, Ore., docks were also the scene of several clashes between strikers and strikebreakers who replaced them, and State troops were called out.

6. Strikes and Violence in 1935

The year that witnessed the enactment of the Wagner Act showed little abatement of employer resistance to union organization. In all parts of the country, in small and large disputes alike, Governors were increasingly inclined to dispatch their troops to cope with strikers. Four disturbances that brought State troops to the strike scene were in coal and metalliferous mining, in addition to two in the lumber industry, and four in textiles. Troops also were sent to a strike in a meatpacking plant in South Dakota, and to another in an engine plant in Freeport, Ill. A streetcar strike in Omaha, Neb., and the general strike in Terre Haute, Ind., accounted for the other incidents. In some States troops were used in more than one dispute. For example, in Kentucky, State troops were sent to both Mannington and Harlan because of disorders at these places in connection with strikes. In Georgia, the Governor sent troops to three textile centers: La Grange, Manchester, and Monroe.[172]

Mining and textiles contributed most of the serious violence in 1935. An attempt to launch a dual union in the anthracite-coal fields caused serious conflict in that area between followers of the new and the old union. Clashes between the adherents of the United Anthracite Miners of Pennsylvania and the United Mine Workers of America resulted in a riot in which two were killed on February 14, and a large number injured. Even more serious was the fight at the Glen Alden collieries at Nottingham, Pa., on May 31, 1936. Five were killed and 21 hurt in this encounter. The United Anthracite Miners finally disbanded in October 1936.[173] Differences between miners and operators in the unorganized areas also led to casualties. On October 28, one was killed and six others shot in St. Clare County, Ala., when they attempted to disrupt operation of a mine operating under nonunion conditions. The next day 10 were shot in Mannington, Ky., when they sought to prevent the opening of a nonunion mine.[174]

In Omaha a clash between striking streetcar men and strikebreakers was responsible for the death of two strike sympathizers and the wounding of a number of others. Governor R. L. Cochran immediately sent troops into the city. Other communities which reported deaths resulting from violence in labor disputes were Rossville, Ga., during a textile walkout, and a strike at the Callaway mills in La Grange, Ga. Two fruit and vegetable strikers were killed in El Centro, Calif. A striking clay worker was killed in Toronto, Ohio, and a brewery picket in Stockton, Calif. The police of Eureka, Calif., killed four pickets in a lumber strike, and a picketing ornamental iron worker was shot to death in Minneapolis. Striking maritime workers in New Orleans, Houston, and Port Arthur, Tex., were killed, as were two striking iron miners in Alabama. Finally, a coal miner in Pikeville, Ky., and a striker at the Motor Products Corp. in Detroit lost their lives while picketing.[175]

Indiana also used its National Guard in labor disputes during 1935. It followed the calling of a general strike in support of 700 striking employees of the Columbian Enameling & Stamping Co., who had left their jobs on March 23, 1935, in support of wage increases and a union shop. When the company brought in strikebreakers and guards from outside the State, 48 unions of the American Federation of Labor called a general strike. On July 22, Governor Paul V. McNutt sent 2,000 National Guardsmen to Columbus. Early the next day the troops charged a long line of pickets with clubs and tear gas. During the next several days almost 200 pickets were arrested by the troops. Martial law was not lifted until the following February.[176]

The violence that was common in the textile industry in 1934 continued into the following year. At La Grange, Ga., the National Guard was sent to maintain order after a disturbance during a strike which started in March. At the Monmouth textile mill in Union, S.C., a foreman and constable were killed during a riot on June 19. At Pelzer, S.C., a woman was killed and 22 persons were wounded when the sheriff and his deputies fired into a crowd of pickets. The sheriff was denounced for his unnecessary use of force. Troops were sent into the area, and a number of deputies were arrested. Later the parties worked out an agreement for ending the walkout.[177]

7. Violence in Labor Disputes in 1936

According to the Chief of the National Guard Bureau of the U.S. War Department, State troops were called out 11 times in 1936 in connection with labor disputes.[178] These troops were used in three textile strikes, in a coal strike, in an Idaho lumber workers strike, in a match factory in Cloquet, Minn., and in a clothing factory in New York State.[179] Troops were mobilized in Pekin, Ill., during a walkout at the plant of the American Distilling Co., but the threat of a general strike prevented their use.

The most violent walkouts in 1936 were in the coal, steel, and textile industries, at least from the point of view of persons killed. A deputy sheriff was killed in a clash with pickets at the Samoset Mills at Talladega, Ala., on July 23. Subsequently another deputy was killed. Nor did the North completely escape. During a strike at the Acme Braid Co. at Closter, N.J., a picket was killed.[180] Equally serious was the clash at the New Boston, Ohio, plant of the Wheeling Steel Co., where a guard was killed and four strikers wounded on June 29, 1936. Two weeks later the strike was settled and the union recognized.[181] The mines were, as usual, a seat of trouble. At the Tennessee Coal & Iron Co. mines around Birmingham, Ala., rioting took place in early June and led to the wounding of five pickets in a gun battle.[182] Two pickets were killed in March 1936 in the strike of loggers at Willamette, Ore.; a striking seaman was killed in Houston, Tex.; and a spectator and picket in front of the plant of the Sun Shipbuilding Co. at Chester, Pa.[183]

8. Violence in Labor Disputes in 1937

By 1937, unions had been for 4 years the beneficiaries of Government legislation to protect their rights to organize and to bargain. Despite this, using the index of people killed in labor disputes, this year was one of the more bloody in the history of American labor violence. One dispute, the Little Steel strike, accounted for 16 deaths and many others seriously injured. In addition, an estimated eight other people died in industrial disturbances.[184]

The worst episode of the steel strike took place "in a stretch of flat, waste, sparsely inhabited prairie land east of and adjacent to the South Chicago plant of the [Republic] steel corporation."[185] From the beginning of the strike, the police interfered with peaceful picketing; however, after Mayor Edward Kelly announced picketing would be permitted, 16 pickets were allowed before the gates. According to his testimony, an anonymous source had informed Capt. James L. Mooney, who was in charge of police in the factory area, that the strikers planned to march into the steel plant on Memorial Day. Because its pickets had been arrested by the police, the union had called a protest meeting on May 30. The meeting was held, and a motion to establish a mass picket line before the plant was adopted. As the marchers reached the police lines, a discussion followed "for a period of from four to ten minutes."[186] Within less than a minute thereafter "the strikers were in full retreat, in haste and confusion, before the advancing police lines. . . . Within that brief space of time, ten of the strikers received fatal gunshot wounds, thirty others were wounded by bullets and some sixty others received lacerations and contusions of varying intensity. Thirty-five police received minor injuries."[187] The Senate committee found—

That the provocation for the police assault did not go beyond abusive language and the throwing of isolated missiles from the rear ranks of the marchers. We believe that it might have been possible to disperse the crowd without the use of weapons. . . . From all the evidence we think it plain that the force employed by the police was far in excess of that which the occasion required. Its use must be ascribed either to gross inefficiency in the performance of the police duty, or a deliberate effort to intimidate the strikers.[188]

On June 19, 1937, the police tried to disperse a small crowd meeting near the Republic mill gate on company property. When the women in the crowd defied the order, the police threw tear gas bombs at them. One was killed. Ten, including four deputy sheriffs, were wounded, and several others injured or overcome by tear gas. James Mayo, the director of the Steel Workers Organizing Committee, claimed the women were sitting peacefully, and when they refused to move at the orders of the police, they were pelted with tear gas bombs.[189] In another outbreak:

At approximately 11 o'clock on the night of July 11, three persons received fatal injuries and an undetermined number were injured by gunfire and gas fumes when special and regular police officers . . . dispersed a crowd of strikers and strike sympathizers at CIO headquarters . . . in the city of Massillon. Witnesses . . . claimed . . . the special and regular police in a murderous and unprovoked assault on CIO headquarters, pursuant to a plan to destroy the union and break the strike.[190]

In Cleveland, Ohio, a picket was killed when a car driven by a strikebreaker crashed into him while he was trying to halt it.[191] Units of the State militia were sent to Canton and Youngstown.

The extent of the violence is summarized in La Follette committee reports. It found that the riots which occurred at Republic Steel Corp. plants during the Little Steel strike of 1937 resulted in the following: total gunshot wounds, 37; injuries other than gunshot, 202; buckshot wounds, 1; birdshot wounds, 17; established and possibly permanent injuries, 19; dead, 16, for a total dead and injured of 283. In addition, one policeman received a bullet wound, two birdshot wounds; injuries, 37; for a total of 40.[192] It was the opinion of Robert Wohlforth, the secretary of the La Follette committee, that during the Little Steel strike—

a mobilization of men, money and munitions occurred which has not been approached in the history of labor disputes in recent times. Although known to be incomplete, the committee has assembled data showing that a total of 7,000 men were directly employed as guards, patrolmen, deputy sheriffs, National Guardsmen, city police and company police on strike duty. Over $4,000,000 was expended directly attributable to the strike. A total of $141,000 worth of industrial munitions was assembled for use.[193]

The violence in the Little Steel strike came largely from the aggressive behavior of the police and company guards. The strike was lost on the picket line and, in this respect, resembled the pattern of past events in the steel and many other industries. However, the union gained recognition and with it collective bargaining was established in Little Steel, as a result of the application and enforcement of the Wagner Act by the NLRB and the courts.

9. Other Violent Events in 1937

There were a number of other violent encounters in 1937, the most serious at the plant of Aluminum Co. in Alcoa, Tenn. Refusal of the company to equalize wages with its Northern plants was the cause of the walkout. On July 7, 1937, a melee started when an effort was made to prevent a truck from entering through the factory gates. Firing began, and 2 were killed and 28 wounded. The dead were a striker and a special policeman, and two of the wounded were police. Troops were sent to the scene, and they restored order. Negotiations were then begun, and the strike was settled on July 11.[194]

Accidents also figured in fatal casualties. For example, in the walkout in June and July, 1937, at the Fein Tin Can Co. at Brooklyn, N.Y., a picket was killed. The United Radio & Electric Workers Union charged it was the result of police brutality, but the evidence indicated that the picket had suffered a fractured skull when he was hit by a flying brick.[195] In another instance, in a strike of furniture workers at Lloyd Manufacturing Co. at Menominee, Mich., a picket tried to prevent a car from entering through the factory gate and mounted the bumper of a car driven by a nonstriking worker. He fell from the bumper and was killed.[196]

Deaths marked other disputes during this year. A picket was killed during a strike at the Moltrop Steel Products Co. of Beaver Falls, Pa., in June 1937 after being struck by a teargas cartridge fired by a deputy seeking to disperse the strikers. Another picket was killed at the gates of the Phillips Packing Co. of Cambridge, Md.[197]

VIOLENCE IN 1938–39

The year 1937 saw the last of the great strike spectaculars in which the clash of armed forces or large-scale assaults led to heavy casualties. Violence continued to accompany some labor disputes, and each year produced new victims, but the level of violence was substantially and permanently lowered. The 1938 strike at the Northwestern Barbed Wire & Rod Co. involved a dispute between the Steel Workers Organizing Committee and an American Federation of Labor union. The former had held a contract with the company which the employer refused to renew. On March 1, a battle between strikers and deputy sheriffs led to the death of one of the pickets, and the serious wounding of two others. One of the latter required the amputation of a leg as a result of wounds. On the next day, workmen who had left their shifts and were on their way home encountered a group of deputy sheriffs. Because the deputies held guns in their hands, the workers mistook them for pickets ready to attack them and the workers opened fire. The deputies defended themselves. Three were wounded, one a deputy. It was agreed after the riot that an

361

election by the National Labor Relations Board was to determine the bargaining agent.[198]

In a riot at the Rice Brothers cannery at Corpus Christi, a battle between pickets and boatmen led to the killing of one and the wounding of another. Chris Clarick, an official of the United Cannery, Pickers & Agricultural Workers Union, who did the shooting, was himself severely beaten and was in serious condition at a Corpus Christi hospital. Clarick was later tried and sentenced to 20 years' imprisonment.[199] In the strike of the Lone Star Bag & Bagging Co. by the Textile Workers Organizing Committee, pickets attempted on March 26, 1939, to block the entrance to the factory and a fight ensued. The employee seeking to block the entrance to the plant left his truck and it rolled down an incline injuring a number of pickets, one of whom subsequently died. The driver of the truck was arrested, tried, and fined $200 and costs.[200]

One striker was killed during the strike at the Del Prado Hotel in Chicago in March 1938, and another before the plant of the Oscar Nebel Hosiery Co. at Hatboro, Pa., in September. In addition to the above incidents, a serious riot took place in front of the Maytag Washing Machine Co. in Newton, Iowa. The rioting brought a proclamation of martial law and State troops into the city. They remained in the community between July 19 and August 15. Order was restored and the CIO union was, in the end, recognized.[201] Troops were also ordered into Sioux City during a strike at the plant of the Swift Packing Co. Charging there existed serious threats to life and property, the National Guard was ordered into the city on October 19, 1938, and they remained until November 19. Eventually the company and the Packinghouse Worker's Union agreed to a contract.[202] In all, there were six deaths in the course of labor disputes in 1938.

In 1939 there was a striking decline in the use of militia in labor disputes. The Kentucky National Guard was sent to protect the Malan-Ellison Mine in Harlan, where a dispute had arisen. Three miners were killed in Harlan and one more elsewhere before the trouble subsided. Another dispute over the signing of a contract led to the wounding of seven men, two of them officers of the Hart Coal Co.[203] The Massachusetts Guard was sent to the Barre Textile plant during a strike of textile workers who were blocking strikebreakers from entering the plant. The Guard restored order.[204] In addition, a member of the Hodcarriers & Common Laborer's Union died during a strike in Millersburg, Ind.; a strike of fishermen in New Orleans and another against the Cairo Meal & Cake Co. were each responsible for the death of one person. Finally, two teamster strikes led to deaths, one in Boston involving a trucking company and the other in an incident growing out of a large chain department store strike.

VIOLENCE IN 1940–46

By 1940, union organizations entered into a new phase of growth and security. Strikes took on more and more their contemporary character of an economic conflict attended with minor violent episodes. This period was one of serious turbulence in the labor market. The shift to war production was accompanied by widespread dislocations. The subsequent reconversion to a peacetime economy was a challenge to the new industrial relations. The continual increase in union membership and union strength resulted in record-high numbers of strikes over important issues at the end of this period.

In 1940, there were seven deaths in labor disputes. While people were killed in most of the subsequent years, the incidents which generated violence were sporadic clashes and usually involved few workers. Private guards were involved in only two fatal disputes in this 7-year period. The first occurred during 1940 in a building trades strike, when a picket was shot in the back by two guards, both of whom were indicted.[205] The other incident, the wounding of a picket who later died, occurred at the Phelps-Dodge plant on July 30, 1946. This was the result of a violent encounter. The union charged that the picket was shot by a guard at the plant; on the other hand, 14 officials of the United Electrical Workers Union were charged with having stormed the company's wharf in an attempt to prevent strikebreakers from going to work.[206]

The coal industry continued to produce a disproportionate share of violence. In 1940, one man was killed and two were wounded while peacefully picketing a coal mine in Ohio. "The tragedy roused the miners to a high pitch and the killer decided to remain in jail for the time being under the protection of the sheriff. He said he fired because one of his brothers was assaulted." [207] In 1942, nine killings took place in three separate incidents in the Kentucky coal mines. In April the president and vice president of the coal company at Middleboro were shot to death along with a miner and a deputy sheriff.[208]

A rising share of violent clashes was caused by jurisdictional disputes. In June 1940, a nonstriking bus driver, who was a member of the Amalgamated Association of Street Railway & Motor Coach Employees, was killed in a jurisdictional dispute with the Brotherhood of Railroad Trainmen. The latter union regretted the violence and "death of a strikebreaker" and claimed that the deceased had "invited a fight, and provoked the assault which resulted in his unfortunate death, and members of the Brotherhood are in no way responsible for the incident." The Amalgamated eventually defeated the trainmen in an NLRB representation election.[209] One of the more grave disputes of 1941 took place in a suburb outside of St. Louis, Mo., and involved a fight between unionized and unorganized building tradesmen. One man was shot to death, four were wounded, and a number of others were beaten in a battle between the two groups.

About thirty shots were fired from pistols, rifles, and shotguns, bricks were thrown and clubs and wrenches swung as two hundred non-union employees of the Schuermann Building and Real Estate Company marched on a line of fifty-nine pickets. The pickets were routed . . . As they approached the picket line, they yelled—"We're going to chase them—law or no law." Thereupon they pushed a few deputies out of the way and walked toward the pickets pounding on automobile tops and smashing windows as they went.[210]

Although the report was that this dispute was between organized and unorganized building tradesmen, it was also reported that—

seven hundred CIO members in automobiles and on foot guarded truckloads of materials being delivered . . . to Country Club Hills, the Schuermann development. . . . The trucks were driven by members of the CIO Quarry Worker's Union Local 261. Joseph Lynch, secretary, said the business agent of the AFL Laborer's Union had warned the CIO drivers not to deliver materials to Schuermann projects. Lynch said more CIO guards would be obtained, if necessary, to continue truck deliveries.[211]

364

The efforts of the Progressive Mine Workers to replace the United Mine Workers ended in the killing of two miners in Kentucky in 1941.[212] The same year also witnessed a fatal stabbing of a picket during a clash between two rival CIO unions, the Playthings & Novelty Workers union and District 65 of the Wholesale and Warehouse Worker's Union[213] and a similar death in Flint, Mich., as a result of differences between an AFL and CIO locals of culinary workers.[214]

The National Guard was seldom employed during this period. Alabama sent the militia to restore order in 1941 at the Utica Mills at Aniston, to Gadsden for 8 days at a strike at the Republic Steel plant there, and on two occasions to police strike activities at the Tennessee Coal & Iron Railroad.[215] The sporadic and at times accidental nature of the remaining violent disputes is readily apparent by enumerating them. An organizer for the International Ladies' Garment Workers' Union in New York City was killed in 1940 after a scuffle with the owner of a nonunion shop.[216] Two months later, a strike at the St. Louis plant of the Century Electric Co., resulted in the death by stabbing of a striker after a fight with a strikebreaker. Local officers of the United Electrical, Radio & Machine Workers charged that the company had armed strikebreakers with knives, sharpened files, and baseball bats.[217] Soon after this, the IBEW conducted a strike at the Triangle Conduit & Cable Co. in Brooklyn, N.Y., where, 7 weeks after the start of the strike, 2,000 pickets tried to prevent the entrance into the plant of strikebreakers. One of the pickets died "of a heart attack brought on by the excitement." Later, several local officers were indicted for rioting.[218]

In 1941 a picket was killed during a strike at the Andrew Jackson Hotel in Nashville, Tenn., while another picket at about the same time died when he was hit by a board at the Currier Lumber Co. yard in Detroit.[219] One striker was killed by a shotgun blast in a strike of the Ed Friedrich Co. in San Antonio. It was claimed that the striker had stoned the home of one man who had remained on the job.[220]

There was only one reported death in a labor dispute in 1942; it occurred during a wildcat strike at the Detroit facility of the Aluminum Co. One employee who refused to join in the unauthorized walkout, which lasted 36 hours, was struck by a striker and died from a skull fracture. The assailant was arrested.[221]

The remaining years in the period 1940-46 showed only modest violence. In Charleston, S.C., a shooting incident in 1943 ended in the death of an individual at a war-housing construction project in the midst of a dispute between the Operating Engineer's Union and building contractors.[212] While no deaths were recorded in 1944, one person lost his life in 1945 in the strike of the Food, Tobacco & Agricultural Worker's Union at the Southern Cotton Co. at Little Rock, Ark.[223] The same union was involved in one of the two fatal strikes in 1946. Negotiations over contract terms broke down and a strike took place at the Muskogee Materials Co. in Oklahoma. One striker was knifed by a strikebreaker and subsequently died. An unusually bloody affair took place at a strike on the Toledo, Peoria & Western Railroad in the same year. The cause of the strike was the attempt of the railroad's president, George McNair, to compel changes in work rules. All service trades and shop employees went out on strike and two of the strikers as well as McNair were killed. The latter was shot by an assailant who was never caught.[224]

THE POST-TAFT-HARTLEY ACT
PERIOD (1947–62)

The passage of the Taft-Hartley Act in 1947 had numerous causes, including a continuing resentment by some employers' groups of the Wagner Act, the postwar strike wave, and patent abuses by some unions. Whatever consequences of the newly imposed legal restraints upon union activities may have been, the Taft-Hartley Act did not in any significant way diminish the protection accorded to unions by the Wagner Act. Public policy in support of the principles and procedures of collective bargaining remained unchanged. Changes in union membership responded more to the level of employment and unemployment than to the changes in the laws governing labor management relations.

Violence, however, was not completely erased from the labor-management scene and several strikes appeared to resemble outwardly the industrial disputes of another day.

However, even those in which violence took place lacked the ferocity of the battles of the pre-Wagner Act days. These incidents seem to demonstrate that the potential for violence is always present in industrial disputes in the United States, but they do not, in most instances, show the relentless bitterness of Homestead, Pullman, Ludlow, and many other affrays which desecrated the industrial landscape of earlier periods. Using fatalities as an index of violence, the comparative numbers are very small considering the high number of labor disputes, and even more the millions of workers who are covered by collective-bargaining agreements peacefully renewed at periodic intervals (see table 8-1).

As in the past, violent strikes in this period exhibit little if any regularity. But some differences emerge that largely confirm certain trends in 1940-46. There is decreasing resort to the National Guard, and assaults on strikers by company guards have been all but eliminated. Industries such as coal that have been a fertile source of past violence have become pacified and no longer provide exceptional

Table 8-1.—Number killed and wounded and number of times militia was called in labor disputes (1947-62)

Year	Location	Killed	Wounded[a]	Militia
1947	....	0	0	0
1948	Maryland..................	1	0	0
	Illinois, Iowa............	3	....	1
1949	Kentucky.................	1	....	....
1950	Tennessee................	1	4	1
	Alabama..................	1	....	....
1951	Georgia..................	1	0	1
	Arkansas.................	1	....	....
	Tennessee................	1	....	....
1952	....	0	0	0
1953	West Virginia............	1	4	....
	Pennsylvania.............	1	....	....
	Southern RR. States......	1	(b)	....
1954	....	....	....	....
1955	Louisiana................	1	....	....
1956	....	....	....	....
1957	Tennessee................	2	7	....
1958	New York................	1	2	....
	Florida..................	2	2	....
1959	Kentucky................	4	....	1
	Louisiana................	1	1	....
1960	Wisconsin................	1	....	....
1961	New York................	1	....	....
1962	Tennessee................	3	....	....

[a] Statistics available usually in connection with strikes involving fatalities.
[b] Several.

bloody episodes. Geographically, violence continues to be widely dispersed, although the data suggest that violence tends to occur more frequently in the South and Midwest and less often in the Northeast and the Far West. Most of the deaths in these strikes were accidental, in the sense that violence was not part of a systematic campaign by either the union or the employer. Some deaths were a result of a brawl between pickets and strike replacements, which has been the single most important source of all strike violence. Indeed, many strikes that had been peaceful were converted to battles on the first day that a back-to-work movement started. Occasionally, violence took place away from the struck facility, sometimes under circumstances in which it is difficult to disentangle personal elements from the labor controversy.

To be sure, there were strikes which had all the hallmarks of past struggles. The national strike of the CIO Packinghouse Workers against several packing companies in 1948 was accompanied by killings, disorder, and the National Guard. In this strike, the police in Kansas City, Kans., raided the union hall, destroyed furniture, and attacked those present. In 1955, during a strike on the Louisville & National Railroad, injuries and a death resulted from clashes between pickets and strikebreakers. Bridges were dynamited and rolling stock damaged, and the railroad was the victim of continual vandalism.

By and large, however, the most publicized strikes in this period, while bitter and prolonged and full of disorder and assaults, did not result in killings. These strike spectaculars—Kohler, Square-D, Perfect Circle, Southern Bell —were all widespread and usually accompanied by minor acts of violence, which in a few cases were quite grave and resulted in more or less extensive amounts of property damage. The worst of these strikes was that involving the Perfect Circle Co. and the UAW, in which both sides were plainly guilty of violence. The Perfect Circle Co. was the only employer of this group that did not settle the strike by beginning or resuming collective bargaining relationships with its union. However, it should be noted that in due time this company eventually recognized the union that had been decertified in three out of its four plants after the strike.

The most informative source of the extent of contemporary violence is found in the records of the National Labor Relations Board. In Section 8(b)(1)(A) of the Taft-Hartley Act, Congress gave the Board power "to proceed against union tactics involving violence, intimidation and reprisal or threats thereof."[225] In interpreting this section, the Board commented that ". . . Congress sought to fix the rules of the game, to insure that strikes and other organizational activities of employees were conducted peaceably by persuasion and propaganda and not by physical force, or threats of force or of economic reprisal."[226] In fiscal 1968, the Board closed 12 cases after the entry of a Board order or court decree in which unions had been found to have engaged in some act or acts of violence. Moreover, 14 Board regional offices for the same period closed informally 38 other such cases.[227] These regions handle roughly half of the agency's total case load and include New England, parts of metropolitan New York and Chicago, the industrial areas of Pittsburgh and Detroit, the Southeastern states, the Midwest, and part of Texas, and the Far West. On the assumption that the unreported half of the United States would have exhibited about the same number of violent labor cases, we may conclude that there were 80 to 100 cases of unlawful acts with some degree of violence committed by labor unions and involving the NLRB in this 12-month period.

1. Informal NLRB Cases of Labor Violence

In 19 of the 38 informally closed cases, the unlawful activities arose out of a strike over the terms and conditions of employment; in nine others the major issue was union recognition. However, the instability of bargaining is reflected in the fact that seven of the economic strikes involved unions which had either just won bargaining rights through a NLRB election or had only negotiated one contract with the charging employer. There were three cases in which rival union claims played a part and the contents of the remaining cases were either unknown or unclassifiable.

2. Violence Arising Out of Disputes Over the Terms of a Contract

An example of present-day violence occurred during a strike between District 50, United Mine Workers, and a manufacturer of iron castings in a small Michigan city. Despite a long history of collective bargaining, a strike of the 85 employees for a new contract that took place on March 13, 1967, lost its peaceful character on March 30 when some pickets were armed with baseball bats. It was alleged that an employer representative and two strike replacements were assaulted by several pickets and formal complaints were made to the police. The employer had been operating the plant at a reduced scale using supervisors and hiring strike replacements from any source. The alleged assailants were not union officers, but the Board imputed agency responsibility to the union on the grounds that this conduct took place under a controlled picket line. The regional office settled the case informally with the union and the employer, on the grounds that the picketing was otherwise peaceful, that no further violence was reported, and that a local court had issued a temporary restraining order directed against the violence. The settlement agreement provided for the usual remedy within the scope of normal Board procedures, that is, the agreement of the union to cease its unlawful activities and post a notice to its members to this effect. The strike continued after the closing of the case and the company's operations remained unaffected by the peaceful picketing.

A different outcome ended another strike in which unlawful activities were more extensive. Machinists began a strike on May 2, 1967, after fruitless bargaining with a manufacturer of industrial tools in a Chicago suburb with whom it had long enjoyed a bargaining relationship. The strike was peaceful, with the 138 nonunion represented employees being permitted free access to and from the plant until September 5 and 6, when 100 union pickets massed in front of the plant gates kept most of them out. Threats were directed at the nonstriking employees such as, "You're not wanted here. Leave while you still can," and "We know you and if you think anything of your family, you will get out of here." There was some shoving by pickets, rock throwing, tearing of sideview mirrors from cars, and several incidents of individual intimidations and harassments. The employer secured a State court injunction on September 18, although the violence had ended more than 10 days before. The region issued a complaint but prior to a formal hearing the company withdrew the charge on December 11, 1967, since a new contract was signed. On the basis that the unlawful activity had terminated, the Board accepted the withdrawal.

The pattern of illegal activities which constitutes violence and coercion subject to the jurisdiction of the Labor Board is rarely changed. Frequently there is some blocking of plant ingress and egress, occasionally the laying of nails "by persons unknown" on the plant driveway, sometimes allegations that sugar or other foreign material is put in the gas tanks of company and nonstriking employees' vehicles, accusations of object throwing which may include rocks, eggs, or paint, some physical scuffling or pushing, and always the making of threats. Damage to company plant is rarely observable in these cases, although vehicles standing in the street appear to be fair game. In very few cases does more violence take place, such as physical assaults or the following and harassing of drivers of company trucks on the highways and at stops. In several cases, union pickets were found in front of the homes of working employees with signs imputing the worst sins of humanity to those who cross picket lines. In all cases but one the union's coercive conduct was limited in time and ceased after the filing of a charge with the Board or the obtaining of a State court injunction. Indeed, in 11 cases of the 38 informally adjusted cases, court orders were obtained by the employer.

In only one instance did unlawful activities continue during the NLRB investigation, and this strike was by far the most violent of 1967 which was closed by the Board. A longtime bargaining relationship was ruptured by a strike for improved conditions of the Papermaker's union at a paper products manufacturing plant in a small town in western Massachusetts. The strike was peaceful from its start on October 28 until November 17, at which time a truck driver crossing the picket line was physically assaulted and his truck damaged. Thereafter mass picketing began, reaching its maximum strength on November 29 and 30, with many threats of physical coercion made. A complete blockage of entrance and exit excluded all employees including clerical, supervisory, and managerial personnel. The violence included some damage to the plant and its appurtenances, assaults with clubs upon some individuals trying to enter the plants, and striking and rocking vehicles in which the attempts were made. The employer obtained a State court temporary restraining order that was exceedingly narrow in scope and limited the court's protection to only three maintenance employees who provided the plant's heat. The judge denied a broader injunction without stating any reason. There were only two officers in the local police force, who were unable to control the situation; their requests for assistance from the State police were unanswered. On December 4, the employer requested that the NLRB obtain an injunction under the authority of section (10)(j) of the act, which was supported by the regional office on December 5, and authorized by Washington on the following day. By December 8 the union agreed to cease all unlawful activities, which it promptly did. The union's agreement was incorporated in an informal settlement agreement. The return of peace led to fruitful negotiations and by December 18 the parties had negotiated a new contract. In light of the postviolent union behavior, the settlement agreement was approved by the Board.

The low level of violence of most of the cases that emerge from stalemated bargaining can be seen by examining an episode involving white-collar workers. A strike of announcers and salesmen at a Detroit radio station resulted in a union agreement with the NLRB not to coerce nonstrikers. The facts which underlay the Board determination of a violation of section (8)(b)(1)(a) included such threats as "I may be your friend, but if you try to cross that line, I will be all over you," and "Well, you better bring your army with you because no one is going to walk in that door tomorrow morning at 8:00." No other "violence" accompanied the strike and the union's coercive conduct was corrected by the normal remedy of agreeing to cease issuing threats.

3. Violence Arising Out of Union Demand for Recognition

The existence of Board machinery for determining a union's representation status has eliminated this issue from its previously predominant role as a cause for strikes. The number of such cases involving coercive union behavior is very low. Two situations involved the International Ladies' Garment Workers' Union which established a number of pickets in front of a small plant during an organizational campaign. In both cases, the sole unlawful activity, which was corrected by the filing of the charge, was interference with free movement to and from the plant.

However, in two other 1967 cases the union's unlawful behavior was overshadowed by illegal employer conduct. A machinist's organizing campaign against a Chicago manufacturer was countered by employer unfair-labor practices which included discharges of seven union supporters and widespread threats of reprisals against other employees. This company's unlawful behavior resulted in a strike by a minority of workers. The cars of some of the pickets were damaged, and their work clothes and other personal property left in the plant were vandalized. Moreover, some strikers received threatening phone calls at their homes. Charges filed by the union with the NLRB resulted in a determination that the company behavior was unlawful and complaints were issued. The employer also filed charges with the Board alleging union violence, which consisted of the scratching of one car by pickets, tampering with the airbrakes on a truck, and one threat to a supervisor. Since these activities constituted a violation of section $(8)(b)(1)(a)$, a non-Board settlement of all charges was agreed upon. Reinstatement and backpay was offered to the dischargees and both the employer and the union agreed to stop all unlawful acts.

In the second case, after an uneventful bargaining history of 16 years, negotiations broke down for a new contract when a Massachusetts employer insisted upon a "word-for-word, comma-for-comma" renewal of the old agreement as a condition for discussing wages. The Textile Workers' Union, after a unanimous vote, went on strike. The employer refused to meet the union after the strike, met secretly with some of the employées, distributed and collected "decertification cards," set up a new union, provided facilities and an attorney for the new union, and recognized and signed a contract with it, after declining to recognize the Textile Workers' Union. The Textile Workers' Union filed charges which the region found to be meritorious. The strike was peaceful except for one incident involving a nonstriking employee who reported being assaulted by three pickets. It seems a scuffle did take place, although the nonstriker was a male who was six foot two and weighed over 220 pounds, while the pickets were women ranging in age from their early fifties to late sixties. Several weeks after this episode, the strike was ended with the renewal of an agreement with the Textile union, the repudiation of the company union, and a withdrawal of all charges.

4. Violence Arising Out of Jurisdictional Disputes in 1967

The disaffiliation of most of the officers and members of a local of Brewery workers to the United Auto Workers in a Michigan factory resulted in a strike led by the UAW. Mass picketing, threats to nonstrikers, and the damaging of vehicles led to filing of charges and the securing of a State court injunction. The union's coercive acts were brief and ceased in compliance with a Board adjustment and the court order.

A conflict between the Carpenters and the Teamsters' Union produced a tangled skein of charges alleging violations by both of many sections of the act. The basic facts indicate that a Chicago firm recognized and executed a contract with the Carpenters Union at a time when that union had no members in the unit, which included drivers and dockmen who were members of the Teamsters. The subsequent Teamster picketing included violations of the act's secondary boycott prohibitions. The teamsters also engaged in threats of physical harm to some employees, rock throwing, and the following and harassing of trucks on the highway. Complaints were issued against both unions and the employer but, subsequent to a hearing, all parties agreed to dispose of the issue by holding of a representation election in the disputed unit. On this basis, all charges were withdrawn.

5. Formal NLRB Cases Involving Violence in Fiscal 1968

Formal cases differ from adjusted NLRB cases in that Board orders and/or court decrees are entered against the respondents. Of course, violations of a court order may constitute contempt of court. Of the 12 cases closed in this category, 8 developed out of a breakdown in negotiations while 4 orginated in organizational efforts. The unlawful activities in these cases do not differ fundamentally from adjusted situations; the pattern consists of threats, mass picketing, blocking and shoving, occasional assaults, damage to cars, rock throwing, and the like. In six of these cases there was no litigation inasmuch as the union consented to the entry of a Board order and court decree on the basis of a written stipulation of facts and the applicable law.

6. Uncontrolled Labor Violence and the Board

The reduction of union-caused violence cannot be exclusively attributed to the impact of section (8)(b)(1)(a), although this section has a direct bearing upon such unlawful acts. With rare exceptions, as is noted in our description of Board cases, local law enforcement agencies supported by State courts are able to control union violence. The power of the State, now as in the past, is usually competent to protect employers' property interests, including the safeguarding of free ingress to and egress from a struck plant. However, in the event of a breakdown of local law enforcement, the Board is empowered under section (10)(j) of the Taft-Hartley Act to secure an injunction from a Federal district court. Since 1947 there have been 11 occasions where such an injunction has been obtained. In all of these cases, uncontrolled mass picketing and large-scale incidents of violence and threats of violence were responsible for the Board's intervention. It also should be noted that the enforcement of a Federal court order is invariably swift and effective. Of course, the significance of section (10)(j) cannot be measured alone by the number of times it was used. The prospect of its use, as observed in one of the Board cases discussed above, is ordinarily sufficient to stop violent behavior.

7. Other Sources of Data on Labor Violence

Attempts were made to secure data on violence from such obvious sources as local police departments and the U.S. Department of Justice. Unfortunately, time limitations forbade any extensive collection of information. Police manuals from a number of cities throughout the country revealed that police departments were highly sensitive to the disorders inherent in labor disputes and a number of cities specified in considerable detail appropriate police procedures. All of these were directed at insuring open picket lines and freedom of movement of people and goods across them. At the same time, police officers were cautioned to maintain neutrality and impartiality in maintaining order. The records of the Labor Board indicate that these instructions were ordinarily executed with considerable fidelity, although the enthusiasm with which police carried out their orders varied with local conditions. There were times when police allegedly turned their backs at minor outbursts of picket line violence; on the other hand, unions charged that the contrary often took place. In one Board case a union representative claimed: "Any time a driver either refused or hesitated to make a delivery, the police showed up." We were given access to the full records of a major northern industrial city's police department which revealed an almost complete absence of labor violence over a 4-year period. During this time only one arrest was made, and that involved a fist fight between a picket and a customer of a struck store.

We were also given summaries of major complaints of labor violence made to the Federal Bureau of Investigation from 1961 to 1967. The Department of Justice informed us that most of the other complaints were about small-scale damage to property whose isolated nature and remoteness in affecting commerce precluded Federal action. Property damage was also the most significant characteristic of the major complaints of labor violence made to the Federal Bureau of Investigation from 1961 to 1967. The use of dynamite was reported in 1961 and 1963 during a jurisdictional dispute on the Great Lakes. Explosions were reported on the Wabash Railroad in 1963, and on the New York Central Railroad in the same year. The most serious incidents of property damage occurred during disputes with employers with extensive and exposed property holdings. A strike of the IBEW against the Alabama Power Co. in 1966 was accomplished by 50 acts of sabotage, including the draining of oil from transformers, placing of chains across powerlines, severing of guy wires on transmission line poles, the destruction of power equipment by gunfire, and the like. Also in 1966 a labor dispute between the Oil, Chemical & Atomic Workers' Union and the United Fuel Gas Co. was followed by dynamiting 24 company pipelines in West Virginia and Kentucky as well as other property damage. A strike at the Illinois Consolidated Telephone Co. also witnessed dynamiting of company facilities at a number of places. Other instances included dynamiting of a construction company's earth-moving and Caterpillar tractors in Huntington, Ind., and dynamite damage to machinery of a California timber company.

In none of the above disputes did personal injuries or deaths occur. Assaults against individuals took place, however, in four strikes. In February 1964, a truck carrying 11 temporary employees of a Chicago firm was overturned by 50 strikers. The injuries were unrecorded. In June of the same year, a Molotov cocktail was thrown through a window of a nonstriking employee in an Illinois strike. Again no information is available for casualties. A strike among employees of a Florida telephone company in 1967 witnessed several dynamiting incidents and the shooting of several employees. The assailants and the circumstances surrounding these incidents are unknown to the writers.

The most serious recent violent strike involved steel hauler owner-operators in 1967, whose dissatisfaction with the Teamsters Union to which they belonged generated more than 50 serious incidents of violence. In their attempt to secure better representation, the dissident Teamsters attempted to intimidate other drivers by acts of violence, including the throwing of fire bombs and rocks. One death and another serious injury were reported.

From time to time the newspapers report outbreaks of strike violence such as in the 1962 Florida East Coast Railroad strike and in the recent dispute between the Steelworkers Union and the Lone Star Steel Co. in Texas. The latter strike has been marked by beatings, shootings, and threats and has required the intervention of the Texas Rangers. It is noteworthy that in describing this strike in its story heading, the *Wall Street Journal* said: "Shades of the 1930's: Violent Steel Strike Rocks a Steel Producer in Texas."[228]

Apart from incidents of sabotage and destruction of property, most incidents of labor violence appear to end up in a NLRB charge. It is clearly in an employer's interest to make such charges, even in the ordinary case of minor coercion where little prospect of a Federal injunction exists. In these situations not only is the employer able to mitigate any legal derelictions of his own, but he can establish his legal right to take reprisals against those strikers guilty of misconduct. This is particularly important since many strike settlements founder on this issue because many employers adamantly refuse to reemploy employees who have participated in violent acts.

8. Other Evidence of the Diminution of Labor Violence

The diminution of the level of violence is attested to by its relatively scant treatment in congressional hearings since 1947. The essential concern of proponents of labor reform during the Taft-Hartley hearings was to deprive employees guilty of violence, threats, sitdown mass picketing, and other forms of intimidation of their reinstatement rights. It should be noted that past court decisions, in some instances overruling the Board, had eliminated the act's protection for employees engaging in the above practices. The McClellan committee's 1956-59 investigation of improper union and employer activities found no evidence of large-scale violence except in few cases such as the Kohler and Perfect Circle cases. However, the Landrum-Griffin Act contains prohibitions against threats and acts of violence and intimidation arising out of the management of internal union affairs. This is one of the least violated sections of the Landrum-Griffin Act. Other Federal statutes which touch upon labor violence, such as the Hobbs Act,[229] have given rise to a handful of cases.

9. The Impact of the National Labor Relations Act Upon Violence

A fundamental purpose of the national labor policy, first enunciated by the Wagner Act and confirmed by its subsequent amendments in the Taft-Hartley and Landrum-Griffin Acts, was the substitution of orderly procedures for trials of combat. But in balancing the public interest in the peaceful settlement of industrial disputes with the freedom of labor and management to work out their problems in light of their needs and experience, the law did not outlaw the exercise of economic force. Indeed, by endorsing collective bargaining, the NLRA explicitly acknowledged that tests of strength, i.e., the infliction of economic harm, with all its costs and hardships, is superior to such alternatives as compulsory arbitration.

However, this approval of the strike, the picket line, and the maintenance of hard bargaining lines by employers and unions was limited by the establishment of specified rules of conduct imposed on all parties. Some subjects were removed as bargaining issues and are not subject to economic pressures. Foremost among these was the question of union recognition and with it the concomitant mutual obligation to bargain in good faith. The wishes of a majority of employees within an appropriate bargaining unit determined whether or not collective bargaining was to begin, and this determination could not be lawfully qualified or limited.

The workings of the majority-rule principle can best be appreciated by applying it to the major disputes of the past. Members of the bargaining committee that approached the Pullman company were fired and Pullman refused to deal with any committee of his employees. Charles Schwab, head of the Bethlehem Steel Co., announced during the 1910 strike, "I will not deal with union committees or organized labor," an attitude reiterated for the entire industry in 1919. This position was taken by employers in Michigan Copper, in the coal industry of Colorado and the major coalfields in West Virginia, and by others in the more violent strikes. Some employer associations were hostile to the principle of dealing with unions, and these groups included the leading firms in many industries. Because employer refusal to meet and deal with unions was the major cause of past violent labor strikes, the effective enforcement of the Wagner Act reduced sharply the number of such encounters.

This diminution of labor violence was not a temporary phenomenon but endured the strains of major and minor wars, a number of business cycles, and substantial changes in national and local political administrations. Moreover, the social and economic environment in post-New Deal America was scarcely conducive to the pacific resolution of disputes of any kind. The reconversion of American industry after World War II brought on the greatest strike wave in our history. Yet, these mammoth strikes were accompanied by virtually no violence, completely at variance with the experience after 1918.

The contribution of the NLRA in sustaining the reduction in the number and severity of sanguinary labor clashes went beyond prescribing enforcible bargaining behavior. The law supported the right to organize of labor unions, but only on condition of avoidance of violence. Violence on a picket line is always latent but tends to surface when the employer recruits replacements and attempts to operate. Today, as always, employers have the legal right to move goods and people freely across a picket line and the duty and practice of police has tended to safeguard this right. Moreover, employees who engage in violence forfeit the protection of the act, which is a restraining influence upon them. The diminution of violence on labor's side has correspondingly lowered the propensity of employers to resort to force as either a defensive or aggressive tactic.

SUMMARY AND CONCLUSIONS

The United States has experienced more frequent and bloody labor violence than any other industrial nation. Its incidence and severity have, however, been sharply reduced in the last quarter of a century. The reduction is even more noteworthy when the larger number of union members, strikes, and labor-management agreements are considered. The magnitude of past violence is but partially revealed by available statistics. One writer estimated that in the bloody period between January 1, 1902, and September 30, 1904, 198 persons were killed and 1,966 injured in strikes and lockouts.[230] Our own independent count, which grossly understates the casualties, records over 700 deaths and several thousands of serious injuries in labor disputes. In addition, we have been able to identify over 160 occasions on which State and Federal troops have intervened in labor disputes.

The most common cause of past violent labor disputes was the denial of the right to organize through refusal to recognize the union, frequently associated with the discharge of union leaders. Knowledge of workers' resentment at their inability to join unions encouraged employers to take defensive measures during strikes and lockouts. These measures often included the hiring of guards who, by their provocative behavior, often created the very conditions they had been engaged to minimize.

The melancholy record shows that no section of the United States was free from industrial violence, that its origin and nature were not due to the influence of the immigrant or the frontier, nor did it reflect a darker side of the American character. Labor violence was caused by the attitudes taken by labor and management in response to unresolved disputes. The virtual absence at present of violence in the coal and copper mines, breeding grounds for the more dramatic and tragic episodes, are eloquent testimony that labor violence from the 1870's to the 1930's was essentially shaped by prevailing attitudes on the relations between employer and employee. Once these were changed, a change accomplished partly by legal compulsion, violence was sharply reduced.

Employer Violence

Employers and unions were both guilty of violence. Employer violence frequently had the cover of law. No employer was legally bound to recognize the union of his employees. He has and always had the right to defend his property and maintain free access to the labor and commodity markets. In anticipation of trouble, the employer could call on the community police force, and depending upon size and financial ability, supplement them with protective auxiliaries of his own. Such actions usually had public support, for the employer was exercising a recognized right to self-defense, despite widespread recognition by many public leaders in and out of Government of the desirability, need, and justice of collective bargaining. In the absence of the authority and effective sanctions of protective labor legislation, many employers fought unionism with every weapon at their command, in the certainty that their hostility was both lawful and proper.

Union Violence

Facing inflexible opposition, union leaders and their members frequently found that nothing, neither peaceful persuasion nor the intervention of heads of government, could move the employer towards recognition. Frustration and desperation impelled pickets to react to strikebreakers with anger. Many violent outbreaks followed efforts of strikers to restrain the entry of strikebreakers and raw materials into the struck plant. Such conduct, obviously illegal, opened the opportunity for forceful police measures. In the long run, the employers' side was better equipped for success. The use of force by pickets was illegal on its face, but the action of the police and company guards were in vindication of the employers' rights.

The effect of labor violence was almost always harmful to the union. There is little evidence that violence succeeded in gaining advantages for strikers. Not only does the rollcall of lost strikes confirm such a view, but the use of employer agents, disguised as union members or union officials for advocating violence within the union, testifies to the advantage such practices gave the employer. There were a few situations, in areas made vulnerable by their openness such as a strike in municipal transportation or involving teamsters, where violence was effective in gaining a favorable settlement. Even here, however, such as in the Teamsters strike in Chicago in 1905, the violence often failed. The most sensational campaigns of the Western Federation of Miners to bring their opponents to heel by the use of force were unsuccessful, and the union was virtually driven out of its stronghold. The campaign of dynamiting of the Iron Workers' Union ended in the conviction of the McNamaras. Subsequent convictions of a number of union leaders, including its president, who were convicted of transporting dynamite and of conspiracy in the Federal courts, almost wrecked the union. The campaign of violence carried on by the molders against the members of the antiunion National Founders Association failed to change the latters' policy.[231]

The right to organize was not retained in Homestead, or won in Pullman, the Colorado metal mines, Coeur d'Alene, or in the steel mills in 1919, although the sacrifice by union members, especially the rank and file members, was great. In fact, the victories gained by violent strikes are rather few, for the use of violence tends to bring about a hardening of attitudes and a weakening of the forces of peace and conciliation. A community might be sympathetic to the demands of strikers, but as soon as violent confrontations took place, the possibility was high that interest would shift from concern for the acceptance of union demands to the stopping of the violence.

It is the violent encounters that have provided organized labor with its lists of martyrs, men and women who gave their lives in defense of the union and collective bargaining. The role of martyrdom is not for us to assay, and may be useful in welding the solidarity of the group. The blood of the martyr may be the seed of the church, but in labor disputes it is doubtful if the sacrifices have been worth the results obtained. The evidence against the effectiveness of violence as a means of gaining concessions by labor in the United States is too overwhelming to be a matter of dispute.

Except for contemporary examples, we have not dealt with the numerous minor disturbances, some of them fairly serious, that were settled by the use of the normal police force. We have also generally avoided the many instances in which organizers and active unionists were denied their right to remain in communities or were the victims of local vigilante groups. We know that union organizers could not enter the closed coal towns, and that labor speakers could neither hire a hall nor speak in a public square in many communities. A number of coal counties in Kentucky and West Virginia built what amounted to an iron wall against the invasion of union organizers. The situation became worse during strikes. In the 1919 steel strike, the mayor of Duquesne, Pa., announced that "Jesus Christ could not hold a meeting in Duquesne," let alone the secretary-treasurer of the American Federation of Labor.

Sitdown Strikes

Some recent apostles of violence as a method of social reform point to the sitdown strikes in the 1930's as proof of the value of such tactics. The sitdown strike was the usual suspension of work, but instead of the employees leaving the premises of their employer, they remained within the plant. The tactic itself is not a violent one, although it is obviously an unlawful trespass upon another's property. However, these tactics were used against employers who had refused to grant recognition to the union, which during the great sitdown strikes in the plants of General Motors and the Chrysler Corp. were in violation

383

of the National Labor Relations Act. As a matter of fact, the sitdown strikes were exceptionally peaceful, given the circumstances, and there was only one serious confrontation between strikers and company guards during the strike at General Motors and, by the standards of the time, it can be described as a minor altercation. The beneficiaries of violence accompanying a sitdown strike are abundantly clear from the events surrounding a conventional recognition strike by the UAW against the Ford Motor Co.'s Rouge plant on April 1, 1941. According to the union, the company—

tried to take an illegal sitdown strike at the plant to discredit the genuine strike and to obscure the legal demands of the Ford workers. A federal conciliator and a Ford advertising director, however, revealed that the sitdowners were a thousand strikebreakers hired by Ford to stage a demonstration of riot and disorder.[332]

The company's attempt to use the sitdown as a basis for State and Federal armed intervention was unsuccessful.

As a matter of fact, violence was used against the automobile workers who used the sitdown tactic. Not only were many discharged for joining the union, but the attack upon Walter Reuther and Richard Frankensteen and others by a group of thugs under the direction of Harry Bennet, in charge of security at the Ford Motors Plant, was one of the more serious incidents in the organization of the industry. In ruling that sitdown strikers lost the protection against discharge for union activity guaranteed by the National Labor Relations Act, the U.S. Supreme Court said: "The seizure and holding of the buildings was a thing apart from any acts of sabotage. But in its legal aspect the ousting of the owner from lawful possession is not essentially different from assault upon the officers of an employer."[233] For our purposes, however, the distinction between a trespass and a physical assault is meaningful and important regardless of their legal equivalence. Once it became known that by participation in a sitdown strike a discharged worker forfeits his reinstatement rights under the law, the use of this tactic virtually ceased, and it has not been widely used since the above decision.

Persistence of Violence

We are, however, confronted with a paradox in that violence in labor disputes persisted even though it seldom achieved fruitful results. With few exceptions, labor violence was the result of isolated and usually unplanned acts on a picket line, or occurred during a prohibited parade or demonstration protesting employer obduracy or police brutality. It might also start by attempts of pickets to prevent the transportation of strikebreakers or goods, and a clash would follow police intervention. Where the employer refused to deal with the union, the possibility of eventual violence was always high. The desire of the American worker for union representation took place in the teeth of employer opposition that was able to impose heavy sanctions for union activity. The reproduction of conditions in which violence is spawned inevitably was followed by outbreaks of violence. Violence could be successfully repressed by superior forces but it could not be eliminated until its causes were removed.

The Reduction in Violence

The elimination in 1933 of the most important single cause of violence, refusal to recognize the union for purposes of collective bargaining, came about at the time when union membership was lower than it had been for 15 years. The first step taken was the adoption of section (7)(a) in the National Industrial Recovery Act, which guaranteed workers in industries operating under codes of fair competition the right to organize and bargain collectively through their own representatives. This provision was only partially effective in protecting the right to organize, but it was a significant beginning. Its successor, the National Labor Relations Act, with its amendments, has now been on the books for 33 years, and it is 31 years since it has been upheld by the Supreme Court. The sharp decline in the level of industrial violence is one of the great achievements of the National Labor Relations Board.

It may have been a fortunate coincidence that the labor laws guaranteeing the right to organize were enacted at the time the character of business management was changing. The professional business executive, who has increasingly come to dominate management, is not inclined to regard his business in the same sense as the head of a family-developed firm. He is more flexible in his thinking and more responsive to social and political changes. It may not be an accident that some of the bitterest contemporary labor disputes—Kohler and Perfect Circle, for example—took place in family-held businesses. The professional business leader is more detached, more pragmatic in his reactions, and knows that American business has sufficient resilience to adapt itself to free collective bargaining. The performance of American industry since the end of World War II demonstrates that union organization and collective bargaining are not incompatible with satisfactory profits and a high rate of technological change.

Violence has greatly diminished, but it has not entirely ceased. Between 80 and 100 proven charges of violence or coercion are closed annually by the National Labor Relations Board. In addition, reports of violence of varying seriousness appear periodically in the press. The charges that come before the Board that we have examined are largely based upon threats and generally minor picket-line incidents. In none of them did deaths or serious injuries occur. Nearly all of them, if they had taken place prior to the 1930's, would have been ignored in our study. Had we taken note of all the threats and picket line incidents prior to the 1930's, our study would have reached unmanageable proportions. Present-day violence is by and large the result of accidental and random events which occasionally erupt in a picket line confrontation.

Prospect of Reversion to Past Patterns of Violence

Has widescale violence been permanently erased from American industry? The reduction in violence in labor disputes has been accompanied by sharp increases in violent behavior in other areas of American life. This is no accident. The conditions that gave rise to past labor violence have been eliminated and a restoration of these conditions would lead to a reversion in conduct. Any tampering with the complex mechanism that governs our contemporary labor policy is an invitation towards unharnessing of the forces of violence and hate that we have successfully mastered.

Can one draw more general conclusions from the labor experience, or are they peculiar to the problems of workers seeking to establish unions in industry? On many occasions the union operated in a hostile community, while minorities carry on their protests in their own friendly neighborhoods. Nevertheless, in both situations the reaction of the majority is likely to be decisive. There have been times where public sentiment was so strongly on the labor side that no matter what violence it committed, it ran no risk of estranging local public sentiment. Such was the case in Virden and in the far more questionable situation in Herrin. Usually, however, violence led to the alienation of public opinion and sometimes to a shift in public sentiment to approval of severe actions against the strike. The evidence is clear that the absence of violence committed by unions would not have retrieved many lost strikes. However, it appears highly probable that the advocacy or the practice of organized and systematic violence on the union side would have prevented the enactment of the New Deal labor legislation.

There is no evidence that majorities will supinely accept violence by minorities. The fact that rioters are fighting for a just cause or reacting to oppression has not, in the case of labor, led to the condoning of violence by the public. The desirability of collective bargaining had, prior to the 1930's, been endorsed by a number of public bodies, and all 20th-century Presidents of the United States. Such views were also sponsored by leading students in the field, legislators, clergymen, and others. Such approval did not save labor from severe repression.

It appears to us that it is a gross confusion of the problem to emphasize the creative character of violence as a guide to the behavior of minorities suffering from serious inequities and injustice. Creative violence obviously refers to the successful revolutions in England, the United States, France, and Russia. It appears to us that such a view is completely irrelevant if it is not vicious and highly misleading. We are concerned not with revolutionary uprisings, which such a view implies, but how a minority can achieve belated justice. Although we believe that minorities can obtain little through violence, we are also convinced, on the basis of labor experience, that violence will continue unless attention is paid to the removal of grievances.

In some respects the violence in the ghettos resembles the kind that surrounded labor disputes; it arises without prior planning and out of isolated instances that may not repeat themselves. It is also highly probable that violence of this kind will be unproductive or even counterproductive, in that it will antagonize many who would normally support the claims of minorities for equal justice and opportunity. Yet the labor analogy with racial minorities can be pushed too far. Labor's grievances were specific and could be met by single or groups of employers with concessions. The adverse effects of granting these concessions were small, injured few people, and employers could generally pass on any added costs to consumers. On the other hand, to the extent that the grievances of minorities are of a general nature and the meeting of their demands impinges upon the privileges of wide sections of the community, the resolution of their disputes is apt to be met with greater opposition.

References

1. For a long period of time strikebreakers were not regarded as replacements.
2. Jean Maitron, *Histoire du Mouvement Anarchiste en France* (Paris: Societe Universitaire D'Editions et de Libraire, 1961), pp. 67-69.
3. Rudolf Rocker, *Johann Most, Das Leben Eines Rebellen* (Berlin: "Der Syndikalist," Fritz Kater, 1924), pp. 127-128.
4. Maitron, *op. cit.*, pp. 103-104; Henry David, *History of the Haymarket Affair* (New York: Russell & Russell, 1958), pp. 63-66.
5. Quotation is from David, *op. cit.*, p. 73; see also John R. Commons and associates, *History of Labour in the United States* (New York: The Macmillan Co., 1918), pp. 291-293.
6. David, *op. cit.*, pp. 98-100; Commons, *op. cit.*, pp. 294-296; Rocker, *op. cit.*, pp. 148-149.
7. See Maitron, *op. cit.*, 168-241, for description of the violence against persons and property and the reaction of the French Government.
8. During World War I many members of the IWW were arrested, and 165 leaders were indicted in the Federal courts in Chicago for conspiring to violate the espionage law. Similar indictments were found against a group tried in Sacramento, Calif., and at Kansas City, Kans. An examination of the record of the trial shows that the prosecution was able to present few instances in which the IWW was guilty of serious violence. Most instances were trivial and, moreover, showed no organized tendency in that direction. William D. Haywood, among others, denied that the IWW advocated such a principle. See Philip Taft, "The Federal Trials of the I.W.W.," *Labor History*, Winter 1962, pp. 57-92.
9. Walker C. Smith, *The Everett Massacre* (Chicago: I.W.W. Publishing Co., 1917), deals with the issue from the IWW point of view. Also, Perlman and Taft, *op. cit.*, pp. 390-392.
10. Ralph Chaplin, *The Centralia Conspiracy* (Chicago: I.W.W. Publishing Co., 1924); *The Centralia Case*, Joint Report on the Armistice Day Tragedy at Centralia, Wash., Nov. 11, 1919, issued by the Department of Research and Education of the Federal Council of Churches, the Social Action Department of the National Catholic Welfare Council,

and the Social Justice Committee of the Central Conference of American Rabbis, 1930; Ben Hur Lampman, *Centralia Tragedy and Trial* (Tacoma, Wash., 1920).

11. Eldridge Foster Dowell, *A History of Criminal Syndicalism* (Baltimore: Johns Hopkins Press, 1939), p. 17.

12. The exchange of letters between Governor Mathews and the President are in *Federal Aid in Domestic Disturbances, 1877-1903*. S. Doc. 209, 57th Cong., 2d session, p. 315.

13. Letters in *ibid.*, p. 317.

14. Gerald G. Eggert, *Railroad Labor Policy* (Ann Arbor: University of Michigan Press, 1967), p. 9.

15. *Report of the Committee to Investigate the Railroad Riots in July, 1877* (Harrisburg: Lane and Hart, State Printers, 1878), pp. 39-40.

16. See Robert V. Bruce, *1877: Year of Violence* (Indianapolis: Bobbs Merrill, 1959); J. A. Dacus, *Annals of the Great Strikes* (St. Louis: Schammell & Co., 1877); Edward Winslow Martin, *The History of the Great Riots* (Philadelphia: National Publishing Co., 1877).

17. *Fifth Biennial Report of the Adjutant General of the State of Kansas, 1885-86*, pp. 53-54.

18. *Investigation of Labor Troubles in Missouri, Kansas and Texas and Illinois*, H. Rept. 4174, 49 Cong. 2d sess., 1887, pp. IV-V.

19. *Biennial Report of the Adjutant General of Illinois to the Governor and Commander-in-Chief, 1885-86*, pp. 21, 22, 27, 30, 32.

20. *Ibid.*, pp. 34-35.

21. *Labor Troubles in the Anthracite Region of Pennsylvania*, H. Rept. 4147, 50th Cong., 2d sess., 1889, p. LXXXV.

22. *Annual Report of the Adjutant General of the Commonwealth of Massachusetts for the Year Ending December 31, 1875*, pp. 17-18.

23. Speech of Gen. C. H. Grosvenor of Athens County to Ohio House of Representatives, Mar. 10, 1875, pp. 3, 9, 15.

24. Quotation is from *Investigation of Labor Troubles*. U.S. S. Rept. 1280, 52d Cong., 2d sess., pp. XII, XIV. See also *Employment of Pinkertons*, H. Rept. 2447, 52d Cong., 2d sess.

25. *Report of the United States Industrial Commission*, Washington, 1901, vol. XII, p. 490; George Edgar French. "The Coeur d'Alene Riots," *Overland Monthly*, July 1895, pp. 33-34; Selig Perlman and Philip Taft, *History of Labor in the United States* (New York: Macmillan Co., 1935), vol. IV, pp. 17-173.

26. *Annual Report of the Adjutant General to the Governor of the State of Ohio for the Fiscal Year Ending Nov. 15, 1894*, pp. 5-6; *Ninth Biennial Report of the Adjutant General of the State of Kansas, 1893-94*, p. 13.

27. *Biennial Report of the Adjutant General of Illinois to the Governor and Commander-in-Chief, 1893 and 1894*, pp. XII, XIII.

28. *Report of the Adjutant General of the State of Indiana for the Year Ending October 31, 1894*, p. 9; *Report of the Adjutant General to the Governor of Iowa for the Biennial Period Ending November 30, 1895*, pp. 19-21.

29. Quotation from Almont Lindsey, *The Pullman Strike* (Chicago: University of Chicago Press, 1942), p. 263. Also see *Federal Aid in Domestic Disturbances*, pp. 194-195. President Cleveland, who had sent troops to Chicago during the strike, believed that "a comparatively insignificant quarrel between the managers of an industrial establishment and their workmen was joined by the large army of the Railway Union. It was the membership of these workmen in the Railway Union . . . that gave it the proportions of a tremendous disturbance, paralyzing the most important business interests, obstructing the functions of the Government, and disturbing social peace." Grover Cleveland, *The Government in the Chicago Strike of 1894* (Princeton: Princeton University Press, 1913), p. 6.

30. Resolution of the General Manager's Association is found in the *Report on the Chicago Strike of June-July 1894 by the United States Commission* appointed by the President, July 25, 1894, under the provisions of sec. 6 of ch. 1063 of the laws of the United States passed Oct. 1, 1888. (Washington: Government Printing Office, 1895), p. 250.

31. *Appendix to the Annual Report of the Attorney General of the United States for Year 1896* (Washington: Government Printing Office, 1896), pp. 221-222.

32. *Report of the Special Committee of Assembly Appointed to Investigate the Causes of the Strike of the Surface Rail Roads in the City of Brooklyn* (Albany: J. B. Lyon, 1895).

33. *Report of the Adjutant General of New York State*, Jan. 8, 1896, app. A.

34. A. C. Hutson, Jr., "The Coal Miners' Insurrection of 1891 in Anderson County, Tennessee," *The East Tennessee Historical Society's Publications*, No. 7, 1935, pp. 103-121.

35. Robert David Ward and William Warren Rodgers, *Labor Revolt in Alabama: The Great Strike of 1894* (Southern Historical Publications No. 9, University of Alabama, 1965), p. 68.

36. *Biennial Report of the Adjutant General of Alabama*, 1894, pp. 52, 62; Ward and Rodgers, *op. cit.*, p. 111.

37. *Biennial Report of the Adjutant General of Illinois to the Governor and Commander-in-Chief, 1899-1900*, pp. 6-7; *Eighteenth Annual Report of the Illinois Bureau of Labor Statistics, 1899*, pp. II-III.

38. See Vernon H. Jenson, *Heritage of Conflict* (Ithaca, N.Y.: Cornell University Press, 1950), pp. 13-14; Selig Perlman and Philip Taft, *History of Labor in the United States, 1896-1932* (New York: Macmillan Co., 1935), vol. IV, pp. 184-186; Report of the United States Industrial Commission, vol. XII, pp. 469-470; *Coeur d'Alene Mining Troubles*, S. Doc. 140, 56th Cong., 1st sess., p. 65; *Coeur d'Alene Labor Troubles*, H. Rept. 1999, 56th Cong., 1st sess., pp. 69-125.

39. The Molly McGuires, a terrorist organization that operated in the anthracite area at this time, was not a bargaining organization. Made up of Irish miners, it exercised vengeance against arrogant mine bosses of British origin and others who came into its disfavor. It did not direct demands for improvements in working conditions, although it issued warnings against oppressors. Whatever its connection with the labor movement may have been, we know that this group was destroyed and many of its leaders hanged.

40. Frank Julian Warne, *The Coal Mine Workers* (New York: Longmans, 1905).

41. *New York World*, Sept. 11-12, 1897; Also see Edward Pinkowski, *The Latimer Massacre* (Philadelphia: Sunshine Press, 1950).

42. *New York Tribune*, Sept. 23, Sept. 27, 1900.

43. *New York Tribune*, Sept. 30, 1902; Perlman and Taft, *op. cit.*, p. 44; Robert J. Cornell, *The Anthracite Coal Strike* (Washington: Catholic University Press, 1957); Frank J. Warne, *The Slav Invasion and the Mine Workers* (Philadelphia: Lippincott, 1904); *Report to the President on the Anthracite Coal Strike of May-October, 1902*, Anthracite Strike Commission (Washington: Government Printing Office, 1903).

44. *A Report on Labor Disturbances in the State of Colorado from 1880 to 1904*, S. Doc. 122, 58th Cong., 3d sess., p. 112.

45. *Ibid.*, pp. 182-187.

46. *Ibid.*, pp. 192-193.

47. *Ibid.*, p. 295.

48. *Ibid.*, p. 325.

49. *Ibid.*, pp. 168-169, 200-201, 205.

50. *Ibid.*, p. 325.

51. See Vernon Jensen, *Heritage of Conflict* (Ithaca: Cornell University Press, 1950); Benjamin McKie Rastall, *The Labor History of Cripple Creek District*, University of Wisconsin Bulletin No. 198 (Madison, 1908).

52. *Coast Seamen's Journal*, Sept. 21, 1901; Ira B. Cross, *History of the Labor Movement in California* (Berkeley: University of California, 1935), p. 243.

53. The information on violence is from the police reports sent to the Bureau of Labor by Frank L. Palmer and Ethelbert Stewart, both of whom were present at different times during the strike in Chicago, and reported regularly to the Commissioner of Labor. These papers were examined in the National Archives, Washington, D.C. They are in the Papers of Ethelbert Stewart.

54. *Coast Seamen's Journal*, Dec. 5, 1909, p. 2; Perlman and Taft, *op. cit.*, pp. 144-149.

55. Statement of James Tyson, a shipper, in *Report of Commission on Industrial Relations*, vol. VII, pp. 5252-5253.

56. *Report of the Adjutant General of the State of New York*, 1902, pp. 61-62.

57. *Report of the Adjutant General, Quartermaster-General and Surgeon General of Rhode Island*, 1902, p. 113.
58. *Report of the Adjutant General of the State of Louisiana*, 1902, pp. 11-13.
59. *Report of the Adjutant General of Connecticut to the Commander-in-Chief*, 1903, pp. VIII, IX.
60. *Nineteenth Annual Report of the Bureau of Labor Statistics, State of Connecticut Public Document N. 23, 1903*, p. 386.
61. The two quotations are from *Street Railway Journal*, July 6, 1907, p. 45, and *The Outlook*, May 11, 1907, p. 88.
62. *The Public*, Mar. 18, 1910, p. 253.
63. Harold J. Howland, "The War in Philadelphia," *The Outlook*, Mar. 5, 1910.
64. *Electric Traction Weekly*, Sept. 10, 1910, p. 993.
65. *Ibid.*, p. 994.
66. *Annual Report of the Adjutant General to the Governor of the State of Ohio*, 1910, p. 5.
67. Louis Levine, *The Women's Garment Workers* (New York: B. W. Huebsch, 1924); *Report of United States Commission on Industrial Relations*, S. Doc. 415, 64th Cong., 1st sess., vol. II, pp. 1031 ff.
68. *The Clothing Workers of Chicago, 1910–1922* (Chicago: Amalgamated Clothing Workers of America, 1922); Perlman and Taft, *op. cit.*, pp. 304-308. A year later, the Cleveland garment workers sought recognition, and their efforts were accompanied by rioting and shooting, including the killing of a picket. C. E. Ruthenberg, "The Cleveland Garment Workers," *International Socialist Review*, Sept. 1911, p. 136.
69. *Peonage in Western Pennsylvania*. Hearings before the Committee on Labor of the House of Representatives, 62d Cong., 1st sess., on H. Res. 90, p. 8.
70. *Report on the Miner's Strike in the Bituminous Coal Field in Westmoreland County, Pa.*, H. Doc. 847, 66th Cong., 2d sess., p. 82.
71. *Report on Strike at Bethlehem Steel Works, South Bethlehem, Pa.*, S. Doc. 521, 61st Cong., 2d sess., pp. 10-16.
72. *Labor Conditions in the Anthracite Regions of Pennsylvania, 1887–1888*, H. Rept. 4147, 50th Cong., 2d sess., pp. 136-167.
73. J. P. Shalloo, *Private Police* (Philadelphia: The American Academy of Political and Social Sciences, 1933), p. 61.
74. See report of the *Committee on Education and Labor Pursuant S. Res. 266* (74th Cong.), *S. Rept. 6, Part 2, 76th Cong., 1st sess.*, 1939; *Report of United States Commission on Relations*, S. Doc. 415, 64th Cong., 1st sess., 1916, pp. 92-98.
75. *Report of the Adjutant General of the State of New Jersey for the Year Ending October 31, 1902*, p. 25.
76. *U.S. H. Doc. 607*, 60th Cong., 1st sess., p. 17.
77. *Ibid.*, p. 22.
78. *Ibid.*, p. 23.
79. *Ibid.*, p. 23. The quotation is from a report of Lawrence O. Murray, Herbert Knox Smith, and Charles P. O'Neil, who were appointed by President Roosevelt to investigate the Goldfield violence.
80. *Report of the Adjutant General of the State of New Jersey for the Year Ending October 31, 1909*, pp. 15-16.
81. *Biennial Report of the Adjutant General of California*, 1910, pp. 50-51.
82. Luke Grant, *The National Erectors' Association and the International Association of Bridge and Structural Iron Workers* (Washington: U.S. Commission on Industrial Relations, 1915), especially pp. 107-148.
83. *Ibid.*, p. 125.
84. *Ibid.*, p. 130.
85. *Ibid.*, pp. 136-137.
86. "A Policy of Lawlessness: A Partial Record of Riot, Assault, Murder, Coercion, and Intimidation Occurring in Strikes of the Iron Molders Union During 1904, 1905, 1906, and 1907" (Detroit: National Founders Association, no date).
87. *Report of the United States Commission on Industrial Relations* (testimony of Charles F. Markham, president of Illinois Central), vol. X.
88. The violence is described in sections dealing with the Harriman and Illinois Central strikes in *ibid*.
89. *Annual Report of the Adjutant General of the State of Louisiana for the Year Ending December 31, 1912*, pp. 7-8.
90. *Annual Report of the State Board of Conciliation and Arbitration in Massachusetts, 1912*, p. 31; *Report of Massachusetts Adjutant General*

for 1912, p. 7; *Report on Textile Strike in Lawrence, Massachusetts,* S. Doc. 870, 62d Cong., 2d session; *Hearings on the Strike at Lawrence, Massachusetts,* H. Doc. 671, 62d Cong., 2d sess.

91. *Report of the United States Commission on Industrial Relations,* vol. 3, pp. 2534, 2547.

92. *Report of the Adjutant General of the State of California,* 1914, pp. 45-46; *Proceedings of the 15th Annual Convention of the Convention of the California State Federation of Labor,* 1914, pp. 72-73.

93. Henry F. Grady, "The Open Shop in San Francisco," *The Survey,* May 25, 1916, p. 193.

94. *Law and Order in San Francisco: A Beginning* (San Francisco Chamber of Commerce, 1916), pp. 8-11.

95. *Report of the Adjutant General of the State of Florida for the Year 1912,* app. B.

96. *Annual Report of the Adjutant General of the State of New York for the Year 1913,* p. 6.

97. *Annual Report of the Adjutant General of the State of New York for the Year 1913,* p. 6; *The Outlook,* Apr. 19, 1913, p. 129.

98. *The Miners' Magazine,* Oct. 1, 1912, pp. 8-9.

99. *The Public,* Jan. 14, 1916, p. 35; Jan. 21, 1916, p. 63; John A. Fitch, "Arson and Citizenship," *The Survey,* Jan. 22, 1916.

100. *The Public,* Aug. 29, 1913, p. 825; Nov. 7, 1913, pp. 1064-1065.

101. *Report of the Indiana Adjutant General of the State of Indiana for the Fiscal Years Ending September 30, 1913 and 1914,* p. 170.

102. *The Survey,* May 3, 1913, p. 163.

103. *The Public,* June 20, 1913, p. 588; J. S. Biscay "The Ipswich Strike," *International Socialist Review,* Aug. 1913, p. 91.

104. *The New York Times,* Jan. 29, Feb. 4, 1913.

105. *The Miners' Magazine,* May 29, 1913, pp. 8-9.

106. Quote is from *The Survey,* Jan. 30, 1915, p. 458; *The Public,* Jan. 29, 1915, p. 107; *New York Times,* June 7, 1913.

107. *The Survey,* July 31, 1915, p. 387.

108. *Literary Digest,* Aug. 7, 1915, p. 237.

109. John A. Fitch, "When a Sheriff Breaks a Strike," *The Survey,* Aug. 7, 1915, pp. 414-415.

110. John A. Fitch, "The Explosion at Bayonne," *The Survey,* Oct. 21, 1916, pp. 61-62; *New York Times,* Oct. 11, 14, 1916.

111. *Strike in the Copper Mining District of Michigan,* S. Doc. 381, 63d Cong., 2d sess.; Perlman and Taft, *op. cit.,* pp. 348-351.

112. *Investigation of Conditions in Paint Creek Coal Fields of West Virginia in Pursuance of S. Res. 37,* S. Rept. 321, 63d Cong., 2d sess., contains the commission's report. Quotation is on p. 238.

113. George P. West, *Report on the Colorado Strike* (Washington: U.S. Commission on Industrial Relations, 1915), p. 31.

114. *Ibid.,* p. 133.

115. West, *op. cit.,* p. 135. West was an investigator for the U.S. Commission on Industrial Relations and was acquainted with the facts. The figure on the dead women from Luke Grant, "The National Erectors Association," p. 131.

116. Perlman and Taft, *op. cit.,* pp. 336-342; Philip Taft, *Organized Labor in American History* (New York: Harper & Row, 1964), pp. 259-262; *Final Report and Testimony Submitted to Congress by the Commission on Industrial Relations,* vols. VI, VIII, IX. Also Barron B. Beshoar, *Out of the Depths* (Denver: Golden Press, n.d.), pp. 180-194.

117. *Monthly Labor Review,* Sept., 1941, p. 569.

118. *Statement by the Mine Operators of the District Arizona Chapter American Mining Congress,* 1917, pp. 8-9.

119. *Transcription of the Hearing of the President's Mediation Board.* Held at Bisbee, Ariz., Nov. 1-5, 1917, pp. 239-240.

120. *Ibid.,* p. 160.

121. *Ibid.,* p. 160.

122. *Journal of the Senate, Third Legislature, First Special Session, State of Arizona,* 1918, p. 11.

123. *Report on the Bisbee Deportations Made by the President's Mediation Commission to the President of the United States,* Nov. 6, 1917.

124. *West Virginia Coal Fields.* Hearings before U.S. Senate Committee on Education and Labor, 67th Cong., 1st sess., pp. 7, 52, 873.

125. *Ibid.,* p. 6. See also Winthrop D. Lane, *Civil War In West Virginia* (New York: Huebsch, 1921).

126. *Biennial Report of the Adjutant General of the State of Colorado*, p. 22.
127. *Quadrennial Report of Adjutant General of Alabama*, 1922, pp. 29-30.
128. *United Mine Workers Journal*, Aug. 15, 1922, pp. 7-8, 9-10.
129. *Monthly Labor Review*, Sept., 1924, p. 570.
130. Paul M. Angle, *Bloody Williamson* (New York: Knopf, 1952) deals with this episode.
131. Quoted by Orville Thrasher Gooden, *The Missouri and North Arkansas Strike* (New York: Columbia University Press, 1926), p. 231. See also Rev. J. K. Farris, *The Harrison Riot or the Reign of the Mob* (Wynne, Ark.: J. K. Farris, 1924), which deals with the strike sympathetically.
132. *Report of the Adjutant General of Missouri*, Jan. 10, 1921.
133. *Annual Report of the Chief of the Militia Bureau*, 1923, pp. 58-65.
134. The information is from the Bill of Complaint Exhibit No. 3, *U.S. Railway Employees Department, American Federation of Labor, etc.*, in the U.S. District Court for the Northern District of Illinois Eastern Division, pp. 123-124.
135. *Ibid.*, pp. 124-128, 139-143.
136. *Appendix to Annual Report of Attorney General of the United States for the Fiscal Year 1922* (Washington: Government Printing Office, 1924), p. 20.
137. *Ibid.*
138. *Ibid.*, p. 21.
139. *Ibid.*, p. 21.
140. *Ibid.*, p. 23.
141. *A History of Organized Felony and Folly, the Record of Union Labor in Crime and Economics* (New York, no publisher, 1923, pp. 62-65). This work claims that the U.S. Attorney General charged that the death of 25 people could be directly attributed to the shopmen's strike.
142. *11th Biennial Report* (Colorado), *Bureau of Labor Statistics*, 1919-20, p. 26.
143. *The Denver Tramway Strike of 1920: Report by Edward T. Devine, Rev. John A. Ryan and John A. Lapp* (Denver: The Denver Commission on Religious Forces, 1921), pp. 2, 21, 32-33.
144. *Annual Report of the Chief of the Militia Bureau, 1922* (Washington: Government Printing Office, 1922), pp. 45-47; *Report of the Adjutant General State of Minnesota*, 1922, pp. 11-14; *Biennial Report of the Adjutant General of the State of North Carolina, 1921-1922*, p. 47.
145. *Annual Report of the Chief of the Militia Bureau, 1922*, p. 47.
146. See Royal E. Montgomery, *Industrial Relations in the Chicago Building Trades* (Chicago: University of Chicago Press, 1927).
147. *United Mine Workers Journal*, Mar. 15, 1926, p. 11; Harriet L. Herring, "12 Cents, the Troops and the Union," *The Survey*, Nov. 15, 1923, pp. 199-200; *Annual Report of the Chief of the Militia Bureau*, 1927, p. 68.
148. Daniel J. McClurg, "The Colorado Coal Strike of 1927—Tactical Leadership of the IWW," *Labor History*, pp. 82-85; *Biennial Report of the Adjutant General of the State of Colorado to His Excellency the Governor*, 1928, pp. 26-28.
149. *Conditions in the Coal Fields of Pennsylvania, West Virginia, and Ohio.* Hearings before the Committee on Interstate Commerce, U.S. Sen., 70th Cong., 1st sess., pursuant to S. Res. 105.
150. *Report of the Adjutant General of the State of North Carolina, July 1, 1926, to Dec. 31, 1927.*
151. *New York Times*, Oct. 3-5, 12, 1929; *The Marion Murder* (New York: National Executive Committee of the Conference for Progressive Labor Action, 1929).
152. *Justice North Carolina Style* (American Civil Liberties Union, 1931), pp. 11-14.
153. *New York Times*, May 6, Nov. 7, 9, 1931, and Feb. 11, Mar. 24-31, 1932; *The Kentucky Miner's Struggle* (New York: American Civil Liberties Union, 1930).
154. *The Struggle for Civil Liberty on the Land* (New York: American Civil Liberties Union, no date), pp. 24-25, 27-28.
155. Walter Wilson, *Call Out the Militia* (New York: American Civil Liberties Union, 1938), p. 27.
156. Captive mines produced coal only for the use of owners, such as steel and public utility companies.
157. *New York Times*, Oct. 5, 10, 11, 1933.
158. *Pittsburgh Press*, July 26-30, Aug. 2-6, Nov. 1-5, 1933.

159. *Violation of Free Speech and Rights of Labor: Private Police Systems, Harlan County, Kentucky,* report of the Committee on Education and Labor pursuant to S. Res. 266 (74th Cong.). A resolution to investigate violations of the right of free speech and assembly and interference with the right of labor to organize and bargain collectively, Feb. 13, 1939, pp. 47-48.
160. *Ibid.,* p. 53.
161. *Ibid.,* p. 79.
162. *Ibid.,* p. 83.
163. *Ibid.,* p. 94.
164. *Ibid.,* pp. 98-104.
165. *Ibid.,* pp. 111-112.
166. *Ibid.,* p. 112.
167. Harriet D. Hudson, *The Progressive Mine Workers of America: A Study in Rival Unionism* (Urbana, Ill.: University of Illinois Press, 1952), pp. 119-120; McAlister Coleman, *Men and Coal* (New York: Farrar & Rinehart, 1943), p. 177.
168. Philip Taft, *Organized Labor in American History* (New York: Harper & Row, 1964), pp. 488-489.
169. *Congressional Record,* Mar. 13, 1958, p. 4098.
170. *Report of the Adjutant General of the State of North Carolina, January 1, 1933–December 31, 1935,* p. 12.
171. *Ibid.,* pp. 447-449. See also *New York Times* through August and September 1934 for detailed coverage of the textile strike situation.
172. Wilson, *op. cit.,* p. 28.
173. *New York Times,* Feb. 1, 15, Mar. 31, May 14, Oct. 27, 1935.
174. *New York Times,* Oct. 29-31, 1935.
175. *Labor Fact Book III,* pp. 173-175.
176. Wilson, *op. cit.,* p. 15.
177. *New York Times,* Sept. 3-8, 1935.
178. *Report of the Chief of the National Guard,* 1936, p. 16.
179. Wilson, *op. cit.,* p. 29.
180. *New York Times,* July 24, Sept. 27, Nov. 30, 1936.
181. *New York Times,* June 30, July 12-13, 1936.
182. *Ibid.,* June 2-4, 1936.
183. *Labor Fact Book,* 1938, pp. 125-126.
184. President Thomas Girdler, of the Republic Steel Co., testified before the La Follette Committee in August 1938, and stated that his industrial relations policy had succeeded. Senator Robert M. La Follette commented: "Mr. Girdler, in connection with the success of his industrial-relations policy, the record of this investigation shows that the steel strike of 1937 cost the country sixteen lives and 307 persons were injured." *Hearings before a Subcommittee on Education and Labor, U.S. Senate 75th Cong., 3d sess.,* pt. 34, p. 13889.
185. *The Chicago Memorial Day Incident.* S. Rept. 46, pt. 2, 76th Cong., 1st sess., 1937, p. 3.
186. *Ibid.,* p. 18.
187. *Ibid.,* p. 18.
188. *Ibid.,* p. 39.
189. *Youngstown Vindicator,* June 20, 1937. See testimony of witnesses on the riot in *Hearings before a Subcommittee of the Committee on Education and Labor, 75th Cong., 3d sess., pursuant to S. Res. 266, 74th Cong.,* pt. 29, pp. 11183-12014.
190. *Hearings Before a Subcommittee of the Committee on Education and Labor, U.S. Senate, 75th Cong., 3d sess.,* pt. 25, p. 10689.
191. *New York Times,* July 27, 1937.
192. *Hearings Before a Subcommittee of the Committee on Education and Labor, U.S. Senate, 75th Cong., 3d sess.,* pt. 34, p. 13968.
193. *Ibid.,* pt. 28, p. 11497.
194. *New York Times,* July 8-12, 1937.
195. *New York Times,* June 26, July 1-3, 1937.
196. *New York Times,* July 1, 1937.
197. *Philadelphia [Pa.] Bulletin,* June 29, 1937.
198. *Chicago Tribune,* Mar. 2, 3, 1938.
199. *Houston [Tex.] Chronicle,* Sept. 15, 1938; *Voice of the Federation,* Sept. 22, 1938.
200. *Houston [Tex.] Press,* July 1, Aug. 5, 1938.
201. *Biennial Report of the Adjutant General of the State of Iowa for the Fiscal Years 1939 and 1940,* pp. 9-10.

202. *Ibid.*, pp. 10-11.
203. *New York Times*, July 17, 28, Aug. 29, Nov. 9, 11, 1939.
204. *New York Times*, Aug. 8, 21, 23, 1939.
205. *Denver Post*, May 23, 1940.
206. *Newark News* (N.J.), Sept. 23, 1946.
207. *St. Louis Dispatch*, July 25, 1940.
208. *New York Times*, Apr. 16, 1941.
209. *Los Angeles Times*, June 9, 1940.
210. *The St. Louis Post Dispatch*, Oct. 23, 1940.
211. *Ibid.*
212. *New York Times*, Apr. 16, 1941.
213. *New York Times*, Apr. 16, 1941.
214. *Ibid.*, Dec. 15, 1941.
215. *Quadrennial Report of the Adjutant General of Alabama*, 1942, pp. 87-88.
216. *New York Times*, May 10, 1940.
217. *St. Louis Dispatch*, July 25, 1940.
218. *Brooklyn Eagle*, Sept. 24, 1940.
219. *Detroit Times*, May 13, 1941.
220. *San Antonio Light*, June 12, 1941; *San Antonian Express*, June 15, 1941.
221. *Detroit Times*, Feb. 16, 1942; Feb. 17, 1942.
222. *Charleston Post*, Apr. 2, 1943.
223. *Arkansas Gazette*, Feb. 2, 1945.
224. *Oklahoma City Oklahoman*, Apr. 21, 1946.
225. *NLRB* v. *Drivers, etc.*, 362 U.S. 274 at 290.
226. *Perry Norvell Co.*, 80 NLRB 225 at 239.
227. We have examined all of the Board's case files in which a finding has been made of union-caused violence or coercion.
228. *Wall Street Journal*, Oct. 30, 1968.
229. The Hobbs Act inhibits the use of or threat of force to transport money in interstate commerce.
230. Slason Thompson, "Violence in Labor Disputes," *World's Work*, Dec. 1904.
231. *Final Report and Testimony of the Commission on Industrial Relations*, S. Doc. 415, 64th Cong., 1st sess. (Washington: Government Printing Office, 1916), vol. I, pp. 242-244.
232. "We Work at Ford's—A Picture History," UAW-CIO Ford Dept., Detroit, Mich., 1955, p. 45.
233. *National Labor Relations Board* v. *Fansteel Metallurgical Corp.*, 306 U.S. 240.

PART IV

PATTERNS AND SOURCES OF
RACIAL AGGRESSION

The history of white aggression against American Negroes has been so thoroughly documented that there is no need to elaborate further upon it here. What is probably most remarkable about the "American Dilemma" of which Gunnar Myrdal and others wrote is that for most white Americans, who have been living with the dilemma since the 17th century, its quotient of frustration has been so minimal. If a dilemma is defined as a situation requiring a choice between two equally undesirable alternatives, one wonders, since the contradiction between the equalitarian American Creed and oppressive behavior has never been resolved, whether Charles Silberman wasn't closer to the mark when he observed that "the tragedy of race relations in the United States is that there is no American Dilemma."[1]

Or perhaps there has been an American dilemma, but one which has more accurately characterized the plight of black Americans, for surely the undesirability of the two alternatives has always been more apparent to them. To acquiesce in slavery and caste meant enduring misery and degradation. But to strike out against the status quo was to invite the rope and faggot. Today, Negro Americans are at long last sharpening the twin horns of the white dilemma, and thereby forcing its resolution. That it will be resolved in favor of the equalitarian creed is by no means certain, for it is possible that under extreme stress American society will choose security over freedom and order over justice.

Whatever the outcome, the contemporary effusion of black militancy poses two closely related questions: What has been the sequence of events that in the 20th century has transformed the Negroes' response to oppression from a defensive to a retaliatory one? And how can we explain the paradox that so many generations of black Americans were relatively quiescent during the epochs of slavery and formal caste, only to explode in wrathful protest just as the physical conditions of life were ostensibly improving?[2]

Racial violence in the 20th century has undergone a fundamental transformation. Interracial riots in the early years of the century were essentially pogroms in which the Negroes were victims of white aggression. In the 1960's the Negroes have been the aggressors; however, in contrast to the earlier riots, deaths have been few, the attacks being concentrated on property rather than persons. Deaths have occurred primarily as the result of conflict between police and Negro civilians, rather than between Negro and white civilians, as had been the case in the early-20th century.

Although black retaliatory violence has been essentially a characteristic only of recent racial rioting, Profs. August Meier and Elliott Rudwick demonstrate in chapter 9 that neither the rhetoric nor the practice of black retaliation is new. They argue that tendencies toward retaliatory violence are correlated to a considerable extent with periods of generally heightened militance among Negroes, and that the reasons for this relationship—as well as for the absence of retaliatory violence during the initial period of growing militance after World War II—are to be found less in external circumstances than in the changing expectations of the black population of the United States.

The historical analysis of Meier and Rudwick is supplemented in chapter 10 by Morris Janowitz's sociological analysis of the transformation of collective racial violence through three stages. First, 50 years ago, the typical race riot in American cities was an interracial clash on the boundaries of expanding black neighborhoods, one in which whites more often than Negroes took offensive action. Second, during World War II, these communal clashes began to give way to large-scale riots, wholly within the black community. Often triggered by a police incident, the outbursts resulted in clash between the local population and officers and agents of the larger society, with implied overtones of political protest. Because the outbursts resulted in widespread looting, they can be described as commodity riots. Third, by the summer of 1968, however, this form of racial violence appeared to be in decline, being replaced by a new form: a more selective, terroristic use of force against whites by small, organized groups of blacks with crude ideological motives.

Each stage in the transformation of racial violence in the United States has carried with it elements of the next stage. Each stage is an expression of the social structure of the United States and the position of the Negro in this social structure. In other words, Janowitz's basic orientation is that the agencies of social change and social control are crucial in accounting for the occurrence and form of urban racial outbreaks. The impact of two such agencies is examined: the patterns of intervention and the consequences of law enforcement crucially condition the sequence and extent of the riot; while the mass media have both an immediate impact on the contagion of riot behavior and a long-term effect on the social structure.

In chapter 11 James P. Comer, a psychiatrist, addresses himself to the paradoxical recent venting of black anger in the face of the demonstrable economic and educational gains made by Negro Americans since 1960. Clearly, the concurrence of accelerated socioeconomic mobility and violence cannot be explained on the basis of any objective and measurable criteria such as the number and quality of jobs and the level of employment or income. The coincidence of black progress and black rage suggests that the latter is in part a legacy of an earlier form of violence: the severe psychic damage wrought by the powerlessness of enslavement and subsequently of caste.

The chronic psychological trauma of slavery and later of caste forced the powerless black community to adapt avoidance and denial mechanisms, which resulted in ignoring or turning anger inward against the self in self-destructive acts, or in projecting or displacing it onto group members and acting aggressively against them rather than toward members of the oppressive group. But social conditions of the past few years have permitted these feelings to be turned outward and directed toward the perceived oppressor. Dr. Comer's psychoanalytical analysis of the relationship of the oppressor and the oppressed over time suggests that the analogy of individual development may largely resolve the apparent paradox.

References

1. Charles E. Silberman, *Crisis in Black and White* (New York: Random House, 1964), p. 10.
2. In addition to the historical, sociological, and psychological answers proposed in the following three chapters, a comparative interpretation is advanced by James C. Davies in chapter 19.

Chapter 9

BLACK VIOLENCE IN THE 20th CENTURY: A STUDY IN RHETORIC AND RETALIATION

By August Meier and Elliott Rudwick*

For most Americans, the increasingly overt talk of retalitory violence among Negro militants, and the outbreaks in the urban ghettos over recent summers, signify something new and different in the history of Negro protest. Actually, retaliatory violence has never been entirely absent from Negro thinking. Moreover, advocacy of retaliatory violence, and actual instances of it, have tended to increase during periods of heightened Negro protest activity.

Thus the past decade of rising Negro militance has been no stranger to the advocacy of retaliatory violence. For example, as far back as 1959, Robert F. Williams, at the time president of the Monroe, North Carolina, branch of the NAACP, came to public attention when the Union County Superior Court acquitted two white men of brutal assaults on two Negro women, but sentenced a mentally retarded Negro to imprisonment as a result of an argument he had with a white woman. Williams angrily told a reporter, "We cannot take these people who do us injustice to the court, and it becomes necessary to punish them ourselves. If it's necessary to stop lynching with lynching, then we must be willing to resort to that method." The NAACP dismissed Williams as branch president, but he remained a leader of Monroe's working-class Negroes, who for several years had been using guns to protect their homes from white Klansmen. In 1961, falsely charged with kidnaping a white couple, he fled from the country. Williams became the most famous of that group of militants existing at the

* August Meier is the university professor of history at Kent State University. He is author of *Negro Thought in America, 1880–1915* (Ann Arbor: University of Michigan Press, 1963), and coauthor with Elliott Rudwick of *From Plantation to Ghetto: An Interpretive History of American Negroes* (New York: Hill & Wang, 1966).

Elliott Rudwick is professor of sociology at Kent State University. His publications include *Race Riot at East St. Louis, July 2, 1917* (Cleveland and New York: Meridian Books, 1966), and *W. E. B. Du Bois: Propagandist of the Negro Protest* (New York Atheneum, 1968).

Professors Meier and Rudwick are senior research fellows at Kent State University's Center for Urban Regionalism.

fringe of the civil-rights movement, who in their complete alienation from American society articulated a revolutionary synthesis of nationalism and Marxism.[1] From his place of exile in Havana, Cuba, Williams undertook the publication of a monthly newsletter, *The Crusader*. In a typical issue, he declared:

Our only logical and successful answer is to meet organized and massive violence with massive and organized violence. . . . The weapons of defense employed by Afro-American freedom fighters must consist of a poor man's arsenal. . . . Molotov cocktails, lye, or acid bombs [made by injecting lye or acid in the metal end of light bulbs] can be used extensively. During the night hours such weapons, thrown from roof tops, will make the streets impossible for racist cops to patrol. . . . Yes, a minority war of self-defense can succeed.[2]

Subsequently Williams was named chairman in exile of an organization known as the Revolutionary Action Movement (RAM),[3] a tiny group of college-educated people in a few major northern cities, some of whose members have been recently charged with plotting the murder of Roy Wilkins and Whitney Young.

Williams, RAM, and the better known Black Muslims[4] were on the fringes of the Negro protest of the early 1960's. More recently violence and the propaganda for violence have moved closer to the center of the race relations stage. Well over 200 riots have occurred since the summer of 1964. The incendiary statements of the Rap Browns and the Stokeley Carmichaels became familiar TV and newspaper fare for millions of white Americans. The Oakland, California, Black Panthers and other local groups espousing a nationalist and revolutionary rhetoric thrived and received national publicity. As has been often pointed out, there is no evidence that the race riots of the 1960's have any direct relations to the preachings of Williams, of these various groups, even of the SNCC advocates of armed rebellion and guerrilla warfare. Yet both the statements of these ideologists, and the spontaneous actions of the masses, have much in common. For both are the product of the frustrations resulting from the growing disparity between the Negroes' status in American society and the rapidly rising expectations induced by the civil-rights revolution and its earlier successes.

Historically, this doctrine of retaliatory violence has

taken various forms. Some have advocated self-defense against a specific attack. Others have called for revolutionary violence. There are also those who hopefully predicted a general race war in which Negroes would emerge victorious. Though seldom articulated for white ears, and only rarely appearing in print, thoughts of violent retaliation against whites have been quite common. For example, Ralph Bunche, in preparing a memorandum for Gunnar Myrdal's *American Dilemma* in 1940, noted that "there are Negroes, too, who, fed up with frustration of their life, here, see no hope and express an angry desire 'to shoot their way out of it.' I have on many occasions heard Negroes exclaim, 'Just give us machine guns and we'll blow the lid off the whole damn business.' "[5]

In surveying the history of race relations during the 20th century, it is evident that there have been two major periods of upsurge both in overt discussion by Negro intellectuals concerning the desirability of violent retaliation against white oppressors, and also in dramatic incidents of actual social violence committed by ordinary Negro citizens. One was the period during and immediately after the First World War. The second has been the period of the current civil rights revolution.

W. E. B. Du Bois, the noted protest leader and a founder of the NAACP, occasionally advocated retaliatory violence, and somewhat more often predicted intense racial warfare in which Negroes would be the victors. In 1916, inspired by the Irish Rebellion, in an editorial in the NAACP's official organ, *The Crisis,* he admonished Negro youth to stop spouting platitudes of accommodation and remember that no people ever achieved their liberation without an armed struggle. He said that "war is hell, but there are things worse than hell, as every Negro knows."[6] Amid the violence and repression that Negroes experienced in the postwar world, Du Bois declared that the holocaust of World War I was "nothing to compare with that fight for freedom which black and brown and yellow men must and will make unless their oppression and humiliation and insult at the hands of the White World cease."[7]

Other intellectuals reflected this restless mood. The postwar years were the era of the militant, race-conscious New Negro of the urban North, an intellectual type who rejected the gradualism and conciliation of his ancestors.

The tone of the New Negro was recorded by Claude McKay, who in 1921 wrote his well-known poem, "If We Must Die": "If we must die/let it not be like hogs; hunted and penned in an accursed spot!/ . . . . If we must die; oh, let us nobly die/dying but fighting back." A. Philip Randolph, editor of the militant socialist monthly, *The Messenger,* organizer of the Brotherhood of Sleeping Car Porters, and later leader of the March on Washington Movements of 1941 and 1963, also advocated physical resistance to white mobs. He observed that "Anglo-Saxon jurisprudence recognizes the law of self-defense . . . . The black man has no rights which will be respected unless the black man forces that respect. . . . We are conseqently urging Negroes and other oppressed groups concerned with lynching or mob violence to act upon the recognized and accepted law of self-defense."[8]

The legality of retaliatory violent self-defense was asserted not only by A. Philip Randolph, but also by the NAACP, which Randolph regarded as a moderate, if not futile organization, wedded to the interest of the Negro middle class. In 1925, half a dozen years after *The Messenger* article, the NAACP secured the acquittal of Dr. Ossian Sweet and his family. The Sweets were Detroit Negroes who had moved into a white neighborhood, and fired on a stone-throwing mob in front of their home, killing one white man and wounding another.[9] More than a quarter of a century later, at the time of the Robert Williams episode, the NAACP in clarifying its position, reiterated the stand that "The NAACP has never condoned mob violence but it firmly supports the right of Negroes individually and collectively to defend their person, their homes, and their property from attack. This position has always been the policy of the NAACP."[10] The views of intellectuals like Du Bois, McKay, and Randolph during World War I and the early postwar years paralleled instances of Negro retaliatory violence which actually triggered some of the major race riots of the period.

The East St. Louis riot of 1917, the bloodiest in the 20th century, was precipitated in July when Negroes, having been waylaid and beaten repeatedly by white gangs, shot into a police car and killed two white detectives. On the darkened street a Negro mob of 50 to 100 evidently mistook the Ford squad car for the Ford automobile containing white "joyriders" who had shot up Negro homes earlier in the evening. The following morning the riot began.[11]

In Houston, several weeks later, about 100 Negro soldiers broke into an Army ammunition storage room and marched on the city's police station. The troops, mostly Northerners, were avenging an incident which occurred earlier in the day, when a white policeman used force in arresting a Negro woman and then beat up a Negro soldier attempting to intervene. A Negro provost guard was pistol whipped and shot at for asking the policeman about the wounded soldier. Even before these events, the Negro soldiers nursed a hatred for Houston policemen, who had attempted to enforce streetcar segregation, frequently used the term "nigger," and officiously partolled the Negro ghetto. The Houston riot was not only unusual because it involved Negro soldiers, but also because white persons constituted most of the fatalities.[12]

By 1919 there was evidence that the Negro masses were prepared to fight back in many parts of the country, even in the Deep South. In an unpublished report to the NAACP Board of Directors, a staff member, traveling in Tennessee and Mississippi during early 1919, noted that "bloody conflicts impended in a number of southern cities." Perry Howard, the leading colored attorney in Jackson, and R. R. Church, the wealthy Memphis politician, both reported that Negroes were armed and prepared to defend themselves from mob violence. Howard detailed an incident in which armed Negroes had prevented a white policeman from arresting a Negro who had become involved in a fight with two white soldiers after they had slapped a colored girl. In Memphis, R. R. Church, fearing armed conflict, privately advised the city's mayor that "the Negroes would not make trouble unless they were attacked, but in that event they were prepared to defend themselves."[13]

The Chicago race riot of 1919 grew out of Negro resentment of exclusion from a bathing beach dominated by whites. One Sunday, while Negroes and whites scuffled on the beach, a colored teenager drowned after being attacked in the swimming area. That attack was the most recent of a long series of assaults against Negroes. A white policeman not only refused to arrest a white man allegedly involved in the drowning, but actually attempted to arrest one of the two complaining Negroes. The officer was mobbed and soon the rioting was underway.[14]

The Elaine, Arkansas riot of 1919 was precipitated when two white law officers shot into a Negro church, and the Negroes returned the fire, causing one death. The white planters in the area, already angered because Negro cotton-pickers were seeking to unionize and obtain an increase in their share-cropping wages, embarked upon a massive Negro hunt to put the black peons "in their place."[15]

The Tulsa riot of 1921 originated when a crowd of armed Negroes assembled before the courthouse to protest the possible lynching of a Negro who had just been arrested for allegedly attacking a white girl. The Negroes shot at white police and civilians who attempted to disperse them.[16]

In each of these conflagrations, the typical pattern was initial Negro retaliation to white acts of persecution and violence, and white perception of this resistance as an organized, premeditated conspiracy to "take over," thus unleashing the massive armed power of white mobs and police. In the Southern communities, Negro resistance tended to collapse early in the riots. After the church incident in the rural Elaine area, most Negroes passively accepted the planters' armed attacks on their homes. At Tulsa, Negroes retreated from the courthouse to the ghetto, and throughout the night held off by gunfire the assaults of white mobs. But after daybreak, many Negroes fled or surrendered before the white onslaught burned down much of the ghetto.[17] One exception to this pattern was the Washington riot of 1919, where it appears that Negroes did not retaliate until the third and last day of the riot.[18]

Negro resistance generally lasted longer in Northern riots than in Southern ones, but even in East St. Louis and Chicago the death toll told the story: in East St. Louis, 9 whites and at least 39 Negroes were killed. In Chicago, 15 whites and 23 Negroes lost their lives. Negroes attacked a small number of whites found in the ghetto or on its fringes. Negro fatalities mainly occurred when victims were trapped in white-dominated downtown areas or residential sections. Negroes were also attacked on the edges of their neighborhood in a boundary zone separating a colored residential district from a lower class white area.[19] In the face of overwhelming white numerical superiority, many

404

armed Negroes fled from their homes, leaving guns and ammunition behind. In East St. Louis, for example, there was a constant rattle of small explosions when fire enveloped a small colored residential district. Perhaps psychological factors contributed to the terrified inactivity of some Negroes. Despite the wish to meet fire with fire, over the years they had become so demoralized by white supremacy and race discrimination that effective armed defense could exist only in the realm of psychological fantasy.

During World War II, the most important race riot erupted in 1943 in Detroit, where nine whites and 25 Negroes were killed. In many respects the riot exhibited a pattern similar to East St. Louis and Chicago. The precipitating incident involved an attack on whites at the Belle Isle Amusement Park by several Negro teenagers who, a few days earlier, had been ejected from the white-controlled Eastwood Park. In the mounting tension at Belle Isle, many fights between Negroes and whites broke out, and the violence spread to the Negro ghetto where patrons at a night club were urged to "take care of a bunch of whites who killed a colored woman and her baby at Belle Isle." Although there had been no fatalities at the park, the night club emptied and revengeful Negroes stoned passing cars driven by whites. They began smashing windows on the ghetto's main business street, where the mob's major attention was directed to destroying and looting white-owned businesses.[20]

It was this symbolic destruction of "whitey" through his property that gave the Detroit holocaust the characteristic of what we may call the "new-style" race riot. It may be noted that in all the riots discussed above, there were direct clashes between Negroes and whites, and the major part of the violence was perpetrated by the white mobs. The riot pattern since the summer of 1964, however, has involved Negro aggression mainly against white-owned property, not white people. This "new style" riot first appeared in Harlem in 1935 and 1943.[21] The modern riot does not involve white mobs at all, and policemen or guardsmen constitute most of the relatively small number of casualties.

One can identify perhaps two major factors responsible for this contrast between the old-style and the new-style riot. One is the relatively marked shift in the climate of

405

race relations in this country over the past generation. On the one hand, whites have become, on the whole, more sensitive to the Negro's plight, more receptive toward Negro demands, and less punitive in their response to Negro aggression. The black masses, on the other hand, have raised their expectations markedly and, disillusioned by the relatively slow pace of social change which has left the underprivileged urban Negro of the North scarcely, if at all, better off than he was 10 or 15 years ago, have become more restless and militant than before.

In the second place, there is an ecological factor. From South to North, the migration of the World War I period was a mere drop in the bucket compared to what it later became. The migration to the North in each of the decades since 1940 has been equal to or greater than the migration of the whole 30-year period, 1910 to 1940. At the same time, owing to the Supreme Court's outlawing of the restrictive covenant in 1948, and the tearing down of the older slums through urban renewal, the Negro population has been dispersed over a wider area, thus accentuating the trend toward the development of vast ghettos. Indeed, compared to the enormous ghettos of today, the Negro residential areas of the World War I period were mere enclaves. Today, of course, Negroes are close to becoming a majority in several of the major American cities.

The character of American race riots has been markedly affected by these demographic changes. Even if white mobs were to form, they would be unable to attack and burn down the Negro residential areas; even in the 19th- and early-20th-century riots, white mobs did not usually dare to invade the larger Negro sections, and destroyed only the smaller areas of Negro concentration. Nor, since the Negroes are such a large share of the population of the central city areas, would white mobs today be in a position to chase, beat, and kill isolated Negroes on downtown streets. More important, from the Negroes' point of view, the large-scale ghettos provide a relatively safe place for the destruction and looting of white-owned property; it is impossible for local police forces to guard business property in the farflung ghettos; even State police and federal troops find themselves in hostile territory where it is difficult to chase down rioters beyond the principal thoroughfares.

It is notable that during the 20th century, both the overt

discussion of the advisability of violent retaliation on the part of Negroes, and also actual incidents of violence were prominent in the years during and after World War I, and again during the 1960's. While there have been significant differences between the outbreaks characteristic of each era, there have been also important similarities. In both periods retaliatory violence accompanied a heightened militancy among American Negroes—a militancy described as the "New Negro" in the years after World War I, and described in the sixties, with the phrase, "the Negro Revolt." In neither case was retaliatory violence the major tactic, or the central thrust, but in both periods it was a significant subordinate theme. However, in both periods a major factor leading Negroes to advocate or adopt such a tactic was the gap between Negro aspiration and objective status. The rapid escalation of the aspirations of the Negro masses who shared Martin Luther King's "dream" and identify vicariously with the success of the civil-rights revolution, while their own economic, housing, and educational opportunities have not improved, is a phenomenon of such frequent comment that it requires no elaboration here.

A comparable situation occurred during and shortly after the First World War. The agitation of the recently founded NAACP, whose membership doubled in 1918-19, the propaganda of fighting a war to make the world safe for democracy, and especially the great Negro migration to the Northern cities which Southern peasants and workers viewed as a promised land, all created new hopes for the fulfillment of age-old dreams, while Negro soldiers who had served in France returned with new expectations. But the Negro's new hopes collided with increasing white hostility. Northern Negroes assigned to southern army camps met indignities unknown at home. They rioted at Houston and came so close to rioting in Spartanburg, South Carolina, that the army hastily shipped them overseas. In the northern cities like East St. Louis and Chicago, Negroes found not a promised land, but overcrowded ghettos and hostile white workers who feared Negro competition for their jobs. The Ku Klux Klan was revived beginning in 1915, and grew rapidly in the North and South after the war ended. By 1919 economic opportunities plummeted as factories converted to peacetime operations. For a while Negroes resisted, protested, fought back, in the South as well as the

North; but the superior might of the whites proved over-powering and the Southern Negroes retreated into old paths of accommodation where they generally remained until the momentous events of the past decade.

There has been no systematic research on Negro advocacy of violence prior to the First World War, but the available evidence supports the thesis that increased overt expression of this tendency accompanies peaks in other kinds of protest activity. For example, it appears likely that Negro resistance to white rioters was minimal in the riots at the turn of the century—at Wilmington, North Carolina, in 1898, and at New Orleans, Akron, and New York in 1900[22]—which took place in a period when the sentiment of accommodation to white supremacy, epitomized by Booker T. Washington, was in the ascendency.

Again, during the ante-bellum period, one can cite two noted cases of incendiary statements urging Negroes to revolt—*David Walker's Appeal* of 1829, and Rev. Henry Highland Garnet's suppressed *Address to the Slaves of the United States of America,* delivered at the national Negro convention of 1843.[23] Both coincided with periods of rising militant protest activity on the part of the northern free Negroes. *Walker's Appeal* appeared on the eve of the beginning of the Negro convention movement, and at the time of intensified Negro opposition to the expatriation plans of the American Colonization Society.[24] Garnet's speech was made at a time when free Negro leaders were disturbed at the prejudiced attitudes of white abolitionists who refused to concern themselves with obtaining rights for the free people of color, or to allow Negroes to participate in the inner circles of the leadership of the anti-slavery societies. Consequently they had revived the Negro national convention movement which had been inactive since 1836. (Garnet's speech was also in part a product of disillusionment with the lack of actual progress being made by the antislavery societies toward achieving abolition.)

We lack any careful analysis of race riots during the 19th century. Some certainly were pogrom-like affairs, in which the Negroes were so thoroughly terrorized from the beginning that they failed to fight back. (Perhaps the Draft Riots, and some of the Reconstruction riots as in Mississippi in 1876 were of this sort.) Yet other riots were characterized by some degree of Negro retaliatory violence, such as the Snow Hill riot in Providence, in 1831, and the Cincinnati riots of 1841. Both appear to have been, like the Chicago and East St. Louis riots, the climaxes to a series of interracial altercations. In the Providence riot, a mob of about 100 white sailors and citizens advanced on a small Negro section; a Negro shot a sailor dead, and within a half hour a large mob descended upon the neighborhood, damaging many houses.[25] In the Cincinnati riot, a pitched battle was fought on the streets; the blacks had enough guns and ammunition to fire into the mob such a volley that it was twice repulsed. Only when the mob secured an iron six-pounder and hauled it to the place of combat and fired on the Negroes were the latter forced to retreat, permitting the rioters to hold sway for 2 days without interference from the authorities.[26] A careful study of interracial violence during Reconstruction will undoubtedly produce evidence of comparable situations. These riots occurred at a time of high Negro expectations and self-assertiveness, and seem to have been characterized by a significant amount of fighting back on the part of Negroes.

One period of marked and rising Negro militance, however, was not accompanied by a significant increase in manifestations of Negro retaliatory violence. This was the one following the Second World War. Indeed, the Second World War itself witnessed far less Negro violence than did the First World War. The reason for this would appear to be that the 1940's and early 1950's were years of gradually improving Negro status, and a period in which the expectations of the masses did not greatly outrun the actual improvements being made. In fact, from 1941 until the mid-1950's the relative position of the Negro workers, as compared to the white wage earners, was generally improving and it was not until the recession of 1954-55, for example, that the Black Muslims, with their rhetoric of race hatred and retaliatory violence, began to expand rapidly.

It would appear that both in the World War I period, and today—and indeed during the ante-bellum era and at other times when manifestations of violence came to the fore—there has been a strong element of fantasy in Negro discussion and efforts concerning violent retaliation. Robert Williams talked of Molotov cocktails and snarling up traffic as devices for a largely poverty-stricken ethnic minority to engineer a revolution. The Black Muslims talk of violence, but the talk seems to function as a psychological safety valve; by preaching separation, they in effect accommodate to the American social order and place racial warfare off in the future when Allah in his time will destroy the whites and usher in an era of black domination. Similarly, in view of population statistics and power distribution in American society, Du Bois and others who have spoken of the inevitability of racial warfare and Negro victory in such a struggle were engaging in wishful prophesies. And Negroes have been nothing if not realistic. The patterns of Negro behavior in riots demonstrate this. In earlier times, as already indicated, those who bought guns in anticipation of the day when self-defense would be necessary usually did not retaliate. And Negro attacks on whites occurred mainly in the early stages of the riots before the full extent of anger and power and sadism of the white mobs became evident.

Negroes of the World War I era resisted white insults and attacks only as long as they had hopes of being successful in the resistance. It should be emphasized that one of the remarkable things about the riots since 1964, in spite of their having been marked by particular resentment at police brutality, is the fact that Negro destruction was aimed at white-owned property, not white lives, even after National Guardsmen and policemen killed scores of Negroes. And in those cases where retaliatory violence has been attempted, Negroes have retreated in the face of massive white armed force. Economically impoverished Negroes press as far as they realistically can; and one reason for the explosions of recent years has been the awareness that whites are to some degree in retreat, that white mobs in the North no longer organize to attack, and that to a large degree the frustrated Negroes in slums like Watts, Detroit, Washington, or Newark, can get away with acts of destruction.

It is impossible of course to make any foolproof predictions for the future. Yet, judging by past experience and present conditions, it is our view that, despite all the rhetoric of engineering a social revolution through armed rebellion and guerrilla warfare, of planned invasions of downtown business districts and white suburbs, the kind of violence we are likely to witness will, at most, continue to be the sort of outbreaks against the property of white businessmen such as those we have witnessed in recent years. The advocacy and use of violence as a deliberate program for solving the problems of racial discrimination remains thus far, at least, in the realm of fantasy; and there it is likely to remain.

References

1. For accounts, see Julian Mayfield, "Challenge to Negro Leadership," *Commentary* Vol. XXXI (Apr. 1961), pp. 297-305; "The Robert F. Williams Case," *Crisis,* Vol. LXVI (June-July-August-September, 1959), pp. 325-329; 409-410; Robert F. Williams, *Negroes With Guns* (New York: Marzani & Munsell, 1962).
2. *Crusader,* Vol. V (May-June, 1964), pp. 5-6.
3. See the RAM publication *Black America* (Summer-Fall, 1965); *Crusader,* (Mar. 1965).
4. C. Eric Lincoln, *The Black Muslims in America* (Boston: Beacon Press, 1961), p. 205.
5. Ralph Bunche, "Conceptions and Ideologies of the Negro Problem," memorandum prepared for the Carnegie-Myrdal Study of the Negro in America, 1940, p. 161.
6. *Crisis,* Vol. XII (Aug. 1916), pp. 166-167; Vol. XIII (Dec. 1916), p. 63.
7. W. E. B. Du Bois, *Darkwater* (New York, 1920), p. 49.
8. A Philip Randolph, "How To Stop Lynching," *Messenger,* Vol. III (Apr. 1919), pp. 8-9.
9. Walter White, "The Sweet Trial," *Crisis,* Vol. XXXI (Jan. 1926), pp. 125-129.
10. "The Robert F. Williams Case," *Crisis,* Vol. LXVI (June-July 1959), p. 327.
11. Elliott M. Rudwick, *Race Riot at East St. Louis* (Cleveland and New York: Meredian Books, 1968), pp. 38-39.
12. Edgar A. Schuler, "The Houston Race Riot, 1917," *Journal of Negro History,* Vol. XXIX (Oct. 1944), pp. 300-338.
13. *NAACP Board Minutes,* Secretary's Report for June 1919.
14. *The Negro in Chicago* (Chicago, 1922), pp. 4-5.
15. *Crisis,* Vol. XIX (Dec. 1919), pp. 56-62.
16. Allen Grimshaw, *A Study in Social Violence: Urban Race Riots in the U. S.,* University of Pennsylvania unpublished doctoral dissertation, 1959, pp. 42-47.
17. *Ibid.*
18. Constance M. Green, *Washington, Capital City, 1879–1950* (Princeton: Princeton University Press, 1962), pp. 266-267; John Hope Franklin, *From Slavery to Freedom* (New York: Alfred A. Knopf, 1947), p. 473; *New York Times,* July 20-22, 1919.
19. Rudwick, *op. cit.,* pp. 226-227; *Negro in Chicago, op. cit.,* pp. 5-10.
20. Alfred McClung Lee and Norman D. Humphrey, *Race Riot* (New York, 1943), pp. 26-30.
21. Roi Ottley, *New World A-Coming* (Boston: Beacon Press, 1943), pp. 151-152; Harold Orlansky, *The Harlem Riot: A Study in Mass Frustration* (New York, 1943), pp. 5-6, 14-15; *New York Age,* Mar. 30, 1935, and Aug. 7, 1943.
22. In the New York riot, however, the precipitating incident was a physical altercation between a white policeman and a Negro; see Gilbert Osofsky, *Harlem: The Making of a Ghetto* (New York: Harper & Row, 1966), pp. 46-52.
23. Herbert Aptheker, *A Documentary History of the Negro People in the United States* (New York: Citadel, 1951), pp. 93-97, 226-233.
24. Founded in 1817 by a group of prominent white Americans, the American Colonization Society officially encouraged colonization as a means of furthering the cause of antislavery. Most Negroes, even most of those who themselves at one time or another advocated emigration to Africa or the Caribbean as the only solution for the Negro's hopeless situation in the United States, denounced the society as a cloak for those attempting to protect slavery by deporting free Negroes.

411

25. Irving H. Bartlett, "The Free Negro in Providence, Rhode Island," *Negro History Bulletin*, Vol. XIV (Dec. 1950), p. 54.
26. Carter G. Woodson, The Negroes of Cincinnati Prior to the Civil War," *Journal of Negro History*, Vol. I (Jan. 1916), pp. 13-15.

Chapter 10

PATTERNS OF COLLECTIVE RACIAL VIOLENCE

*By Morris Janowitz**

Race riots are the dramatic hallmark of the injustices of race relations in the United States. They have an explosive, destructive, and amorphous character which makes generalization very difficult. As a form of "collective behavior," their natural history is not easily recorded or analyzed. Students of race relations believe that one of the most adequate and comprehensive studies of a particular race riot still remains that prepared by the Chicago Commission on Race Relations on the Chicago rioting of 1919—the result of the careful work of the late Charles S. Johnson, which was done under the supervision of Robert E. Park of the University of Chicago.[1] Nevertheless, it is the purpose of this paper to present a sociological interpretation of changed patterns of collective racial violence in the United States over the last century. The history of race riots reflects not only the expanded aspirations of the Negro but also the techniques that have been used to maintain his inferior social position. The history of race relations in the United States has been grounded in a system of law enforcement that has denied to Negroes due process and equal protection, and that therefore has weakened the legitimacy of the agents of law enforcement, especially in the lowest Negro income areas.

The purpose of this paper is to trace the transformation in the patterns of collective racial violence in urban areas

* Morris Janowitz is professor of sociology at the University of Chicago and has written on many aspects of social and political change. Two of his numerous books are *Social Change and Prejudice*, with Bruno Bettelheim (New York: The Free Press, 1964), and *The Military in the Political Development of New Nations* (Chicago: University of Chicago Press, 1964).

over the last 50 years through three different phases. First, the typical race riot of the period of World War I and thereafter, the communal riot, was an interracial clash, an ecologically based struggle at the boundaries of the expanding black neighborhoods. Second, during World War II, communal riots began to give way to large-scale outbursts within the black community. These riots represented a form of collective behavior against the agents and symbols of the larger society. They can be described as commodity riots because of the extensive looting that gives symbolic meaning to these outbursts. Third, the commodity-type riots that reached a high point during the period of 1964-67 have shown signs of being replaced by a new form of racial violence, a more selective, terroristic use of force with political overtones, again mainly against whites, by small organized groups of blacks.

The form and extent of collective racial violence, it is assumed, are expressions of the social structure and the agencies of social change and social control. Therefore, in particular, the role of the police and law enforcement agencies and of the mass media in fashioning patterns of collective urban violence will be explored.

A central "sociological assumption" supplies a point of departure. There is a considerable body of evidence to support this assumption, but it is best to consider it as an assumption. Social tensions generated by discrimination, prejudice, and poverty offer essential but only partial explanations of Negro mass rioting in the urban centers of the United States. Social conditions conducive for collective violence have been much more widespread than the actual selective outbursts. Allen Grimshaw, one of the most careful students of race riots, concluded in 1962 that "there is no direct relation between the level of social tension and the eruption of social violence."[2]

It is not necessary to accept all that this proposition implies because the evidence is not that solid, and more important, because significant "indirect relations" may well have operated. It is enough to reemphasize the obvious fact that, in the United States, social tensions exist where riots break out, and to accept his alternative formulation that "in every case where major rioting has occurred, the social structure of the community has been characterized by weak patterns of external control."[3] Because of the widespread potentials for racial violence, in the language of sociology, the agencies of social change and social control are crucial in accounting for actual urban racial outbreaks. Moreover, the manner in which outbursts are handled and controlled deeply influences race relations and subsequent patterns of violence. It is well to keep in mind that the supporting evidence for this basic assumption rests on the events before the mid-1960's, when a new and intensified wave of urban racial violence broke out in the United States.

On the whole, statistical studies designed to account for which cities have been struck by riots have not been highly rewarding. However, one carefully matched comparison of riot and nonriot cities by Stanley Lieberson and Arnold R. Silverman of 76 race riots between 1913 and 1963 confirms and amplifies this perspective.[4] For the period before the new wave of riots of the mid-1960's, they found (a) no support for the contention that rapid population change accompanies riots; (b) no confirmation for the hypothesis that unemployment level is a direct factor, but rather that encroachment of Negroes on the white occupational world evidently tends to increase chances of riots; and (c) no support for the notion that race riots are a consequence either of low Negro income or relatively large Negro-white discrepancies in income. Nor, for that matter, does poor Negro housing serve to distinguish riot cities from nonriot cities.

However, their evidence supports "the proposition that the functioning of local government is important in determining whether a riot will follow a precipitating incident." Thus, (a) cities with more racially integrated police forces had fewer riots; (b) cities which had more representative forms of local government (e.g., citywide election of councilmen versus district elections) had fewer riots; and (c) cities were less riot prone that had a large percentage of Negroes who were self-employed in retail trade, such as store, restaurant, or tavern owners—that is, cities that had stronger independent middle-class business groups. In short, these measures were indicators of the articulation of the Negro into the social and political fabric of the metropolitan community, reflecting stronger and more viable patterns of social control.

In addition, if one is interested in the institutional aspects of race riots, it is necessary to focus attention on (a) the professional and organizational limitations of law enforcement agencies, and (b) the impact of the mass media. The record of law enforcement agencies over the last half century has been one of inadequate equal protection for minorities and limited capacity for dealing with urban disorders, with noteworthy exceptions and with slowly and definitely increasing levels of professionalization. Likewise, the growth of the mass media, especially television, has not been accompanied by increased standards of performance. The impact of the mass media, in its lack of a constructive role in describing problems of social change, plus its imagery of violence and its treatment of riots and law enforcement agencies, has made a positive contribution to violence.

FROM "COMMUNAL" TO "COMMODITY RIOTS

Racial violence has a history as old as the nation itself. The institution of slavery was rooted in ready resort to violence. After the Civil War, the political control of the freed Negro was enmeshed in a variety of illegal forms of resort to violence. For the purposes of this analysis, however, the particularly devastating and explosive outbreak of collective mass racial riots can be thought of as a distinct phenomenon, although any effort at categorization is a tricky and elusive intellectual effort. The draft riots of the Civil War had clear racial overtones. But "modern" riots can be traced to the racial outbreaks that were generated during the period of World War I and again during World War II. There were, of course, riots during the interwar period, but the heaviest concentration was during wartime years. The riots of this historical era need to be distinguished from the outbursts that took place during the 1960's.

During World War I and its aftermath, the modern form of the race riot developed in Northern and border cities where the Negro was attempting to alter his position of subordination. These outbreaks had two predisposing elements. First, relatively large numbers of new migrants—both Negro and white—were living in segregated enclaves in urban centers under conditions in which older patterns of accommodation were not effective. The riots were linked to a phase in the growth and transformation of American cities. Second, the police and law enforcement agencies had a limited capacity for dealing with the outbreak of mass violence and often conspired with the white rioters against the Negro population. The historical record indicates that they did not anticipate such happenings.

The riots of this period could be called "communal" riots or "contested area" riots. They involved ecological warfare, because they were a direct struggle between the residents of white and Negro areas. The precipitating incidents would come after a period of increasing tension and minor but persistent outbursts of violence. For example, the Chicago riot of 1919 was preceded by 2 years of residential violence in which more than 27 Negro dwellings were bombed. Typically, the precipitating incident would be a small-scale struggle between white and Negro civilians—often in a public place such as a beach or in an area of unclear racial domain. In the major riots of the large cities, tension and violence would spread quickly throughout various parts of the larger community. Thus, deaths and injuries were the result of direct confrontation and fighting between whites and Negroes.

Within a few hours the riot was in full swing, and continued intermittently with decreasing intensity for a number of days. Whites invaded Negro areas and very often the riot spread to the central business district where the white population outnumbered the Negroes. Much of the violence took place on main thoroughfares and transfer points as Negroes sought to return to their homes or sought some sort of refuge. Symbolically, the riot was an expression of elements of the white community's impulse to "kick the Negro back into his place."

Despite the wide areas that were engulfed and the number of casualties inflicted, the whites involved were limited to very small groups or nuclei of activists, often encouraged by vocal bystanders to take the initiative. White youth gangs and their leaders were in the forefront in a number of cities. The Negroes fought back in time, but they seldom invaded white areas. According to available documentation, the whites were mainly armed with bricks and blunt sticks, and they fought with their fists. There were a limited number of handguns (pistols) and rifles. On occasion, Negroes were better armed because they had more of

416

these weapons and knives as well. These riots had many incidents of direct, personal, and brutal struggle between the contestants. The personalized aspect of the violence can be inferred from reports such as that of the Chicago Commission report, which stated that "Without the spectators, mob violence would probably have stopped short of murder in many cases."[5]

Gunshots were directed at specific and visible targets, often where one side had the overwhelming superiority. Nevertheless, deaths by beating and mauling greatly outnumber those from gunshots. Newspaper reports of snipers were exaggerated. In the East Chicago riots of 1917, there was only one case of repeated gunfire, and in Chicago in 1919, the Commission found one such serious incident and a number of more scattered occurrences, as Negroes sought to retaliate against white marauders passing by in automobiles. In fact, instead of the term "sniper" fire, the reports of the period around World War I speak of occasional "volley firing."

During these riots, rumors about specific incidents of racial strife were spread by word of mouth. Newspapers contributed to racial tension by frequently and repeatedly publishing inflammatory reports such as one that Negroes slaughtered a defenseless white child. Since the riots often lasted for several days, news reports served to recruit white activists from other parts of the city and even from out of town. Editorial efforts to calm public opinion and to demand effective law enforcement developed slowly and hardly balanced the presentation in news columns.

The restoration of civil order required the police to separate the two groups and to protect the enclaves of Negroes from whites. Frequently the police were very deficient in their duties and occasionally assisted the white rioters. In any case they were not prepared for such outbreaks. The state militia or federal troops were used repeatedly and generally displayed a higher level of professional standards. Without overlooking the casualties that were caused by the police themselves, the fundamental anatomy of these riots was a communal clash between Negroes and whites.

During World War II, the pattern of rioting underwent a transformation which took full form with outbreaks in Harlem and Brooklyn in 1964, in Watts in 1965, and in

Newark and Detroit in 1967. For lack of a better term, there has been a metamorphosis from "communal" riots to "commodity" riots.[6] The Detroit riot of 1943 conformed to the communal or contested area pattern. It involved concentrations of recently arrived Negro migrants, and the precipitating incident occurred in a contested area, Belle Isle. The violence spread rapidly and produced clashes between Negroes and whites. However, the Harlem riots of 1943 contained features of the new type of rioting. The Negro population was composed of a higher concentration of long-term residents in the community. Most important, it was a riot that started within the Negro community, not at the periphery. It did not involve a confrontation beween white and Negro civilians. It was an outburst against property and retail establishments, plus looting—therefore the notion of the commodity riot in the Negro community. These establishments were mainly owned by outside white proprietors. The deaths and casualties resulted mainly from the use of force against the Negro population by police and National Guard units. Some direct and active participation by white civilians may take place in such a riot, as was the case in Detroit in 1967, but this is a minor element.

THE NATURAL HISTORY OF COMMODITY RIOTS

There have been repeated efforts to describe the various stages in the natural history of race riots, especially the commodity-type riots.[7] Two considerations need to be held in mind in pursuing this goal. The style of intervention by the law enforcement officers has deeply influenced the anatomy of race riots in the United States. During the period of the initial communal riots, the effectiveness of local police forces varied greatly, reflecting their high degree of decentralization. The increased ability of local police to seal off contested areas reduced the prospect of communal riots. Since the riots of World War I, there has been a gradual growth in the capacity of local police to prevent riots at the periphery of the Negro community, but not without conspicuous exceptions. The use of radio communications and motorized local police forces have been the essential ingredients of control. Most Northern cities have witnessed a steady and gradual expansion of the Negro residential areas, accompanied by bitter resentment and continuous minor outbreaks of violence, including bombings. But the police almost daily contain these tensions, which could explode into communal riots if there were defects in their performance. But the capacity of local enforcement agencies to deal with "border" incidents has not been matched with a capacity for controlling the resort to violence within the Negro community. The outbreak of commodity riots produced very different police responses in various communities, ranging from highly effective and professional behavior to weak and irresponsible action that exacerbated rioting and prolonged tension. Thus, the stages of a riot are not predetermined but reflect the pattern of intervention of law enforcement agencies.

Second, it is, of course, very difficult to assemble accurate documentation in order to describe the natural history of a riot and especially the behavior of rioters in a commodity riot. The riots of the 1960's have produced a number of official inquiries and a variety of private studies, but there are few adequate analyses in depth.[8]

The President's Advisory Commission on Civil Disorders (Kerner Commission) sponsored a variety of social research studies that focused mainly on the attitudes of the public and the rioters. The methodology of the sample survey was emphasized, which does not make possible a full analysis of the dynamics of the "collective behavior" of a racial riot. While teams of investigators are required to collect basic documentation, the natural history and anatomy of a riot is still best assessed by a single person who is concerned with cross-checking sources. Brig. Gen. S. L. A. Marshall has demonstrated how a single investigator can reconstruct a complex and fluid battle by afteraction group interviews. This procedure has not generally been applied to race riots. Perhaps the most analytic account of a commodity riot was presented by Anthony Oberschall, a Yale University sociologist.[9]

From all sources, one conclusion emerges, namely the absence of organized conspiracy in commodity riots. However, the absence of organized conspiracy does not mean the absence of a pattern of events. Thus, Jules J. Wanderer's analysis of 75 riots during the period 1965-67 demonstrates the pattern of events in these outbursts. By means of the Guttman scale techniques, he demonstrated the consistent cumulation of a very similar configuration of violence from low to high intensity.[10] The difference from one outburst to another involved the extent to which each one proceeded through the various stages of increased and intensified collective behavior.

The motivation of contemporary commodity riots is clearly not desperation generated by the anticipation of starvation, such as in food riots in India during famine times. One is struck by the repeated reports of the carnival and happy-day spirit that pervades the early stages of a commodity riot. The new type of rioting is most likely to be set off by an incident involving the police in the ghetto where some actual or believed violation of accepted police practice has taken place. The very first phase is generally nasty and brutish: the police are stoned, crowds collect, and tension mounts. The second stage is reached with the breaking of windows. Local social control breaks down and the population recognizes that a temporary opportunity for looting is available. The atmosphere changes quickly, and this is when positive enthusiasm is released. But all too briefly. If the crowds are not dispersed and order restored, the third stage of the riot is the transformation wrought by arson, firebombs, and sniper fire and the countermeasures taken by police and uniformed soldiers.

There can be no doubt that the countermeasures employed deeply influence the course of rioting—even in some cases prolonging the period of reestablishing order. One is, of course, struck by the great variation in local response to escalated rioting and in the skill and professionalism of the forces in their counterefforts. Differences in police strategy have been partly accidental and partly the result of conscious policy, because law enforcement officials have a past record to draw on, and are continuously alerted to the possibility of riots. Thus, for example, there were wide differences in response patterns to early manifestations of disorder by local police in the 1960's. In Detroit, Ray Girardin, a former police reporter who became police commissioner, explicitly acknowledged that he followed a loose policy in the early phase of the Detroit rioting, assuming that local civilian Negro leadership would contain the disorder. He cited his previous experience in which this approach worked effectively. In his theories of riot behavior, he made frequent recourse to "sociological" terms.

By contrast, the operational code of the police in New York City under Commissioner Howard Leary and in Chicago has been to intervene with that amount of force judged to be appropriate for early stages of the confrontation. The objective was to prevent the spread of contagion. Special steps were taken to prevent routine police performance from developing into incidents which might provoke tension. However, if an incident became the focal point for tension and the collection of a crowd, the police responded early and in depth in order to prevent the second stage from actually expanding. Numerous police were sent to the scene or kept in reserve nearby. The police sought to operate by their sheer presence, not to provoke further counteraction. They sought to prevent the breaking of windows and the starting of looting that would set the stage for an escalated riot. If actual rioting threatened, one response was the early mobilization of local National Guard units and their ready reserve deployment in inner city garrisons. In part, this was designed to reduce the time required for their deployment on city streets and in part it was policy that enables the local police to commit their reserves with the surety of having a supporting force available.

Whereas the communal riot involved a confrontation between the white and the black community, the commodity riot, especially as it entered into the third and destructive phase, represents a confrontation between the black community and law enforcement officials of the larger society. The question of the extent of the exchange of gunfire emerged as one of the most problematic dimensions. The reports in the mass media of the use of weapons during and immediately after the riots by the rioters were exaggerated, according to the investigations of the Kerner Commission.[11] In fact, the deaths inflicted by sniper fire were few. For example, it is reported that 5 of 43 deaths during the Detroit disorder were linked to sniper fire, and in Newark, 2 of 26 deaths.[12] These observations did not involve comparisons with earlier riots or an assessment that the gunfire contributed to conditions in which extensive arson developed. In fact, direct comparisons with the communal type riots underline the greater dispersal of

421

firearms and the much more intense use of fire power. They are escalated riots because of the more extensive but still scattered use of weaponry.

A distinguishing characteristic of commodity riots is not only the widespread dispersal of small arms and rifles among the rioters, and correspondingly, the increased capacity of the local police to concentrate armed personnel in a given area. There are no adequate statistics on the distribution of weapons in the hands of participants before any particular riot started. However, there is clear evidence that, over the years, the sale and home storage of firearms has continually increased, made possible by affluence, the absence of adequate gun control legislation, and stimulated by fears of racial violence. These trends have taken place both in the white and in the Negro community. As Zimring has demonstrated in the case of personal violence, the sheer availability of weapons has tended to escalate racial conflict.[13] In addition to the already available arms, a significant stock of weapons appears to have been accumulated during the actual rioting in particular areas. Important sources of supply have been looted including sporting goods stores, general merchandise establishments, and pawnshops.

Available documentation indicates that during the third phase of the commodity riots, when sniper fire developed, it usually involved single individuals, occasionally groups of two or three persons. There is little evidence of forethought by rioters in the deployment of weapons for effectiveness or mutual fire support. Supporting fire by such snipers could render them much more destructive. In isolated cases, there is evidence of limited coordination and planning of firepower. But these cases are of minor importance in accounting for the firepower involved or its destructiveness. The crucial impact of the sniper fire derived from its interplay with arson activities. Sniper fire immobilized firefighting equipment, which permitted widespread destruction by fire, which in turn contributed to more rioting and sniper fire. In this sense, the commodity riots were escalated in intensity and sheer destruction as compared with the communal outbreaks. They were escalated also in the sense that the mass media rapidly disseminates the image and reality of mass fires and widespread looting on a scale not found in the earlier ones. The spread of fire was frequently facilitated by various incendiary bombs of a home-made nature. These firebombs have been used as anti-vehicle bombs, but generally with little effectiveness.

The phase of scattered sniper fire is, in some respects, a type of quasi-military situation, but the notion of an insurrection has little meaning, for snipers had no intention or capability for holding territory, nor were they part of a scheme to do so even temporarily. Frequently the sniper fire exposed police officers and National Guard units without experience to dangers with which they were not accustomed. Personal risk was clearly present. The scattered source of fire often enveloped the law enforcement units. It was this envelopment fire, especially from behind, which has led to the use of the term "guerrilla tactics," but the guerrilla concept is also not relevant since guerrillas are part of an organization, proceed with a plan, prepare paths of withdrawal, and develop sanctuaries.

Overresponse and excessive use of firepower by police and National Guard units in turn contributed to the escalation of the rioting.[14] The police were at times surrounded and, in the absence of effective command and control, were exposed to an environment that most had not previously experienced. Their behavior was conditioned by the sheer feeling of the unreality of the rioting situation and the physical disruption that takes place. They often responded with indiscriminate and uncontrolled fire. The immediate result was that they exposed numerous civilians to danger. Such fire does not suppress snipers, who can only be eliminated by carefully directed fire and counter-sniper procedures. In fact, the initial counterfire actually mobilized new rioters.

The summers of 1964 through 1967 demonstrated wide variations in the capacity of National Guard units to respond to and assist local police. On the whole, National Guard units had received little specific training in riot control and the content of any such training did not appear to have been particularly germane to actual problems. The level of National Guard effectiveness derived from their military preparedness in general. The performance of National Guard units in Newark and in Detroit has been judged by expert observers to be deficient. By contrast, the behavior of the National Guard units in Maryland and in Wisconsin (Milwaukee) has been reported to be much more in accordance with the requirements of the constabulary function; namely, the minimum use of force to restore civil law and due process. The basic question is fire control and an effective communications network. By contrast, federal troops used in Detroit were highly professional units with extensive training, who clearly displayed a higher degree of unit control and were less prone to employ unnecessary fire. The superiority of the federal troops reflects past experience and indicates that more effective military training per se (even without additional civil disorder training), and more effective officers, produces more appropriate responses.

There is some evidence that one index to National Guard effectiveness is the extent of integration of units. Because of its fraternal spirit, most National Guard units have been able to resist Federal directives and Negroes accounted for less than 2 percent of its personnel in 1967. In those cases where integration took place, it meant that the units were seen as more legitimate by the local population. Moreover, units that were forced to integrate were more likely to be concerned with problems of conflict in the unit and developed an officer corps concerned with these issues. For example, units in Detroit and Newark were not integrated while Chicago-based units that were employed during the summer disturbances of 1965 were integrated and had Negro officers.

PARTICIPATION IN COMMODITY RIOTS

The extent of participation and the social characteristics of the riots are revealing indices of underlying factors in the social structure that condition these collective outbursts. There is every reason to believe that in the commodity riots of the 1960's, a larger number of Negroes and a greater percentage of the population of riot-torn communities actively participated in the outbursts than was the case during the older, communal-type confrontations. The commodity-type riots take place within the confines of the black ghettos, which have grown greatly in size and population since World War I. Within these massive ghettos during the hours of the most intensive outbursts, it appears as if social controls were momentarily suspended. The sheer size of the ghettos and the greater remoteness of the outer community contribute to this breakdown and to the "mobilization" of numbers. It is understandable that in the second phase of milling and looting, many residents were swept up by the sheer contagion of events, especially where law officers stood by passively while stores and shops were being entered.

It is also necessary to emphasize that the societal context had radically changed during the period of transition to commodity riots. Through the mass media, the demands of the Negro population had received widespread and favorable publicity and there was considerable sympathy in the nation for their plight. The civil-rights movements had achieved strong legitimacy. Within the black community there was strongly increased sensitivity about minority status. All these factors contributed to the intensity and participation during actual rioting.

The size of the groups rioting and their percentage of the available population, as well as their social characteristics, became matters of public debate. The Kerner Commission devoted efforts to probing these questions and refuting the claim that only a very tiny percentage—for example, less than 1 percent—of the Negro population was involved in riot-torn communities.[15] The Commission argued that the riots included a much larger active group who were generally representative of lower class slum dwellers and therefore could not be characterized as a tiny criminal element. The size of the rioting group could be estimated from direct observation, a most hazardous approach; from extrapolations from arrest data—a technique that probably underestimated the number of the activists; or from self-reports gathered by sample surveys after the riots—an approach that grossly overstated the case. On the basis of different sources, it was estimated that between 10 to 20 percent of the potential population was involved in the riots of 1967. The lower figure of 10 percent appears to be more accurate, although even this estimate is open to serious question. Aside from the reliability of the data, the question hinges on the differing definitions of participation. To speak of even 10 percent participation is to include those persons who were caught up in the collective processes of the riot as the contagion spread.

Although there are numerous statistical and methodological weaknesses in the various analyses of the arrest data and sample surveys, the findings are relevant for describing the social characteristics of the rioters. All sources agree that women were a significant minority of the activists in the commodity riots, reflecting a broadening of the base of involvement as contrasted with the communal riots, which were mainly a men's affair. Interestingly enough, the police tended to arrest few women, either because their infractions of the law were minor or because they believed that women were not at the core of the riot.

As expected, the bulk of the rioters were young males between the ages of 15 and 34 who skill levels were low. In a social profile of the 496 Negro males arrested in Detroit, the typical participant has been characterized as "a blue collar worker in a manufacturing plant where he earned about $120.00 a week. Although currently employed, he had experienced more than 5 weeks of unemployment in the past year. He had not participated in a government training or poverty program." In some groups of arrested Negro youths, the unemployment level reached almost 40 percent.[16] In addition, among samples of those caught up in the riots and arrested in 1967, previous arrest records comparable to the equivalent age groups in the black population at large were found. The explanation for this finding is that it is very common for young Negro males to have an arrest record—in some categories, a majority.

Clearly, these data indicate that the activists were not a tiny minority of chronic law offenders nor highly unrepresentative in terms of selected social background characteristics. The full personal and social dynamics will probably never be adequately described, for involvement relates not merely to the demographic and social characteristics but to the patterns of primary and informal group structures of the ghetto community, as well as social personality and attitude. Some clues can be drawn from the observation of various surveys that the participants over-represented single men, who frequently lived outside of family units. These were persons who were less subject to the informal group structure linked to family life and more to informal street and community life. Anthony Oberschall is one of the few analysts who sought to probe the role of youth gangs in riots, in his case, Watts:

Another informant who has been close to some of the gangs in South Los Angeles reported, however, that gang members, in an effort to prove their claims upon leadership in a certain territory and in competition with each other, were vying for leadership over the crowds during the riots, and this meant among other things actively participating in the skirmishes against the police, breaking into the stores and setting them on fire.[17]

In other cities, especially in Chicago in 1968, gang leaders were active in seeking to dampen tensions and violent outbursts. Fogelson reports on the social difference between those arrested as disorderly persons—who tended to be younger, unemployed, and native born in the locality —and the looters, who tended to be older, less unemployed, and Southern born.[18] In other words, the looters, who joined the riots after they were underway, were more integrated into the adult occupational world.

In contrast to the criminal interpretation, the alternative formulation of the commodity riots as a form of political insurrection appears equally inadequate, if by insurrection is meant an armed social movement with an explicit set of goals. The very absence of evidence of prior planning—either rightist or leftist—would weaken such an interpretation. In 23 disorders studies by the Kerner Commission, none were "caused by, nor were they the consequence of any plan or conspiracy."[19] But more important, it is striking that during the riots of 1964 to 1967, there was a remarkable absence of visible leadership—either existing or emergent—that sought to press for collective demands. It is, of course, clear that the leadership and support of the civil-rights movement were not centrally involved in the riots. The emphasis of the civil-rights leaders on issues such as school integration, access to public accommodation, and voting rights were less directly relevant to the immediate lives of slum dwellers, who were mainly concerned with the welfare system and with immediate employment opportunities. The impact of the riots of 1967 on the civil-rights movement was drastic in that it made the movement's demands more militant. But clearly the leaders of the civil-rights movement were not activists in these outbursts. If anything, they occurred because of the inability of the civil-rights movement to accomplish sufficient social change in the slums, although the movement made a decisive contribution in intensifying aspirations and group consciousness.

Many participants, after the riots, could consciously verbalize their social and economic dilemmas and link their situation to their behavior. In interviews, they had a tendency to highlight "police brutality" as the underlying cause. Of course, many who participated merely took the events as a given fact of life and offered little explanation for their involvement.

In contrast to the communal riots, where the Negro response was a direct and primitive struggle for survival, the commodity riots had overtones which might be called parapolitical, in the sense that group consciousness pervaded this particular form of collective behavior. In balance it can be said that the commodity riot by 1967 was a form of collective action, which on occasion was large scale and included a broadly representative segment of the lower socioeconomic class of the urban community. Regardless of the amount of sympathetic interest they mobilized among middle-class Negroes, the commodity riots were a "violent lower class outburst."[20]

A final aspect of participation has been the active involvement of those in the Negro community who sought to dampen or inhibit the spread of the riot. In official reports, they have come to be described by the awkward and unfortunate term, "counterrioters." In the communal riot, such a role was not possible and, paradoxically, such behavior by Negroes during a riot was a consequence of an increase in integration of the Negro into the larger social structure as compared with the period of communal rioting. Already in the Harlem riot of 1943, more than 300 Negroes were given Civilian Defense insignias and armbands, and used as deputies. For the summer of 1967, the Kerner Commission reported that in all but 6 of 24 disorders they investigated, Negroes were actively on the streets attempting to control rioters.[21]

In some cities, political and community leaders sought to address gathering crowds. On other occasions, religious leaders and community workers walked the streets urging persons to disperse, while still other local residents assisted police and firemen in their tasks. Some of these activities were officially recognized and even sanctioned by the local authorities, but the bulk of the efforts seem to have been without official sponsorship. It is very difficult to evaluate the effectiveness of these efforts, especially in communities

428

where extensive rioting broke out. However, it does appear that such activities had the greatest effect in communities which were on the verge of rioting and in which rioting was avoided.

SUMMER RIOTS OF 1968

It will remain for future historians to assess whether the summer of 1968 was in fact a turning point in the era of communal riots. The trend in racial conflict from 1964 to 1967 was one of continued, and even expanded, outbreaks that appeared to reach one high point with the massive destruction of Newark and Detroit.

In the winter and spring months of 1968, the outlook for the summer of that year was bleak. Racial tensions remained high. Extremist and even moderate leaders anticipated even higher levels of violence, and a variety of analysts were thinking in the same direction. One of the writers for the Kerner Commission, assessing public opinion polls, stated "on the eve of the summer of 1968, these responses are anything but reassuring."[22] The tensions of the Vietnam crisis continued. There was no new massive national response to the social and economic needs of the black community, except in the important employment sector where industrial corporations started to abandon rigid recruitment and training procedures and to engage an increasing number of inner city personnel who would develop their qualifications on the job. Community relations were made more difficult by extremist statements by some individual police officers, who spoke of the necessity of a "tough" policy and of their plans to use heavier hardware for control purposes. The tragic assassination of Dr. Martin Luther King, Jr., served as a final element in the prelude to the summer of 1968.

However, race relations during the summer had a different character from these anticipations. In October 1968, the Department of Justice released a report by Attorney General Ramsey Clark which revealed a decline in the scope and intensity of racial riots. Quantitative measures of riots are difficult to construct, but these appear to be of relatively high validity. The definitions were carefully worked out and the same data collection procedures used to compare the months of June, July, and August, 1967, with the same months of 1968. The results showed a decline in "major" disturbances from 11 to 7, and of "serious" ones from 35 to 18, while minor outbursts increased slightly from 92 to 95. The most dramatic indicator of the decline was the drop in deaths from 87 to 19. To some degree, these data understate the full decline from 1967 to 1968, since the category "major" riots included all riots which lasted longer than 12 hours and included more than 300 persons. The very large-scale riots such as Newark and Detroit were absent in 1968. This is reflected in part in the marked decline in estimated property damage, from $56 million in 1967 for three riots in Cincinnati, Newark, and Detroit to $4 million for all damage during June, July, and August of 1968. It is, of course, very possible that no new long-term trend was at work. One hypothesis to account for the short-term and immediate pattern was the development of new tactics and new organizations that permit more effective expression of black interests and black solidarity. Another hypothesis is that improved police-community relations and higher levels of police professionalism contributed to the decline. These data seem to indicate that, while minor outbreaks continued, interaction between the police and the black community was able to reduce and contain larger and more widespread riots.

Under pressure of political and community leadership, many police took initial steps to improve communications with the Negro community through devices such as special conferences, the assigning of special officers of community relations, and improved police training. The criticism of the police in some communities and the relative success in other areas led to more professional behavior. The advocates of deescalation had more and more influence; the slogan became "manpower and not firepower." Older doctrines of riot control, which emphasized weaponry and technical characteristics, gave way to new and more flexible approaches. Police departments sought to improve their internal communications and their ability to mobilize manpower. They sought to strengthen supervision and control in the field and emphasized the need for restraint. There was a much more professional response to the problem of sniper fire, in that police were instructed not to respond with indiscriminate firepower. There was some progress toward deescalation of police response to more appropriate levels. Despite the publicity given to those few police officers who spoke about the need for tanks and Mace, the major trend in local police work was in the opposite direction.

National Guard and federal troops were deeply involved in the events of the summer of 1968. The lack of professional competence on the part of the local police to deal with problems of urban racial violence in part reflects the particular system of law enforcement that developed in the United States. Deeply influenced by British institutions, the nation did not develop a national police force that had responsibility for the control of civil disorder, in contrast to France for example. However, the United States has had extensive civil disorders throughout its history and the country found its equivalent to a gendarmerie in the state militia and later in the National Guard. The National Guard especially was organized and trained for national defense purposes, so that it seldom developed professional standards for local police support. The result has been that in both labor disputes and in race riots, federal troops have performed with high levels of effectiveness, not because of their specialized training for the task but because of generally higher organizational effectiveness.

But the division of responsibility between local, state, and federal agencies greatly complicates the conditions under which federal troops will intervene in a riot. In the Detroit riots of July 1967, federal troops were not deployed on the basis of the request of State and local authorities, but only after the Presidential representative, former Assistant Secretary of Defense Cyrus Vance, had personally inspected the city and certified the need for federal troops. There was local criticism that this procedure unduly delayed the dispatch of necessary troops. The office of the President has had to struggle to avoid premature commitment of federal troops whenever local authorities feel under pressure, but at the same time maintain the credibility of swift federal intervention if required. As a result, the Department of the Army established a Directorate for Civil Disturbance Policy and Operations to oversee such involvements. Greater use was made of federal troops in 1968 than in 1967. These troops underwent specialized training, but it was their general organizational effectiveness and command structure that enabled them to operate with the greatest restraint. They very seldom made use of their weapons; their sheer presense was mainly responsible for limiting riot behavior. (For example, in the Washington, D.C., operation, at most 15 bullets were fired.) In fact, there were numerous occasions in which the local population welcomed the arrival of federal troops, with the clear implication that they preferred not to be policed by local personnel.

With reliance placed on the National Guard, it became abundantly clear during the summer of 1967 that racial integration in these units had to be pressed with much greater vigor. It had been federal policy to encourage such integration, and in fact all Negro units were disbanded, but the recruitment of Negroes into the National Guard lagged. Where integration of the Negro into the National Guard had taken place, it was the result of state and local political leadership. Therefore, on August 10, 1967, the President's Commission on Civil Disorders unanimously issued a set of recommendations to produce short-term improvements in riot control. These recommendations called for increased recruitment of Negro personnel into the National Guard, the establishment of standards for eliminating inferior officers, and greater reliance on specialized training. During the next year, these federal policies began to have an effect, especially in the area of improved training.

NEXT STAGE: POLITICAL VIOLENCE

Each stage in the transformation of racial violence already carries with it the elements of the next stage. In the midst of the mass rioting of 1967, there was anticipated marked decline in such outbursts and an emergence of a more selective, more delimited form of violence.[23]

The social position of the Negro in American society was changing, with an effect on patterns of racial tension. In our open society, it is necessary to underline that the commodity rioting of 1964-67 bears a parallel to one explanation of the outbursts of militancy in the trade union movement in the 1930's. The unions displayed their vigor not during the depth of the depression but during 1936 and 1937, a period of halting but increasing prosperity. It may well be that the ghetto outbursts, especially of 1965-

67, were linked to the first stages—slow and incomplete—in new levels of opportunity and achievement for the Negro community. If social and economic progress were to continue, the conditions conducive to tension would then start to decline.

Although the topic is outside the scope of this paper, continued improvement of the relative socioeconomic position of the Negro in American society depends on a variety of elements of social change. Much social learning has taken place since the initial phase of the "war against poverty." The main lines of effective innovation are beginning to emerge: federal assistance in family planning, radical modification of the present welfare system including a negative income tax, special youth work training enterprises, and decentralization, plus improved quality of public education. Of special importance are the efforts to locate employment opportunities in depressed areas. Experience to date indicates that such industrial establishments become training stations that serve to incorporate youngsters into the labor market for the first time and that, after a period of work experience, they develop incentives to seek additional training or better employment in the wider labor market. No doubt, regardless of their limited immediate impact, some of the community organizations being developed in Negro areas with foundation, trade union, and federal funds serve as a learning experience for training new leadership.

Any anticipation of a continued decline of commodity riots is also based on the assumption that a more professional police force would both extend more equal protection and would be more effective and more humane in avoiding collective outbursts. Likewise there would be a more equitable judicial system that would accord more due process to the Negro community. Thus the likelihood of destruction on the level of Newark and Detroit declines, although the escalated riot remains a possibility in any area of heavy Negro population concentration. Likewise, as Negro enclaves develop in suburban areas, forms of communal riots between Negroes and whites become a reality in these areas.

However, the essential trend was that escalated rioting and the rioting of commodity looting appeared in 1967 to be giving way to more specific, more premeditated, and more regularized uses of force. It was as if the rioters learned the lesson emphasized in the mass media, that mass destruction achieves too few tangible benefits. New outbursts appeared to be more goal directed—a diffuse goal at times, at other times a very specific one. It is almost appropriate to describe these outbursts as political violence or political terror, or even conspiratorial violence. It is not inaccurate to describe this shift as one from expressive outburst to a more instrumental use of violence. Those involved were persons who came to believe that white society cannot be changed except with violence.

The participants were likely to be persons who have taken part in previous outbursts. There was an element of organization, at least to the extent that activists are concerned with personal survival and avoidance of the police. There was an element of organization to the extent that the target seems to be selected, and the patterns repeated for a specific purpose. The local school was a particular target. The form of violence can be the harassment of a group of white schoolteachers active in union work, an assault on teacher picket lines during a strike, or a small-scale outburst at the neighborhood schoolyard and on occasion sniper fire against the police. Housing projects, especially integrated housing projects, were repeatedly subject to rifle fire and fire bombing. These incidents are created for the purpose of developing solidarity in local gangs and in paramilitary groups. The United Automobile Workers Union reported the use of terror tactics, including knifings and physical assault, against both white and black workers in the Detroit area. The union identified a group, League of Revolutionary Black Workers, in its documentation.[24]

The object seems to be to establish a vague political presence. Conspiratorial overtones are involved and the assaults spill over against social agencies and local political leaders. The line between random outbursts and these forms of political violence or political terror is difficult to draw. However, these outbursts often take place with the explicit appeal of Black Power. Traditional youth gang activities tend to resist political orientations, but signs of conscious orientation become more visible.

Dramatic manifestations of the third phase of political violence, or conspiratorial violence, were the shootouts which occurred with police personnel during the summer of 1968 in New York City, Cleveland, Pittsburgh, Oakland, Los Angeles, and elsewhere. The amount of prior planning is difficult to ascertain, but focused selection of police personnel as specific and delimited targets is obvious. In some cases the action appears to have been a response to presumed harassment by the police. In other cases the police were responding to a call for help. In still other cases police cars were attacked without warning. For example, on September 29, 1968, a man wearing a "black cape lined with orange walked up to a police car in Harlem early yesterday and without provocation, opened fire on two patrolmen, wounding them both. . . ."[25] Other incidents developed around a police action such as the removal of a disabled vehicle. Generally these incidents seem to involve loosely and informally organized groups. It is much rarer but perhaps indicative of emerging trends that a formal organization such as the Black Panthers finds itself in repeated gun battles with the Oakland police. The shootout in Cleveland on July 26, 1968, created such community tension that Mayor Carl B. Stokes responded by the unprecedented withdrawal of white police officers and deployment of Negro officers and 500 black community leaders to maintain peace. This procedure was rapidly terminated.[26]

Such activities appear to be a new form of "defiance" politics. In the past, organized racketeers, including groups which penetrated political party organizations, made use of violence to extract a financial toll from slum communities. These traditional groups confined violent outbursts to the maintenance of their economic privilege. Practitioners of political violence and political terror are now more open in advocating violence and opposition to the larger society. They represent an effort to achieve goals much broader and vaguer than those of the racketeer. There are crude ideological overtones and especially a desire to carry violence into the white community.[27]

It is very difficult to contain terroristic eruptions of political violence. The toll is small at a given point and therefore does not produce a violent public reaction. The tactics and organizational plans are more secret and only official surveillance and covert penetration supplies an effective technique of management. The forms of organization are those of a combination of a conspiratorial and predatory gang and a paramilitary unit with overtones of a "liberation" outlook. The more secret and cohesive the

435

group, the greater the problems of surveillance. Even though many of these paramilitary groups will break into factions, the task of control will become extremely difficult. It bodes ill when it is necessary to rely on covert operators. The control of secret operations is at best difficult; in the United States, it is very difficult.[28] The task becomes even more complex and troublesome when these surveillance agencies develop the conception, as they often do, that to collect information is not enough. They begin to believe that they must act as active agents of control, particularly in spreading distrust within these organizations. The task becomes endless and dangerous if the operators play a game without an end or develop an interest in maintaining the groups whom they are supposed to be monitoring.

The failure of the larger society to meet the needs of the black community would contribute to an environment in which conspiratorial violence will continue to flourish. However, such violence has a life of its own. Small groups of terrorists have on historical occasion been able to achieve important goals and political objectives. It is hazardous to even speculate about the conditions under which they are able to succeed. In the past, they appear to have succeeded when they were struggling against a political elite that ruled by terror and without a broad base of support. They have also succeeded when terror is merely an opening step in a broad political campaign. Neither of these conditions seems applicable. Instead it may well be the case that political violence will have counterproductive features. Only limited amounts of political violence can be employed before a point of diminishing return is reached for both the user and the social order in which it is applied.[29]

THE IMPACT OF THE MASS MEDIA

Another important institution of social control that has special relevance for collective racial violence is the mass media. A debate on this issue has raged among social scientists since the early 1930's when the Payne Foundation underwrote a group of University of Chicago social scientists in the first large-scale study of the impact of the mass media, in this case, the consequences of movies for young people.[30]

The mass media both reflect the values of the larger

436

society and at the same time are agents of change and devices for molding tastes and values. It is a complex task to discern their impact because they are at the same time both cause and effect. Controversies about the mass media focus particularly on the issue of their contribution to crime and delinquency and to an atmosphere of lawlessness. Among social scientists, it is generally agreed that consequences of the mass media are secondary as compared with the influence of family, technology, and the organization of modern society. But differences in the meaning and importance attributed to this "secondary factor" among social scientists are great. "Secondary" can mean still important enough to require constructive social policy, or "secondary" can mean that a factor is trivial and unimportant.

Two separate but closely linked issues require attention. First, what are the consequences of the mass media, with its high component of violence, on popular attitudes toward authority and on conditioning and acceptance of violence in social relations? Second, what have been the specific consequences of the manner in which the mass media have handled escalated rioting since the period of Watts? The managers of the mass media run their enterprises on a profit basis and one result has been that the content of channels of communication, especially television, in the United States have a distinct "violence flavor" as contrasted with other nations. This content emphasis continued to persist as of the end of 1968 despite all the public discussion about this standard of the mass media.[31] In this respect, self-regulation of the mass media has not been effective except to some extent in the comic book industry.

In my judgment, the cumulative evidence collected by social scientists over the last 30 years has pointed to a discernible, but limited, negative impact of the media on social values and on personal controls required to inhibit individual disposition into aggressive actions. Other students of the same data have concluded that their impact is so small as not to constitute a social problem.

Many studies on media impact are based on limited amounts of exposure, as contrasted to the continuous expose of real life. Other studies made use of ex post facto sample surveys that are too superficial to probe the psychological depths of these issues. More recent research employing rigorous experimental methods has strengthened the conclusion that high exposure to violence content in the mass media weakens personal and social controls.[32] These new findings are based on probing fantasy and psychological responses of young people after exposure to violence content. They have special importance for lower class groups because of the high exposure of these groups to television. These lower class groups have less involvement in printed media, which has less violence material.

The issue runs deeper than the concentration of materials on violence in the mass media. It involves as assessment of the mass media's performance in disseminating a portrayal of the Negro and social change in depth. It also involves the access that the mass media extends to the creative talent of the Negro community. The Kerner Commission emphasized the lack of effective coverage of the problems of minority groups by the mass media and the absence of minority group members, especially Negroes, in operating and supervisory positions in these enterprises. The events of the riots and the recommendations of the Kerner Commission on this aspect of the mass media produced "crash" programs to recruit and train minority group personnel. The contents of the media have become more integrated, including advertising, and a long-run impact on public opinion is likely to be felt, especially in younger persons.

It is also necessary to assess the coverage of the riots themselves by television and the impact of this coverage on social control. For example, the National Advisory Commission on Civil Disorders sought to probe the immediate impact of the mass media coverage of the riots of the summer of 1967 both on the Negro community and on the nation as a whole. They commissioned a systematic content analysis study which, despite its quantitative approach, did not effectively penetrate the issue or even satisfy the Commission itself. The content study sought to determine if "the media had sensationalized the disturbances, consistently overplaying violence and giving disproportionate amounts of time to emotional events and militant leaders."[33] The conclusion was negative because of findings that, of 837 television sequences of riot and racial news examined, 494 were classified as calm, 262 as emotional, and 81 as normal. "Only a small proportion of all scenes analyzed showed actual mob action, people looting, sniping, setting fires or being killed or injured." In addition, moderate Negro leaders were shown on television more frequently than were militant leaders. Equivalent findings were reported for the printed media.

But such a statistical balance is no indicator of the impact of the presentation. Even calm and moral presentations of the riots could have had effect on both black and white communities; more certainly, persistent presentation of "hot" messages, even though they constitute only a part of the coverage, would have an impact. Therefore, the Commission modified and in effect rejected its own statistical findings and more appropriately concluded that (1) "there were instances of gross flaws in presenting news of the 1967 riots;" and (2) the cumulative effect was important in that it "heightened reaction." "What the public saw and read last summer thus produced emotional reactions and left vivid impressions not wholly attributable to the material itself." The Commission concluded that "the main failure of the media last summer was that the totality of its coverage was not as representative as it should have been to be accurate."

The national crisis produced by escalated riots warranted massive coverage according to existing standards of mass media performance. The coverage was so extensive that there was an imbalance in presentation of the total scene in the United States, and in particular, a failure to cover successful accomplishments by community leaders and law enforcement agencies. In fact, there were overtones in the coverage of racial violence which conformed to the "crime wave" pattern of news. The result was to bring into the scope of coverage violent events that would not have been reported under "normal" circumstances.

Television has served as the main instrument for impressing the grim realities of the riots onto the mass consciousness of the nation. On-the-spot reportage of the details of the minor riots and their aftermath was extensive and was buttressed by elaborate commentaries. If the fullest coverage of these events is deemed to be necessary as a basis for developing constructive social policy, the costs of such media coverage should not be overlooked. It is impossible to rule out the strong contention that detailed coverage of riots has had an effect on potential rioters. Such a contention does not rest on the occasional instance in which the television camera focused on the riot scene and led either rioters or police to play to the television audience. Of greater importance is the impact of pictures of the rioting on a wider audience. Again we are dealing with a process of social learning, especially for potential participants. Rioting is based on contagion, the process by which the mood and attitudes of those who are actually caught up in the riot are disseminated to a larger audience on the basis of direct contact. Television images serve to spread the contagion pattern throughout urban areas and the nation. Large audiences see the details of riots, the manner in which people participate in them, and especially the ferment associated with looting and obtaining commodities which was so much at the heart of riot behavior. Television presents detailed information about the tactics of participation and the gratifications that were derived.

A direct and realistic account of the tactical role of the mass media, in particular television, can be seen from specific case studies, such as reported in depth by Anthony Oberschall on the Watts riot. He writes:

> The success of the store breakers, arsonists, and looters in eluding the police can in part be put down to the role of the mass media during the riot week. The Los Angeles riot was the first one in which rioters were able to watch their actions on television. The concentration and movements of the police in the area were well reported on the air, better than that of the rioters themselves. By listening to the continuous radio and TV coverage, it was possible to deduce that the police were moving toward or away from a particular neighborhood. Those who were active in raiding stores could choose when and where to strike, and still have ample time for retreat. The entire curfew area is a very extended one.[34]

The media disseminate the rationalizations and symbols of identification used by the rioters. The mass media serve to reenforce and spread a feeling of consciousness among those who participate or sympathize with extremist actions, regardless of the actions' origins. In particular, television offers them a mass audience far beyond their most optimistic aspirations. Knowledge of the riot would spread in any case, but immediate extensive and detailed coverage both speeds up the process and gives it a special reality. On balance, I would argue that these images serve to reenforce predispositions to participate and even to legitimate participation. To be able to generate mass media coverage, especially television coverage, becomes an element in the motivation of the rioters. The sheer ability of the rioters to command mass media attention is an ingredient in developing legitimacy. In selected highbrow intellectual circles in the United States, a language of rationalization of violence has developed. The mass media serve to disseminate a popular version of such justification. The commentaries on television were filled with pseudo-sociological interpretations and the rioters themselves given ample opportunity to offer a set of suitable rationalizations.

In the past, when rioting was of the contested area variety, the newspapers were the major mass media. In many areas they developed an operational code, informally and formally, to deal with news about rioting. The practice was to apply an embargo on news about a riot during the actual period of the riot. After the event, it would be covered. The goal was to prevent the newspapers from serving as a means for mobilizing rioters, as was the case in the riots of Chicago in 1919. With the growth of television and the intensification of competition between the press and television, this practice broke down.

It is difficult to estimate the short- and long-term effects of the mass media portrayal of riots on white and Negro opinions. However, the riots projected a new element in the mass media imagery of the Negro, if only for a limited period of time. In the past, the mass media served to reenforce the system of segregation by casting the Negro exclusively in a minority position as well as by describing and characterizing him as weak. The portrait of the Negro as weak in the mass media served to mobilize and reenforce aggressive sentiments and emotions against these groups. The extremely prejudiced person is more disposed to release his aggression if he believes that the object of his aggression is too weak to respond to his hostile feelings and emotions.[35]

Since the end of World War II, the mass media have been helping to modify the imagery of the Negro and thereby to weaken the prejudiced symbolism. The advances of the Negro in economic, social, and political life have supplied a basis by which the mass media could project a more

441

realistic and more favorable picture of the Negro. The reasoned and moral arguments in defense of racial equality by black and white leaders provide the subject for extensive editorial commentary in the mass media. Mass media images of the Negro were enhanced by the role of Negro troops in the Korean conflict and by the increasing presentation of the Negro as policemen. Regardless of Negro leadership opinion on the war in South Vietnam, the Negro soldier's role has served to modify in a positive direction the image of the Negro in both white and Negro communities. The early phase of the civil-rights movement, with its emphasis on orderly and controlled demonstrations, served also to alter the symbolism of the Negro from that of a weak, powerless figure. The climax of this phase of change, as presented by the mass media, was the dramatic March on Washington led by the late Dr. Martin Luther King, Jr. As an event in the mass media, it was unique. The national media were focused on a predominantly black assemblage moving in an orderly and powerful fashion. In a real sense, it was a symbolic incorporation of the Negro into American society, because of the heavy emphasis on religion and the setting in the nation's capital.

In the elimination of prejudiced imagery, the Negro in the United States obviously has had to face much greater psychological barriers than any other minority group. Hostility and prejudice formed on the axis of color runs deep. Nevertheless, the secular trend in negative stereotypes toward the Negro from 1945 to 1965 has showed a dramatic decline, and the mass media have had an effect in this trend.

Even in the absence of adequate psychological studies in depth, some speculation is possible about the image projected by the riots. The view of Negroes as a group growing in strength and direction was for the moment shattered. Instead, a partial image of explosive irrationality has been dramatized. The use of sheer strength for destructive purposes rather than to achieve a goal that the white population could define as reasonable and worthwhile has served only to mobilize counter hostility and counteraggression. No doubt these images fade away as the mass media focus on reporting in depth the realities of the black community and the processes of social change that are at work.

442

Thus, in conclusion, the history of the race riot is more than an account of the change from communal to commodity type conflict. It is more than the history of the gross inadequacies of the system of law enforcement and the limitations in the performance of the mass media. It is in part an answer to the question posed by Ralph Ellison, the Negro novelist, "But can a people live and develop for over three hundred years simply by reacting?"[36] The Negro outbursts have been more than a reaction to police brutality and a double standard of legal justice. In a symbolic sense, they are expressions of energies to participate in and transform the larger society. In all phases of life, the Negro is not merely reacting but acting.

References

1. Chicago Commission on Race Relations, *The Negro in Chicago: A Study of Race Relations and a Race Riot* (Chicago: The University of Chicago; 1922). For another riot that has been documented in depth, see Elliott M. Rudwick, *Race Riot at East St. Louis* (Carbondale: Southern Illinois University Press, 1964).
2. Allen D. Grimshaw, "Factors Contributing to Color Violence in the United States and Great Britain," *Race*, May 1962, p. 18. See also Robin M. Williams, "Social Change and Social Conflict: Race Relations in the United States, 1944-1964," *Social Inquiry*, Apr. 1965, pp. 8-25.
3. Allen D. Grimshaw, "Actions of Police and Military in American Race Riots," *Phylon*, Fall 1963, p. 288.
4. Stanley Lieberson and Arnold R. Silverman, "Precipitants and Conditions of Race Riots," *American Sociological Review*, Dec. 1965, pp. 887-898.
5. The Chicago Commission on Race Relations, *op. cit.*, p. 23.
6. See also Allen D. Grimshaw, "Lawlessness and Violence in the United States and their Special Manifestations in Changing Negro-White Relationships," *Journal of Negro History*, Jan. 1957, pp. 52-72.
7. See for example, Hans Mattick, "The Form and Content of Recent Riots," *Midway*, Summer 1968, pp. 3-32.
8. See Allen A. Silver, "Official Interpretations of Racial Riots," *Urban Riots: Violence and Social Change, Proceedings of the Academy of Political Science*, vol. XXIX, No. 1, July 1968, pp. 146-158.
9. Anthony Oberschall, "The Los Angeles Riot of August 1965," *Social Problems*, pp. 322-334.
10. Jules J. Wanderer, "1967 Riots: A Test of the Congruity of Events," *Social Problems*, Fall 1968, pp. 193-198.
11. National Advisory Commission on Civil Disorders, *op. cit.*, p. 180.
12. Arnold Katz, "Firearms, Violence and Civil Disorders," Stanford Research Institute, July 1968, p. 10.
13. Frank Zimring, "Is Gun Control Likely to Reduce Violent Killings?" *The University of Chicago Law Review*, Summer 1968, pp. 721-737.
14. Louis C. Goldberg, "Ghetto Riots and Others: The Faces of Civil Disorder in 1967," *Journal of Peace Research*, p. 120.
15. Robert M. Fogelson and Robert B. Hill, "Who Riots? A Study of Participation in the 1967 Riots," *Supplemental Studies for the National Advisory Commission on Civil Disorders*, July 1968, pp. 221-248.
16. *The Detroit Riot: A Profile of 500 Prisoners*, Department of Labor, Mar. 1968, 28 pp.
17. Anthony Oberschall, *op. cit.*, p. 335.
18. National Advisory Commission on Civil Disorders, *Supplemental Studies*, p. 239.
19. *Ibid.*, p. 89.
20. Anthony Oberschall, *op. cit.*, p. 329.
21. National Advisory Commission on Civil Disorders, p. 73.
22. *Ibid.*, p. 243.

23. Morris Janowitz, *The Social Control of Escalated Riots* (Chicago: The University of Chicago Press, 1967).
24. *New York Times,* Mar. 13, 1969, p. 22.
25. *New York Times,* Sept. 29, 1968.
26. For a list and analysis of 25 reported sniping incidents in July and August 1968, see *Riot Data Review* (Lemberg Center for the Study of Violence), No. 3 (Feb. 1969), pp. 1-38.
27. See Harold Cruse, *The Crisis of the Negro Intellectual* (New York: William Morrow, 1967), pp. 347-401, for an analysis of the ideologies of violence in the black community.
28. Paul Blackstock, *The Strategy of Subversion* (Chicago: Quadrangle Books, 1964).
29. Paul Blackstock, "Anarchism, Manipulated Violence and Civil Disorder," unpublished manuscript, 1968.
30. See W. W. Charter, *Motion Pictures and Youth* (New York: Macmillan, 1933).
31. See *Christian Science Monitor,* Oct. 4, 1968 for details of a survey conducted by that newspaper's staff.
32. Leonard Berkowitz, Ronald Corwin, and Mark Heironimus, "Film Violence and Subsequent Aggressive Tendencies," *Public Opinion Quarterly,* vol. XXVII (Summer 1963), pp. 217-229.
33. National Advisory Commission on Civil Disorders, p. 202.
34. Oberschall, *op. cit.,* pp. 335-336.
35. For a discussion of this psychological mechanism, see Bruno Bettelheim and Morris Janowitz, *Social Change and Prejudice* (New York: The Free Press, 1964).
36. Ralph Ellison, *Shadow and Act* (New York: Random House, 1964), p. 315.

Chapter 11

THE DYNAMICS OF BLACK AND WHITE VIOLENCE

*By James P. Comer, M.D.**

When black and white violence again struck urban America in the early 1960's, social scientists and government leaders looked around hurriedly for a quick solution. The obvious cause, to many, was the low social and economic conditions of black Americans. In spite of multiple efforts to improve this situation, violence mounted to a frightening peak in 1967. While interracial violence decreased sharply in 1968, the polarization of the races pointed up in the *Report of the National Advisory Commission on Civil Disorders* is continuing to take place. Thus

* James Comer is assistant professor of psychiatry at the Yale Child Study Center. His publications include "The Social Power of the Negro," *Scientific American* (Apr. 1967), and "Black Rebellion and Individual Development: Some Parallels," *Midway* (Summer 1968).

the possibility of future and even more malignant violence, such as guerrilla tactics, remains a possibility, if not a probability.

If the social and economic conditions of a group are the primary determinants of group violence and potential violence, civil disorder on the part of blacks is a paradox.[1] While the irrelative economic position remains low, social and economic gains directly experienced by black Americans from 1960 through 1968 have been more rapid and substantial than ever before in American history.[2] The number of nonwhites, 92 percent black, at the poverty level as defined by the Social Security Administration has declined from 10.9 million in 1964 to 8.3 million in 1967. The unemployment rate for blacks has declined from 12.4 percent of the labor force in 1961 to 6.8 percent for the first 6 months of 1968. A 31 percent drop in underemployment was recorded between 1966 and 1967, compared with a 17 percent decline for whites.

In 1960 there were only 3 million blacks in the better job categories, while 46 million whites held such jobs. Between 1960 and 1967 there was a 47 percent increase in the number of blacks in white-collar jobs, craftsmen, and operatives (the better jobs), compared to a 16 percent increase by whites. There was an 80 percent increase in the number of black professional and technical workers between 1960 and 1967, compared with a 30 percent increase among whites. There was a 77 percent increase in the number of black clerical workers as compared to a 23 percent increase for whites; a 49 percent increase in craftsmen and foremen in the nonwhite category, compared with 13 percent of whites. There was a corresponding decline in private household workers, 17 percent for nonwhites compared with 23 percent among whites; a 7 percent decline was registered among black nonfarm laborers, compared with a 2 percent decline among whites. Because so few blacks held relatively good occupational positions prior to 1960, these changes are not as dramatic as they appear, yet represent substantial improvement.

During the summer of 1967, it became clear that the socioeconomic explanation for black and white violence was inadequate.[3] Observations made after the disorders following the assassination of Dr. Martin Luther King, Jr., suggest the same. A *Wall Street Journal*[4] report read:

Arrest records suggested that the adults who looted were for the most part Negroes with comparatively good education who held jobs and had not been arrested before. Few expressed a conscious desire to revenge Dr. King's slaying. . . . In many cities, the violence apparently originated with Negroes in their early teens, or even all the way down to kindergarten age—those who had the least reason to revere, or even know of, Dr. King, and those who scorned the moderate civil rights approach Dr. King espoused.

A black militant in Baltimore responded to the question of what sparked the riots with this comment, "You did, Whitey. You did it by treating us like animals. The black man in Baltimore is tired of his life, tired of his low pay, tired of being kicked about. King was just an excuse." The National Advisory Commission on Civil Disorders, while stating the problem differently, agreed that white racism was the basic cause of black and white violence. Both explanations—racism and poverty—view intergroup violence as a simple reaction to an unhappy set of circumstances.

A third explanation of black and white violence is of even more limited value. Some social scientists have contended that persons with impulse-control difficulties as a consequence of black family disintegration have been heavily involved in precipitating urban violence.[5] Recent studies have both challenged the notion of black family disintegration and shown that such persons are just as likely to be nonparticipants as they are to be participants.[6] The complexity of intergroup violence is further revealed in some of the incongruous events which occurred during several 1967 disturbances. A group of black youngsters in Washington, D. C., escorted their white teacher out of the danger area, but hurried back to throw rocks at the passing cars of "white honkies." In Detroit, blacks and whites sat together in a friendly atmosphere and bid on the plunder recovered in disturbances which occurred only a few months before.

Obviously there is no simple explanation. Racism, poverty and personal-control problems are not enough to explain the complexities and incongruities of current black-white conflict—although all three factors are involved. A more useful approach is to recognize intergroup violence as primarily a product of specific social system malfunctioning. It is a natural and predictable phenomenon—although largely preventable—related to the nature of man and his basic human tasks. It occurs and recurs when an individual or group is denied the opportunity to meet their basic and man-made needs.

The human animal is born with drives and needs which conflict with those of other human beings.[7] Some form of social organization that will regulate the manner in which these drives are expressed and needs are met have always been necessary. In all societies, parents, caretakers, and socializers of one kind or another are charged with the responsibility of meeting the child's basic needs and helping the young convert drive energy into "tools" which will help them cope with the demands of an adult society. Libidinal energy becomes "the stuff" of exploration, learning, and work.[8] Without satisfactory transformation, these energies may result in a variety of troublesome forms of personal behavior, including self-destructive action and unwarranted conflict and violence against people and property. When the young are adequately developed and socialized and are able to cope as adults, they enjoy a sense of adequacy and security. Being able to cope and as a result receiving the respect and acceptance of significant peers is the primary way an individual meets basic and man-made needs. When a sufficient number of members of a society feel relatively adequate and secure, a high level of peace and stability can exist in families and the society without force and repression of individuals or groups.[9]

It is the task of the leaders of a society to establish social policy that facilitates optimal individual development and adequate socialization of the young. Failure to do so constitutes social violence, resulting in damage to individuals, groups, and the society, which is far more harmful and lasting than overt physical violence. In a representative society where groups must organize and participate in the political and administrative system in order to obtain opportunities that will facilitate the optimal development of their members, the obstructive and unjust exercise of power—physical or social—by another group constitutes a crippling form of violence. The victimized group, when healthy, struggles against the unjust and oppressive situation. This struggle in the face of resistance frequently results in overt physical violence. In addition, when the leaders of a society sanction social exploitation of a group, they concomitantly encourage physical violence toward that group. Thus the

447

historical American situation of slavery or legal social violence toward blacks; white physical violence and relatively little black retaliation;[10] finally a legal and nonviolent struggle now punctuated with black violence is an understandable sequence.[11]

There is an aspect of the pattern—black restraint—which, on the surface, is difficult to explain. Given the level of social violence toward blacks, the logical question now should not be "Why black violence?" but "Why has black initiated and retaliatory violence been so little and so late?" The record of provocation certainly is extreme.

During slavery, whippings and other abusive acts were frequent. Because of the economic value of the slave, it was usually only after abortive slave revolts or "unpardonable" offenses that the killing of slaves took place. Freedmen, North and South, who found themselves in economic competition with whites frequently fared less well. After slavery when the 4 million blacks in the South came into direct economic competition with the 5½ million poor whites and were no longer of value to the white planters, the severity of violence toward blacks increased. Beatings, torture, and murder in order to disfranchise blacks, decrease economic competition, and maintain a caste system for economic and psychological advantage became the pattern of the day. It has been estimated that between 1865 and 1955 over 5,000 blacks were lynched by white mobs.[12] Official U.S. Census Bureau statistics show that over 3,000 were lynched between 1882 and 1935.[13] Legal lynchings, "kangaroo court" action, and unreported murders are not included in these totals. Black schools and homes were frequently burned in the early postslavery period. Between 1865 and 1940, over 500 blacks were killed in race riots and massacres. Many more were injured and abused. Relatively few whites were killed in these disturbances. Finally, the burning and bombing of black property and the murder and intimidation of blacks and their white supporters involved in civil-rights activities since the early 1950's is well known.

Despite this abusive and oppressive pattern, black reaction was generally not violence but nonviolence. Aptheker and other historians have pointed out that there were slave uprisings and rumors of uprisings, but they certainly did not approximate the frequency or severity of black slave uprisings in South America. Even after slavery there was generally an under response to the level of oppression. Historians and revolutionaries have often puzzled over and despaired about this situation.

Certainly the overwhelming power of the dominant group is a factor. But it is not enough to explain the phenomenon. Often slaves and freedmen greatly outnumbered their masters and sometimes did attack and kill them, but not very often. Subsequent events have demonstrated that inherent docility and passivity and the other explanations for extreme black restraint were inaccurate. This is evidenced by the remarkable change in black reaction to white control efforts in a short period of time. Only 15 years ago a black family stood fearful and powerless as whites, without legal authority, dragged their black youngster from his home and murdered him. Today the arrest of a black man by a white policeman in a black neighborhood carries with it the risk of touching off a violent disturbance. Obviously there are important psychosocial forces at play in black and white violence which go beyond simple unhappiness and reaction to racism or poverty. These forces can best be delineated through a review of the critical aspects of black and white reaction over time.

Slavery, the initial contact of most blacks and whites in America, set the stage for continuing conflict. Many students of slavery have been preoccupied with the question of whether it was largely a harsh and cruel or pleasant and humane system. This is an interesting but relatively unrewarding focus. The most important consideration here is the effect of the system on the social and psychological development of individual blacks and whites and on the functioning of the respective groups in the society at large. The effects of the system were enormous indeed and still "haunt" us over 100 years since the demise of the "peculiar institution."

The issue of who was to blame, the black chiefs or middlemen in Africa or slavers, is likewise not important here. The point which is critical to this discussion is that established social systems were interrupted and new and traumatic ones were imposed on the victims. Socialization, which was meaningful and enabled individuals to meet basic needs and prepare to cope as adults in the African society, was no longer useful nor possible. The socialization which was necessary to cope as a slave was traumatic and harmful to the psychological and social development of blacks—an extreme form of social violence.

In West Africa, blacks were socialized in a way to meet the needs of individuals and the respective societies.[14] Children were provided with nurturance and physical care in a family or kinship system which oriented them to their immediate world of kin, the community, society and to their own feelings. Cultural and subcultural goals and values were transmitted to the children and interpersonal skills, modes of feeling, thinking, and working were developed. Contact with parents, elders, chiefs, warriors, medicine men, traders, etc.—one of which they were destined to become—gave the children a sense of direction, purpose, and meaning.

Ritual and ceremony deepened the meaning of individual existence and gave testimony to the importance of societal functions. The circumcision and naming ceremonies of the Dogon tribe were very important exercises with lifelong significance to the individual. Indeed it is only through the naming ceremony that a member of that tribe became a part of the society. In the Ibo, Zulu, Dogon, and other tribes of West Africa, children were brought into the adult cultural milieu through age-group organizations. Every function in the society brought these groups together and a sense of belonging and participation resulted. The transference from age group to age group was marked by meaningful ceremony.

Specific expectations and responsibilities were laid down and had to be met before a young person could receive additional responsibilities and privileges. The individual received approval and acceptance from important people in his society through the accomplishment of societal tasks and developed a sense of adequacy and self-respect for his achievement. The universal outcome of adequate socialization which permits one to cope as an adult is a sense of security. This is not to say that there were no injustices, insecurity, or uncertainty within the African system. But in general the operation of the tribes and tribal nations fostered the development of a sense of security and a positive self and group concept. Slavery radically changed this situation.

The objective of socialization in slavery was not to develop the individual to a point that he or she might perform as a fully adequate, competent, full participant in adult society. The socialization and management of slaves was designed to maintain the master's power and control over them and to increase his benefits. Even humane treatment has its "master's twist." An ex-slave from Louisiana said, "Marse always say being mean to the young-uns make them mean when they grows up and nobody gwine to buy a mean nigger."[15]

The slaves were powerless for two major reasons. Their legal status was that of chattel without rights in court and without the protection of any institution. The master was all-powerful and had the right to control every aspect of slave life from birth to death, from sex to settling disputes. His power was enhanced by additional factors. Black slaves in a predominantly white controlled land were readily identifiable. The slaves were not of a single tribal origin with a long group history and a resultant cohesive bond. They were far from home and generally unwanted except for economic exploitation. They were not able to maintain the organizational elements of their respective previous cultures—kinship ties, family organization, religion, government, courts, etc.[16] Thus they were not able to run away en masse; to turn in on their own culture for psychological support or to effectively organize to attack their oppressors.

Economic and social policies were not determined by the slaves. The provision of food, clothing, and shelter for a family was not the task of the black male. Often a family structure or kinship structure did not exist at all. Protecting the family and tribe from assault was not the role of a black warrior, groomed from childhood for the task and honored for his feats by ritual and ceremony. The naming ceremony meant nothing any more. Males were often referred to by the master they worked for and the woman they had a sexual liaison with. . . . Mr. Barber's boy or Sophie's man. The master provided for basic human needs and regulated basic human functions. For everything the slaves were forced to look to the master.

Obviously the slavemaster functioned as "father," ruler, and God. Indeed slaves were often taught to "obey thy master as thy God." Even when the slave resisted, he was relating to a master, for it was not resistance in the name

451

of a people or a tribe or a tribal nation. It was one to one, slave to master. The condition of total power and complete powerlessness, with the master providing and regulating basic needs—thus providing all the security a black slave could know—resulted in an intense emotional bond or tie between the black slave and the white master. Because slaveholdings in this country averaged 5 to 15 persons, this bond was much more intense than in South American countries where the slaveholdings were much larger and a greater degree of black self-identity and culture were maintained.

After the first generation, children were born into the system and prepared from birth for a life of subservience. Nurturance and physical care came from an adult but not in the interest of a family, kinship group, or tribe, but in the interest of a master. (This is probably the reason that so many adults cared so little for children—a point which confounded slaveowners and observers.) Children were not destined to become elders, chiefs, warriors, traders, etc. Their future was that of a despised slave. Ritual and ceremony did not give testimony to the importance of their own lives and that of their people. The master, or parents doing his bidding, set expectations. Approval and acceptance from fellow slaves was based on the degree to which the child achieved goals acceptable to the master.

Children were taught what they could and could not do in relation to whites. They were taught to obey and respect whites. The Bible and the whip reinforced their parent's teaching. Frequent references in the literature of slavery indicate that black children were taught to knuckle under to the little white tyrant of the same age, one in training to become the master and the other to become the slave. There could be no black-group goals for children to inculcate. Blacks did not exist as a group with goals of their own. They were given organization, goals, and direction by the master. They existed for his benefit and by his permission.

Some ran away to the Indians, to Canada, and to freedom in the North.[17] But most could not. Most had to adjust to the circumstances, for man does not exist in groups without some form of social organization. Some led a passive-aggressive existence in relationship to whites—working as little as they could without being punished,

452

sabotaging property, and generally provoking the master. Some used religion to establish a relationship and existence in which they had an importance and purpose beyond the master and their lowly slave position. Some established a life style which was a carbon copy of the master. Some adjustments were extremely harmful to individual development and others were less so. All, however, had to identify and relate to the master or the white power group. This led to an identification with the aggressor or oppressor—an adaptive mechanism of generally adverse consequences to blacks.[18]

It is understandable under the condition of powerlessness, dependency and rejection inherent in the nature of American slavery that wisdom and adequacy became associated with the master. Eventually these attributes were extended to all white persons. All whites had the right to abuse and exploit blacks without fear of serious censure or consequences. Blackness was associated with inadequacy and subservience and the notion was transmitted to black and white children during their earliest developmental years. The message was driven home well. Benjamin Botkin's collection of slave narratives shows many instances of slave guilt for not working hard or disobeying the master. This suggests that the values of the master were internalized by the slaves. Slave narratives also indicate very clearly that they were rendered dependent on the powerful master and many developed feelings and attitudes toward him parallel to the parent-child relationship. The large number of slaves who could not or would not leave the plantation after slavery indicates the degree of psychological dependency that was developed.

Identification with the master was of serious psychological consequence to the slaves. Attitudes about blacks held by whites became the feelings or attitudes blacks held for themselves and each other as a group. Hatred of self, anger toward the self, presumption of black incompetence, etc., are a legacy of slavery reinforced by residual and later social practices—segregation and exclusion. Independent black achievement was almost nonexistent during slavery.[19] Success was being like whites, being with whites, or being white. Often the black ideal or goal was to be white or to become white.[20] Students of behavior have repeatedly documented the adverse psychological effect of these "impossible strivings."[21]

Given the circumstances, dependency and identification with the master is an understandable outcome. But such a relationship is always an ambivalent one. Man in such situations enjoys the security of dependency but rebels against the price, external control. He despises the person of power but attempts to be a part of him. The goals and ideals of the powerful can easily become those of the powerless. In such a relationship, anger or action against the powerful and protective person or group is a blow against part of the self of the dependent and powerless person or group. It is not surprising then that many blacks would have some difficulty expressing anger toward whites during slavery and for a long period thereafter. The psychological tie of powerless blacks to powerful whites was as important a deterrent of black retaliation as the probable physical consequences.

Had blacks become an acceptable part of the total society after slavery, the significance of racial differences would have been greatly changed. Race would not have remained as a symbol or a sign of goodness and badness, success or failure. Blacks would not have been denied employment, education, ownership and entreprenurial opportunities. The masses could have received a basic sense of adequacy by simply providing for their families and receiving recognition as desirable parents and citizens. The talented could have moved to positions of leadership and registered high-level achievement. Without the atmosphere of white rejection of blacks at every level, the latter could have identified with achievers, leaders, goals, and values which were American rather than black or white. Black children would have aspired to a wide range of goals rather than those open to blacks. But blacks were not accepted into the total society and the consequential psychological outcome was different.

After slavery, blacks were immediately closed out of the economic, political, and educational mainstream of American life.[22] The program of federal Reconstruction failed to provide blacks with a solid economic base and was, as a consequence, gradually eroded as an adjustment tool. None of the organizational aspects of the African culture remained to provide a basis for group stability and direction. Only remnants of previous African life styles and behavioral residuals remained, greatly modified by the American experience and of little value in promoting adjustment in the postslavery period. As a result of these factors, blacks remained economically, socially, and psychologically dependent on whites who retained almost complete economic and social control. Over 50 percent of the black population remained in a condition of serfdom until the early part of the 20th century. While some were able to directly express anger and advocate rejection of and attacks on the perceived oppressor—as some did in slavery —most were not able to do so. Not only had their training been effective but to express hostility toward whites on which many were dependent was to risk the loss of a major source of a sense of security.

The circumstances reflected an extremely unhealthy state of affairs. As a group, blacks were unable to obtain opportunities which would facilitate the optimal development of large numbers of their members. Public education was long delayed and often inadequate. They were employed at the lowest level of the job market. They were rapidly closed out of business and government. Yet because many had been trained to accept white control, their lack of education and skills, the level of antagonism toward blacks, and their dependency tie to whites with power, many blacks—although woefully oppressed—were unable to struggle against the unjust exercise of power they experienced. This combination of circumstances did not exist for any other excluded group in America.

Although powerless after slavery with still little sense of community other than being a despised, rejected part of a larger community, blacks were forced to turn in on themselves anyway. Segregation, which rapidly developed as a social policy after slavery, made this necessary. With the end of the control and exploitation of blacks by their masters, legislation, judicial and extra-legal control (intimidation, violence, economic reprisals) were established. Control and authority had now been extended to all whites, most of them more economically vulnerable and in need of psychological scapegoats than the more wealthy slave-owning class.[23] Whites outside the planter class were more likely to act in an unjust and violent fashion toward blacks. Black parents had to prepare their children to live in such

455

a setting. Aggressive styles had to be crushed lest they lead to conflicts with whites. Such socialization led to the destruction and/or diminution of the capacity for exploration, learning, and work in many blacks.

A strict social etiquette developed which symbolized white privilege and black subservience.[24] Children learned the rules of the game through subtle and overt ways. In the 1930's when a black youngster in Texas was beaten by white adult males for entering a bus before a white woman, his father did not protect or console him but angrily counseled, "You ought to know better than to get on the bus before the white folks."

The implication of segregation, as it was practiced, was clear: blacks are inferior and incapable of participation in the total society. This rejection occurred to a people generally trying desperately to belong. Denied the tools and opportunity for personal achievement and the resultant sense of adequacy and security achievement brings, belonging to a group which met these needs was most important. Blacks made various adaptations to meet adequacy and security needs in a society in which they were now "free" but still rejected and bused.

Blacks who had used religion as an adaptive mechanism during slavery now embraced it more firmly. The church became a substitute society.[25] "Walking and talking with Jesus" was more than a metaphor. It was an important method of being a valued person. In many black communities, a sense of relatedness born of the need for mutual support necessary to survive in a theatening society began to develop. Sharing and mutual aid became a style of life for many. Many informal and formal Afro-American mutual support organizations developed after slavery, reflecting the great need. Other blacks became paid employees of their former masters and maintained a carbon-copy style of life and identified strongly with whites. Some wandered disorganized and hopeless for several years after slavery. Some were without social organization, goals, and direction, and were largely pleasure oriented, responding to their inadequately controlled sexual and aggressive drives in a way that led them into conflict with the larger society. Such behavior was not viewed as a failure of the society to establish social policy which promoted adequate social and psychological development but was seen as "the way the niggers are." Similar behavior among whites was not viewed as "white behavior."

Because blacks did not respond to oppression with violent retaliation did not mean that they did not experience anger. It was generally turned against the self or others like the self.[26] Passive, self-destructive modes of behavior are, in part, a product of the reaction to self-hate and low self-esteem. The excessive use of drugs and alcohol are but a few examples. Violent behavior against other blacks—often a displacement of anger toward whites—is a familiar pattern. The assault on " a friend" over a dime or a bottle of wine is an indication of the low self-esteem. The disproportionately high violent crime rate of blacks is, in part, a manifestation of displaced anger. A black student at an Ivy League school angrily contested a black professor after it was obvious that the student was in error. He readily accepts similar comments from whites. Low aspiration level and high family-conflict rates among some blacks is often a byproduct (or partially so) of anger against the self. Because many blacks have very little power to effect change, overwhelming obstacles and hopeless surrender produce high social and psychological depression rates. Only occasionally and only recently has rage and anger been turned against whites.

The circumstances of black and white interaction has also had an impact on the white psyche.[27] Until recent years, many whites have felt justified in their abuse and exploitation of blacks. Leaders of the society—a U.S. Congressman as late as the early 1900's—threatened greater violence toward blacks if favorable legislation for them was passed. During Reconstruction, many white leaders urged the white masses to attack blacks and often joined in the fun. It is small wonder that a cavalier attitude (indeed a collective superego defect) developed with regard to white abuse of black. It was wrong to murder unless it was a nigger out of his place—his place being determined by whites.

Inherent superiority was taught and is still taught to white youngsters through denial and by ignoring the accomplishments of blacks in the face of overwhelming obstacles. Institutional denial—exclusion of blacks from textbooks, communications media, and white institutions—facilitated individual denial. White youngsters were taught white superiority and black inferiority through direct and inadvertent means. A white youngster of marginal intelligence had learned from his father that he should be nice to blacks, otherwise they would not want to work for him when he grew up—an assumption of a superior status in spite of the fact that the youngster was less prepared to be a high-level achiever than many blacks. A golf caddy who wanted to work for two black physicians without taking his turn asked them to tell the pro in charge that they worked for his father. A white suburban child looked at a black youngster in town and said, "Look Mommy, a baby maid!" White people act consciously and unconsciously on these feelings in relationship to blacks. These attitudes and conditions are clearly changing under the pressure of new social forces but many undesirable conditions still exist. Such attitudes and reactions are, in part, a basis for continued black and white conflict.

In spite of the many psychological and social forces which inhibited normal black reaction to oppression, the basis for such a reaction has been gradually developing for a long time. It began when slavery was ended and the policy of racial segregation forced white leaders to prepare or permit some blacks to prepare themselves to take care of their own. This "crack" in the pattern of forced dependency was the beginning of the development of a positive black group identity and eventually a normal reaction to oppression. Many blacks, as preachers, teachers, physicians, and other professional service people, began to develop skills which gave them a sense of adequacy and the capacity to cope. In the South in particular, successful business communities developed. Black youngsters were able to identify with people like themselves in positions of leadership and respect. Obviously the level of respect was limited by the implications of a segregated system, but nonetheless it was of value in enhancing black self-esteem. More among the black masses were better able to earn enough money to take care of their families and as a result were able to develop a sense of personal adequacy. Involvement in two world wars and achievement in entertainment, athletics and other areas, and the exposure facilitated by mass migration began to change the black American's feelings toward the self. A positive sense of self began to replace the previous negative self concept.[28]

458

Today's young adult blacks and teenagers grew up observing the heroics of Jackie Robinson and Jimmie Brown. They watch Sidney Poitier and listen to Aretha Franklin. They observe better trained blacks achieve and move to positions of high responsibility. They test themselves against white youngsters on the gridiron, in the military service, and occasionally in the classroom, and often find that they can perform just as well. When this is not the case, it is often clear that limited opportunity and not a lack of ability is the probable cause. The black nurse's aide and practical nurse often realize that with the same educational development and training, they could hold the nurse's job, more often held by whites.

For good reasons, blacks began to raise critical questions. Why is the White American entitled to special opportunity and privilege? Why have we been denied political, economic, and educational opportunity? Why should we despise blackness, indeed, hate aspects of ourselves? Having rejected notions of inferiority, there is no good answer. In spite of this, blacks continue to experience excessive white resistance to pressure for justice and opportunity.

Many of the young black leaders of today were part of the sit-in movement of a decade ago. Many attended racially integrated schools while being harassed, intimidated, and attacked by white hoodlums while "responsible authorities" turned their heads. Many watched "Bull" Connor bring out the dogs to interfere with the peaceful protest of unjust laws and practices. Many looked in vain for action by the legislative, judiciary, and executive branches of government to remove obstacles to first-class citizenship. Most troublesome, they watched white public officials, clearly violating the law, be elected to offices of high trust and responsibility because they stood for the unjust exercise of power against blacks.

The reaction to resistance could now be different. Blacks are no longer largely employed in Southern agriculture and consequently vulnerable to economic reprisal for any self-interest activities—political, economic, or social. Black adequacy and competence is now built on more than white approval and assurance of acceptance as a child of God with a reward in heaven. A significant number of black parents no longer teach their children to accept white authority, right or wrong. Many whites, now economically more secure and better educated, no longer need or approve of the scapegoating of blacks. The tie that bound—black social, economic, and psychological dependence on an almost totally rejecting white community—has now been broken.

With the breaking of the dependency bond came expected responses. A greater number of blacks could experience anger and rage in response to denial and injustice.[29] In addition, blacks could now seek an identity free of the implications of the aggressor and/or oppressor (the white power structure which denied opportunity to blacks on the basis of a rationalization—inferiority). An intense search for a positive black identity followed.

The breaking of the dependency bond, acceptance of blackness, and a sense of outrage is an energizing and potentially explosive set of psychological developments. The potency is increased by the fact of a continued high level of resistance. The black American experiences intense and ambivalent feelings as a result and is confronted with numerous questions and conflicts. Should he attempt to become a part of the mainstream of his society—now changing but once so abusive and rejecting—or is he obliged to retaliate and/or reject it? Indeed, does manhood require retaliation and rejection? Can he trust a white America which has never before demonstrated itself trustworthy with regard to recognizing and protecting the human rights of black Americans? These developments and circumstances have created the tension and potential for black violence, retaliatory and black initiated.

The ambivalence and uncertainty is reflected in the wide range of black community responses. The shooting of a black man in connection with a jay-walking traffic violation in Washington, D.C., recently prompted a violent, retaliatory black community mood, necessitating a massive police confrontation. In St. Louis, black churchmen made angry demands for an apology when a white cashier referred to the group of men as "boys." Any expression of white superiority or excessive control evokes a strong reaction from many blacks. Obviously new ground rules for black and white interaction are being established and blacks are sensitive to violations.

A black student was ordered off the lawn at his predominantly white college campus by a white policeman. To be a man—a black man—he had to hit the policeman, a symbol of oppression. But it was a "minor incident" and to avoid difficulty he had to hold back. In fury, rage, and confusion he smashed his arm through a plateglass window a few minutes later. Such feeling occasionally results in a loss of control after "trigger incidents" (reflecting white superiority and black helplessness) with attendant burning of property. With a breakdown in personal control, blacks, employed and unemployed, loot and plunder the "symbolic enemy." Such reactions on the part of oppressed groups have been reported throughout human history.

In the one-to-one black and white relationship where mutual respect exists, interaction is less difficult, perhaps better than ever before. It is the battle against the symbolic enemy that permits black youngsters to escort their white teacher to safety and stone the cars of passing white strangers a few minutes later.

Black reactions are manifest in other ways. A distinguished banker in New York has said that "I am a black man first and an American second." The new black bank president in Chicago identified himself in reverse order. Both accept the values and styles of the total society but want to change the society to meet the needs of more among the black masses. On the other extreme are blacks so angry and alienated that they advocate the establishment of a separate state. One group has already emigrated to Africa. Two black Olympic athletes raised their fists in a symbolic black power salute and another waved an American flag. Black militants and intellectuals ponder the question of whether entrance into the American mainstream is possible or desirable, whether constructive modification of the American system is a realistic aim or whether revolution is necessary, possible, or suicidal.

Some black college students are so "hungup" on these issues that they are unable to concentrate on course work which is irrelevant by comparison. The feelings have filtered down to youngsters, as young as 3 or 4 years of age. Just as young members of the Klan are taught that it is permissible to abuse blacks, some young blacks are being taught that it is permissible to abuse whites. The level of awakening and concern is now so pervasive and reaches such a young age group that one can only anticipate growing presure for justice—the fair exercise of power. This level of uncertainty, ambivalence, anger and confusion, and resistance cannot persist for long without a drift toward a more malignant reaction—guerrilla warfare and vigilante-type responses.

There is no easy answer to the problem of black and white conflict and violence. The energy released by black awakening and the development of a positive group concept is profound. If channeled, it can be a powerful force for black community development, pride and forceful but nonviolent (or minimally violent) pressure for constructive change within the present social system. But before it can be channeled, it must be clear to blacks that support of the present system and participation in it is in the interest of justice for the black masses. To support a social system that continues to formulate social policy which does not permit adequate development of individual blacks as well as the community and permits blatant disregard for the rights of blacks is to support the conditions that promote intolerable rage and anger.

The nation is a race against time. Constructive attitudinal and economic changes have been made. In many places, members of the white power structure have shown an unprecedented interest in facilitating black entrance into the mainstream of American life. The interaction is establishing new and more healthy ground rules for black and white relations. But often the complex factors related to emergence from a dependent, despised position to full participation in the society are not well understood—nor are the many subtle forms of resistance and racism.

Only when blacks are competent performers in much more significant numbers with access to every area and level of human endeavor within the society will the impression of white power, superiority, and independence and black powerlessness, inferiority, and dependence be destroyed. One alternative now is to attempt to achieve these ends within the society, as a part of the society and through methods deemed acceptable by the society. Another, most likely to develop if white resistance to full black participation persists, is to move against the society—violently. Logic or concern for the consequences cannot stay passion generated by the desire to satisfy basic human needs. Government, industry, educators, and every group responsible for establishing social policy must make it clear through

462

rapid and enlightened action that manhood, respect, adequacy, and security are possible within this society or black and white conflict and violence will become more malignant.

References

1. In an analysis of the feelings, attitudes, and behavioral interaction between black and white Americans, a basic methodological problem exists. Primary documents relating conditions and reactions from the loss of the organizational elements of the original black culture through subjugation are generally available from the slaver and master and not the slaves—save a limited number of narratives. Yet behavior under certain conditions is somewhat predictable and understandable even in retrospect. Combining historical, sociological, and psychological data can give us a greater depth and breadth of understanding of current behavior than documentable historical evidence alone. After all, to say that what cannot be completely documented did not happen is to limit progress in understanding critical problems. I have combined my backgrounds in social science, public health, child, adult, and social psychiatry as well as a vast amount of work in disorganized and low-income black community areas to develop the thesis presented in this paper.
2. U.S. Department of Labor and U.S. Department of Commerce, *Recent Trends in Social and Economic Conditions of Negroes in the United States*, Current Population Reports, Series P-23, No. 26 BLS Report No. 347, July 1968.
3. U.S. Riot Commission Report, *Report of the National Advisory Commission on Civil Disorders*, Mar. 1968.
4. *The Wall Street Journal*, Apr. 10, 1968, p. 1.
5. Richard Komisaruk and Carol Pearson, "Children of the Detroit Riots: A Study of their Participation and Mental Health," Lafayette Clinic and Wayne State University, unpublished.
6. Gerald Caplan, "A Study of Ghetto Rioters," *Scientific American*, vol. 219:12 (August 1968), pp. 15-21.
7. Anna Freud, *Normality and Pathology in Childhood* (New York: International Universities Press, Inc., 1965).
8. Albert J. Solnit, "Some Adaptive Functions of Aggressive Behavior," *Psychoanalysis—A General Psychology* (New York: International Universities Press, Inc., 1966).
9. Theodore Lidz, *The Family and Human Adaptation* (New York: International Universities Press, Inc., 1963).
10. See Morris Janowitz, "Patterns of Collective Racial Violence," in this report.
11. See August Meier and Elliott Rudwick, "Black Violence in the Twentieth Century: A Study in Rhetoric and Retaliation," in this report.
12. Tuskeegee Institute Report, Tuskeegee, Ala., Apr. 1959.
13. Bureau of the Census, *Historical Statistics of the United States, Colonial Times to 1957* (Washington, D.C.: U.S. Government Printing Office, 1960), p. 218.
14. James L. Gibbs, Jr. (ed.), *Peoples of Africa* (New York: Holt, Rinehart & Winston, Inc., July 1966).
15. Benjamin A. Botkin, *Lay My Burden Down, A Folk History of Slavery* (Chicago: The University of Chicago Press, 1945), p. 126.
16. Stanley M. Elkins, *Slavery* (Chicago: The University of Chicago Press, 1959), pt. III.
17. George Frederickson and Christopher Lasch, "Resistance to Slavery," *Civil War History* (Fall 1967), pp. 293-329.
18. Urie Bronfenbrenner, *Child Development*, 1960, 31, pp. 15-40.
19. Kenneth B. Clark, *Prejudice and Your Child* (Boston: Beacon Press, 1955).
20. Bertram P. Karon, *The Negro Personality* (New York: Springer Publishing Co., Inc., 1958).
21. Mary Ellen Goodman, *Race Awareness in Young Children* (Reading, Mass.: Addison-Wesley Press, 1952).
22. John Hope Franklin, *Reconstruction After the Civil War* (Chicago: The University of Chicago Press, 1961).

463

23. C. Vann Woodward, *The Strange Career of Jim Crow* (Oxford: Oxford University Press, 1955), pp. 44-60.
24. John Dollard, *Caste and Class in a Southern Town* (New York: Oxford University Press, 1938).
25. E. Franklin Frazier, *The Negro Church in America* (New York: Schocken Books, 1963).
26. Alvin F. Poussaint, "The Negro American: His Self-Image and Integration," *Journal of the National Medical Association; vol. 58, No. 6* (Nov. 1966), pp. 419-423.
27. Dollard, *op. cit.*
28. Thomas F. Pettigrew, *A Profile of the Negro American* (Princeton, N.J.: D. Van Nostrand Co., Inc., 1964), pt. III.
29. William H. Grier and Price M. Cobbs, *Black Rage* (New York: Basic Books, Inc., 1968).

PART V

PERSPECTIVES ON CRIME IN THE UNITED STATES

Whether the stark assertion that violence is "as American as cherry pie" has any historical validity, the recent spate of political assassination, urban rioting, and a crime wave of allegedly epidemic proportions has clearly convinced many Americans that their persons and property are endangered to an unprecedented degree. While the wave of assassination and ghetto rioting that has plagued the 1960's is manifestly unsettling to our restive society, it is probable that the fear of personal assault—the dark spectre of the stranger lurking in the night—currently instills the greatest sense of terror in the collective American psyche.

The essays in this section are addressed to three broad clusters of questions concerning the magnitude of violent crime in America. First, how unprecedented is the contemporary upsurge of violent assault? How valid is the apparently popular assumption that the curvilinear ascent of violent crime reflects the evolution of American society from a relatively stable and quiescent agrarian order to our present metropolitan disarray? Central to this view is a pervasive strain of agrarian suspicion and mistrust of the sinister city. This instinctive animosity owes much of its respectability to the romantic naturalism of Crevecoeur, Franklin and Jefferson, Emerson and Melville, but it has persisted even in the cosmopolitan thought of such urbane figures as Henry James, John Dewey, and Theodore Dreiser. Frank Lloyd Wright wanted to demolish the city. Henry Ford explained that "We shall solve the City Problem by leaving the City." [1] How much historical validity is there to the defeatist corollary implicit in this intellectual antiurbanism—that spiraling crime is an inevitable companion to metropolis?

If criminologists, like most students of contemporary society, are burdened today by a surfeit of statistical evidence, historians of American crime have been severely hindered by the scarcity of data. There is simply insufficient evidence available from which to reconstruct a complete historical model of national trends in violent crime. Whatever the social and political virtues of a federal system which has historically vested the police power in state and local government, the implication for historians has been that a definitive history of American crime remains impossible of achievement. Even so, sufficient if fragmentary records have been kept by a variety of local and state jurisdictions to permit a cautious generalization from a defensible sample. Possibly the best such state sample is the Commonwealth of Massachusetts, which during the 19th century experienced in microcosm the great American transition from an agrarian-commercial to an urban-industrial society. Roger Lane's analysis in chapter 12 brings sharply into question the conventional American assumption that spiraling criminal disorder is inherently a child of the city.

A second concern, one imminently more compelling to our generation, is whether the alarm expressed over the current crime wave is warranted by the facts. Writing in 1960, the sociologist Daniel Bell concluded after a "somber look at the problem" that "there is probably less crime today in the United States than existed a hundred, or fifty, or even twenty-five years ago, and that today the United States is a more lawful and safe country than popular opinion imagines." [2] This reassuring view was reaffirmed as recently as 1968 by Robert M. Cipes, a lawyer and consultant to the President's Commission on Crime in the District of Columbia. Cipes concluded that "in fact there is no crime wave," but rather that "current statistics simply reflect the fact that we are digging into the reservoir of unreported crimes." [3] Academic criminologists have generally shared this optimistic assessment. They have periodically debunked the rising crime index of the Federal Bureau of Investigation. How can we reconcile this analysis with the frenetic outcry of an aroused public, and that of the politicians who echo their alarm?

Criminal statistics have been collated nationally only since 1933, when the Federal Bureau of Investigation began systematic publication of its crime index. Far from bringing consensual order to the statistical void—or chaos—the FBI's crime index has provoked a running controversy over its credibility. Critics have argued that the Bureau had a vested interest in magnifying the magnitude of criminal activity in order to substantiate its bureau-cratic demands for increased appropriations. Furthermore, the Bureau's system of statistical collection has suffered from the decentralized and multiform nature of the American police function. Some police jurisdictions rewarded their districts and precincts for reporting a high rate of criminal activity, which might substantiate demands for greater manpower; others rewarded low reporting, which allegedly reflected police efficiency. Finally, "crime" was reported according to no uniform criteria.

Although the FBI has periodically revised and tight-ened its data-gathering system, critics continued into the late 1960's to insist that the FBI's perennially soaring Uniform Crime Reports (UCR) largely reflected self-serving "paper crime waves." Fred P. Graham, an at-torney and legal correspondent for the Washington Bureau of the *New York Times,* weighs the evidence in a critical analysis in chapter 13 that concludes on a somber note.

The final question concerns regional variations in pat-terns of criminal violence. Whether the aggregate national crime rate has been rising or falling, it is clear from even the static evidence that there have been significant vari-ations in regional patterns of criminal violence in the United States. What light can an analysis of this regional variation shed on the origins of criminal violence? More specifically, can a purely sociological analysis of regional violence suffice to account for these differences, in the ab-sence of a historical analysis of the evolution of what may be called distinctive regional subcultures?

Although historical analysis of national trends in violent crime has been retarded by a lack of data, and the con-temporary calculus of crime is rendered problematical by the uses to which the relative abundance of data is put, the studies of Lane and Graham suggest that while rising crime is not an inevitable concomitant of urbanization, rapid urbanization *may* be accompanied by alarmingly spiraling rates of crime, depending upon the form that urbanization takes. Whereas latter-19th-century urbaniza-tion was accompanied by a vast industrial expansion which provided a channel for upward socioeconomic mobility, contemporary urbanization has crowded young males, often Negro migrants from the rural South, into deteriorating

inner cities from whence whites and an increasingly auto-
mating industry are fleeing.

Since violent crime, while not inevitably a by-product
of urbanization, is clearly accelerated by the ghettoization
of the nation's inner cities, logic would suggest that rates
of criminal assault would be highest in the more rapidly
urbanizing North and West than in the more rural South.
Such a prediction would be reinforced by a corollary to
the frontier hypothesis—that rates of personal assault
should decline as the frontier's environment gives way to
a more settled and ordered civilization. Yet the data
reveal a somewhat contrary pattern: of all regions in
America, the traditional Southeast manifests substantially
the highest incidence of personal assault, followed by the
post-frontier Southwest. In chapter 14, Sheldon Hackney
seeks to explain this paradox by bringing both sociological
and historical analysis to bear on the persistence of violence
in the South.

References

1. For a lucid analysis of this tradition, see Morton and Lucia White, *The
   Intellectual Versus the City* (Cambridge: Harvard University Press, 1962).
2. Daniel Bell, "The Myth of Crime Waves: The Actual Decline of Crime in
   the United States," ch. 8 of *The End of Ideology* (Glencoe: The Free Press,
   1961), p. 151 of the Collier edition.
3. Robert M. Cipes, *The Crime War* (New York: New American Library,
   1968).

Chapter 12

URBANIZATION AND CRIMINAL
VIOLENCE IN THE 19th CENTURY:
MASSACHUSETTS AS A TEST CASE*

*By Roger Lane***

America is now an urban nation, but Americans are still
afraid of cities. There are many dimensions to this fear,

* This Chapter is copyrighted by the *Journal of Social History*, 1968; reprinted by permission of the copyright owner.
** Roger Lane is associate professor of history at Haverford College. His
publications include *Policing the City: Boston, 1822-1855* (Cambridge, Mass.:
Harvard University Press, 1967), and "Crime and Criminal Statistics in Nineteenth Century Massachusetts," *Journal of Social History*, vol. II (December
1968). This article is reprinted here in revised form by permission of the
Journal of Social History.

but one of them is especially direct, and starkly physical. The current concern with "safety in the streets" echoes a belief, as old as the Republic, that the city is dangerous, the breeding ground of vice and violence. Observers of varying sophistication have pointed out that dark streets hide dark deeds, and that the anonymity and freedom of urban society, its temptations and frenzied pace, all contribute to encourage criminal behavior. From this it is easy to conclude that with metropolitan growth and the multiplication of all these conditions, the rate of violence crime is inexorably multiplied also.

But constant repetition of a myth is no substitute for proof. Under some circumstances it does in fact seem clear that migration to the metropolis has been accompanied by disruption and violence. This does not mean that there is a necessary or inevitable connection between the growth of cities and the growth of crime. In fact the existing historical evidence suggest the very reverse, that over a long-term urbanization has had a settling, literally a civilizing, effect on the population involved.

The statistical evidence for such a long-term trend is necessarily fragmentary and local. But for this purpose local studies may well be more reliable than national. Figures for the United States as a whole, compiled by the Federal Bureau of Investigation, have been available only since 1930. Based on the records of police departments with widely varying standards of accuracy, these have provided a generation of criminologists with material for argument.[1] Analyses of crime rates in individual urban areas, on the other hand, are less complicated by discrepancies in definition and in police practice. While few of these reach back to any period before the FBI's Uniform Crime Reports, these few are significant. None points to any clear proportional increase in serious crime within particular cities. And the more recent suggest, on the contrary, a sometimes striking proportional decrease.[2]

Both the decrease and some of the explanation for it may be demonstrated since it is necessary to choose a single area to represent the whole—by an examination of 19th-century Massachusetts. A stable Eastern state, with one growing metropolis and a number of thriving smaller cities, this Commonwealth had a fairly typical experience with industrial urbanization. As a result of the legislature's enormous appetite for statistical information, its official records, including all those relating to criminal behavior, are probably better than any kept elsewhere.[3] And while criminal statistics are notoriously difficult to deal with, and by themselves offer no firm conclusions, the history of the Commonwealth has been abundantly studied, and may be used to help interpret the raw numerical data. Together, the statistics and the social record can illuminate several aspects of the history of criminal violence in America. These include: the changing incidence of disorder itself, the relation of this change to urban growth, the special conditions which may upset this relation, and lastly the problem of public attitudes or concern.

While all criminal statistics are subject to some doubt, the central conclusion about the figures from Massachusetts may be stated with confidence: serious crime in metropolitan Boston has declined sharply between the middle of the 19th century and the middle of the 20th. This often ragged downward trend does not, of course, apply equally to all offenses, but it does to most of the more serious common-law crimes. Three independent studies, by a lawyer, a historian, and a sociologist, confirm this basic direction.[4] While the three cover different periods, and employ somewhat different methods, they do fit together, and all are based essentially on police arrest statistics, the index most widely used by contemporary criminologists.[5] The most comprehensive, covering the years from 1849 to 1951, shows a drop of nearly two-thirds in those crimes which the FBI classifies as "major."[6]

But only half the story, at best, can be told through the figures from the metropolis alone. Our concern is with the whole society. And it has been argued that the difference in crime rates between urban and nonurban areas may be great enough so that a drop in the incidence of criminality in the cities is more than offset by the fact that a continually greater percentage of the population is living in them.[7] It is necessary, to meet this problem, to look at the statistics for Massachusetts as a whole.

For most of the 19th century, the use of police records is neither possible nor desirable on a statewide basis.[8] But other indices of real criminal activity are available. And four of them may be used to establish the changing incidence of "serious" crime, defined as that which involves real injury to persons or loss of property.[9] These four are lower court cases, jail commitments, grand jury cases, and state prison commitments, all involving the major common-law offenses against persons or property. The first date for which two of these indices were published in trustworthy form is 1834; the first year for which all four were compiled is 1860. The figures for these periods, expressed in 3-year averages, may be compared with those for the end of the century in the table 12-1:[10]

Table 12-1—Average yearly incidence of cases
per 100,000 population

	1834-36	1860-62	1899-1901
Lower Court cases		777	707
Jail commitments		333	163
Grand jury cases	89	117	63
Imprisonments	16.8	11.9	5.9

The decline in the officially recorded crime rate is unmistakable here. And it is strongly probable that the real decline is greater than the statistics indicate. The key problem in the interpretation of criminal statistics is posed by "the dark figure," representing those illegal activities or incidents which never come to the light of official attention. But since in later years, as will be discussed below, there was both an increasing intolerance of crimnal activity and a great growth in the numbers of police and investigative agents, all evidence suggests that this "dark figure" was growing proportionately smaller as the century progressed. Thus table 12-1 considerably understates the real decline.

For purposes of explanation, it is almost equally important to note the pattern of this decline. The table lists offenses in the order of their severity: lower court cases generally involve the least important crimes, jailings the next, indictments next, and imprisonments the most. And with one exception—the relative rise in indictments between the 1830's and the 1860's, which will be considered later—it is especially notable that the recorded drop in the crime rate is directly proportional to the seriousness of the offense. This is generally true also when the four indices used are examined further and broken into subcategories. Thus

471

for example the combined rate of commitments for homicide, rape, armed robbery, and arson in 1860-62 was 6.8 per 100,000; by 1900 it has dropped to 2.9 per 100,000.[11] Most of the other data point in the same direction—not only a fall over time but a fall most marked in the most serious categories.

Meanwhile, however, while the serious crime rate was falling, the total crime rate—or the officially recorded total —was actually rising. This apparent paradox results from the fact that the downward curve described above may be wholly reversed simply by adding a third official category, "Crimes Against Public Order," to the two above. When these offenses are added in—drunkenness is by far the largest of them—the results for the lower courts may be indicated as follows:[12]

Table 12-2—Yearly incidence of cases per 100,000 population.

	1840	1860	1900
Total lower court cases	595	1,869	3,317

The pattern for these minor crimes is the obverse of that for serious offenses, in that the more trivial the degree of the offense the larger its proportional increase over time. While virtually no indictments or imprisonments resulted from third-class offenses, their addition makes less difference in the case of jailings than of lower court cases:[13]

Table 12-3—Yearly incidence of cases per 100,000 population

	1841	1860	1900
Total jail commitments	419	548	969

This upward curve in total offenses does not have the same importance as the other, downward curve in the incidence of serious crime. The latter represents the basic statistical conclusion, in that it reflects a real situation, a real decline in the rate of criminal activity. But the former, while it is merely statistical, is nonetheless important. There is a complementary relationship between the two trends, and the nature of this relationship helps account for much that underlies the numbers.

The entire increase in the criminal statistics of Massachusetts, during the period covered, may in fact be attributed wholly to the rise in cases of drunkenness. Indeed this one offense, together with simple assault, its constant companion, may serve as a focus for much more. To understand the reasons for the rise in drunk arrests is to understand much about the social changes occurring in the 19th century, changes which affected all of its criminal patterns.

It is clear, first, that the mounting total of cases fed into the official machinery of justice does not reflect a real increase in the consumption of alcohol. The misuse of drink was throughout the 19th century a problem of enormous dimensions. The continuing debate about the nature of drunkenness, although some of it anticipated the best of current thinking, was on the whole punitive, and tended to blame the use of alcohol for virtually every individual and most social evils.[14] But even the most ardent spirits in the temperance movement did not usually suggest that there was any long-term rise in drunken behavior. They and their opponents generally united in agreeing that the situation, in ragged fashion, was improving with time.[15] Because much of the alcohol was made and sold illegally, especially in the countryside, it is difficult to investigate this statistically. But certainly in the metropolis and probably elsewhere the evidence does suggest a decline. Early in the century even ministerial ordinations, to say nothing of less grave occasions, were frequently bibulous affairs.[16] By the 1830's a substantial portion of the middle class had renounced the use of hard liquor. The prohibition was extended later to all drinks, and its champions carried on a continuous political and educational campaign against it. In the 1830's, and again in the 1850's, law enforcement officers estimated that 1 in every 65 inhabitants of Boston —men, women, and children—were selling alcohol for a living, in the latter period in defiance of a state law which prohibited all private sales.[17] Certainly neither this proportion nor this widespread evasion of the law was matched later in the century; by about 1880 the ratio was down to 1 seller in 150 and rising fast.[18]

On one level, the rising statistics of drunk arrests simply reflect an increase in the numbers of professional police and in the penal apparatus. It was not until 1837 that Boston organized a squad of full-time professionals, and for many years these were the only ones in the Commonwealth. But by 1860 all of the larger cities had organized forces of varying sizes, and these had grown and spread to the smaller towns well before 1900.[19] The effect of this, and of a proportionate increase in the rest of the agents of justice, is easily demonstrated. In the absence of police, ordinary citizens were expected to make complaints on their own, and to call on constables only to execute warrants already sworn. But while private individuals may make the effort to initiate the processes of justice when directly injured, professionals are required to deal, in number, with those whose merely immoral or distasteful behavior hurts no one in particular. It takes real cops, in short, to make drunk arrests.

Again on this level, the relative shortage of official agents of law enforcement accounts for one of the most striking characteristics of table 12-1 above. The farther back the figures go, as noted, the higher is the relative proportion of serious crimes. The authorities, with limited resources, obviously had to deal with felony first, indictable crime next, and misdemeanor only when resources permitted.

Conversely it is notable that as time advanced and it became easier for injured citizens to complain to a policeman, the tables indicate that proportionately fewer such complaints were being made. In the city of Boston, at least, the result was a progressive decrease in the number of annual arrests made by each patrolman: in 1855, the average was 71 per man, while by 1885 this had dropped to 37.[20]

Drawn as a model, this development may explain the only apparent anomaly in table 12-1, already referred to. This is the fact that between the 1830's and the 1860's the figures show both a fall in prison commitments and a rise in grand jury indictments. Perhaps—the subject will be investigated further—there is no great paradox at all. District attorneys in the 1830's, faced with a high incidence of truly violent criminal behavior, may have had to concentrate on the more important prisonable offenses, to the neglect of others, even indictable ones. As their resources were increased, and as the real crime rate fell, they would be able by the 1860's to catch up on lesser indictments.

But there remains a more fundamental level of explanation. To account for the rise in lesser offenses or the drop in more serious crimes simply in terms of the expansion of police, courts, and prosecutors is to misplace the emphasis. The expansion is not cause but symptom. The machinery of justice was increased because of a felt need, a growing intolerance of behavior which had earlier been tolerated, coupled with a belief that the state and not the individual citizen was required to do the necessary job.

This process is most evident in Boston itself. Leading citizens and governmental officials were always proud of their reputation for maintaining a tidy and well-governed "order" in the city. But the definition of what constituted "order" changed considerably with time.

Josiah Quincy, one of Boston's first mayors, was also the first to boast that in on other city "of equal population, are there fewer instances of those crimes, to which all populous places are subject."[21] He had in fact assumed charge, in 1823, of a newly incorporated city of about 45,-000 inhabitants, which officially issued some 697 liquor licenses and ignored the existence of a large number of illegal sellers. Relatively little attention was paid to such common offenses as simple drunkenness and assault. The night watch, largely concerned with the danger of fire or arson, was afraid to enter some of the more notorious neighborhoods. No one patrolled anywhere in the daytime. Quincy's several terms of office were marked by frequent battles between rival gangs of firemen, whose hunger for looting threatened the whole institution of fire insurance. When, after one of the city's numerous "riots, routs, and tumultuous assemblies" had spluttered on for a full week during the long hot summer of 1825, Quincy was forced to take personal charge of a posse of citizens to put it down. This was clearly an unusual action, and the mayor refused later opportunities to risk his limbs and authority in physical combat, preferrring to let mob violence burn out by itself. Nevertheless, neither he nor the voters were unduly alarmed by the prevailing level of disorder. Citizens were traditionally supposed to take care of themselves, with the help of family, friends, or servants when available. An organized professional police would certainly be expensive and might be a threat to valued freedoms. And Quincy was proud to point out, at the end of his official career, that he had not added a single constable or watchman to Boston's part-time corps of peace officers.

By the 1880's, when an aldermanic committee echoed Mayor Quincy's earlier claim that Boston was the most orderly of America's larger cities, the situation had changed considerably.[22] In 1837, after three major riots in 4 years, the city had acquired a police force.[23] Since then it had been growing steadily, at a rate faster than the population. By the Civil War, the citizens had abandoned their objection to uniforms, with their paramilitary connotations, and the patrolmen had begun to carry guns.[24] By the 1880's the force had acquired most of its familiar modern characteristics and functions.[25] And the demand for more men continued—despite the fact that the crime rate had been dropping for some time, and with it the workload for each man on the force.

The demand for more men, then, reflected not a worsening situation but higher standards, a change in attitude. Really violent crime brought more severe retribution than formerly; the same offenses which had earned 2-year sentences in the 1830's were now punished by 3 to 4 years or more in the state penitentiary, and the average was still going up.[26] While the police stations were still being built for "defensibility," there had been—and would be—no large-scale riot for years.[27] It is impossible to imagine a late-century mayor wrestling with mobs as did Quincy in the twenties and Theodore Lyman in the thirties. All of the city had been brought under more or less effective patrol, and the voters were demanding that the streets be cleared not only of arsonists but of drunks, peddlers, and truants. Traffic problems were settled not by teamsters with their fists but by officers with whistles. The responsibility for individual safety had been decisively shifted to these agents of the law; uniformed men with revolvers were stationed not only in potentially dangerous areas but in the quiet confines of the public library.[28] And the end result, reflected in many arrests for minor breaches of conduct, was a degree of "order" which would have astonished and perhaps dismayed an earlier and rougher generation.

The progressive heightening of standards of propriety, and with it the increasing reliance on official law enforcement, were processes which, while most sharply visible in Boston, were common to the whole society. Traditionally, criminologists have interpreted the zigs and zags of recorded criminal statistics in terms of individual events or situations—war, for example, or depression. But the change in social behavior reflected in the two dominant curves of

476

criminality in Massachusetts is so long term and so wide-spread as to suggest a connection with the most fundamental of contemporary social processes, that of industrial urbanization itself. The nature of that connection has never been studied in detail, but it may at least be outlined.

Massachusetts in 1835 had a population of some 660,-940, 81 percent rural, overwhelmingly preindustrial and native born.[29] Its citizens were used to considerable personal freedom. Whether teamsters, farmers, or artisans, they were all accustomed to setting their own schedules, and the nature of their work made them physically independent of each other. None of the more common occupations provided any built-in checks against various kinds of personal excess. Neither fits of violence nor bouts of drunkenness disrupted any vital patterns. Individual problems, sins or even crimes, were not generally cause for wider social concern.

Under these circumstances, while scarcely a frontier, the Commonwealth could afford a fairly high degree of lawlessness. No city in the state boasted a professional police, and the machinery of justice was not equipped to handle many cases. Many of the more common forms of violence or crime were simply not reported to the agents of law, as those affected either shrugged off their injuries or struck back directly.

But the impact of the twin movements to the city and to the factory, both just gathering force in 1835, had a progressive effect on personal behavior throughout the 19th century and into the 20th. The factory demanded regularity of behavior, a life governed by obedience to the rhythms of clock and calendar, the demands of foreman and supervisor. In the city or town, the needs of living in closely packed neighborhoods inhibited many actions previously unobjectionable. Both blue- and white-collar employees in larger establishments were mutually dependent on their fellows; as one man's work fit into another's, so one man's business was no longer his own.

The results of the new organization of life and work were apparent by 1900, when some 76 percent of the 2,805,346 inhabitants of Massachusetts were classified as urbanites.[30] Much violent or irregular behavior which had been tolerable in a casual, independent society was no longer acceptable in the more formalized, cooperative atmosphere of

477

the later period. The private, direct response to criminal injury was no longer necessary or approved. All cities and most towns had acquired police forces, constantly expanding to meet greater expectations. Throughout the state, the victims of violence and theft were conditioned to seek official help. The move to the cities had, in short, produced a more tractable, more socialized, more "civilized" generation than its predecessors.[31]

The trend in the direction of higher standards and a lower level of violence may be measured from the early 19th century through much of the 20th. But what is true in the long run is not necessarily evident in the short. While the process of urbanization has helped to raise standards of personal behavior, it may not do so by itself. And there is some indication in the history of 19th-century Massachusetts that under unfavorable conditions migration to the cities may at some times have increased the incidence of violently unsocial behavior. This may well be true, at least, of the long generation between 1835 and 1860.

The existing statistics, alone, are no sure guide to what was actually happening during these crucial early decades. The Boston arrest figures were not kept until 1849. For the state as a whole, much of the remaining evidence remains ambiguous. As explained above, the two main indices, the rate of grand jury indictments and of imprisonments for felony, point stubbornly in opposite directions. But there is good reason to suspect that the period from the mid-1830's to the Civil War illustrates at least a partial, and important, exception to the general developments previously sketched.

From the war on to the end of the century and beyond, the industrial development of Massachusetts, however painful for those involved, was at least proceeding at a pace and along lines already laid out. The era just before was the one which witnessed the turbulence of transition. No similar timespan in fact encompassed a more rapid increase in the urban population. Between 1835 and 1860, while the total population was growing from 660,940 to 1,231,-066, the proportion of city dwellers leaped from 19 to 44 percent of the total.[32] At the same time, too, the major railroad lines were laid in patterns still existing. As steam began to replace waterpower as the major source of industrial energy, the factories, earlier confined to rural sites near waterfalls, began to move into the cities.

Social dislocation, meanwhile, accompanied economic. All through the period, and especially during and after the "hungry forties," heavy Irish immigration exacerbated all of the problems of city living. By 1855, some 68,100 of the 168,031 residents of Boston were natives of Ireland.[33] Uprooted from a rural setting, wholly without skills, the newcomers experienced the kind of culture shock, prejudice, and alienation which would plague other waves of migrants later. Crowded into stinking hovels, some of them underground, their miserable conditions of living strained all of the city's institutions of charity and police. Smallpox, once virtually eliminated, became again a problem, cholera struck hard, and the death rate about the middle of the century climbed to the highest point in the city's recorded history.[34]

In terms of its effect on behavior, all of these rapid and wrenching changes promoted the worst aspects of living in the city without benefit of its compensations. It must be stressed that economic developments were not fully able to keep pace with migration. Between 1837 and 1845, it has been estimated, the amount of large-scale or factory employment did not increase at all.[35] And in the 15 years following, while the total of factory employees grew to something like 25,000 or 30,000, the number of outright paupers in the metropolitan area was increasing at an even faster rate, to reach a peak of nearly 13,000 in 1860.[36] Without the discipline imposed by regular employment, this first large-scale flow of migrants into the city was a kind of mutual disaster. The raw arrivals from the countryside, Yankees as well as Irish, had not yet learned to weave warily through crowds, with their arms held in close. Often radically insecure, in neighborhoods still unstable, they sought release in drink. But to drink with strangers requires different rules, and more restraints, than drinking in more familar situations. In this era of swinging elbows, bewilderment, and desperate unemployment, it is hard to find evidence that the level of violence was declining.

Indeed it is easy to find the opposite. During this whole period Massachusetts was wracked by political instability, aggravated by one unpopular war and the overhanging threat of another one.[37] The 1850's, in particular, witnessed a resurgence of mob violence as Know-Nothings and Irishmen, opponents and defenders of slavery, all found occasions to take to the streets.[38] These clashes, superimposed on and partly resulting from the already unhealthy social condition of Boston, were deeply disturbing to the inhabitants. If the real incidence of criminal behavior was not actually rising at this time, then surely it was not falling at the rate apparent in the generations following the Civil War.

All evidence points to the long-term drop in criminal activity as normative, and associated with urbanization. But the process was not complete without the accompaniment of rapid industrial development also. It was this which provided the means of absorbing raw migrants, of fitting them into a "system" which socialized and accommodated them into more cooperative habits of life. Without this other process, migration to the city alone, simply by multiplying human contacts, may very well multiply the incidence of criminally violent interaction among inhabitants unsuited to its demands.

Because of its clear connection with ethnic prejudice, and its dangerous political and social implications, the violent state of Boston during the 1850's was the source of considerable public concern. But the relation between concern about violence and violence itself is not always so uncomplicated. Both in the 19th and the 20th centuries, the attitudes of newspapers, scholars, and the public generally have been various and volatile, the product often of special interests or misinformation. This makes such attitudes difficult to measure. But they are nevertheless crucially important to the study of criminal disorder.

In the long run and in the short, popular concern has a direct effect on the shape of criminal statistics. As it was changing public standards which accounted for the rising total of arrests during the 19th century, so police departments still concentrate on those offenses of greatest current interest. Moreover, it is not simply the actual level of criminal activity, but the balance between this and social attitudes, which determines how much violence is a "problem" at any given time.

While public "attitudes" are slippery concepts to compare, it does seem that in the sense above the state of Massachusetts, and the United States in general, had a criminal problem less worrisome in the 19th century than in the 1960's. The citizens of the Commonwealth, still close to their rural antecedents, were indeed afraid of cities, which one legislative committee called "the common sewers of the state."[39] And one major source of this fear was the "poverty, vice, and crime" commonly associated with Boston, in particular.[40] But hostile critics were more interested in the first two than in the last, and reformers endlessly debated the causal relation between them. The charge that the city had lost control of its "dangerous classes" was used in several attempts to limit self-government in Boston, but mob action was the only form of violence which generally figured in these complaints, and "crime" was used typically as a synonym for "vice."[41] It is significant that the laws concerning drink, especially, were subject to constant revision, but except for a reduction in the number of cases involving the death penalty, the general criminal code was not.[42] Legislative action or inaction mirrored public concern in this case. As the sons and daughters of Massachusetts migrated to the metropolis, the image conjured by the fearful was the rake or tempter, not the robber or rapist.

Nevertheless, however overshadowed by other issues, there were periodic outbursts of concern about violence or other crime. Often these occurred in response to some new development, or threat, for which the public or authorities were unprepared. In fact, the history of these threats, and the responses to them, comprise much of the history of criminal law enforcement.[43]

Thus the multiplication of banks and bank notes, through the 1820's, provided golden opportunities for counterfeiters. The nature of the problem, in this case, required a network of private bankers' agents to cooperate, across state and even national boundaries, with the appropriate public authorities. Anti-Catholic rioting, in the 1830's, was a principal spur to the development of professional police. During the 1870's, the growing sophistication of professional criminals, dramatized by a spectacular series of bank robberies, led to an overhaul of existing detective methods in many American cities. During the same period, bands of healthy native vagrants, fugitives from the new industrial age, were a subject of great concern to the readers of sensational newspapers, who feared the violent potential in these "wild-eyed" strangers. The response in this case was harsher police action, and a tightening of the rules governing charity and soup kitchens.

These concerns were at any rate real, and had often lasting effects, although they had little to do with the overall crime rate. Another and more frequent kind of scare resulted not from some genuinely new problem but from sudden attention focused on an old one. Lincoln Steffens, as a cub reporter in New York, learned how easy it was to manufacture a "crime wave," with techniques still familiar.[44] Thus a particularly brutal murder or a series of muggings could touch off a wave of arrests "on suspicion."[45] Often it was simply an investigation or expose of some endemic form of crime which generated a sudden excitement, during which the public was assured that Boston was facing a threat of unprecedented proportions.

But it is impossible, from these brief scares, to get any clear sense of direction. While the definition of the tolerable was altering with time, it was altering slowly and imperceptibly. And there is no evidence that, as the century progressed, the gap between the level of order expected and the level actually obtaining was changing in any constant direction. It is true that the police often felt that they were faced with problems of unprecedented magnitude, and chiefs decades apart warned that the level of juvenile delinquency, and the general breakdown of authority, threatened the very basis of society.[46] Other observers too, perhaps beguiled by the image of a more peaceful golden age in the past, sometimes asserted that crime was growing faster than the population. But this tendency to fear was balanced throughout the century by pride in growth and progress. And the many apocalyptic statements may be countered with an equal number of others, more optimistic. Thus even in the troubled year of 1859, the State's attorney general could declare that "at no time in the history of Massachusetts have life, liberty, and property been more secure than at present."[47]

In short, while it is possible now to discover a long-term drop in the level of violence, contemporaries were simply not aware of this. The degree of public concern has never been, nor is it now, an accurate index of the degree of criminal activity. Indeed the reverse is often true. And it is doubly ironic that a drop in the actual incidence of disorder has been accompanied by—and contributed to—a heightened sensitivity to disorder. Such sensitivity, by leading to a more demanding standard of conduct, has been essential to the functioning of an interdependent urban society. But unless the process is recognized and understood, it may have unsettling effects. There are times when for various reasons the level of violence overbalances current expectations. In such situations the social pressure to maintain and extend high standards, and to enforce them universally, may result in frustration. The frustration may translate into fear. And this fear, in turn, may focus on the very urban process which helped to create those standards, on the growth of cities itself.

References

1. See *The Challenge of Crime in a Free Society: A Report by The President's Commission on Law Enforcement and The Administration of Justice* (Washington, 1967), p. 29.
2. Four studies are especially germane: Harold A. Phelps, "Frequency of Crime and Punishment," *Journal of the American Institute of Criminal Law and Criminology*, vol. XIX, No. 2 (Aug. 1926), pp. 165-180, which covers Rhode Island between 1897 and 1927; Sam Bass Warner, *Crime and Criminal Statistics in Boston* (Boston, 1934), "Crime as a Function of Anomie," *Journal of Criminal Law, Criminology, and Police Science* (June 1966), covering Buffalo from 1854 to 1956; and Theodore Ferdinand, "The Criminal Patterns of Boston Since 1849," *The American Journal of Sociology* (July 1967), pp. 84-99, which runs to 1951. These all differ in purpose and sophistication, and none is directly concerned with the long-term decline, which helps to make their results the more striking.
3. A survey of many of the official and criminal records of Boston and Massachusetts is contained in Roger Lane, *Policing the City: Boston, 1822-1885* (Cambridge, Mass.: Harvard University Press, 1967), pp. 225-229 and 239-241.
4. See the works by Ferdinand, Warner, and Lane, in footnotes 2 and 3, above. There is no attempt, in these or in this paper, to measure the extent of statutory or white-collar crime.
5. Thorstein Sellin and Marvin E. Wolfgang, *The Measurement of Delinquency* (New York, 1964), p. 31.
6. Ferdinand, "Criminal Patterns of Boston," p. 87. Together with roughly similar results in Powell's study of Buffalo, these figures suggest that the main conclusions of the present paper, which is largely confined to the 19th century, may be projected up to the founding of the Uniform Crime Reports and beyond.
7. Ferdinand, "Criminal Patterns of Boston," p. 99.
8. Statewide arrest figures were not compiled until very late in the 19th century, and comparing those for different cities involves many of the same problems as plague students of the Uniform Crime Reports.
9. In this paper except where specifically noted, no distinction is made between violent crimes—against the person—and other serious offenses. Such terms as "crime" or "disorder" are used to cover both.
10. For references in this table, see Roger Lane "Crime and Criminal Statistics in Nineteenth Century Massachusetts," *Journal of Social History* (December 1968), footnote 8.
11. For references, see *ibid.*, footnote 8.
12. For references, see *ibid.*, footnote 10. 1840 is the first year for which these figures are available.
13. For references, see *ibid.*, footnote 11. The year 1841 is the first for which these figures are available.
14. Compare *The Challenge of Crime*, p. 235, and Lane, *Policing the City, passim*, especially pp. 112-113.

15. For testimony of both reformers and conservatives, see especially Massachusetts House Document No. 415, *Reports on the Subject of a License Law . . . Together With a Stenographic Report of the Testimony* (Boston, 1867), *passim*.
16. Alice Felt Tyler, *Freedom's Ferment: Phases of American Social History to 1860* (Minneapolis, 1944), ch. 13, especially p. 311.
17. Lane, *Policing the City*, pp. 41 and 71.
18. *Ibid.*, p. 211.
19. Unfortunately, neither the federal nor the state census permits an accurate statewide count of policemen during the 19th century.
20. Lane, *Policing the City*, pp. 230-232. The trend has continued. Modern police, despite the introduction of patrol cars and call wagons, make fewer arrests, in general, than did their predecessors, especially when the whole class of minor auto violations is eliminated.
21. Quoted in *ibid.*, p. 25. For the other information in this paragraph see ch. 2 *passim*.
22. *Ibid.*, p. 204.
23. *Ibid.*, pp. 29-35.
24. *Ibid.*, pp. 104-105.
25. *Ibid.*, p. 224.
26. These figures for the average sentences to the state penitentiary. The range of offenses listed remained about the same through the century. For references, see Lane, "Crime and Criminal Statistics," footnote 14.
27. *Annual Report of the Commissioners of Police of the City of Boston for . . . 1885* (Boston, 1885), pp. 28-30.
28. Lane, *Policing the City*, p. 173.
29. Population figures are from *The Census of Massachusetts . . . 1905* (Boston, 1909), vol. 1, p. xxxi. The urban definition is based on a population of 8,000.
30. *Ibid.*
31. It should be noted that after the 1880's, when Boston already had nearly 2 policemen per 1,000 inhabitants, which is close to the present nationwide average for major cities, it was the smaller places only where the arrest rate continued to climb dramatically. Boston, because of its very small geographical area, was ahead of most American cities in this respect. It was still possible in other places to raise the arrest figures by extending patrol and demanding higher standards in previously neglected areas, such as outlying slums. This process, and the reduction of the "dark figure" which results from better policing in general, may account for many apparent "rises" in crime rates which occur right up to the present.
32. See footnote 29.
33. Oscar Handlin, *Boston's Immigrants: A Study in Acculturation* (rev. ed., Cambridge, 1959), p. 244.
34. *Ibid.*, pp. 114-116.
35. *Ibid.*, p. 74.
36. *Ibid.*, pp. 74 and 256.
37. For political conditions in Massachusetts, see William Gleason Bean, "Party Transformation in Massachusetts, 1848-1860, with Special Reference to the Antecedents of Republicanism" (unpublished Ph.D. dissertation, Harvard University archives, 1922), *passim*.
38. Lane, *Policing the City*, pp. 72-74, 90-91, and 94-95.
39. *Ibid.*, p. 132.
40. First used by Josiah Quincy in his "remarks on some of the Provisions of the Massachusetts Affecting Poverty, Vice, and Crime" (Cambridge, 1822), these last four words became a stock phrase among the Commonwealth's reformers.
41. Lane, *Policing the City*, especially pp. 122-125, 128-134, 142-156, and 213-219.
42. *Ibid.*, *passim*. For the criminal code, summed up in revisions compiled in 1835, 1859, 1881, and 1900, see p. 239.
43. For references in the following paragraph, see *ibid.*, pp. 55-56, 29-35, 142-156, 157-160, and 193-195.
44. Lincoln Steffens, *Autobiography* (New York, 1931), pp. 285-291.
45. In 1865, inspired by a fear of returning veterans much like that following World War II, the police made some 2,532 such arrests. See Lane, *Policing the City*, p. 149.
46. See, e.g., *ibid.*, pp. 68, 137, and 34.
47. *Ibid.*, p. 117.

Chapter 13

A CONTEMPORARY HISTORY
OF AMERICAN CRIME*

By Fred P. Graham**

The land is full of bloody crime and the city is full of violence.
—Ezekiel VII: 23

On a rainy night last June a "frost notice"—a word-of-mouth warning system used by the U.S. Marines to inform personnel of emergency situations—went out to all Marines in and around the Washington, D.C., area. It concerned the fashionable Georgetown section of residential Washington, a stately neighborhood of tree-lined streets and expensive townhouses where such citizens as Allen Dulles, Averell Harriman, Dean Acheson, and Abe Fortas have their homes.

"It would be inadvisable to frequent the Georgetown area currently," the frost notice warned the Marines, "and in general exercise caution and restraint in Washington." The reason for the warning was that in the early hours of that morning, June 5, two young Marine lieutenants had stopped in Georgetown for coffee in an all-night hamburger shop, had exchanged remarks with a trio of black militants who had come from California for the Poor Peoples' Campaign, and had been shot dead. Only 3 nights earlier an 18-year-old high school senior had been shot to death after a bumping incident with a stranger outside a pharmacy two blocks away. In the 6 weeks before that, the area had been plagued by a series of vicious muggings.

The spectacle of Marines being warned away from Washington's most prestigious neighborhood (all the crimes were within shouting distance of the familiar townhouse from which John F. Kennedy had announced his Cabinet appointments in 1960) was only one of a number of bizarre incidents that seemed to show that violence had become more prevalent and threatening than before. Bus drivers in Washington and Baltimore had gone on strike in protest against being required to carry change, because a number had been beaten and one had been killed by robbers. An all-night grocery chain in Cleveland had issued free food vouchers to policemen so that their comings and goings would frighten away potential robbers. Pistol practice had displaced ladies' bridge clubs as the center of social activity in some suburban communities. A book by a former Ice Follies performer on judo and self-defense for ladies was selling briskly, along with such titles as "How To Avoid Burglary, Housebreaking, and Other Crimes," and "How To Defend Yourself, Your Family, and Your Home."

Small wonder that in the summer of 1968 the Harris poll found 81 percent of the people believing that law and order had broken down, and that all of the presidential candidates were promising to do something about it.

"Crime is rising nine times faster than the population" was a stock punch line of Richard M. Nixon's all-purpose campaign speech. Vice President Humphrey noted that the annual number of homicides was lower than it was in 1930, but he, too, campaigned from the assumption that the crime rate is getting out of hand. George Wallace never failed to warn his listeners that they might get hit on the head on the way home by a thug who would probably be out of jail before they got out of the hospital.

With most Americans from the President down believing that crime has risen to emergency proportions, there has emerged a puzzling paradox: many of those who have given the subject the most study have, until recently, concluded that it is not so.

Attorney General Ramsey Clark became the whipping boy of the 1968 political campaign because he had expressed the belief in an unguarded moment that "there is no wave of crime in this country." In 1968 Robert M. Cipes, a lawyer and consultant to the President's Commission on Crime in the District of Columbia, published a book, "The Crime War," which proceeded from the thesis that "in fact there is no crime wave," but rather that "current statistics simply reflect the fact that we are digging into the reservoir of unreported crimes." Intellectuals who were not specialists in the field also tended to accept this view. Dr. Karl Menninger, founder of the famed Menninger

Clinic of psychiatry, concluded after writing a book on crime and punishment that—

No crime statistics are dependable: most crime is not reported. Most violent crime takes place in the home. Most nonviolent crime crime takes place in department stores. My own belief is that there is less violence today than there was 100 years ago, but that we have a much better press and communications to report it.

The President's Commission on Law Enforcement and Administration of Justice, reporting in 1967, could not say after an 18-month study if the crime rate is higher than it has been before, or if Americans have become more criminal than their counterparts in earlier times.

At the center of this controversy had been the ever-rising crime index of the Federal Bureau of Investigation. This index, which has been widely accepted by politicians, policemen, and editorial writers as the official barometer of crime, has also been described by Harvard crime expert Lloyd E. Ohlin as "almost worthless—but it is the only thing there is." Thornstein Sellin, the dean of American criminal statisticians, has been quoted in *Life* magazine as saying that the United States "has the worst crime statistics of any major country in the Western world." The *New York Times* quoted Sophia M. Robinson of the Columbia School of Social Work as saying that "the FBI's figures are not worth the paper they are printed on." Other experts were quoted to the same effect in the press.

Until the last few years, it was fashionable for criminologists to debunk the crime index in this vein when periodic flaps over the FBI's figures erupted and the news media solicited the academicians' views. However, their quoted statements were decidedly more critical than the articles that these same experts were writing for their fellow professionals. Whether they were being quoted out of context (as some claimed) or whether they were victims of betrayed innocence by reporters who did not bother to cushion the professors' true opinions in qualifying padding, the outcome was that the academicians' criticisms of the FBI's statistics were overstated in the mass media. The result was that while the general public tended erroneously to accept the crime index as gospel, the sophisticated readers who delved far enough into news articles to find the scholars' comments were usually persuaded that the statistical proof of rapidly increasing crime was almost certainly wrong. Most of the academic experts did not intend to go that far—but the most respected ones agreed, at least until 1967 or 1968, that the FBI had not proved its case.

This division of opinion was most pronounced with regard to violent crimes. The President's Crime Commission stressed repeatedly that while thefts and other property crimes were rising rapidly, the increase in the type of violent crime that most people fear was lagging far behind. All of this doubt and division cast an aura of unreality about the political dialogue over such suggested reforms as Nixon's demand for changes in the Supreme Court's confessions decisions, Humphrey's call for a tenfold increase in law enforcement spending, and Wallace's suggestion that Federal judges' lifetime tenures be ended.

So long as some of the most thoughtful crime specialists in the country questioned whether violent crime was rising at an unusual or unexpected rate, there was every reason to hold back on any institutional changes, and especially such drastic ones. But since the President's Crime Commission issued its report in February 1967, events have occurred which have convinced most of the previously skeptical experts that violent crime is rising dangerously, and that the increase can be expected to continue for a decade, at least. The exact nature and extent of this rise is still blurred. But that it is occurring—that the dark prophecy of the crime statisticians and the politicians is coming true—is no longer disputed by the experts.

This has come about in a curious way. In the early 1960's, the academicians could see that a crime scare was being launched on the basis of questionable conclusions drawn from unreliable statistics. Many of them committed themselves publicly then to the proposition that the statistical "crime rise" was overblown. The Crime Commission hinted as much, although it stopped short of laying the blame at the doorstep of J. Edgar Hoover and the FBI, where most of it belonged. Yet after the Commission issued its report in early 1967, crime reports from around the country and special studies in key urban areas have satisfied the most serious doubts of the academic skeptics. In effect, these data have confirmed the conclusions about rising violence that Mr. Hoover had been drawing all along—unjustifiably, the experts thought—from the earlier data.

Despite the circumstances, the justification of J. Edgar Hoover and his crime statistics is certain to have a profound impact on the future of the law-and-order controversy, and possibly of the Supreme Court. The controversy over the mathematics of crime will continue over the meaning of the statistics and the manipulations and distortions to which they are subjected, but the frame of reference has shifted in a dramatic way. Crime—violent crime—is increasing rapidly, and few criminologists will now deny it.

There were three good reasons why, prior to release of the 1967 statistics, thoughtful crime experts bridled at the assumption that violent crime was in a dangerous spiral. First, history shows that there has been a rhythm to criminal violence in the United States, and that its rate has probably been higher at times in the past than it is now. Second, the crime scare had been generated by crime statistics that were so questionable that some critics considered them unworthy of belief, and by distortions and exaggerations of those statistics. Finally, even those statistics did not show an alarming rise in violent crime until 1967.

Attempting to put the recent spurt of lawlessness in perspective, the Crime Commission said:

There has always been too much crime. Virtually every generation since the founding of the Nation and before has felt itself threatened by the spectre of rising crime and violence.

A hundred years ago contemporary accounts of San Francisco told of extensive areas where "no decent man was in safety to walk the street after dark; while at all hours, both night and day, his property was jeopardized by incendiarism and burglary." Teenage gangs gave rise to the word "hoodlum"; while in one central New York City area, near Broadway, the police entered "only in pairs, and never unarmed." A noted chronicler of the period declared that "municipal law is a failure . . . we must soon fall back on the law of self preservation." "Alarming" increases in robbery and violent crimes were reported throughout the country prior to the Revolution. And in 1910 one author declared that "crime, especially its more violent forms, and among the young is increasing steadily and is threatening to bankrupt the Nation."

Crime and violence in the past took many forms. During the great railway strike of 1877 hundreds were killed across the country and almost 2 miles of railroad cars and buildings were burned in Pittsburgh in clashes between strikers and company police and the militia. It was nearly a half century later, after pitched battles in the steel industry in the late thirties, that the Nation's long history of labor violence subsided. The looting and takeover of New York for 3 days by mobs in the 1863 draft riots rivaled the violence of Watts, while racial disturbances in Atlanta in 1907, in Chicago, Washington, and East St. Louis in 1919, Detroit in 1943 and New York in 1900, 1935, and 1943 marred big city life in the first half of the 20th century. Lynchings took the lives of more than 4,500 persons throughout the country between 1882 and 1930. And the violence of Al Capone and Jesse James was so striking that they have left their marks permanently on our understanding of the eras in which they lived.

No comprehensive crime figures were collected prior to 1933, but studies of individual cities have been made, and they show that crime characteristically has its ups and downs, rather than a steady growth along with the population. James Q. Wilson, a crime expert at Harvard, has said that the early studies "agree that during the period immediately after the Civil War the rate of violent crime in the big cities was higher than at any other time in our history." Almost all of the available data also indicate that the crime rate rose rapidly during the post-World War I period and the economic boom of the twenties, and that it nosedived within a year or so after the bust in 1929. Although no national figures were collated prior to 1933, figures were available for many cities for 1930-32, and they all show that the downward trend had begun from a crime rise that peaked before 1930. Studies in Boston, Chicago, New York, and other individual cities have shown that the rates were higher in the World War I years and the twenties than they were in the forties, and a detailed analysis of crime in Buffalo, N.Y., showed that crime peaked in the 1870's and at the end of World War I, then dipped in the 1940's.

These studies differ in the timing of the crime peaks, but they all show the steep downswing in crime in the forties. The only available national crime statistics that predate 1933, homicide figures collected by the Department of Health, Education, and Welfare, confirm this slump in the forties. (See Fig. 13-1.) Although the FBI's figures cannot indicate the height of the peak prior to 1933, they suggest the same pattern as shown by graphs drawn by the Crime Commission from FBI data, and bear out the impression that crime rates, like women's skirts,

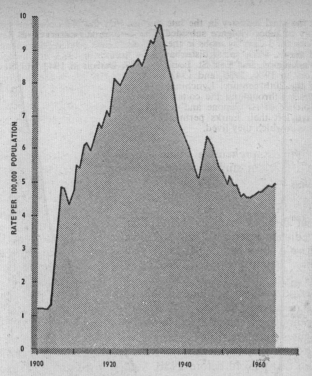

Figure 13-1.—Homicide rates, 1900-64.

go up in periods of prosperity. (See Fig. 13-2.) However, when the FBI publishes its own crime charts, it always slices off the downward years, showing only the upward side, which seems to bear out its claim of "record highs" in crime, even in mild years. One reason for this is that the FBI's statistical system was overhauled in 1958, and the Bureau doesn't consider the pre- and post-1958 figures to be entirely fungible. Yet as a result of slicing off the earlier years, the FBI gets this skyrocket effect. (See Fig. 13-3.)

The crime index has given "law and order" an important element in common with the other political issues that have stirred the emotions of the modern electorate— the proposition that things are bad and are likely to get worse can be demonstrated by statistics. Figures on paper

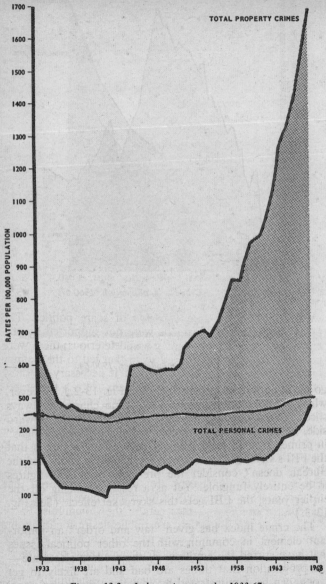

Figure 13-2.—Index crime trends, 1933-67.

492

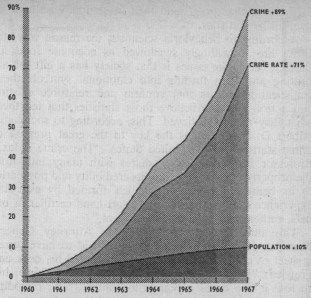

Figure 13-3.—Crime and population, 1960-67.

were not always a *sine qua non* of scare politics. The prosecutions of the Mormons were not supported by statistical evidence that polygamy was deleterious; there were no figures to support the Red scare that led to the Palmer raids in 1919, and nobody thought it necessary to show on paper that the Japanese-Americans were a threat before the Nisei were rounded up after Pearl Harbor. But since World War II, Americans have not easily been persuaded that evil threatens unless the threat could be reduced to figures on paper. One of the pioneers of statistical politics, Senator Joseph McCarthy, demonstrated that this requirement need not cramp a statesman's style. For so long as the figures are sufficiently obscured that they cannot be absolutely refuted ("I have here in my hand a list of 205 . . . members of the Communist Party . . ."), they usually satisfy the public desire for quantum proof. That this was not some political witchcraft peculiar to Senator McCarthy was later demonstrated by John F. Kennedy during his missile-gap stage and still later by Lyndon B. Johnson, who discovered an alarmingly large category of the "poor" and then substantially reduced its size, all by statistics.

According to behavioral scientists, the reason why statistics are so willingly swallowed as adequate food for thought on public issues is that society has a gift for accepting and then turning into emotional symbols those statistical indicators that confirm and reinforce existing conceptions. People believe those statistics that tell them what they already believed. This, according to sociologist Albert D. Biderman, is the key to the great prestige of crime statistics in the United States. "The crime index," Professor Biderman says, "shares with many indicators the property of owing much of its credibility and popularity to its being consistent with beliefs formed by everyday experience. . . . [It] serves as a short-hand certifier of beliefs, rather than as a shaper of them."

This once became so galling to Attorney General Nicholas deB. Katzenbach that he is said to have seized a sheet of crime statistics one day, pounded his desk and growled: "It's bad enough to lose the war on crime, but to lose it five times a year is too much!" The offending paper was one of the most predictable of Government documents—the latest report by the Federal Bureau of Investigation on crime. These compilations of crime statistics from local police departments, released to the public in the form of four quarterly reports and a fifth annual recapitulation, are known as Uniform Crime Reports. For the past decade they have been truly uniform in at least one sense—they have invariably declared that crime is rising at a terrifying rate.

By 1966, the year of Mr. Katzenbach's outburst, the periodic crime increase announcement had become a familiar Hoover's Comet that burst upon the national scene at regular intervals, always followed by a trail of indignant editorials and congressional speeches deploring rising crime. In 1968—a typical year—the reports produced these headlines in the *New York Times*: "Major Crimes up 16 percent in '67," "First-quarter Rate of Crime in U.S. Rise 16%," and "Crime Rise of 19% Reported by FBI." After a decade of this steady drumbeat of crime rises, many, if not most, Americans have become conditioned to feel that as a function of the law of averages, their chances

494

of escaping rape, murder, or mugging much longer must be about to run out.

As the federal official primarily responsible for contending with the problem of crime, Mr. Katzenbach had good reason to be irked, for the FBI's stewardship of the nation's crime statistics has resulted in a hysteria that seems more beneficial to the FBI as a crime-fighting public agency than to the public's enlightenment. Three elements appear to have combined to puff the crime picture out of shape, and the FBI could at least have ameliorated two of them.

First, the figures themselves are easily the most suspect statistics published under the imprimatur of the U.S. Government. They are highly susceptible to reporting vagaries, do not allow for built-in increases due to shifting age ratios in the population, and do not clearly separate crimes against property from more serious offenses against people.

These flaws are built into the system and the FBI is not necessarily responsible for them, but in its zest for bearing bad news the Bureau has compounded the mischief that is inherent in the system. The FBI, with its flair for publicity, has managed five times a year to wring the maximum amount of public terror out of a statistical system that was conceived (by the International Association of Chiefs of Police) as a technique for keeping lawmen informed of the trends of their trade. It has consistently emphasized the alarming implications of the statistics (even in good years, such as 1959 and 1961, when crime declined in relation to the population), and has not adequately pointed out their inadequacies.

Finally, the FBI's statistical image of a rising national crime rate has been translated into a personal threat in the minds of many Americans through the instant shared experience of television coverage of a few spectacular crimes and riots. The Crime Commission found that this has created a pervasive "fear of strangers." It noted the interaction between crime statistics and vivid exposure of a few events:

Many circumstances now conspire to call greater attention to crime as a national, rather than a purely local, problem. Concern with crime is more typically an urban than a rural phenomena and the rural population of the country is declining. At one time, for a majority of the population, reports of crime waves related only to those remote and not quite moral people who inhabited cities.

Now, also, more people are informed by nationally oriented communications media and receive crime reports from a much wider territorial base. In recent years news of the violent and fearful mass killing of eight nurses in a Chicago apartment, five patrons of a beauty shop in Mesa, Arizona, and 13 passersby on the University of Texas campus in Austin received detailed coverage throughout the country. The fear of the people of Boston in 1966 of the brutal attacks of the "Boston Strangler" must have been sympathetically shared and understood in many homes across the land. Some part of the public fear of crime today is undoubtedly due to the fact that the reports of violent crime we receive daily are drawn from a larger pool of crime-incident reports than ever before. But perhaps most important has been the steady stream of reports of rising crime rates in both large and small communities across the Nation. From all this has emerged a sense of crisis in regard to the safety of both persons and property.

The political effects of this have already been profound. During the 1968 Presidential campaign a reporter for the *New York Times* polled the citizens of Webster City, Iowa, which calls itself "Main Street, U.S.A." He found the overriding issue to be "crime in the streets," with particular concern about riots and unruly demonstations. But when the interviewer inquired about crime in "Main Street, U.S.A.," the complaints were that youngsters were drinking beer, driving fast, and breaking an occasional window. Pressed further, the city fathers complained that trucks hauling turkey feathers through town were unlawfully failing to cover their cargoes to keep from littering Main Street. Another reporter, who found the citizenry of Garnett, Kansas, up in arms over crime, discovered that there hadn't been a rape there for 12 years, nor a murder for 21, and that the only person in jail was a 17-year-old hotrodder.

To understand how this exaggerated image of "crime" gained currency, long before the academic experts agreed that violence was climbing, it is necessary to comprehend the mechanics of the Uniform Crime Reports. Local police departments voluntarily report to the FBI the volume of crimes known to the police, offenses cleared by arrest, persons held for prosecution, and persons released or found guilty of offenses. Of the 29 different crimes reported, the FBI uses only 7 in its crime index. The "index" crimes, chosen because they are serious and are thought to be bellwethers of criminal activity, are murder, forcible rape, robbery (muggings, armed robbery, and theft by threat of force), aggravated assault (assault with intent to kill or seriously injure), burglary (breaking and entering to steal), larcency of $50 or more and auto theft. From this the FBI publishes the famous crime index, which is simply the rate of these offenses per 100,000 people.

The Uniform Crime Reports are naturally suspect because the FBI's crime index reflects only *reported* crime. There is known to be so much crime that is either not reported to the police, or not reported by them to the FBI, that only slight changes in reporting habits could have a yo-yo effect on the crime index. The Crime Commission learned from house-to-house surveys that the volume of unreported crime is far greater than anyone had imagined —double, triple, and even 10 times the volume of offenses that are actually reported, depending on whether the crime involved is the type that shames the victim or whether it is the kind the police are thought likely to solve.

Because there is so much unreported crime, it is theoretically possible to have a "crime wave" on the index charts, when in fact nothing but reporting habits have changed. Thus a crime scare could result from victim sophistication—a realization that only reported thefts can become valid income tax deductions or insurance claims, or a new willingness by nonwhites to report crimes to the police.

The same crime "rise" can occur when the police become more diligent in reporting crime. For years the police of Chicago reported many times more robberies than the city of New York, which has more than twice as many people (in one year, Chicago reported eight times as many robberies). Finally, in 1949, the FBI stopped including New York's statistics because it did not believe them. New York has since been reinstated, but periodically its police have slipped back into their old ways of neglecting to report painful facts.

There seem to be two principal reasons for this tendency by the police to "fudge" on crime reports. One is that much of the crime occurs in Negro neighborhoods, between Negroes, and there has sometimes been an easygoing tolerance of it by the police. It was neither investigated nor reported as carefully as crime was elsewhere. The other reason is that increasing crime is political trouble for city administrations, and they like to give the impression that it is under control. Ambitious police officials realize that their superiors want crime kept down, with the result that complaints sometimes get "lost." The Crime Commission found a secret "file 13" in one city containing a catalog of complaints that were not officially reported, and a single precinct in Philadelphia once had 5,000 more crime reports on file than it had officially recorded.

Some experts suspect that both motives for underreporting are losing their validity, and that a good portion of the crime bulge in certain cities is due to the new official willingness to tell all about crime. In recent years more Negro policemen have been hired and more attention given to ghetto crime. This concern has probably dissipated the feeling that Negro complaints are not worth reporting. Also, with the Supreme Court and not the police being widely blamed for the increase in crime, some resentful policemen are said to be reporting crime with a vengeance. The late Police Chief William Parker of Los Angeles once startled a visiting Federal official by his candid discussion of the huge chart on his wall depicting the rise of crime. Each crime peak was topped with the title of a Supreme Court decision in favor of defendants' rights. Chief Parker explained that the police had seen, years before the Court issued its landmark rulings, that a crime boom was coming despite their best efforts—and that they had been lucky to have the Supreme Court to serve as a lightning rod for the criticism. He said that this was partially responsible for his decision to begin making speeches and writing articles about the connection between crime in the streets and judicial decisions.

Jerome Daunt, the chief of the FBI's crime statistics operation, concedes that some of the index crimes are subject to wide reporting fluctuations, but he points out that some are not. Mr. Daunt, a lean, serious man who learned his crime statistics on the job as an FBI agent, makes the point that certain crimes by their nature are almost always reported: bank robberies, because none is too insignificant to report; assault by gun, because the law requires physicians to file reports; murder, because there is a body to be explained.

Bank robberies have increased even faster than the general index, with a rise of 248 percent from 1960 to 1967. Assault by gun rose 84 percent in the 5 years from 1962 to 1967. Much has been made of the fact that criminal homicide has actually declined by 70 percent since 1933, but Mr. Daunt has an explanation for this: "Police response, ambulance response, and improved medical techniques," he says. "It's like the decline in the relative number of war wounded who die—because they get better, quicker treatment."

"Trends—it is the trends in crime statistics that count," declares Mr. Daunt, "and we have been right on the trends." The FBI has indeed been right on the trends (except that its gloomy projections of future crime levels have invariably fallen short of reality) and this has been due in some part to its painstaking efforts to eliminate error—especially by checking for reporting failures whenever reports began to run suspiciously counter to expectations. But part of this success must also be attributed to the melancholy fact that in dealing with crime, if one predicts disaster long enough, events will finally bear him out.

The most valid complaint against the FBI is not that its figures have been soft, but that the Bureau has not presented them honestly to the public. When the FBI first began to sound the alarm about rising crime a decade ago, the overall increase was small and the violent crime rate was actually frequently in decline. In 1961, for instance, the crime rates for violent offenses decreased across the board. Murder, forcible rape, robbery, and aggravated assault all declined. Yet the overall crime index rate rose by 3 percent because of a modest increase in property crimes. J. Edgar Hoover darkly announced that "major crimes committed in the United States in 1961 have again reached an all-time high," adding that during the year there were "four serious crimes per minute." The reason for the rise was that then, as now, about 9 out of 10 offenses included in the crime index do not involve violence, so that even a modest rise in property offenses can lift the entire crime index. Currently, murders, rapes, and assaults make up only 8 percent of the crimes reported in the index.

If robberies are included as "violent crimes" (about one-fourth of them result in injuries to the victims), it is still true that more than four-fifths of the index crimes are non-violent thefts of property—burglary, larceny of $50 or more, and car theft. Since the crime rates for these offenses were, until recently, consistently higher than the rates for violent crimes, they inflated the overall crime index and gave the impression that violent crime was rising faster than it actually was. This has led to the charge that the FBI's crime index is really a gage of "joyriding" by youngsters in other peoples' cars. In any year the number of auto thefts in the crime index will far outnumber all of the violent crimes taken together, and because 9 out of 10 cars are recovered and returned to their owners, the fearsome "crime rate" is far less a reflection of the pain of victims of rape and assault than the temporary aggravation of those who left their keys in their cars.

Another complaint about the FBI's crime-reporting system is its tendency to tempt exaggeration, oversimplification, and even manipulation of the crime increase. By taking the population increase (1½ percent per year) over a given stretch of years and dividing it into the percentage of crime increase, it can be said that crime is growing many times faster than the population. For instance, if the population increased by approximately 10 percent over a 7-year period, but the number of reported index offenses grew by 88 percent, it could be said that "crime outpaced the population growth by almost nine to one"—J. Edgar Hoover's latest assessment of the recent crime rise. Once announced, this slightly exaggerated calculation from the highly suspect crime index can be cited as government proof that "crime is growing nine times faster than the population." And when the public recalls that only 1 year earlier Mr. Hoover used the multiple of 7 to describe the increase, and that 2 years before that he used the figure 5, it is given an avalanche impression of "crime"—the threat of attack by strangers—that is puffed out of any relation to the actual threat that any individual will become a victim of violent crime.

An even more warped impression is given by the "crime clocks" that the FBI publishes each year. This baffling presentation, year after year, of the shrinking average interval between the commission of various offenses across the country, seems to have no purpose other than sheer terror. Because the population is growing, the interval between crimes would necessarily narrow each year, even if the crime rate was not increasing. Thus the hands of the FBI's "crime clocks" invariably show fewer minutes between crimes than for the previous year. The "crime clock" device lends itself to shocking conclusions that mean nothing, as a published interpretation of the 1966 figures show: "An American woman is raped every 12 minutes. A house in the United States is burglarized every 27 seconds. Someone is robbed every 4½ minutes in this nation."

By reducing crime to these terms, the "fear of strangers" syndrome is justified in a way that is not borne out by the risks of everyday life. Statistically, the risk of attack by strangers is one of the least likely hazards that the average person encounters. The risk of death from willful homicide in any given year is about 1 in 20,000, and almost three out of four murders are committed by family members or friends. The result is that a person's likelihood of being killed in a car crash is almost 15 times the chances that he will be murdered by a stranger. His risk in any given year of being attacked by a stranger and hurt badly enough to require any degree of hospitalization is about 1 in 4,500 —and this is an average possibility: If he lives away from high-crime areas his risk is much lower. As Ramsey Clark used to put it, the average individual's chance of being a victim of a crime of violence is once in 400 years, and Clark always added that if one wished to improve his odds he could avoid his relatives and associates—since they are statistically the most likely to do him harm.

What this shows is that extremely subjective conclusions can be drawn from the basic crime data in this country and that the FBI has consistently presented it in a way that tends to make little old ladies stay indoors and strong men look over their shoulders. As one observer pointed out, rather than publishing the fact that some unfortunate individual is murdered every 48 minutes, the FBI could have told the country that the average citizen's chances of becoming a murder victim on any given day are about 1 in 2 million, and that then he might well be willing to brave those odds without hedging on personal freedom of movement or the country's traditional scheme of personal rights.

As slippery as these figures can be in the hands of crime experts, politicians can turn them to quicksilver. During the 1968 Presidential campaign, Richard Nixon observed that crime had increased 88 percent under the Democratic administration. Attorney General Clark went on television with the reply that crime had risen 98 percent during the Eisenhower period. Aghast, the Republican Task Force on Crime fired back with this statement:

501

. . . crime in the 8 Eisenhower years between 1953 and 1960 did not increase by 98 percent. That charge is simply inaccurate.

Crime reported in 1960, the last year of the Eisenhower administration, was 63 percent greater than in 1952, the last year of the Truman administration.

This, of course, covers 8 years. If the experience of 1967 holds true this year, the 8-year Kennedy-Johnson record will show a whopping 118 percent increase for the comparable period, or almost double the rate under a Republican administration. Parenthetically, if only a 7-year frame of reference is used, they fare even worse. During the first 7 years of the Eisenhower administration the crime increase was 43 percent, less than half of the 88 percent recorded during the 7 years thus far under Kennedy and Johnson.

Vice President Humphrey said he deplored this crime numbers game—and added that if he were inclined to play it he could point out that the eight States with the highest crime rates all had Republican Governors.

Because the FBI's crime index was so frequently abused, because its figures were suspect, because even those figures showed the crimes of violence lagging far behind, and possibly because they were liberals indulging in wishful thinking, the academicians refused throughout most of the sixties to admit that serious criminal-violence problem had been proved.

The first break in the familiar statistical pattern came when the 1967 crime reports from across the country were tabulated by the FBI. The usual pattern of relatively low violent-crime rates and high property offenses was shattered by a 16-percent overall increase, composed of a 16-percent rise in violent crimes and a 17-percent increase in property offenses.

But most startling to crime experts was the 28-percent jump in the crime of robbery, which many criminologists consider the bellwether offense in the crime index. Since robbery always involves a treat of force, if not its use, it gives an indication of the public's proclivity toward violence. And since the offender and the victim are usually strangers, the family-quarrel element does not distort the picture. For that reason, criminologists were shocked to see robbery suddenly increasing as rapidly as the property crimes (Fig. 13-4). Preliminary figures for the first 6 months in 1968 confirmed the trend: robbery increased another 29 percent over the high 1967 level.

Meanwhile, new studies showed what Professor Ohlin

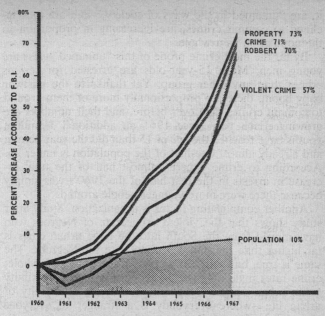

Figure 13-4.—The rising U.S. crime rate.

termed "a pronounced increase in the readiness in people to resort to armed attack." In Philadelphia, where the volume of robberies fluctuated up and down after 1960, the rate of persons injured in robberies began to rise in 1962 and climbed steadily. "Perhaps it is because the robbers tend to be younger, and the young are more likely to use violence," concluded criminologist Marvin E. Wolfgang; "but there has been a considerable increase in the level of violence in robberies."

Ronald H. Beattie, chief of California's Bureau of Criminal Statistics, who had declared as late as 1966 that the available crime statistics "indicate no substantial increase in aggressive crimes during recent years," took another look in 1968 and said that violent crime was growing even faster than crimes against property. Most experts now believe that this rapid surge in crime, with its new heavy component of crimes of violence, will continue and perhaps will accelerate, at least for the next 10 years. The reason is that the types of people who, as one observer put it, are "untamed in the ways of society," and are thus inclined to commit crimes, are increasing in proportion to the population as a whole.

By far the most crime prone of this "untamed" class are young men. More 15-year-olds are arrested for serious crimes than any other group. Yet thanks to the postwar baby boom, there are proportionally more of them around to commit crimes than ever before, and their numbers are growing. Each year since 1961 an additional 1 million youths have reached the age of 15 than did the year before, and already almost one-half of the population is under 25. According to crime experts, almost half of the total increase in arrests in the first half of the 1960's was simply because there were more younger people around.

Another complicating factor is urbanization. Study after study shows that the violent crime rate of Negroes who have moved from the South into the large urban cities is far higher than the national crime rate for Negroes. The same is true, but with less emphasis, for cities as a whole; crime rates invariably rise in proportion to the proximity to an urban center. Concomitant with the anonymity of urban life—where everybody is a stranger to everyone else and the fear of detection and shame of arrest are diminished—a familiar pattern of bold, casual criminality has developed.

There are other indices, all of them pointing upward. Statistics show that communities with large transient populations experience high crime rates, and demographers predict increasing population mobility in the coming years. High crime and narcotics addiction accompany each other, and the narcotics arrests (although heavily weighted with marihuana cases) almost doubled in 1967 over 1966. Some scientists believe that overcrowding alone can cause antisocial behavior, and the decrease in living space is obvious. It is sad but not surprising that Professor Wilson concludes, "We shall be fortunate if we can even slow the rate of increase in crime; we shall be impossibly blessed if we can actually reduce the level of crime."

504

Chapter 14

SOUTHERN VIOLENCE*

By Sheldon Hackney**

Violence has always been a facet of human experience and a problem for human society. For those interested in determining the causes of violence, and perhaps constructing cures, nothing could be more important than the fact that different societies and different eras produce widely varying rates of violence. Unfortunately for the investigator, even moderately reliable data are available only for the recent past and only for relatively modernized countries. This limits the possibility of cross-national comparisons. For this reason, regional variations within modernized nations become an extremely important source for the comparative analysis of the ecology of violence. The most fruitful area within the United States for such a study is the South, a region with a pattern of violence that stands in striking contrast to that of the nation at large and about which there is a well-developed scholarly literature.

A tendency toward violence has been one of the character traits most frequently attributed to Southerners.[1] In various guises, the image of the violent South confronts the historian at every turn: dueling gentlemen and masters whipping slaves, flatboatmen indulging in a rough-and-tumble fight, lynching mobs, country folk at a bear baiting or a gander pulling, romantic adventurers on Caribbean filibusters, brutal police, panic-stricken communities harshly suppressing real and imagined slave revolts, robed night riders engaged in systematic terrorism, unknown assassins, church burners, and other less physical expressions of a South whose mode of action is frequently extreme.[2] The image is so pervasive that it compels the attention of anyone interested in understanding the South.

H. C. Brearley was among the first to assemble the quantitative date to support the description of the South

* This Chapter is copyrighted by the American Historical Association, 1969; reprinted by permission of the copyright owner.

** Sheldon Hackney is assistant professor of history at Princeton University. This essay is a revised version of his article, "Southern Violence," *American Historical Review*, Vol. LXXIV (February, 1969), pp. 906-925. It is reprinted here by permission of the *American Historical Review*.

as "that part of the United States lying below the Smith and Wesson line."[3] He pointed out, for example, that during the five years from 1920 to 1924 the rate of homicide per 100,000 population for the Southern states was a little more than two-and-one-half times greater than for the remainder of the United States. Using data from the *Uniform Crime Reports* concerning the 1930's, Stuart Lottier confirmed and elaborated Brearley's findings in 1938. He found for this period also that homicide was concentrated in the Southeastern states. Of the 11 ex-Confederate states, Louisiana showed the lowest homicide rate, but it was 74 percent greater than the national average, and no non-Southern state had a higher rate. Interestingly, while under and assault were oriented to the Southeastern states, robbery rates were highest in the Central and Western states.[4] These findings were replicated in 1954 using data on crime for the years 1946 through 1952.[5] The pattern of high rates of serious crimes against persons and relatively lower rates of crimes against property for the South is consequently quite stable.

At the time that Brearley was setting forth the evidence for Southern leadership in physical aggression against people, another statistical study primarily of American suicide rates revealed that the South was the area whose people had the least propensity to destroy themselves.[6] Austin Porterfield in 1949, using mortality tables from *Vital Statistics,* brought the murder and the suicide indices together and showed that there was a general inverse relationship between the two rates among the states, and the Southern states ranked highest in homicide and lowest in suicide.[7] In 1940, the national average rate of suicide per 100,000 population was 14.4 and of homicide was 6.2, but the old and cosmopolitan city of New Orleans had a suicide rate of 11.1 and a homicide rate of 15.5. Even though some Southern cities exceed some non-Southern cities in suicide rates, the New Orleans pattern of more homicides than suicides is typical of the South but not of the nation. Porterfield comments that "suicide in every non-Southern city exceeds homicide by ratios ranging from 1.19 to 18.60, while suicide rates exceed homicide rates in only 8 of the 43 Southern and Southwestern cities, 5 of those being in the Southwest."[8]

Violence in the South has three dimensions. Relative to

the North, there are high rates of homicide and assault, moderate rates of crime against property, and low rates of suicide. The relationship between homicide and suicide rates in a given group is best expressed by a suicide-homicide ratio (SHR = 100 (suicides/suicides + homicides)).

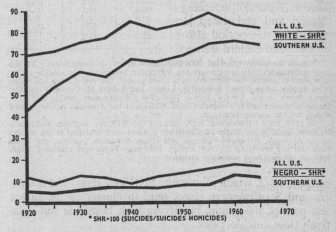

Figure 14-1.—Suicide-homicide ratios.

The closer the SHR approaches 100, the greater is the proportion of the total number of homicides and suicides accounted for by suicide. The European pattern, shared by white Northerners but not by Negroes or white Southerners, is for suicides to far outnumber homicides so that the SHR is in excess of 80. The ratios in table 14-1, displayed graphically in figure 14-1, measure the difference between Southerners and other Americans with regard to violence.

Because the statistics for "the United States" include the statistics for the Southern states, the differences between Southern and non-Southern suicide-murder ratios are understated. Even so, the differences are significant. In the North and the South, but more so in the South, Negroes commit murder much more often than they commit suicide. Among white Americans, Southerners show a relatively greater preference than do non-Southerners for murder rather than suicide. The latter pattern is evident

Year	U.S. white SHR	Southern white SHR	U.S. Negro SHR	Southern Negro SHR
1915	77.4	[b]62.9	23.7	[b]11.3
1920	69.3	[b]43.4	11.2	[b]05.6
1925	70.9	[b]53.5	09.2	[b]05.0
1930	75.0	[b]61.1	11.9	[b]06.0
1935	76.2	59.9	11.4	06.3
1940	83.3	68.5	09.6	06.5
1945	80.3	66.4	11.1	06.8
1950	82.4	69.8	12.4	09.3
1955	88.3	73.1	15.6	09.7
1960	82.0	74.4	17.0	12.2
1964	81.1	73.2	16.7	11.1

[a] Suicide-homicide ratio = 100 (suicides/suicides + homicides). As the ratio approaches 100, it registers the increasing preference for suicide rather than murder among the members of a given group. The ratios were computed from figures taken from: Forrest E. Linder and Robert D. Grove, *Vital Statistics Rates in the United States, 1900-1940* (Washington, 1943), and U.S. Department of Health, Education, and Welfare, *Vital Statistics of the United States,* for the appropriate year.

[b] In 1915, only Virginia was represented in the SHR for Southern whites and Negroes. In 1920, all of the ex-Confederate states were included in the figures except Alabama, Arkansas, Georgia, and Texas. Arkansas, Georgia, and Texas were still not reporting in 1925, but by 1930 only Texas was excluded. From 1935 on, all Southern states are included.

in figure 14-2, which plots white SHR's by state. The Southern and Southwestern states tend to cluster in the upper left part of the graph, signifying high homicide but relatively low suicide rates.

High murder and low suicide rates constitute a distinctly Southern pattern of violence, one that must rank with the caste system and ahead of mint juleps in importance as a key to the meaning of being Southern. Why this should be so is a question that has puzzled investigators for a long time, and their answers have been various. When one loyal Southerner was asked by a probing Yankee why the murder rate in the South was so high, he replied that he reckoned there were just more folks in the South that needed killing.

Few apologies surpass this one in purity, but there is a more popular one that tries to explain the high homicide rates in the Southern states by the extremely high rates of violence among Negroes who constitute a large part of the population. As table 14-1 indicates, however, Southern whites considered by themselves vary from the national norm in the same direction as Negroes, though to a much lesser extent. In addition, Porterfield points out that for the 12 Southern states with the heaviest Negro population, the coefficient of correlation between serious crimes and

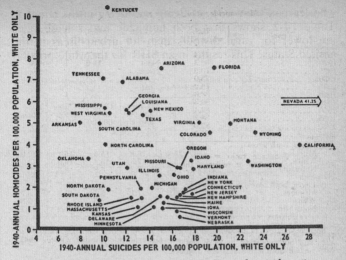

Figure 14-2.—*Regional homogeneity in homicide-suicide ratios.*

the percentage of Negroes in the population is —0.44. There is actually a tendency for states to rank lower in serious crimes as the percentage of Negroes in the population increases.[9]

A more sophisticated theory is that Southern white society contains a larger proportion of lower status occupations so that the same factors that cause lower status groups in the North to become more violent than the rest of society have a proportionately greater effect on the South. The difference in rates would then be accounted for by the numerical bulge in the high risk group, and only the stratification of society would be peculiarly Southern. Unfortunately for this theory, Southern cities, in which whites show the distinctive pattern of Southern violence, actually have greater percentages of the white population in higher status jobs than do Northern cities.[10] It is not the class structure that causes the Southern skew in the statistics.

In the same way, the agricultural nature of Southern life might account for the pattern of Southern violence. The fact that the peculiar configuration exists in Southern cities as well as in the countryside could possibly be accounted for by the large migration into the city of people who learned their ways of living and dying in the country. Table 14-2 shows that both homicide and suicide rates are lower for rural districts than for urban areas in the United States. This results in an SHR for the white popula-

Table 14-2.—Homicide and suicide rates by race and by size of population group, United States, 1940

	U.S.	Cities 100,000 and Up	Cities 10 to 100,000	Cities 2,500-10,000	Rural
Suicide (all ages, both sexes):					
All races	14.4	16.8	15.6	15.1	12.0
White	15.5	17.8	16.4	16.0	13.3
Nonwhite	4.6	7.2	5.8	4.5	3.0
Homicide (all ages, both sexes):					
All races	6.2	7.1	5.7	7.3	5.7
White	3.1	3.2	2.5	3.7	3.3
Nonwhite	33.3	43.3	43.0	51.9	23.1

Source: Forrest E. Linder and Robert D. Grove, *Vital Statistics Rates in the United States, 1900-1940* (Washington: Government Printing Office, 1943). Table 24, pp. 534-553.

tion of rural districts considered by themselves of 80.1, as compared with an SHR of 83.7 for the white population of the nation as a whole. The SHR of 68.8 in 1940 for Southern whites, both urban and rural, is significantly lower than the national ratios and indicates that Southern whites were much more given to acting out their aggressions than the white population of either the cities or the countryside in the rest of the nation.

Another way of testing the notion that the rurality of the South may be the root of its strange configuration of violence is summarized in table 14-3, a comparison of the SHR's of the 11 ex-Confederate states with those of the 11 most rural non-Southern states. The non-Southern states, mostly Western, are closer in time to frontier days and are currently much more subject to instability caused by inmigration than are the Southern states, but otherwise the two sets of states are similar enough for purposes of comparison. The percentage of population living in the urban areas of the Southern states ranged from 13.4 percent to 36.7 percent with the mean falling at 26.1 percent, while in the 11 non-Southern states the degree of urbanization ranged from 13.6 percent to 36.7 percent, with the mean at 31.2 percent. In order not to distort the comparison more than necessary, Nevada, with an extraordinary suicide rate of 41.3 per 100,000 population, is omitted from the comparison. At the same time, Virginia and Florida, with very non-Southern SHR's, are retained in the Southern sample. The results still show a significant difference between the suicide-murder ratio of the Southern states and that of the most rural non-Southern states. The strange bent of Southern violence cannot be accounted for by rural nature of Southern society.

Poverty is also a logical factor to suspect as the underlying cause of the South's pattern of violence. Howard Odum computed that the Southeast in 1930 had 20.9 percent of the nation's population but only 11.9 percent of the nation's wealth.[11] Whether or not the region was poor before it was violent is an undetermined matter. Even more to the point, poverty alone cannot explain high homicide rates. The decline of homocides during business depressions in the United States underlines this argument, as does the fact that crime rates among second-generation immigrants are much higher than among first-generation immigrants despite the fact of increased material welfare.[12]

Table 14-3.—Suicide and homicide rates and suicide-homicide ratios for Southern states and 11 most rural non-Southern states, 1940

Population group	Suicide-homicide ratio
Southern nonwhite	6.7
National nonwhite	12.2
Southern white	68.8
Non-Southern, white rural (11 states)	79.0
National white rural	80.1
National white	83.7

Southern states	White		Rural non-Southern states	White	
	Suicide rate	Homicide rate		Suicide rate	Homicide rate
Alabama	11.7	6.9	Arizona	15.2	7.5
Arkansas	8.0	5.1	Idaho	17.7	3.3
Florida	19.8	7.5	Iowa	15.2	1.3
Georgia	12.1	5.6	Kansas	13.0	1.1
Louisiana	12.4	5.5	Montana	21.1	4.8
Mississippi	10.1	5.7	Nebraska	16.8	.7
North Carolina	10.4	4.0	New Mexico	14.2	5.7
South Carolina	9.7	5.0	North Dakota	9.7	1.4
Tennessee	10.0	7.1	South Dakota	10.5	1.8
Texas	13.6	5.3	Vermont	16.7	.8
Virginia	18.4	5.0	Wyoming	23.5	4.5
Average	12.4	5.6	Average	15.8	4.2

Source: Forrest E. Linder and Robert D. Grove, *Vital Statistics Rates in the United States, 1900-1940* (Washington: Government Printing Office, 1943), Table 20. All rates per 100,000 population.

One study has found no significant correlation between crime rates and the proportion of the population on relief by county in Minnesota, whereas there was a strong correlation between crime rates and the degree of urbanization. Like the rural poor in Minnesota, the Japanese of Seattle were poor but honest and nonviolent.[13]

Nevertheless, though the data are extremely questionable, there is a significant positive correlation between the SHR for the 56 world polities for which information is readily available and almost every measure of modernization that can be quantified.[14] It is difficult to determine whether it is underdevelopment or the process of change that accounts for this, for scholars have noted that the process of modernization generates conflict and violence of various sorts.[15] For developing as well as for industrialized nations, education is the most powerful predictor of a country's SHR, but indices of industrial and urban activity, along with reflections of the society's general welfare are also significantly correlated with the SHR. This is true for the 56 world polities considered together as well as for the European nations considered as a group and for the non-European countries taken together. That Southerners over the past half century have been growing more similar to non-Southern Americans in their tastes in violence as the gap between the nation and the South in economic development has slowly narrowed also argues that there may be no increment of violence in the South that is not "explained" by the relative slowness of the region's development.

Multiple regression analysis offers a technique for testing the possibility that variations in the key indices of modernization operating in an additive fashion might account for the South's particularity in rates of violence. Six independent variables measuring the four factors of wealth, education, urbanization, and age are included in this analysis. Except where indicated below, their values are taken from the *United States Census* of 1940. Urbanization is stated as the percentage of the population living within towns of 2,500 or more; education is measured by the median number of school years completed by persons 25 years old and older; "income" is the state's per capita personal income in dollars for 1940; unemployment is expressed as the percentage of the working force out of work; "wealth" is the state's per capita income in dollars in 1950; and age is the median age of the population. The values of each variable except "income" are recorded by race. "South" is a dummy variable included in the analysis in order to see if any of the unexplained residue of the dependent variable is associated with the fact of its occurring either inside of or outside of the South. All of the ex-Confederate states were assigned the value of one, while all non-Southern states were recorded as zero. The dependent variables that require "explaining" are the suicide rate, the homicide rate, the sum of the suicide rate and homicide rate, and the suicide-homicide ratio. Even though these rates are taken from the most reliable source, *Vital Statistics for the United States,* there may well be large errors between the published rates and the true rates. Some violent deaths are never recorded, and many are improperly classified, but there is no reason to suspect that there has been a long-term, systematic bias in the collection and recording of the statistics for the Southern states. For the purposes of the crude comparison between South and non-South, the *Vital Statistics* are acceptable.

The results of the analysis are summarized in table 14-4. The coefficient of correlation between each of the independent variables and the dependent variable is found in the column labeled "simple." The percentage of the variation in the dependent variable that is associated with, and thus "explained" by, the variation in the independent variable is found by squaring the coefficient of correlation. For example, education is the best single predictor of the white suicide rate. The simple coefficient of correlation of 0.62 between education and suicide in table 14-4 indicates that approximately 30 percent of the variation in the white suicide rate among the 48 states in 1940 is associated with variations in the educational level of the populations. The fact that the correlation is positive means that the suicide rate tends to rise from one state to the next as the educational level rises. Conversely, the negative coefficients of correlation between each of the independent variables, except region, and the white homicide rate indicates that the homicide rate tends to decline as the indices of development rise.

The effect on the dependent variable of all of the independent variables considered together is measured by the

513

Table 14-4.—Multiple regression analysis—violence, development, and sectionalism in the United States, 1940

Dependent variable by state	R² variation explained	Urbanization		Education		Income		Unemployment		Wealth		Age		South	
		Simple	Partial	Simple	Partial	Simple	Partial	Simple	Partial	Simple	Partial	Simple	Partial	Simple	Partial
White suicide rate............	*0.72	.25	*-0.64	*0.62	.52	*0.56	0.14	0.22	0.33	*0.53	0.35	*0.55	*0.59	-0.31	*0.42
White homicide rate...........	*.52	*-.45	-.24	-.17	.09	-.42	.23	-.13	.26	-.42	-.12	*-.58	.24	*.54	*.49
White homicide-suicide rate ...	*.57	.07	*-.59	.52	*.44	.36	.20	.15	.35	-.34	.22	-.30	*.41	-.09	*.50
White homicide-suicide rate ...	*.72	*.53	-.02	*.40	.11	*.63	-.24	.25	-.18	*.62	.29	*.76	*.49	*-.68	*-.53
Nonwhite suicide rate.........	.30	.08	-.13	.30	.25	*.47	.26	.15	-.09	.34	-.00	.13	-.04	-.34	.08
Nonwhite homicide rate........	.25	-.07	-.28	-.19	-.25	-.11	.18	-.17	.21	-.09	-.04	.04	*.40	-.28	*.37
Nonwhite homicide-suicide rate...	.22	-.02	-.30	-.03	-.12	.13	.27	-.08	.15	.09	-.04	.10	.35	.09	*.37
Nonwhite suicide-homicide rate ...	.35	.27	.36	.36	.31	*.43	.18	.30	-.11	.36	-.10	.12	-.40	-.36	-.09

* The chances that a random ordering of the data would produce a relationship this strong are less than 1 in 100.

coefficient of multiple correlation, R. Thus 72 percent of the white suicide rate and 52 percent of the white homicide rate are explained by the seven independent variables operating in an additive fashion. The coefficient of partial correlation expresses the relationship of each independent variable with the unexplained portion of the dependent variable after the independent variables acting collectively have done all the explaining possible. The coefficient of partial correlation for the dummy variable, South, is the most important yield of the multiple regression analysis.

Even though the seven independent variables acting together explain 72 percent of the variation of the white SHR among the 48 states in 1940, 28 percent ($r = -0.53$) of the remaining portion of the variation of the white SHR is associated with the South. This means that the white SHR is lower in the South than can be accounted for by the lower indices of urbanization, education, wealth, and age. Similarly, there is a significant portion of the variation from state to state in the white homicide rate, and in the white suicide rate, that is unexplained by variations in measures of development but that is explained by Southernness.

If the deviation of the South from the national norms for violence cannot be attributed to backwardness, or at least not to the static measures of underdevelopment, there are other possible explanations that should be considered. The concept of anomy, developed by Emil Durkheim in his study, *Suicide,* in 1898, is frequently mentioned as an explanation of both homicide and suicide. Anomy has meant slightly different but not contradictory things to different investigators. It is most generally understood to be a social condition in which there is a deterioration of belief in the existing set of rules of behavior, or in which accepted rules are mutually contradictory, or when prescribed goals are not accessible through legitimate means, or when cognition and socialization have been obstructed by personality traits that cluster about low ego strength.[16] In its manifestation in the individual, in the form of anomy, it is a feeling of normlessness and estrangement from other people. An anomic person feels lost, drifting without clearly defined rules and expectations, isolated, powerless, and frustrated. In this state, there is a strong strain toward deviant behavior in various forms. The problem is that both homicide and suicide are thought to be related to it, and the theory does not predict what sorts of people or what groups will favor one form of behavior rather than another.

To look at Southern violence as the product of anomy in any case would involve a great paradox. The most popular explanation of the high rates of American violence as compared to Europe places the blame on the rapid urbanization, secularization, and industrialization of the United States and on the social characteristics associated with this remarkable growth: geographic and status mobility, an emphasis upon contractual relationships and upon social norms rather than upon personal relationships, competitive striving, and a cultural pluralism that involves a high level of dissonance among the values that everyone tries to put into practice.[17] The South has traditionally served as the counterpoint to the American way of life for the reason that it seemed to differ from the North in these very aspects.[18] Southerners have a greater sense of history than Northerners, a greater attachment to place, and more deferential social customs. By all reports, Southerners place more emphasis on personal relations and on ascribed statuses than do Northerners. Not only do Southerners prize political and social cohesion, but by most measures the South is much more homogeneous than the non-South.[19] Yet, though the South differs from the North on so many of the factors that supposedly contribute to anomy and thus to violence, the South is the nation's most violent region.

There is one body of theory that would seem to predict higher rates of violence precisely because of the South's homogeneity. Reformulating the observations of George Simmel and Bronislaw Malinowski, Lewis Coser writes that "we may say that a conflict is more passionate and more radical when it arises out of close relationships." "The closer the relationship," so the reasoning goes, "the greater the effective investment, the greater also the tendency to suppress rather than express hostile feelings. . . . In such cases feelings of hostility tend to accumulate and hence intensify." Such a theory fits the empirical observation that individuals who express hostility retain fewer and less violent feelings of antagonism toward the source of their irritation.[20] But Coser himself states that, though conflicts within close relationships are likely to be intense when they occur, "this does not necessarily point to the likelihood of

516

more *frequent* conflict in closer relationships than in less close ones." There are situations in which accumulated hostilities do not eventuate in conflict behavior and may even serve to solidify the relationship.[21]

The frustration-aggression hypothesis involves similar perplexities.[22] For example, one of the alternative ways of adapting to frustration is to turn the frustration inward upon the self. In extreme cases this can result in suicide.[23] A psychoanalyst has concluded after an extensive study that a major portion of Sweden's very high suicide rate is caused by the frustrations arising from a highly competitive, success-oriented society.[24] The general rise in suicide rates in the United States during economic downturns argues that the same mechanism is at work among some segments of the population. Consequently, nothing in the frustration-aggression hypothesis predicts the direction the aggression will take.

There are currently two theories that attempt to explain the generally inverse relationship between homicide and suicide as reactions to frustration. The first, developed by Andrew F. Henry and James F. Short, Jr.,[25] is based on the assumption that both homicide and suicide are the result of frustration-aggression and builds upon Porterfield's initial suggestion that the strength of the relational system might have something to do with an individual's choice of either homicide or suicide.[26] Henry and Short adduce data on the relationship of homicide and suicide rates to the business cycle and to certain statistically distinct groups. They reason that overt aggression against others "varies directly with the strength of external restraint over the behavior of the adult—external restraint which is a function of strength of the relational system and position in the status hierarchy."[27]

Martin Gold has pointed out, however, that contrary to the assumption of Henry and Short, upper status people are likely to be more restrained by the expectations of others than are lower status people. Even more damaging is Gold's demonstration that the Henry and Short hypothesis does not correctly predict the greater preference of women for suicide rather than homicide,[28] nor does it correctly predict the fact that suicide rates are lower among the middle classes than at either extreme of the social scale.

The second theory, fashioned by Martin Gold, attempts

517

to relate differences in child rearing practices to preferences for hostility or guilt as an accommodation to frustration. Specifically, Gold shows that there is a positive correlation between the incidence of physical punishment commonly used in the child-rearing practices of certain groups and the rate of homicide for that group. His conclusion is that physical disciplining of children leads to aggression against others rather than against the self.[27] To confound the theory, restrictive child-rearing practices in Europe evidently do not lead to the physical violence that such practices among the lower classes in America are supposed to produce. There is also considerable doubt that there is a significant class differential in the degree of physical punishment used to discipline children.[30] William and Joan McCord found in their study of juveniles that there was no strong relationship between disciplining methods and criminality except when a child is rejected by his parents or when his parents provide him with a deviant role model. Harsh discipline does less damage than neglect.[31] That there is some causal relationship between the socialization of aggression and a group's SHR in reason enough to suppose that it will provide a fruitful line of research, but before it can be a useful ingredient of an explanation of Southern violence, anthropologists and historians need to know much more about regional differences in child-rearing techniques.

Whether or not the cause can be located in child-rearing practices, several bodies of evidence point to the conclusion that Southern violence is a cultural pattern that exists separate from current influences. For instance, several commentators have suggested that the habit of carrying guns in the South made murder a much more frequent outcome of altercations among Southerners than among Northerners. This argument is buttressed by a 1968 survey, reported in table 14-5, which showed that 52 percent of Southern white families owned guns, as opposed to only 27 percent of the white families of the non-South. It may be, however, that this differential in gun ownership is the result of a violent turn of mind rather than the cause of violence. This is the implication of the fact that when the House of Representatives in 1968 passed a weak gun-control bill to restrict the mail-order sale of rifles, shotguns, and ammunition by the overwhelming vote of 304-

518

118, representatives of the 11 ex-Confederate states none-theless voted 73-19 against the bill.[32] It should be noted too that some Southern states have relatively strict firearms laws without dramatically affecting their homicide rates.[33] Furthermore, the assault rate is extremely high in the South, indicating that Southerners react with physical hostility even without guns.

A glance at table 14-4 reveals that for Negroes either the data are grossly skewed or there is little relationship between violence and the selected indices of social wel-

Table 14-5.—Percent of families owning firearms

	Yes	No	Not sure
Total white..............................	34	65 ·	1
South................................	52	45	3
Non-South............................	27	72	1
Total nonwhite..........................	24	70	6
South................................	34	61	5
Non-South............................	15	78	7

Source: Survey of national statistical sample by Opinion Research, Inc., for a Columbia Broadcasting System program Sept. 2, 1968.

fare. There is the barest hint that, controlling for the selected factors, there is some explanatory value in sectionalism, a conclusion that has independent verification. Thomas F. Pettigrew and an associate found that the major correlate of the rate of Negro homicide in the North was the proportion of Negroes in a given area who had been born and raised in the South and that this was in addition to the effect of migration itself. It had long been known that homicide was much less frequent among Northern than among Southern Negroes, but this finding suggests that violence in the South is a style of life that is handed down from father to son along with the old hunting rifle and the family Bible.[34]

The great contribution to the discussion of Southern violence made by Wilbur J. Cash in his book, *The Mind of the South,* was precisely this, that Southern violence is part of a style of life that can be explained only historically.[35] According to Cash's own poetic and impressionistic rendering, violence grew up on the Southern frontier as naturally as it grows up on any frontier. Violence was an integral part of the romantic, hedonistic, hell-of-a-fellow personality created by the absence of external restraint that is characteristic of a frontier. The cult of honor, with its insistence on the private settlement of disputes, was one form taken by the radical individualism of the South, but there were other influences at work. The plantation, the most highly organized institution on the Southern frontier, reinforced the tendency toward violence that had been initiated by the absence of organization. This was so, Cash argues, for two reasons. In the first place, whites on the plantation exercised unrestrained dominance over blacks. In the second place, whites were generally raised by blacks and consequently were deeply influenced by the romantic and hedonistic Negro personality. Cash does not explicitly say what forces produced this Negro personality, but the implication is that Negro personality is fixed by the laws of genetics. But if the more likely position is taken that Negro and white personalities are shaped by environment and experience, then the reader is left with yet another Cashian paradox: violence in the white personality stems at the same time from the effect of being unrestrained and from imitating the Negro personality which was formed out of a situation of dependency and subordination.

It may be that the mediating variable that brings together the various inconsistencies in Cash's explanation of how violence came to be established in the late ante-bellum period as part of the Southern personality is the absence of law. Not disorganization nor individualism, not dominance nor submission, not lack of restraint—none of these forces played as important a role as the absence of institutions of law enforcement in forcing Southerners to resort to the private settlement of disputes. Cash makes this explicit in his treatment of Reconstruction, the second frontier.

During Reconstruction, according to Cash, Southern whites resorted to individual and collective violence because the courts were dominated by carpetbaggers and scalawags. Though this is logical, it is not consistent with Cash's earlier argument that the growth of law had been inhibited on the ante-bellum frontier by the desire of Southerners to provide their own justice. Apparently the direction of causation in the relationship between law and violence changes in accordance with the needs of Cash's interpretation.

Just as the first and second Southern frontiers simultaneously promoted social solidarity and individualism, the third Southern frontier, Progress, changed the South in the direction of the American norm of Babbittry while at the same time accommodating continuity in the basic traits of the Southern mind. A further paradox is involved in the impact of progress on the pattern of violence. Because violence originally arose from individualism, Cash says, the growth of towns should have brought a decrease in rates of violence. This decrease did not materialize because progress also brought poverty and poverty destroys individualism. Cash in effect argues that individualism produced violence in the ante-bellum period and the loss of individualism produced violence in the 20th century.

Though Cash failed to produce a coherent theory of Southern violence, he did focus on two factors that are obvious possibilities as the chief motive forces of Southern violence: the frontier experience and the presence of the Negro. The American frontier did spawn violence, but it seems improbable that the frontier could have much to do with the fact that in the 20th-century Southern states on the Eastern seaboard have much higher rates of violence than the nation at large. There is also considerable difficulty with the notion that the presence of large numbers of Negroes accounts for the great propensity of whites for violence. There is, in fact, very little interracial homicide,[36] and there is no reason to question John Dollard's hypothesis that Negroes murder and assault each other with such appalling frequency because of their daily frustrations in dealing with white men. Because aggressions against whites would call forth extreme negative sanctions, frustrated Negroes display their aggressive feelings to other Negroes.[37] If this is the case, it is difficult to see how high rates of violence among the dominant white group would also be attributed to the white-Negro relationship, especially when the presence of Negroes in the North is not accompanied by a proportionate rate of violence among the whites. It is also interesting that whites in South Africa who also experienced frontier conditions and a subordinate nonwhite population have a homicide-suicide ratio almost identical to the ratio for the American North but quite different from that of the Southern whites.

Subservience, rather than dominance, may be the condition that underlies a pattern of low SHR's. Franz Fanon, in his controversial book, *The Wretched of the Earth,* suggests that the oppressed status of a colonial people produced a pattern of aggressiveness directed against fellow colonials and a need to achieve manhood through violence. That task of revolutionaries is to mobilize the aggressive drives, provide them a sustaining ideology, and direct them against the oppressors.[38] The South's defeat in the Civil War and its position as an economic dependency of the industrial Northeast qualifies it for consideration as a violent colonial region. In addition to the difficulty of separating the effects of subserviency from the effects of sheer underdevelopment, the problem with this line of reasoning is that the heroic myths created about the "Lost Cause" and the relatively early return of home rule after the Civil War may have mitigated the trauma of defeat and social dislocation. It would be difficult to maintain that the South's historical experience as a region is the equivalent of the sort of cultural conflict that leads to the loss of self-esteem, disrupts the processes of socialization, and initiates the cycle of self-crippling behavior within the subordinate group.[39] Furthermore, American Indians have responded to their experience of defeat and repression with higher rates of suicide and other intrapunitive behavior rather than with aggression against others. Similarly, while industrialization was transforming and disrupting its established folk culture, Harlan County, Ky., had the highest homicide rates in the country, but a study of community growth in New England finds suicide and depressive disorders highly correlated with the disruptive impact of geographic mobility.[40]

Though the social sciences offer no clearly authenticated hypothesis that predicts the relationship in different populations between homicide and suicide rates,[41] there are some potentially illuminating investigations currently in progress. Assuming that depressed mental patients are people who have turned anger inward through the mechanism of introjection and guilt when under chronic stress, while paranoid patients are those who have turned anger outward through the mechanism of denial and projection, one study has found an interesting association between the pattern of intrafamily communication and the direction taken by mental pathology when it occurred. Depressed patients in this study came from families in which the children were forced to try by themselves to attain the desired forms of behavior through positive, "ought" channels. Children in the families of paranoid patients were forced into acceptable modes of behavior by negative "ought not" procedures.

"In families of *depressed* patients the child comes to view his environment as non-threatening to him physically. It is something to be manipulated by him in order to bring about the desired effects that will win approval. There is directionality here, and it is *from* the child *toward* his environment. On the other hand, in families of *paranoid* patients the child comes to view his environment as having potentially harmful properties that he cannot control and that must be avoided in some way. Here the directionality is *from* the environment *toward* the child."[42]

The hypothesis is that a manipulative attitude toward the environment will be associated with intrapunitive behavior and that a passive attitude toward the environment, with the absence of the internalization of a feeling of responsibility for the self, will be correlated with a greater use of projection in ego-defense.

There are firm indications that cultural patterning as well as child-rearing techniques will affect the perception of the environment and the orientation of the personality on the paranoia-depression continuum. In Burma, a hierarchical and age-graded society, the social and physical environment is typically perceived as potentially harmful, and Burma has one of the highest homicide rates in the world.[43] There is also the possibility of a connection between the high rates of violence among Afro-Americans and the recent diagnosis that the Negro psyche has been rendered paranoic by the hostile American environment.[44]

Testing the hypothesis that a paranoidal perception of the environment is the root cause of the pattern of violence in the white South is a problem for future scholarship. The most immediately useful technique would be an opinion survey of attitudes toward violence, perceptions of the environment, feelings of personal efficacy, and other measures of alienation. There may be regional differentials in these categories as well as class, age, and sexual differentials. A rigorous comparison of rates of violence in perhaps a Kentucky county and an Ohio county at comparable stages of settlement is also a promising approach. The records of the county court, the reports of the state attorney general, and newspaper surveys might produce useful data on individual as well as collective violence. Some effort must be made to determine when the South became violent. The timing may reveal much about the relationship of slavery to violence. The possible effects of Scotch-Irish immigration, population density, temperature, and religious fundamentalism should be investigated with quantitative methods. Even though the SHR's of Australia and Canada fit the European mold, some insight may derive from pursuing such comparative cases in a detailed manner. There is much that can be done.

Meanwhile, in the search for a valid explanation of Southern violence the most fruitful avenue will probably be one that seeks to identify and trace the development of a Southern world view that defines the social, political, and physical environment as hostile and casts the white Southerner in the role of the passive victim of malevolent forces. When scholars locate the values that make up this world view and the process by which it was created and is transmitted, the history of the South will undoubtedly prove to have played a major role. The un-American experiences of guilt, defeat, and poverty will be major constituents of the relevant version of that history,[45] but perhaps they will not loom so large as the sense of grievance that is at the heart of the Southern identity.

The South was created by the need to protect a peculiar institution from threats originating outside the region. Consequently, the Southern identity has been linked from the first to a siege mentality. Though Southerners have many other identities, they are likely to be most conscious of being Southerners when they are defending their region against attack from outside forces: abolitionists, the Union Army, carpetbaggers, Wall Street and Pittsburgh, civil-rights agitators, the Federal Government, feminism, socialism, trade unionism, Darwinism, communism, atheism, daylight saving time, and other byproducts of modernity. This has made for an extreme sensitivity to criticism from outsiders and a tendency to excuse local faults as the products of forces beyond human control or beyond local control. If the South was poor, it was because the Yankees stole all the family silver and devastated the region in other ways after the Civil War. If industrialization seemed inordinately slow in the South, it was because of a conspiracy of Northern capitalists to maintain the South as an economic colony. Added to this experience with perceived threats has been the fact that almost every significant change in the life of the South has been initiated by external powers. This is even true of industrialization. Though there was a fervent native movement to sponsor industrialization, absentee ownership has been characteristic. Furthermore, the real qualitative change in the Southern pattern of low value-added industry came as a result of World War II and the activities of the Federal Government.

Being Southern, then, inevitably involves a feeling of persecution at times and a sense of being a passive, insignificant object of alien or impersonal forces. Such a historical experience has fostered a world view that supports the denial of responsibility and locates threats to the region outside the region and threats to the person outside the self. From the Southern past arises the symbiosis of profuse hospitality toward strangers and the paradox that the Southern heritage is at the same time one of grace and violence.

References

1. For example, see Charles O. Lerche, Jr., *The Uncertain South: Its Changing Patterns of Politics in Foreign Policy* (Chicago, 1964), pp. 48-49. Representative comments can be found in: John Richard Alden, *The South in the Revolution, 1763-1789* (Baton Rouge, 1957), pp. 34-35, and 41; Clement Eaton, *A History of the Old South* (2d ed., New York, 1966), pp. 260, 395, 404, 407, and 415; John Hope Franklin, *The Militant South, 1800-1861* (Cambridge, Mass., 1956); David Bertelson, *The Lazy South* (New York, 1967), pp. 101-113, and 241; and H. V. Redfield, *Homicide, North and South: Being a Comparative View of Crime Against the Person in Several Parts of the United States* (Philadelphia, 1880).
2. A stimulating essay on this theme is Frank Vandiver, "The Southerner as Extremist," in Frank Vandiver, ed., *The Idea of the South* (Chicago, 1964), pp. 43-56. A lighter treatment of the same subject is Erskine Caldwell, "The Deep South's Other Venerable Tradition," *New York Times Magazine* (July 11, 1965).
3. "The Pattern of Violence," in W. T. Couch, ed., *Culture in the South* (Chapel Hill, 1934), pp. 678-692; and *Homicide in the United States* (Chapel Hill, 1932).
4. Stuart Lottier, "Distribution of Criminal Offenses in Sectional Regions," *Journal of Criminal Law and Criminology*, vol. XXIX (Sept.-Oct. 1938), pp. 329-344.
5. Lyle Shannon, "The Spatial Distribution of Criminal Offenses by States," *Journal of Criminal Law and Criminology*, vol. XLV (Sept.-Oct. 1954), pp. 264-273.
6. Louis I. Dublin and Bessie Bunzel, *To Be or Not To Be: A Study of Suicide* (New York, 1933), pp. 80 and 413.
7. Austin Porterfield, "Indices of Suicide and Homicide by States and Cities: Some Southern-Non-Southern Contrasts with Implications for Research," *American Sociological Review*, vol. XIV (Aug. 1949), pp. 481-490.
8. *Ibid.*, p. 485.
9. Austin Porterfield, "A Decade of Serious Crimes in the United States," *American Sociological Review*, vol. XIII (Feb. 1948), pp. 44-54. See also

James E. McKeown, "Poverty, Race, and Crime," *Journal of Criminal Law and Criminology*, vol. XXXIX (Nov.-Dec. 1948), pp. 480-483.

10. Norval D. Glenn, "Occupational Benefits to Whites From the Subordination of Negroes," *American Sociological Review*, vol. XXVIII (June 1963), pp. 443-448. See particularly table 1.

11. *Southern Regions of the United States* (Chapel Hill, 1936), p. 208.

12. Edwin H. Sutherland and Donald R. Cressey, *Principles of Criminology* (6th ed., New York, 1960), pp. 92 and 146-149.

13. Van B. Shaw, "The Relationship Between Crime Rates and Certain Population Characteristics in Minnesota Counties," *Journal of Criminal Law and Criminology*, vol. XL (May-June 1949), pp. 43-49.

14. Simple intercorrelations were run between the indices of homicide and suicide and measures of social and economic activity using data from: Bruce M. Russett *et al.*, eds., *World Handbook of Political and Social Indicators* (New Haven, 1964); and Statistical Office of the United Nations Department of Economic and Social Affairs, *Demographic Yearbook, 1963* (New York, 1964), table 25, pp. 592-611.

15. Richard S. Weinert, "Violence in Pre-Modern Societies: Rural Columbia," *The American Political Science Review*, vol. LX (June 1966), pp. 340-347; Harry Eckstein, ed., *Internal War* (New York, 1964); E. J. Hobsbawm, *Primitive Rebels* (New York, 1959). An important synthesis and statement of theory is Ted Gurr, "Psychological Factors in Civil Violence," *World Politics*, vol. XX (Jan. 1968), pp. 245-278.

16. Herbert McCloskey and John H. Schaar, "Psychological Dimensions of Anomy," *American Sociological Review*, vol. XXX (Feb. 1965), pp. 14-40.

17. David Abrahamsen, *The Psychology of Crime* (New York, 1960), pp. 18-21 and 177-183. These relationships are greatly illuminated by the discussion in David M. Potter, *People of Plenty: Economic Abundance and the American Character* (Chicago, 1954).

18. William H. Taylor, *Cavalier and Yankee: The Old South and American National Character* (Garden City, N.Y., 1963); C. Vann Woodward, "A Southern Critique for the Gilded Age," *The Burden of Southern History* (Baton Rouge, 1960), pp. 109-140.

19. Jack P. Gibbs and Walter T. Martin, *Status Integration and Suicide: A Sociological Study* (Eugene, Ore., 1964), particularly table 6, p. 54.

20. Lewis A. Coser, *The Functions of Social Conflict* (New York, 1956), pp. 57, 62, and 71; Albert Pepitone and George Reichling, "Group Cohesiveness and Expression of Hostility," in Neil J. Smelser and William T. Smelser, *Personality and Social Systems* (New York, 1963), pp. 117-124.

21. Coser, *The Functions of Social Conflict*, p. 72.

22. John Dollard, Neil E. Miller, Leonard W. Doob, O. H. Mowrer, and Robert R. Sears, *Frustration and Aggression* (New Haven, 1939); Leonard Berkowitz, *Aggression: A Social Psychological Analysis* (New York, 1962); Aubrey J. Yates, *Frustration and Conflict* (New York, 1962).

23. Karl Menninger, *Man Against Himself* (New York, 1938), p. 23. The assumption that homicide and suicide are simply aggressions manifested in different directions is the basis of the concept of the suicide-homicide ratio.

24. Herbert Hendin, *Suicide and Scandinavia: A Psychoanalytic Study of Culture and Character* (Garden City, N.Y., 1965), ch. 5.

25. *Suicide and Homicide: Some Economic, Sociological, and Psychological Aspects of Aggression* (Glencoe, Ill., 1954).

26. Porterfield, "Indices of Suicide and Homicide by States and Cities," p. 488.

27. Henry and Short, *Suicide and Homicide*, p. 119.

28. Martin Gold, "Suicide, Homicide, and the Socialization of Aggression," *The American Journal of Sociology*, vol. LXIII (May 1958), pp. 651-661. Gold organized the SHR, which he called the suicide murder ratio.

29. *Ibid.*

30. Melvin L. Kohn, "Social Class and the Exercise of Parental Authority," in Smelser and Smelser, *Personality and Social Systems*, pp. 297-314; Martha Sturm White, "Social Class, Child Rearing Practices, and Child Behavior," *ibid.*, pp. 286-296; Bernard C. Rosen and Roy D'Andrade, "The Psychosocial Origins of Achievement Motivation," *Sociometry*, vol. XXII (1959), pp. 185-215, cited in Marshall B. Clinard, ed., *Anomic and Deviant Behavior: A Discussion and Critique* (New York, 1964), pp. 260-261. Bernard Berelson and Gary A. Steiner, *Human Behavior: An Inventory of Scientific Findings* (New York, 1964), pp. 479-481.

31. William McCord and Joan McCord, *Origins of Crime: A New Evaluation of the Cambridge-Somerville Youth Study* (New York, 1959), pp. 172 and 198.
32. *New York Times*, July 25, 1968.
33. Carl Bakal, *The Right to Bear Arms* (New York, 1966), pp. 346-353.
34. Thomas F. Pettigrew and Rosalind Barclay Spier, "The Ecological Structure of Negro Homicide," *The American Journal of Sociology*, vol. LXVII (May 1962), pp. 621-629.
35. Wilbur J. Cash, *The Mind of the South* (New York, 1940, Vintage edition, 1960), pp. 32-34, 44-52, 76, 115-123, 161, 220, 424.
36. Marvin E. Wolfgang, *Patterns in Criminal Homicide* (Philadelphia, 1958), pp. 222-236.
37. John Dollard, *Caste and Class in a Southern Town* (3d ed., Garden City, N.Y., 1949), ch. 13.
38. Franz Fanon, *The Wretched of the Earth* (New York, 1963).
39. Thomas Stone, Dorthea C. Leighton, and Alexander H. Leighton, "Poverty and the Individual," in Leo Fishman, ed., *Poverty and Affluence* (New Haven, 1966), pp. 72-96.
40. Paul Frederick Cressey, "Social Disorganization and Reorganization in Harlan County, Kentucky," *American Sociological Review*, vol. XIV (June 1949), pp. 389-394; Henry Wechsler, "Community Growth, Depressive Disorders, and Suicide," *The American Journal of Sociology*, vol. LXVII (July 1961), pp. 9-16.
41. Jack O. Douglas, *The Social Meanings of Suicide* (Princeton, 1967), pp. 3-160.
42. Hazel M. Hitson and Daniel H. Funkenstein, "Family Patterns and Paranoidal Personality Structure in Boston and Burma," *The International Journal of Social Psychiatry*, vol. V (Winter 1959).
43. *Ibid.*
44. William H. Grier and Price M. Cobbs, *Black Rage* (New York, 1968).
45. C. Vann Woodward, "The Search for Southern Identity," *The Burden of Southern History*, pp. 3-26.

PART VI

INTERNATIONAL CONFLICT AND INTERNAL STRIFE

Psychoanalysts no sooner popularized the concept of displacement than some scholars made an analytic leap of faith to propose that wars represented a displacement of aggressions within the community onto foreign enemies. Conflict theorists, relying more on reason than faith, suggested that in the face of external conflict, members of a community were likely to join ranks and minimize their differences. Some factually oriented sociologists and political scientists pointed out that unsuccessful wars had frequently led to revolutionary movements: for example, in Russia in 1918, in Bavaria the next year, and Italy several years after that. Opponents of the war in Vietnam have suggested that the increase in domestic turmoil in recent years is the work of those who take their cues from the international actions of the government.

Some cautions, but no definitive answers, for grand theorizing about connections between external and internal conflicts are suggested by the examination of the historical and contemporary experience of the United States in the following two chapters. Robin Brooks points out that some of the wars the United States has fought have been accompanied by direct internal protest, others not. When specifically antiwar protest has occurred, its immediate sources have been the belief that a particular war was unjust, and resentment against its contingent requirements of conscription and material support. Opposition on both grounds was especially widespread during the Civil War, in both the North and the South; during World War I; and during the Vietnam war. In the latter two wars the protesters seldom resorted to violence on their own initiative. They were however frequent targets of retaliatory violence by groups of outraged citizens and by the police and military. Despite the historical continuity of American antiwar protest, and especially of the patterns of severe governmental response, Brooks concludes that the contemporary anti-Vietnam protest is of such an unprecedented magnitude and reflects such a broad constituency that historical guidelines have little to tell us.

Raymond Tanter examines systematically the relations between the Vietnam involvement and the incidence of various forms of domestic turmoil. His evidence supports the obvious connection: that periods of escalation were accompanied by a high incidence of antiwar protest. Less obviously, opposition has not increased consistently with the absolute level or duration of the war. Brooks' paper provides an important qualification to the last point: although the incidence of war protest may not have increased as the war has dragged on, the most militant protesters have come increasingly to challenge the legitimacy of the political system that conducts the war and to assert their willingness to use violence to oppose it.

The evidence for an association between the Vietnam war and the supposed breakdown of norms that has led to domestic turmoil other than antiwar protest is inconclusive, in Professor Tanter's judgment. Crimes, strikes, and urban riots have seasonal fluctuations that are more striking than any correspondence with events in Vietnam. Urban riots were most numerous in the years of escalation, but it is at best a hypothesis that the phenomena are related.

Chapter 15

DOMESTIC VIOLENCE AND AMERICA'S WARS: AN HISTORICAL INTERPRETATION

*By Robin Brooks**

INTRODUCTION

This essay analyzes the domestic protest and violence that erupted in response to American involvement in the

* Robin Brooks is associate professor of history at San Jose State College, where he specializes in the American Revolution and the Early National period. His publications include "Alexander Hamilton, Mclancton Smith, and the Ratification of the New York Constitution," *William and Mary Quarterly,* 3d series, vol. XXIV (Oct. 1967).

nine major wars carried on by the United States since 1775: the Revolution, the War of 1812, the Mexican War, the Civil War, the Spanish-American War, World Wars I and II, the Korean war, and the current war in Vietnam. The focus is further limited to include only those conflicts with a clearly antiwar component—e.g., the New York City Draft Riots of 1863—while excluding the racial violence of World Wars I and II and the ghetto rebellions of the last 4 years. Violence initiated by opponents of the war or by those who support it—whether civilians, police, or military—is examined, but not technically nonviolent events like the legal repression of draft resisters or the relocation of Japanese-Americans in 1942. Further, a distinction is made between violence that in effect represents support for the other side in internecine conflicts like the Civil War or the American Revolution, and violence arising from opposition to war beyond America's borders or to the means by which it is carried on. The inquiry seeks to understand why there have been so few antiwar riots in the American past, despite much opposition to American wars, and to draw some conclusions about similarities and differences between antiwar violence during the present conflict, and that in our past.

HISTORICAL RETROSPECT

Opposition to the Revolution

The American Revolutionary era is replete with violence involving mobs and unofficial bodies of men. Before the actual outbreak of the Revolution, numerous violent outbreaks occurred: the Boston Massacre, the Gaspé incident, the Regulator movement, tenant riots in Westchester County, N.Y., and the mobbing of Stamp Act collectors, to cite just a few. During the war itself, bloody conflicts between Tories and Whigs occurred frequently in New York, the Carolinas, and along the frontier. But these seemed to have involved less opposition to the war itself than a taking of sides in a civil war. None of them, I believe, fits the criteria of an antiwar riot.

The so-called "Fort Wilson" riot, in Philadelphia, October 4-6, 1779, is somewhat more difficult to categorize. The origins of the Fort Wilson riot might be described as a popular movement to punish some opponents of war, but it quickly moved beyond that limitation. After the British evacuated Philadelphia, early in 1779, popular resentment against suspected Tories mounted. The suspects included some Quakers, at once conscientious opponents of war, but also British sympathizers and wealthy merchants. When the Pennsylvania government's appointed committee did not seem to be acting effectively, the popular militia moved to take the law into its own hands. Its committee, composed of one man from each company, moved swiftly against Tories—and also against "engrossers, monopolizers, and those who sympathized with them, as well as certain lawyers who had appeared as counsel for the accused at the Tory trials."[1] Placards appeared, denouncing several prominent leaders of the Revolution, among them Declaration of Independence signers Robert Morris (speculating in flour) and James Wilson (lawyer for the Tories).

The militia committee and its sympathizers, after attempting in vain to find leaders among prominent radicals like painter Charles Wilson Peale, set out to punish the evildoers. After arresting several suspects, including a number of Quakers, they headed toward the home of James Wilson. Wilson's friends, among them some of the most prominent Philadelphia Whigs, had armed and barricaded themselves in his house. The mob approached, and one of its leaders, a ship's joiner, disclaimed any intention of attacking Wilson, he explained that they supported the constitution of Philadelphia, but that "the laboring part of the city had become desperate from the high price of the necessaries of life."[2] The procession marched on and had mostly passed Wilson's house when a member of the garrison, a Captain Campbell, opened a window and waved a pistol at the crowd. Who fired first is not known, but in the exchange of shots Campbell was mortally wounded. A battle ensued with casualties on both sides, quelled only when the Philadelphia Light-Horse Cavalry, led by Gen. Joseph Reed, the state's chief executive, charged upon and dispersed the mob.

Twenty-seven of its number were jailed, while Wilson and his fellow defenders left town. Many returned—Wilson prudently accepted his friends' counsel to stay away—to organize plans for dealing with the militia, whose officers had proposed violent measures to free their friends. This action was forestalled when the militiamen were set free on bail, and General Reed managed to conciliate both sides. Ultimately no one was prosecuted, as the Assembly declared an Act of Amnesty for all implicated persons. In summation, the riot was only peripherally connected with opposition to war, and more clearly a case of class or economic conflict.[3]

In Dutchess County, N.Y., during July 1776, and again in Columbia County in August 1777, farmers took up arms against Revolutionary authorities, and were suppressed after some fighting. But is it not possible to discern from the fragmentary surviving records whether they acted out of opposition to the war per se, which fell harshly upon them in requisitioning goods and supplies and in sometimes requiring military service as proof of loyalty, or whether their actions were simply an expression of economic grievances or of loyalty to His Majesty George III.[4] Nor can we find clear-cut evidence of civilian riots against the British authorities occupying New York and other cities. On balance, it appears there was very little antiwar violence of any kind that might usefully be compared to that of our own time.

The War of 1812 and the Mexican War

The War of 1812, in contrast, is neatly organized for the purposes of our study. It furnished one major and one

minor riot, plus a fine scholarly explanation of the sources of social cleavage of the day.

The Baltimore Federalist newspaper, the *Federal Republican,* published a harsh critique of President Madison and the Republican Party for the declaration of war against Britain, just a few days after the event. A loyal mob promptly destroyed the editor's house and his press, forcing him to flee to the District of Columbia. But other Baltimore Federalists, taking a principled stand for freedom of the press and their right to express their antiwar opinions, arranged to have another issue of the paper (published in Washington) circulated in Baltimore and carrying a Baltimore address on the masthead. They shut themselves up in the house they named, armed, and prepared to defend their rights. On July 27, 1812, the mob attacked the twenty defenders. After a sharp battle, in which some of the attackers were killed or wounded, the mob brought up cannon. The mayor's intervention, with cavalry, halted the action. He then persuaded the Federalists to go to jail to await trial. Inexplicably, the troops protecting the jail were called off—other members of the city militia had refused to serve—thereby exposing the prisoners to renewed attack. The mob—led by two butchers—broke into the jail, took out the prisoners, and beat them savagely. Eight were beaten into insensibility and tossed into a heap in front of the jail, from where the mob refused to allow them to be removed until noon the next day. General Lingan, a hero of the Revolution, was beaten to death. Gen. Henry Lee, former Governor of Virginia, colleague of Washington, and father of Robert E. Lee, nearly suffered the same fate; almost 2 months later he could neither talk nor eat solid food. Other Federalists were manhandled and tortured for hours before finally escaping or being released. No punishment was visited upon the mob.[5]

In direct response to this event, New Englanders opposed to the war took revenge on one of their own. On August 3, 1812, Massachusetts Congressman Charles Turner, who had voted for war, returned to his home in Plymouth. In addition to being a Republican Congressman, he was also Chief Justice of Sessions for Plymouth County. This made no difference to his antiwar Federalist neighbors, who seized him on the main street and kicked him through the town.[6]

Neither Henry Adams, in his great history of the period, nor the histories of any of the major towns record any other mob action during the War of 1812. But Roger N. Brown, in *The Republican in Peril: 1812* offers an explanation of the bitter cleavage in politics. He contends that Federalists and Republicans were deeply divided, each certain that the other side had the worst motives—for going to war or for opposing it—in mind, and that each side was prepared to go to almost any lengths to frustrate its enemies: "Republican and Federalist views of party opposites are largely false . . . wild parodies of the truth." Such views stem from "personal inexperience with political parties that encouraged men to identify opponents with their fears." What experience they had, "derived as it was from history and the factional contests of the colonial period, instinctively presumed prolonged opposition to rest on selfish, even traitorous motives. . . . Eighteenth-century political thought extolled the blessings of the harmonious commonwealth and condemned sustained organized party activity" for ignoring the common good in pursuit of power.[7]

Given such sharp polarization as Brown describes, why do we find such little violence during the War of 1812? One explanation might lie in the comparatively high degree of consensus within each section; e.g., Baltimore was overwhelmingly Federalist, so that no opposition dared raise its head after the riots. But such an explanation does not explain why violence did not flare up in the marginal areas. Perhaps a more useful explanation might run counter to Brown's, to suggest that many people did not care much about the war one way or the other, while the open, legitimate, and effective channels of expression—the press and the political system—afforded adequate outlets for the concerned minorities.

At least this is the explanation offered by Charles G. Sellers for the lack of antiwar riots during the Mexican War.[8] (There may have been some such incidents, but a sampling of the press and periodicals, diaries, town histories, and other secondary accounts does not reveal any of which I am aware.) The Mexican War also elicited sectional cleavage, very similar to that of 1812, with New England largely opposed and the South and West largely in favor. But because political opinion could easily be translated into effective protest and political movements, Sellers suggests, there would be little cause for riots on the part of those opposed to the war. Since the actual fighting from the outbreak of the war until the capture of Mexico City lasted less than 18 months and produced an uninterrupted string of U.S. victories, we might speculate that antiwar protests would be less than desperate while prowar groups could afford to be tolerant of misguided scrupulousness.

THE CIVIL WAR

The Civil War, of course, is quite another matter. Replete with all sorts of violence arising from opposition to the war, both North and South, it confronts the historian with the need to make fine distinctions about the purposes of the participants. Only a few days after the firing on Fort Sumter had initiated the conflict, some 10,000 Confederate sympathizers in Baltimore, carrying the Stars and Bars at their head, attacked approximately 2,000 Union troops from Massachusetts and Pennsylvania who were passing through "mobtown" en route to Washington, D.C. The soldiers opened fire to protect themselves, but it took the resolute action of the Baltimore police to enable them to escape the fury of the mob. At least 12 citizens and 4 soldiers died in the affray. Yet this conflict belongs properly to the history of the Civil War itself, rather than to the category of antiwar violence.[9] Subsequently French S. Evans, who had been a well-known newspaper editor before the war, fled Baltimore to escape an irate mob prepared to punish him for the expression of pro-Union sentiments.[10]

Similarly, many actions of Unionists in the South might properly fall within the category of pro-Northern demonstration rather than that of antiwar protest. Georgia Lee Tatum's *Disloyalty in the Confederacy* tells us that in almost every State of the Confederacy, conscription roused bitter opposition among the poor whites. The German areas of Texas, the mountains of Appalachia and the Ozarks, and the swamps of Florida all became centers for deserters and the disaffected from which guerrilla warfare emanated and into which Confederate recruiting officers and provost marshals could venture only with the escort of the Army. Let us consider three events which might be considered as reflecting in some measure antiwar violence.

Western North Carolina was originally a source of loyalty to the Confederacy. But when the conscription law omitted owners of 20 or more slaves from its purview, disaffection flared up. W. W. Holden, editor of the Raleigh *Standard,* became the leader of the antiwar movement in the state, writing editorials that came perilously close to treason in the eyes of many. On September 9, 1863, a detachment of Georgia troops en route through Raleigh attacked the office of the *Standard.* The next day a Unionist mob attacked and destroyed the Raleigh *State Journal,* the pro-Confederate paper in town. Although Governor Vance maintained a neutral attitude during this period of strife, Holden ran against him as a peace candidate for Governor in 1864. Those voting for Holden in some areas where pro-Confederate sentiment still ran strong found them-selves subjected to what one of the state's historians euphemistically called "violent unpopularity."[11]

German settlers around Austin, Texas, generally op-posed the Confederate cause. Draftees at Industry, Texas (in Austin County), in December 1862, attacked a Con-federate officer and drove him away, after they organized armed bodies to defend themselves, threatening to destroy those of their fellow Germans who were loyal to the Con-federacy.[12] At the same time, citizens of Randolph County, in northern Alabama, defied the Conscription Act. Led by their very active Peace Society, an armed mob raided the county jail forcibly to free arrested deserters.[13]

Opposition to conscription proved to be the major source of mob violence in the North, too. German immigrants in Port Washington, Wisconsin, attacked a draft commis-sioner, destroyed draft machinery, and sacked the homes of prominent Republicans until dispersed by troops. This story could be repeated in almost every midwestern state. One enrolling officer was killed in Indiana, another in Wis-consin. An Irish mob in Chicago manhandled a U.S. marshal.[14]

But the most notorious case of all was the great New York City Draft Riot, of July 13-17, 1863, one which dwarfs by comparison all contemporary racial or antiwar violence. Estimates of the size of the mobs, which fought police, militia, and federal troops, run as high as 50,000. Its most recent chronicler suggests total deaths were as many as 1,300 and damage above $5 million, while ac-knowledging that these must remain imprecise estimates. Official records list 18 persons killed by the rioters, 11 of them Negroes; but more than 70 persons, most of them Ne-gro, were reported missing, and many of them were never accounted for. Nor is there agreement about the general causes of the riot. The Conscription Act, of course, pro-vided the occasion, as it went into operation only 2 days be-fore the eruption of the riots. But the vicious persecution of blacks by the mobs, largely made up of poor Irish immi-grants, indicates that the identification of the Civil War with the cause of Emancipation was a major factor, compounded by competition for jobs and status at the bottom of the urban pecking order. Class animosity entered into the equation, too, because the $300-exemption clause made the war into "a rich man's war but a poor man's fight."[15]

New York City was not the only center of antidraft rioting in the East. Irish miners in the anthracite coalfields of Pennsylvania rioted; so did Connecticut draftees.[16] But the draft was not the only source of antiwar violence during the Civil War; the organized peace movement in the North also led to violence.

Clement Vallandigham, Ohio Peace Democratic Congressman, proved the main focus of antiwar agitation in the North. On May 1, 1863, Union troops arrested Vallandigham in his hometown of Dayton for a speech denouncing the war. A mob of his sympathizers burned down the proadministration paper, the Dayton *Journal* (and when the fire got out of hand, a good bit more of the town). Federal troops were called in to quell the rioting, and did so after killing one member of the mob. In Indianapolis that same month, a pro-Vallandigham rally was broken up by armed soldiers with considerable violence erupting, none of it fatal.[17]

Many antiwar demonstrations and rallies suffered a similar fate. As early as August 16, 1861, veterans (of 3 months' service) broke up a peace meeting in Saybrook, Connecticut. At Stepney, in the same state, loyalists from Bridgeport led by P. T. Barnum and sewing-machine heir Elias Howe, Jr., attacked a meeting and tore down its peace flag. Returning to Bridgeport, despite the pleas of Barnum and Howe, the mob, now swelled to over 8,000, destroyed the Copperhead Bridgeport *Farmer*.[18] Other Copperhead papers like the Columbus [Ohio] *Crisis*, the Dubuque [Iowa] *Herald*, and the Chicago *Times* suffered from attacks by soldiers and civilians. But in both Connecticut and in the Midwest, federal crackdowns on the peace movement —involving violation of due process for those arrested by suspension of habeas corpus and arbitrary incarceration without trial—succeeded in destroying organized peace activity in the North.[19] David Donald has ascribed the greater ability of the North than the South to suppress opposition to an excess of democracy in the Confederacy; I suspect that the victories of Grant and Sherman in 1863 and 1864 also played a large part, insofar as "nothing succeeds like success."[20]

The Spanish-American War—John Hay's "splendid little war"—was effectively over in 3 months. It had been enormously popular to begin with, and cost only 379 battle casualties (although more than 5,000 Americans died from disease and food poisoning), so it should be no surprise to discover that there was no antiwar violence. Curiously, there was considerable opposition in high places to the war's imperial fruits—the annexation of Puerto Rico, the Philippines, etc. Mark Twain, Andrew Carnegie, William James, House Speaker Thomas Reed, and E. L. Godkin, editor of the *Nation,* were all active in the Anti-Imperialist movement. But none of these men could have—and none showed the slightest interest in—organized popular antiwar violence, and none was forthcoming from any other source.[21]

World War I

Opponents of War, 1917-1918, by H. C. Peterson and Gilbert C. Fite, provides an outstanding treatment of anti-war violence during World War I. The persistence and scale of violence, as well as the social base of opposition to this war, make it the nearest thing to a parallel with the present situation. But it differs sharply with the present in that almost every case of violence occurred when patriotic mobs attacked opponents of war. From the long and appalling list of incidents compiled by Peterson and Fite, I could find only the following two in which the initiative for violence appeared to originate with the antiwar movement.

An anticonscription meeting of 2,000 persons in New York City on June 15, 1917, almost led to a riot. Word that soldiers and sailors had surrounded the hall and intended to question members of the audience as they came out caused a near panic. According to the New York *Times* report, the servicemen who tried to block the doors were hit by flying wedges of the audience, and cursed by more than 10,000 more onlookers outside the hall.[22]

More serious was the "Green Corn Rebellion" of eastern Oklahoma. Before the outbreak of war, poor tenants and sharecroppers had formed the Working Class Union, a syndicalist organization associated with the Industrial

Workers of the World. In August 1917, several hundred of these farmers assembled, intending to march on Washington, take over the Government, and stop the war. They expected to be joined by many thousands more who objected to the war and the draft across the country. While waiting for other WCU members to rally to them, they subsisted on unripe green corn. They had cut some telegraph wires and attempted without success to destroy railroad bridges, when they were attacked and dispersed by patriotic posses. Some 450 antiwar farmers were arrested; many were released but minor offenders were sentenced to incarceration from 60 days to 2 years, and the leaders drew 3- to 10-year sentences.[23]

In all the other cases Peterson and Fite record, violence was initiated by patriots. In Boston, in July 1917, 8,000 Socialists and other radicals staged an antiwar parade. Sailors and soldiers, attacking in regular formations upon command by an officer, broke up the parade; the paraders were beaten and the Socialist Party headquarters raided. None of the approximately 10,000 persons involved in the attack was arrested; 10 of those attacked were.[24] In Collinsville, Illinois, a young man of German birth, registered as an enemy alien and professing Socialist leanings—but with no record of having opposed the war overtly—was lynched by a drunken mob. When its leaders were indicted, their attorneys called their act a "patriotic murder," and the local jury acquitted them after 25 minutes' deliberation.[25]

At Rutgers University, in the only case of a campus riot I have found prior to the present conflict, fellow students demanded that Samuel Chovenson, an antiwar Socialist, speak at their Liberty Loan rally. When he refused, they stripped him, covered him with molasses and feathers, and paraded him through New Brunswick.[26] Berkeley, California, also had its riot, although it was not primarily a campus affair: a mob attacked religious pacifists, burned down their tabernacle (a tent), and dunked them in their baptismal tank— whereupon the authorities arrested the pacifists and jailed them.[27]

A major source of opposition to World War I was the People's Council of America for Peace and Democracy. Its meetings were broken up in Philadelphia, Wilmington, and Chicago. When pacifist minister Herbert Bigelow, a Socialist, attempted to speak under the Council's auspices in Newport, Kentucky, a mob seized, bound and gagged him, drove him 20 miles into a forest and lashed him repeatedly with a blacksnake whip on his bare back. The assistant Attorney General of the United States commented that no statement against the attackers would be considered unless it was by a "responsible citizen," while the dean of the University of Minnesota Law School, denouncing the People's Council, said that "wartime was no time to quibble about constitutional rights and guarantees."[28] When Irish opponents of the war paraded carrying a red flag in Butte, Montana, on June 6, 1917—the day after the draft law went into effect—patriotic citizens, reinforced by the police and by the state militia with fixed bayonets, dispersed the demonstration. Twenty arrests were made, all of demonstrators.[29] Elsewhere, sailors and soldiers broke up a Philadelphia anticonscription meeting.[30]

The Industrial Workers of the World, advocates of direct action and sabotage in the interest of revolutionary syndicalism, pose a special problem of interpretation. They had been the most militant and violent opponents of the American capitalist system, especially in the West, before the war. As revolutionaries, they were hardly pacifists, but they sharply opposed the war as a war for big business. In this circumstance patriotism became the cover under which the enemies of the IWW could destroy it. Mass jailings, beatings, and deportations of "Wobblies" took place in Arizona, Montana, and other states. In Butte, patriotic vigilantes seized IWW organizer Frank Little, dragged him through the streets tied behind their automobile until his kneecaps were scraped off, then hanged him to a railroad trestle. The New York *Times* commented, on August 1, 1917, that the lynching was "deplorable and detestable," but noted that "IWW agitators are in effect and perhaps in fact, agents of Germany. The Federal government should make short work of these treasonable conspirators against the United States."[31]

For the *Times,* then and subsequently, the only alternative to lynching was federal suppression and dissent against the war. The *Christian Science Monitor* agreed. It editorialized on May 4, 1918: "The most regrettable thing about the whole matter is that, owing to the failure of the state and federal courts to deal adequately with the problem, private citizens are left, in self-protection, to take the law into their own hand." Governor Lowden of Illinois, U.S. Attorney General Gregory, and other members of the Cabinet, and many Senators and Congressmen agreed. The upshot was the Sedition Act, a sweeping amendment to the Espionage Act, aimed to muzzle all except "friendly" criticism of the Government, the armed forces, the Constitution, the flag, and the war. Its signature into law by President Wilson on May 16, 1918, led to some 1,500 arrests, effectively superseding mob action against opponents of war as it effectively wiped out all expression of dissent.[32]

Peterson and Fite provide an appropriate conclusion: they note that "a strong minority bitterly resented the war and conscription," but (as Attorney General Gregory said) "their propaganda was almost immediately suppressed and destroyed."[33]

World War II

World War II was totally unlike World War I. Norman Thomas, veteran Socialist and pacifist leader, reported in 1943:

Now it is true that there has been almost no interference by legal authorities or by mobs with public meetings. There has been . . . no parallel to the wholesale arrests under the Espionage Act. . . . In every previous war in which we have engaged there has been organized opposition of various strength. Last time, despite rigorous suppression, opposition was persistent and by no means confined to enemy sympathizers. Opposition to active participation in this war, strong before Pearl Harbor, completely dissolved after the surprise attack by Japan and the Japanese and German declarations of war against the United States. . . .

Roger Baldwin, director of the American Civil Liberties Union (itself formed to protect pacifists in their expression of antiwar opinions during World War I), agreed fully with Thomas. He noted that firm, effective Government action had "tended to allay fear and to create the conviction that any movements obstructive of the war are well in hand."[34] As a result, he found, "we experience no hysteria, no war-inspired mob violence, no organization of virtuous patriots seeking out seditious opinion, and no hostility to persons of German or Italian origin." He did note the hostility to persons of Japanese origin, but commented that "while painfully in evidence, [it] is largely confined to the Pacific Coast and smaller communities in the West."[35]

Attorney General Earl Warren of California, testifying before a congressional hearing concerned with the forcible removal of these same Japanese-Americans, warned that "my own belief concerning vigilantism is that the people do not engage in vigilante activities so long as they believe that their Government through its agencies is taking care of their most serious problem." Only if they believe that that is not happening do they "start taking the law into their own hands." Mr. Warren, in asking for this racist action— Japanese removal—was also making an important point about our treatment of serious dissent in wartime: either the Government suppresses it legally, or the people will suppress it violently. Despite the long, uncertain course of World War II, its origins guaranteed that there would be such little dissent that the people could tolerate what the Government did not suppress.[36]

The Korean War

The Korean war appears as an excellent example of consensus through crackdown. Like the War of 1812, the Korean war generated one brief flash of opposition. On August 2, 1950, New York City opponents of the war, mostly leftist, held a rally despite refusal by the police to grant them a permit. The rally drew a few thousand people, but they were quickly dispersed by a heavy police force. The New York *Times* reporter noted that "some of the demonstrators who refused orders to disperse were badly beaten by the police. Some were charged by mounted police who rode onto crowded sidewalks. On the whole, however, the police used restraint."[37] There were two other newsworthy incidents, both comparatively minor: Four workers in the Linden, New Jersey, plant of General Motors attempted to hand out antiwar leaflets at the plant. Their fellow employees beat them and threw them out of the plant, GM refused to rehire them, and the United Auto Workers expelled them from the union.[38] In San Francisco, a meeting of Harry Bridges' Longshoremen's Union erupted into a riot when Bridges tried to substitute a peace resolution for one supporting the actions of the United States in Korea. (A Senate committee reported that it was seeking ways to jail Bridges, and his deportation hearing followed almost immediately.)[39] Unlike other conflicts, the Korean war began during a period of greater peacetime repression than the country had ever known; as a result the Government itself, with committees of the House and Senate playing a role equal to or greater than that of the administrative branch, played an enormous role in quashing dissent, leaving very little room for the efforts of would-be vigilantes.[40]

The War in Vietnam

And so we come down to the present. Violence in the early stages of the war in Vietnam resembled the model of the Korean war and most American wars, in that peaceful demonstrators were attacked by citizens or by the police. In October 1965, demonstrators in Berkeley, California, declared their intention to close down the Oakland Army Terminal by massive, nonviolent action. They were easily turned aside, without violence, by the massed Oakland police on the borders of that city. Violence erupted when members of the Hell's Angels motorcycle gang attacked seated demonstrators, but this was quickly quelled by the same Oakland police. Subsequently, nonviolent pickets were attacked repeatedly while picketing the Port Chicago, California, naval facility, and draft-card burners in Boston were beaten by a Boston mob. As late as April 1967, anti-war demonstrations took the form of peaceful protest marches (with no violence in San Francisco, and very little in New York), but there was a reversion to type during the summer of 1967, when pickets protesting the appearance of President Johnson at the Century-Plaza Hotel in Los Angeles were badly beaten by police. The demonstrators were overwhelmingly a nonviolent group, although they did include a few activists who provoked the police onslaught by jeers and intemperate language.[41]

But the events of "Stop-the-Draft Week"—October 16-22, 1967—appear to be something of a watershed. In California, radical student leaders announced that they would close the Oakland Selective Service Induction Center "by any means necessary." But tactical divisions reflecting opposing principles within the anti-Vietnam movement led to a division of labor. On Monday, October 6, members

543

and sympathizers of "the Resistance" sat in nonviolently and were arrested nonviolently. On Tuesday, several thousand students and other radicals attempted physically to seal off the induction center, and were violently dispersed by the Oakland police. Few were arrested, but many were beaten or gassed in response to their token resistance (those who resisted nonviolently, and newsmen, seemed to bear the brunt of the police onslaught). Wednesday saw a return to nonviolence, and when Thursday passed almost without any demonstration, it appeared that the protesters faced an inglorious defeat. But inexplicably, Friday became a day of new, escalated tactics by the militants. Instead of trying to stand up to the police, some 15,000 activists dispersed all over the neighborhood in the vicinity of the induction center. They dragged parked cars into intersections and overturned them there or deflated their tires; they blocked traffic with potted plants and trash cans; and by fleeing and regrouping they easily avoided the superior power of the police. These mobile tactics succeeded in sharply reducing physical violence against the demonstrators.

If "the capture of intersections" delayed the work of the induction center scarcely an hour or two, the demonstrators regarded their actions as a moral victory. Beyond their ingenious tactical innovations, the militants had also embarked on a new stage in opposition to the war: no longer was the leadership of the movement in the hands of the nonviolent opponents of war, but rather the initiative lay with the activists who, in words at least, claimed the right to self-defense and even to take the offensive against the enemy—although in fact they were singularly unsuccessful in effectively opposing police violence with violence of their own.

The crowning event of Stop-the-Draft Week was "The Siege of the Pentagon," on Saturday and Sunday, October 21-22. Here again, a classically nonviolent demonstration, numbering 50,000-100,000, had to share the stage with demonstrators who proclaimed their intention to use force, though the advocates of violence were in much smaller proportion to the rest than at Oakland. Most of the action during the day was nonviolent, but in the small hours of the night, soldiers and federal marshals beat many of the young demonstrators severely.[42]

544

Taken together, the Oakland and Pentagon riots indicate a change in focus on the part of radical opponents of the war. Until then most opponents of the war had tacitly accepted the legitimacy of American institutions by submitting voluntarily to the penalties for civil disobedience; now, however, many of the dedicated radical opponents of the war had denied legitimacy to the institutions as well as to the war, thus expressing their rejection of the notion that justice is to be found at the heart of the American system.[43]

This new tendency dominated the events of the next months, as the scene of violence shifted to the campus. Beginning with a riot which developed when police broke up a demonstration against Dow Chemical Co. at San Jose State College, in November 1967, violent confrontations between students and police occurred repeatedly, with recruitment by Dow Chemical, the CIA, and the Armed Forces triggering the action. Among the sharper struggles were those at the Universities of Wisconsin and Iowa, Cornell, Long Beach State College, and San Francisco State College, culminating in the Columbia riots of May 1968. Two points may be noted:

(1) The student protesters verbally expressed their determination to stop Dow et al. by any means necessary, thereby inviting the violence.

(2) In almost all cases the students committed violence against property, whereas the police beat up the (ineffectually) resisting students.[44] Certainly this new pattern obtained in the two major riots of 1968: the Columbia riots of May, where radical students, acting in cooperation with blacks, seized buildings and were violently dispossessed, and in the Chicago convention riots of August 1968. The last are particularly instructive as examples of the new pattern.

A handful of militant activists uttering vocal threats to "destroy the system" succeeded in provoking massive police attacks against an irresolute mass of young people who shared the militants' description of the illegitimacy of "the system," but were not seriously prepared to move beyond rhetorical dedication to revolutionary goals. Whether this state of affairs will long obtain is open to question, but at present there appears to be an enormous gap between the perception by tens of thousands of radical students that both the war and "the system" are illegitimate, and their readiness—however stridently proclaimed—to act in accordance with that perception. Their inability to act is not so much a matter of attitude as it is a matter of their lack of effective power. But this in turn rests on the present unwillingness of other millions of American college students (who agree with the radicals about the wrongness of the war, as shown by their support of Eugene McCarthy and other peace candidates) to act outside "the system" (and their support of McCarthy, who insisted he was trying to give them an alternative within it, shows this point, too).[45]

The present equilibrium is quite unstable. It is highly unlikely that large numbers of students can be persuaded to accept the legitimacy of the present war. Therefore, continuation of the status quo in Vietnam is likely to have the effect of persuading them to accept the radicals' proclaimed identity between the war and "the system." In such a case, violent repression like that which took place at Chicago will only increase their acceptance of the legitimacy of violent resistance—though the facts of power in America may limit such actions to one or another form of guerrilla tactics like those of Oakland's Friday, October 30, 1967, riots. On the other hand, rapid termination of the war in Vietnam—by negotiated peace and withdrawal—would serve effectively to isolate the radicals by apparently undermining the major premise of their argument that war and imperialism are necessary concomitants of "the system."

CONCLUSION

Violent conflict arising from opposition to the Vietnam war has followed a course quite different from that in earlier wars, the only possible exception being antiwar violence in the Confederacy. For the crucial fact seems to be that antiwar rioting shows no signs of diminishing. In attempting to explain this fact, the study of the past is of some help, if only to point up contrasts. Other wars have been unpopular, at least in some sections—the War of 1812, the Mexican War, and the Spanish-American War—without evoking significant violence. But each of these was relatively short. Furthermore, in each there were effective channels for opposition short of violent protest; today opponents can demonstrate peacefully, but such demonstrations seem to make little inroads upon an unresponsive political structure (the failure of the peace candidacies of McCarthy and Kennedy, which had promised to open such channels, will undoubtedly heighten the sense of frustration which is one component of violent protest). Unresolved minority tensions, like those of the Civil War, undoubtedly heighten the intensity of domestic conflict. Apart from the War of 1812 and the Korean war (and of course the Confederacy), American arms have won decisive victories, and both of these conflicts came to a halt much more rapidly than the present conflict. Other wars have had prestigious people in opposition, or have been opposed by dedicated and well-organized radicals, or by a large part of a social group (workers in World War I), or by significant ethnic or sectional minorities—the Vietnam conflict has all of these in tandem.

But there is much that is without historical parallel. In no previous American war have youth and students been significantly in opposition; previously they were a major source of patriotic sentiments. And with the single exception of the losing effort of the Confederate South, in no previous war have its opponents been able to see their case gaining increasing popular support. Nor is there any example of such widespread opposition to an American war coming from the academic and literary community.

For a conclusion we might look to St. Thomas Aquinas. He defined a just war as one meeting three qualifications: the ruler must be legitimate; the cause must be just; and the means employed must be proportionate to the ends in view. Apart from civil wars, there has seldom been any question about the legitimacy of American Government. Every American war has produced a few opponents who thought the cause unjust, but (perhaps duration is of siggificance in this equation) these have been relegated to one section or ethnic group without greatly changing the attitudes of large patriotic majorities—again the civil wars are an important exception. Proportionality of means to ends first became a question at the beginning of the century, when Mark Twain and other intellectuals denounced the torture of prisoners in the Philippines. But atrocity stories only heightened American patriotism during World War I, World War II, and the Korean war, because Americans or neutrals were the victims of enemy barbarities. Violent opposition to the Vietnam war seems to have begun with the question of proportionality—the questions of napalm, defoliation, saturation bombing, etc.—and to have escalated to the point where a large minority of the American people question the justice of this war, and some begin to question the very legitimacy of "the system" that, in the minds of radical opponents of the war, has produced these effects.

History teaches, when it does, by analogy. That is, we look for similarities in the causal sequence of events which produce like effects. So Americans facing mounting civil disorder and riots during a period of war, arising out of opposition to that war, seek to understand this phenomenon by searching through our past wartime experience. Unfortunately, the past does not have much to tell us; we will have to make our own history along uncharted and frightening ways.

References

1. J. Thomas Scharf and Thomas Westcott, *History of Philadelphia 1609-1884* (3 vols., *Philadelphia: L. H. Everts & Co.,* 1884) I, p. 401.
2. *Ibid.*
3. *Ibid.,* pp. 401-403. A few weeks later a mob of sailors, complaining of low pay, rioted in Philadelphia, *ibid.,* p. 403. Jesse Lemisch, "Jack Tar in the Streets: Merchant Seaman in Revolutionary America," *William & Mary Quarterly,* 3d ser., vol. XXV (July 1968), pp. 371-407, lists many sailors' riots, but the only one which was an antiwar riot during wartime was a 3 day anti-impressment riot in Boston, Nov. 17, 1747, during King George's War (p. 391).
4. *Journal of the Provincial Congress* . . . (2 vols., Albany: T. Weed. 1842), vol. II, pp. 309-311: *Minutes of the Committee* . . . *for Detecting Conspiracies* . . . (2 vols., New York: New York Historical Society 1924-25), II, pp. 442-443. In the 1776 action the revolutionary authorities described the rioters as Tories. See also Richard M. Brown, "Historical Patterns of Violence in America," elsewhere in this volume.
5. J. Thomas Scharf, *History of Maryland From the Earliest Times to the Present Day* (3 vols., Hatboro, Pa.: Tradition Press, 1967; reprint of 1879 ed.), vol. III, pp. 3-25. See also Henry Adams, *History of the United States during the First Administration of James Madison* (New York: C. Scribner's Sons, 1890), vol. II, pp. 405-408 (vol. VI of Adams' great *History* of the period 1800-17), says the "well-organized" mob consisted mainly of "low Irish and Germans."
6. Adams, *History,* vol. II, p. 400.
7. Brown, *The Republic in Peril: 1812* (New York: Columbia University Press, 1964), pp. 181-183.
8. Sellers, personal conversation, Sept. 30, 1968. Professor Sellers is presently completing his study of the Polk administration.
9. Scharf, *History of Maryland,* vol. II, pp. 403-413.
10. Charles L. Wagandt, *The Mighty Revolution: Negro Emancipation in Maryland, 1862-1864* (Baltimore: Johns Hopkins Press, 1964), p. 28.
11. Georgia Lee Tatum, *Disloyalty in the Confederacy* (Chapel Hill: The University of North Carolina Press, 1934), pp. 115, 122, 132-133, citing H. G. De Roulhac Hamilton.
12. *Ibid.,* p. 46.
13. *Ibid.,* p. 58.
14. Frank L. Klement, *The Copperheads in the Middle West* (Chicago: University of Chicago Press, 1960), pp. 26-27, 78-80. See also Ella Lonn, *Desertion During the Civil War* (Gloucester, Mass.: Peter Smith, 1966, reprint of the 1928 ed.), p. 204; and George Fort Milton, *Abraham Lincoln*

and the Fifth Column (New York: Collier Books, 1962; paperback reprint of 1942 edition), pp. 72-73, 116.

15. James McCague, *The Second Rebellion: the Story of the New York City Draft Riots of 1863* (New York: Dial Press, 1968), pp. 177-179 and *passim*.

16. Milton, *Lincoln and the Fifth Column*, pp. 109-111; John Niven, *Connecticut for the Union: the Role of the State in the Civil War* (New Haven: Yale University Press, 1965), p. 90.

17. Klement, *Copperheads*, pp. 92, 98. Klement argues that the peace movement was in no way related to any organized pro-Southern scheme; Northern Republican soldier-politicians foisted that canard on the public and on history.

18. Niven, *Connecticut*, pp. 300-302.

19. Klement, *Copperheads*, pp. 88, 320; Niven, *Connecticut*, p. 302.

20. David Donald, "Died for Democracy," in Donald, ed., *Why the North Won the Civil War* (New York: Collier Seeks, paperback 1965; reprint of 1960 ed.), pp. 87-90.

21. Robert L. Beisner, *Twelve Against Empire: the Anti-Imperialists, 1898-1900* (New York: McGraw-Hill, 1968), 10-12 and *passim*. I have not discovered any antiwar riots arising from opposition to the longer and more severe war of "pacification" of the Philippines, 1899-1902.

22. Peterson and Fite, *Opponents of War, 1917-1918* (Madison, Wis.: University of Wisconsin Press, 1957), pp. 30-31.

23. *Ibid.*, pp. 40-41.

24. *Ibid.*, pp. 45-46. James Weinstein, *The Decline of Socialism in America, 1912-1925* (New York: Monthly Review Press, 1967), pp. 139-141, list other cases of mob violence against Socialists.

25. Peterson and Fite, *Opponents of War*, pp. 202-204. The Washington *Post* commented: "In spite of excesses such as lynching, it is a healthful and wholesome awakening. . . ."

26. *Ibid.*, p. 199.

27. *Ibid.*, pp. 197-198.

28. *Ibid.*, pp. 74-79; Weinstein, *Decline of Socialism*, p. 145, identifies Bigelow as a Socialist.

29. Peterson and Fite, *Opponents of War*, p. 28.

30. *Ibid.*, p. 32.

31. *Ibid.*, pp. 48-60.

32. *Ibid.*, pp. 211-230.

33. *Ibid.*, pp. 41-42.

34. Richard Polenberg, ed., *Americans At War: the Home Front, 1941-1945* (Englewood Cliffs, N.J.: Prentice-Hall, 1968), pp. 94-95, citing Thomas' article in *Common Sense*, vol. XII (May 1943), pp. 156-159.

35. Polenberg, *Americans At War*, pp. 92-94, citing Baldwin, "Freedom in Wartime," *Report of the American Civil Liberties Union* (June 1943), pp. 3-6.

36. Polenberg, *Americans At War*, p. 102, citing Warren's testimony before the House of Representatives, *National Defense Migration Hearings* (Washington, 1942), vol. XXIX, pp. 11010-11019.

37. *New York Times*, Aug. 3, 1950, p. 1. There is no secondary account of this period that treats this issue.

38. *Ibid.*, Aug. 1, 1950, p. 13; Sept. 15, 1950, p. 18.

39. *Ibid.*, July 12, 1950, p. 16; July 13, 1950, p. 22.

40. Two incidents will help to illustrate the temper of the times. Four men and one woman drew 6-month and 1-year jail sentences for having painted the words "Peace" and "No H-Bomb" on a Brooklyn park entrance—before the outbreak of the Korean war. The judge accused them of stabbing our men fighting in Korea in the back. (*New York Times*, Aug. 2, 1950, p. 6). The Social Science Research Council accepted a $100,000 grant from the Markle Foundation to devise a test for detecting traitors (New *York Times*, Nov. 19, 1951, p. 25).

41. The riots growing out of our involvement in Vietnam are so much a part of our time (and more fully cataloged in other studies) that I have not documented them separately. The *New York Times Index* is the best guide. I have also used clippings from the San Francisco *Chronicle*. Radical and underground papers like the *Guardian* (formerly the *National Guardian*), the Berkeley *Barb*, the *Mid-Peninsula Observer*, and the Los Angeles *Free-Press*, as well as journals like *Ramparts* and *Liberation*, give the demonstrators' view of events—some of which I observed at firsthand.

42. Norman Mailer, *The Armies of the Night* (New York: New American Library, 1968), Irving L. Horowitz, "The Struggle Is the Message: An Analysis of Tactics, Trends, and Tensions in the Antiwar Movement" (unpublished MS, 1968), p. 42, notes that "the level of violence is greatest on the West Coast and in the Berkeley-Oakland-San Francisco area."
43. *Ibid.*, p. 10, Horowitz says: "The anti-war movement can be considered as an ideology in search of a tactic." I think Horowitz exaggerates the role of ideology in the antiwar movement, while underestimating its nihilism, personified by some of the culture heroes of the New Left: Bob Dylan, the Doors, Arthur Brown, and the Rolling Stones—note the Stones' recent hit, "Street-Fighting Man."
44. Compare Horowitz, p. 43.
45. *Ibid.*, pp. 35-36. By "the system," antiwar radicals denote the interrelated complex of political, economic, social and cultural institutions of the United States and the ideology which supports them. (Daniel Walker) *Rights in Conflict* (New York: Bantam Books, 1968).

Chapter 16

INTERNATIONAL WAR AND DOMESTIC TURMOIL: SOME CONTEMPORARY EVIDENCE

By Raymond Tanter*

Consider a typical issue of a U.S. newspaper; it may carry news on such events as the Vietnam war, demonstrations on university campuses, urban riots, labor strikes, and violent crime. Is the United States on the offensive abroad and on the retreat in the face of the young, the black, the poor, and the criminal at home?[1]

The media carries the message of the violent ones. "Draft Beer, Not Boys," "Hell no, we won't go," and "Burn, Baby, Burn!" echo in the streets and are faithfully recorded by the press. But coexisting with these expressions of dissent, and similarly recorded, are shouts like "Commie-Fink" and demands for "Law and Order" to get rid of "Crime in the Streets."

Most Americans assume, from the militant protests and backlashes by the "forgotten Americans," that turmoil of various kinds is on the increase at home as well as abroad. What are the connections between the intensity of the Viet-

* Raymond Tanter is associate professor of political science at the University of Michigan and author of many articles on internal and foreign conflict. In 1967, he was the Deputy Director for Behavioral Sciences of the Advanced Research Projects Agency, Department of Defense.

nam war and the level of turmoil in America? Do they rise and fall together over time? What does the theoretical literature suggest regarding international war and domestic turmoil in general?

THEORY AND PRIOR ANALYSIS

Scholars such as Georg Simmel and Lewis Coser have theorized about conflict within and between groups in general:

(1) The unity of a group is frequently lost when it does not have an opponent.[2]

(2) Hostilities help maintain group boundaries and are frequently consciously cultivated to guarantee existing conditions.[3]

(3) If a group with a basic consensus regarding its preservation engages in outside conflict, internal cohesion is likely to increase.[4]

(4) Groups may look for enemies to help maintain and/or increase internal cohesion.[5]

(5) Exaggeration of the danger of an enemy serves to maintain group structure when it is threatened by internal dissension.[6]

These propositions from Simmel and Coser suggest that international war may offer alternatives to domestic turmoil; they do *not* seem to anticipate a situation in which international war may provoke domestic turmoil. Proposition (3) above is a partial exception in its suggestion that a basic consensus is an intervening variable; that is, if a group without a basic consensus regarding its preservation engages in outside conflict, internal turmoil may follow. Simmel and Coser, however, do not deal directly with international war.

A growing number of students of international politics do focus on the relations between foreign and domestic conflict behavior. Quincy Wright is one of them, and seems to agree with Simmel and Coser when he suggests:

By creating and perpetuating in the community both a fear of invasion and a hope of expansion, obedience to a ruler may be guaranteed.[7]

Rulers have forestalled internal sedition by starting external wars.[8]

In the later stages of the Napoleonic Wars, Napoleon began to appreciate the value of war as an instrument of internal solidarity.[9]

In addition to Wright, Richard Rosecrance asserts that over time there is a tendency for international instability to be associated with the domestic insecurity of elites.[10] Moreover, Ernst Haas and Allen Whiting suggest an explanation of this relationship. They contend that the elites become fearful of losing their domestic positions during periods of rapid industrialization and widespread social change; they then try to displace the attention of the disaffected population onto some outside target. The authors suggest, however, that this form of self-preservation rarely leads to war.[11]

Rosecrance's finding of a correlation between international instability and domestic insecurity of elites contrasts with evidence reported by Samuel Huntington, who concludes that a decrease in the frequency of interstate conflict is likely to lead to an increase in the level of domestic violence.[12] Both Rosecrance and Huntington, however, have the international system as their unit of analysis rather than the individual nation.

A study using the nation as a unit of analysis identified a small negative relationship between internal subversion and foreign conflict behavior among 77 nations during 1955-57. That is, nations with high levels of subversion tend to avoid issuing threats to other nations and have relatively few antiforeign demonstrations.[13] Rudolph Rummel also found a consistently positive, though low, relationship between measures of turmoil (riots, demonstrations) and such foreign conflict variables as threats, accusations, protests, and antiforeign demonstrations in a country.[14] In a replication of the Rummel study for later years, the author of this paper also found a small positive relationship between indicators of turmoil and measures of diplomatic conflict activity. For example, the number of riots and the frequency of troop movements within a country were positively associated ($r = 0.40$) among 82 nations during 1958-60. In general, though, both the Rummel and the author's studies showed only slight positive relationships between foreign and domestic conflict behavior, which increased with a timelag between the two.[15]

A longitudinal study by Pitirim Sorokin inspired the

Rummel-Tanter cross-national efforts. He visually examined data for a number of nations across 14 centuries, A.D. 525 to 1925, and found a small positive association between unsuccessful external wars and later internal disturbances. Sorokin concludes, however, that international war and domestic disturbances are independent of one another.[16]

In summary, the theorists generally agree that there should be an inverse relationship between internal and external conflict behavior. Some cross-national studies find a negative relationship between subversion and foreign conflict behavior and a positive relationship between turmoil and diplomatic conflict. Moreover, a longitudinal study concludes that unsuccessful wars tend to be followed by revolutionary disturbances. This type of longitudinal study has implications for the present study of the Vietnam war and turmoil in the United States. If Sorokin's findings are generalized to the United States, one would expect that the longer the Vietnam war lasts without apparent success, the greater would be the level of domestic turmoil. Now let us turn to Vietnam and American turmoil.

THE VIETNAM WAR AND U.S. TURMOIL

In March 1965 the United States made an extensive commitment of forces to South Vietnam. One indicator of escalation is the rate of change in U.S. troop strength in Vietnam. Although U.S. casualties increased from 1965 to 1968 at approximately the same rate, the increases were of different magnitudes. For this reason, and because disorder seems most likely to have fluctuated with the troop buildup, the troop strength data are used as the indicator of escalation.[17]

Indicators of domestic turmoil fall into two categories. Most important for this paper is the Movement in both its antiwar and civil-rights phases. A secondary set is labor and criminal activity. Most of the subsequent discussion focuses on a comparison of the Movement with the war. Primary turmoil indicators are the frequencies, rates of change, and populations participating in antiwar protests; levels of urban riots; and participation in civil-rights demonstrations. Secondary indicators are the number of labor strikes and levels of violent crime.[18]

The tentative hypotheses are as follows:

(1) As U.S. troop commitments to Vietnam increase, domestic turmoil increases.

(2) The longer the period of time in which the United States is engaged in Vietnam, the higher the frequency of domestic turmoil, or, alternatively, the fewer the total incidents of domestic turmoil, but the more intensive are individual incidents.

Table 16-1 lists annual totals of U.S. force levels in Vietnam and domestic turmoil indicators. The secondary measures of labor and criminal activity are important because of their coverage of a long period, which enables a comparison of their trends before and during U.S. involvement in Vietnam. For example, strikes for 1961-68 and violent crime for 1961-67 show trends in those incidents before, as well as during, the Vietnam war. The percentage increase in strikes from 1964 to 1965 is 7.6 percent; for 1965 to 1966 it is 11.9 percent; and for 1966 to 1967 it is 2 percent. Comparable increases for violent crimes are 6 percent, 11 percent, and 16 percent. While the incidence of crimes is increasing, the aggregate changes are not very dramatic. The talk about crime rates in the context of a bipartisan law-and-order political campaign in 1968 implied that even sharper increases had occurred.

A second set of observations about the turmoil indicators is that they all are seasonal within years, and they appear to be unrelated to Vietnam commitments. Figures 16-1 to 16-7 chart the indicators for the war and for turmoil over time. Figure 16-1 is the plot of the cumulative total of U.S. Department of Defense (DOD) forces in South Vietnam. Figure 16-2 juxtaposes the antiwar protests and the urban riot indicators. Figure 16-3 shows the rate of change in the frequency of antiwar protests. Figure 16-4 is the number of participants in antiwar protests, figure 16-5 the number of participants in civil-rights demonstrations. Figures 16-6 and 16-7 are the frequencies of labor strikes and violent crimes, respectively.

Note that the curve for the war (16-1) looks much different from the other curves. Specifically, the seasonal fluctuations of the domestic turmoil indicators contrast sharply with the smooth increase and then decrease of the rate of U.S. buildup in Vietnam. Let us examine specific indicators. A glance at figure 16-2 illustrates that the fre-

Table 16-1 Annual totals of indicators of U.S. domestic turmoil and Vietnam troop commitments, January 1961–July 1968

Indicator	1961	1962	1963	1964	1965	1966	1967	1968
Indicator of troop commitment:								
U.S. DOD strength in Vietnam (000)[a]			15	23	184	385	486	537
Indicators of domestic turmoil:								
Antiwar protests:								
Antiwar protests[b]					57	53	58	17
Participants in antiwar protests (000)[c]					222	137	385	329
Urban riots/clashes[d]				16	23	53	82	65
Participants in civil rights demonstrations (000)[e]					117	51	37	42
Labor strikes (00)[a,f]	34	36	34	37	39	44	45	26
Violent crime (000)	1,926	2,048	2,259	2,604	2,780	3,243	3,802	h

See footnotes 17 and 18 for all data sources.

(a) Data recorded from Jan. 1, 1963, to July 31, 1968. Figures are for the end of the calendar years. Department of Defense (DOD) includes all U.S. forces assigned to Vietnam.

(b) Data recorded from Jan. 1965 to Sept. 1, 1968.

(c) Data recorded from Jan. 1965 to Sept. 1, 1963.

(d) Data recorded from Jan. 1965 to May 31, 1968.

(e) Data recorded from Jan. 1965 to May 31, 1968.

(f) Data for 1967 are preliminary.

(g) Data recorded to June 30, 1968; data for 1968 are preliminary.

(h) Data unavailable at this writing. The first quarter of 1968 shows a 17-percent increase over the same period of 1967.

quency of antiwar protests exhibits a seasonal fluctuation with the academic year. This probably reflects the fact that many of the participants are associated with the academic community, and may react more strongly to the requirements of the academic year than to the international conflict they oppose.

Consider the trends in the data over specific periods of time, rather than their monthly fluctuations. A relationship between antiwar protests and international conflict emerges. The heavy line in figure 16-3 is the slope or line of "best fit"[19] for the incidence of the antiwar protests for January 1965 to November 1965; it indicates the rate of change over time in the number of protests. This is the period during which the United States made its first large increase in troops, and this line is approximately the same as the line of best fit for increasing troop strength. But the absolute number of antiwar protests declines after November 1965. It appears, then, that antiwar protests were a response to a *change* in U.S. forces, rather than a response to their actual magnitude. The mean frequency of antiwar protests decreases from 4.56 per month during the entire escalation phase (approximately January 1965-January 1967) to 3.55 per month during the leveling-off phase (about February 1967-July 1968). (No significance tests are applied to these data.)

Jeffery Milstein and William Mitchell[20] observe a similar relationship between U.S. bombing and the rate of North Vietnamese infiltration.

. . . U.S. bombing of North Vietnam may physically decrease infiltration, but escalation of the bombing is matched by North Vietnamese escalation of troop commitments. Thus, the North Vietnamese appear to be reacting to proportional changes in U.S. bombing rather than to actual levels. . . . In fact, escalation of the bombing produces subsequent counterescalation, as predicted by the Richardson hypothesis. Once a high level of bombing is attained, however, Communist troop commitments are subsequently at a lower level.

Escalation of troop strength is one thing. What about the effect of the war's length on the magnitude of protests? Looking at the number of participants in antiwar protests (figure 16-4) over this same period of time, we find a different tendency. The rate of change (slope omitted) of the number of protest participants during the initial Viet-

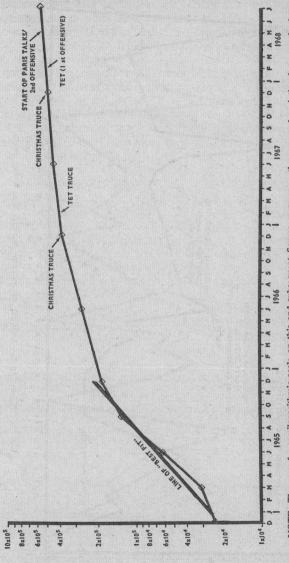

NOTE: The use of a semilogarithmic scale on this and subsequent figures compresses the range of variation between the lows and highs on the graph, as is apparent from an examination of the numbers on the vertical axis.

Figure 16-1.—Department of Defense strength in South Vietnam.

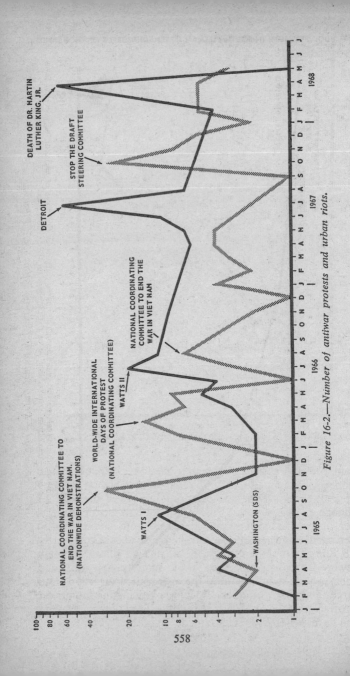

Figure 16-2.—Number of antiwar protests and urban riots.

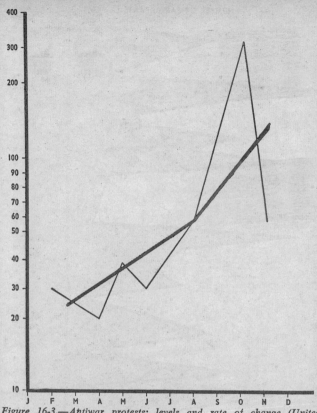

Figure 16-3.—*Ahtiwar protests: levels and rate of change (United States, 1965).*

nam escalation period appears negatively related to the slope of Vietnam escalation. That is, the higher the rate of change in Vietnam escalation, the lower the rate of change in protest participation. In addition, the mean number of protest participants increases from about 14,400 per month during the escalation phase to approximately 38,700 per month during the leveling-off phase. Though fewer demonstrations were held, more people attended them, which may be due to the aggregation of groups into larger units. The number of people participating in antiwar protests thus may be a response to the level of commitment, the duration of U.S. involvement, or both.

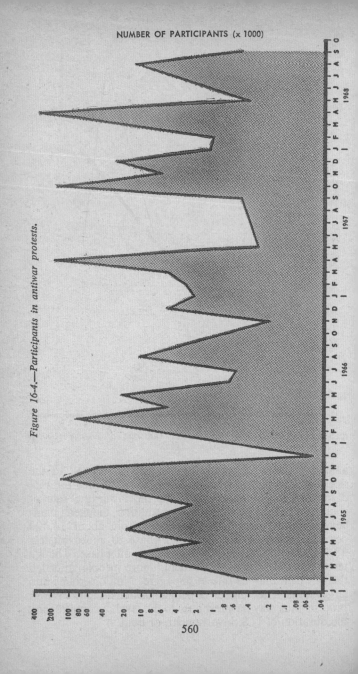

NUMBER OF PARTICIPANTS (x 1000)

Figure 16-4.—Participants in antiwar protests.

NUMBER OF PARTICIPANTS (x1000)

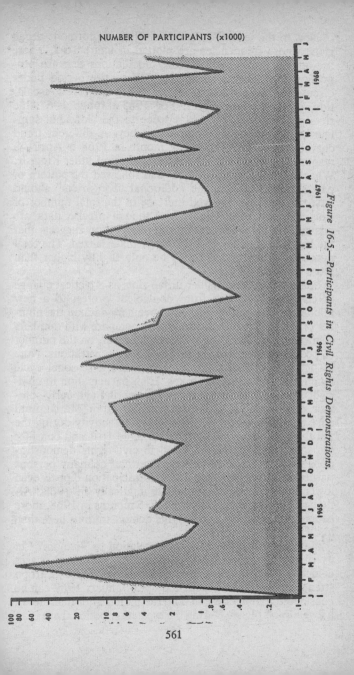

Figure 16-5.—Participants in Civil Rights Demonstrations.

561

Now to the second indicator of domestic turmoil: urban riots, whose frequencies are plotted in figure 16-2. There are annual cycles with monthly fluctuations that are proportionately constant throughout the entire period under discussion, independent of either U.S. force levels, escalation, or length of the war. For 1965 through 1967, the riots peak in July, giving credence to the "long hot summer" proposition of common currency. A different trend characterizes 1968. The peak month in 1968 is April—a response to the assassination of Dr. Martin Luther King, Jr. What if the frequency of riots had followed the pattern of past summers? Then, the additional "King riots" should have resulted in a marked increase in the total number of riots in 1968 over 1965-67. Although precise data are unavailable here, impressionistic observation suggests that the long hot summer of 1968 never materialized. The total number of riots in 1968 may be only slightly higher than those of previous years.

Some observers consider urban riots as a tactical change of civil-rights activity from nonviolent protest to a new militancy. The author does not have here data on the number of civil-rights demonstrations to compare with numbers of urban riots. Data are available, however, on the number of people participating in civil-rights demonstrations. Note in figure 16-5 that there appears to be a seasonal cycle much like that of labor strikes. High participation in civil-rights demonstrations seems to be a spring and early-summer phenomenon, with peak activity from March until June. For 1967, however, there is more activity during the fall than the spring. Refer back to table 16-1 and consider the sharp drop in participation in civil-rights demonstrations from 1965 to 1966. Less than half as many persons participated in 1966 as in 1965. Participation dipped even lower in 1967, but increased dramatically in 1968. Although the data cover only the first 5 months in 1968, more people participated in civil-rights demonstrations here than in all of 1967.

Now what about civil rights in relation to Vietnam? Let us divide the civil-rights participation into two phases coincident with the escalation and leveling off of U.S. troop strength in Vietnam. The period up to January 1967 can be considered a time of escalation, the period after that month a leveling-off phase. During the escalation period there is an average of about 6,700 participants in civil-rights demonstrations monthly, contrasting to the mean of perhaps 5,000 per month in the leveling-off phase, a decrease of 26 percent. The levels of participation may be related to the escalation but not to the absolute level of troop strength, similar to our interpretation of the evidence concerning Vietnam escalation and the antiwar protests.

We observed that the level of antiwar protests decreases slightly from an average of about four to three per month from the escalation to levelling off in Vietnam. The average number of people protesting the war, however, increases from approximately 14,400 to 38,700 per month. One interpretation of the slight decrease in the average number of war protests is that the groups began to merge into larger, more sophisticated combinations. But does this account for the increase in protesters? Assuming that the universe of white activists is fairly constant, from where do the extra protesters come? Perhaps some shifted away from civil-rights activity as integration gave way to Black Power as a dominant theme. The ex-rights activists became available for the war protests in a kind of "Movement Migration." A slight radicalization of the black bourgeoisie, moreover, might account for the increased number of participants in civil-rights activity in 1968 despite the loss of some of their "blue-eyed soul brothers."

Figures 16-6 and 16-7 chart the frequencies of labor strikes and violent crimes over time. As with the primary indicators, there is definite annual periodicity. At no point do any events connected with either escalation or absolute level of U.S. forces in Vietnam seem to compare with the fairly stable annual strike cycles. The shape of the curve appears determined by the dates on which union contracts expire. Like the frequency of violent crimes, labor strikes maintain approximately the same annual cycle throughout the period of U.S. involvement in Vietnam, though in fact the absolute number of strikes increases slightly over time. When the number of participants involved in labor strikes is plotted, the curve is similar though not as smooth as the curve for the number of strikes. The number of participants increases slightly over time, as does the number of strikes, but the same annual cycle repeats itself regardless of U.S. force levels in Vietnam in any particular year. (The plot of participation in labor strikes is not presented here.)

NUMBER OF LABOR STRIKES IN EFFECT

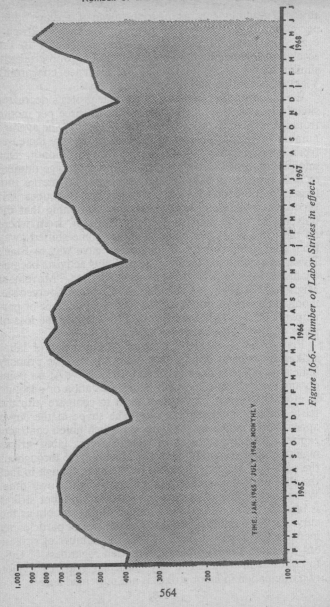

Figure 16-6.—Number of Labor Strikes in effect.

564

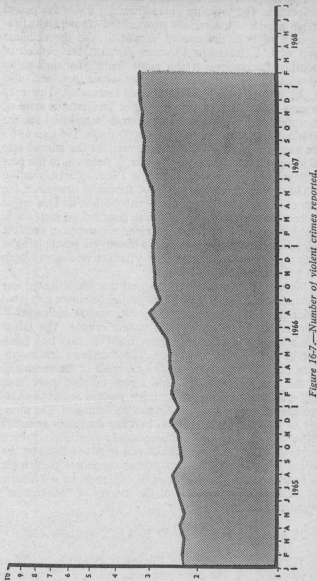

Figure 16-7.—Number of violent crimes reported.

The frequency of violent crimes also exhibits annual periodicity. The monthly fluctuations for the entire period under consideration remain proportionately constant irrespective of both the rate of escalation and the absolute level of U.S. forces in Vietnam. Though the pattern of monthly fluctuations is the same, each year brings an increase in the number of crimes committed and also in the rate at which the number is increasing. This may suggest that as the war continues, it facilitates a state of "normlessness" in which traditional strictures against criminal acts lose their effectiveness. From 1961 to 1963 the absolute number of crimes as well as the annual rate of increase rose. There is, however, a decrease in the percentage increase between 1964 and 1965. Initial escalation of U.S. forces in Vietnam did not appear to strengthen the rate of increase in crimes, nor even maintain it. This might be because the escalation of forces required an increase in the draft call and therefore removed a number of possible offenders from the population without yet resupplying it with a proportionate amount of Vietnam veterans to keep the population stable.

Figures 16-1 to 16-7 thus suggest that the Vietnam war escalation and the length of U.S. participation are unrelated generally to the secondary domestic turmoil indicators—numbers of labor strikes and violent crimes. The initial rate of change in antiwar protests, however, may be a function of the Vietnam escalation. The change in demonstrations declines, moreover, with a decrease in the escalation of the war, although the U.S. forces number more than half a million. A somewhat similar pattern seems to characterize urban riots and civil-rights participation. The number of participants in antiwar protests fluctuates annually enough to say that any increase would probably not be a response to any "atmosphere of violence" sustained by the length of the war. The fact that more people participate in fewer activities perhaps can be explained by a dynamic of social movements, that of the merger of "Movement" organizations.

QUALIFICATIONS AND POLICY RELEVANCE

The tentative findings of this study should be qualified in several ways. The correspondence between the concepts and their measures may not be exact. For example, the indicators of the war and turmoil levels may not be adequate to the task. Justifications for using these indicators include their high correlation with other measures and their prior use in earlier systematic studies. U.S. casualties might have been used as an indicator of escalation rather than forces sent to Vietnam, but because these two variables are closely correlated, they can be used interchangeably. The indicators used for turmoil are justified by the results of a series of systematic studies. There is considerable evidence regarding the defining characteristics of turmoil. Factor analysis, a data-reduction method, yields a "turmoil" factor across several studies, consisting of demonstrations, riots, and general strikes. Although these studies are cross-national, the longitudinal results are not likely to differ substantially because different cross sections yield a similar turmoil factor.[21]

Another basis for qualifying the tentative findings is the reliability of the data. The accuracy required of data depends upon a study's purposes. Because this study focuses on the extent to which escalation and the length of the war relate to indicators of turmoil over time, a fairly high degree of error can be tolerated: the relative magnitude of each series is more important than their absolute levels. A more serious problem arises if there is a systematic bias introduced as a consequence of changing definitions and/or means of acquiring information, which may be the case with the violent crime statistics. Even here, however, error would have to be extremely large each month, and in the same direction, for the author to have accepted the violent crime data as having confirmed his initial hypotheses.

A third basis of qualification is the level of aggregation of data. For example, as regards crime information, it may be necessary to separate urban versus rural violent crimes and to plot urban crimes separately. An assumption of this study, however, is that this need not be done because most violent crime does in fact occur in urban areas.

The following statement of policy relevance of the tentative findings is suggestive rather than definitive. The initial escalation of the Vietnam war may be a primary cause of breakdown in social order. Rates of increase in several important indicators of domestic turmoil are related to the escalation of the war. Based on past patterns, a policy of further escalation abroad by the new administration in Washington may result in an increase in the turmoil at home. Furthermore, correctives to turmoil should take into account the relative decline in the rates of increase in turmoil that parallel the slowdown in the Vietnam buildup.

References

1. Acknowledgments are made to Patricia Kwik for assistance in data acquisition, analysis, and interpretation; to Ted Robert Gurr, Irving L. Horowitz, Bryan T. Downs, and Stephen W. Burks for the use of their data; and to the National Science Foundation for a grant to the Comparative International Processes project.
2. Georg Simmel, *Conflict and the Web of Intergroup Affiliations* (Glencoe, Ill.: The Free Press, 1955), p. 97.
3. *Ibid.*, p. 97.
4. Lewis A. Coser, *The Functions of Social Conflict* (Glencoe, Ill.: The Free Press, 1957), pp. 92-93.
5. *Ibid.*, p. 104.
6. *Ibid.*, p. 106.
7. Quincy Wright, *A Study of War, II* (Chicago: University of Chicago Press, 1942), p. 1016.
8. Wright, *I*, p. 140.
9. Wright, *II*, p. 725.
10. Richard N. Rosecrance, *Action and Reaction in World Politics* (Boston: Little, Brown, 1963), p. 304.
11. Ernst R. Haas and A. S. Whiting, *Dynamics of International Relations* (New York: McGraw-Hill, 1956), pp. 61-62.
12. Samuel P. Huntington, "Patterns of Violence in World Politics," in S. P. Huntington (ed.), *Changing Patterns of Military Politics* (New York: The Free Press, 1962), pp. 40-41.
13. Rudolph J. Rummel, "Testing Some Possible Predictors of Conflict Behavior Within and Between Nations" in *Peace Research Society (International) Papers,* III, 1964, p. 17.
14. Raymond Tanter, "Dimensions of Conflict Behavior Within and Between Nations, 1958-1960," *Journal of Conflict Resolution,* X (March 1966), pp. 41-64, 46.
15. Tanter, pp. 61-62.
16. Pitirim Sorokin, *Social and Cultural Dynamics, III* (New York: American Book Co., 1937), pp. 487, 492.
17. Department of Defense Strength: 1965-1966, from John Voevodsky, *Quantitative Behavior of Warring Nations,* Mar. 27, 1968, mimeo; 1967-1968, Department of Defense, Unclassified Statistics on Vietnam, table 6. Department of Defense strength is the total number of U.S. military (Army, Navy, USMC, USAF, USCG) personnel in South Vietnam. All data are for the end of the period.
18. Data sources:
    (a) Antiwar protests: Computed from a list of all protests with a stated antiwar purpose in Irving L. Horowitz, Washington University, "The Struggle Is the Message: Tactics, Trends, and Tensions in the Anti-War Movement." Position paper prepared for the National Commission on the Causes and Prevention of Violence. Third draft: Sept. 23, 1968, mimeo.
    (b) Urban riots: Bryan T. Downs with Stephen W. Burks, "The Black Protest Movement and Urban Violence," paper read at the annual meeting of the American Political Science Association, Washington, D.C., Sept. 1968, mimeo.
    (c) Labor strikes: Computed from Department of Labor "Table E-1. Work Stoppages Resulting From Labor-Management Disputes," *Monthly Labor Review,* September 1968.
    (d) Violent crime: Computed from Federal Bureau of Investigation, U.S. Department of Justice, *Crime in the United States—Uniform Crime Reports* (1961-68).

    (e) Civil-rights demonstrations: Ted Robert Gurr, "Civil Rights and School Integration Demonstrations," June 1963 to May 1968, unpublished list.

19. Briefly, the line of "best fit" is drawn through the mean of the observations so as to minimize the sum of the distances from any point to the line.

20. Jeffery Milstein and William Mitchell, "The Dynamics of the Vietnam Conflict: A Quantitative Analysis and Predictive Computer Simulation," paper prepared for delivery to the Peace Research Society (International) Conference to study the Vietnamese war, June 3-4, 1968, Cambridge, Mass.

21. Raymond Tanter, "Dimensions of Conflict Behavior Within Nations, 1955-60: Turmoil and Internal War," *Peace Research Society (International) Papers*, III (1965), p. 174.

PART VII

COMPARATIVE PATTERNS OF STRIFE AND VIOLENCE

A historian who contributed to this volume remarked, before editorial consultation, that it was difficult, perhaps impossible, to judge the relative levels of violence among nations. The chapters of this and the next part demonstrate that some instructive comparisons can be made. One kind of comparison, exemplified in the following two chapters, abstracts some general qualities or quantities from many occurrences of group violence in order to make general statements about all such cases. Such comparisons have two purposes: to describe, and to explain.

Such descriptions and explanations can provide answers, partial ones at least, to some worrisome questions Americans pose to one another. Is the United States truly a "violent society" by comparison with other nations? The first of the following studies by Ted Robert Gurr, shows collective protest and violence in the United States in the mid-1960's to be greater, in relative terms, than in most of the European democracies but much less than in many other of the 114 nations studied. Moreover, civil strife in the United States shares the general characteristics of strife in other modern, democratic, and Western nations, but is strikingly dissimilar from strife in other groups of nations. Even the ethnic character of much American protest and group violence is paralleled by the experience of other Western nations. The unsatisfied demands of ethnic, regional, and other communal minorities are chronic sources of turmoil in many other Western nations, and relatively more common in Western nations than in most non-Western nations. Most of the results of this comparative study are reported here for the first time.

Is there some unique seed of evil at the heart of the American social order that nonetheless makes the tumult of recent years inexplicable in general terms? Both of these studies measure some general "causes" of strife and violence and determine their importance by comparing them statistically with measures of the extent of violence. Neither of them suggests that American violence is incomprehensible. Rather the evidence is that the same kinds of things have gone wrong in the United States that have gone wrong in many other nations, Western and non-Western, with predictable kinds of consequences. Americans may be unique in their wealth and uncommon in their immigrant heritage, but they are scarcely uncommon in their ability to mismanage their social affairs.

For example, Ivo and Rosalind Feierabend and Betty Nesvold inquire into the general connections between social change and political violence. Almost every desirable facet of our material and social lives are the products of massive and ongoing socioeconomic change. But anguish and violence as well as progress have been among the consequences of change in Western and non-Western societies —violence by those whose stable circumstances of life were disrupted, violence by those whose hopes for personal achievement were disenchanted. The authors identify patterns of change that are usually peaceful, others that are likely to generate the systemic frustrations that dispose men to violent political action. They then examine some types of change in 84 nations over a 30-year period and ask how they are related to violence in those nations, and to many of the nations' other characteristics. Political violence is least in traditional and modern societies, greatest in societies in the process of more or less rapid social change that we call "modernization." The evidence is that the more rapid are economic, social, and political change, the greater is political unrest—but with significant qualifications and exceptions. Among modernizing societies, for example, political instability is highest where education is rapidly expanding but economies are stagnant. The relations between change and disorder are complex, but their complexity is comprehensible and open to empirical examination. So far as the United States is concerned, it has the socioeconomic and political characteristics associated with civil peace in most other nations. But some specific groups are caught up in cycles of social change that resemble those of transitional societies both in their nature and in their violent consequences.

Does the United States have a potential for revolution commensurate with the fantasies of a few militants and the nightmares of some defenders of "law and order?" Quantitative assessment of some general causes of strife in the study by Professor Gurr demonstrates that the United States now has the general conditions associated with turmoil in other nations: intense, persisting discontents among some groups and a tumultuous history that provides justification enough for violent collective protest and violent defense. The comparisons also indicate that the nation has many of the social and political conditions that make revolutionary explosions of discontent unlikely in other countries. Yet all these conditions are subject to change. The direction and nature of their change will determine the future extent and forms of violence in America. But one principle seems evident from the comparative statistical evidence: whatever the historical, political, or social character of a nation, its citizens are likely to resort repeatedly to public protest and violence so long as they have severe and persisting grievances.

. Chapter 17

A COMPARATIVE STUDY OF CIVIL STRIFE[1]

*By Ted Robert Gurr**

Group protest and violence is episodic in the history of most organized political communities and chronic in many. No country in the modern world has been free of it for as much as a generation. Sorokin analyzed the histories of 11 European states and empires over a 25-century span and found that they averaged only four peaceful years for each year in which major outbreaks of civil strife were in progress.[2] A comparison of average levels of disturbance, from the 6th to the 19th century, indicates that the most violent century, the 13th, had only twice the level of violence of the 18th, the most peaceful century.[3]

* The author is assistant professor of politics and faculty associate of the Center of International Studies at Princeton University. His publications include *Why Men Rebel* (Princeton University Press, forthcoming); *The Conditions of Civil Violence: First Tests of a Causal Model*, with Charles Ruttenberg (Princeton: Center of International Studies, 1957); *American Welfare*, with Alfred de Grazia (New York University Press, 1961); and a number of articles.

Between 1900 and 1965, Calvert estimates that 367 revolutions occurred, defining revolution as forcible intervention to replace governments or change their processes. Of these, 135 occurred between 1946 and 1965, an average of 6.75 a year compared with an average of 5.56 a year for the entire 65-year period.[4] The Feierabends found that between 1948 and 1961, collective antigovernmental action occurred in all but one of 82 independent countries.[5] Between 1961 and 1967, some form of civil strife is reported to have occurred in 114 of the world's 121 larger nations and colonies.[6]

Relatively few occurrences of strife are "revolutionary." Most are manifestations of opposition to particular policies of governments or of hostilities between competing groups. Moreover, certain kinds and levels of civil strife are more likely to occur in some kinds of nations, and under some kinds of socioeconomic conditions, than under others. The kinds of systematic evidence mentioned above have been used not only to determine differences in the types and extent of civil strife among nations but to test various explanations of its causes. This paper summarizes some results of a comprehensive study of civil strife in 114 nations and colonies during the years from 1961 through 1965. This information is used in the first two sections, below, to make descriptive comparisons between characteristics of civil strife in the United States and other nations, and finally to estimate the relative importance of different causes of strife.

LEVELS AND TYPES OF CIVIL STRIFE AMONG CONTEMPORARY NATIONS

In this study, "civil strife" means all collective nongovernmental attacks on persons or property that occur within a political system, but not individual crimes. We included symbolic attacks on political persons or policies such as political demonstrations and political strikes. Their inclusion does not reflect a normative judgment about their desirability or their legality; demonstrative protests are legal under some conditions in some countries, illegal in many others. Whatever their legal status, they are essentially similar to violent forms of protest: they are collective manifestations of substantial discontent that typically occur outside institutional frameworks for action. The violence used by regimes to maintain social control is not included as an aspect of civil strife because we are concerned with the extent to which ordinary citizens, not officials, resort to force. Regime coercion and violence can be both a cause of and a response to civil strife, and for the purposes of this study is analyzed in those terms, not as an integral part of strife.

Three general kinds of civil strife were distinguished in the study, in addition to more specific kinds:

Turmoil.—Relatively spontaneous, unorganized strife with substantial popular participation, including political demonstrations and strikes, riots, political and ethnic clashes, and local rebellions.

Conspiracy.—Highly organized strife with limited participation, including organized political assassinations, small-scale terrorism, small-scale guerilla wars, coups d'état, mutinies, and antigovernment plots.

Internal war.—Highly organized strife with widespread popular participation, accompanied by extensive violence and including large-scale terrorism and guerilla wars; civil wars; "private" wars among ethnic, political, and religious groups; and large-scale revolts.

Information was collected on all such events reported in general news sources for 114 nations and colonies from 1961 through 1965. More than 1,000 events were identified, counting waves of demonstrations, riots, or terrorism over related issues as single "events." For each reported event or group of related events, we recorded such information as the kinds of socioeconomic groups involved, the approximate number of people who took part, their apparent motives or grievances, whom or what they attacked, how long they persisted, the severity of governmental response, and the costs of the action in terms of damage, casualties, and arrests.

Two kinds of comparisons of this information are reported here. The first, discussed in the following section, is based on summary measures of the magnitude of civil strife for each country. The "magnitude" of strife is a combined measure that takes into account its duration, pervasiveness, and a relative intensity. Additional data were collected for the United States, to update and increase the accuracy of some of the comparisons. Statistical comparisons in which the United States is shown separately are based on relatively precise American data for the 5-year period from June 1, 1963, through May 31, 1968, related to the 1961-65 data for other countries. Specific procedures used in collecting and summarizing the American and foreign data are described in appendix I, and the actual scores for 114 countries listed.

The second kind of comparison, discussed in the second section below, takes into account differences among groups of countries in the socioeconomic classes of people that typically initiate civil strife, their motives, their targets, and relative levels of violence. For this set of comparisons the countries of the world are divided into groups according to their economic, political, and regional characteristics. Appendix II describes the basis for each grouping and lists the groups in which each country was included.

Characteristics of American and Foreign Civil Strife

More than 2 million Americans resorted to demonstrations, riots, or terrorism to express their political demands and private antagonisms during the 5 years that ended in May 1968. No more than a fifth of them took part in activities prescribed by law, but their actions reportedly resulted in more than 9,000 casualties, including some 200 deaths, and more than 70,000 arrests. As table 17-1 shows, civil-rights demonstrations mobilized about 1.1 million Americans, antiwar demonstrations about 680,000, and ghetto riots an estimated 200,000. Riots were responsible for most of the consequent human suffering, including 191 deaths, all but a few of them Negroes. Almost all other deaths, an estimated 23, resulted from white terrorism against blacks and civil-rights workers. There is no direct way of determining whether these 5 years were the most tumultuous in American history. Some suggestive comparisons can be made with other nations in the contemporary era, however. Tables 17-2, 17-3, and 17-4 provide comparisons of some of the quantifiable information on strife in the United States against the characteristics of strife in other nations in the years 1961 through 1965.

The United States in the mid-1960's experienced relatively more civil strife than the majority of nations in the world, but far less than some. Compared with all other nations, it ranks 24th in total magnitude of strife. When the measures that make up the "magnitude" scores are

Table 17-1.—Characteristics of major types of civil strife in the United States, June 1963-May 1968[a]

Type of event	Number of events identified[b]	Estimated number of participants[c]	Reported number of casualties[d]	Reported arrests[e]	Total magnitude of events[f]
Civil rights demonstrations[g]	369	1,117,600	389	15,379	7.53
Antiwar demonstrations[h]	104	680,000	400	3,258	5.62
Student protests on campus issues[i]	91	102,035	122	1,914	4.02
Antischool integration demonstrations[j]	24	34,720	0	164	1.66
Segregationist clashes and counter-demonstrations[k]	54	31,200	163	643	3.24
Negro riots and disturbances[l]	239	(200,000)	8,133	49,607	8.30
White terrorism against Negroes and rights workers[m]	213	(2,000)	112	97	2.48
All turmoil[a]	.....	2,174,655	9,285	.....	13.40
All conspiracy[a]	.....	2,040	122	.....	3.00
All strife[a]	.....	2,176,695	9,407	.....	13.64

[a] The data in this table include many estimates; all are imprecise. A number of less extensive forms of strife are not specifically shown, among them interracial clashes not involving civil-rights activities; terrorism within the Black Muslim movement; organized black terrorism against whites (negligible in this period); the local rebellion of Mexican-Americans in New Mexico in June 1967; and labor violence. Data on these events are included in the summary measures of magnitudes of strife.

b As reported in news sources, with the inclusions and exclusions listed in footnotes (g) to (m). Demonstrations and riots that last for more than 1 day are counted as one. Simultaneous demonstrations in several neighborhoods or cities are counted separately.

c Despite the apparent precision of some of the figures, the component figures for many events are rough estimates and in some instances "guess-estimates" assigned by coders. Figures in parentheses are especially tentative.

d Including deaths and injuries. Riots reportedly resulted in the deaths of 191 persons; white terrorism in the deaths of 23. Injury reports are of questionable reliability, since there are no standard reporting practices for them. Minor injuries usually are unreported.

e People reported in news sources to have been detained. No totals are shown because of incomplete data on arrests for types of strife not separately listed.

f The magnitude scores are not additive. Scores should be expanded to their fifth power to determine the actual average of their component Pervasiveness, Intensity, and Duration scores. Procedures by which magnitude scores are derived are described in app. I.

g As reported in the New York Times Index, including civil rights and school integration demonstrations. Excluded are events involving less than 100 people, boycotts, and demonstrations that become riots or clashes with segregationists. Also see (i), below.

h Based on data reported by Irving Louis Horowitz, "The Struggle Is the Message," paper prepared for the Task Force on Group Protest and Violence, National Commission on the Causes and Prevention of Violence, Sept. 1968, tables 1, 2, and 3. The Horowitz data were revised to maintain comparability with other data by elimination of events involving less than 100 people and by exclusion of indoor rallies and protest meetings. Also see (i), below.

i Student demonstrations on issues other than civil rights and peace, as reported in the New York Times Index. Student civil-rights protests are included under civil-rights demonstrations; student antiwar protests are included under antiwar demonstrations.

j Demonstrations opposing busing, integration, and local control of schools by Negroes, as reported in the New York Times Index. Excluded are demonstrations involving less than 100 people; and boycotts, strikes, and walkouts.

k Demonstrations by white segregationists opposing civil-rights demonstrations and collective public attacks by segregationists on rights demonstrators, as reported in the New York Times Index. Excluded are events in which less than 100 white demonstrators or attackers were involved.

l "Hostile outbursts" initiated by blacks, as reported by Bryan T. Downes with Stephen W. Burke, "The Black Protest Movement and Urban Violence," paper read at the annual meeting of the American Political Science Association, Washington, D.C., Sept. 1968, pp. 12-15.

m Small-scale, clandestine acts of terror and violence, including bombings, arson, shootings, beatings, and major cross-burning incidents, as reported in the New York Times Index. Ordinarily no estimates of the number of participants are available.

Table 17-2.—Some general characteristics of strife in the United States, 1963-68, compared with strife in other nations, 1961-65

	United States[a]	Average for 17 democratic European nations[b]	Average for 113 polities[c]
Proportion of population that participated (pervasiveness).....................	1,116 per 100,000	676 per 100,000	683 per 100,000
Pervasiveness rank of the United States compared with..................	....	7	27
Casualties from strife as proportion of population (intensity).................	477 per 10,000,000	121 per 10,000,000	20,100 per 10,000,000
Intensity rank of the United States compared with........	....	3	53
Duration rank of the United States compared with[d]	....	1	6
Rank of total magnitude of strife in the United States compared with...................	....	1	24
Rank of magnitude of turmoil in the United States compared with...................	....	1	6
Rank of magnitude of conspiracy in the United States compared with...................	....	2	38

[a] The population estimate used for weighting participation and casualties from strife in the United States is 195 million. Information for the United States is more detailed than for other countries; as a consequence the U.S. data is somewhat inflated by comparison with the non-U.S. data.

[b] Nations used in this comparison are Australia, Austria, Belgium, Canada, Denmark, Finland, France, Greece, Ireland, Italy, Netherlands, New Zealand, Norway, Sweden, Switzerland, United Kingdom, and West Germany.

[c] All polities included in the study except the United States.

[d] Duration is the total number of days of all strife events in a country, not weighted by population, hence no comparative proportional measures are shown.

examined, the United States ranks 27th among nations in the pervasiveness of strife; about 11 out of 1,000 Americans took part in strife, compared with an average of 7 per 1,000 in all other countries. The relative intensity of strife in the United States has been considerably lower, its proportional casualties ranking 53d among 114 nations; its duration very high, ranking 6th among all nations. Most civil strife in the United States was turmoil, in magnitude of which the country ranks 6th among nations. The magnitude of conspiracy, which in the United States took the form of interracial terrorism, ranks 38th among all nations.

Nation	Pervasiveness (participants per 100,000)[a]	Duration (sum of all events)[b]	Intensity (casualties per 100,000)[c]	Total magnitude of strife[d]
Selected European and Latin nations:				
Sweden..........	0	0	0	0.0
U.S.S.R..........	10	3 months	.5	3.6
Canada..........	40	5 months	.5	4.9
Mexico..........	150	1 week	2	4.7
United Kingdom..	80	1 year	.5	5.4
Japan...........	300	2 months	1.0	5.9
Brazil...........	1,100	4 months	.5	7.4
Belgium..........	6,700	1 month'	6	10.5
France..........	2,200	2 years	4	12.1
United States.....	1,100	5 years	5	13.8
Venezuela........	1,300	5 years+	120	20.3
Other nations:				
Jamaica.........	20	1 day	0	1.5
U.A.R. (Egypt)...	70	1 month	.5	3.9
Malaya..........	650	1 day	.5	4.5
Pakistan.........	200	3 months	1.5	6.3
Ghana...........	550	1 month	8	7.9
South Africa......	600	2 years	3	10.0
Ecuador.........	1,100	3 months	12	10.1
India...........	1,600	4 years	1	11.0
Rhodesia.........	150	2 years	50	16.4
Algeria	900	4 years	150	19.5
Indonesia........	1,300	5 years	[e]4,000	33.7

[a] Total estimated participants in all strife events identified, weighted by population. All figures shown here are rounded to reflect their relative imprecision.
[b] Sum of the duration of all events identified, rounded to reflect the imprecision of the data.
[c] Sum of estimated deaths and injuries in all events identified, weighted by population, rounded to reflect the imprecision of the data.
[d] See footnote (f), table 17-1, and app. I.
[e] This figure is probably grossly inflated because it includes an unrealistic estimate of injuries associated with the massacre of several hundred thousand Indonesian Communists. (See app. I.)

The most meaningful standard of comparison is provided by the 17 other democratic nations of Western Europe and the British Commonwealth—the nations against which Americans typically judge their cultural, political, and economic progress. In magnitudes of all strife, and of turmoil, the United States ranks first among these nations, though only slightly ahead of France, Italy, and Belgium; Italy alone had a greater degree of conspiracy in this period. These overall rankings are made more meaningful when the component measures are examined. Strife was more pervasive in six of the European nations than in the United States and more intense in two. Only in the relative duration of strife does the United States markedly surpass all other Western nations.

Specific comparative information on characteristics of strife in 20 Western and non-Western nations is shown in table 17-3. It is apparent from these data, as it is from the listing of magnitude-of-strife scores in appendix II, that some countries in all regions of the world, at all levels of economic development, have had less domestic conflict than the United States. With few exceptions, the countries more strife torn than the United States have experienced internal wars, like Venezuela, Algeria, and Indonesia.

Generally, civil strife in the United States has been somewhat more pervasive and of much longer total duration than strife in the majority of nations, but of average intensity. The relative human cost of strife has been much less than in countries wracked by internal wars, and less

Table 17-4.—*Average magnitudes of civil strife, 1961-65, by type of nation*[a]

	Magnitude of turmoil	Magnitude of conspiracy	Magnitude of internal war	Total magnitude of strife
Average for 114 nations.............	5.2	3.0	3.3	9.1
United States, 1963-68.............	13.4	3.0	.0	13.6
Nations grouped according to level of economic development:[b]				
High (37)[c]	3.8	1.8	.7	5.5
Medium (39)......	6.5	3.8	4.3	11.6
Low (38).........	5.1	3.4	4.0	9.9
Nations grouped according to type of political system:				
Polyarchic (38)[c] ...	4.9	1.8	1.0	6.5
Centrist (28)......	4.2	2.9	2.1	7.2
Elitist (32)........	5.4	3.5	6.8	12.4
Personalist (16)....	6.5	4.9	3.9	11.4
Nations grouped according to geocultural region:				
European (27)c....	3.6	1.2	.2	4.6
Latin (24).........	5.6	4.0	2.9	9.6
Islamic (21).......	5.4	3.2	3.7	9.7
Asian (17).........	5.2	2.4	5.7	10.7
African (25).......	6.1	4.2	5.1	11.7
Nations grouped according to racial homogeneity[d]				
Multiracial societies (39)........	6.0	3.5	4.3	10.7
Other societies (81).	4.8	2.8	2.9	8.4

[a] See footnote (f), table 17-1, and app. I. Total magnitude of strife scores for each country are shown in app. II.

[b] The bases on which countries are grouped are indicated in app. II.

[c] Including data on the United States for 1961-65.

[d] For this comparison, "multiracial" societies are those whose population in the early 1960's included 5 percent or more of at least two of the following "racial" groups: Orientals, Amerindians, East Indians, Polynesians, Europeans, Negroes, Semites. The category includes all Latin American countries except Haiti, Argentina, Uruguay, and Paraguay; white-ruled Southern African countries and territories; Ethiopia, Sudan, Chad, and Niger; Algeria and Saudi Arabia; Malaya, Singapore, Cambodia, and Thailand; Israel, United States, Puerto Rico, and New Zealand.

than that of several Western democratic nations. On the basis of this evidence, America has been in recent years a more tumultuous nation than any other Western nation, but not a more violent one. It has had frequent and widespread turmoil, most of it peaceful and legal, but relatively little of the intense, organized violence that accompanies widespread conspiratorial and revolutionary movements.

Differences in Magnitudes of Strife Among World Regions

The forms and magnitudes of civil strife vary greatly among types of nations, as is shown in table 17-4.[7] The most developed nations have considerably less turmoil and conspiracy than others, and almost never undergo internal wars. The most strife-torn countries are the "developing nations," not the least developed. Differences are equally great among nations grouped by type of political system. The most peaceful nations are the "polyarchic," those which approximate Western democratic forms and processes of government. The centrist countries, those which have autocratic one-party or no-party governments, are only slightly more prone to violence. Strife is likely to be far more pervasive and violent in countries ruled by small, modernizing elites and in nations characterized by unstable, "strong-man" rule. It is noteworthy, though, that turmoil is very nearly as great among the democratic nations as it is among all nations; the establishment and survival of democracy are associated with the minimization of conspiracy and internal war, but not of the kinds of demonstrative and riotous protest that have characterized the United States in the past decade.

The countries of Eastern and Western Europe, combined with Israel and the English-settled countries outside of Europe, have had the lowest relative levels of all forms of strife, when compared either with other geocultural regions or the economic and political groupings. When strife does occur in these nations, it is highly likely to take the form of turmoil, internal war almost never. Asian and African nations have the highest levels of internal war and total strife, Latin and Islamic nations somewhat less. Conspiratorial movements are substantially more common in Latin America and tropical Africa than elsewhere.

The final set of comparisons groups nations according to their "racial" homogeneity. Multiracial societies tend to have greater levels of strife of all kinds, not merely turmoil, but the differences are moderate, not great. It is by no means certain that ethnic conflicts are responsible even for these differences. Countries with ethnic diversity also are more likely than others to have regional and political diversities, which also tend to generate internal conflicts.

None of these comparisons necessarily implies a causal connection between economic development, type of political system, or geocultural region and levels of civil strife. It could be argued, for example, that polyarchic nations can maintain democratic processes and institutions because of a lack of intensely violent internal conflict, and that intense conflicts within the elite give rise to "personalistic" patterns of government rather than vice versa. However, the results of the groupings do make it possible to anticipate the kinds and levels of strife specific kinds of countries are likely to experience. Such statements do not apply inevitably to specific cases, of course. Examination of the American data provides a striking illustration. The prospects for domestic peace are greatest for a nation that is highly developed, democratic, and European by geographical location or settlement. The United States meets all three criteria, yet has higher levels of turmoil and total strife than the average for any group of nations. The prospects for domestic violence are greatest for Asian and African nations that have low or medium levels of development and elitist or personalist political systems. Cambodia, the Ivory Coast, and Malagasy meet these criteria, yet have had lower levels of strife than any of the averages shown in table 17-4. General differences in economic development, political forms, and cultural heritage affect levels of civil strife; they do not determine them in any absolute sense.

ACTORS, OBJECTIVES, AND HUMAN COSTS

The measurable aspects of magnitudes of civil strife are not the only nor necessarily the primary determinants of strife's impact on political systems. Nor are they the only characteristics of collective protest open to systematic cross-national comparison. The socioeconomic classes and organizations that participate in strife are as important in evaluating its causes and effects as the number of people who take part. Their motives, and the men and institutions against which they act, are likely to be as consequential for the survival of their societies and governments as the intensity of action itself. Some of the evidence on differences among nations in these characteristics of strife is summarized below, and the American experience interpreted by reference to it.

Group Participation in Civil Strife

People of almost all walks of life have taken part in civil strife in the United States in the past decade. Civil rights and peace demonstrations have included tens of thousands of workers, students, and professional people. Ghetto rioters have included relatively large proportions of unskilled workers, but also many of the unemployed, skilled workers, and a few members of the black bourgeoisie.[8] "Backlash" protest and violence have mobilized both working- and middle-class whites. Only public employees have participated relatively little, aside from the tacit support some police have given to white vigilante groups and the violent responses of police and soldiers to some riots and some demonstrations.

Comparative evidence suggests that cross-class participation in strife is not exceptional; it is the norm, in European nations even more than others. Table 17-5 summarizes some of the evidence. An examination of turmoil events in all nations shows that working-class people take part in about three-quarters of them. However, the middle groups of society participate almost as often, in 60 percent of cases. Students are the middle group most often involved, but members of the business and professional classes also are present in substantial numbers in at least a fifth of all events. Even the nominal members of the political establishment, the "regime classes," occasionally take to the streets. A noteworthy difference emerges when group participation in all countries is compared with group

Table 17-5.—*Specific socioeconomic classes that participated in civil strife, 1961-65, by type of strife*

| Type of socioeconomic class | Percentages of events in which specified classes are reported to have participated[a] | | | | |
| | Turmoil | | Conspiracy | | Internal war all nations[b,c] |
	All nations[b]	European nations[c]	All nations[b]	European nations[c]	
Working classes:					
Peasants, farmers....	18	17	4	n.d.	93
Urban workers, unemployed..........	40	41	5	n.d.	36
Any working-class groups[d]	73	67	25	62	100
Middle classes:					
Students............	45	54	5	0	27
Petite bourgeoisie....	8	11	7	10	24
Professionals.......	11	12	18	20	33
Any middle-class groups[d]	61	70	41	46	63
Regime classes:					
Military, police......	1	2	50	23	31
Civil servants.......	3	5	7	0	23
Political elite........	3	7	32	8	31
Any regime groups...	7	13	70	23	48
Percentage of events in which 2 or more of the 3 general classes participated...	39	47	30	30	76

n.d. = no data (computations not made).

[a] Percentages for specific classes are based on events for which specific information on participation is reported. Percentages for the 3 general types of classes are based on events for which either specific or general information is reported. A class is said to have participated if it apparently made up more than a tenth of the rank and file or more than a third of the leadership of an event.

[b] Data for events in 114 nations and colonies.

[c] Data for events in 27 Eastern and Western European nations plus developed English-speaking countries elsewhere, including the United States. Only two internal wars occurred in these countries, too few to justify inclusion of separate group-participation data.

[d] These percentages include a large number of events for which general but not specific class participation is known, hence they are not directly comparable with the percentages shown for specific class participation.

participation in the European nations: in these countries, including the United States, middle classes are just as likely to participate in turmoil as are the working classes, and the regime classes are twice as likely to do so as they are in the world at large. It also should be noted that turmoil throughout the world usually—in three cases out of four —involves members of only one general class, whereas in European nations two or more classes participate in nearly half the events. These comparisons do not take into account the relative or absolute numbers of people from different classes involved in turmoil. They do strongly suggest, however, that turmoil in the contemporary world is not solely or primarily a lower-class phenomenon but a cross-class form of protest that is likely to mobilize discontented people whatever their social status.

Class participation is conspiratorial activity presents a distinctly different picture when all cases are examined. The conspiracy—terrorism, bombing, revolutionary plotting—is usually the work of middle and regime classes, not the lower classes. In the European nations, however, the pattern of participation is similar to that of turmoil: the working classes are more likely to participate than the middle classes, the middle classes more likely to do so than regime classes. The comparison is somewhat questionable,

Table 17-6.—Group contexts for civil strife, 1961-65, by type of nation

Type of nation	Percentages of strife events known to have been initiated by groups of the specified types[a]					
	Communal groups[b]	Economic groups[c]	Political groups[d]	Governmental groups[e]	Clandestine groups[f]	Other groups[g]
All nations (114)......	20	7	42	10	15	6
Nations grouped according to level of economic development:						
High (37)........	22	9	45	5	14	5
Medium (39).....	17	7	47	9	13	6
Low (38).........	23	5	27	16	21	7
Nations grouped according to type of political system:						
Polyarchic (38)...	19	8	50	5	13	5
Centrist (28).....	28	5	34	4	21	8
Elitist (32)........	26	5	38	13	12	5
Personalist (16)...	4	12	45	18	17	4
Nations grouped according to geocultural region:						
European (27)....	34	9	40	1	14	3
Latin (24)........	2	12	55	13	12	6
Islamic (21)......	18	7	34	11	20	10
Asian (17).......	19	3	47	11	16	4
African (25).....	32	5	33	11	14	5

[a] Based on data for approximately 1,020 strife events of all types. Of these events, 113 were clashes between nongovernmental groups, for example, between two political or communal groups; only the group that initiated each clash is counted. Groups of several general types participated in some other strife events; only the largest group was coded in such cases.

[b] Percentages of events in which initiators acted as members of territorial, religious, ethnic, or linguistic groups, whether or not formally organized.

[c] Percentages of events in which initiators acted primarily as members of organizations of workers, the unemployed, craftsmen, traders, or employers.

[d] Percentages of events in which initiators acted as members of open political organizations, including political parties, politically oriented nterest groups, and crowds at political meetings.

[e] Percentages of events in which initiators acted as members of the executive, administrative, or legislative structure, including military and police units, and the official party in one-party states.

[f] Percentages of events in which initiators acted as members of prescribed political or nonpolitical groups.

[g] Percentages of events in which initiators acted either as members of unstructured crowds or apolitical groups.

since participants could be identified in only 13 European cases, compared with 233 in the world at large.

Patterns of class participation in internal war are intermediate between those of conspiracy and turmoil. The lower classes took part in all the 54 internal wars for which we have information, as would be expected by the definition of such events. The leaders and cadres of internal wars are more likely to include members of the middle classes than regime classes: very often both are involved.

Random crowds seldom initiate civil strife. We also can examine differences and similarities among nations in the kinds of organizations that provide the cohesion that is necessary for collective action. Group cohesion may be provided by communal organization, or simply by people's awareness that they belong to the same ethnic, religious, or territorial community. Group contexts for action may also be provided by economic organizations, such as trade unions and cooperatives; by legal political organizations, such as political parties and issue-oriented groups like anti-war organizations; by clandestine groups like guerrilla and terrorist movements; and by the governmental hierarchy itself, including the civil service and military establishment. The type of group context for civil strife was identified in more than a thousand of the civil-strife events and series of events in 1961-65; table 17-6 summarizes some of the data.

Several general patterns can be noted. Among nations generally, political groups most often mobilize people for strife, in 42 percent of cases, compared with communal groups in 20 percent of events and clandestine groups in 15 percent. Strife in the more developed and democratic nations is more often organized by legal political groups than in other nations and is less often carried out by clandestine groups. The implications are that strife is a recurrent facet of the political process and that the effect of economic development and political democratization is to channel it into the political process rather than to insulate politics from violence. At the same time the intensity and seriousness of violence in politics tends to decline. The most developed nations also experience substantially less strife within the governmental hierarchy than do other nations; that is, fewer plots, mutinies, and attempted coups by dissatisfied members of the political establishment. Such strife is also very infrequent in both democratic and centrist (au-

586

thoritarian) nations, though presumably for different reasons. There also is a tendency for strife by economic organizations to increase as development increases.

Another significant contrast is provided by the relative frequency with which communal groups initiate strife. They are more often involved in strife in the most and least developed nations than in developing countries, and most often so in European and tropical African nations—in a third of events in both groups. Their relative preponderance in Africa is a manifestation of the unresolved tribal and ethnic cleavages that afflict that continent. In the European nations they seem to be residual group hostilities, ones that have persisted beyond the resolution of fundamental political and economic group conflicts. It is highly likely that increases in economic well-being and popular political participation for majority groups in European nations exacerbate the hostilities of regional and ethnic minorities that do not have what they regard as a fair share of those benefits. The United States, of course, manifests the problem to a striking degree; the evidence here suggests that it is also common in other Western nations.

Apparent Objectives of Civil Strife

With few exceptions, the demands or apparent objectives of participants in civil strife in the United States have been limited ones. Civil-rights demonstrators have asked for integration and remedial governmental action on Negro problems; they have not agitated for class or racial warfare. Peace marchers vehemently oppose American foreign policy and some of the men who conduct it; none of them have attempted to overthrow the political system. Black militants talk of revolutionary warfare; such sentiments are rarely voiced by those who participate in ghetto riots. By the testimony of most of their words and actions, they have been retaliating against the accumulated burden of specific grievances: inconsistent and coercive police control, economic privation, and social degradation. The United States has experienced chronic conspiratorial violence in the past decade, but it has been almost entirely defensive. Southern Klansmen and Northern vigilante groups have not opposed the existing socioeconomic or political system so much as they have tried to protect their conception of it and their position in it from Negroes, Jews, criminals, Communists, and a host of other perceived enemies. There are vociferous advocates of guerrilla, class, and racial warfare in the United States, and some of them have begun to take the lead in some antigovernment demonstrations and university rebellions. Nonetheless their objectives seem shared by few of their fellow participants. Their actions are comparable to those of rioters and demonstrators the world over, not those of guerrillas or revolutionary conspirators.

The comparative evidence summarized in tables 17-7 and 17-8 suggests that the dominant objectives of Americans who participate in strife more closely resemble the objectives of those in the European nations than elsewhere. Several characteristics of the worldwide patterns of demands or objectives of strife should be pointed out. In 93 percent of the events we examined, some kinds of political objectives were apparent. These political demands are twice as common as social ones, and social more than twice as common as economic ones. This does not necessarily imply that economic and social grievances are less important than political ones. It does suggest that when economic and social grievances are expressed, they are voiced in political terms.

Another general characteristic is that the objectives of turmoil are typically more limited than those of conspiracy and internal war. The objectives usually expressed in turmoil are opposition to particular governmental policies and actors, and the promotion of a group's particular social interests. Conspirators by contrast more often want to seize political power than attain any other specific objective. Internal wars usually manifest a variety of unlimited objectives, almost always including the seizure of regional or national power, often on behalf of a particular class or communal group. Internal wars also are more likely to reflect explicit economic objectives than are turmoil or conspiracy.

The objectives of particular kinds of strife in European nations differ somewhat from those of all nations. Turmoil in European nations is somewhat more likely to be based on opposition to or demands for specific governmental actions than turmoil elsewhere, and considerably more likely to include explicit social objectives. Ideological issues and promotion of the interest of a particular community, for

Table 17-7.—Objectives manifested in civil strife, 1961-65

Type of motive	Percentages of events in which specified objectives were expressed or apparent from actions[a]				
	Turmoil		Conspiracy		Internal war, all nations
	All nations	European nations	All nations	European nations	
Political objectives:					
Retaliation	4	3	2	7	4
Seize political power	1	0	37	4	25
Increase political participation	2	1	0	0	2
Oppose competing political group	6	4	2	11	0
Promote or oppose a specific governmental policy	23	33	7	21	0
Promote or oppose a political actor	8	4	13	14	0
Oppose a foreign nation's policies or actors	20	13	3	11	0
Several or diffuse political objectives	26	26	32	33	67
Any political objectives	90	85	98	100	98
Economic objectives:					
Retaliation	1	0	0	0	0
Seize economic goods	2	1	3	0	9
Change economic distribution patterns	7	10	4	0	7
Several or diffuse economic objectives	8	11	1	0	19
Any economic objectives	18	22	8	0	36
Social objectives:					
Retaliation	5	7	3	7	5
Promote or oppose belief systems	11	17	10	15	5
Promote or oppose an ethnic, linguistic, religious, or regional community	15	23	7	33	30
Increase social goods	1	19	2	4	2
Several or diffuse social objectives	11	6	9	0	43
Any social objectives	43	71	32	59	87
Number of events	653	136	294	27	55

[a] Objectives are those attributed to participants in news sources or apparent from the nature of the event. For example, peace demonstrations in the United States and Spanish student riots against governmental bans on student organization would be coded "promote or oppose a specific governmental policy"; a civil-rights demonstration would be coded both "promote or oppose a specific policy" and "promote or oppose a community"; a French general strike against a government wage freeze would be coded both "promote or oppose a specific policy" and "change economic distribution patterns"; white attacks on civil-rights demonstrators would be coded "retaliation" under "Social Objectives"; and so forth. Coding categories are defined in Gurr with Ruttenberg, app. A. Only primary objectives were coded, but in many cases, especially in internal war, participants had several major objectives of each type. For example, an antiwar demonstration at a speech of a U.S. Cabinet member would be coded "several political objectives" because it reflects opposition to the individual and a policy he supports. Percentages shown for each subheading do not necessarily add to the total because of rounding errors.

example, are relatively common issues of conflict in European nations. Explicit demands for "social goods" such as removal of social barriers to mobility, rights of equal treatment, free association, and more and better education are much more common in European nations than elsewhere.

Type of nation	Percentages of events in which specified types of objectives were expressed or apparent from action[a]						
	Seize political power	Increase participation or oppose competitors	Promote/ oppose policies or actors	Promote oppose community	Any political objectives	Any economic objectives	Any social objectives
All nations (114)........	13	6	26	13	93	16	33
Nations grouped according to level of economic development:							
High (37)..........	6	6	56	13	92	16	46
Medium (39).......	12	5	40	10	92	15	36
Low (38)...........	22	6	27	17	94	18	49
Nations grouped according to type of political system:							
Polyarchic (38).....	6	6	49	14	91	16	47
Centrist (28)........	8	5	38	10	91	10	51
Elitist (32)..........	17	8	33	18	93	20	45
Personalist (16).....	22	2	44	5	98	16	20
Nations grouped according to geocultural region:							
European (27)......	1	7	49	25	87	18	69
Latin (24)..........	22	4	55	0	96	15	4
Islamic (21)........	10	3	34	13	96	13	66
Asian (17)..........	6	1	47	13	95	17	52
African (25)........	22	12	23	18	86	17	40

[a] Categories of objectives are combinations of categories shown in table 17-7. "Increase participation or oppose competitors" combines "increase political participation" and "oppose competing political group." "Promote/oppose policies or actors" combines "promote or oppose a specific governmental policy," "promote or oppose a political actor," and "oppose foreign nation's policies or actors."

The objectives of conspiratorial activity in European nations are sharply different from conspiratorial objectives elsewhere; they are relatively limited and resemble the objectives of European turmoil. European conspirators seldom want to seize political power, but are much more likely to oppose particular political policies and actors. They also are quite likely—in 59 percent of the 27 instances—to have explicit social objectives, usually ideological or communal ones.

When all types of strife are combined and their objectives compared, in table 17-8, some of these relationships become more sharply apparent. The seizure of political power is rarely an objective of strife among highly developed democratic, or European nations. When nations are grouped according to their level of ecnomic development, it is apparent that the lower the level of development, the more common are attempts to seize power. The higher the level of development, however, the more likely does strife represent opposition to specific policies and individuals. Demands for increased political participation, a common student grievance in the United States and elsewhere, for example, are relatively uncommon and do not vary greatly among nations according to levels of economic development; they do tend to be more common in African and European states than in others.

There are substantial differences among groups of nations in social objectives for civil strife. They are substantially more common in European and Islamic nations than in others, and very infrequent in Latin American nations. This does not necessarily mean that Latin Americans lack social grievances, only that they seldom are voiced in specific demands in strife. It should be pointed out that, by contrast, the groups of nations do not differ substantially in the relative frequency of political or economic objectives for civil strife. Political objectives predominate, being salient in at least 86 percent of the events in each set of nations. Economic objectives are relatively uncommon, characterizing between 10 and 20 percent of events in each group.

One specific category of social objectives, promotion of or opposition to interests of specific communities, is separately shown in table 17-8 because it includes the explicit demands of American civil-rights demonstrators, the implicit demands of ghetto rioters, and the sometimes violent resistance of white Americans to those demands. This kind of social objective is more common in civil strife in the European nations than any other, being specifically identifiable in a quarter of all occurrences of strife. Country-by-country examination of the evidence suggests that the relative frequency of such motives in the European nations is only partly the result of the inclusion of the United States in this group. More important, it indicates that incomplete assimilation of minority groups into national life is one of the pervasive unresolved problems of the Western nations. Examples are the conflicts between French- and English-speaking Canadians, the Flemish and the Waloons of Belgium, Coloureds and whites in England, Catholics and Protestants in Northern Ireland, Arabs and Jews within Israel. Other manifestations are the chronic and sometimes violent separatist activities of German-speaking Italians, Basques and Catalonians in Spain, Welsh nationalists,

| Type of target | Percentage of events in which specified primary targets are identifiable[a] | | | | |
| | Turmoil | | Conspiracy | | Internal war, all nations[b,c] |
	All nations[b]	European nations[c]	All nations[b]	European nations[c]	
Property targets:					
Public.................	15	18	26	36	76
Private................	18	22	17	36	69
Foreign................	17	14	7	7	24
Any property...........	37	39	36	64	82
Political actors:					
Public figures...........	28	27	56	39	2
Military and police.......	16	14	9	4	13
Private political groups...	8	4	2	7	2
Several of the above......	16	23	16	18	76
Foreign public figures and military personnel......	20	21	4	11	25
Any political actors......	83	83	85	75	93
Nonpolitical actors:					
Communal groups........	14	22	3	4	36
Economic actors.........	4	2	—	—	—
Several groups, and random victims........	3	6	7	4	44
Any nonpolitical actors (including others)......	21	31	11	11	80
Number of events..........	666	136	315	28	55

[a] The primary targets are the places or people on which violence, threats, or demands are focused. For example, the Watts riot of 1965 was coded as directed against private and public property, the police, and several types of nonpolitical actors (both white storekeepers and random white victims). Peace marches were coded as directed against public figures, since they constituted demands made on political leaders. Percentages do not necessarily add to subtotals because the subcategories shown here are not all mutually exclusive or exhaustive.

[b] See footnote (b), table 17-5.

[c] See footnote (c), table 17-5.

Bretons in France, Ukrainians in the Soviet Union, and the people of the Swiss Jura. Such conflicts tend to be low keyed; if they are not resolved, however, they can flare up repeatedly in intense strife, as they have in the United States, Belgium, and Spain.

The Targets of Civil Strife

Even the members of a rampaging mob are selective in the targets they attack. They, along with demonstrators, conspirators, and rebels, focus their actions on the objects and people that symbolize their grievances. Table 17-9 shows that there is little difference among the primary targets of turmoil when the European nations are compared with all nations. Property is attacked in about 4 cases out of 10, private property slightly more often than public. Political actors are by far the most common objects of verbal and physical attack. Demonstrations are typically directed against the political figures who are held responsible for grievances by their sins of commission or omission; riots usually include attacks on several kinds of political actors, including both officials and the police. A fifth of turmoil events are focused on foreign political actors, usually representatives of governments with unpopular foreign policies. The United States has been the target of many such demonstrations and riots throughout the world; Americans also have taken to the streets to oppose actions of the governments of the Soviet Union, Cuba, and other countries. Nonpolitical actors—usually members of ethnic groups—are attacked in about a fourth of turmoil events, somewhat more often in the European nations than in others.

The objects of conspiratorial attacks do vary substantially between European and other nations. The European conspirator is much more likely to vent his anger on property, less likely to attack public figures. The statistical differences reflect the fact that European conspirators more often resort to symbolic and indirect political opposition— for example, bombing public buildings and police barracks —than to direct attacks on the lives and governments of political leaders. Conspiratorial attacks on members of ethnic or other nonpolitical actors are rare. The reemerging American phenomenon of terroristic attacks by white vigilantes on Negroes and their white supporters, and the new phenomenon of black-militant attacks on whites, have relatively few parallels among either Western or non-Western nations. Such group hostilities elsewhere usually inspire riots, not terrorism.

Internal wars by their very nature involve attacks on many targets: property, public and private; politicians, national and foreign soldiers and police; and nonpolitical opponents and victims of all sorts. Turmoil is more likely than internal war to be focused on a few objects and individuals, while conspiracy is likely to be even more narrowly focused.

The Human Costs of Civil Strife

Americans have been shocked by the occurrence of nearly 200 deaths in ghetto riots, by political assassinations, and by several dozen killings by black and white terrorists in recent years. By comparison with most nations, however, the proportional loss of American lives in civil strife has been low. Table 17-10 summarizes comparative informa-

Table 17-10.—The human costs of civil strife, 1961-65, compared with the United States, 1963-68

Type of nation	Percentages of events with casualties[a]		Average number of deaths per event[b]			Deaths per million population[c]
	Turmoil	Conspiracy	Turmoil	Conspiracy	Internal war	
All nations (114)	59	42	18.1	17.2	13,900	238
United States, 1963-68[d]	—	—	—	—	—	1.1
Nations grouped according to level of economic development:						
High (37)[e]	56	38	3.5	9.2	160	1.7
Medium (32)	59	45	28.4	22.1	12,000	264
Low (38)	69	39	17.2	18.9	18,500	841
Nations grouped according to type of political system:						
Polyarchic (33)[e]	61	33	8.8	8.3	3,600	12
Centrist (28)	54	52	38.9	23.1	2,200	19
Elitist (32)	58	44	16.2	20.6	20,000	1,604
Personalist (16)	62	40	12.0	17.5	4,300	223
Nations grouped according to geocultural region:						
European (37)	61	25	11.5	0.4	220	2.4
Latin (24)	63	44	5.9	16.2	2,900	76
Islamic (21)	53	45	19.2	23.5	6,500	222
Asian (17)	45	42	42.6	25.7	35,000	357
African (25)	64	43	18.5	17.5	4,900	539

[a] Percentage of events of each type in which any deaths or injuries were reported among initiators, their opponents, or victims. Executions of initiators are included. All internal wars result in casualties, hence no separate percentages are shown. Also see (d), below.

[b] Based on totals of all reported deaths. Only rough and questionably reliable estimates of deaths are available for most internal wars. The averages are rounded to reflect this imprecision. Also see (d), below.

[c] Total reported deaths for the countries in each group divided by the total population of the countries in that group.

[d] Percentages and deaths per event for the United States, 1963-68, are not reported because the data are not comparable. Many turmoil events counted in the 1961-65 period are waves of related outbreaks, each wave counted as one "event." Strife events in the United States, 1963-68, were recorded on an occurrence-by-occurrence basis without attempting to categorize them in waves.

tion on the human costs of strife. An estimated 750,000 people lost their lives in civil violence between 1961 and 1965, the great majority of them victims of internal wars. Although almost all types of civil strife in the United States resulted in casualties, the relative loss of life has been comparable to that of other developed nations and of other European nations. Both turmoil and conspiracy lead to relatively few deaths in the highly developed nations, in democratic countries, and in the European and Latin

American nations. The loss of life tends to be greatest in turmoil and conspiracy events in the developing nations, centrist nations, and Asian countries.

By far the most striking differences among groups of nations are in deaths per million population. The rate in the least-developed nations, 841 per million, is 500 times the 1.7 rate in the most developed nations. The rates in the democratic and centralized countries, 12 and 19 per million, respectively, are about one one-hundredth of the 1,604 rate in the new nations that are characterized by elitist leadership and relatively weak and unstable political institutions. When nations are grouped according to geocultural region, civil-strife death rates appear to vary with the regions' relative levels of economic development. The rate is substantially the lowest in the European nations, 2.4 per million; some 30 times greater in Latin America, which is considerably less developed; and 150 to 200 times greater in the underdeveloped Asian and African states.

It is not justifiable to conclude from these figures that increasing economic development leads directly to decreasing deaths from civil violence. It is a truism that people discontented with their poverty are more likely to rebel than people whose economic desires are satisfied, but even these descriptive data suggest that their political environment has a major influence on the consequences of rebellion. Democratic and centrist countries are likely to have both the coercive capacity to restrain strife with minimal loss of life and the institutional structures that can provide alternatives to and solutions for violence. The least-developed countries that have relied on elitist or personalistic leadership, however, confront two interrelated and almost insoluble problems. Their economies produce too little to satisfy the economic aspirations of many of their citizens. Their leaders, for lack of will, ability, or resources, are often unable to establish strong and pervasive means of coercive and institutional control. When civil strife does occur in these countries, the regimes are usually strong enough to resist it but lack the capacity either to suppress it or to remedy its causes. The consequence is likely to be an escalating spiral of inconsistent and ineffective repression and increasing popular resistance, culminating in the peace of the charnel house that is statistically manifested in the death rates shown in table 17-10.

COMPARATIVE EVIDENCE ON THE CAUSES OF CIVIL STRIFE

Some Psychological Preconditions of Civil Strife

The popular and sociological cliché is that "frustration" or "discontent" or "relative deprivation" is the root cause of rebellion. Cliché or not, the basic relationship is as fundamental to understanding civil strife as the law of gravity is to atmospheric physics: relative deprivation, the phrase used in this research, is a necessary precondition for civil strife of any kind. The greater the deprivation an individual perceives relative to his expectations, the greater his discontent; the more widespread and intense is discontent among members of a society, the more likely and severe is civil strife. Relative deprivation is not whatever the outside observer thinks people ought to be dissatisfied with. It is a state of mind that I have defined as a discrepancy between people's expectations about the goods and conditions of life to which they are justifiably entitled, on the one hand, and, on the other, their value capabilities—the degree to which they think they can attain those goods and conditions.

This is not a complicated way of making the simplistic and probably inaccurate statement that people are deprived and therefore angry if they have less than what they want. Two characteristics of value perceptions are more important than this "want-get ratio": people become most intensely discontented when they cannot get what they think they deserve, not just what they want in an ideal sense; and when they feel they are making inadequate progress toward their goals, not whether they have actually attained them or not.

Underlying the relative deprivation approach to civil strife is the frustration-aggression mechanism, apparently a fundamental part of our psychobiological makeup. When we feel thwarted in an attempt to get something we want, we are likely to become angry, and when we become angry the most satisfying inherent response is to strike out at the source of frustration. Relative deprivation is, in effect, a perception of thwarting circumstances. How angry men become in response to the perception of deprivation is determined partly by the relative importance to them of the expectations to which they are striving; the number of alternatives they have yet to try; and the degree of the discrepancy itself. If angry men believe that collective protest or violence are legitimate responses to anger, and if they think that protest or violence will help alleviate their discontent, the impetus to civil strife is strengthened. If they believe that strife is unjustified and unlikely to succeed, they are more likely to contain their anger or to divert it into other activities.

In brief, the basic psychological factors in the genesis of civil strife are the intensity and extent of deprivation-induced discontent in a group, and people's attitudes about the justifiability and utility of collective protest and of collective violence in response to discontent.[9] To evaluate the relative importance of these psychological variables as causes of civil strife, we devised indirect measures of deprivation and justificatory attitudes about strife for a large number of national populations, and related them statistically to measures of the magnitude of civil strife. Some of the procedures and results are summarized here.

Relative Deprivation as a Cause of Civil Strife

The first step toward assessing deprivation-induced discontent among nations was to identify general patterns of social conditions that cause it. Four patterns of conditions likely to cause discontent are shown in figures 17-1 through 17-4. In the first (fig. 17-1), group deprivation results when expectations increase without an accompanying increase in the potential for their satisfaction. The pattern has been called the "revolution of rising expectations." To test its importance, we assumed that expectations should be increasing most rapidly in countries in which education has been expanding most rapidly, and that expectations should be highest in countries with the highest educational levels. To take account of differences in capabilities, we hypothesized that discontent would be greatest in countries in which educational levels were expanding more rapidly than the economy.

Measures of educational levels, and of educational levels

597

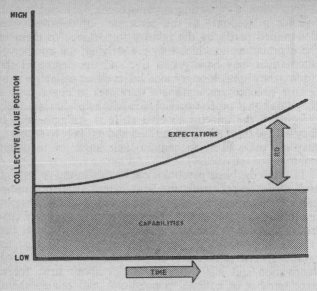

Figure 17-1.—Aspirational deprivation.

Note

"Relative deprivation (RD)" is men's perception of discrepancy between their value expectations and their value capabilities.

"Collective value position" is the average level or amount of goods and conditions of life that members of a collectivity have or expect to attain.

"Value expectations" are the average value positions justifiably sought by members of a collectivity.

"Value capabilities" are the average value positions members of a collectivity perceive themselves capable of attaining or maintaining.

and changes relative to economic levels and changes, were constructed for 119 nations and correlated with measures of magnitude of civil strife for 1961-63. As predicted, we found that the countries with the most rapidly expanding educational systems experienced the greatest strife, but the correlation for all nations was relatively weak, +0.16. When education was related to economic conditions, however, the results contradicted the assumptions and hypotheses. For example, we found that strife was high in countries with high economic growth but stable or declining education, and lower in countries with relatively

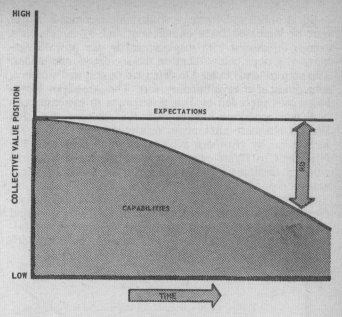

Figure 17-2.—Decremental deprivation.

little growth but expanding education. We also found that, in the developing nations, the greater the relative increase in higher and technical education compared to the level of development, the less likely was turmoil and the lower the magnitude of strife. These and other findings all point to one general conclusion: In both developed and developing societies, but not in the least developed, *the expansion of educational opportunities is less likely to raise expectations to an unsatisfiably high level than it is to provide ambitious men with an increased sense of capacity to attain their expectations.*[10] There almost certainly are circumstances in which exposure to new and better ways of life increases men's expectations beyond the possibility of attainment and to point of violent reaction; expanding education appears to meliorate rather than reinforce them.

The pattern of deprivation-inducing conditions in figure 17-2 is one of declining capabilities in the presence of stable expectations. Such "decremental deprivation" is experienced, for example, by people deprived of long-held political liberties; by groups with stable incomes who are hurt by increased taxes or inflation; and by middle-class groups threatened with displacement by the upward mobility of groups below them on the socioeconomic ladder. The pattern tends to lead to defensive protest and violence, sometimes of a revolutionary sort. The American Revolution was preceded by British attempts to increase political and economic control over the colonies; the Civil War by Northern attempts to restrict slavery; the first Ku Klux Klan by Northern subjugation and Negro mobility after the Civil War; current vigilante activity in Northern cities by declining law and order and expansion of Negro neighborhoods.

The pattern that seems most often associated with revolutionary movements is shown in figure 17-3: a period of substantial increase in capabilities or satisfactions followed by a substantial relative decline. Prolonged experi-

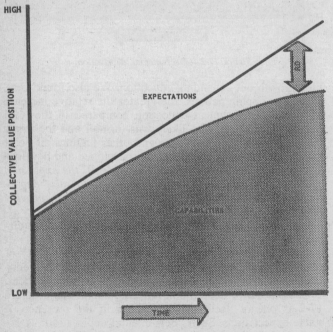

Figure 17-3.—*Progressive deprivation.*

ence of increasing well-being generates intense expectations about continued increases; if changing circumstances make those expectations seem unsatisfiable, the likely consequence is intense discontent.[11]

For the purpose of estimating the extent and importance for strife of these two kinds of deprivation, we developed many measures of short-term deterioration in political and economic conditions among nations in the 1950's and early 1960's. The assumption was that any short-term decline in economic conditions, and any governmental policies that restricted political activity or reduced people's socio-economic status, increased deprivation. Both the relative degree of decline and the proportion of a national population likely to be affected were estimated. (No attempt was made to distinguish between the two patterns for the purpose of cross-national comparison.) We hypothesized that the greater the degree and scope of all such relative declines in a nation, the greater its magnitude of strife.

The pattern in figure 17-4 represents persisting depriva-

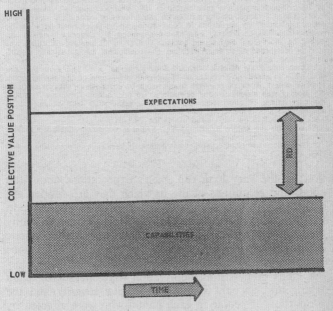

Figure 17-4.—Persisting deprivation.

Type of nation	Correlations[a] between short-term deprivation and magnitudes of—			Correlations[a] between persisting deprivation and magnitudes of—		
	Turmoil	Conspiracy	Total strife[b]	Turmoil	Conspiracy	Total strife[b]
All nations (114)[c]	32	45	47	27	30	35
Nations grouped according to level of economic development:						
High (37)[c]	50	38	57	30	28	34
Medium (39)	29	55	58	28	46	29
Low (38)	*04	41	23	*19	*07	31
Nations grouped according to type of political system:						
Polyarchic (38)[c]	28	49	46	48	29	46
Centrist (27)[d]	47	63	55	37	*31	52
Elitist (32)	*15	49	58	33	*14	37
Personalist (16)	58	*05	*21	*10	52	*35
Nations grouped according to geo-cultural region:[e]						
Anglo-Nordic (10)[c]	73	82	80	65	83	80
Western Europe (11)	*16	*08	*30	59	*-31	*41
Eastern Europe (8)	78	*-05	79	*37	*-47	*-05
Latin (24)	43	*28	51	59	43	42
Islamic (21)	37	37	*22	*-06	*26	47
Asian (17)	*25	53	56	*30	*15	*28
African (23)	*15	50	55	*15	*11	*22

[a] The figures shown are product-moment correlation coefficients multiplied by 100. A perfect positive relationship is 100; a perfect negative relationship, −100. The differences among nations in magnitudes of strife that are statistically "explained" by variations in deprivation can be determined by squaring each correlation coefficient. For example, among all nations, variations in extent of short-term deprivation explain $(0.47)^2$ or 22 percent of differences in total magnitude of strife. Asterisked (*) coefficients are statistically significant at less than the 0.10 level.

[b] Total magnitude of civil strife, including internal war. The groups of nations vary so greatly in frequencies of internal war—some groups having none, 1, or 2, others 20 or more—that comparisons of correlations with magnitudes of internal war among groups of nations are misleading. Among all nations the correlations of short-term and persisting deprivation with magnitude of internal war are, respectively, 0.34 and 0.24.

[c] Including data on the United States for 1961–65.

[d] Excluding the colony of Papua-New Guinea, which was included in this group in preceding tables.

[e] The nations are grouped somewhat differently here than in preceding tables. (See app. II.)

tion. In the very long run, men's expectations about the goods and conditions of life to which they are entitled are likely to adjust to what they are capable of attaining. In the medium run, however, some groups may persistently demand and expect such conditions as greater economic opportunity, political autonomy, or freedom of religious expression that their societies will not or cannot provide. Six kinds of persisting deprivation were measured, again taking into account both their relative severity and the proportion of people in each nation who were affected by them: economic and political discrimination, political separatism, dependence on foreign economies, lack of educational opportunity, and religious divisions. A combined measure was devised to facilitate simple comparisons with magnitudes of civil strife.[12]

Some results of the correlation analysis are summarized in table 17-11. With few exceptions, both short-term and persisting deprivation are significant causes of the various forms of civil strife among groups of nations. Among highly developed nations, for example, differences in short-term deprivation explain $(0.57)^2$ or 32.5 percent of differences in total magnitude of strife; and differences in persisting deprivation account for $(0.32)^2$ or 10 percent of differences in strife. Two qualifications reinforce the significance of these findings. One is that the relationships are relatively strong, despite the fact that deprivation was measured only partially and indirectly, often on the basis of suspect data. The fact that the correlations between deprivation and strife in the least-developed countries are somewhat weaker than in the developed countries, for example, may reflect the unreliability of economic and other data for these countries. A second qualification is that, generally, deprivation is an apparent cause of all major forms of strife, and of most forms in most groups of countries. This general similarity of results strongly supports the underlying theoretical argument.

Some differences among groups of nations also should be noted. Short-term deprivation is more important as a cause of turmoil than of conspiracy in the most developed nations, whereas it is more important as a cause of conspiracy in the less-developed nations. This difference also is apparent among the geocultural regions: short-term deprivation leads to conspiracy in the least-developed, Asian and African nations; and to turmoil in the more-developed, European and Latin nations. We pointed out above that conspiracy is usually organized by the upper and middle classes. The inference is that in less-developed countries, deprivation of the kinds indexed in this study is more strongly felt by these groups than by the working classes. The deprivations that give rise to turmoil in the less-developed countries may be those caused by the social dislocations of socioeconomic development itself, which are not well represented in these measures.

An unusual pattern is apparent when the "Anglo-Nordic" and the other two groups of European nations are compared. The correlations between deprivation and strife in the Nordic and English-speaking countries are far higher than in any other group of nations. Differences in deprivation account for almost all their differences in strife. The findings reflect partly the close connection between the degree and extent of discriminatory deprivation in countries like South Africa, Rhodesia, and the United States and high levels of ethnic strife in them, and the relative lack of discrimination and negligible strife in the Nordic countries, Australia, and New Zealand. To the same point, we found in an earlier study of the causes of civil violence in 1961-63 that the proportional size of groups subject to discrimination, however intense, correlated 0.30 with magnitude of strife in 119 nations.

In the other Western European nations, persisting deprivation is more closely related to turmoil than short-term deprivation. This is consistent with the findings, discussed above, that persisting deprivation is a source of chronic disorder throughout the Western community, not only in the United States. On the other hand, the lack of relationship between short-term deprivation and magnitudes of strife has two possible explanations. One is that the immediate causes of strife in Europe are of a specific and idiosyncratic kind not represented in general measures of deprivation. Another is that much European strife is a manifestation of tactical political motives more than of intense discontent. One observation supports the second interpretation: the fact that the political demonstration, riot, and strike are established tactics of both leftwing and rightwing groups in the three European countries with highest magnitudes of strife—Italy, France, and Greece. Both explanations probably apply, and are relevant to other countries as well: the resolution of a nation's most critical problems may lead to heightened awareness of other problems, and in some circumstances to the institutionalization of turmoil as a response to them.

In the Eastern European nations, deprivation is rather closely related to turmoil, the only consequential form of strife that occurred in the Communist countries in the 1961-65 period. This may seem surprising, given the common assumption that collective expressions of opinion are so carefully controlled by the Communist regimes that demonstrative protest occurs only at times and places when control is deliberately or accidentally loosened. Other analyses show, however, that turmoil is substantially lower in these nations than in other European nations. Totalitarian control seems to minimize absolute levels of strife, but in spite of it intense discontents are likely to be given some public expression even in the short run.

Legitimacy and Tradition of Strife as Causes of Civil Strife

It is all but impossible, without opinion survey evidence, to ascertain men's attitudes about the justifiably and utility of collective protest and violence. Historical and survey evidence suggests that Americans as a whole are more favorably disposed to violence as a solution to problems than many other national groups.[13] For purposes of cross-national comparison, we used two indirect measures to represent these attitudes. A measure of the legitimacy of the political system was devised, on the theoretical assumption that people are less likely to attack their political leaders, or to engage in violence against others, if they have a high positive regard for the political system. Highest legitimacy scores were given to nations whose political system was developed solely by indigenous leaders, rather than borrowed or imposed from abroad, and which had endured for the longest time without substantial structural change.

The second measure is of levels of collective violence in the period from 1946 to 1959. The assumption is that the greater strife has been in a country's past, the more likely some of its citizens are to regard it as justifiable, and -the more likely some of them would have found it partially successful in the past, and hence regard it as potentially useful in the future. A history of civil strife should thus facilitate future strife, a relationship that is historically documented in detail for the United States in other contributions to this volume.

The correlations between the measures of legitimacy and past levels of strife are shown in table 17-12. Among nations generally, and among most groups of nations, the legitimacy of the political system does inhibit magnitudes of violence, and historical levels of strife do facilitate future strife. But these conditions are not as important, for all nations, as are differences in levels of deprivation, as a comparison with table 17-11 indicates. Comparison of groups of nations suggests why: there are striking differences among them in the efficacy of legitimacy in reducing strife, and in the facilitating effects of past strife on future events.

Legitimacy most strongly inhibits civil strife in the developing nations; in the democratic and the personalist nations; in the non-Communist Western nations; and in Latin, Islamic, and Asian nations. It has relatively weak effects in the most- and least-developed nations; the nations governed by modernizing elites; and in African and Communist nations. In centrist (authoritarian) regimes it tends to inhibit conspiracy but has no effect on turmoil. Historical levels of strife very strongly facilitate subsequent strife in the most-developed, democratic, and Western nations. Their effects are inconsequential or negative in the developing, personalist, and Eastern European nations.

Many special interpretations could be made of these results. Only some general ones are suggested here. Legitimacy presumably has little inhibiting effect on strife in the new, least-developed nations and in the authoritarian nations because their regimes generally have low legitimacy. Only high degrees of loyalty to leaders and institutions are likely to inhibit strife under conditions of intense deprivation. We know that the dislocations associated with nation-building and socioeconomic development generate intense conflict within nations. The regimes of developing nations, including a number of Latin and Islamic nations, have high apparent legitimacy; Chile, Costa Rica, Morocco, and Iran are examples. The efficacy of legitimacy in minimizing strife in these kinds of countries is manifest in the relatively high correlations for these groups of countries in table 17-12.

The close connection between past and future strife in the developed, democratic, and Western nations supports the conclusion of the preceding section that a number of these nations are, in effect, inherently tumultuous. This is partly the result of persisting deprivations, and also of the existence of historical traditions that sanction protest and violence as justifiable responses to a variety of grievances and conflicts. The lack of connection between past and

Table 17-12.—*Legitimacy of the political system and historical sanctions for strife as determinants of magnitudes of civil strife, 1961-65, by type of nation*

Type of nation	Correlations[a] between legitimacy and magnitudes of—			Correlations[a] between historical levels of strife and magnitudes of—		
	Turmoil	Conspiracy	Total strife[b]	Turmoil	Conspiracy	Total strife[b]
All nations (114)[c]	-30	-29	-38	29	23	29
Nations grouped according to level of economic development:						
High (37)[c]	*-10	*-23	*-20	57	48	65
Medium (39)	-44	-34	-52	*-23	*18	*01
Low (38)	*-24	*-11	*-23	38	*14	37
Nations grouped according to type of political system:						
Polyarchic (38)[c]	-46	*-18	-45	51	61	64
Centrist (27)[d]	*10	-32	*-08	*11	*-04	*-07
Elitist (32)	-36	*-05	*-26	29	*13	53
Personalist (16)	-66	-43	-58	*16	*09	*-28
Nations grouped according to geo-cultural regions:[e]						
Anglo-Nordic (10)[c]	*-45	-72	-61	59	*34	57
Western Europe (11)	-50	*-25	-57	77	57	87
Eastern Europe (8)	*-27	61	*-29	*49	*-49	*07
Latin (24)	-40	*-16	-39	*27	55	37
Islamic (21)	-46	49	-37	46	*09	*29
Asian (17)	*-33	*-19	-63	*-07	56	*39
African (23)	*-25	*-08	*-24	47	36	43

[a] See footnote (a), table 17-11. Asterisked (*) coefficients are statistically significant at less than the 0.10 level.

[b] See footnote (b), table 17-11. In all nations the correlations of legitimacy and historical levels of strife with magnitudes of internal war are, respectively, -0.26 and +0.15.

[c] Including data on the United States for 1961-65.

[d] See footnote (d), table 17-11.

[e] See footnote (e), table 17-11.

future strife in the developing nations almost certainly reflects the current tensions of socioeconomic change, tensions that in most of them became severe only in recent years, when the pace of change increased.

Social Control and Facilitation as Determinants of Magnitudes of Civil Strife

The extent and intensity of relative deprivation, and justificatory attitudes about protest and violence, are psychological determinants of the potential for civil strife. Whether or not men act on their dispositions to collective action depends partly on some structural characteristics of their societies. Three general kinds of societal characteristics were examined in the cross-national study: the nature of coercive control; the strength of political and economic institutions; and the availability of physical, organizational, and material support for dissidents.

Coercive control.—Conventional wisdom and studies of riots and revolutions all emphasize the importance of actual or threatened coercion in minimizing the occurrence and extent of strife. If men are sufficiently afraid of the consequences, the argument goes, they will not riot. Comparative studies of civil strife, and psychological theory, both suggest that the relationship is not so simple: some kinds of coercion are more likely to increase than to deter strife. Several cross-national studies show that strife tends to be greatest in countries that have medium-sized military and security forces, lowest in those with either small or very large forces.[14] Another study suggests that political instability is greatest in countries that exercise intermediate degrees of political control, lowest in those that are either highly democratic or totalitarian[15] The proposed explanation for these findings is that medium levels of coercive threat and control are more likely to increase men's anger and will to resist than to restrain them from strife. The consistency with which coercion is used is probably even

Table 17-13.—*Coercive control, institutionalization, and facilitation as determinants of the total magnitude of civil strife, 1961-65, by type of nation*

Type of nation	Correlations[a] between total magnitude of civil strife and—			
	Coercive control		Strength of institutions	Facilitation
	Relative size of forces	Size weighted by loyalty		
All nations (114)[b]	*-13	-51	-34	66
Nations grouped according to level of economic development:				
High (37)[b]	*-12	-53	-29	59
Medium (39)	*-18	-49	*-02	58
Low (38)	*14	-31	-32	67
Nations grouped according to type of political system:				
Polyarchic (38)[b]	n.d.	-55	-36	65
Centrist (27)[c]	-57	-44	*-26	57
Elitist (32)	*25	-44	-35	76
Personalist (16)	*27	*-29	52	*27
Nations grouped according to geo-cultural region:				
Anglo-Nordic (10)[b]	*-39	-68	-75	*-44
Western Europe (11)	74	*-18	*-14	58
Eastern Europe (8)	*03	*17	*23	*-12
Latin (24)	*-08	-56	*-03	*33
Islamic (21)	*05	-61	*-29	71
Asian (17)	*-08	-74	*15	80
African (23)	*18	*-19	-45	82

n.d. = no data (computations not made)
[a] See footnote (a), table 17-11. Asterisked (*) coefficients are statistically significant at less than the 0.10 level.
[b] Including data on the United States for 1961-65.
[c] See footnote (d), table 17-11.

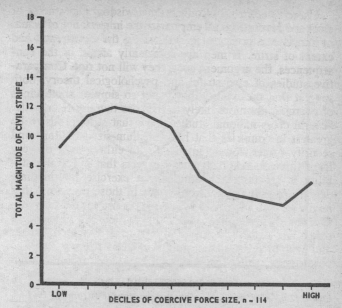

Figure 17-5. Coercive force, size, and magnitudes of civil strife, 1961-65.

more important than the degree of control. Coercion is "consistent" to the extent that all the "guilty" are subject to sanctions in proportion to the seriousness of their action, and the "innocent" not sanctioned. The literature of civil strife provides many examples of cases in which random or terroristic coercion by troops or police intensified violence, transforming peaceful demonstrations into riots, riots and conspiracies into revolutionary movements.[16]

Two measures of coercive control were used in the cross-national study. One indexed the size of military and internal security forces relative to the adult population. The second weighted the relative size of such forces according to their loyalty to the regime, on the assumption that the greater their historical and contemporary loyalty, the more likely they would be to make consistent use of force and the less likely they would be to use illegal force against the regime.[17] Some correlational results are shown in the first two columns of table 17-13. As expected, the size of forces is weakly and inconsistently related to magnitudes of strife. The strongest relationship is found in the Western

609

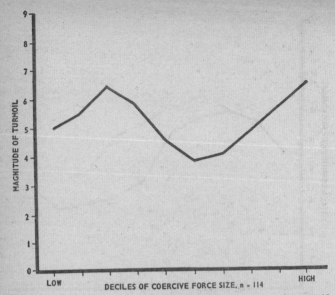

Figure 17-6.—Coercive force, size, and magnitudes of turmoil, 1961-65.

European nations, in which the larger are coercive forces, the greater is strife. Positive relationships of this sort also are apparent in the elitist and personalist nations, and in the least-developed nations. But when the loyalty of the military establishment, and the implied consistency of coercion, are taken into account, a definite inhibitory effect on strife is apparent in most nations. When coercive forces are both large and loyal, the magnitude of strife tends to be low, with the apparent exceptions of Africa and Eastern and Western Europe.

Evidence regarding the inconclusive effects of reliance on large military and police establishments alone to maintain domestic order is shown in figures 17-5 through 17-8. Figure 17-5 relates coercive force size to total magnitude of civil strife for all nations. It is evident that total strife is likely to be highest in countries with low-to-medium-sized coercive forces, but not those with very small forces. Moreover, at the very highest levels of coercive force size there is a slight tendency for magnitudes of strife to increase. Such an S-shaped curve is considerably more pronounced in the comparison of coercive force size with mag-

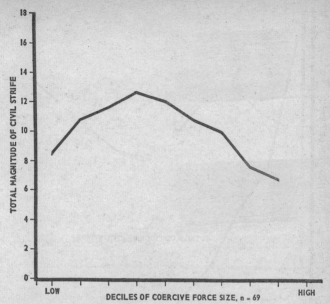

Figure 17-7.—Coercive force, size, and magnitudes of civil strife, 1961-65, 69 low-conflict politics.

nitudes of turmoil; turmoil peaks at both moderate and very high force levels.

Two other factors should be considered in interpreting these results. It is likely that countries with protracted political violence expand their coercive forces to counteract it. It also is plausible that armies in countries facing foreign threats cause less dissatisfaction—by their presence or actions—than armies in states not significantly involved in international conflict. Countries with one or both of these characteristics were removed and the relationship plotted for the remaining 69 countries, with the results shown in figure 17-7; the curvilinear relationship is again clearly evident.

The graph in figure 17-8 shows the relationships between coercive force loyalty and, respectively, total strife and turmoil. The relationships are essentially linear, though in neither instance does the level of strife approach zero when size and loyalty approach their maximum. For turmoil in particular, the results at the outer end of the "loyalty" scale are inconclusive.

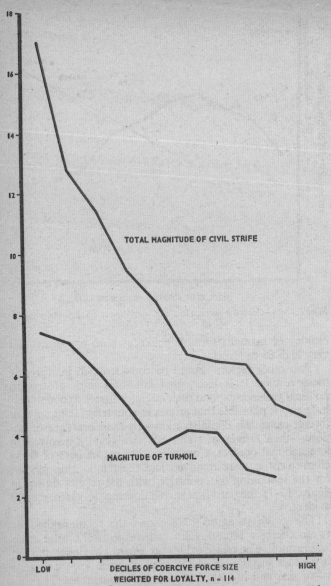

Figure 17-8.—Coercive force, size, weighted for loyalty and magnitudes
of civil strife, 1961-65.

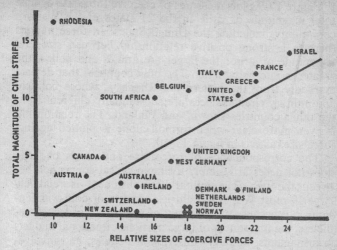

Figure 17-9—Coercive force, size, and magnitudes of civil strife in the Western community, 1961-65.

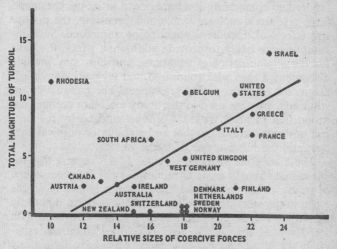

Figure 17-10—Coercive force, size, and magnitudes of turmoil in the Western community, 1961-65.

Figure 17-9 plots measures of coercive force size against total magnitude of strife in the 21 states of the Western community, including the United States. In these nations there is a strong positive relationship between size and magnitude of strife: the larger are armies and police, the greater is internal conflict. The only countries that deviate markedly from the pattern are Rhodesia, whose political and military circumstances are substantially different from the other countries shown, and Finland. The relationship is even more clear when turmoil alone is plotted against force size, as it is in figure 17-10.

The correspondence of force size and levels of strife does not necessarily imply a simple causal connection between the two. The military establishment is relatively large in most Western countries because of cold-war tensions, not because of the threat of internal disorder. Nonetheless, the investment of large portions of national budgets in armaments; military conscription policies; and involvement in foreign conflict have directly generated widespread popular opposition in the United States and France in the past decade, and may have provided a similar though less dramatic impetus to public protest in other Western nations.

Strength of institutions.—If social institutions beyond the family and community level are broad in scope, command large resources, and are stable and persisting, the disruptive effects of discontent ought to be minimized. Such institutions are likely to provide additional, peaceful means for the attainment of expectations, and also may provide discontented men with routinized and typically nonviolent means for expressing their grievances. The measure of institutional strength used in this study took into account the proportion of gross national product utilized by the central government; the number and stability of political parties; and the relative size of trades unions.

The results summarized in table 17-13 suggest that institutional strength tends to minimize strife in some groups of countries but not in others. Strong institutions have this effect in the most-developed, democratic nations, especially the Anglo-Nordic countries. They also are associated with low levels of strife in the least-developed countries, especially the elitist and African states. They have little effect on strife in the developing or Latin American nations, how-

614

ever, and in the nations with personalistic political systems, strong institutions apparently facilitate strife. The probable cause of these discrepancies is that the efficacy of strong nongovernmental institutions in minimizing strife depends on their political orientations. If the leaders of political parties and trade unions are strongly opposed to political leaders and their policies, they are likely to direct their organizations into demonstrative and sometimes violent opppositional activity. In Latin America and in some continental European nations, for example, such activity by political parties of the left and right and by unions is quite common. The establishment or reinforcement of strong and stable organizations thus does not necessarily minimize the potential for civil strife; the determining factors are likely to be the discontents and loyalties of the members of those organizations.

Facilitation.—A great many social and environmental conditions may facilitate the outbreak and persistence of strife. It is easier to organize collective action in organizations of likeminded individuals. Ideologies may provide the discontented with the belief that violent responses to depriving circumstances are justified. Jungle or mountain fastnesses can provide secure base areas for rebels. Three kinds of facilitation were measured in this study: the size and status of Communist parties (except in countries in which they were in power); the extent of isolated terrain; and the degree of foreign refuge, training, and supplies provided to rebels during the 1961-65 period.[18]

The last of these characteristics was expected to be an especially strong determinant of the magnitude of internal wars. This partly accounts for the high correlations shown in table 17-13 between facilitation and magnitudes of strife; the correlations are highest in the elitist, Islamic, Asian, and African nations, those in which internal wars have been most common. The high correlations between facilitation and strife in the polyarchic (democratic) and Western European nations reflects primarily the oppositional activities of Communist parties in them, only secondarily foreign support for rebels. Generally, extremist political activity by both left and right in the Western nations in the 1960's has led to turmoil of limited objectives, not to the guerrilla or revolutionary activities that attract and require material foreign support. One noteworthy finding was that facilitation, as measured in this study, has a statistically insignificant association with magnitudes of strife in Latin American countries. Despite dramatic cases of Communist instigation of revolutionary movements in Latin America, Communist activity and support apparently had little systematic effect on levels of Latin American strife in the early and mid-1960's.

Levels of Explanation of Civil Strife

Most of the causal variables used in this study have the predicted effects on levels of civil strife. To determine their combined explanatory power, the seven major variables discussed above were used in multiple correlation analyses, with the summary results shown in table 17-14. On the average, nearly three-quarters of the differences among nations in levels of civil strife are explained, in a statistical sense, by the conditions measured. The Latin nations are the only ones for which the level of explanation seems low. It is low, however, only by comparison with the other results. All the measures used in the study are relatively imprecise and indirect. Differences within nations, and their unique historical and contemporary characteristics, all play significant and largely unspecified parts in the genesis of civil strife. Given these limitations on this kind of study, the levels of explanation shown in table 17-14 are surprisingly high. These "explanations" are only statistical. Nonetheless they are persuasive evidence for the essential accuracy of most of the underlying theoretical arguments that dictated the measures to be used, and also suggest that the variables used represent many if not all the consequential, general causes of civil strife.

Some forms of strife in some groups of nations are less well explained than others. Turmoil, for example, is best accounted for when nations are grouped on the basis of geocultural similarity, poorly explained when they are grouped by level of economic development. A general interpretation is that the causes of turmoil are more closely linked with cultural differences than with stages of economic development or with type of political system. In other words, the cultural heritage of a nation may tell us more about the conditions to which discontented men are sensitive than information about its economic or political

616

Type of nation	Percentages of variation explained in magnitudes of—			
	Turmoil	Conspiracy	Internal war	Total strife
All nations (114)[b]...............	28	39	47	64
Nations grouped according to level of economic development:				
High (37)[b]...................	49	.41	45	66
Medium (39)..................	50	58	62	71
Low (38)....................	45	22	57	82
Nations grouped according to type of political system:				
Polyarchic (38)[b].............	45	63	41	64
Centrist (27)[c]...............	60	67	50	81
Elitist (32).................	45	32	71	74
Personalist (16).............	70	63	65	71
Nations grouped according to geo-cultural region:[d]				
Western community (21)[b,d]....	66	57	74	74
Latin (24)..................	62	45	22	49
Islamic (21)................	60	73	65	67
Asian (17).................	56	61	79	87
African (23)................	64	42	76	81
Average variation explained among groups[e]....................	53	52	59	72

[a] Results multiple correlation analysis using the 7 major explanatory variables discussed previously: short-term and persisting deprivation, legitimacy, historical levels of strife, coercive force size weighted by loyalty, institutionalization, and facilitation. The figures shown as percentages are multiple correlation coefficients squared (R^2), which represent the variation in magnitudes of strife in each group of nations that is statistically explained by the measures taken together. The R^2 statistic is always less than the sum of the separate, squared correlation coefficients because the causal variables themselves are intercorrelated. The correlation matrix for all polities is reported in Gurr, "A Causal Model of Civil Strife."

[b] Including data on the United States for 1961-65

[c] See footnote (d), table 17-11.

[d] Multiple correlation coefficients are distorted in the direction of perfect "explanation" when the number of variables used approaches the number of cases (countries). To minimize this effect the Eastern European group (8 nations) is excluded from this table and the Anglo-Nordic and Western Europe groups are combined.

[e] The average of the percentages for the 12 groups of nations.

system. Conspiracy is poorly explained in the least-developed nations, and also in the elitist and African nations, most of which are among the least developed. Conspiracy in many of these nations may reflect the largely dispassionate tactics of men seeking political power in situations in which there is little else worth seeking. Discontented they may be, for lack of power, but their discontents are not easily determined by the procedures used in this study, and the likelihood of their expression is probably influenced strongly by many unique rather than a few common circumstances. The minimal explanation provided for internal wars in Latin America, and the relatively weak accounting for all Latin strife, suggests that Latin American strife has causes distinctively different from those of other groups of nations. The common observation that strife in Latin America is "institutionalized" is one approach to the explanation of the difference.

One other pattern in the results worth noting is that the magnitudes of the specific forms of strife are less well explained than total magnitudes of strife in almost all groups of nations. There are partial, technical explanations for this. The most likely substantive explanation is that, despite its widely different manifestations and consequences, all civil strife has fundamentally similar causes, and that distinctions among its general or specific forms are somewhat arbitrary. Our general interpretation, which is largely supported by the results of this study, is that strife is predicated on intense discontents. The precise nature of those discontents, the forms in which they are expressed, their objects, and their immediate consequences are mediated by specific historical and social circumstances. But there seems to be an inescapable social dynamic to collective discontent. Societies in which there are intense and widespread discontents have a potential for disruptive internal conflict that sooner or later will find expression, whatever is done to control or divert it, short only of alleviating its causes.

A COMPARATIVE INTERPRETATION OF CIVIL STRIFE IN THE UNITED STATES

The United States unquestionably has experienced strife of greater intensity and pervasiveness in recent years than all but a very few other Western democracies. It is equally certain that violence in America has been less extensive and less disruptive than violence in a substantial number of non-Western nations. Americans have not experienced any strife whose scale or threat to the political order approaches the internal wars of countries like Venezuela, Colombia, the Sudan, or Iraq, much less the grim, nationwide bloodletting of the Congo, Indonesia, South Vietnam, or Yemen. Americans also have had little experience of the chronic revolutionary conspiracy and terrorism that characterizes countries like Algeria, Syria, Guatemala, or any of a dozen other nations. But this is merely to say that conditions in the United States could be worse. They pro-

618

vide little comfort when the tumult of the United States is contrasted with the relative domestic tranquility of developed democratic nations like Sweden, Great Britain, and Canada, or with the comparable tranquility of nations as diverse as the Soviet Union, Yugoslavia, Turkey, Malagasy, and Malaya.

Probably the most important general conclusion suggested by the descriptive evidence of the first part of this paper is that civil strife in the United States is different in degree but not in kind from strife in other Western nations. Turmoil is by far the most common form of strife in the United States and in the nations against which we compare ourselves in political, cultural, and economic terms. The antigovernment demonstration and riot, the violent clash of political or ethnic groups, and the student protest are pervasive forms of protest and conflict in modern democracies. Other nations have them in good measure also, but they also are much more likely to have serious conspiratorial and revolutionary movements. Such activities have been no more common in the United States than in other Western nations, despite the lip service given them. A comparative study of revolutionary movements would suggest that few of the advocates of "revolution" in the United States or most other Western countries have the dedication or skills to organize and sustain an effective revolutionary movement.

There also are distinct similarities between the classes and groups of people who participate in strife in the United States and those who participate in other European countries. Strife in the European countries is a cross-class phenomenon: it is quite likely to mobilize members of both the working and the middle classes, but rarely dissatisfied members of the political establishment. Strife also is likely to occur within or on the periphery of the normal political process in the Western nations, rather than being organized by clandestine revolutionary movements or cells of plotters embedded in the political and military hierarchy. All evidence suggests that some overt strife is an inevitable accompaniment of social existence. If so, it is certainly preferable—from the viewpoint of maintaining a semblance of social order—that it take the form of open political protest, even violent protest, rather than concerted, violent attempts to seize political power.

Similarities between the United States and other Western countries are also apparent in the comparative information on the human costs of strife. Civil strife in the United States has been chronic and pervasive, and has resulted in many bloodied heads, but the consequent loss of life has been proportionally no greater than in most European nations and substantially less than in many democratic nations.

One obvious and distinctive characteristic of civil strife in the United States is the extent to which it is a manifestation of ethnic hostilities. We repeatedly found evidence of parallel problems in other developed, European, and democratic nations. The unsatisfied demands of regional, ethnic, and linguistic groups for greater rights and socioeconomic benefits are more common sources of civil conflict in Western nations than in almost any other group of countries. This is apparent from the relative frequency with which such communal groups initiate strife in Western countries; the frequency with which communal objectives are expressed in strife; and the frequency with which strife includes attacks by members of communal groups on one another. The partial or discriminatory distribution of rights and benefits to minority groups, and the lack of national tolerance for their desires for establishing their own satisfying ways of life, appears to be a pervasive unresolved problem among modern nations. It is a problem that has persisted in many Western countries long beyond the solution of fundamental questions about the nature of the state, the terms of political power and who should hold it, and economic development. Such problems are also found in less-developed and non-Western countries, where they often lead to intense and protracted civil wars or to massive communal rioting. Their manifestations in Western nations are usually less severe. It is nonetheless ironic that nations that have been missionaries of technology and political organization to the rest of the world, nations that claim to provide more satisfying lives for the majority of their citizens than any others in human history, have thus far been unwilling or unable to provide satisfactory conditions of life for all their citizens.

The comparative evidence on the causes of civil strife takes account of three levels of causation. The fundamental cause of civil strife is deprivation-induced discontent:

the greater the discrepancy between what men believe they deserve and what they think they are capable of attaining, the greater their discontent. The more intense and widespread discontents are in a society, the more intense and widespread strife is likely to be. The specific nature of discontents and the patterns of social conditions that create and intensify them vary widely within and among societies. Nevertheless it is possible to identify and measure some of the general economic, political, and social conditions that are associated with short-term and persisting deprivation. Findings summarized above show that differences in the extent and degrees of deprivation among nations are responsible for a substantial part of their differences in magnitudes of strife. Among the Anglo-Nordic nations, including the United States, differences in persisting deprivation—especially the deprivation associated with discrimination—are very closely related to strife: two-thirds the variation in magnitudes of strife among them is explainable by differences in the degree and extent of persisting deprivation.

People's attitudes about the legitimacy of their political system and the justifiability of civil strife represent a second level of causation: such attitudes significantly influence the extent to which intense discontents are expressed in collective action. Evidence of this study demonstrates that the greater the apparent legitimacy of political regimes, the lower are all forms of strife in almost all groups of nations. The relationship is especially strong among the Anglo-Nordic countries. People's historical experience of strife is a significant determinant of justificatory attitudes about future strife. Among the developed, Western, and the democratic nations, those with the highest historical levels of civil violence are quite likely to have high levels of contemporary strife. The United States is no exception to the rule: along with countries like France and Italy, it has had a tumultuous past and a tumultuous present.

The third level of causation comprises the structural characteristics of nations and their governments that facilitate or minimize violent responses to discontent. One of the more striking findings of this study is that the size of military and police establishments has no consistent effects on strife. For nations generally, strife tends to be highest when coercive forces are of moderate or very large size proportional to population, lowest when they are either small or relatively large. The dubious value of large military and police establishments for minimizing civil strife is especially evident in the 21 nations of the Western community: among them, the larger the military and police establishment, the greater the magnitudes of strife. Other evidence suggests that the consistency with which coercion is employed is more important in minimizing strife than the size of the forces that employ it.

Another social characteristic associated with low levels of strife is the existence of strong and pervasive political and economic institutions. The Anglo-Nordic nations with large trade unions, stable political party systems, and large governmental sectors are more free of strife than those that lack these characteristics. The United States has the second of these three characteristics; compared with other Anglo-Nordic nations, however, unionization and the governmental sector are relatively small.[19] Facilitating social conditions, like the existence of extremist political organizations and the provision of external support for rebels, are important conditions of high magnitudes of violence in most types of nations but not in the Anglo-Nordic nations.

When measures of the three kinds of causal conditions of civil strife are all taken into account, most of the differences among nations in magnitudes of strife are accounted for. In the 21 nations of the Western community, 74 percent of the differences are statistically explained, for other groups of nations an average of 72 percent. One question that remains to be answered is, Which are the most important and immediate causes of strife? A series of causal analyses, reported elsewhere, was made in an attempt to answer this question.[20] When total strife in all nations was examined, we found that the immediate causes are, in declining order of importance, facilitation, persisting deprivation, short-term deprivation, and legitimacy. When magnitudes of turmoil in all nations were analyzed, only three conditions were directly related to current strife: persisting deprivation, historical levels of strife, and legitimacy. When the nations of the Western community were examined as a separate group, the results were similar: the immediate determinants of magnitudes of strife are historical levels of strife, long-term deprivation, facilitation, and legitimacy, in that order of importance.

These results do not indicate that conditions such as institutionalization and coercive capacities are irrelevant to strife, but that they are indirect causes. If institutionalization is high, coercive potential is likely to be high, if both are high, facilitation is likely to be low, and strife as a consequence is also likely to be low. The effects of short-term deprivation on magnitude of turmoil also are largely controlled by the immediate causes: if past strife and facilitation are low and coercive potential high, short-term deprivation is not likely to lead directly to turmoil. On the other hand, if past strife and facilitation are high and coercive potential low, the relationship of short-term deprivation to strife is magnified.

These findings have some general implications for explaining and resolving civil disorder in the United States. The United States has several of the conditions that in other nations lead directly to civil strife. Persisting deprivation characterizes the lot of most black Americans, whatever lipservice and legal remedies have been given to equality. Repeatedly we found evidence that comparable deprivation is a chronic and all but inevitable source of strife among other nations. If the general relationship holds for the United States, then the country is likely to be afflicted by recurrent racial turmoil as long as ethnic discrimination persists. The United States also has a history of turmoil, which increases the likelihood that all Americans, white and black, will respond to discontent with demonstrative and sometimes violent behavior. Traditions of violence are unalterable in the short run; the discontents whose disruptive effects are magnified by such traditions are susceptible to change.

The United States also has certain characteristics that in other countries tend to minimize the most destructive manifestations of discontent. Most Americans have a high regard for the legitimacy of their political system, however much they may object to some of its policies. If that legitimacy is maintained and reinforced, discontent is unlikely to lead to conspiratorial and revolutionary movements. On the other hand, if policies of government anger enough people badly enough, legitimacy is likely to be undermined. American political and economic institutions are also relatively strong by comparison with most countries of the world, if not by comparison with some Anglo-Nordic nations. Coercive potential also is high: the military and police are numerous and unlikely to support civil violence. Facilitative conditions are low: extremist political organizations have been few and small, and material foreign support for civil strife was and is nonexistent. Such generalizations nonetheless conceal major internal variations. Americans in many cities and regions have been underorganized and underserved by local governments. Police tactics have in many cases been inconsistent and repressive, intensifying rather than minimizing discontent. These conditions can be corrected by strengthening local organizations and improving the quality and training of police. Such policies may reduce levels of violence; if the experience of other nations is a guide, only the resolution of the underlying discontents that give rise to strife will eliminate it.

In conclusion, the United States has many of the conditions that in other nations lead to high levels of turmoil, but it also has the conditions that minimize the more intense and disruptive forms of civil strife. Both kinds of conditions are subject at least to limited change. If governmental legitimacy and military loyalties are seriously undermined and popular discontents persist and intensify, revolutionary movements are a distinct possibility. They occur in other countries under just such circumstances. If legitimacy, institutional capabilities, and the consistency of techniques of social control are increased and intense discontents alleviated, turmoil is likely to subside. A society in which intense discontents are manifest in riotous outbreaks and demonstrative public protest can count itself fortunate that they are not expressed in concerted revolutionary action. The members of that society at least have warning and time to ward off the more destructive manifestations of discontent, if they can and will treat its causes rather than its symptoms.

References

1. The research reported in this paper was supported in part by the Center for Research in Social Systems (formerly SORO) of the American University, and by the Advanced Research Projects Agency for the Department of Defense. This support implies neither sponsor approval of this article and its conclusions nor the author's approval of the policies of the U.S. Government toward civil strife. The assistance of Charles Ruttenberg and Diana Russell in research design, data collection, and analysis is gratefully acknowledged. Robert Van den Helm replicated and corrected the correlational analyses. Mary Fosler, Joel Prager and Lois Wasserspring assisted in data collection. Research was conducted at the Center of International Studies, Princeton University.

2. *Social and Cultural Dynamics, Vol. III: Fluctuation of Social Relationships, War, and Revolution* (New York: American, 1937), p. 504.
3. *Ibid.*, pp. 383-506.
4. Peter A. R. Calvert, "Revolution: The Politics of Violence," *Political Studies*, vol. XV (No. 1, 1967), p. 1.
5. See Ivo K. and Rosalind L. Feierabend, "Aggressive Behaviors Within Polities, 1948-1962: A Cross-National Study," *Journal of Conflict Resolution*, vol. X (Sept. 1966), pp. 249-271; and Betty A. Nesvold, "A Scalogram Analysis of Political Violence"; *Comparative Political Studies*, vol. II (July 1969).
6. Data for 1961-63 for 119 polities are reported in Ted Gurr with Charles Ruttenberg, *The Conditions of Civil Violence: First Tests of a Causal Model* (Princeton: Center of International Studies, Princeton University, Research Monograph No. 28, 1967). Data for 1961-65 for 114 polities are summarized in appendices to the present paper.
7. Note that the magnitude scores greatly understate the actual differences among and within nations, as explained in app. I. Scores should be expanded to their fifth power to determine the actual average of their component Pervasiveness, Intensity, and Duration scores.
8. For studies of ghetto riot participation, see *Report of the National Advisory Commission on Civil Disorders* (New York: Bantam Books, 1968), pp. 127-135; Governor's Select Commission on Civil Disorder, State of New Jersey, *Report for Action* (Trenton: State of New Jersey, 1968), pp. 129-131; Nathan E. Cohen, "The Los Angeles Riot Study," in Shalom Edleman, ed., *Violence in the Streets* (Chicago: Quadrangle, 1968), pp. 333-346; and Robert M. Fogelson and Robert B. Hill, "Who Riots? A Study of Participation in the 1967 Riots," *Supplemental Studies for the National Advisory Commission on Civil Disorders* (Washington, D.C.: National Advisory Commission on Civil Disorders, 1968), pp. 217-248.
9. The theoretical argument is made systematically and empirically documented in Ted Robert Gurr, *Why Men Rebel* (Princeton: Princeton University Press, in press), chs. 2, 3, 6, and 7. The relevance of frustration-aggression theory to civil strife is proposed in Gurr, "Psychological Factors in Civil Strife," *World Politics*, vol. XX (Jan. 1968), pp. 245-278.
10. The analyses are reported in Gurr with Ruttenberg, *The Conditions of Civil Violence*, pp. 71-76. But also see the paper by the Feierabends and Nesvold, elsewhere in this volume, which reports contradictory findings.
11. This pattern was first proposed by James C. Davies, "Toward a Theory of Revolution," *American Sociological Review*, vol. XXVII (1962), pp. 5-19. He provides evidence that the pattern preceded the Russian Revolution, Dorr's rebellion in Rhode Island in 1842, and the Egyptian revolution of 1952. Also see his paper elsewhere in this volume.
12. Evidence for the deprivation measures were obtained from a variety of news, historical, and statistical sources. Procedures and sources are described in Gurr, "A Causal Model of Civil Strife: A Comparative Analysis Using New Indices," *American Political Science Review*, vol. LXII (Dec. 1968).
13. Some suggestive survey evidence to this point is summarized in Gurr, *Why Men Rebel*, ch. 6. The historical evidence is amply provided by other papers in this volume.
14. See Douglas Bwy, "Political Instability in Latin America: The Cross-Cultural Test of a Causal Model," *Latin American Research Review*, vol. III (Spring 1968), pp. 17-66 and Gurr with Ruttenberg, *The Conditions of Civil Violence*, pp. 81-85.
15. Jennifer G. Walton, "Correlates of Coerciveness and Permissiveness of National Political Systems: A Cross-National Study," M.A. thesis, San Diego State College, June 1965.
16. Some of this evidence is reviewed in Gurr, *Why Men Rebel*, ch. 8. Also see the comparative study of governmental uses of coercion in Cuba and Venezuela by Gude, elsewhere in this volume.
17. Procedures used to construct these measures are described in Gurr, "A Causal Model of Civil Strife." The basic data for size of forces are military personnel per 10,000 adults and internal security forces per 10,000 adults, which were rescaled, weighted equally, and combined; the maximum possible score for a country is 30, the minimum 3. The U.S. score is 22. The "loyalty" scores used to weight these estimates take into account the length of time since the last forceful intervention of the military or police against the regime, and the frequency with which they resorted to illicit force in the 1961-65 period.

18. The facilitation measures are described in Gurr, "A Causal Model of Civil Strife." A better measure of organizational support for civil strife would take account of the size and status of all extremist political organizations; comparative data were available only for Communist parties.
19. Country data supporting this judgment are reported in Gurr, *New Error-Compensated Measures for Comparing Nations: Some Correlates of Civil Violence*, Research Monograph No. 25 (Princeton: Center of International Studies, Princeton University, 1966).
20. See the causal model analyses in Gurr, "A Causal Model of Civil Strife," and Gurr, "Urban Disorder: Perspectives from the Comparative Study of Civil Strife," in Louis H. Masotti and Don R. Bowen, eds. *Riots and Rebellion: Civil Violence in the Urban Community* (Beverly Hills: Sage Publications, 1968), pp. 51-67.

APPENDIX I

PROCEDURES USED IN COLLECTING AND SUMMARIZING CIVIL STRIFE DATA

Civil strife is defined as all collective, nongovernmental attacks on persons or property that occur within the boundaries of an autonomous or colonial political unit. By "nongovernmental" is meant acts by subjects and citizens who are not employees or agents of the regime, as well as acts of such employees or agents contrary to role norms, such as mutinies and military coups d'état. Operationally the definition is qualified by the inclusion of symbolic attacks on political persons or policies, e.g., political demonstrations, and by the exclusion of turmoil events in which less than 100 persons take part.

To obtain systematic data on civil-strife events, a set of coding sheets and a coding manual was devised for recording a variety of information about any strife event. The coding sheets and coding manual are published in Ted Gurr with Charles Ruttenberg, *Cross-National Studies of Civil Violence* (Washington, D.C.: Center for Research in Social Systems, The American University, 1969, in press), app. A.

A large number of sources were scanned and coded to get as full as possible a record of the strife events that occurred in 114 polities in the 1961-65 period. Three sources were systematically searched: the *New York Times; Newsyear* (the annual volumes of *Facts on File*); and *Africa Digest*. This information was supplemented from a variety of other sources, among them *The Annual Register of World Events; Africa Diary: Weekly Record of Events in Africa; Hispanic-American Report*; and country and case studies. Some 1,090 strife events were thus identified, coded, and the data punched on IBM cards. Many small-scale strife events, and some larger ones, probably were unreported in these sources and hence are not included. Moreover, much reported and estimated data are inaccurate in varying degrees. However, neither random nor systematic error seem great enough to affect substantially the analyses or conclusions reported here.

It was not always possible or desirable to record full information on each single event identified. When a number of related events occurred in a country over a single issue, like the series of antiwar demonstrations in the United States, they were summarized in a single record and tabulated as a single "event."

Data often were not available from the sources. For characteristics like class participation, motives, targets, and arrests, estimates were made on the basis of indirect evidence when possible, otherwise coded "no basis for judging." Data estimation procedures were used when numbers of initiators and numbers of casualties were not reported precisely. Methods used to estimate number of initiators serve as examples. The coding sheet contained two "number of initiators" scales. The first was a modified geometric progression of two, used to record proximate estimates of initiators; its first interval was 1 to 40, its highest 55,001 to 110,000. For purposes of summing such estimates to obtain total number of initiators, the midpoint of each interval was used. The second scale was used for recording rough estimates, sometimes coder estimates, of number of initiators, ranging from "less than 100" (set equal to 40 for purposes of computing totals) to "10,001 to 100,000" (set equal to 40,000). Data for events for which no estimate could be made were supplied by calculating and inserting means for the appropriate subcategory of event. For example, riots with no data on initiators were assumed to have the average number of initiators of all riots for which estimates were available.

Casualties were coded similarly to number of initiators, the principal missing-data component being estimates of injuries. The ratio of injuries to deaths was calculated for all events of each subcategory (e.g., all riots, all nonpolitical clashes) for which both data were available, and was used to estimate injuries for all such events for which "deaths" estimates but not injuries estimates were given. The general ratio for all well-reported strife was 12 injuries for each death.

"Duration" of strife events was almost always determinable from sources. It was coded on a geometric progression whose first two intervals were "one-half day or less" and "one-half to one day," and whose upper intervals were 4 to 9 months, 9 to 15 months, etc. No event was assigned a duration of more than 5 years, though some began before and/or persisted after the 1961-65 period.

To estimate relative magnitudes of civil strife, three kinds of summary measures were calculated from this data:

Pervasiveness: The extent of participation in civil strife in a polity, operationally defined as the sum of the estimated number of participants in all acts of strife as a proportion of total population, expressed as participants per 100,000 population.

Intensity: The human cost of strife, indexed here by the total estimated casualties, dead and injured, in all strife events in a polity as a proportion of total population, expressed as casualties per 10 million population.

Duration: The persistence of strife, indexed here by the sum of the spans of time of all strife events in each polity, whatever the relative scale of events, expressed as total days of strife.

Pervasiveness, Intensity, and Duration scores were calculated separately for each of three major forms of strife in each country: turmoil, conspiracy, and internal war. They also were calculated for all strife taken together for each polity. All these scores were converted into logarithms using a log $(X+1)$ transformation. To obtain combined magnitude scores for turmoil, conspiracy, internal war, and total strife (TMCS), the three component logged scores for each form were added; divided by 8 to obtain their eighth root; and the antilog used as each country's magnitude score. Country TMCS scores and ranks are shown in table 17-15, below. *It should be emphasized that these combination procedures result in scores that are not additive. To compare magnitudes of strife between countries with TMCS scores of 3.0 and 10.0, for example, the scores should be expanded to their fifth power (3.0^5 and 10.0^5) to determine the actual average of their respective Pervasiveness, Intensity, and Duration scores* The component scores are highly skewed, which makes this transformation necessary for a variety of statistical tests used in the study.

Additional data on the types, number of events, and characteristics of civil strife in the United States were collected for the period June 1, 1963, through May 31, 1968, using the sources and guidelines specified in the footnotes to table 17-15. Estimates of number of participants, casualties, and duration were obtained on an event-by-event basis to increase the precision of the magnitude scores. Classes of participants, motives, targets, and coercive response were not separately coded. The magnitude-of-strife scores for the United States in the comparisons in the first section of this paper are based on this information Comparisons of groups, motives, and targets of action in the first section are based on the summary of 1961-65 data for the United States, as are the correlation results in the second section.

Appendix Table 17-15.—List of polities, total magnitude of strife (TMCS) scores, 1961-65, and groupings

Polity	TMCS		Bases for grouping[a]		
	Score	Rank	Economic development	Political system	Geocultural region
Congo-Kinshasa[b] ...	48.7	1	Medium	Elitist	African
Indonesia[b]	33.7	2	Medium	Elitist	Asian
South Vietnam.....	32.8	3	Low	Elitist	Asian
Rwanda[b]	28.2	4	Low	Elitist	African
Yemen.............	23.6	5	Low	Elitist	Islamic
Angola.............	22.1	6	Low	Centrist	African
Dominican Republic	21.9	7	Medium	Personalist	Latin
Iraq..............	20.5	8	Medium	Personalist	Islamic
Venezuela..........	20.3	9	High	Polyarchic	Latin
Sudan.............	20.2	10	Low	Elitist	Islamic
Algeria............	19.5	11	Medium	Centrist	Islamic
Syria..............	17.8	12	Low	Personalist	Islamic
Colombia...........	16.9	13	Medium	Polyarchic	Latin
Rhodesia...........	16.4	14	Medium	Centrist	African/European
Uganda............	15.6	15	Low	Elitist	African
Zambia............	15.5	16	Medium	Elitist	African
Bolivia............	15.2	17	Medium	Polyarchic	Latin
Cuba..............	15.2	18	Medium	Centrist	Latin
Kenya.............	15.0	19	Medium	Elitist	African
Guatemala.........	14.5	20	Medium	Personalist	Latin
Israel[b]	14.0	21	High	Polyarchic	European
Burma.............	13.9	22	Medium	Elitist	Asian
Nigeria............	13.8	23	Low	Elitist	African
Argentina..........	13.2	24	High	Personalist	Latin
Ethiopia...........	13.2	25	Low	Centrist	African
Camerouns........	13.1	26	Low	Elitist	African
Italy..............	12.3	27	High	Polyarchic	European
Peru..............	12.3	28	Medium	Personalist	Latin

Polity	TMCS		Bases for grouping[a]		
	Score	Rank	Economic development	Political system	Geocultural region
France	12.1	29	High	Polyarchic	European
Tunisia	11.8	30	Medium	Elitist	Islamic
Greece	11.6	31	Medium	Polyarchic	European
Malawi[b]	11.6	32	Low	Elitist	African
Singapore	11.5	33	Medium	Polyarchic	Asian
Papua-New Guinea	11.3	34	Low	Centrist	Asian
India	11.0	35	Medium	Polyarchic	Asain
Burundi	10.9	36	Low	Elitist	African
Belgium	10.5	37	High	Polyarchic	European
Nepal	10.3	38	Low	Centrist	Asian
Thailand	10.3	39	Medium	Personalist	Asian
South Korea	10.2	40	Medium	Personalist	Asian
United States[c]	10.2	41	High	Polyarchic	European
Ecuador	10.1	42	Medium	Personalist	Latin
South Africa	10.0	43	High	Centrist	African/European
Mozambique	9.8	44	Low	Centrist	African
Guinea	9.5	45	Low	Elitist	Islamic
Panama	9.5	46	Medium	Personalist	Latin
Nicaragua	9.4	47	Medium	Personalist	Latin
Portugal	9.3	48	Medium	Centrist	Latin
Iran	8.4	49	Medium	Centrist	Islamic
Honduras	8.3	50	Low	Personalist	Latin
Mali	8.3	51	Low	Elitist	Islamic
Philippines	8.3	52	High	Polyarchic	Asian
Ceylon	8.2	53	Low	Polyarchic	Asian
Jordan	8.1	54	Medium	Centrist	Islamic
Ghana	7.9	55	Medium	Elitist	African
Somalia	7.9	56	Low	Elitist	Islamic
Haiti	7.8	57	Low	Personalist	Latin
Dahomey	7.7	58	Low	Elitist	African
Brazil	7.4	59	Medium	Polyarchic	Latin
Chad	7.2	60	Low	Elitist	African
Morocco	6.7	61	Medium	Polyarchic	Islamic
Liberia	6.6	62	Low	Centrist	African
Sierra Leone	6.5	63	Low	Elitist	African
Libya	6.3	64	Low	Polyarchic	Islamic
Pakistan	6.3	65	Low	Elitist	Islamic
Tanganyika	6.2	66	Low	Elitist	African
Uruguay	6.2	67	High	Polyarchic	Latin
Japan	5.9	68	High	Polyarchic	Asian
Lebanon	5.8	69	Medium	Personalist	Islamic
Niger	5.8	70	Low	Elitist	Asian
China	5.7	71	Medium	Centrist	Asian
East Germany	5.5	72	High	Centrist	European
El Salvador	5.4	73	Medium	Personalist	Latin
United Kingdom	5.4	74	High	Polyarchic	European
Czechoslovakia	5.3	75	High	Centrist	European
Spain	5.2	76	High	Centrist	Latin
Senegal	5.1	77	Low	Elitist	Islamic
Paraguay	5.0	78	Medium	Personalist	Latin
Turkey	5.0	79	Medium	Polyarchic	Islamic
Canada	4.9	80	High	Polyarchic	European
Chile	4.9	81	High	Polyarchic	Latin
Mexico	4.7	82	High	Polyarchic	Latin
West Germany	4.6	83	High	Polyarchic	European
Malaya	4.5	84	Medium	Polyarchic	Asian
Togo	4.1	85	Low	Elitist	African
Bulgaria	3.9	86	High	Centrist	European
U.A.R.	3.9	87	Medium	Centrist	Islamic
Cambodia	3.8	88	Low	Elitist	Asian
U.S.S.R.	3.6	89	High	Centrist	European
Poland	3.3	90	High	Centrist	European
Yugoslavia	3.3	91	High	Centrist	European
Austria	3.1	92	High	Polyarchic	European
Puerto Rico	2.9	93	High	Polyarchic	Latin
Hungary	2.8	94	High	Centrist	European
Costa Rica	2.7	95	Medium	Polyarchic	Latin

Polity	TMCS		Bases for grouping[a]		
	Score	Rank	Economic development	Political system	Geocultural region
Australia............	2.6	96	High	Polyarchic	European
Ireland.............	2.3	97	High	Polyarchic	European
Finland.............	2.1	98	High	Polyarchic	European
Afghanistan........	2.0	99	Low	Centrist	Islamic
Ivory Coast........	1.8	100	Low	Elitist	African
Jamaica............	1.5	101	Medium	Polyarchic	Latin
C.A.R.............	1.3	102	Low	Elitist	African
Switzerland.........	1.2	103	High	Polyarchic	European
Saudi Arabia.......	1.1	104	Low	Centrist	Islamic
China-Taiwan......	.0	105	High	Centrist	Asian
Denmark...........	.0	106	High	Polyarchic	European
Hong Kong.........	.0	107	Medium	Centrist	Asian
Malagasy...........	.0	108	Low	Elitist	African
Netherlands........	.0	109	High	Polyarchic	European
New Zealand......	.0	110	High	Polyarchic	European
Norway............	.0	111	High	Polyarchic	European
Romania...........	.0	112	High	Centrist	European
Sweden............	.0	113	High	Polyarchic	European
Volta..............	.0	114	Low	Elitist	African

[a] Economic development level was assessed on the basis of conditions in the late 1950s and early 1960s, the type of political system on the basis of conditions in the early 1960s. Some polities would be reassigned on the basis of conditions in them in the late 1960s.

[b] These scores are believed to be unrealistically high because of data estimation procedures used.

[c] The United States is ranked on the basis of 1961-65 civil-strife data. On the basis of June 1963-May 1968 data, it ranks 24th, with a TMCS score of 13.6.

APPENDIX II

PROCEDURES USED IN SELECTING AND GROUPING COUNTRIES FOR CROSS-NATIONAL COMPARISON

The universe of analysis includes all distinct national and colonial political entities that had a population of 1 million or more in 1962, excluding four countries for which data were judged un reliable (Albania, Mongolia, North Korea, and North Vietnam) and one (Laos) on grounds that it was a state in name only during the period in question. The remaining 114 polities include more than 98 percent of the world's population.

The 114 countries were grouped in several different ways to permit comparison of the effects of different levels of economic development, types of political system, and geocultural region on characteristics of strife. The bases of the groupings are as follows:

ECONOMIC DEVELOPMENT

Mary Megee, "Problems of Regionalizing and Measurement," *Peace Research Society: Papers,* vol. IV (1965), pp. 7-35, identified several factors underlying various measures of economic development for 153 nations and territories. The two major factors found were "industrial development" and "social overhead (infrastructure) and government expenditures." Countries were plotted according to their scores on these two dimensions into four quadrants: those low on both factors (very underdeveloped); those low on one of the factors (developing); and those high on both. A similar set of "regions" (groupings) also identified by Megee included one very underdeveloped set of nations, three sets of developing nations, a number of developed nations, and several dozen "isolated cases." We used the latter set of grouping, with certain modifications: Megee's "very underdeveloped" constitutes our "low economic development" group; her three groups of developing nations were combined into our "medium" group; and the developed nations constitute our "high" group. Megee's "isolate" polities were assigned to one of these three groupings on the basis of their quadrant locations. Six nations that fall just inside the "developed" quadrant we reclassified in the "medium" group: Cuba, Jamaica, Portugal, Greece, Turkey, and Indonesia. China-Taiwan was reclassified to the "high" group because of its very high industrialization score. Some apparent errors in her classifications also were corrected on the basis of her own and other data. Finally, a few polities not included by Megee were assigned to our categories on judgmental grounds. The economic groups of the 114 polities are shown in table 17-15.

TYPE OF POLITICAL SYSTEM

The background conditions for civil strife were expected to vary markedly from one type of political system to another, suggesting that polities be grouped on the basis of their political characteristics. The grouping used is based on the results of a Q-factor analysis of 68 specifically political variables for 115 nations, by Arthur S. Banks and Phillip M. Gregg, "Grouping Political Systems: Q-Factor Analysis of *A Cross-Polity Survey,*" *American Behaviorial Scientist,* vol. IX (Nov. 1965), pp. 3-6. The component variable are measures of such conditions as the degree or nature of ideological orientation, interest articulation, power distribution, role of the military, colonial tutelage (if any), and many others.

The factor analysis distinguished five classes of nations, each characterized by rather distinct patterns of political behavior and rule. We have used the authors' labels for them: *polyarchic,* nations the approximate Western democratic political structures and processes; *centrist,* Communist and other non-Latin American authoritarian regimes; *elitist,* recently indepedent, predominantly African states with relatively small, modernizing elites: *personalist,* predominantly Latin regimes characterized by unstable personalistic political leadership; and *traditional,* four nations such as Yemen. We reclassified polities from the traditional class to the larger group they most closely resembled. We also judgmentally assigned polities included in our 114 but excluded by Banks and Gregg to the remaining four groups. The political groups are shown in table 17-15.

GEOCULTURAL REGIONS

Assignment of nations to geocultural region was made on judgmental grounds, with some guidance from a factor analytic study by Bruce M. Russett, "International Regions and International Integration: Homogeneous Regions," Yale University, Department of Political Science, 1965 (mimeo). The groups were distinguished as follows:

Latin (24): All Latin American and Caribbean nations, plus Puerto Rico, Spain and Portugal.

Islamic (21): Countries whose populations are 50 percent or more Muslim, including the North African and Middle Eastern nations, Lebanon, and Saharan and sub-Saharan African countries of Guinea, Mali, Niger, Senegal, Somalia, and Sudan.

African (23): Non-Islamic African states and colonies. In the analyses of the first two sections of this paper, South Africa and Rhodesia were added to the group; in the correlation analyses in the third section, they are included in the Anglo-Nordic group, below.

Asian (17): Non-Islamic nations and colonies of mainland Asia and its periphery, including Papua-New Guinea but excluding Australia and New Zealand.

European (27): The countries of Eastern and Western Europe (except Spain and Portugal), plus the United States, the English-settled states of the British Commonwealth, and Israel. For the correlational analyses, these countries were divided into three more homogenous groups:

Anglo-Nordic (10): The three Nordic nations, Great Britain, the United States, and the English-settled states of the British Commonwealth, to which were added South Africa and Rhodesia.

Western Europe (11): Other non-Communist European states, plus Israel.

Eastern Europe (8): The European Communist nations.

Specific country designations are shown in table 17-15.

Chapter 18

SOCIAL CHANGE AND POLITICAL VIOLENCE: CROSS-NATIONAL PATTERNS

By Ivo K. Feierabend, Rosalind L. Feierabend, and Betty A. Nesvold*

This study examines selected aspects of social change and their effect upon political violence and the internal

* Ivo Feierabend is professor of political science; his wife Rosalind, associate professor of psychology at San Diego State College. Dr. Nesvold is assistant professor of political science at the College. The Feierabends have written a number of articles and papers based on their comparative studies of political instability, including "Aggressive Behaviors Within Polities, 1948-1962: A Cross-National Study," *Journal of Conflict Resolution,* vol. X (Sept. 1966), pp. 249-271. Their work received the American Association for the Advancement of Science's 1966 Socio-Psychological Prize for research in the behavioral sciences. Dr. Nesvold is the author of "A Scalogram Analysis of Political Violence," *Comparative Political Studies,* vol. II (July 1969).

political stability of nations.[1] The inquiry is predominantly empirical rather than speculative in nature. It is also extensive in scope, scrutinizing 84 nations in an attempt to discern broad global patterns of both change and violence.

In general, the study compares nations for their relative levels of political stability or instability, modernization, and rates of socioeconomic change. By means of these comparisons, the study approaches the question: In what ways are social change and development related to political violence within the sample of 84 nations at mid-20th century?

This broadly comparative, cross-national approach has its shortcomings. Important depth and detail are lost in the panoramic overview that would be more thoroughly preserved in intensive exploration of a single country. On the other hand, the advantage of the broader method lies in its scope. The examination of many cases can reveal patterns that may go unnoticed, or that may be obscured, in the unique circumstances of a specific case.[2]

THEORETICAL CONSIDERATIONS

The notion of social change is complex. It refers to movement through time of a variety of ecological, socioeconomic, political, structural, cultural, and ideational aspects and conditions of social existence. The problem is not only to clarify those aspects of social reality that are changing but also to specify the nature of the change. Is the social universe changing slowly or swiftly; is change continuous or discontinuous, or perhaps accelerating in some aspects and lagging in others? Elusive notions such as progress, growth, decline, and decay all entail some particularized view of change. Assumptions as to the direction of change are implicit in the concept of development, which suggests that change proceeds from one stage to another, or perhaps through several developmental phases. Withdrawal from one stage and movement toward another is referred to as "transition." The entire notion of change is sometimes identified with such periods of transition.[3]

Social Change and Violence

The assumption of a relationship between change and violence is based on arguments that are intuitively persuasive. Change, especially extensive, rapid, and abrupt change, is an unsettling and bewildering human experience. It is likely to create strain in the psyche of the individual and crisis in the social order. Old ways, familiar environments, deep-seated habits, and social roles become obsolescent, while a new way of life and a new routine are not yet clearly established. Social change is perhaps analogous to the experience of the individual who moves suddenly from one community to another. He lives in a new dwelling, interacts with a new set of individuals, faces new and strange situations that require an inordinate amount of difficult adjustment.

To project this example to a broader social base, one might argue that massive change that moves people physically into new environments, exposes their minds to new ideas, and casts them in new and unfamiliar roles is very likely to create collective bewilderment. This bewilderment may find its expression in turmoil and social violence. However, there are other, conflicting theoretical speculations that are equally persuasive. These suggest that change has beneficial and pacifying social consequences. If social change is perceived as bringing gratification, if it fulfills aspirations, there is no reason to expect social crisis in its wake. On the contrary, obstructing such change, or slowing its pace, should result in social discontent registered in protest movements and violence.[4]

Given these contradictory insights, the idea of change alone is not sufficient to explain the occurrence of violent political behavior. It is only when change brings with it social circumstances that breed discontent and strain, that it may be assumed to be responsible for social turmoil. Other modes of change will not so qualify. On the contrary, they may have a stabilizing effect on the political order. The blanket assertion that change breeds violence is too simplistic.

Our theoretical assumption linking change to violence begins with the notion that political turmoil is the consequence of social discontent. This commonsense assumption is predicated on a motivational rather than a structural orientation. And it reaffirms the often-repeated insight that political protest and revolution begin in the minds of men. Nevertheless, structural and processual variables are intimately a part of the wider view, since men's experience of change in the ecological, social, or political universe may create the revolutionary state of mind. In other words, although our assumptions are based on psychological, motivational factors, we are nevertheless interested in analyzing change in environmental, structural circumstances of political systems. What is required is some refinement of the idea of discontent and strain. Also needed is an effort to identify those modes of change and development that can be presumed to lead to the discontent that is the necessary precondition of political instability and violence.

Change, Systemic Frustration, and Aggression

While the concept of aggression has received extensive elaboration within psychology, the frustration-aggression hypothesis seems the most useful for our purposes.[5] In its most basic and fundamental formulation, this hypothesis maintains that aggression (as well as some other specified behaviors) is the result of frustration. Frustration itself is defined as the thwarting or interference with the attainment of goals, aspirations, or expectations. On the basis of frustration-aggression theory, it is postulated that frustration induced by the social system creates the social strain and discontent that in turn are the indispensable preconditions of violence. The commonsense assertion that revolutionary behavior has its root in discontent, and the more technical postulate that frustration precedes aggression, are parallel statements indicating a common insight.

The concept of frustration is often thought more appropriate to individual than to social circumstances. We believe, however, that the notion of *systemic frustration* makes the concept applicable to the analysis of aggregate, violent political behavior within social systems.[6] We define systemic frustration in reference to three criteria: (1) As frustration interfering with the attainment and maintenance of social goals, aspirations, and values; (2) as frustration simultaneously experienced by members of social aggregates and hence also complex social systems; and (3) as frustration or strain that is produced within the structures and processes of social systems. Systemic frustration is thus frustration that is experienced simultaneously and collectively within societies.

Guided by this definition, we may adopt two basic propositions from the frustration-aggression hypothesis and restate them with reference to social systems: (1) Violent political behavior is instigated by systemic frustration; and (2) systemic frustration may stem, among other circumstances of the social system, from specific characteristics of social change.

Four general hypotheses further qualify the notion of systemic frustration: (1) Systemic frustration at any given time is a function of the discrepancy between present social aspirations and expectations, on the one hand, and social achievements, on the other. (2) In addition, present estimates or expectations of future frustrations (or satisfactions) are also responsible for level of present frustration (or satisfaction). (3) Uncertainties in social expectations in themselves increase the sense of systemic frustration. (4) Conflicting aspirations and conflicting expectations provide yet another source of systemic frustration.

The first hypothesis focuses on the discrepancy between aspirations, expectations, and attainments within the present situation. This discrepancy is a result of the interplay between these factors in the present, and level of frustration is postulated to be a function of the number of aspirations involved, their level of valuation, their frequency of occurrence within various population strata, their expected level of attainment, and the degree of certainty with which these expectations are held. Similar criteria apply to the notion of social attainment. It should also be pointed out that it is perceived rather than actual social attainment that is important.

The distinction between aspirations and expectations needs clarification. In simplest definition, aspirations are the goals that people wish to attain. Also included in the definition are presently valued possessions that people desire to maintain. Expectations, on the other hand, include only the portion of aspirations which we expect to achieve. Strictly speaking, expectations refer always to the future. Yet expectations are disappointed (or fulfilled) in the context of the present. And this is the measure of systemic frustration as formulated in the first hypothesis.

The expectation of future frustration or satisfaction may also intensify or counteract present predicaments. The second hypothesis recognizes this possibility, hence uses the term "expectation" in a somewhat different sense. It does not refer to expectations regarding the present situation, but present expectations of future occurrences. The third hypothesis singles out uncertainty as yet another source of frustration. Uncertainty is a special quality of expectations. Ambiguity as to whether the future will bring disaster or salvation should be considered a distressful experience, adding to the present sense of frustration. Only in the case of disaster is certainty likely to be judged as more frustrating than uncertainty. Finally, the fourth hypothesis sees conflict as a systematically frustrating circumstance. Conflict is considered a specific case of frustration in which an individual's alternative motives, aspirations, and expectations work at cross-purposes, blocking one another.[7] The notions of intensity, scope, and distribution of aspirations are as relevant in this context as in the previous one.

Patterns of Social Change and Discontent

These theoretical propositions refine the general notion of systemic frustration and social discontent, but the important question still remains: What modes of change and development may we assume to lead toward systemic frustration? Let us point to a few studies in the recent literature of political violence, in order to identify objective social situations that are presumed to create a sense of systemic frustration.

Davies, in his analysis of several revolutions, concludes that, contrary to Marxian expectations, revolutions do not occur during periods of prolonged abject or worsening situations of social deprivation.[8] Neither does the evidence sustain the insight of de Tocqueville and others, that revolutions are perpetrated during periods of relative prosperity and improvement. Instead, Davies postulates a J-curve of socioeconomic development, whereby revolution occurs in social systems in which social well-being has been continually raised for an extended period of time, followed by an abrupt and sharp setback. His explanation is in accord with our notion of discontent and systemic frustration. We may suggest that certainty of social expectations was reinforced during the period of continued socioeconomic development. The sharp reversal in social fortunes creates an intolerable discrepancy between achievement and expectation. It is also possible that the unexpected reversal in attainment creates an alarmist expectation of continued severe decreases in levels of achievement. Such a fear for the future, possibly an exaggerated fear, motivates present actions as much as do actual present conditions.

Figure 18-1 graphically portrays Davies' hypothesis of the J-curve pattern of change. Furthermore it takes into account not only the sense of frustration that is created by disappointed expectations in the present, but also depicts estimates of the future. If men still anticipate future gratifications (depicted by line A in fig. 18-1), political violence is less likely to occur in the present. If, on the other hand, they anticipate intensified frustration (depicted by line B), the likelihood of violence is strengthened. In the latter case, the sense of frustration resulting from disappointed expectations in the present is intensified by the gap between present level of achievement and an even more pessimistic estimate of the future.

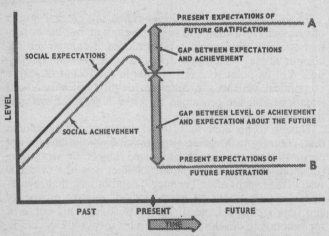

Figure 18-1.—J-curve change model—deterioration pattern.

Another type of J-curve may be equally productive of social discontent. A sudden and unexpected improvement in social circumstances may give rise to hopes of better things to come. If actual improvement is not sufficiently high to meet the newly aroused expectations, an intolerable gap between expectation and attainment will ensue, constituting systemic frustration. Again the argument is based on a contrast effect, one that give impetus to expectations. The novelty of gratification following a long history of deprivation may give the aspect of reality to long-suppressed aspirations. It is exaggerated hope for the future, in this case, which inevitably breeds disappointment.[9]

Figure 18-2 illustrates this situation. As shown, the social achievement line intersects the line of expectations at time t_1, or shortly after achievement exceeds expectations. Hence this is the point of social satisfaction. Yet at t_2, where achievement does not keep pace with soaring, newly awakened expectations, a gap occurs comparable to that in Davies' J-curve model. Expectations regarding the future in this model also may either detract or add to the present sense of systemic frustration.

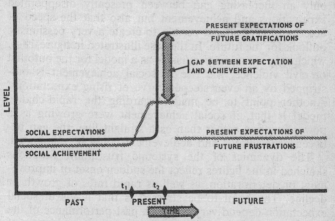

Figure 18-2.—J-curve change model—improvement pattern.

These models of social change indicate the dynamics of motivational factors stipulated in the first two hypotheses. There are also social circumstances that can be judged as unlikely to stimulate social discontent. Examples in the social process are situations in which objective achievement remains constant, no matter what that level may be, or situations in which acceleration or deceleration of change are either consistent or slight. Situations in which a minimal, gradual, or constant amount of change is experienced are the least likely to introduce striking discrepancies between present social expectations and present levels of achievement. Also, by avoiding contrast effects in achievement, expectations about the future are held fairly realistically in line with attainments. These social situations are represented in figure 18-3.

terioration is gradual and constant. On the other hand, very rapid social deterioration should have the consequences postulated in the J-curve of Davies: a discrepancy between expectations and achievements is created by rapid decline in social attainments. It is also conceivable that a rapidly improving situation could follow the pattern of the J-curve in figure 18-2.

This impact of rapid and consistent change is illustrated in figures 18-4 and 18-5. The model in figure 18-4 assumes that a rapidly deteriorating level of attainment creates not only an increasing gap between presently disappointed expectations and achievement but also that the speed of deterioration is almost certain to create a very pessimistic outlook for the future. In the case illustrated in figure 18-5, which may seem less persuasive as a model for the outburst of civil violence, the rise in social achievement is outstripped by an even steeper curve of rising expectations. Another point to be made regarding the rapid-change model is that, if social achievement were growing as a power function rather than as a straight line, the gap between expectations and achievement could be eliminated.

The dynamics of the systemic frustration situations sketched in the figures reflect the sudden onset of improvement or deterioration, as well as rapid rates of growth or decline. The point to be stressed is that levels of social expectation depend very much on past performance of the social system. Men who experience a constant history of either frustration or satisfaction will develop learned expectations consistent with their experience. Abrupt change in objective circumstances, especially a reversal of direction but also, at least at the outset, a very rapid rise or decline, will have a sharp and sometimes unrealistic impact on expectations. The consequent lack of alignment between expectations and attainments creates the intolerable discrepancy which is postulated as the motivational antecedent to political violence.

Unrealistic expectations regarding the future may also be pinned to a major change in circumstance that is clearly certain to occur at a particular point in time. The irreality

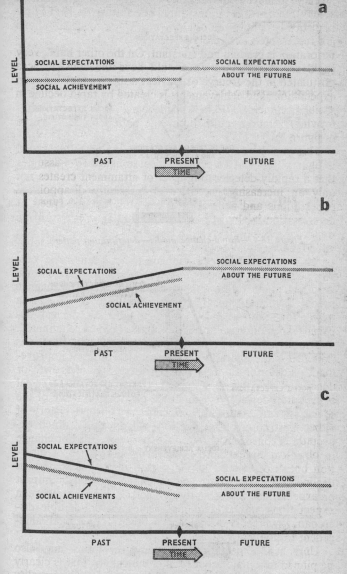

Figure 18-3.—Minimal changes model.

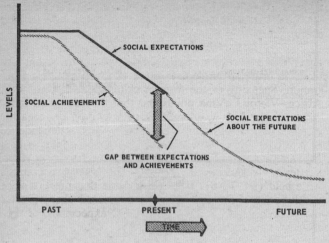

Figure 18-4.—Rapid-change model—deterioration pattern.

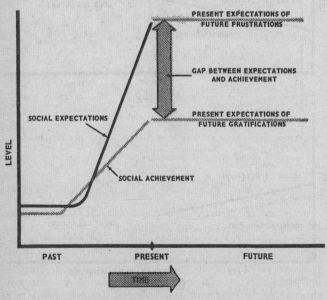

Figure 18-5.—Rapid-change model—improvement pattern.

of such expectations is that a variety of other changes are also anticipated concomitant with the single, clearly stated event.

There are situations in the present century in which exaggerated expectations regarding some future event are likely to bring an immediate sense of sharp systemic frustration. Speaking of the trauma of independence in West Africa, Victor LeVine points out that the advent of independence is often counted upon to provide a panacea for all the social ills besetting a country.[10] When independence does occur, however, it falls far short of providing a perfect solution to all problems. This experience proves a shattering frustration if, in fact, such high expectations were held (fig. 18-6). It is indisputable that the extent of revolutionary behavior in Africa increased sharply after independence was granted. It was the expectation of momentous change that proved illusory.

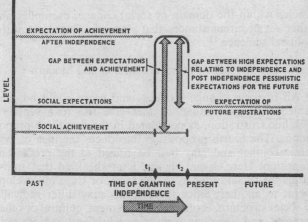

Figure 18-6.—Disappointed expectations tied to future events.

In figure 18-7, flux in social and economic performance or policy is postulated as creating social discontent and political violence. Flux is likely to create ambiguity and uncertainty of expectations, as suggested in the third hypothesis. Discontinuous economic growth, that is, alternating periods of relative prosperity and economic slump in short succession, or conflicting policies simultaneously pursued or sequently administered, as well as other inconsis-

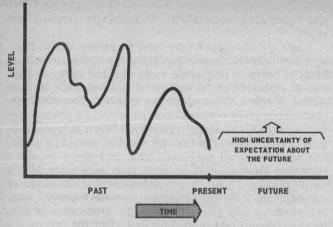

Figure 18-7.—*Fluctuation change model.*

tencies within the domain of social change, exemplify another set of circumstances that ripen the impulse toward political violence.[11]

Conflict Between the Traditional and Modern

All of these change models—and more could be generated[12]—suggest situations that give rise to a sense of systemic frustration, as postulated in the first three propositions. The fourth proposition introduces the idea of systemic conflict and may best be traced to the process of transition. Here, social change is of the kind that transforms the social order from one form, or stage of development, to another. Since these forms may differ radically in social structure, economic achievement, culture, or other respects, and since one form is receding and another only slowly gaining ground, a large area of struggle and conflict between the new and the old is likely to occur. Indeed, conflict may be seen as indispensable to the very notion of transition and transformation. If the new and the old were similar and harmonious, if little or no change were required, it would be superfluous to speak of transition.

The notions of development, stages, and transition are familiar themes, as is the idea that political violence is associated with the transitional process. In different periods of history, the process of transition has been conceptualized in different ways; for example, as a change from religious to secular society or from small principalities to nation-states. The dominant contemporary view stresses the process of modernization, which is seen as engulfing the less-developed nations of today's world. In this view, nations may be classified into three groups: modern societies, traditional societies, and modernizing societies. The latter are passing through the transitional stage from traditional society to modernity. Generally, this period of transition is regarded as one that entails an inordinate amount of strain, tension, and crisis.[13]

On the evidence, members of transitional societies aspire to the benefits of modernity, yet modern goals may be blocked by the values inherent in traditional society.[14] Any modicum of modernity introduced into traditional society will conflict with its traditions. The farther the process of transition progresses, the more likely and the more intense the conflicts between modern and established patterns. The situation may be depicted as a massive conflict, reflected in myriad individual psyches of different strata of the population and infecting different domains of the social process. It may lead to intergroup conflict between more traditional and more modern strata with conflicting social roles, structures, and expectations.

Figure 18-8 attempts to schematize the pattern. If we assume that many traditional patterns are in fact incompatible with modernity, then the midpoint of the transitional process is the point of highest intensity of conflict

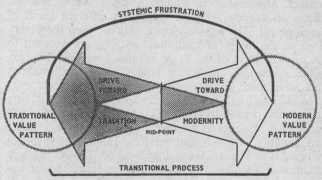

Figure 18-8.—Systemic—conflict model of transition.

and hence the point of highest systematic frustration. The stage of transition is also the one most likely to be characterized by a high incidence of violent activity. It is at this midpoint that the accomplishments of modernity equal those of tradition, and the drive toward modernity is offset by the contradictory and equal attraction of traditional ways. This should be the stage of the most intense struggle between the traditional and the modern. Figure 18-8 symbolizes this systemic conflict situation with two intersecting arrows representing traditional and modern drives. The closer the transitional process to the stage of modernity (tradition), the stronger the modern (traditional) drive, and the weaker the traditional (modern) drive. (This strengthening and weakening of drives is depicted by the varying width of the two arrows.) The forces determining the strength and weakness of the two drives are specified by the psychological hypothesis that postulates a strengthening of drive with proximity to the goal.[15] Hence the closer the transitional country to either modernity or tradition, the less the systematic conflict. As a country approaches either end of the transition continuum, the attraction toward the closest value pattern overcomes the drive in the opposite direction.

The Processes of Modernization

It can be argued that all of the conditions conducive to systematic frustration are produced by the modernization process, in addition to the occurrence of systematic conflict. Modernization, especially since World War II, affects an uneven array of nations at different levels of development. The less-developed nations, even those very close to the image of traditional society, are exposed to the modern ways of the more advanced nations. This exposure alone may create new aspirations and expectations and leave them unmatched by social achievements.

Modernity itself denotes a very specific mode of culture and social organization. It includes the aspiration and capacity in a society to produce and consume a wide range and quantity of goods and services. It includes high development in science, technology, and education, and high attainment in scores of specialized skills. It includes, moreover, a secular culture, new structures of social organization and more specialized and differentiated participation, new sets of aspirations, attitudes, and ideologies. Modern affluent nations with their complex economic, political, and social systems serve best as models of modernity to nations emerging from traditional society.

The adoption of modern goals, although an integral aspect of modernity, is hardly synonymous with their attainment. The arousal of an underdeveloped society to awareness of complex modern patterns of behavior and organization brings with it a desire to emulate and achieve the same high level of satisfaction. But there is an inevitable lag between aspiration and achievement. The more a country is exposed to modernity and the lower its level of development, the greater the discrepancy between achievement and social aspirations. It is postulated that the peak discrepancy between systematic goals and their satisfaction, and hence maximum systemic frustration, is likely to occur during the transitional phase. Highly modern and truly traditional nations should experience less systemic frustration—in the modern nations, because of their ability to provide a high level of attainment commensurate with modern aspirations; in the traditional nations, unexposed to modernity, because modern aspirations are still lacking. Figure 18-9 depicts the increasing and de-

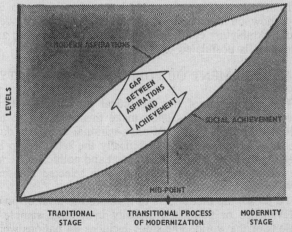

Figure 18-9.—Model of uneven growth of modern aspirations and achievement during transition.

647

creasing gap between modern aspirations and modern achievements.

A similar logic is applicable not only to social aspirations but also to social expectations. Furthermore, there may also be a feedback effect stemming from modern social attainment. It could be argued that the satisfaction of modern wants and aspirations reinforces the expectation of further satisfaction. As modern aspirations are formed through the process of exposure to modernity, if even a few aspirations are satisfied, these few satisfactions may create the drive and expectation for more, thus adding to the sense of systematic frustration. If so, it could be assumed that the faster the rate of modern achievement, the greater the feedback effect and the more thorough the "revolution of rising expectations." It is in this sense that rapid rates of change, as opposed to gradual change toward modernity, could lead to more rather than less frustration, the situation postulated in the model in figure 18-5. At the same time, rapid achievement could reduce the gap between aspirations and attainment and hence reduce the sense of frustration. Rapid rate of change in the establishment of modernity in this estimation then could have contradictory effects.

The aura of uncertainty also hangs over the entire process of social change, a consequence of its conflicts and confusions. There is ambivalence of attitudes to old ways now on the wane, as well as toward the modern future. Ambiguity epitomizes the transitional process, and ambiguity is postulated to increase frustration.

MEASUREMENT OF POLITICAL INSTABILITY

The complexity of the theoretical propositions elaborated in the previous section make them difficult to test precisely through the use of cross-national aggregate data. We may, however, assess empirically the relationship between levels or stages of development and political violence, as well as between violence and some selected measures of rate of socioeconomic change.[16]

To do so, the first task is to measure the level of political violence or political instability in a large sample of nations of the world. The study includes 84 nations which are examined for an 18-year period, 1948-65. Every reported event relevant to political instability that occurred in these countries during the time period is recorded to form a cross-national data bank of political instability events. (See the appendix for a detailed description of the data.)

Events are scaled in terms of an intensity weighting that assigns values on a seven-point scale. The scale ranges from 0, extreme stability, to 6, extreme instability. In assigning scale values to events, the criteria used are the amount of violence accompanying the event, the number of persons involved in the event, its duration, the political significance of persons involved in the event, and an estimate of the political repercussions of the event upon the society as a whole. Typical scale positions assigned to events are the following: regularly scheduled election, 0; dismissal or resignation of cabinet official, 1; peaceful demonstration or arrest, 2; assassination (except of chief of state) or sabotage, 3; assassination (of chief of state) or terrorism, 4; coup d'etat or guerrilla warfare, 5; civil war or mass execution, 6.

Countries are profiled in a number of different ways. One basic technique is to assign countries to groups on the basis of the event with the highest scale value experienced during the time period under investigation. Within these intensity groupings, countries are ranked according to both frequency and intensity scores. The types of profiles yielded by this grouped intensity and frequency technique are illustrated in table 18-1. Table 18-1A shows country instability profiles for the entire 18-year period, 1948-65, grouped according to the single most violent event experienced. It will be noted that the distribution is highly skewed, with most countries falling at scale position 5 and quite a few at scale position 6. This profiling tells us that, within this relatively long time period, a large number of countries experienced a high level of instability, although perhaps only temporarily. It also shows that there is a smaller number of countries that did not experience a single severely unstable event in the entire 18 years. If instability scores are averaged for three six-year subperiods within the 18 years, as in table 18-1B, a more normal distribution is obtained. In this profiling, countries that have experienced severe internal turmoil, but only briefly, have their scores tempered by the periods of relative quiescence.

Table 18-1A.—National Political Instability Profiles, 1948-65
(Grouped scores, n = 84)

1 — Stability

Luxembourg	1:012

2

Finland	2:056
Australia	2:026
Netherlands	2:021
Sweden	2:020
New Zealand	2:015

3

U.K.	3:112
W. Germany	3:087
Canada	3:084
Libya	3:069
Romania	3:060
Switzerland	3:042
China (Taiwan)	3:039
Norway	3:034
Ireland	3:031
Iceland	3:026
Saudi Arabia	3:018

4

United States	4:318
Spain	4:284
Iran	4:237
Pakistan	4:231
Italy	4:192
U.S.S.R.	4:165
Belgium	4:162
Chile	4:156
Ceylon	4:152
Japan	4:123
Mexico	4:111
Ghana	4:106
Uruguay	4:100
Yugoslavia	4:077
Bulgaria	4:071
Albania	4:067
Israel	4:064
Austria	4:057
Liberia	4:036
Denmark	4:030
Afghanistan	4:029

5

France	5:435
Venezuela	5:429
So. Africa	5:422
India	5:360
Syria	5:329
Guatemala	5:234
Lebanon	5:212
Brazil	5:209
Haiti	5:205
Peru	5:196
Morocco	5:134
Portugal	5:190
Turkey	5:179
Poland	5:152
Thailand	5:152
Egypt	5:145
Jordan	5:117
Ecuador	5:117
Malaya	5:108
Philippines	5:105
Nicaragua	5:096
El Salvador	5:079
Cambodia	5:071
Ethiopia	5:034

6 — Instability

Argentina	6:445
Indonesia	6:413
Bolivia	6:318
Korea	6:291
Cuba	6:283
Iraq	6:274
Colombia	6:214
Greece	6:236
Burma	6:213
Dom. Rep.	6:195
Sudan	6:189
Paraguay	6:141
E. Germany	6:138
Laos	6:129
Tunisia	6:126
Cyprus	6:123
Hungary	6:113
Honduras	6:105
Panama	6:101
Czech.	6:100
China (mainland)	6:086
Costa Rica	6:058

Table 18-1B.—Political Instability Profiles of 84 Countries (1948-65)
(Stability Score Shown for Each Country is Grouped Score, Averaged)

1	2	3	4	5	6
			France 13435		
			Union of South Africa 13422		
			Brazil 13209		
			Morocco 13194		
			Portugal 13190		
			Turkey 13189		
			Poland 13179		
			Thailand 13152		
			Jordan 13145		
			Cyprus 13123	Argentina 16445	
			Hungary 13113	Bolivia 16318	
			Philippines 13105	Cuba 16283	
			Czechoslovakia 13100	Iraq 16274	
			China (Mainland) 13086	Colombia 16244	
			Cambodia 13071	Burma 16213	
			India 12360	Venezuela 15429	
			Iran 12237	Syria 15329	
			Pakistan 12231	Korea 15291	
			Sudan 12189	Haiti 15205	
			U.S.S.R. 12165	Peru 15196	
			Ecuador 12117	Greece 14236	
			Nicaragua 12096	Guatemala 14234	
		Belgium 10162	United States 11318	Lebanon 14212	
		Chile 10156	Spain 11284	Egypt 14152	
	U.K. 07112	Mexico 10111	Dom. Rep. 11195	Paraguay 14141	
	Ghana 07106	Uruguay 10100	Ceylon 11152	East Germany 14138	
	Austria 07057	Israel 10064	Japan 11123	Laos 14129	
	Denmark 07030	Liberia 10036	Malaya 11108	Tunisia 14126	
	Iceland 07026	Ethiopia 10034	Yugoslavia 11077	Honduras 14105	
	W. Germany 06087	Italy 09192	Bulgaria 11071	Panama 14101	
	Finland 06056	Libya 09060	Albania 11067	El Salvador 14079	Indonesia 18416
	China (Taiwan) 06039	Romania 09060			
	Australia 06026	Costa Rica 09058			
	Sweden 06020	Afghanistan 09029			
	Ireland 05031	Canada 08084			
	Saudi Arabia 05018	Switzerland 08042			
Netherland 04021	New Zealand 05015	Norway 08034			
Luxembourg 03012					

Stability ———————————————————————————— Instability

651

Only Indonesia remains in scale position 6, indicating that it has experienced civil war during each of the three sub-periods.

Another method of profiling nations on political instability is to sum the scaled events for the entire time period without grouping the nations. The profiles yielded by this method rank countries somewhat differently than previously. Frequency of events, though weighted for intensity, is a more dominant factor than in the grouped scoring method. A final scaling method uses only violent events. The profiling of nations with these violent events (scored by the Guttman technique, see appendix) is presented in table 18-2.

It should be pointed out that all of these scaling methods show a high level of agreement, while at the same time shifting the position of specific countries in response to different emphases in the scaling criteria. The United States, for example, is at the midpoint of the 84 countries in tables 18-1A and 18-1B, but among the most unstable 25 percent of countries in table 18-2.

Table 18-2.—Political Violence Profiles of 84 Countries (1948-65)
[Sources Derived from Guttman Scalogram]

Country	Score	Country	Score	Country	Score
Finland	0	Yugoslavia	27	Dominican Republic	70
Luxembourg	0	China (mainland)	28	Sudan	71
Denmark	1	El Salvador	28	Laos	72
Iceland	1	Belgium	31	Greece	73
New Zealand	1	Albania	32	Paraguay	74
Saudi Arabia	1	Japan	32	Haiti	77
Netherlands	2	Czechoslovakia	33	Pakistan	77
Norway	3	Mexico	33	Portugal	77
Sweden	3	Ghana	35	Morocco	79
Australia	4	Malaya	36	U.S.S.R.	81
Afganistan	7	Chile	38	Lebanon	83
Austria	7	East Germany	39	Burma	87
Ireland	7	Cyprus	41	France	95
Switzerland	7	Ecuador	41	Colombia	96
Israel	8	Jordan	41	United States	97
China (Taiwan)	9	Honduras	42	Guatemala	109
Canada	10	Panama	42	Syria	111
Liberia	15	Hungary	45	Iran	114
Uruguay	16	Nicaragua	48	Bolivia	120
United Kingdom	17	Ceylon	51	Iraq	120
Ethopia	19	Philippines	51	Spain	121
Italy	19	Poland	54	Cuba	123
Romania	20	Tunisia	54	India	124
West Germany	20	Egypt	56	Korea	125
Costa Rica	21	Brazil	57	Argentina	134
Cambodia	24	Peru	64	Venezuela	153
Bulgaria	25	Thailand	65	Union of South Africa	158
Libya	25	Turkey	65	Indonesia	190

In subsequent sections of the study in which we analyze the relationships among measures of development, rates of change, and political instability and violence, we use

these several techniques of qualifying the notion of instability and violence. In all of the studies, a consistent patterning of relationships is found, no matter which measure
of instability is used. In most of the analyses, data are used
from the entire time period, 1948-65. In some cases, however, a particular subperiod of time is selected because of
its relationship to measures of the ecology of the system.

LEVEL OF DEVELOPMENT AND POLITICAL VIOLENCE

The hypotheses stated in the theoretical portion of this
paper are that modern and traditional nations tend toward
stability, while transition leads to political turmoil and
violence. Also, the closer a country to some theoretical
midpoint between tradition and modernity, the stronger
the impulse to political instability. This is the logic of the
conflict model of the transitional process, as well as of the
exposure-to-modernity model.

In order to test these hypotheses, some cross-national
measure of modernity is necessary, to compare levels of
political violence. Given the complexities of the notion of
modernity and the process of modernization, the measurement task is an exceedingly difficult one. Our measurement cannot embrace all aspects of modernity. It is confined to a specific set of indicators which, in combination,
yield a rough indication of developmental level.

Economic Development

Let us turn first to a rather narrow definition of modernity, assuming that the difference between a modern and
a traditional country lies in their relative wealth. Highly
affluent modern nations are those capable of producing
great quantities of goods and services and of providing
their citizens with high standards of living, high incomes,
adequate education, health, and other socioeconomic benefits. With this approach, modernity may be measured in
terms of the degree to which a nation enjoys some very
specific commodity such as per capita gross national product (GNP), caloric intake, telephones, physicians, etc.
These indices of modernity may be used singly, to indicate
that particular aspect of modernity, or they may be com-

bined, indicating a more comprehensive and summary view of modern development. In this study, a set of separate indicators is employed, as well as a composite modernity index. The modernity index combines GNP per capita, caloric intake, telephones, physicians, newspapers, radios, literacy, and urbanization.[17]

Level of modernity is thus assessed quantitatively: those countries scoring high on the selected indicators are judged modern, while the median range denotes the transitional group of nations. It should be pointed out that a country which is low on these indicators may be a traditional country, but not necessarily. A further criterion for distinguishing a traditional society is that it is static and unchanging. By this definition, a traditional country must not only be low in its level of development, but it must maintain this low level over time. A tendency toward improvement in economic conditions places it in the transitional group. In terms of this criterion, we have very few if any traditional countries in our sample. This lack is inevitable since a traditional country in this sense will not collect statistical data and so not be amenable to study in terms of our empirical approach. This is not to say that there are no extremely underdeveloped countries among our sample of 84. On the contrary, there are a number that are characterized by minimal industrialization, almost total dependence on agriculture or extractive industry, and a very thin stratum of educated persons within the population.

While we have predicted that very little political unrest will occur in the most traditional nations, with violence increasing with modernization to reach a peak among nations at midpoints of development, and then subsiding again among modern, industrial states, this complete pattern may not be evident in our cross-national sample. If, in the present analysis, most of the nations are either caught in the midst of transition to modernity or have achieved a high level of industrialization, we would expect the prevailing relationship to show a consistent trend of decreasing political unrest with increasing development.

Let us look first at the relationship between the composite index of modernity and political unrest. In table 18-3, countries are classified into three groups: modern, transitional, and so-called traditional states, and further

Table 18-3.—*Relationship Between Modernity and Political Instability, 1948-65*
(Grouped Scores)

	I. Traditional	II. Transitional	III. Modern	
Unstable (5:105-6:445)	Bolivia Burma China (mainland) Haiti India Indonesia Iraq Jordan Laos Malaya Morocco Philippines Sudan 13	Brazil Colombia Costa Rica Cuba Cyprus Dom. Rep. Ecuador Egypt Greece Guatemala Honduras Hungary Korea	Lebanon Panama Paraguay Peru Poland Portugal Syria Thailand Tunisia Turkey Union of South Africa Venezuela 25	Argentina Czechoslovakia East Germany France 7	42
Stable (1:012-5:096)	Afghanistan Cambodia China (Taiwan) Ethiopia Ghana Iran Liberia Libya Pakistan Saudi Arabia 10	Albania Bulgaria Ceylon Chile El Salvador Italy Japan Mexico Nicaragua Romania Spain Yugoslavia		Australia Austria Belgium Canada Denmark Finland Iceland Ireland Israel Luxembourg	Netherlands New Zealand Norway Sweden Switzerland United Kingdom United States Uruguay U.S.S.R. West Germany 20	42
	23	37		24	84

Table 18-4.—Relationship Between Economic Development and Political Instability, 1948-65*

	I. Traditional Primitive	II. Traditional Civilization	III. Transitional	IV. Industrial Revolution	V. High Mass Consumption
Unstable (5:105–6:445)	Burma Laos Sudan	Bolivia China (mainland) Haiti India Thailand	Dominican Republic Ecuador Egypt Guatemala Honduras Indonesia Iraq Jordan Korea Morocco Paraguay Peru Philippines Portugal Syria Tunisia Turkey	Argentina Brazil Colombia Costa Rica Cuba Cyprus Czechoslovakia East Germany Greece Hungary Lebanon Malaya Panama Poland Union of South Africa Venezuela	France
	3	5	17	16	1
Stable (1:012–5:096)	Afghanistan Ethiopia Libya	Cambodia Liberia Pakistan	Albania Ceylon China (Taiwan) El Salvador Ghana Iran Nicaragua Saudi Arabia	Austria Bulgaria Chile Finland Iceland Ireland Israel Italy Japan Mexico Romania Spain Uruguay U.S.S.R. Yugoslavia	Australia Belgium Canada Denmark Luxembourg Netherlands New Zealand Norway Sudan Switzerland United Kingdom United States West Germany
	3	3	8	15	13
	6	8	25	31	14
					42
					42
					84

* These categories of economic development are from Russett et al, *op. cit.*

subdivided into stable and unstable categories.[18] We see that the modern countries are predominantly stable (20 stable and 4 unstable). Transitional countries, on the other hand, are unstable by a ratio of 2:1. And among so-called traditional countries (which are those lowest in development level), instability also predominates but by a less striking ratio of 13:10. Very similar results are obtained using Russett's five-level classificatory scheme of economic development, shown in table 18-4.[19]

We may also determine socioeconomic conditions that represent critical threshold levels of political stability and instability. The possibility of finding such threshold values is illustrated in table 18-5, which presents eight tables based on environmental indicators (literacy, GNP per capita, radios, newspapers, telephones, physicians, calories, and urbanization).[20] From these empirical tables, a composite picture of the stable country emerges: it is a society which is 90 percent or more literate; with 65 or more radios and 120 or more newspapers per 1,000 population; with 2 percent or more of the population having telephones; with 2,525 or more calories per day per person; with not more than 1,900 persons per physician; with a GNP of $300 or more per person per year; and with 45 percent or more of the population living in urban centers. If all of these threshold values are attained by a society, there is an extremely high probability that the country will achieve relative political stability. Conversely, to the extent that gratifications are less than these threshold values, the greater the likelihood of political instability.

To complete this picture of the relationship between economic modernization and political instability, we may look at a further set of economic, social, and political indicators of development and their relationship to the level of political violence within society.[21] The emphasis in this case is on violence with the scoring of political unrest based solely on violent events (as illustrated in table 18-2).

The following were selected as broad indices of industrialization and development in the economy: (1) percent of the population living in urban centers; (2) percent of the gross domestic product (GNP) that comes from agriculture; (3) percent of the labor force engaged in agriculture; and (4) GNP/capita. To supplement these data, other attributes of society were also examined, such as the

A. Percent literacy

	Low (below 90%)	High (above 90%)	Total
Unstable	48	5	53
Stable	10	19	29
Total	58	24	82

Chi square = 25.93, $p < 0.001$
Yule's $Q = 0.90$

B. Radios per 1,000 population

	Low (below 65)	High (above 65)	Total
Unstable	45	6	51
Stable	9	20	29
Total	54	26	80

Chi square = 25.02, $p < 0.001$
Yule's $Q = 0.887$

C. Newspapers per 1,000 population

	Low (below 120)	High (above 120)	Total
Unstable	48	5	53
Stable	6	10	16
Total	54	15	69

Chi square = 17.34, $p < 0.001$
Yule's $Q = 0.88$

D. Percent of population owning telephones

	Low (below 2%)	High (above 2%)	Total
Unstable	35	6	41
Stable	7	18	25
Total	42	24	66

Chi square = 19.68, $p < 0.001$
Yule's $Q = 0.875$

E. Calories per capita per day

	Low (below 2525)	High (above 2525)	Total
Unstable	39	10	49
Stable	8	20	28
Total	47	30	77

Chi square = 17.43, $p < 0.001$
Yule's $Q = 0.81$

F. People per physician

	Low (below 1900)	High (above 1900)	Total
Unstable	40	13	53
Stable	6	19	25
Total	46	32	78

Chi square = 11.41, $p < 0.001$
Yule's $Q = 0.81$

G. GNP per capita (in U.S. dollars)

	Low (below 300)	High (above 300)	Total
Unstable	36	8	44
Stable	9	18	27
Total	45	26	71

Chi square = 14.92, $p < 0.001$
Yule's $Q = 0.80$

H. Percent of population living in urban centers

	Low (below 45%)	High (above 45%)	Total
Unstable	38	6	44
Stable	11	15	26
Total	49	21	70

Chi square = 13.08, $p < 0.001$
Yule's $Q = 0.79$

spread of modern communications (newspapers, radios, and mail); the distribution of social benefits (education, literacy, life expectancy); and the level of participation in politics (voting, executive stability). We find that these indicators of economic, social, and political modernization are a clue to the level of political violence within a society. Economic modernity, modern communications, health, education, and political participation are all associated with lower levels of political violence, although the relationships are not equally strong in all cases. (The correlation values for these relationships are given in the appendix.)

In combination, these analyses demonstrate some of the hypothesized relationships between level of socioeconomic development and political unrest and violence: modern countries show a lower level of political unrest, less-developed countries a higher level.

Political Development

To supplement the findings relating economic development to political instability, we sought an assessment of developmental level that would depend more on political than on socioeconomic factors. A broad framework was provided by judgments regarding democracy-authoritarianism made by Almond and Coleman for 45 nations. These authors classified nations into several groupings. Table 18-6 presents these groupings arranged to indicate increasingly concentrated authority structures.[22] If these groupings can be considered indicative of political development, as well as indicative of increasingly democratic political structures, one can see among them a pronounced relationship to economic and social development. Calculating the average scores on GNP per capita and on percentage of the population literate within each level of political development, a clear pattern emerges. The higher the level of political development of a society, the higher the level of the population on both income and literacy.

On the other hand, a different tendency is apparent when average scores for political violence are calculated. In table 18-6 it may be seen that conservative and traditional oligarchies are relatively stable, while significant increases in political violence are noticeable in the modernizing oligarchy, the tutelary democracy, and the Latin American

Political system	GNP/captia	Percent literate	Political violence	Instability grouped-averaged	Instability grouped
Developed and/or European (n = 23)	$943	98.5	6	07116	3087
Latin American competitive (n = 5)	379	80.1	28	10156	5203
Latin American semicompetitive (n = 5)	262	55.7	37	14101	5196
Asia and Africa political democracy (n = 7)	220	47.5	43	12360	5108
Latin American authoritarian (n = 9)	189	39.4	57	14141	5429
Asia and Africa tutelary democracy (n = 4)	136	17.5	55	15169	6169
Asia and Africa modernizing oligarchy (n = 6)	119	16.4	56	13650	5241
Asia and Africa conservative oligarchy (n = 6)	99	16.2	22	12654	4604
Asia and Africa traditional oligarchy (n = 3)	92	2.5	5	09029	4029

* Median scores, 1948-65.

authoritarian groups. Declining instability appears in the political democracy group, followed by the Latin American semicompetitive and competitive groupings. A return to relative political stability is apparent in the developed notions.

From these data one can infer that with growth in the economic and social sectors of society, the political system also undergoes change. Concomitant with these changes, there is an increasing amount of manifest conflict within society. On the other hand, once the system approaches full modernization (as indicated by almost universal adult literacy) and its economy approaches the high mass-consumption level (as indicated by a GNP per capita well above the subsistence level), political stability tends to reemerge.

Coerciveness of Regime

A second technique for evaluating the structure of authority in the political system is to develop a typology of the coerciveness-permissiveness patterns of the regime. A six-point classification scheme was applied to the nations in this sample, rating each for level of coerciveness of regime.[23] The resultant groups are arrayed in table 18-7. As

Table 18-7.—Level of Coerciveness

1. Highly permissive	2. Permissive	3. Mildly coercive	4. Moderately coercive	5. Coercive	6. Highly coercive
Australia	Belgium	Austria	Bolivia	Afghanistan	Albania
Canada	Costa Rica	Brazil	Colombia	Argentina	Bulgaria
Denmark	Finland	Burma	Ecuador	Cuba	China (mainland)
Netherlands	Ireland	Cambodia	El Salvador	Egypt	China (Taiwan)
Norway	Iceland	France	Ghana	Ethiopia	Czechoslovakia
Sweden	Israel	Greece	Honduras	Haiti	Dominican Republic
Switzerland	Italy	India	Guatemala	Korea	East Germany
United Kingdom	Luxembourg	Japan	Indonesia	Morocco	Hungary
United States	Mexico	Malaya	Iran	Nicaragua	Poland
	New Zealand	Pakistan	Iraq	Paraguay	Romania
	Uruguay	Panama	Jordan	Portugal	U.S.S.R.
	West Germany	Philippines	Laos	Saudi Arabia	Yugoslavia
		Turkey	Lebanon	Spain	
			Liberia	Union of South Africa	
			Libya	Venezuela	
			Peru		
			Syria		
			Sudan		
			Thailand		
			Tunisia		

661

may be seen, the most coercive group of nations comprises primarily the Communist bloc and the most permissive group the Western democracies.

On the composite modernity index, the Western democracies are the most modern nations in the world. Some of the Communist nations also score relatively high in modernity, but others are closer to the midpoint on the index. If one tests for patterning of modernity within levels of coerciveness, the pattern demonstrated in table 18-8 emerges. The highly coercive nations are not as modern as the permissive or highly permissive nations, but clearly tend to be more modern than those nations at midlevels of coerciveness. The least modern nations are those that are coercive, but not at the extreme of coerciveness. The same patterning occurs between coerciveness and political violence. Violence is lowest among permissive states. It increases with increasing coerciveness of regime, but subsides to some degree with extreme coerciveness. When one compares this patterning to that in table 18-6, it is apparent that the coerciveness dimension is not identical to Almond and Coleman's typology of political development. On the latter, economic and political development go hand in hand. On the former, economic development is high among nations at both extremes of coerciveness-permissiveness. Political violence, however, shows the same relationship to both coerciveness and political development.

Table 18-8.—*Modernity, Political Violence, and Coerciveness of Political Systems**

Levels of coerciveness-permissiveness	Modernity	Political violence	Instability grouped-averaged	Instability grouped
1. Highly permissive ($n = 9$)	1.54	4.0	07030	3083
2. Permissive ($n = 12$)	.70	12.0	08042	3574
3. Mildly coercive ($n = 15$)	−.36	51.0	13071	5108
4. Moderately Coercive ($n = 21$)	−.49	65.0	14105	5209
5. Coercive ($n = 15$)	−.40	77.0	13427	5194
6. Highly coercive ($n = 12$)	.55	32.5	11680	4672

* Median scores.

In summary of the relationship between development and political violence, we find that with increased levels of economic modernity there is a tendency toward lower levels of political unrest. Countries in the transitional stage of economic modernization are the most beset by political turmoil. Among the very few countries that might be characterized as yet untouched by the process of economic change, there is a tendency toward political quiescence. Regarding political development, we find in these results and others that permissive, democratic regimes, by and large, experience low levels of political unrest. This is also true of repressive, totalitarian governments that are capable of effectively suppressing the overt political expression of popular dissatisfaction. It is governments at midlevels of coerciveness and political development that experience the most political turmoil. And these governments also tend to be at a midpoint of economic modernization.

SOCIETAL CHANGE AND POLITICAL VIOLENCE

The final question, which was raised at the outset of this paper, is whether empirical relationships can be discovered between patterns of socioeconomic change within society and levels of political unrest. We now seek to go beyond an assessment of attained levels of socioeconomic development, to examine the rates at which these levels were achieved. Are countries that modernize gradually less susceptible to political violence than those in which change is rapid? Some of our hypotheses suggest this relationship, although others do not.

In order to measure rate of change, we confined ourselves to the same types of socioeconomic indicators adopted for measuring levels of development.[24] Data were gathered on these indicators for the time period 1935-62, for all of the 84 countries. An average annual percentage rate of change for each country was calculated on each indicator and a combined rate-of-change index was developed by pooling the country's separate change scores.[25] Differences in percentage change rates among countries were then compared to political instability profiles. To the procedures for measuring political violence discussed above, we added another which seemed particularly applicable to assessment of rate of change. This is a dynamic, rather than a static, scoring of political unrest, yielding a measure of change in instability level over time.[26] (See appendix.)

The results obtained from interrelating percentage rates of change on the environmental indicators and levels of political instability indicate, in general, that the faster the rate of socioeconomic change within a society, the higher the level of political unrest. The combined rate-of-change index shows a strong relationship to political instability, as do change rates on many of the indicators taken singly.[27] Looking at the dynamic instability measures, we find a similar set of relationships (see table 18-9). Countries with the lowest socioeconomic rate of change show a trend toward political stability; countries with the highest rate of socioeconomic change are beset by increasing instability; and countries experiencing intermediate rates of change toward modernization are also intermediate in instability pattern.

These general findings point to the fact that we cannot assume that modernization will bring political stability in its wake. While highly modern countries tend to be politically stable, the process of attaining modernity is one that is rife with political unrest. Furthermore, the more rapid the modernization, the greater the impact in increasing political violence. Only after certain threshold socioeconomic values have been attained may the stabilizing political benefits of modernity be experienced.

The rationale for these findings may be found in the models presented in the theoretical section of this paper, particularly in figures 18-2, 18-5, 18-8, and 18-9. There it was hypothesized that rapid change will serve to increase the gap between expectations and achievements. The feedback effect of a few satisfactions will increase the demand for more accomplishments, beyond the level that can possibly be attained within the society. Also, the conflict between traditional and modern ways of life will be intensified by rapid transition between the two patterns, allowing less time for adjustment.

If we look at the socioeconomic indicators individually, however, we find that they do not all have the same impact upon society. For example, while a rapid increase in percent of the population being educated does entail a higher level of political instability, a rapid increase in percent of the population owning telephones is accompanied by more stability within the society. Similarly, rapid increase in national income brings a lessening of political unrest.[28]

Furthermore, for theoretical reasons, we are particularly interested in examining the relationships between rates of

Table 18-9.—Relationship Between Mean Rate of Change on Ecological Variables, 1935-62, and Change in Stability as Measured by Variance and Slope, 1945-62

Mean rate of change on ecological variables	Stable — Low variance and either- Negative slope or Zero slope	Indeterminate — Low variance/positive slope or High variance/negative slope	Unstable — High variance and either- Positive slope or Zero slope	Total
Low change	Norway, New Zealand, West Germany, Australia, Denmark, Iceland, United States, Canada, Sweden, Switzerland, Netherlands, Luxembourg, Israel — 13	Great Britain, Austria — 2	Belgium — 1	16
Moderately low change	Ireland, Guatemala, Bulgaria, China (Taiwan), Finland, Italy, Chile, Philippines — 8	France, Union of South Africa, Mexico, Pakistan, Greece, Argentina, Uruguay, Spain, Ecuador — 9	Cuba, Paraguay, Hungary — 3	20
Moderately high change	0	Thailand, Colombia, Egypt, Ceylon, Poland, Costa Rica, Ghana, Turkey, India — 9	Peru, Portugal, Panama, Brazil, Haiti, Iraq, Japan, Yugoslavia, Tunisia, Burma, U.S.S.R. — 11	20
High change	Syria — 1	Korea, Malaya — 2	El Salvador, Bolivia, Venezuela, Dom. Rep., Cambodia, Morocco, Honduras, Indonesia — 8	11
Total	22	22	23	67

change on these various socioeconomic indicators and level of political unrest among the transitional group of countries. It was postulated at the outset of this paper that this group of countries suffers the most deleterious effects of change. Change occurring at a higher level of development presumably does not mean change in the sense of developing new patterns and new ways of life; it may simply be an intensification or logical extension of existing patterns. Moving from a low to a high level of development, however, entails conflict and discrepancies between aspirations, expectations, and attainments.

Some of the findings at this midlevel of development confirm expectations based on the wider analysis. Among transitional countries, those experiencing a faster rate of change in proportion of population receiving primary education, 1935-62, also experience a higher level of political instability at some time during 1948-65, and show a trend toward greater instability over time during this period.[29] Furthermore, if we control for the maximum value attained on ratio of population receiving primary education, we find that the relationship between an increase in this ratio and political instability is still high.[30] This is significant, since it tells us that it is actually the rate of increase in education as well as the maximum number of educated persons in the society that is important for political unrest. Using the dynamic measure of political unrest, we corroborate the tendency for change in proportion of the population receiving primary education to be positively associated with an increase in political instability over time.[31] Again, change, per se, emerges as important.

We also find that, within this group of countries, percentage change in income (gross domestic product (GDP) per capita), 1951-59, shows the opposite relationship to political unrest: the faster the increase in income, the less the political instability. This indicates that a percentage increase in GDP per capita is associated with a decrease in level of political unrest. If we control for attained level of GNP per capita within the society, we gain find that rapid change in increasing incomes is important in reducing instability, apart from the impact of the absolute level of income achieved.[32]

The most detrimental combination of factors appears to

be a rapid increase in proportion of the population receiving primary education, but a slow rate of percentage change in GDP per capita. This set of circumstances is most conducive to political unrest among the transitional group of countries.[33]

The relationship between these two change indicators and political instability fits a number of the models proposed at the outset of this paper. Education, like literacy, is a means of arousing awareness of modern goals and hence of raising aspirations within a society. It is also likely that education raises expectations regarding the fulfillment of these aspirations. GDP per capita, on the other hand, is an achievement indicator; it provides gratification of aroused aspirations. A society in which the trend is toward increasing numbers of educated persons within the population, without an increase in their level of income, is a society in which rates of change are widening the gap between aspirations/expectations and their satisfaction. This would appear to be particularly explosive for the transitional society.

The challenge in these findings is whether it is possible to avoid an imbalance between number of educated in the population and opportunity for increased income. Unfortunately, it would seem that the process of modernization makes this imbalance highly probable. Education is a necessary first step to infusing the society with the skills appropriate to industrialization. But the lag between this first step and the second—that of developing the industrial society—is hazardous indeed. Huntington speaks of the dangers of education in the underdeveloped society, a danger that many leaders of nonindustrialized states themselves recognize.[34] He particularly stresses the pitfalls of an increasingly educated population for a society in which political opportunity is lacking. While the political and economic aspects of society are clearly interrelated, our findings suggest that if economic opportunities were immediately available to the newly educated, the lack of political opportunities might not be so disruptive.

A second challenge in these findings relates to a proposition advanced by some economists, that widespread psychological discontent is a precondition for economic growth within society.[35] This view stresses, as a psychological antecedent for modernization, the type of discontent that certainly is fostered by increased education. Again, in this view it seems that a lag between aspiration and achievement is inevitable within societies in transition, a period of hiatus that is particularly violence prone.

The question is whether, in fact, an optimal combination of all relevant conditions is feasible: a sufficient level of psychological discontent to foster change, a sufficient level of education to supply the society with a skilled population, a sufficient level of development to provide jobs and income to match popular skill levels, and a political system sufficiently open to offer access to an educated people. To maintain an optimum balance among these factors, especially during a period of rapid change, may be difficult indeed. Typically, it is education that is expanded most rapidly in response to expressions of popular discontent, an expansion that creates the discrepancy between skill and opportunity.

CONCLUSIONS

To interpret the relationships that we have uncovered between levels of development, rates of socioeconomic change, and political violence, we must return to some of the initial questions raised in this study. The first of these concerns the meaning of social change. As has been pointed out, change is a complex concept that cannot simply be identified with increases, decreases, or fluctuations in the economic characteristics of a society. If these quantifiable ecological traits do have bearing on the question, it must be because they reflect a wide variety of other, unmeasured, qualitative societal factors. The validity of this assumption, that quantifiable economic change is a clue to other types of change, may depend upon the historical era under investigation. As discussed earlier, the prevailing insight of contemporary social science is that the process of modernization provides the pathway of change in the postwar world. This process is generally regarded as socioeconomic and amenable to quantification.

This, however, is not the only interpretation. For example, quite a different view is presented by Sorokin, from the perspective of a major portion of human history. In this light, our 20-year span of analysis is but a wave in a much larger cycle.[36] Sorokin's view of change is essentially ideological or attitudinal, not economic. Civilizations vary between an emphasis on material ("sensate") culture and an absorption in ideological ("ideational") concerns. Sensate culture is accompanied by a rise in economic conditions, which is only to be expected since such a culture deems these economic factors of importance. Ideational culture, however, is generally accompanied by a low level of material success, since material welfare is not a valued commodity and material concerns are considered of secondary importance. Sorokin traces the rates of change in the general economic situations of the ancient world of Greece and Rome from 600 B.C. to A.D. 400, of France from 800 to 1926, and of Germany from 700 to 1932. These curves show considerable fluctuation, tending to be low during eras which Sorokin identifies as ideational and high during periods of sensate culture. In this long-range view, the 20th century is the epitome of sensate culture. From this we may deduce that change is inevitable, since Sorokin's model is a cyclical one in which the penultimate realization of the goals of either type of culture inevitably breeds the conditions of its own decline. Transition then sets in, a period of social disruption and violence in which the dominant cultural theme begins to move in the opposite direction.

If this Hegelian, "poison-fruit" approach is correct, we would be led to a different investigation of change than we have pursued in this study. In the Sorokin view, disruptive change will occur at the highest levels of modernity, when sensate culture is at its peak. Some intuitive and empirical support might be found for this view in the apparently restless dissatisfaction of intelligentsia and student elements within American society, a phenomenon that Sorokin identifies as typical of the last stages of sensate culture. On the other hand, our examination of the economic situation of the postwar world certainly indicates that the economic decline of modern countries is not yet in sight. Also, it shows that the highest levels of turbulence occur at lesser levels of development.

Thus, while Sorokin's broader vision may prove to be correct in the long run, the crisis of transition in our era still seems to be tied to the effort at achieving the higher levels of economic well-being sought by members of a materially oriented culture. And it is a particular attribute of the modernization process that its quality can be indexed not only in quantitative, but specifically in socioeconomic terms. With sufficient ingenuity, other attributes of society, even ideational, could conceivably be reduced to observable, quantifiable indicators.[37] With the process of modernization, however, this effort at ingenuity is superfluous since economic levels and stages of development are well nigh synonymous.

Interest in the relationship between economic development and political violence has characterized a number of recent investigations. All begin with the common insight that the more advanced countries are less subject to political disturbances. This finding is corroborated by those who define development in political terms, as well as by those who define it in economic terms.[38] The kernel of agreement among these investigators is that the highest level of development is accompanied by a decrease in violence, while levels that fall short of modernity are more prone to political unrest. The consistency of this general relationship has been corroborated using quite different measures of violence and different samples of nations. Its stability as a finding may be due to the fact that there is a sufficient sample of identifiable modern and transitional nations in the present-day world.

It is not equally clear whether, in the relationship between development and violence, the least-developed countries show less of a tendency to violence than states at mid-levels or transitional stages of development. The problem of discovering the direction of the relationship between violence and development at the low end of the modernity continuum is largely due to the fact that extremely few countries now qualify as traditional, in the sense that they are unaware of modernity. We have suggested earlier in this report, and elsewhere,[39] that such countries do not report data to the United Nations, which makes it difficult to include them in this type of empirical study. Nevertheless, if we are willing to base our assessments on a very few cases, we find that countries at the lowest levels of development are less prone to political instability than are countries at the next higher stages of modernity. Political development, in combination with economic development, shows this pattern (tables 18-6 and 18-8), as does economic development alone, but to a lesser degree (tables 18-3 and 18-4). Again, this slight tendency has been found by other researchers.[40] If it is an actual trend, it corroborates theoretical insights regarding the gap between aspirations/expectations and their achievement, the effects of uncertainty of expectations, and the occurrence of motivational conflict elaborated in the theoretical section of this study. All of these hypotheses point to the transitional stage of development as the most frustration ridden. Neither lower nor higher levels of development will be as prone to violence.

Since this study is specifically concerned with rates of change, it may be asked why so much attention has been paid to attained levels of development. The answer is twofold. On the one hand, an assessment of level of development gives a cross-sectional view of the same process that, in longitudinal perspective, is indexed by rates of change. It is true that knowledge of the present level of development of a nation cannot tell us how rapid or slow, how continuous or discontinuous was the process of attainment. But we may infer from the relationship between development and violence that as countries become more modern, they will also become more politically stable. This inference may be correct in broadest perspective, but it may also be misleading regarding the impact of change on a society that is still far removed from the threshold economic values accompanying political stability (table 18-5).

Therefore, the second point regarding the importance of attained modernity lies in the interrelationships between the static levels and rates of socioeconomic change. It is suggested that rates of change have different implications for societies that differ in modernity level. Furthermore, different indicators, and rates of change on these indicators, have varying impacts on society. There are thus three factors that must be taken into account in assessing the relationship between change and political instability: attained level of development, the nature of the specific socioeconomic indicator, and the rate of change.

This more detailed approach may help to explain some of the conflicting claims of researchers who have explored this problem. For example, in our own first investigation of the question, we found that the faster the rate of socioeconomic change, the higher the level of political unrest.[41]

We also noted that rate of change, measured in percentage terms, was strongly related to attained level of development. Modern countries showed smaller percentage change rates; less-developed countries showed higher percentage change rates. At the same time, we discovered that on one indicator, national income, the relationship was reversed: the faster the rate of increase on this variable, the lower the level of political unrest. Furthermore, rate of change in national income, unlike change rates on the other indicators, was related to modernity level in such a way that modern countries showed the highest percentage change rates while underdeveloped countries showed the lowest.

A similarly complex set of findings regarding the relationship between rate of economic change and political violence occurs in the work of other researchers. Alker and Russett find that the highest annual growth rates occur at midlevels of per capita income.[42] Furthermore, the higher the level of income within a society and the greater the growth in income levels, the lower the level of political unrest. Gurr, on the other hand, finds no relationship between measures of civil violence for 119 countries, 1961-63, and growth rate in per capita income, 1953-62.[43] Using only Latin American countries, Bwy finds that the higher the rate of annual growth of GNP per capita, 1950-59, the lower the levels of both organized and anomic violence.[44] Since his study is limited to countries beyond a suggested threshold level of attained development, Bwy speculates that for countries at lower levels of modernity, the relationship may operate in the reverse direction. Finally, Tanter and Midlarsky assess the relationship between rate of increase in GNP per capita in the 7 years immediately prior to the outbreak of revolution, and the number of deaths from domestic group violence in all successful revolutions occurring between 1955 and 1960.[45] They find more revolutionary violence with higher economic growth rates in 10 revolutions occurring in the Middle East and Asia, but the opposite relationship in 4 Latin American revolutions. For all 14 cases combined, there is some indication of greater numbers of persons killed in revolutions preceded by higher annual growth rates in GNP per capita.

It is suggested that the resolution of these contradictions will be found in an approach that differentiates between rates of change on different types of indicators and among nations at different levels of development. A beginning in this direction has been made in this study and further work is intended. Our preliminary efforts have been directed toward distinguishing indicators in terms of their implications for the members of a society. This categorization is based upon the distinction between social aspirations/expectations and social achievement. Change on one type of indicator may imply greater gratification for society; change on another indicator may simply broaden aspirations and expectations.

Evidence in support of this interpretation comes from the finding that a rapid increase in primary school enrollment is positively related to political violence, while a rapid increase in GNP per capita is negatively related. One change increases the level of political unrest; the other tends to decrease it. Furthermore, the impact of both change rates was separately analyzed among countries at the transitional stage of development. We find that for these nations, the combination of factors most closely associated with political violence is a rapid spread in society of an awakened population, combined with a slow rise in income.

As a final application of this study, we may ask whether our findings have any bearing on the occurrence of violence within our own society. In socioeconomic terms, the United States is the most modern nation in the world, showing the highest attained level on almost all indicators. On the other hand, it is not among the most politically stable societies, although neither is it among the most violent. Using various methods of measurement for the 18-year period, 1948-65, the United States falls generally at the median position of world violence: half of the nations exceed our violence level; half do not attain it. There is thus some discrepancy between our economic level and our level of political unrest, given the expected form of relationship.

It should also be pointed out that the occurrence of violence in the United States has increased during the 1960's. In the previous two decades, the internal aggression profile of the United States was lower and generally more in line with the majority of Western democratic political systems. During 1955-61, for example, the United States was among the group of nations at position 3 on the seven-point instability scale. It ranked 24th among 84 states, falling within the more stable third of the sample. In the subsequent period, however, it moved into the 4th scale position, joining nations experiencing more severe internal turmoil. From 1961 to 1965, 12 percent of this country's events were at scale position 4.

In terms of the factors discussed in this paper, the rise in political unrest in the United States could be explained in several quite different general ways. This is not to say that these explanations are necessarily contradictory or mutually exclusive. Rather, they may reinforce each other. On the one hand, if Sorokin is correct, we may be witnessing a transitional stage which few if any other nations have yet experienced: the passing of material culture based on an advanced technology. It would not be surprising that the United States should be among the first nations to enter this phase, in view of its most advanced technological standing. This probably is the most speculative, and perhaps most imaginative, among the possible explanations.

On the other hand, a different explanation is perhaps more plausible, based as it is on familiar contemporary notions of transition. The United States, as a large heterogeneous society, is an aggregate of subcultures not all of which share the advanced way of life of the majority. A large portion of specific instability events in the United States arise directly from the problems of racial and other minority cultures within the wider society. The average newspaper reader is aware of passive resistance, demonstrations, and urban ghetto riots. To this picture we may add that half of the 12 assassinations (successful or attempted) that occurred in this country during the 1960's can be attributed to issues of minority conflict.[46]

Nor is it simply the domain of majority-minority conflict that must be blamed. Also relevant are notions of modernity and participant, egalitarian society. Our aggregated measures are not sensitive to these internal variations, since they assign one score to an entire nation. We may nonetheless suggest that forces of tradition are now undergoing transition in our society and that we have in microcosm the processes evident in the global pattern. We can perhaps think of the current "Black Revolution" as a transition process that involves both the white and the black communities. A previously isolated, tradition-bound stratum is becoming politically significant and participant, reaching

674

toward modern goals. This stratum is subject to the revolution of rising expectations and its consequent systemic frustration. Undoubtedly the entire society is involved in the systemic conflict that accompanies the passing of an established pattern of social relationships and institutions.

Another point is that the combination of a rapid increase in educational level and a smaller increase in per capita income may be as virulent a mixture of conditions for groups within our society that are seeking to emerge from traditionalism, as it is for so-called transitional societies. There is support for this view in some of the findings regarding the participants in recent riots in the United States.[47] Interviews with rioters in Newark and Detroit provide a picture of the rioter as young, native to the ghetto, educated, and underemployed. The interpretation proposed by the investigators is one of "blocked opportunity." It is a case of an increasing gap between education and income, between aspirations and satisfaction. Education may also serve to strengthen the sense of legitimacy of demands and expectations. The educated person feels qualified and entitled to betterment in his conditions of life.

It may further be speculated that the transitional process within our own society was intensified by the demonstration effect of the global process of transition at mid-20th century. Its most salient aspect may have been provided by the emergence of a number of nations from colonial bondage to gain independence. Perhaps an additional and powerful impetus to the transition witnessed within our society is a function of the logic of social change depicted in figures 18-2, 18-5, and 18-6. Figures 18-2 and 18-5 postulate that both abrupt and rapid improvement in social achievement may, paradoxically, bring violence in their wake. Figure 18-6 suggests that when unrealistic hopes are pinned to an occurrence, these hopes are often disappointed. The scheduled event itself takes place, but the concomitant changes foreseen as accompanying it do not occur.

Some striking developments in the 1940's and 1950's heralded the lessening of racial discrimination in this country. For example, the series of Supreme Court decisions, legislative and Federal measures, including the desegregation of the Armed Forces, may have been instrumental not only in bringing satisfaction to the Negro population but also in raising expectations for the future. Greater equality, more abundant opportunities, and social and economic betterment all may have been foreseen. When actual conditions did not provide satisfaction for these expectations, a strong sense of systemic frustration predictably followed. Note that none of these hypotheses assumes a setback in achievements. Frustration may result from the lack of realization of what prove to be exaggerated expectations. Furthermore, the greater the certainty with which fulfillment is expected, the greater the disappointment when it fails to materialize.

In the broadest view, then, much violence in the United States may be interpreted as resulting from a transitional stage of modernization characterizing specific groups within the society as a whole. During this stage of improving conditions, violence may actually rise, and this will be especially likely if increases in achievement do not keep pace with increases in aspirations and expectations. The question of whether this disparity can be avoided is particularly challenging. It may be discussed specifically in terms of a gap between increases in education and increases in income. At first glance, it would seem that this imbalance is highly likely, if not inevitable, at least in the short run, since training for skills is a necessary prerequisite to taking one's place in the industrial society. It may be, however, that the lag could be shortened.

A second, more provocative proposition discussed above is that widespread psychological discontent within a society is a necessary precondition to economic growth. At the individual level, this implies that only when his discontent has reached a certain level will the individual be motivated to seek the training and skills that eventually gain him admission to the modern way of life. This is not to ignore the fact that minority groups within our society have historically been excluded and discouraged from embarking upon this path. Rather, it is to stress that for all individuals, regardless of origin, the motivation necessary to raise one's goals arises from a dissatisfaction with present attainment. Thus discontent is a basic prerequisite for effort expended. And if the effort is not eventually rewarded, the outcome is very apt to be aggression, directed against the perceived barriers to accomplishment.[48]

As a prognosis for the future, this analogy tells us that once certain socio-economic threshold values have been reached by relatively deprived persons within our society, violence will subside. On the other hand, the process of transition will be tumultuous, especially in the short run, as education becomes more prevalent and outstrips opportunity. It must be remembered, of course, that these insights are only suggestive, and based on cross-national studies of political violence and change. They have not been validated by an intensive or historical empirical analysis of American society.

References

1. We are grateful for the support of the National Science Foundation (Grant No. GS-1781), which made it possible to collect and analyze the data on internal political aggression as well as the underlying conditions of political instability.
   We wish to thank Rosemary J. Roth and Antonia E. Williams for their help in constructing tables for this manuscript, and Franz Jaggar for the computer analyses.
2. Cross-national quantitative analysis of political and social variables is a relatively recent development. For an overview, see Richard L. Merritt and Stein Rokkan, eds., *Comparing Nations: The Uses of Quantitative Data in Cross-National Research* (New Haven: Yale University Press, 1966). Two impressive cross-national data collections and analyses should also be mentioned: Arthur S. Banks and Robert B. Textor, *A Cross-Policy Survey* (Cambridge: MIT Press, 1963), and Bruce M. Russett, Hayward R. Alker, Jr., Karl W. Deutsch, and Harold D. Lasswell, *World Handbook of Political and Social Indicators* (New Haven: Yale University Press, 1964). Among the few cross-national analyses of internal political violence we may mention: Harry Eckstein, *Internal War: The Problem of Anticipation* (a report submitted to the Research Group in Psychology and the Social Sciences, Smithsonian Institution, Washington, D.C., Jan. 15, 1962); Ted Gurr with Charles Ruttenberg, *The Conditions of Civil Violence: First Tests of a Causal Model*, Research Monograph No. 28 (Princeton: Center of International Studies, Princeton University, Apr. 1967); Rudolph J. Rummel, "Dimensions of Conflict Behavior Within and Between Nations," *General Systems Yearbook*, vol. VIII (1963), pp. 1-50; Raymond Tanter, "Dimensions of Conflict Behavior Within and Between Nations, 1958-60," *Journal of Conflict Resolution*, vol. X (Mar. 1966), pp. 41-65; Ivo K. and Rosalind L. Feierabend, "Aggressive Behaviors Within Polities, 1948-1962: A Cross-National Study," *Journal of Conflict Resolution*, vol. X (Sept. 1966), pp. 249-271; and Betty A. Nesvold, "A Scalogram Analysis of Political Violence," *Comparative Political Studies*, forthcoming, July 1969.
3. For a sample of contemporary literature using these notions, see Gabriel A. Almond and James S. Coleman, eds., *The Politics of the Developing Areas* (Princeton: Princeton University Press, 1960); David E. Apter, *The Politics of Modernization* (Chicago: University of Chicago Press, 1965); H. R. Barringer et al., *Social Change in Developing Areas* (Cambridge: Schenkman, 1965); Karl W. Deutsch, "Social Mobilization and Political Development," *American Political Science Review*, vol. LV (Sept. 1961), pp. 493-514; Samuel P. Huntington, "Political Development and Political Decay," *World Politics*, vol. XVII (Apr. 1965), pp. 386-430; Everett E. Hagen, *On the Theory of Social Change* (Homewood: Dorsey Press, 1962); Daniel Lerner, *The Passing of Traditional Society* (Glencoe: Free Press, 1958); W. W. Rostow, *The Stages of Economic Growth* (Cambridge: Cambridge University Press, 1960); Pitirim A. Sorokin, *Social and Cultural Dynamics*, vol. III: *Fluctuation of Social Relationships, War, and Revolution* (New York: The Bedminster Press, 1937, 1962); and George K. Zollschan and Walter Hirsch, eds., *Explorations in Social Change* (Boston: Houghton Mifflin, 1964).
4. The theme that social change carries with it political crisis and turmoil is commonly acknowledged in the literature, as is the contradictory insight. See the literature cited in footnote 2.

5. For the classic theoretical statement of the frustration-aggression hypothesis, see John Dollard et al., *Frustration and Aggression* (New Haven: Yale University Press, 1939). Also, there are several more recent general restatements, among them Leonard Berkowitz, *Aggression: A Social Psychological Analysis* (New York: McGraw Hill, 1962), and Arnold H. Buss, *The Psychology of Aggression* (New York: Wiley, 1961).

6. In the literature of political science, Ted Gurr systematically applies the frustration hypothesis and modifies its terms to develop a coherent empirical and multivariate theory of political violence. His use of the concept of relative deprivation comes very close to our use of systemic frustration. Also, we believe that the broad insights, hypotheses, and models presented in this section would generally be sustained by his theoretical constructs, although they might be couched in different terminology. See Ted Robert Gurr, *Why Men Rebel* (Princeton: Princeton University Press, 1969, in press), and "Psychological Factors in Civil Violence," *World Politics*, vol. XX (Jan. 1968), pp. 245-278.

7. In the most recent literature on revolution, David Schwartz uses the notion of conflict, as well as of cognitive dissonance, to build a processual model of revolution; see his "Political Alienation: A Preliminary Experiment on the Psychology of Revolution's First Stage," paper presented at the annual meeting of the American Psychological Association, Washington, D.C., 1967. The psychological literature on which these applications are based may be found in F. Heider, "Social Perception and Phenomenal Causality," *Psychological Review*, vol. LI (1944), pp. 358-374; Theodore Newcomb, "An Approach to the Study of Communicative Acts," *Psychological Review*, vol. LX (1953), pp. 393-5; and Leon Festinger, *The Theory of Cognitive Dissonance* (New York: Harper & Row, 1957).

8. See James C. Davies, "Toward a Theory of Revolution," *American Sociological Review*, vol. XXVII (Jan. 1962), pp. 5-19.

9. The notion of a marked contrast among sets of ecological conditions having a greater effect on expectations and behavior than would a continuous series can be viewed as an application of adaptation level theory. See Harry Helson, *Adaptation-Level Theory: An Experimental and Systematic Approach to Behavior* (New York: Harper & Row, 1964). According to this view, a cohesive set or series of stimulus conditions creates adaptation; a contrast within the stimulus conditions triggers response.

10. Victor LeVine, "The Trauma of Independence in French Speaking Africa," paper presented at the Midwest Conference of Political Scientists, 1967.

11. Robert LeVine observes that, in sub-Saharian Africa, those colonial powers that over the decades consistently denied self-rule to the indigenous populace, or those which consistently fostered such a goal, experienced the lowest incidence of anti-European violence. Those regimes that vacillated between the two policies of permissiveness and coerciveness were often subject to intense outbreaks of violence. See his article, "Anti-European Violence in Africa: A Comparative Analysis," *Journal of Conflict Resolution*, vol. III (Dec. 1959), pp. 420-429.

12. These models are given fuller elaboration in I. K. Feierabend, R. L. Feierabend, and B. A. Nesvold, "Political Violence and Social Discontent," in David C. Schwartz, ed., *Revolution Studies*, forthcoming.

13. For example, Lucian W. Pye, in *Aspects of Political Development* (Boston, Little, Brown, 1966), identifies six such crises that hamper smooth political processes: the identity crisis, the legitimacy crisis, the penetration crisis, the participation crisis, the integration crisis, and the distribution crisis.

14. Apter, *op. cit.*, among other authors, describes these more or less intense conflicts, especially in the African context and on the Gold Coast. Destruction of the traditional culture may ensue if the indigenous culture is entirely hostile to innovation and the acceptance of modernity. On the other hand, if the traditional culture is more instrumentally oriented, the conflict may be less intense. Apter also speaks of the appropriate political systems that may follow from these situations.

15. This is the goal-gradient hypothesis, which derives from psychological learning theory and has wide applicability to both animal and human behavior. It maintains that the impulse to action, or the strength of attraction, varies as a function of the distance (spatial or temporal) between the organism and the goal. The closer the individual comes to attaining a desired goal, the stronger the level of attraction and the greater the impulse to action. The further the individual is from a goal, the less the attraction and the weaker the impulse to action. See N. E. Miller, "Experimental Studies of Conflict Behavior," in J. McV. Hunt, ed., *Person-*

ality and the Behavior Disorders (New York: Ronald Press, 1944), and C. L. Hull, *Principles of Behavior* (New York: Appleton-Century-Crofts, 1943).

16. Other researchers have also attempted to measure stages of development and rates of change for the purposes of cross-national study of political violence. For example, see Seymour M. Lipset, *Political Man: The Social Basis of Politics* (Garden City: Doubleday, 1960); Russett et al., *op. cit.*; Gurr with Ruttenberg, *op. cit.*; Raymond Tanter and Manus Midlarsky, "A Theory of Revolution," *Journal of Conflict Resolution*, vol. XI (Sept. 1967), pp. 264-280; Douglas Bwy, "Political Instability in Latin America: The Cross-Cultural Test of a Causal Model," *Latin American Research Review*, vol. III (Spring 1968), pp. 17-66.

17. Betty A. Nesvold, "Modernity, Social Frustration, and the Stability of Political Systems: A Cross-National Study" (San Diego: San Diego State College, Master's thesis, June 1964). Data on these indicators were collected for the 84 nations from United Nations sources. The country raw scores were converted into standard scores and a mean standard score was calculated for each country as a measure of level of development.

18. The cutting points for these three groups are to some extent arbitrary. The 24 countries that are highest on the modernity index are selected as the modern group. The traditional group is set equal in size to the modern group, while ranking at the opposite end of the modernity continuum. The remaining countries, falling between the modern and traditional groups, are designated transitional. As already pointed out, the countries designated "traditional" are simply less modern than those classed as "transitional," but they have nonetheless been exposed to modernity.

19. Russett et al., *op. cit.* The correlation coefficient between our Modernity Index and Russett's level of development, which is based on GNP per capita, is $r = 0.90$.

20. The cutting points on these modernity indicators were chosen in such a way as to maximize the loading of countries in one set of diagonal cells and minimize it in the other. In this way, threshold values may be determined.

21. Data for these measures of development were taken from the compilations in Russett et al., *op. cit.*

22. Nations were rated according to characteristics of participation in governmental and political groups and the existence of a viable legislative body and freedom of the press. The underlying assumption of the classificatory scheme was that when an agency such as the military or a political party fills a specialized role in the polity, the conditions for democracy, or pluralism, are present. If, on the other hand, a few such agencies monopolize policymaking, the conditions for elite authority structures are generated. Within this classification scheme, Latin American nations are trichotomized into competitive, semicompetitive, and authoritarian political systems. The Asian and African classifications contain seven such groupings: political democracy, tutelary democracy, modernizing oligarchy, conservative oligarchy, and traditional oligarchy. Of the remaining nations in our study that were not rated by Almond and Coleman, 23 qualify as Western European, developed nations. One can assume that these latter nations served as a model for Almond and Coleman's original typology and that it would be reasonable to classify them as highly competitive political systems. See Almond and Coleman, *op. cit.*

23. Information regarding such matters as the competitiveness of the political system, the protection of free speech, and the degree to which police actions inhibit the freedoms of the citizenry were used to assign nations to one of the six categories. Case studies were examined for 84 nations for the time period 1948-60. See Jennifer G. Walton, "Correlates of Coerciveness and Permissiveness of National Political Systems: A Cross-National Study" (San Diego: San Diego State College, Master's thesis, 1965). Also I. K. Feierabend and R. L. Feierabend, "The Relationship of Systemic Frustration, Political Coercion, International Tension and Political Instability: A Cross-National Study," paper presented at the annual meeting of the American Psychological Association, Sept. 1966.

24. The initial analyses using these data concentrated on nine indicators: urbanization (percent of the population living in localities of 100,000 or more inhabitants); percent of the population literate; primary education (ratio of total school enrollment to total population age 5-14); post-primary education (percentage of total population enrolled in all educational institutions beyond the primary schools); national income in local currencies; cost-of-living index; calories per capita per day; infant mor-

tality rate; and total number of radios per 1,000 population. See Wallace W. Conroe, "A Cross-National Analysis of the Impact of Modernization Upon Political Stability" (San Diego: San Diego State College, Master's thesis, 1965), and Feierabend and Feierabend, "Aggressive Behaviors Within Polities."

25. The yearly percent rate of change on the ecological variables was calculated by subtracting the lowest value of the variable in the 28-year period from the highest value attained, dividing by the lowest value to convert to a percentage change, and then dividing by the number of years spanned to obtain the yearly percentage change. The advantage of the combined rate of change index, assuming substitutability of indicators, is that it makes it possible to compensate for missing data. The index is based on data for six or more indicators per country.

26. Stability scores for the 84 nations were calculated on a year-by-year basis and plotted as a function of time. To characterize the time function, two measures were used: the slope of a best-fit line, indicating the average instability trend over the time period; and amplitude of change from year to year, as estimated by variance.

27. The correlation with the combined rate of change index is Pearson $r = 0.66$, using the seven-point scaling of political instability for the 1948-65 time period.

28. The correlation between rate of change in primary education and scaled level of political instability is $r = 0.49$. The corresponding correlation for rate of increase in percent of the population owning telephones is $r = 0.44$, for increase in national income, $rho = -0.34$ with the static measure of stability, and -0.45 with the dynamic measure.

29. The correlation is $r = 0.50$ with the static level of instability and $r = 0.31$ with the dynamic measure.

30. The partial correlation technique makes it possible to access the degree of relationship between two variables, with the influence of a third variable statistically controlled or removed. The partial correlation in this case is 0.49.

31. The partial correlation is 0.29.

32. The correlation with political instability level, 1948-65, is $r = -0.34$ and with trend in instability over time it is -0.37. Controlling for GNP per capita in 1957, the partial correlation is -0.40 with scaled instability and -0.37 with trend in instability. Growth rate in GDP per capita, 1951-59, is taken from "World Tables of Economic Growth," Economics Department, MIT, mimeographed.

33. The multiple correlation is $r = 0.56$ using the static measure of instability and $r = 0.44$ using trend in instability over time.

34. Samuel P. Huntington, *Political Order in Changing Societies* (New Haven: Yale University Press, 1968), especially pp. 47-49.

35. See, for example, Ronald G. Ridker, "Discontent and Economic Growth," *Economic Development and Cultural Change,* vol. XI (October 1962), pp. 1-15.

36. Sorokin, *op. cit.* Cyclical and historicist conceptions of history are, of course, not peculiar to Sorokin. They are especially current in 19th-century literature, but also span earlier and later times. Marx and Engels' conceptions are the best known and certainly the most influential. Other names that come immediately to mind are Gobineau, Hegel, Spengler, and Toynbee.

37. Efforts in this direction today are associated with the tremendous increase in awareness of the possibilities of social data. See, for example, Eugene Webb et al., *Unobstrusive Measures* (New York: Wiley, 1967).

38. See, for example, Lipset, *op. cit.*; Philip Cutright, "National Political Development: Measurement and Analysis," *American Sociological Review,* vol. XXVIII (April. 1963), pp. 253-264; Gurr with Ruttenberg, *op. cit.*; Hayward R. Alker, Jr., and Bruce M. Russett, "The Analyses of Trends and Patterns," in Russett et al., *op. cit.*; Feierabend and Feierabend, "Aggressive Behaviors Within Polities"; and Bwy, *op. cit.*

39. Feierabend and Feierabend, "Aggressive Behaviors Within Polities."

40. Alker and Russett, *op. cit.*; Gurr, *op. cit.*; Bwy, *op. cit.*

41. Feierabend and Feierabend, "Aggressive Behaviors Within Polities," and Conroe, *op. cit.*

42. Alker and Russett, *op. cit.*

43. Gurr with Ruttenberg, *op. cit.*

44. Bwy, *op. cit.*

45. Tanter and Midlarsky, *op. cit.*

46. See I. K. Feierabend, R. L. Feierabend, B. A. Nesvold, and F. J. Jaggar, "Political Violence and Assassination: A Cross-National Assessment," report prepared for the Task Force on Assassinations of the National Commission on the Causes and Prevention of Violence, Nov. 1968.
47. Nathan S. Caplan and Jeffery M. Paige, "A Study of Ghetto Rioters," *Scientific American*, vol. CCXIX (Aug. 1968).
48. The question of the target of aggression has received considerable attention in all psychological theories of aggression. The forces underlying displacement of aggression from one target to another are given precise formulation in Miller, *op. cit.*

APPENDIX

POLITICAL INSTABILITY

DATA COLLECTION

The data on political instability are extracted from two sources, *Deadline Data on World Affairs* and the *Encyclopedia Britannica Yearbooks*. Events are classified into 28 nonoverlapping categories: elections, dissolution of legislature, resignation, dismissal, fall of cabinet, significant change of law, plebiscite, appointment, organization of opposition party, governmental action against specific groups, strike, demonstration, boycott, arrest, suicide of significant political persons, martial law, execution, assassination, terrorism, sabotage, guerrilla warfare, coup d'état, civil war, revolt, and exile.

Each event is coded on 16 characteristics: country, date, whether a composite or noncomposite event, whether or not event is accompanied by violence, location (capital city, urban, rural, etc.), duration, number of persons involved, number of persons injured, number of persons killed, number of persons arrested, amount of property damage, nature of tension, whether or not significant persons are involved, outcome, scale value (in terms of the intensity scale devised by the investigators), and data source. Where sufficient data are not available to characterize the event in absolute terms (e.g., absolute number of persons involved), an alternative judgmental scale is used (e.g., "few, many," etc.). Each event is recorded on a separate IBM card. The Data Bank of Political Instability Events, covering the years 1948-65, now contains some 8,000 events. A major portion of the bank, including the years 1948-62, is on file with the Inter-University Consortium for Political Research, Ann Arbor, Mich.[49]

DATA RELIABILITY

Deadline Data on World Affairs is a news abstracting service that draws its information from a variety of leading world newspapers. It is an abbreviated and hence selective source of event coverage. Data obtained from this source, therefore, may exhibit systematic biases both due to reporting in the original news source and in *Deadline Data,* as a result of press censorship and notions of newsworthiness of particular countries or regions of the world.

We have assesed the reliability of the political instability data bank, both by comparing it to similar work of other researchers and to information on particular political events drawn from other sources. Also, we have examined the empirical relationship between both press censorship and population size (the latter used as a rough indicator of country importance and hence newsworthiness) and both overall level of political instability and incidence of selected violence events. We find evidence that our data provide a representative picture of the comparative levels of instability and violence of the nations in the sample, although the bank undoubtedly does not include every single relevant event which occurred in the 84 nations over the past 18 years.

Our first comparison is with a comparable effort by Ted Gurr to assess the level of civil violence among the nations of the world from 1961-65. Gurr drew his data from the *New York Times, Newsyear, The Annual Register of World Events, Asian Recorder, Africa Diary, Africa Digest, Africa Report, East Europe,* and *Eastern Europe.* His scoring of these events is weighted for extent of participation, duration, and intensity of violence.[50] Although Gurr uses different data sources and a different scoring method, we find a correlation of $r = 0.7$ between our nation instability profiles and his nation violence scores for the same time period.

If we select a particular type of violence, assassination, and compare national profiles on this variable as drawn from *Deadline Data* and from the *New York Times,* we find a correlation of $r = 0.8$, although three times as many assassinations were reported in the latter source. We may say that the relative frequency of reported assassinations remains largely the same among nations, although absolute frequency varies with the source.[51]

Furthermore, we find a correlation of $r = 0.51$ between ratings of press censorship and levels of political violence, indicating that, contrary to expectations regarding news suppression, the higher the level of press censorship within a country, the higher the level of political violence.[52] Evidently news of major internal conflict does reach the press. This positive relationship may be explained in terms of the relationship between coerciveness of political regime (of which press censorship is one facet) and level of political violence. That is, nations with highly coercive regimes that censor the press tend to have much more political violence than less coercive, non-censoring regimes.

Finally, we find little or no evidence of relationship between population, size and political violence. Across the entire sample of nations, the correlation of these variable is $r = 0.12$, indicating a lack of systematic bias in underreporting of news from smaller countries. Undoubtedly less news is included from these states, but since violence is in itself newsworthy, the events in which we are interested are likely to be reported from all states.

DATA SCALING

The seven-point intensity scale of political instability described in the text is based on construct validity and consensual validation. High consensus on the operationalization of such a complex variable as political instability is, however, only one way of validating a measuring instrument. An alternative approach is to subject the instability data to a statistical method for ordering data, such as the Guttman scaling technique. A basic assumption inherent to this method is that there is a common characteristic present to a greater or lesser degree in each of the events.[53] The common characteristic, or underlying dimension, within our data is presumed to be the intensity of violence. In applying this method, only violent events were used. These were grouped into four classes: (1) riots and demonstrations, boycotts against the government, political arrests, governmental action against specific groups, and sabotage; (2) martial law, coups d'etat, and revolt; (3) guerrilla warfare, assassination; (4) execution and civil war. These four classes were conceived as denoting sets of increasing violent events.

Essentially, a Guttman scale is present if occurrences of events in the most extreme class are accompanied by events in each of the other classes. Similarly, if there are no events in the most extreme group, but events occur in the next most extreme class, they are expected to be accompanied by events in the two classes denoting lesser violence. This pattern should repeat itself with each step of decreasing violence. A perfect scale is perfectly reproducible from a knowledge of the most extreme event on the scale. For example, knowledge that the most extreme event experienced within a polity was among those grouped in class (2)—e.g., martial law—would also convey the knowledge that events designated in class (1) are present. No events from class (3) or (4) should be found, however. Since perfect scales are unlikely to exist in empirical data, a reasonable approximation of a perfect scale may be determined by counting the "errors" in scale position that occur within the data and calculating a coefficient of reproducibility. As a rule of thumb, if 90 percent of the behaviors are scalable and 10 percent or less constitute "errors," one may use the scaling technique to order the data and to weigh the events. This criterion was met with our violence data with a coefficient of reproducibility of 0.97, indicating that only 3 percent of the events did not fit the pattern. The profiling of nations with these violent events scored by the Guttman technique is presented in Table 18-2. These summed scores were correlated with the summed scores from the original seven-point scaling of political instability, yielding a coefficient of $r = 0.95$, an empirical validation of the scale.[54]

DEVELOPMENT AND POLITICAL INSTABILITY

Table 18-10 presents the correlation coefficients between the measures of economic, social, and political devolpment and the summary score of political violence calculated by the Guttman scale technique. Also included are the correlations with each of the classes of events indicating increasing intensity of violence: Turmoil Events (type 1), Revolt Events (type 2), Guerrilla Warfare Events (type 3), and Civil War Events (type 4). The magnitude of the relationship between indicators of modernization and political violence is consistently the highest with frequency of Revolt Events (type 2). It is generally the lowest using Turmoil Events (type 1).[55]

Table 18-10.—Development and political instability

A. Relationship Between Industrial Development and Political Instability

	Percent urban	Percent GDP in agriculture	Percent labor in agriculture	GNP per capita
	1	2	3	4
Summary score of instability.............	−0.191	0.285	0.360	−0.343
Frequency of type 1.......	0.044	−0.006	0.064	−0.105
Frequency of type 2.......	−0.273	0.352	0.368	−0.357
Frequency of type 3.......	−0.249	0.279	0.318	−0.259
Frequency of type 4.......	−0.147	0.309	0.245	−0.148

B. Relationships Between Modern Communications and Political Instability

	Newspapers per 1,000 population	Radios per 1,000 population	Domestic mail per capita
	1	2	3
Summary score of instability.............	−0.452	−0.288	−0.373
Frequency of type 1.......	−0.210	−0.064	−0.096
Frequency of type 2.......	−0.418	−0.325	−0.452
Frequency of type 3.......	−0.359	−0.285	−0.335
Frequency of type 4.......	−0.118	−0.056	−0.342

Table 18-10.—Development and political instability—Continued

C. Relationships Between Social Development and Political Instability

| | Higher education per 1,000 population | Primary and secondary enrollment | Percent literate | Life expectancy | Death rate |
	1	2	3	4	5
Summary score of instability	-0.169	-0.267	-0.306	-0.483	0.477
Frequency of type 1	0.027	-0.027	-0.080	-0.194	0.325
Frequency of type 2	-0.256	-0.351	-0.344	-0.599	0.522
Frequency of type 3	-0.134	-0.331	-0.360	-0.442	0.359
Frequency of type 4	-0.064	0.033	0.013	0.001	-0.095

D. Relationships Between Political Development and Political Instability

| | Percent voting | Executive stability |
	1	2
Summary score of instability	-0.297	-0.232
Frequency of type 1	-0.263	-0.034
Frequency of type 2	-0.281	-0.296
Frequency of type 3	-0.066	-0.198
Frequency of type 4	0.082	-0.108

MEASUREMENT OF RATE OF
SOCIOECONOMIC CHANGE

The rate at which socioeconomic change appears to occur is a function of the base level attained by the society, especially if rate is calculated in percentage terms. A high value of percentage rate of change depends on a low base value, and vice versa. Thus less-developed countries, with much smaller base levels on all indicators, will show high percentage increases, while modern countries will appear to be low changers. The relationship between the rate of change index, based on percentage change, and level of development is $r = -0.82$, using our modernity index, and $r = -0.75$, using GNP per capita in U.S. dollars, 1957.

In view of the strong inverse relationship between attained level and percentage rate of change, we sought to measure change in a different fashion. The slope of a regression line through the change points was selected as logically independent from the initial base level. This technique of measurement, which was also used to assess increases and decreases in instability over time, indicates the absolute rate of change, in contrast to the percentage rate. We find, however, that it also relates to modernity level but in two different ways, depending on whether we are dealing with ceiling or non-ceiling indicators. A ceiling indicator is one which has a logical upper limit. Indicators that are themselves percentage calculations, such as literacy level, show this characteristic. Most modern nations, for example, are around 90 percent literate, and as they approach the 100 percent ceiling, their rate of change reaches a standstill. This same is true of primary education, reported as the percentage of school-age children actually enrolled. Caloric intake also has a limit beyond which humans can no longer consume additional food.

There are other indicators, however, which have no such logical bounds or, at least, for which the saturation point is still not reached even by the most developed contemporary nations. These nonceiling indicators include such variables as radios, newspapers, telephones, and national income per capita.

On indicators with an intrinsic ceiling, an absolute measure of change yields the same pattern as a percentage rate of change. Countries low in development appear as high changers, while the reverse is true of highly modern countries. On nonceiling indicators, however, the absolute measure yields the reverse pattern: the modern countries are the high changers; the underdeveloped nations are the low changers. In effect, we have found that on nonceiling indicators modern countries continue to show large absolute gains although their percentage rate remains low. Less-developed states, with a much smaller base level on the indicators, show high percentage increases but their small absolute advancement may be interpreted to mean that they are not really moving as fast as might appear. This reversal pattern makes it apparent that change is dependent on level of modernity.

This patterning helps us to classify ceiling and nonceiling indicators. They may be identified either on the basis of the direction of relationship to level of development, or the relationship between the results obtained from percentage and absolute methods of calculating change. For example, over the whole sample of countries, both percentage and absolute rates of change in primary education are inversely related to level of development, $r = -0.61$ and -0.40, respectively. The same direction of relationship is found with calories consumed daily. Absolute change on this variable correlates $r = -0.45$ with level of development, while the correlation based on percentage rate of change is $r = -0.24$. On the other hand, the increase in radios per 1,000 population shows a positive relationship of $r = 0.66$ to modernity level, if measured in terms of absolute change rate. With percentage rate of change, the relationship to development is reversed and the correlation is $r = -0.51$. The same reversal of relationship is apparent with change rates on percentage of population owning telephones: using an absolute change measure, the correlation to modernity is $r = 0.88$, while with a percentage change measure, the correlation is $r = -0.35$.[56]

Given this patterning, the relationship between the two types of change rates and level of instability may also be predicted. Percentage change rates or rates of change on ceiling indicators will be positively related to instability, indicating that the faster the rate of change, the greater the political violence. Absolute change rates on nonceiling indicators, however, will show the reverse pattern: a rapid rate of change will be associated with political stability. In view of the relationship between change rates and developmental levels, however, it is not clear that it is change, per se, that produces political unrest. It may be the level of attained development.

To extricate rate of change from level of development, we have controlled for the influence of level of modernity through the use of the partial correlation technique. Also, we have restricted the range of development of the sample of nations used to those classed as "Transitional." This group, as mentioned earlier, was seselected for theoretical reasons. An added advantage is that the countries within this group show the greatest range of rates of change, measured in either percentage or absolute terms.

References

49. For more detailed information on the data bank, see Ivo K. Feierabend and Rosalind L. Feierabend, *Cross-National Data Bank of Political Instability Events (Code Index)* (San Diego: Public Affairs Research Institute, San Diego State College, 1965).
50. See Ted Gurr, "A Causal Model of Civil Strife: A Comparative Analysis Using New Indices," *American Political Science Review*, vol. LXII (Dec. 1968), pp. 1104-1124; also *op. cit.*
51. Feierabend, Feierabend, Nesvold, and Jaggar, *op. cit.*
52. The press censorship ratings were based on information derived primarily from John C. Merrill, *A Handbook of the Foreign Press* (Baton Rouge: Louisiana State University Press, 1959); I.P.I. Survey, *The Press in Authoritarian Countries* (Zurich: The International Press Institute, 1959); and Associated Press Surveys of World Censorship.
53. Louis Guttman, "The Basis for Scalogram Analysis," in Samuel A. Stouffer et al., *Studies in Social Psychology in World War II*, Vol. IV: *Measurement and Prediction* (Princeton: Princeton University Press, 1950). For a further explanation of this and other techniques of scaling, see Warren S. Torgerson, *Theory and Methods of Scaling* (New York: Wiley, 1958).
54. For a further elaboration of these procedures, see Nesvold, *op. cit.*
55. See Betty A. Nesvold, *Turmoil to Civil War: A Cross-National Analysis.* Ph. D. dissertation, University of Minnesota, 1968.
56. For a more detailed discussion of methods of measuring socioeconomic change, see Norman M. Howard, "Modernity, Rate of Change and Coerciveness of Political Systems: A Cross-National Study" (San Diego: San Diego State College, master's thesis, 1966).

PART VIII

PROCESSES OF REBELLION

We are struck by uniqueness when we examine the circumstances of a single instance of political violence. At very close hand, each riot, each revolution appears *sui generis*. When several are compared, though, we begin to detect common patterns and processes. The contributors to the preceding part compared some causes and characteristics of violence in the aggregate. The next two chapters offer parallel case studies of some processes that lead to political violence and that determine its course and outcome.

Two conventional "explanations" of rebellion and revolution have been used popularly to explain the militancy and violence of some black Americans in recent years. One is that men rebel when they are suddenly awakened, perhaps by "agitators" or "promises," to their dismal status in life. The other is that men are especially prone to violence "when things are getting better," either because the taste of progress generates exponentially increasing expectations for more progress or because they intensely resent the few remaining barriers they face. James C. Davies suggests a different and more general pattern of change preceding rebellion, one illustrated by his case studies of the French Revolution, the American Civil War, the Nazi revolution, and the uprisings of black Americans in the 1960's. In all these cases, revolt was preceded by a long period of improvement in conditions followed by a more or less sharp decline. The dynamic is that rising socioeconomic or political satisfactions generate in people expectations that improvements will continue. If such expectations are substantially frustrated for many people, group conflict is likely to increase and popular uprisings to occur.

This J-curve pattern of rising and then declining satisfactions is reflected in the economic and political conditions of the bourgeoisie, urban workers and peasants in France during the decades before 1789, in the changing political and economic status of Southerners vis-a-vis the North before the Civil War, and in the conditions of Negro Americans after 1940. The economic condition of Negroes, compared to white Americans, increased very substantially toward equality between 1940 and the early 1950's; nearly half the relative gains of that period had been lost by the early 1960's. At that same time the obdurate resistance of some white Americans to the expansion of Negro rights and opportunities, especially in the South, seemed to demonstrate that further progress was blocked. The behavior of black Americans would have been less explicable had they not reacted as they did to a situation that paralleled the situations of rebellious Frenchmen, white Southerners, and Germans in earlier eras.

The uses of public force influence strongly the course and outcomes of riots, as Morris Janowitz pointed out in chapter 10. It similarly influences revolutionary movements, which Edward Gude demonstrates in his comparative study below, of the uses of insurgent force and regime counterforce in two extreme situations: the successful Cuban revolutionary movement of 1956-59 and the unsuccessful Venezuelan revolutionary movement of the early 1960's. An editorialist recently wrote that "Force empowers its own destruction."[1] The Cuban and Venezuelan cases demonstrate unmistakably that under certain circumstances the use of violence does indeed empower its adversaries. The most crucial circumstance is the popular legitimacy attributed to the use of violence, whether by governments or their opponents. In Cuba, guerrilla activity inspired a terroristic overresponse from the military and police that undermined middle-class support for the Batista regime, and at the same time strengthened popular support for the 26th of July movement. In Venezuela, where the circumstances of the regime and of the insurgents closely paralleled those in Cuba, the Betancourt government responded cautiously to insurgent terrorism, using intensive force only after terrorism had alienated the insurgents' potential supporters and had led to increased public support for retaliatory action by the regime. In the Cuban case, governmental force engendered its own destruction. In Venezuela, insurgent force ultimately proved self-destructive.

1. Roy Pearson, "The Dilemma of Force," *Saturday Review*, Feb. 10, 1968, p. 24.

Chapter 19

THE J-CURVE OF RISING AND DECLINING SATISFACTIONS AS A CAUSE OF SOME GREAT REVOLUTIONS AND A CONTAINED REBELLION

By James C. Davies*

The J-curve is this: revolution is most likely to take place when a prolonged period of rising expectations and rising gratifications is followed by a short period of sharp reversal, during which the gap between expectations and gratifications quickly widens and becomes intolerable. The frustration that develops, when it is intense and widespread in the society, seeks outlets in violent action. When the frustration becomes focused on the government, the violence becomes coherent and directional. If the frustration is sufficiently widespread, intense, and focused on government, the violence will become a revolution that displaces irrevocably the ruling government and changes markedly the power structure of the society. Or the violence will be contained within the system, which it modifies but does not displace. This latter case is rebellion. The following chart (figure 19-1) shows what happens as a society heads toward revolution.[1]

This is an assertion about the state of mind of individual people in a society who are likely to revolt. It says their state of mind, their mood, is one of high tension and rather generalized hostility, derived from the widening of the gap between what they want and what they get. They fear not just that things will no longer continue to get better but—even more crucially—that ground will be lost that they have already gained. The mood of rather generalized hostility, directed generally outward, begins to turn toward government. People so frustrated not only fight with other

* The author is professor of political science at the University of Oregon. He is author of *Human Nature in Politics* (New York: Wiley, 1963), editor of *When Men Revolt—and Why* (New York: The Free Press, forthcoming), and has written several influential articles on collective and revolutionary behavior.

1. I wish to note that Janice Rademaker and Hendrik van Dalen gathered most of the statistical and many of the factual data presented here. Their work was indispensable to the completion of this paper. Ted Gurr made some generous and acute comments on an earlier draft that helped the reader to get more easily to the heart of the matter.

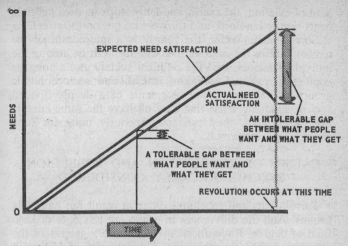

Figure 19-1.—Need satisfaction and revolution.

members of their families and their neighbors. They also jostle one another in crowds and increase their aggressiveness as pedestrians and bus passengers and drivers of cars. When events and news media and writers and speakers encourage the direction of hostilities toward the government, the dispersed and mutual hostility becomes focused on a common target. The hostility among individuals diminishes. The dissonant energy becomes a resonant, very powerful force that heads like a great tidal wave or forest fire toward the established government, which it may then engulf.

This phenomenon of synergic unification of a public when frustration becomes widespread and deep is awesome in its tendency to erase hostility between people. It is akin to the feeling that develops in a quarrelsome household at times. A fighting family may just barely manage to hold together. The father may be unemployed and frequently drunk the mother worn to a frazzle, the children quarrelsome as they displace the tensions generated by poverty and the frustrations of their fighting parents. The father, no longer able to provide for his family, may lose his authority within the family and strike out at those nearest to him. But when the landlord knocks on the door and announces that the rent must be paid by 10 o'clock tomorrow morning on pain of eviction, the family suddenly stops its own fighting, beats up the landlord, and throws him out on the street.

Such tension within the family is a microcosm of the tension within the national community; that is, among the individual members of the political society and among its conflicting regional, religious, racial, and socioeconomic groups. When the various segments of a deeply divided society suddenly sense that they all have the same enemy, the government, they can spontaneously unite for long enough to overthrow it.

CAUSES OF REVOLUTION AND REBELLION, PSYCHOLOGICALLY CONSIDERED

Revolutions and rebellions differ in result but have like origins. And the differences in origin are less ones of kind than of degree. Revolutions involve more segments of the population than do rebellions. The intensity of feeling in revolutions is probably greater and has taken a longer time to develop than in rebellions. The violent phase of a revolution is longer and more savage. The bitterness that lingers after the violence is likely to endure for decades or centuries after a revolution.

The difference is not in causes and the violent action or even in the long-range consequences so much as it is in the immediate result. Rebellions do not remove the established government but instead are contained, partly as the consequence of the use of violent force in large enough amounts to override the rebels' anger at the government. The rebels may choose to live with their frustrations rather than endure the blows of the police and the army and the dull, sick anguish of imprisonment. But rebellions also are contained within the established system to the extent that the government pays heed to the grievances that led to the rebellion. If the only response to extralegal violence is legal violence, then hatred of oppression becomes deeply imprinted in the minds of the momentarily silenced rebels. The hatred lingers and deepens like embers in dry tinder after firefighters have tried to beat to death a small fire.

As the American Declaration of Independence said in 1776, people do not for "light and transient causes" make a rebellion or revolution. What then are the grave and enduring conditions that produce frustrations in a broad

692

and varied citizenry, that in turn produce the revolutionary state of mind?

The common condition appears to be the denial of satisfaction of those needs that are basic to all human beings. Not all needs (as for a new automobile) are basic, and not all basic needs are of equal revolutionary potential. Abraham Maslow has argued that man's basic needs are arranged in sequence, from the most to the least powerful. The most potent are the physical needs, which must continuously be satisfied for all people during their entire life. But when a person gains their satisfaction—as an infant, a child, and an adult—he does not then, animal-like, remain content with satisfying just these bodily needs. Soon after birth he demands affection and, if he gets it, he reciprocates affection toward others. But his physical needs persist, and if he is forced to choose, he will first satisfy his need for food and then his need for affection.

In early childhood the individual who has been regularly gratified in his physical and affectional needs does not then rest content with this mental state of affairs. He begins, usually no later than when he is 8 or 10 years old, to demand recognition as an individual who is worthy of his own regard for himself and of others' regard for him. In early childhood people begin to demand that others accord them respect. The respect of others is necessary if people are to acquire self-respect.

It is this kind of demand that lies so close to the surface of the Declaration of Independence, in the statement that all men are created equal and in the specific indictments of British rule—for example, in the great indignation expressed at the quartering of troops in private homes without the consent of the homeowners, and at the removal of trials at law from the Colonies to England. This demand is evident in the Declaration's "decent respect to the opinions of mankind," whose approval the American rebels sought.

And once these successive needs—the physical, the social-affectional, and the equal esteem or dignity needs—are sufficiently gratified, humans are not even then content: they then begin to look for that kind of activity that is particularly suited to them as unique individuals. Whether their competence is to be a ditchdigger, a powershovel operator, a construction foreman, a civil engineer or a building contractor, an architect, a mother, a writer, or a politician—they must do these things when they have become rather sure in the gratification of their even more basic physical, social, and esteem needs.

The crucial point is this: no human being so long as he lives is ever completely gratified in the satisfaction of his needs. Up to the moment of his death, he must eat and sleep, he must be with people; he has to be acknowledged as a distinct person; and he must realize his individual potential. When he ceases to do these things, he ceases to live. All of these needs of his have got to be gratified; they ultimately can be denied only by natural or by violent death. Armies and police forces can quash these natural and irrepressible human needs only by reducing human beings to animals and then killing them. The logic of this was stated in fictional form by George Orwell, in describing what was necessary for the perpetuation of dictatorship: "a boot, stamping in a human face, forever."

The Maslow need hierarchy is a necessary part of a psychological explanation of the causes of revolution. Marx to the contrary, revolutions are made not only by economically depressed classes and their leaders but by the joint effort of large numbers of those people in all social groups who are experiencing frustration of different basic needs. People deprived of career opportunities may join in revolt with people who have suffered indignities at the hands of employers, landlords, police, or military troops. They also may join with people who have suffered no indignities but are for the moment simply hungry.

The common characteristic of potential revolutionaries is that each of them individually senses the frustration of one or more basic needs and each is able to focus his frustration on the government. After this need frustration is generated, people begin to share their discontents and to work together. But preceding this joint action, there is no more conspiracy than there is among trees when they burst into flame during a forest fire.

THE J-CURVE AND PARTICULAR REVOLUTIONS

On the level of general theory, one can say precisely the same thing—in abstract terms—about each revolution and rebellion. But in some ways each revolution is unlike every other revolution. And from the practical research standpoint, directly comparable data are not available for all revolutions, particularly when they took place decades or centuries ago. In many nations now, the seeds of revolution are sprouting. But established governments in these nations are not likely to welcome social scientists in search of data by conducting public opinion surveys inquiring about attitudes toward the government.

In the interest of arriving at some conclusions and of arriving at the understanding that they are tentative, we can profitably consider particular revolutions.

The French Revolution of 1789

The French Revolution is the first of the great modern postindustrial revolutions. It is the first grand revolution after that grandest of all modern revolutions, the 16th-century Protestant Reformation.

The position of the various major social classes in France gives a major clue as to how the revolution came about. The relationship between these classes help explain also why liberty, equality, and fraternity did not arrive on the day they were declared to be human rights. The major segments of French society in the late 18th century were the well-known three estates: the clergy, the nobility, and then everybody else, who collectively were called the third estate for lack of a more precise term.

What is less well known are the proportions that each of these estates comprised of the total French population of about 23 million. There were, according to George Lefebvre, perhaps the greatest historian in 20-century France of the French Revolution, about 100,000 Frenchmen in the clergy (less than half of 1 percent); about 400,000 in the nobility (about 2 percent); and over 23 million in the third estate. The third estate included the high bourgeoisie, an economically, socially, and politically active group of merchants, bankers, and manufacturers. Also in the third estate were the petty bourgeoisie—small merchants, bakers, artisans in wood and metal, and the growing body of skilled government bureaucrats. Finally, the third estate included workingmen, many of them the sons of peasants, and also the vast body of peasants. France, beginning its industrialization somewhat later than England, was still overwhelmingly an agricultural nation.

Even less well known than the proportions of each of the three estates in the total population is the proportion of land which each estate owned. Again, according to Lefebvre, the clergy owned about 10 percent of the land, the nobility somewhat less than 20 percent, the bourgeoisie about 20 percent, and the peasants all the rest. The heavy imbalance of landownership reflects only the most evident part of the land-tenure picture. Anywhere from 20 to 75 percent of the rural households in France before the revolution did not own any land. These peasants were either working as tenants to save money to buy land, or they had given up and were working as paid farm laborers. And in massive numbers they were drifting into cities to find work.

These peasants who aspired to landownership or who had achieved it saw themselves as facing an unending struggle to survive and to get a little ahead. As the industrial economy began to develop rapidly, the demand for farm products increased because so many people who once tilled and lived off the soil now worked for money in cities, which —as everywhere in developing nations undergoing industrialization—made ever-increasing, insatiable demands on the countryside to feed their people. Peasants, seeing the chance thus to move up the ladder from farm labor or land rental, were beset by a variety of inhibitors. There were the feudal dues (payment to landlords for the use of his flour mill, the exclusive right of landlords to hunt and fish, the reversion of land to a landlord if the peasant died without proper heirs, etc.); the duty to perform physical labor for public purposes (building public roads and other structures); the tithe (a 10-percent tax due to the church); and a variety of taxes payable directly to the national government through its local representatives and more specifically to the local collector, who took his lawful share of what he was able to extract from the peasant.

Peasants did not, in short, believe that they were beloved objects of solicitude of other segments of French society. Neither did their sons who went into the cities to work in factories and small shops or into mines to dig coal. Wages went up slowly in the 18th century, as we shall see later, and prices went up rather rapidly. Better off than when they left the countryside, they were nevertheless gradually getting worse off than they had been in years past in the city.

That portion of the bourgeoisie containing skilled artisans suffered some of the same taxing pains as did the landowning peasants. Their guilds were heavily taxed and so were their incomes. The high bourgeoisie, growing in wealth and power, suffered the disadvantage that the more systematically they ran their enterprises and kept record of profits and losses, the more they had to pay in taxes. And they believed the government was becoming increasingly subservient to the nobility.

The nobility saw the government as increasingly subservient to the bourgeoisie. With no respect for the dignity of inherited title, the government for a price was adding pseudonoble titles to wealthy men of no family, arrogantly designating these arrivistes as "nobles de robe" to distinguish them from the natural-born "nobles d'épée." The old nobles observed the new nobles buying country estates from increasingly vestigial but still very sworded noblemen. The nobles of the robe were enfolding, smothering, the nobles of the sword.

Old nobles, looking through dusty old documents, discovered a way to be with but not be of the modern mercantile-industrial world. They found that services and payments in kind were due them from peasants, many of whom had for centuries been free peasants. (Serfdom was first abolished, according to Tocqueville, in Normandy in the 13th century and was virtually nonexistent on the eve of the great 18th century revolution.) In short, landlords, seeing their economic advancement, their political power, and their prestige all threatened and actually diminished by the energetic and of course unhonorable bourgeoisie, began in the mid-18th century to reassert long-dead "rights" against peasants, who thereby saw not only their freedom, power, and prestige but also their economic welfare threatened and diminished.

The sworded nobles furthermore had little to do—few, if any functions in society to give their lives meaning. The government gradually was taking away—efficiently, effectively, and thoroughly—such governmental powers as nobles had possessed before kings could successfully establish national power. They were no longer needed to keep the peace, to adjudicate disputes among vassals and serfs, and most particularly to protect from violence their people, their peasants, their onetime serfs. Now the government acted, or tried or professed to act, directly in the behalf of the population at large. So the old nobles, sensing their loss of position in society as the new nobles of the robe began to emulate the sword-bearing style of life, began to emulate the new nobles in their wealth. And this meant evading such taxes as the capitation, by law payable by all people with incomes. It also meant using documents to enforce feudal dues, in many cases centuries after the reason for the dues had been reduced to legal paper, which now was hard to read and harder to justify.

The clergy, that one-half of 1 percent of the population, had a few functions to perform. They kept records of births and deaths. They baptized. They warned souls of the need for grace and invoked God's grace. And they prayed, managed estates, and bottled wine, extracted the tithe from the peasants. And, for their recordkeeping and their divine intervention, they were freed of any tax payments.

These then were the major segments of society, each of which eyed every other segment and its members with suspicion and envy. Was that a tax collector coming? Was that a secret hoard of grain which that peasant or that landlord so hurriedly covered up? Where was that set of books of the merchant that were a true report of how rich he was getting? How much did that fat father pay the government to get his bright but unprincipled son the job as secretary to the resident government commissioner?

If individuals in each estate tended to suspect and envy individuals in all other estates, they all mistrusted and condemned the government. The monarchy asserted in the mid-15th century (during the reign of Charles VII) the power to tax anyone without the consent of any estate. In the 18th century, the crowd was intermittently, and more frequently, beginning to use the power. It had to. France engaged in a nearly unbroken series of expensive wars in the 18th century. Good for members of all estates, as businessmen, landowning lords and peasants and the small class of workers, the wars were bad for businessmen and peasants as taxpayers. Starting in 1781, the government increased—but with an infirm hand—its efforts to collect taxes, demanding even that the nobility actually pay the taxes nominally due from it.

The government was thus disappointing the popular expectation of continued prosperity without cost. And until the French intervention in the American War of Independence, the wars were lost. The intervention in America gave France pride in somewhat vicariously defeating England, which by 1763 had virtually knocked France out of North America except for Louisiana. The financial crisis—which threatened and actually deprived high bourgeoisie, nobles, and now even clergy of wealth they had come to expect as their due—got worse. Inflation intensified. Lefebvre has calculated the rise in the cost of living thus: in about 50 years before the revolution, prices went up some 65 percent and wages went up some 22 percent. Whether rich or poor, most people had enough excuse to displace at least some of their inter-state hostility onto the government. And in addition they had reason enough also to dislike and condemn the government, which either lost its wars or was unable to pay for the one war that it assisted in winning.

These growing tensions, increasingly directed toward government, were aggravated by events that amounted to bad luck at best and gullibility at worst. In 1786 France made a trade treaty with the England it had helped to defeat 3 years earlier in America. France agreed to reduce the tariff on textiles, which helped the then more efficient and mass-market-oriented English mills. In return, England agreed to reduce tariffs on wines and brandies, which England did not produce anyhow but imported from Portugal and France. The trade treaty went into effect in 1788.

In 1778, the French harvest of grain suffered from bad weather. That is, the weather was bad for grain and good for the vineyards. There was thus a nearly catastrophic shortage of grains for bread and a large surplus of wine to flood the English market after the lowering of the trade barriers. And the opening of war of Turkey against Russia and Austria diminished these countries as markets for French textiles, which now faced competition in French stores from cheap English cloth.

Unemployment rose along with the reduced demand for textiles. The abundant grape harvest dropped wine prices somewhat. Peasants who produced wine had to buy their food at higher prices. These economic dislocations chain reacted to reduce the demand for everything but jobs and bread—the two goods that were in scarcest supply. Bread had never been so expensive since the end of the reign of Louis XIV in 1715, and so bread riots broke out in the major cities, and people in the cities began restlessly roaming out into the countryside to get food. Long-term rising expectations of a prosperous and peaceful economy and effective government were quickly disappointed. In the spring of 1789 and into the summer, the growing interclass hostility and growing hostility to government quickly burst into revolution, when the fear of physical deprivation quickly became real and immediate. The 18th-century developments are shown in figure 19-2.

The J-curve helps explain the French Revolution. The growing frustration of the land expectations of peasants, of the dignity expectations of landlords who wanted the status-wealth of the high bourgeoisie, and of the dignity-and power expectations of the high bourgeoisie are all closely comparable to developments in other nations that have had revolutions. And so is the effect of sudden economic dislocation following long-term economic growth.

But the J-curve is not a total explanation of the French Revolution. At least in its intensity, the interclass hostility in France, not as such related to the J-curve, was unique. More or less independently of frustrated rising expectations in the 18th century, French society was already deeply fragmented. The internal war of all against all had already begun. The absorption of these forces, in conflict between classes and individuals, did temporarily deflect them from the government. But in the end the sheer hostility, as it became more intense, turned toward the government.

And in addition to the disappointed expectations and deflected interclass hostility, there was in France in 1789 the visible and exciting example of the successful American revolution. In 1968 French students followed the example of students in Japan, America, and elsewhere by rebelling against French universities and government. But this was only the second time the American revolutionary example had been followed: it had already been followed almost 180 years before.

The American Civil War of 1861

The difference between the terms "revolution," "rebellion," and "civil war" may be nothing more than this:

revolution succeeds, rebellion fails, and civil war leaves the question open. All involve violence. In the Gettysburg Address of 1863, Lincoln referred to the ongoing conflict as "a great civil war"; at other times he called it rebellion and he never acknowledged the sovereign independence of the 11 Southern States that asserted it. It is not quite clear even a hundred years later that it was a rebellion or that it failed, but it is clear that the American Civil War did not end in Southern independence. It remains hard to characterize this most savage conflict. In proportion to the population of the time, this civil war produced the most catastrophic loss of life and property that America has ever suffered. The awesome depth of the conflict makes it important to explain.

The American Civil War is in some ways the French Revolution of 1789, and in others like the Nazi revolution of 1933 examined in the next section. As in the French Revolution, the middle-class, entrepreneurial, and industrializing part of the nation was arrayed in battle against the landed aristocracy. Southern plantations fought a change in social institutions that would make them more suitable to the profound changes which capitalism and industrialization brought with them. But the American Civil War is unlike the French Revolution in the absence of joint action by both American bourgeoisie and landlords against the national government. If Southern landlords and Northern industrialists had combined against the government, it is quite possible the civil war would have resembled the Nazi revolution. It could have established an oligarchical dictatorship of the urban upper-middle-class and rural landlords, as in many 20th-century developing nations.

The American conflict does resemble the Nazi revolution in that it was intiated by conservative segments of society that were restive with the pace and direction of change. In both America before the Civil War and Germany before nazism, an agrarian economy was being rapidly replaced by industry, and the hegemony of landed aristocrats was threatened by the growing political power of merchants and industrialists. Industrialization was about as recent in both countries—about two generations, though its growth rate in Germany was greater. But the principal difference between America in 1861 and Germany in 1933 was in

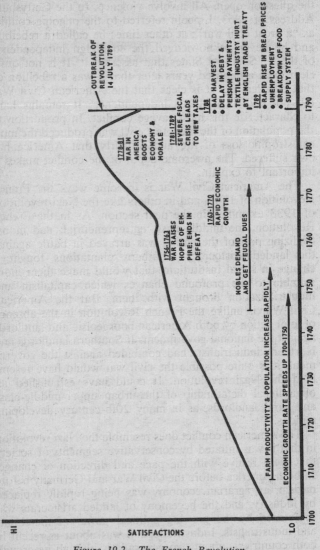

Figure 19-2.—The French Revolution.

OUTBREAK OF REVOLUTION, 14 JULY 1789

1781-1789 SEVERE FISCAL CRISIS LEADS TO NEW TAXES

1778-81 WAR IN AMERICA BOOSTS ECONOMY & MORALE

1788
- BAD HARVEST
- DELAY IN DEBT & PENSION PAYMENTS
- TEXTILE INDUSTRY HURT BY ENGLISH TRADE TREATY

1789
- RAPID RISE IN BREAD PRICES
- UNEMPLOYMENT
- BREAKDOWN OF FOOD SUPPLY SYSTEM

1763-1770 RAPID ECONOMIC GROWTH

1756-1763 WAR RAISES HOPES OF EMPIRE; ENDS IN DEFEAT

NOBLES DEMAND AND GET FEUDAL DUES

FARM PRODUCTIVITY & POPULATION INCREASE RAPIDLY

ECONOMIC GROWTH RATE SPEEDS UP 1700-1750

HI

SATISFACTIONS

LO

1700 1710 1720 1730 1740 1750 1760 1770 1780 1790

the orientation of the two revolutions: the latter was more progressive in its orientation in that there was a strong and real appeal in nazism to those people who felt they had been denied equal opportunity to acquire education and technical skills. In America the South denied the desirability of education and anything other than agricultural technology.

The gradual rise and rapid decline in gratifications in Pre-Civil War America occur in two cycles, one contained within the other. There had been a very long cyclical rise in expectations of Americans generally, from the beginnings of colonization, through independence, and down to the great growth of wealth in the early-19th century. There also was a shorter term cycle in Southern expectations, which rose from about 1789, when the national government was established, and began to decline in the mid-1850's. That is, there was a roughly 200-year cycle and within it a 70-year cycle of rising and falling gratifications. The latter cycle is set forth in figure 19-3.

The colonization of America in the 17th and 18th centuries provided a steady rise in expectations and gratifications until the 1750's and 1760's. But a common pattern of growth in the various colonies and a common determination on independence concealed some growing differences. In the northern colonies, from New England down to Pennsylvania, the dominant settlers were religious dissenters, radically modern in their individualism and anticorporatism. The democratic New England town meetings emerged from the institution of theoretical democracy in the New England church congregations. This democracy was an antithesis of the hierarchy in church and government that were so typical of England. This style of rule appeared also in Pennsylvania, dominated as it was by Quakers and their radically democratic ideology.

In Maryland, Virginia, the Carolinas, and Georgia, fewer of the settlers were democratically and individualistically oriented dissenters. Indeed there was a substantial influx of both Roman Catholics and their institutional cousins, Episcopalians. They were more accustomed to hierarchy and order established from above and they carried with them the nondissenting, establishment orientation of their English ancestors. There were, in addition, influxes of poor people with more individualistic and less establishment-

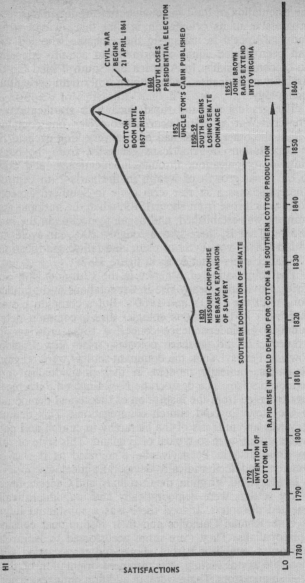

Figure 19-3.—Southern satisfactions before the Civil War.

704

oriented religious views, but they rarely were a major influence in the South, politically or socially, at any time before the Civil War, and they shared with the establishment-oriented plantationer class a dedication to the rectitude of slavery and to the virtues of the rural life.

Differences in institutions and values if anything became greater with the passage of time. Big cities of commerce and industry grew in the North and, with the exception of the great port city of New Orleans, never developed in the South. Agrarian development in the North was typified by family-sized farms. With their highly individualistic outlook, farmers had appreciable political power in the Northern state governments from the beginning of national independence. Agrarian development in the South was on the surface of things like growth in the North. There were far more family-sized farms in the South than there were plantations, but the plantationers dominated Southern politics, using the issue of black inferiority to all white men very effectively in maintaining acquiescence by poor whites in the rule of the large landholders and slaveowners.

Inevitably, as industrialization and commerce developed in the North it began to urbanize rapidly. This process included not just a division of labor between farmers and city dwellers, but also a rapid growth in population. Correlatively and inevitably, an agrarian society like that in the South experienced a slower growth in population. The growth toward political equalitarianism in the North became more and more fundamentally opposed to the oligarchical domination of politics by the plantationers. And so began—more exactly, continued—the widening of the gulf between economic and social values and ways of life between North and South.

In national politics, the question of who should rule echoed continuously across the ever-eroding canyon between South and North. The Virginia dynasty was not a legend but a reality for a generation after independence. Excepting the brief and not very portentous administrations of John Adams (1797-1801) and his son John Quincy Adams (1825-29), there was an unbroken line of Southern Presidents of the United States, from Washington through Jefferson, Madison, Monroe, and Jackson. John Calhoun of South Carolina served as Vice President during J. Q. Adams' administration and the first term of Jackson's. From 1789 to 1837 the Presidency was almost continuously Southern.

This Southern domination became increasingly more romantic. The Southerners who became Presidents acted nationally, not sectionally. In Congress, the Missouri Compromise settled and unsettled (in 1820) the conflict over sectional representation. By this Compromise the South won the votes in Congress of the border state of Missouri, which was to be admitted as a slave state, and lost the free opportunity to expand its political power westward. The South did continue to dominate the Senate for another generation, judging at least by the 1854 Kansas-Nebraska Act, which, repudiating the Missouri Compromise, allowed slaves to come into these territories. Indeed the Senate was not just the last retreat of the South but also the only part of the government that did not reflect the ever growing social and economic dominance of the North.

The regional growth comparisons are awesome. In one decade, from 1850-60, the population of the South grew greatly—about 23 percent; in the same decade the non-Southern population increased a fantastic 43 percent. Although adequate economic trend data over time are hard to come by, in 1860 the North was producing over 90 percent by value of all manufactured goods. The proportion produced by the North had apparently been increasing rapidly as the war approached. The North was even exporting food (grains and livestock) to the agricultural South. And free farmers were saying politically that they did not want to compete, economically or socially, with plantationers whose fieldhands worked without pay.

These developments suggest, at least in hindsight, that the South was made to suppose that it could win a war against the growing industrial and commercial Yankee giant. But the South itself was enjoying, early in the 1850's, unprecedented prosperity. There was an almost insatiable world demand for cotton, of which the South had close to a world monopoly in production. The average annual production during the 1840-50 decade was 2.2 million bales; it increased to 3.4 million in the next decade. At the same time the average annual price during 1840-50 was about 8 cents per pound, rising more than 30 percent, to 10.6 cents, in the final prewar decade. Along with this—and an improvement in profit from tobacco and sugarcane production—came an increase in the price of prime field hands, the most commonly valuable category of slaves. Their price doubled during the 1850-60 decade, reaching as high as $1,500 per head, and the demand was enormous. It was not easy for Southerners to concede the rightness or the efficiency of an economy based on free labor.

But the little-diversified agrarian Southern economy was fragile. A particular weakness was the plantationers' custom of buying on credit advanced before the sale of their crops. Even before the 1775 War of Independence, it was common for Southern planters to be thus in long-range debt to English merchants. After 1783 there was one change: the creditors were now Northern merchants, mainly in New York. The South quite simply remained money-poor up to 1861 (and beyond). On a sellers' market, which the South enjoyed with some ups and downs until 1857, the system of credit worked well enough for Southern planters. And it worked even better for Northern creditors. To protect themselves from market uncertainties—and from individuals who were poor credit risks—Northern dealers would charge Southern buyers higher than normal prices. Southern buyers, when they were paid by credit paper at harvesttime, would sell the paper at a discount to pay their bills. So they paid twice at least: in the form of higher prices for the goods they bought, and lower prices for the credit paper they sold to pay off their annual debt.

This chronic low-intensity economic crisis, in the face of seemingly endless prosperity, is akin to the situation that producer the looting and burning of white-owned stores by Negroes in the 1960's—more than a century later: the Southern plantationers developed no affection for the big Yankee houses that had the goods and sold them at a price higher than a Yankee would have to pay. They were unable to set fire to the New York stores and say "Burn, Baby, Burn." But they did try to destroy the Union.

Near the end of this cycle of rising and then declining political gratifications was the more immediate and very threatening economic crisis of 1857. It was an epitome of the Southern dependence on the North, of the dependence of any raw-material-producing colony on the financial and other economic circumstances of the diversified "mother country." In 1857 the South was hit by a panic in the New York commodity exchange market. For a time money exchange with England virtually ceased, and so did the effective demand for cotton in England. Although the Liverpool price was 18 or 19 cents a pound for cotton, in contrast to 10 cents a pound in New York, Southerners for the most part had to sell in New York. Many of them had already committed their crop to New York buyers and so were stuck, many who had not committed their crop needed money badly and were in virtually the same bind as those who had already sold their crops for future delivery. A Southern Senator in Washington saw the situation with a clear intelligence and passed his judgment: a cotton crop that could have sold for $100 million went for $65 million. To save irresponsible and selfish Northern speculators—who perhaps blamed the system for producing the money crisis—the South lost $35 million.

This was the final critical downturn in the gratifications of Southerners. They had lost political power that they had exercised so successfully in nearly a half century of Southern but Nation-minded Presidents of the United States. They had neared the final loss of their dominant power in the Senate, where so often they held a veto over laws demanded by Northerners. And now, in a process that so starkly showed their economic thralldom to the North, they had to save their economic masters to the tune of a loss of a third of the value of their major crop—and the nation's major export.

The growing and now enormous tensions found release in secession. The eventual outcome of the 1854 Kansas-Nebraska Act, which in 1854 still offered some hope of restoring the balance of sectional power in the Senate, soon became clear. An honest referendum on the slavery issue indicated an 8-to-1 majority in Kansas in favor of entering the Union as a free state. After liberating a few slaves in Kansas, that madman and self-styled liberator, John Brown, in 1859 made a raid in search of arms on the U.S. arsenal at Harpers Ferry. But Harpers Ferry was not in Kansas; it was in Virginia. And it was clear where John Brown now proposed to commence the liberation of slaves.

So the South began to secede. South Carolina was the first to take the step, on December 20, 1860. And South Carolina fired the first shot, on the federal Fort Sumter in Charleston Harbor, on April 21, 1861. The Civil War had begun as the ever-romantic South came to the end of its neofeudal dream. Its expectations of freedom to continue to expand its wealth and way of life were shattered by the events of the late 1850's, in Congress and in the mercantile houses of New York.

The Nazi Revolution of 1933

The Nazi revolution was a German and a world catastrophe. It led to the partial destruction and the partition of a population that had been growing in unity, civilization, and recognition since the Protestant Reformation that Luther led, since the tremendous spurt in industrialization in the late-19th century, and since the surge of nationalism that took the form of empire building and then, in 1914, of war.

Germany was the first to experience a successful reformation, that major advance toward establishing the equalization and individuation of men. For whatever reasons, it was the last major European nation to undergo that profoundest of modernizers: industrialization. In one sense the first modern popular revolution took place in Germany in the 16th century, before industrialization had developed anything like its modern factory system anywhere. In another sense Germany never had a postindustrial revolution comparable to the French Revolution. The German Reformation was universalist in its equalitarian principles and so was the French Revolution. There was a messianic quality to the equalitarian beliefs of the German Reformation of the 16th century, the French Revolution of the 18th, and the Russian of the 20th. These revolutions spawned and nurtured many popular movements in the world. But the Nazi revolution—the nearest counterpart to the postindustrial French Revolution—was not universalist. It was particularistic, intensely nationalistic, and imperialistic, proposing to subject and exploit both Slavic and Gallic peoples to the control and enrichment of the Germanic. It was a kind of revenge for the world recognition that came to France and Russia after their universalist revolutions, renown that had stifled Germany between two peoples that felt their own superiority to Germans.

The growth in vitality of German society and culture was relatively steady and continuous, perhaps for centuries up to 1918. Surely it was continuous since the tariff union (developing from 1819-1844) that intensified the trend, under Prussian domination, toward economic unity. With the growth of an enormous iron and steel industry, the basis was laid for building warships, artillery, and rifles. Construction of these commodities made war and expansion a euphoric dream that called for realization. In 1870, in battle, Germany defeated the France that had been the terror of Europe just two generations before. Within months, in January 1871, came the siege and surrender of Paris. Within days after the surrender of Paris came the formal inauguration of the unified German empire, when the Prussian king was crowned Emperor William I. The curves of rising expectations and gratifications were steadily rising, for Germans as individuals and as a nation.

In such a short analysis it is not possible to specify steps in the progress of Germany upward to its dismaying and unacknowledged defeat in world war in November 1918. It is clear enough that the long-range trend, accelerating rapidly after the tariff union and the 1871 unification, was upward. It is clear that the 1918 defeat came as a profound shock. It was sufficiently stunning and ambiguous to be regarded as only a temporary setback by those elitist individuals who believed in an imperial destiny and by those ordinary Germans who had a deep pride in their country. All these had entrusted basic decisions to the government. Under two emperors and such gifted paternalistic rulers as Bismarck and the Krupp family, the government had given them economic prosperity, social security, and world prestige.

Again, as in the analysis of the American Civil War, there was a centuries-long J-curve and a decades-short one. For present purposes, we can commence the analysis of the final rise and decline with the ambiguous 1918 defeat, recalling only that the advances up to 1918 had been real and enormous and remained in the memories of perhaps most Germans.

Both the French and the German Nazi revolutions were preceded by military defeat. But the former nation could not so easily turn the blame outward as could the latter. In the French case, the Seven Years' War, ending in 1763, was a virtually total defeat by England in North America. The vicarious French victory over England at Yorktown in 1781 produced independence for the United States and near-bankruptcy for France. The military action was far from France. England did not make demands intimately affecting Frenchmen in France in 1763 and the government's financial crisis in 1781 could hardly be blamed by Frenchmen on the defeated British.

With Germany after the 1918 Armistice it was different. The Allies blockaded German ports and then occupied just enough German territory to hurt pride and business badly. German Communists, exalted by the Russian example, threatened their countrymen with total destruction of the established system, already shaken by the loss of the emperor. Germans therefore could readily displace blame and thereby dissociate the glories of an ever-greater German nation from the trickeries of external and internal enemies who sought only their own aggrandizement and German degradation. This hope for restoration of recently and meanly lost greatness was a very central part of the mental outlook of perhaps most Germans in the 1920's.

The continuation of hope and of pride in being German formed a cement that kept the nation from the disintegration that France experienced in the late-18th century. There was not quite the war of all against all that characterized prerevolutionary French society. Internal hostility was less personal and the enemies were more symbolic. The Allies, the French, the Communists, the Jews, the capitalists were the enemies rather than one's neighboring peasants, one's landlord, one's boss in the shoe factory, or the arriviste wealthy bourgeois who bought one's estate.

The impersonal contacts with enemies in Germany were such as to reinforce displacement of the internal tensions of an economy that had suffered the consequences of vast military expenditure, in an all-out war from 1914 to 1918. It was easier to forget the sanctions (governmental and industrial) against industrial strife than the more comfortable fact of punitive and unrealistic reparations. It was the government that initiated currency inflation. But the effect of the inflation on the internal economy could be overshadowed in people's minds by its effect on the French enemy, especially since the inflation was an effort to defeat the French and Belgian military occupation of the Ruhr Basin, starting in January 1923, by watering down the high price of reparations. German workers, who did strike in large numbers in this period, often regarded the French and Belgian occupying forces (and their attendant business experts who took over management control of the big enterprises) as the enemy. And then they could also blame those German capitalists, many of them Jews, who skillfully made fortunes out of the inflation. Because their customs made them stand out—particularly in the abstract—the Jewish capitalists were easier to blame than the German ones. And middle-class Germans could blame the Communists as agitators of the proletariat. In many such plausible ways, blame for Germany's ills could be projected outward. These plausible and sufficiently genuine external and internal enemies limited the tendency, which was never notably strong, of Germans to blame themselves for their problems, which in the 1920's indeed became severe.

The underlying optimism (a continuing heritage from the imperial and Reformation eras) and the surface displacement of responsibility for contemporary problems probably combined to encourage an irrepressible optimism in the mid-1920's. The inflation was a trauma. It began in August 1922 and ran wild for more than a year, until November 1923 when efforts at drastic monetary reform were undertaken. But the 1920's nevertheless were times of hope and progress in Germany. If the inflation wiped out private savings and insurance policies, it also wiped out internal public debt, and in April 1924 the Dawes plan promised a large influx of external capital for reconstruction. Though there were peaks of unemployment (1.5 million in January 1923, 2 million in February 1926, and 1.4 million in January 1928), the trend in jobs was generally upward. Taking the prewar year 1907 as a base of 100, by 1925 the number of gainfully employed had increased to about 127, and by 1933 had increased to 128. Again taking 1907 national population as a base of 100, by 1925 it had increased only to 102 and by 1933 to 106. In short, the proportion of of the population that had jobs, roughly a decade after World War ended, was a fourth larger than a decade before the war ended.

Up to 1929, economic conditions in Germany generally improved. And then, starting in July 1929, there was a steady, unremitting increase in unemployment until some time in the first quarter of 1933—that is, until after Hitler came to power on January 30, 1933. At the peak of unemployment, sometime in 1932, between 5.6 million and

7.3 million were unemployed. This was about three times the previous peak of about 2 million in February 1926 and 10 times as high as the 560,000 people who were out of work in July 1928.

The depression hit hard in other ways. Germans, who as we noted had lost all their savings in the inflation, had begun to save again. Savings had increased by about half between 1928 and 1930. In the next year, 1931, the amount of money in savings accounts declined about 6 percent. This hurt many kinds of people, perhaps most seriously the lower middle class. And the shortage of work, statistically a cold figure, became a chilling reality, particularly for the working class. Germans on the average in 1928 worked 7.7 hours per day. By 1932, the hours worked per days had declined to 6.9—roughly by 10 percent.

What this adds up to, in summary, is that fewer people were working; those who worked were working fewer hours. And more money had to be drawn out of savings than could be put in. The sense that work and thrift would pay off, as Germany and Germans rose out of the defeat in war and the disgrace in postwar inflation and occupation, was rapidly replaced with despair. The gap between expectations and gratifications yawned wide, for perhaps a large majority of Germans. The gap was filled first with Nazi words and then with deeds as the economy was revived and geared toward war.

We have become so sensitive to the impact of ideology— perhaps as a consequence of the enormous amount of it generated and broadcast throughout the world since the 1917 Russian Revolution—that we tend to explain the success of the Nazis in terms of the racist, irrational rhetoric that stems from *Mein Kampf*. However nicely it fit the German mood in the late 1920's, the words would have found few ears if there had not been recurrent and at last catastrophic economic crisis. Figure 19-4 shows the series of crises.

The physical needs of millions of people were deeply denied. The standard diet of the unemployed consisted largely of potatoes and margarine. Working-class people might have been a force to oppose the racist or at least antiproletarian appeals of the Nazis. But unemployed people, particularly when they have suffered for several years, are more inclined toward apathy than activity. Those whose

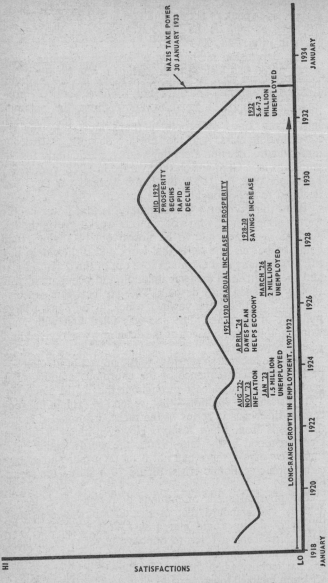

Figure 19-4.—*Economic satisfactions and Nazi Revolution.*

714

physical survival was not so directly endangered—those who had enough to eat—were threatened in virtually all walks of life with a regression to the economic level of 1919-23.

Interclass conflict took different form in pre-1933 Germany from that in pre-1789 France. In the German instance, intergroup conflict seems to have been less pronounced, at least on anything approaching the personal level of hostility that prevailed in France in the last-18th century. Nevertheless various segments of the society did show hostility toward others, however vague its form and ill defined its object. There was a high degree of symbolic hostility between labor and capital in Germany, but the number and intensity of strikes declined greatly from 1925 on. At first this decline was probably due to the rather general prosperity of the mid-1920's. Later (1920-32) it was probably due to the acuteness of unemployment, which led men to fear a strike because they would then be faced with a diet of potatoes and margarine. The conflict between labor and capital was thus more abstract and ideological than real, and took place more in politics than outside factory gates. As such it was inevitably attenuated. Its savagery diminished to a rather generalized hostility, perhaps on both sides.

The petty bourgeoisie, the *Kleinbügertum,* is now almost fabled as the hard core of anti-Semitism. Indeed it may be that from this social group came those who formed the mobs that quite concretely smashed Jewish shops. In any case, the frustrated expectations of the petty bourgeoisie must have been compounded of the loss of their savings along with the fear that they would retrogress into the mass of pitiably poor people, whence they thought they had emerged by a combination of thrift and hard work.

One major segment of German society that saw its expectations frustrated were those who hoped for a resurgence of the nation that had fought so valiantly in the World War. This segment consisted principally of two groups—the military elite, those who were indeed Junkers or who styled themselves as such; and the returned veterans who after the war were met not with victory parades but often with contempt and derision. Even more crucially, veterans were often faced with unemployment or unemployability—the latter including many of those for whom military life had been their first successful occupation. They had no GI bill to train or retrain them for useful work. Thinking themselves heroes returned, they often found themselves drifters and bums. From this subgroup came many of the early Nazi rank and file. From the other subgroup, the officer caste, came those who first supported more traditionally nationalist political parties than the Nazis, who then stood by and observed the arrant Nazis with mingled contempt and envy, and who at last became the willing instruments of the Nazis when the glorious war clouds gathered again.

The pervasive German attitude in the late 1920's seems to have been one of bafflement rather than of active support for the Nazi movement or widespread intergroup hostility. Labor was inhibited by fear of loss of jobs. Many of the middle class were disconcerted by their recurrent failure to better themselves. Members of the upper middle class could not believe that things were getting as bad for so many people as clearly was the case. And the old aristocracy remembered only the glories of feudalism and war or of the sheltered academic life.

It is this stunned state of mind that produced a high measure of political apathy or of active contempt for the inadequate efforts of the republican, parliamentary government to govern. The Nazi revolution was just a coup d'etat: it had broad popular support. But it did depend for its rise to power on the growing political irresoluteness of people who had hitherto been politically more self-confident (labor and the upper middle class). And it depended on a high degree of involvement and participation on the part of those whose frustrations—whether military or economic—coincided with the medley of themes played by the Nazis. The Nazi revolution depended on the support of people whose desperation and consequent dissociation from reality led them to ignore, tolerate, and even take part in violence they would otherwise have abhorred.

The Black Rebellion of the 1960's

The black uprisings in America in the 1960's clearly amount to a rebellion, but they are not in any precise sense a revolution like those of France in 1789 or Russia in 1905 and 1917. However, the differences between these revolutions and the black rebellion are largely quantitative. The latter involves a widespread joint commitment to rather fundamental change among all segments of Negro society in the country: change in the political power structure of the country in all political units—cities, counties, states, and nation. And these changes, involving all blacks and all parts of the political community, have been accompanied by the violence that is a universal element of revolution.

The differences between revolution and the black rebellion derive from several facts: Negroes constitute only about 11 percent of the national population and therefore are numerically incapable of enforcing changes to the same degree as in a nation where a substantial majority is frustrated by the established government. The constitutions and laws of the national and most state governments have not contained many restrictions that discriminate against people on racial grounds—quite the contrary.

So there has been no basic change in principles. The Constitution and law of the land have been used or developed in ways that make them instruments to achieve changes in the nonlegal social practices and customs of discrimination. And there has been a sufficiently developed sense of commitment to equality as a major social value to make the equalizing of opportunities for black people a process against which most whites could not readily fight. They could not readily deny the applicability of their principles to those who newly have demanded equality. And that portion of the nation which frankly accepted the principle of racial inequality lost the savage Civil War. The very slow struggle for racial equality and human dignity for blacks commenced with Lincoln's 1863 Emancipation Proclamation and the military defeat of the South 2 years later.

What is striking, in a comparison of this (and other) contained rebellions with the great revolutions, is that the Negro rebellion appears to have been preceded by the same J-curve of expectations that are at first gratified and then frustrated. The same reaction patterns of this level of analysis appear to have developed in the minds of American blacks as have developed in the minds of those who have become revolutionaries in previous eras and other countries.

The difficulty in seeing this likeness relates to the vast gap between what whites and blacks have gotten in America. This gap has made it hard to see just what advances blacks have made and when. Those who as blacks and whites believe in equality have emphasized the vast and continuing inequalities. Black or white, they do not see what advances have been made. In the 1960's, when conditions were better than in the 1860's or than in the 1930's, the expressions of discontent have been at their maximum. The new words and deeds of discontent can be understood only if one appreciates that profoundly deprived people are often incapable of expressing their discontent. In short, to understand why the black rebellion has occurred, it is necessary to see how black people had already developed.

At the end of the Civil War, Negroes were perhaps as near to minimal survival in the psychological sense, as human beings, as they had been since their initial transportation from Africa. They had lost the security of provision for food, clothing, shelter, and physical safety that had been fairly well assured them as long as they docilely accepted their position as slaves. They could no longer be sure that the master would provide for them. They had, often, to forage for themselves, like war refugees everywhere when crops have been destroyed and normal patterns of collaboration in productive work have been shattered. Overjoyed at their emancipation, they could use their freedom no more effectively than could concentration camp inmates in Germany when the doors at last swung open in early 1945. They could concern themselves really with only the satisfaction of their physical needs, which freedom is not and equality and dignity are not.

Those who must concentrate only on survival usually do not revolt: they are too hungry. This preoccupation simply with staying alive if anything strengthened in the late decades of the 19th century as the practice of lynching—the killing by mobs rather than by lawfully or other systematically employed force—continued. Between 1882, when records of lynchings were first kept, down to 1941, lynchings averaged 78 per year. The constant fear that one might be arbitrarily killed, maimed, or injured was one of the day-to-day facts of life for most blacks, particularly until the early 1920's. Lynching and physical injury could be said to have declined to a relatively minor worry—comparable perhaps to the level of worry about automobile accidents in the 1960's—in the late 1930's and the 1940's:

the average for 1937-42 was five per year and for 1943-48 less than three per year. But the level of general health remained low and so did life expectancy.

The process of moving up off the even, flat plane of survival itself was of course continuous. But it was so slow that it seems best to date the first major upturn, from concern for mere survival for most blacks, as the beginning of the Second World War. Responding to the threat of a large demonstration, a repetition of something akin to the 1932 veterans' march on Washington, Franklin Roosevelt in 1941 issued an Executive order prohibiting discriminatory hiring practices in all defense industries, and establishing the Fair Employment Practices Commission (FEPC) to administer the order. Though it worked unevenly and in many cases not at all, it nevertheless was a major basis for advance above subsistence for Negroes. By war's end, some 2 million blacks were employed in war industry, and the FEPC reported that 1,300,000 of these had gotten jobs in consquence of its efforts.

What could have been a cataclysmic frustration of rising expectations for blacks at war's end turned out not to be. The successful efforts to avoid a postwar recession, which would have witnessed the old (and still common) practice of discharging Negroes first, benefited blacks as well as whites. There was no widespread and sudden drop in Negro employment. Instead, the pace of rising economic opportunity continued. In 1946 the CIO and AFL tradeunion organizations undertook a drive to organize Negro workers in the South and to integrate them into existing unions. By 1948, FEPC legislation had been passed in six states, taking up some of the slack when the ending of war contracts removed the protection of the wartime FEPC. Symbolically, and a bit more, the first Negro was admitted in 1947 to major league baseball, Jackie Robinson; there were 14 major league Negro players in 1951; by 1954 all but 3 of the 16 major league teams were integrated. Racially integrated low-cost public housing after the war began the breakdown of discrimination in this basic concern of life. In 1956 all public housing in Washington, D.C., was desegregated. In 1962 President Kennedy issued an order prohibiting discrimination in any housing that was either financed or had mortgage insurance under a Government program. It was estimated that this affected a fourth of all future housing construction in the nation.

These advances relate to jobs and housing and therefore to the physical needs, but they also—notably in the case of sport participations—have overtones of equal dignity. Advances that more directly related to this profound, non-physical need for equality included the following:

The admission of Negroes into the category of commissioned officer: 500 Negro officers in the Army in 1943, 7,500 by war's end; and 28 officers in the Navy in 1944, 50 by war's end;

The integration of 90 percent of all Negro army personnel into unsegregated units by 1953 and complete integration a year later;

The first desegregation of interstate buses in 1946, of railway dining cars in 1950, and of railway passenger cars in 1952;

The long series of steps designed to desegregate education, commencing with the court order to the University of Oklahoma in 1948 to admit on a segregated basis a graduate student who was black, to the University of Texas in 1950 to admit on a non-segregated basis a Negro to the law school, down to and beyond the landmark 1954 case which ordered the integration of public secondary and primary schools "with all deliberate speed";

The similarly long series of steps to end discrimination in the voting process, starting with the court invalidation in 1944 of the white primary closed to blacks and continuing with the 1954, 1964, and later civil-rights acts, which increasingly protected and enforced the right of blacks to register and vote in all elections.

The range and number of national and state legislative and judicial and administrative efforts to see that black people were accorded equal dignity is very large indeed. Repeatedly in the 1940's, 1950's, and early 1960's it gave evidence to Negroes that progress was being made. Their expectations inevitably rose from the near-ground level before the second World War to what proved increasingly to be excessively optimistic. Acts of legislatures, court, and administrative agencies—and of private groups and citizens—to equalize life opportunities for black people have never quite fulfilled their initial purpose. This brings us to the matter of promise and performance, to assessment of the gap between the expectations aroused by legislation, Executive order, and court decision, on the one hand, and realization of equality, on the other.

The killing by lynch mobs dwindled to one case in 1947 and two in 1948. A new kind of killing of blacks began and at times something like the old lynch mob operated again. In 1952 a top state NAACP official in Florida who organized a campaign to secure the indictment of a sheriff charged with killing a Negro prisoner was killed by a bomb. After the 1954 commencement of public school integration, there were some 530 cases of violence (burning, bombing, and intimidation of children and their parents) in the first 4 years of integration. Schools, churches, and the homes of black leaders were bombed and many people were killed in these bombings. Federal troops were brought into Little Rock in September 1957 to integrate the high school; during the following school year (1958-59), public schools were closed in Little Rock.

In short—starting in the mid-1950's and increasing more or less steadily into the early 1960's—white violence grew against the now lawful and protected efforts of Negroes to gain integration. And so did direct action and later violence undertaken by blacks, in a reciprocal process that moved into the substantial violence of 1965-67. That 3-year period may be considered a peak, possibly the peak of the violence that constituted the black rebellion. It was violence mostly against white property and black people. It merits reemphasis that during this era of increased hostility, progress continued to be made. Indeed, the occurrence of some progress intensified both the white reaction to it and the black counteraction to the reaction, because every time a reaction impeded the progress, the apparent gap widened between expectations and gratifications.

Direct (but not violent) action by Negroes began in late 1956 when the bus boycott in Montgomery, Alabama, which endured for over a year and succeeded. It was precipitated when a Negro woman got on a city bus, sat down in a front seat, was ordered to give up her seat to a white man, and refused. The bus boycott soon came under the leadership of Dr. Martin Luther King, Jr., whose belief in nonviolent resistance—and the mild temper of blacks in Montgomery at the time—succeeded in keeping the action relatively peaceful.

Direct violent action began in April 1963 in Birmingham, Alabama, in what may be called the first full-scale concerted violent encounter of blacks and whites in recent years. Seeking integration of such facilities as lunch counters, parks, and swimming pools, the blacks in Birmingham, most of them young, were met with water hoses, police dogs, and violent acts of police and white people. The numbers of demonstrators increased to some 3,000 and there were 1,000 arrests. The repressiveness of the police united a hitherto-divided black community in Birmingham. And it produced perhaps the first major case since the second World War in which Southern blacks threw rocks and bottles at police. From this time on, violence deepened and spread among blacks. The Birmingham riots immediately touched off a response in other cities—according to one estimate, 758 demonstrations in the 10 weeks following the Birmingham violence. And in 6 weeks of that 1963 summer, blacks (in Birmingham and elsewhere) succeeded in gettings some 200 lunch counters and other public facilities desegrated.

The combined effect of substantial, though slow, progress in employment, housing, education, and voting did not have the effect of quieting blacks or stopping the Negro rebellion of the 1960's. The full-fledged riots of Los Angeles in 1965 and Newark and Detroit in 1967 have been amply studied, at least from the descriptive viewpoint. But there is a tendency to see these events in isolation. It is recognized that riots in one place will touch off riots in another or—more likely—in several others, but the social-contagion theory (including the contagion of seeing African nations liberated after the Second World War) by no means gets to the roots of the rebellion. And neither does the notion that blacks are frustrated and are striking out rather blindly at the centuries of repression. If 300 years of repression have been too much, why were 200 or 280 not enough to produce rebellion?

What is striking is the time sequence of events. As in major historic revolutions, the events relating to the 1960's rebellion consist of a rather long period of rising expectations followed by a relatively brief period of frustration that struck deep into the psyches of black people. And I suggest that from the 17th to the early-20th century there has been very little development beyond mere physical survival for virtually all black people in America (and in Africa). It is significant to note that in the prosperous 1960's, there was no sharp or sudden rise in unemployment of blacks. There was no marked deprivation of material goods to which blacks had become accustomed. But there was, starting notably in 1963, not the first instance of violence against blacks but a sudden increase in it. This resurgence of violence came after, and interrupted, the slow but steady progress since 1940. It quickly frustrated rising expectations.

This increase in violence, commencing so to speak with the firehoses and police dogs in May 1963 in Birmingham, affronted not only the physical safety of the demonstrators, thereby reactivating anxiety and fear of bodily harm itself —the most basic of human concerns. This increase in violence also affronted the dignity of black people as human beings. Black people sensed that their various and continuously rising expectations, now confronted with violence, were to rise no more.

In addition to this violence between whites against blacks and of blacks against whites, there has been an explosive growth of private acts of violence of blacks against blacks. This has newly activated the fear for physical safety itself. And the ever-growing congestion in the slums has worsened housing conditions.

White people who fail to understand their own past and their own ever-rising expectations (if we have one car, we must have two; if we finished 4 years of college, our son must become a doctor or a lawyer) are puzzled at the dissatisfaction of blacks who have made such considerable progress since the Second World War. But what would be odd about blacks, and indicate that they indeed had some special nature, would be for them to be satisfied in present circumstances. The very rapidity of their advance makes them expect to continue its pace. The very low point from which they started makes them expect to reach equality within a few years or at the very most a few decades. Their mental processes are operating in an altogether normal manner. They would be less than human if they acted otherwise.

Figure 19-5 and Table 19-1, the latter devised by Harmon Zeigler with the assistance of Jerry B. Jenkins, represent one striking index of the origin and time sequence of black frustrations. He chooses, as the items to form his index, average family income and average years of schooling. He divides the former by the latter, for the total U.S. population and for the nonwhite population (which is about 95 percent black), from 1940 to 1967, using U.S.

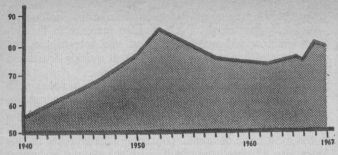

Figure 19-5.—Index of nonwhite economic satisfaction, 1940-67.[a]
[a] For data see table 19-1.

Census Bureau data. The increase and decrease in the gap between what an average family and a nonwhite family of given educational level gets in income becomes Zeigler's measure of frustration.

If black and white workers with the same amount of education were earning the same income, there would be no difference in the indexes between the two categories of people. As the chart indicates, nonwhites were closest to earning the same amount as the total population in 1952. They rose from 58 percent in 1940 to 86 percent in 1952, but declined after 1952 to a low of 74 percent in 1962. They did not return to their relative status of 1940, but they lost substantial ground compared with where they were in 1952.

If the education-income relationship were the only one involved in producing frustration in people as their expectations and gratifications diverge, we could have expected a peak of unrest sometime in the mid-1950's. It came later —by my reckoning in 1963. This suggests that the gap formed from the increased incidence of violence on the part of police and white citizens provided the quantum of energy necessary to raise black frustrations to the point of rebellion. Figure 19-6 shows the developments.

Two ways are possible of resolving the problem that arises when the expectations-gratifications gap develops— and perhaps there are others. One way to close the growing gap is to attempt to deprive blacks in America of all the gains that they have made since at least the beginning of the Second World War. These gains have been mostly in the satisfaction of their physical needs (in jobs and housing); their social and their dignity needs are beginning to gain prominence. In George Orwell's phrase, we may call this the technique of the boot stamping in a human face forever. If white people were to attempt and even succeed in so reducing black people to a life that consisted of trying to stay alive—the life they lived under slavery and, most of them, for two to four generations after emancipation—black rebelliousness could be contained. In the process white people would be reduced to the same animal-like behavior that they themselves were imposing on blacks, just as concentration camp guards and concentration camp inmates came to resemble each other in appearance and behavior.

A second way to resolve the problem is to recognize and help them to satisfy their expectations, which fundamentally are the expectations which degraded white people in decades and centuries long past have themselves achieved —notably the recognition of their equal dignity and worth. It is not to be supposed or hoped that black people then will at last become satisfied, any more than white people who achieve dignity become satisfied. But at least those blacks who have achieved dignity will then be that much closer to becoming fulfilled human beings, able at last to realize themselves in the climate of self-respect that is necessary for people to grow.

Student Rebellions of the 1950 and 1960's

These rebellions seemingly commenced first among university students in Japan and then began in the United States and in Western and Central Europe. Partly because of space limitations, it is impossible to assess the J-curve as a device for explaining these particular rebellions. Part of the reason for deferring an attempt to do so lies in the continuing complexity of related events.

It is true, for example, that living quarters and classrooms for French students were getting progressively worse as the postwar French wave of newborn children reached university age. Expectations rose and were frustrated, contributing to the May 1968 riots. It is true that the 1964 Berkeley riots followed soon after enforcement of a previously unenforced rule against on-campus fund solicitation for off-campus organizations. Expectations had risen and

725

Table 19-1—Origin and time sequence of black frustrations.

Exp. anation

Col. 1: $\dfrac{\text{Social want satisfaction}}{\text{Social want formation}}$ = systemic frustration

Col. 2: $\dfrac{\text{Social want satisfaction (nonwhite)}}{\text{Social want formation (nonwhite)}}$ = frustration (nonwhite)

Col. 3: Index of satisfaction (nonwhite)   Col. 4: Index of frustration (nonwhite)

	1	2	3	4
	Average family income divided by average years of schooling for—		Nonwhite satisfaction	Nonwhite frustration
Year	Total population	Nonwhite population	Nonwhite percentage of total population frustration level (100 percent would represent equality of want satisfaction relative to want formation between nonwhites and total)	Percentage difference between nonwhite population and that of total population (derived by subtracting col. 3 from 100 percent)
1940[a]	$\dfrac{\$1{,}231}{8.4}$ = 146.3	$\dfrac{\$489}{5.8}$ = 84.3	$\dfrac{84.3}{146.3}$ = 57.5	42.5
1947	$\dfrac{\$3{,}031}{9.0}$ = 336.8	$\dfrac{\$1{,}614}{6.9}$ = 233.9	$\dfrac{233.9}{336.8}$ = 69.4	30.6
1950	$\dfrac{\$3{,}319}{9.3}$ = 356.9	$\dfrac{\$1{,}869}{6.8}$ = 274.9	$\dfrac{274.9}{356.9}$ = 77.0	23.0
1952	$\dfrac{\$3{,}890}{10.1}$ = 385.1	$\dfrac{\$2{,}338}{7.1}$ = 329.3	$\dfrac{329.3}{385.1}$ = 85.5	14.5
1957	$\dfrac{\$4{,}971}{10.6}$ = 469.0	$\dfrac{\$2{,}764}{7.7}$ = 359.0	$\dfrac{359.0}{469.0}$ = 76.5	23.5
1960	$\dfrac{\$5{,}620}{10.6}$ = 530.2	$\dfrac{\$3{,}233}{8.2}$ = 394.3	$\dfrac{394.3}{530.2}$ = 74.4	25.6
1962	$\dfrac{\$5{,}956}{11.4}$ = 522.5	$\dfrac{\$3{,}330}{8.6}$ = 387.2	$\dfrac{387.2}{522.5}$ = 74.1	25.9
1964	$\dfrac{\$6{,}559}{11.7}$ = 560.6	$\dfrac{\$3{,}839}{8.9}$ = 431.3	$\dfrac{431.3}{560.6}$ = 77.0	23.0
1965	$\dfrac{\$6{,}957}{11.8}$ = 589.6	$\dfrac{\$3{,}994}{9.0}$ = 443.8	$\dfrac{0.5740}{0.7627}$ = 75.3	24.7
1966	$\dfrac{\$7{,}436}{12.0}$ = 619.7	$\dfrac{\$4{,}628}{9.2}$ = 503.0	$\dfrac{0.6223}{0.7666}$ = 81.2	18.8
1967			78.9	20.2

[a] 1940 income figures are actually for 1939, and are for families and un-related individuals.

SA: 1952. (73d ed.), p. 111: median school years (1947, 1957, and 1964-67).
SA: 1965. (86th ed.), p. 112: median school years 1960.
SA: 1966. (87th ed.), p. 340: median family income: (1947, 1950, 1952, 1957, 1959, 1960, 1962, and 1964).

NOTE—The frustration index and tables were devised by Harmon Zeigler with the help of Jerry B. Jenkins

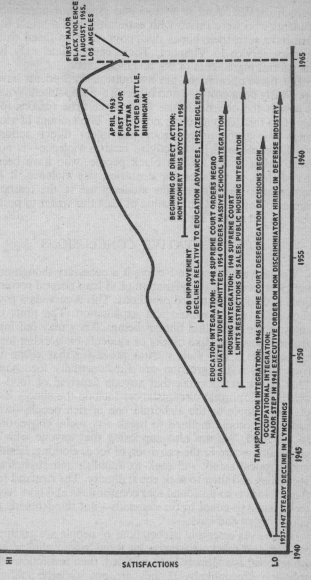

Figure 19-6.—*The black rebellion of the 1960's.*

727

were frustrated. And it is true that American university students who were raised with expectations of a bright future have seen their hopes disappointed when faced with military service in Vietnam. These explanations may be the central ingredients of the rebellious mood.

But these phenomena are not quite new. Students have previously been crowded and otherwise disappointed. What is new is the occasional use of violence. The reasons for resort to this technique are not clear. The amount of violence—as distinguished from nonviolent direct action, which people tend incorrectly to read as violence—is not great but it is real. When black people, who have been the victims of violence for centuries, use violence, it is comprehensible. When white students use it, the reasons remain obscure enough to cause at least this writer to postpone an attempt to explain.

SOME TENTATIVE CONCLUSIONS

We have seen that the J-curve is a necessary though not sufficient part of the explanation of at least several revolutions and some contained rebellions. This J-curve is a psychological, not a sociological explanation. The units of analysis are individual human beings. They may fall into visible categories (like blacks or students or working men or peasants), but their mental processes that relate to frustration and aggression are fundamentally the same. That is, we are positing that anyone deprived of food—whether his normal circumstances include the simple diet of poor people or the elaborate one of rich people—will suddenly become inclined to break any social convention to get food. We are also supposing that anyone who is physically secure in the provision of food, clothing, health, and physical safety will seek to establish and strengthen social ties and then to seek equal dignity. The demand for these things is so profound that constitutions and laws have to be made to adapt to the demands—not the demands to constitutions and laws.

If the ever-emerging expectations of people are gratified without too much resistance by those whose similar expectations have already been gratified, then revolution and rebellion are unlikely. If they are not, orderly political processes are displaced by violence. It was that way with

our ancestors; it is that way now. And it is that universal
a phenomenon. Lawmakers as well as clerks, businessmen
as well as laborers, professors as well as students would
react the same if suddenly deprived of the goods and dignity they had come to expect in the normal course of life.
They would be less than human if they too did not become
angry.

References

References on the French Revolution

Ralph W. Greenlaw, ed., *The Economic Origins of the French Revolution,*
Boston: D.C. Health, 1958. A very useful collection of essays.
Georges Lefebvre, *The Coming of the French Revolution* (1939), New York:
Vintage Books, 1957. Probably the best single volume to date on the causes
of the French Revolution.
Alexis de Tocqueville, *The Old Regime and the French Revolution* (1856),
New York: Doubleday Anchor Books, 1955. This hundred-year-old classic
is still the best starting point for studying origins of the French Revolution.

References on the Civil War

W. J. Cash, *The Mind of the South* (1941), New York: Vintage Books, 1960.
A penetrating, passionate, and fairminded view of the outlook of Southerners
before and after the Civil War.
M. B. Hammond, *The Cotton Industry: An Essay in American Economic History,* New York, 1897. A valuable statistical source.
Robert R. Russel, *Economic Aspects of Southern Sectionalism: 1840-1861,*
Urbana: University of Illinois Press, 1924. An excellent economic analysis
of the pre-Civil War South, demonstrating the very rapid growth of that
economy before the war.
U.S. Bureau of the Census, *Historical Statistics of the United States: 1789-
1945,* Washington, D.C.: U.S. Government Printing Office, 1949. An invaluable statistical source.

References on the Nazi Revolution

Theodore Abel, *The Nazi Movement* (1938), New York: Atherton Press, 1965.
An excellent, careful explanation of the socioeconomic and psychic appeal
of nazism, based on direct and systematic reports of 600 Germans who chose
nazism freely.
Hadley Cantril, *The Psychology of Social Movements,* New York: Wiley, 1941.
Still a classic study of why people join fascist (and other social) movements.
Statistischen Reichsamt, *Statistisches Jahrbuch für das Deutsche Reich,* Berlin.
The volumes from 1920 on are an official source of a wide variety of
crucial statistical data.
Gustav Stolper, *The German Economy, 1870-1940,* New York: Reynal &
Hitchcock, 1940. A source of economic indexes from the imperial to the
Nazi periods.

References on the Black Rebellion

There are excellent sources of bibliography in such primary sources as the
Report of the National Advisory Commission on Civil Disorders. Data used
here came from the *Encyclopaedia Britannica Book of the Year* (1938-68)
and from the U.S. Census Bureau's *Current Population Reports.*

General References on Revolution and Rebellion

Crane Brinton, *The Anatomy of Revolution* (1938), New York: Vintage Books, 1955. This oft-revised classic is the best introduction to the study of revolution.

James C. Davies, "Toward a Theory of Revolution," *American Sociological Review,* vol. XXVII (Feb. 1962), pp. 5-19. This is the original statement of the J-curve.

James C. Davies, *Human Nature in Politics,* New York: Wiley, 1963. The first two chapters develop a politically oriented theory of human needs; the concluding chapter relates to growth processes that relate to revolution.

James C. Davies, "The Circumstances and Causes of Revolution," *Journal of Conflict Resolution,* vol. XI (June 1967), pp. 247-257. A critical view of the state of knowledge about revolution in the mid-1960's.

John Dollard et al., *Frustration and Aggression,* New Haven: Yale University Press, 1939. This is the initial and still basic statement of the frustration-aggression nexus, necessary for understanding revolution psychologically.

Harry Eckstein, "On the Etiology of Internal Wars," in George H. Nadel, ed., *Studies in the Philosophy of History,* New York: Harper Torchbooks, 1965, pp. 117-147. Like the Laqueur essay below, a good brief starting point.

Frantz Fanon, *The Wretched of the Earth,* New York: Grove Press, 1968. The most intimate analysis of the roots of political violence that I have seen. Based on the author's psychiatric work with patients in Algeria who had experienced or used violence during the final years before Algeria's independence.

Walter Laqueur, "Revolution," *International Encyclopedia of the Social Sciences,* vol. 13, New York: Macmillan, 1968, pp. 501-507. A good, brief starting place.

O. Mannoni, *Prospero and Caliban: The Psychology of Colonization,* New York: Praeger, 1964. A brilliant study of the tensions resulting from the confrontation of individuals from an advanced cultural state with those from an undeveloped condition. The effects on both the dominant and the subordinate individuals are elegantly analyzed.

Abraham H. Maslow, "A Theory of Human Motivation," *Psychological Review,* vol. L (July 1943), pp. 370-396. The first statement of the hierarchy of basic needs, a theory that is very helpful in understanding why people varying from poor to rich, educated and uneducated, can join together to overthrow a government.

Mancur Olson, Jr., "Rapid Growth as a Destabilizing Force," *Journal of Economic History,* vol. XXIII (Dec. 1963), pp. 529-552. An economist's statement of what happens when an economy causes people to get dislocated and less poor because the economy is developing rapidly. Applies to some of the effects not only on American blacks but also on developing nations.

Thomas F. Pettigrew, "Social Evaluation Theory: Consequences and Applications," in David Levine, ed., *Nebraska Symposium on Motivation,* Lincoln: University of Nebraska Press, 1967, pp. 241-315. A synthesis of research and theory relative to how people see each other in the eyes of others. If self-esteem is indeed not separable from others' esteem of self, then this is a major theoretical contribution. It applies to the black rebellion particularly and to the mental outlook of potential revolutionaries, anywhere and any time.

George Wada and James C. Davies, "Riots and Rioters," *Western Political Quarterly,* vol. X (Dec. 1957) pp. 864-874. Based on riots that took place in the relocation centers for Japanese in this United States during the Second World War, this study distinguishes the riot participants from the nonparticipants on grounds of the social marginality of the former.

Chapter 20

BATISTA AND BETANCOURT: ALTERNATIVE RESPONSES TO VIOLENCE

By Edward W. Gude*

Governmental response to violence is of both theoretical and practical importance. On the most obvious level, it takes two parties to generate a cycle of violence—insurgents and government forces. Police-type action in response to terrorism is at one end of the coercive response scale, military counterinsurgency at the other. All such responses interact with those of the insurgents in the revolutionary processes. On the practical level, governmental response is the side of the equation over which governments obviously have some control.

Much analysis has focused upon the strategy and tactics of revolutionaries, as a means for assessing how governments ought to respond. This focus assumes that government forces are reactive, neglecting the important effect the government forces themselves have on the course of strategy and tactics of insurgents. In actuality, revolutions are made by both insurgents and governments. Mistakes or excesses committed by government forces are as responsible for the collapse of established regimes as are the tactics of the insurgents. This essay examines one aspect of the revolutionary process—governmental responses—in two cases: Cuba under Batista and Venezuela under Betancourt.

THEORETICAL CONSIDERATIONS

It can be argued that revolutionary politics are but an extension of violent politics of less severity. Revolutionary politics exaggerates the implications of governmental actions in such a way as to make clearer the implications of this part of the equation. Some argue that violence signals the end of politics and that force becomes the sole arbiter.

* The author is assistant professor of political science at Dartmouth College and author of "Political Violence in Venezuela: 1958-1964," in James C. Davies, ed., *When Men Revolt—and Why* (New York: The Free Press, forthcoming).

This military view of politics sharply differentiates the normal nonviolent processes of governing societies from those involving force. This view usually does not differentiate between means, in this case violence, and process, in this case politics. Certainly when violence is introduced, a new form of communications and bargaining emerges on both sides. Symbols are partially displaced by violence as the means and substance of politics, but the processes of maintaining legitimacy continue to be the task of governing.

In the military view of violence in politics, the most important criterion of success is usually violent confrontation of military and paramilitary forces. When this becomes the overwhelming objective, the political implications of the use of force become lost. Kill ratios are substituted for support ratios. In the political view, conflict is basic to politics and is handled in more peaceful times by the process of allocation of resources in response to various demands in such a way that a government maintains support, a sense of legitimacy, and an adherence to these more peaceful means. This allocation of resources involves both substantive and symbolic rewards. While in these more peaceful times the allocation of symbolic and substantive rewards is accomplished by bargaining and communication whose primary content is symbols, in less peaceful times violence becomes part of this process. The goals of government, however, remain the same: to maintain support and a sense of legitimacy.

Before violence can become a factor, there must be a governmental failure to maintain support or legitimacy; otherwise there would be no basis for a serious threat to it. Even a few hundred dedicated revolutionaries would be captured in short order if no portion of the community was willing to provide them some protection. Any willingness to give such protection is an indication of decline of support and legitimacy of government. Any government in such a situation must conduct itself so as not to increase the loss of support and legitimacy. Organized violence in this sense is a signal of political trouble within regimes, not only a signal of the existence of a group dedicated to changing the means and content of the political process. It signifies that a government has failed to maintain adherence to more peaceful means.

In this perspective a government must do more than

eliminate a few revolutionaries, for if there has been a decline in popular support and legitimacy, they can be easily replaced. A government so threatened by violence must continue to seek its political goals. It is potentially disastrous to lose sight of political objectives in the effort to stop violence.

Two important concepts have a bearing on this problem: legality and legitimacy. Officials naturally tend to see problems in legal perspective, in terms of the prescribed rules governing peaceful political bargaining as well as personal behavior. A legal system can function, however, only so long as there is popular consensus and legitimacy for that system of laws and rules. The introduction of violence as a means in the political process indicates that there has been at least a partial breakdown in support. To view events only in conventional legal terms at such a time is to exclude from consideration the attitudes of a significant portion of the polity. In a situation in which the legal system has partially broken down, it is important to shift the perspective from the formal legal level to the underlying sense of legitimacy. Only when legitimacy becomes the locus of concern is it possible to pursue the political objective of maintaining support.

If actions are categorized as they are in the following table, there is an inherent bias against recognizing the broader threat of violence. The legal perspective leads to consideration only of cells I and IV in the chart: government actions are assumed to be legal, insurgent actions illegal. This is further complicated by the fact that govern-

	Acts of—	
	Government	Insurgents
Legal	I	II
Illegal	III	IV

ments are primarily responsible for the promulgation of law.

Violence becomes a factor in politics either when some individuals recognize the illegality of their acts yet consider them legitimate, or when they recognize the legality of government acts yet consider them illegitimate. By replacing the concept of legality with legitimacy, we can more easily see the problem facing a regime:

	Acts of—	
	Government	Insurgents
Legitimate	I	II
Illegitimate	III	IV

In this formulation it is possible to define relatively peaceful political times as those in which most acts of violence are perceived to be on the I and IV axis. But the greater the number of people who attribute legitimacy to acts of insurgents and illegitimacy to acts of government, the more threatening the situation is for government. This formulation is independent of the actual level of violence; violence is significant when citizens' perceptions fall in the II-III axis. Thus a shift in popular attitudes from the I-IV axis to the II-III axis signals the introduction of violent politics. This can be summarized in a proposition: Political stability varies directly with the proportion of citizens whose perceptions fall on the governmental axis (I-IV), and inversely with the proportion whose perceptions are on the insurgent axis (II-III). The greater the rate of change from the governmental to the insurgent axis, the greater the decline in stability. It is the nature and rate of change in perceptions of legitimacy that are crucial for stability, not the absolute level of violence. This relationship may be stated more precisely, as follows: Political stability is equal to the rate of change of perceptions from the I-IV axis to the II-III axis, or

$$PS = \frac{d}{dt} \left[\frac{(I + IV)}{(II + III)} \right]$$

This formulation provides a basis for evaluating the impact of governmental and insurgent actions in the course of violent politics. It subsumes several other important factors such as outside support for either party, degree of organization of the revolutionary movement, particular ethnic or class differences within the polity, terrain, ethical tradition, and many others. For the purposes of comparative analysis, they might well be tested only as they affect the overall perceptions by significant groups of the legitimacy of the acts of governments and of insurgents. The one other factor that might be singled out for attention is the degree of revolutionary organization and skill, which is important for assessing whether a government was lucky or skillful in defeating an insurgent movement. After all, revolutionaries can make critical mistakes as well as governments.

One way to look at the impact of the organization and skill of revolutionaries is to assess the impact of this factor on the probability of successful revolution. To do this we might consider figure 20-1. The probability of successful revolution is a function of the position of the curve, which in turn is dependent on the degree of revolutionary skill and organization. At a given level of political stability (A) we have differing probabilities of successful revolution (B, C), depending on the curve for a particular level of skill and organization. The upper curve denotes a higher level of skill and organization than the lower.

As we have developed these concepts, it is obvious that a government has more control over the level of political stability than revolutionary organization. Thus it is less able to affect the position of the curve than the position of point A. Effective police and military tactics, especially intelligence, can affect the skill and organization of the revolutionaries, but the fundamental fact is that these must be carried out in such a way as to keep point A stationary or move it to the right of the chart. Governmental actions frequently do reduce the effectiveness of revolutionaries, but if this is accompanied by a shift toward governmental illegitimacy, and a consequent shift in level of political stability in the direction of D, the probability of revolutionary success is not reduced.

The primary focus of this essay, then, is to examine the political and military actions of governments under threat of violence, with reference to their effects first on the degree of political stability and on revolutionary organization and skill, and finally on the overall probability of successful revolution. This is at least as much a political problem as a military one: the determining factor, according to this analysis, is the perception of the legitimacy of acts by significant groups within the polity.

Violent politics characteristically involve only a few active participants. The number of revolutionaries is never large in comparison with the population as a whole. Similarly, the number actively involved on the governmental side is small. The large majority of citizens are not mo-

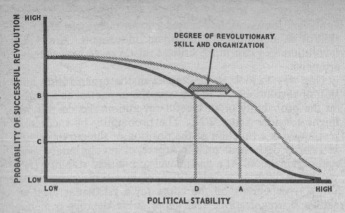

Figure 20-1.—Probability of successful revolution.

bilized to the struggle. One of the primary tasks of a regime is to avoid losing further support; the goal of the insurgents is the converse. The decline in political stability that characterizes the revolutionary situation inclines many people to take a hesitant and more critical attitude toward the regime than is usually the case. They frequently develop a skeptical "wait and see" attitude, which makes the task of government that much more difficult. A regime needs positive support if it is to get the necessary intelligence and cooperation needed to weather a revolutionary situation. The insurgents, on the other hand, need only for the majority to withdraw support from the government. In the early phases they do not need positive revolutionary support.

In pursuit of these objectives, insurgents attempt through violence to demonstrate that the government cannot provide public safety. This is a relatively simple task for terrorists. A more important objective involves the attempt to induce the regime to commit acts against the uncommitted so that they will withdraw their support from the government. This involves inducing a government to overrespond and commit acts that citizens will consider illegitimate (even though they may be technically legal). In the battle for differential political mobilization, the task of the government is enormously delicate and requires political leadership of tremendous sophistication to avoid falling into the traps set by revolutionary violence.

736

If the assumptions that underlie this analysis are correct, then the political tasks of a government faced with revolutionary violence must determine and take precedence over the military tasks. Excessive military action can lead to a reduction in the organization and skill of an insurgent movement, but if done at the cost of increasing the number of people who perceive the acts of government as illegitimate, it is a pyrrhic victory.

The cases of Cuba under Batista and Venezuela under Betancourt provide a useful comparative test of these ideas. The analysis in this essay is of necessity incomplete, but nevertheless sheds some light on the relationship of violence to politics. The relationship of political processes dominated by largely symbolic communications and bargaining to those in which violence becomes a factor is most clearly illuminated by discussing extreme cases of revolutionary potential, which these are. Similar analysis could be used to discuss the earlier phases of violent politics, in which the shift to violent means initially occurred. The same demands, pitfalls, and opportunities exist.

CUBA UNDER BATISTA

When Fulgencio Batista seized power in the coup of March 1952, shortly before a scheduled election, he set in motion the violent processes that led to his flight on New Year's Day in 1959. Batista was an obscure sergeant when he led his first revolt in 1933, against the regime of Gerardo Machado. He dominated the government for the next 10 years, until his voluntary retirement in 1944. In 1952, during his attempt at a legal comeback, the election polls found him a poor third. This apparently motivated his trip to Camp Columbia, Cuba's most important military base, to lead his second coup. Although the popular outcry was great, little opposition immediately devolped. Fidel Castro, who had been a candidate for Congress when the coup interrupted the campaign, attempted to challenge the legality of the move but the courts refused to consider the issue. These events convinced many that the peaceful route to social or political change was rather a losing proposition. The attack on the Moncada barracks on July 26, 1953, was the first step in Castro's rise to power. Although the attack was an absolute failure militarily, it became the symbol of resistance and provided as well the name of Castro's organization, the July 26th Movement.

Much has been written of how Castro, after release from prison, went to the hills and organized a peasant revolution. This myth has been most recently enshrined in the writings of Regis Debray. While it is true that Castro landed with 82 men in 1956, after a period of training and organization in Mexico, only 12 of this group reached the mountains. The others were killed or captured and tortured. In the Sierra Maestra base he was able to build a group of some 180 men by the spring of 1958—certainly not a formidable band compared with the 30,000 American-trained troops at Batista's disposal. Even late in 1958 the total rural guerrilla force numbered about a thousand, with some 7,000 in the urban underground. It was this latter group that became the backbone of the revolutionary movement.

The Castro forces themselves did engage in some terrorism and raids on supply stores, but they did not constitute a serious military threat. In fact, even to the end they avoided a large-scale military confrontation with the Army. It is certainly true that Castro became an important symbol of the revolution via his frequent radio broadcasts over clandestine stations and other publicity he received both in and out of Cuba. In order to achieve even this base of support, it was necessary for the guerrilla band to develop friendly relations with local peasants for logistics and intelligence. This Castro certainly did.

How could a band of several hundred, finally a thousand, guerrillas bring down a government? Clearly they did not do so alone. Operating in almost all urban areas were significant underground organizations led by numerous leaders, mostly unheralded. These forces harassed and terrorized the government, provoking the most brutal of responses. It is clear that counterterror became the strategy of the Batista government.[1] Everyone suspected of the slightest disloyalty was subjected to the threat of arrest, torture, and even death. The urban underground was not comprised solely of middleclass ex-students, the mainstay of the Castro forces. Its members included much of the political and professional elite of the country, as well as many skilled workers.

Batista's forceful accession to power had deprived him

of much of the legitimacy normally associated with a constitutional government.[2] With marginal support from the start, he apparently did not think it necessary to seek a broader base of political support. Through his police he succeeded in alienating much of the middle class, who otherwise were not totally unsympathetic to the government's efforts to restore law and order. When police efforts focused on the sons of the middle class, this potential support evaporated. Batista acted as though he accepted Mao's dictum that power comes out of the barrel of a gun.

The record of the Batista police and military is impressive if only for its thoroughness. Approximately half of the government forces were tied down with the urban problem, some 15,000 troops. It has been estimated by some that as many as 20,000 civilians were tortured or killed by the government from 1956 until the end of 1958. This is a victor's figure, but even if exaggerated by a factor of 2 or 3, it represents a tremendous number for such a small country. It is not difficult to see how so many families could be affected. Throughout this struggle the question of legality seemed to lose importance—there was little legality anywhere. The overriding consideration became the legitimacy of guerrilla terror and governmental counterterror. The rebel forces took great care to develop tactics that alienated as few people as possible. Thus when burning sugarfields brought great hardship on the peasants as well as the landowners, it was discontinued. The government lacked this sensitivity and continued to use tactics that offended many.

The acts of the insurgents were not so much considered legitimate, as the governmental acts illegitimate. This affected the shift from the stable axis (I-IV) to the unstable axis (II-III): the political consequences of the governmental use of force significantly increased the probability of successful revolution. At the same time the rural and urban resistance groups gained experience that increased their ability to operate in a police state and their sensitivity to popular reactions and cooperation.

This process must be understood in the context of full-scale revolutionary violence. In addition to the selective raids for military supplies, the insurgents carried out numerous assassinations of particularly hated figures of the Batista regime and other serious acts of terrorism. Students made an abortive attempt on the dictator's life in March 1957 that brought particularly severe reprisals. Other acts of revolutionary terrorism were carried out to demonstrate that the government could not provide physical security for the population.

Another revolutionary stratagem was a general strike called for April 8, 1958. The strike was a debacle, since it exposed so much of the revolutionary organization to police reprisals. The refusal of Communists to cooperate in the strike insured its failure. It was not until the pact of Caracas, signed in July 1958, that the various revolutionary groups were able to agree to a degree of cooperation necessary to avoid such failures. The agreement brought the several groups under the nominal leadership of Castro, by then the best known of the leaders. The weakness of this coalition is revealed in the rapid factionalization that occurred after January 1959, in which the rural (but decidedly not peasant) faction gained tentative ascendancy.

The actions of the police during 1957 and 1958 were significant in that they served to alienate significant factions from the government. Because the revolution was primarily middle class in composition, counterterrorism particularly affected that class: This was particularly counterproductive because the police and military themselves were soon affected. Military morale and discipline rapidly declined to the point that the spring offensive of 1958, which pitted 10,000 or-more troops against the few hundred Castro forces in the mountains, failed completely. This failure seemed to signal to the populace that the government was no longer viable.[3]

Given its internal divisions, lack of meaningful coordination, poor communications, and extremely limited numbers, it is difficult to see how the revolutionary movement succeeded except as a consequence of the ineptitude of Batista. He repeatedly fell into the trap set by the insurgents by reacting viciously with his own forces. The insurgents demonstrated that the government could not prevent violence; the police and military then proceeded to engage in counterterror perceived by many as illegitimate. In the race for differential mobilization, the regime fared badly.

Having only limited popular support after the 1952

740

coup, Batista tried "free" elections, amnesty, and similar moves to bolster his regime. All of these failed to attract significant popular support, however, and as a result many Cubans were uncommitted before revolutionary violence began. The significant events of the revolution were the steps by which this uncommitted group shifted increasingly to the side of the insurgents.[4] The Batista regime appeared unable to control the revolutionary violence, no matter how violent its own response, promising only civil war for the future. The popular relief at Batista's flight probably reflected as much a hope for an end to violence as it did positive support for the insurgents, but this just as surely represents the failure of government.

In summary, the Cuban revolution can be interpreted as a case in which a middle-class insurgency in both urban and rural areas, without substantial peasant or working class participation, brought down a regime. The trigger of terrorism and violence of the insurgents opened the floodgates of police and military reprisals, which alienated the significant uncommitted segment of the population. This sealed the fate of the regime by tipping the scales of political mobilization in favor of the insurgents.

VENEZUELA UNDER BETANCOURT

Romulo Betancourt gained power under the most difficult of circumstances in February 1959. The dictatorship of Perez Jimenez had brought both economic and political havoc to the country. The tens and probably hundreds of millions of dollars lost in graft had left the nation in a state of bankruptcy. Oil resources had been squandered through new concessions that never reached the national treasury, public works projects had been established to appease labor with no meaningful program of payment, and there was lavish spending on the military to maintain their support. The country was in the most serious of crises in terms of maintaining its ability to govern.[5] When students and others finally brought down the Perez regime in early 1958, the intervening junta was hesitant to act decisively since its members had programed a return to civilian rule within the year. This meant an additional year in which conditions did not improve.

In addition to the difficult economic position, the factions that had momentarily united against Jimenez reappeared. A considerable faction within the military felt threatened by the end of the military rule. Throughout the immediate postcoup period there were recurrent rumors of plots and several actual attempts at overthrow. Castro Leon, almost pathologically opposed to the possibility of rule by Romulo Betancourt and the Acción Democrática (AD) Party, which won the election of December 1958, was particularly active in antigovernment activity. There were serious attempts in July and September of 1958, October of 1959, and April 1960. All of these attempts involved the classic techniques of the military coup. They did not involve the mobilization of the population; the dynamics of political violence as we have defined them were not involved. Such seizures of government, if successful, present the public with a fait accompli with little chance to intervene.

When the Acción Democrátia Party was first in power, in 1945, Betancourt was not sufficiently sensitive to support from the military and the party was thrown out in 1948. In 1959 the newly elected President was wiser, carefully courting the advice and support of the various leaders in the military. It was his success in holding the majority of the military to his side that led to the failures of some right wing military leaders.

Leftwing political violence dates from a split in the AD party. A younger faction of the party had been active in the underground during the Jimenez regime, while leaders such as Betancourt were in exile. In this period members of the faction had worked actively with the radical faction of the Communist Party. Becoming disenchanted with the pace of reform under Betancourt, this group broke with the party in 1960 and formed the Movement of the Revolutionary Left (MIR). Members of this group became convinced that violence was the only route to the type of reform they demanded.[6] Against the advice of more seasoned and older Communist leaders, the MIR almost immediately launched a campaign of urban violence, which reached its peak in November 1960. The failure of this attempt at fomenting large-scale riots and strikes resulted in a plan for developing a full revolutionary situation in 1962. The Communist leadership attacked the assumptions, timing, and general plan of the MIR insurgents, causing considerable conflict within the radical movement. Nevertheless the frequency of attacks increased during the ensuing months. The 46 reported serious attacks attributed to it in 1960 may not appear numerous, but the MIR had become a factor to be reckoned with in Venezuelan politics.[7] These early attempts were quite random, probably being used as training missions. Random terrorism takes less planning and skill than robbery or sabotage. Table 20-1 indicates the types of violence used by the MIR during the 1960-63 period. Random terrorism declined in

Table 20-1—Leftwing violence in Venezuela, 1960-63.[9]

Type	Percentage distribution of reported leftwing political violence by means employed			
	1960	1961	1961	1963
Riot	17	3	13	5
Assassination	4	9	12	6
Robbery	0	6	9	12
Terrorism	63	60	50	42
Sabotage	5	7	6	2
Other	11	15	10	33
Cases reported	100%	100%	100%	100%
	46	33	120	181

[1]From El Universal.

proportion over this period and more purposive violence such as robbery and sabotage increased. The initial terrorism, in addition to possibly providing training, communicated most distinctly the concerns and commitment of this group.

Throughout 1961 the government was active in attempting to capture the terrorists, though the tactics terrorists used made detection particularly difficult. However, Betancourt was careful not to employ police tactics in an indiscriminate manner so as to alienate innocent victims. During this period there was also the development of significant leftwing support within the military itself. This was manifested in June 1962 with serious risings at Carupano and Puerto Cabello. These risings were used as a pretext by the government to suspend some constitutional guarantees and band the Communist Party and the MIR. However, the government waited to carry out large-scale public measures against the insurgents until the public had been sufficiently frightened by the seriousness of the uprisings at Carupano and Puerto Cabello. That is, Betancourt waited until the illegitimacy of the insurgent actions was well accepted before making a major move. In this manner he was able to maximize support for the government action. In addition, he did not use the opportunity of suspended constitutional guarantees to attack other political opposition. On the 31st of July 1962, the guarantees were restored.

Continued insurgent activity led, however, to a second suspension on the 7th of October. This time the government went out of its way to enlist the support of major groups within the society. The strong measures against the insurgents were accompanied by successful appeals for support from the military and groups such as labor. Betancourt accelerated action against the insurgents only as the public demands for such action warranted, and was extremely careful to maintain popular and institutional support for his use of counterforce against the insurgents. In this manner he avoided the problem of alienating the innocent who might otherwise have been affected by repression.

The Communist Party became more and more disenchanted with the program of violence, which they regarded as counterproductive.[8] The threat from the left actually increased support for the government. Many factions that might otherwise have been more vocal in opposition united under the threat of violence. In fact, Betancourt was not unmindful of this phenomenon and used it repeatedly in appeals for unity, action, and support. One of the strategies advanced by the insurgents was an attempt to stimulate a military coup against the AD government. They judged that a return to military dictatorship would make recruitment into the revolutionary ranks easier, since it would unite the moderate left with the violent left.[9] Again, Betancourt used the existence of this plan to convince the military that they must at all costs remain loyal to avoid falling in with the plans of the insurgents themselves. Restraint again was the characteristic of the government action. Throughout the entire period of violent threat, the reported frequency of government acts of violent reactions was closely correlated with the reported acts of the insurgents. This apparently contributed to the impression of legitimacy of the police and military responses. The insurgents during 1962 did not significantly increase the base of their support and the government did not suffer significant defections.

As the elections of December 1963 approached, violence increased rapidly. The insurgents felt that it was necessary either to induce a military coup or to force the government into overreaction before there was a successful transfer of democratic power. Again Betancourt was careful not to overstep his support, and he appeared in public to be responding less forcefully than many would have wished. His was an unstable tightrope to walk, because he was exposed to failure from insufficient action as easily as from excessive action. Because the insurgents were unsuccessful in expanding their scope of operation, the threat against the government did not increase as rapidly as it did in Cuba. A vicious attack on an excursion train in September 1963 provided an opportunity for a very forceful response with large-scale popular support. Betancourt took advantage of this situation to arrest MIR and Communist Party deputies, to use regular military troops in urban areas, and to pass emergency measures. These actions were carried out with the strong support of the military and the public at large. As previously, the Betancourt response to insurgent activity appears to have been commensurate with public judgements about what was appropriate.

As in the case of Cuba, violence remained primarily a middle-class phenomenon. The labor movement, though its members had voted against the AD Party and were a potential base of insurgent support, remained neutral or progovernment during the entire period in spite of the fact that the Communist Party had gained control of the union movement during the Jimenez era.[10] The significant difference in the experience of the two countries lies in the continued support for the government from the Venezuelan middle class, including the military and police.

While the insurgents in Venezuela were probably less highly skilled than the Cubans, the government did not make their job easier by overresponding and thus alienating important middle-class support. Had the government lost the support of this important sector, it is entirely possible that the skill and success of the insurgents would have increased sufficiently to overthrow the government or stimulate a military coup.

The cadre of the insurgents was about a thousand men, more than Castro had in the mountains until the fall of

1959 but less than the combined urban and rural force of insurgents in Cuba. The split between Castro and the Communists was similar to the split in Venezuela. The revolutionary testing ground of the Jimenez period was similar to that of Batista. Given all these similarities it is difficult to assess finally the causes of the failure of the insurgents in Venezuela. It is clear that maintaining support from the middle class as well as labor and the peasants was critical for Betancourt's success. With less political adroitness and more intensive police response, this support could easily have been lost. The AD government was successful in maintaining popular perceptions that the acts of violence fell on the I-IV axis of stability rather than the II-III axis of instability. In addition, the government responses did not lead to significant defections that could have increased the skill and organization of the revolutionary movement. There is one last qualification to this analysis. It is entirely possible that Betancourt was able to minimize the factionalism of his own coalition, the moderate left opposition, and the military by the very threat of the insurgents. Had that threat not existed, Betancourt might not have been able to govern successfully. If so, it is strange irony for the insurgents.[11]

CONCLUDING COMMENTS

In this essay we have examined two cases of revolutionary violence. In one instance—Cuba—the insurgents were successful, in the other—Venezuela—unsuccessful. We have looked at the tactics of the respective governments in terms of the underlying strategy, either political or military; the perception of the legitimacy of acts of violence; and the differential political mobilization that occurs as a consequence. If this analysis is correct, it suggests that a predominately military strategy of eliminating insurgents at all costs is fraught with pitfalls that can benefit the insurgents. It suggests that primary issues for scholarly and policy analysis are popular perception of the legitimacy of the acts of violence committed by insurgents and responded to by government forces, the impact of governmental actions on the organization and skill of the insurgents, and the continuance or withdrawal of support of the largely uninvolved sectors of the population. There are, of course, other relevant factors that would be necessary for a complete comparison of these cases. Outside support, popularity of the existing regime, terrain, objective economic conditions, and others are all of importance. What is argued here is that they are not so critical to the dynamics of the political processes involving violence as the ones chosen for this analysis.

The cases selected were, in addition, ones in which the objectives of the insurgents were the complete overthrow of the regime and system in power. In such cases the dynamic relationship between the violence of both sides and the political process is clearly defined. In cases in which violence is used as a tool of reform rather than revolution, it is likely that the same dynamic relationship exists, although not so clearly evident. The argument is based on the assumption that the critical variable is the perception of the legitimacy of the act of violence, not its legality. Violence in this sense may represent a breakdown in the legal system but not necessarily of politics. No political process is as delicate as one involving significant levels of violence. To lose sight of the political implications of force and violence is to toy with dangerous consequences. Governments can no more hide behind the legality of their acts than insurgents can assume they will have large-scale support. In this dynamic relationship, the violence of governments is more amenable to control than that of insurgents. At the least a government should be able to avoid counterproductive consequences of its own actions.

References

1. David D. Burks, *Cuba Under Castro* (New York: Foreign Association, 1964), p. 8.
2. George I. Blanksten, "Fidelismo and Its Origins: Fidel Castro in Latin America," in Robert Tomasek, ed., *Latin American Politics: 24 Studies of the Contemporary Scene* (Garden City, N.Y.: Doubleday, 1966), p. 369.
3. See Federico Gil, "Antecedents of the Cuban Revolution," *The Centennial Review*, vol. VI (Summer 1962), p. 383.
4. Douglas P. Bwy, "Discerning Casual Patterns Among Conflict Models: A Comprehensive Study of Political Instability in Latin America," unpublished MS., p. 35.
5. Robert J. Alexander, *The Venezuelan Democratic Revolution* (New Brunswick: Rutgers University Press, 1964), pp. 42-43.
6. Atlantic Research Corp., *Castro-Communist Insurgency in Venezuela* (Alexandria, Va,: author, Dec. 31, 1964), pp. 39-53 (mimeo).
7. As reported in the Caracas daily, *El Universal*.
8. See Atlantic Research Corp., *op. cit.*, p. 38.
9. For an important statement of the thinking of the leftists, see Walter H. Slote, "Case Analysis of a Revolutionary," in Frank Bonilla and Jose A. Silva Michelena, *The Politics of Change in Venezuela*, vol. 1: *A Strategy*

for Research on Social Policy (Cambridge: M.I.T. Press, 1967), pp. 241-311.

10. Alexander, *op. cit.*
11. See Edward W. Gude, "Political Violence in Venezuela: 1958-1964," in James C. Davies, *When Men Revolt—and Why* (New York: The Free Press, forthcoming), for a fuller treatment of this point.

PART IX

ECOLOGICAL AND ANTHROPOLOGICAL PERSPECTIVES

No scholarly discipline has a primary, much less an exclusive, claim to expertise in explaining the nature, processes, and consequences of violence. Psychiatrists, psychologists, criminologists, and sociologists have all contributed substantially to the understanding of individual violence. The analysis of collective protest and violence has proceeded from the viewpoints of these disciplines as well as those of history and political science. The inadequacy of our understanding of the phenomena of violence is only partly the result of insufficient research. In fact we know a great deal about the subject, as the contributions to this volume testify. One lack is an integrated theoretical and empirical approach to the subject in its entirety, one that overcomes the essentially arbitrary division of conventional academic discourse and gives unified, systematic attention to all aspects of the human dispensation to do violence to other humans. The two chapters in this section do not attempt any cross-disciplinary theoretical integration. Rather, they demonstrate the relevance—perhaps a critical relevance—of research in the supposedly more esoteric biological and social sciences for a comprehensive explanation of violence.

It is sometimes assumed that man is an infinitely adaptable being. Whether or not he has an innate disposition to aggression—a matter of dispute among psychologists and students of animal behavior—it usually is held that human aggression is socially determinable, if not entirely socially determined. What is sometimes neglected in analyses based on such assumptions is that there may be a fundamental interaction between men's biological nature and ecological circumstances that increases aggressiveness. The work of Lorenz. Ardrey, and others on territoriality and aggressiveness in animal populations points to one such relationship. In the first of the following chapters, George Carstairs draws on laboratory studies of animal behavior, evidence on the incidence of mental disorder, and the history of millenarian social movements to demonstrate that overcrowding seems to have biological concomitants that heighten disruptive behavior, behavior that is reinforced but not solely caused by social disorganization. The evidence is suggestive, not definitive. It does imply some devastating social consequences of unchecked increases in the density and concentration of human populations.

How do groups respond when they experience external threat or deprivation that seems to threaten their cultural integrity? Perhaps the first answer suggested by a reading of American history is the resort to retaliatory or defensive violence. White Southerners, Northern immigrants, and American Indians all have done so in response to varied external stresses. When the threatened group is relatively powerless, however, quite a different response occurs: its members often attempt to establish and preserve their cultural identity by non-violent defensive techniques. Bernard J. Siegel describes the nature of these defensive adaptations in the second chapter below. In the American context, examples of groups that have adapted defensively include Pueblo Indians of New Mexico, the Black Muslims, and religious bodies like the Amish, Hutterites, and Mormons. All such groups have certain characteristics in common: in response to perceived stress they develop and enforce details and rigorous codes for the regulation of their members' behavior, they increase cultural integration by emphasizing and elaborating a few key cultural values, and they intensify communication within the group and minimize communication with outsiders. The two most general questions raised by the study of defensive groups for the contemporary problems of the United States are these: What effects do they have on the disposition to individual and collective violence? and What are their consequences for the attainment of the American ideal of a culturally and socially integrated national society? The following anthropological analysis implies that they minimize the former but at the cost of raising serious barriers to the latter.

The disciplines represented by these contributions have given relatively little attention to questions of the etiology and consequences of violence. In view of the significance of the findings in hand, how great an increment in knowledge might we have if these and other little-studied aspects of violence were thoroughly examined?

Chapter 21

OVERCROWDING AND HUMAN AGGRESSION

By George M. Carstairs*

When statisticians warn us about the inevitable consequences if recent population trends are allowed to continue
unchecked during the next few generations, our first concern has naturally been over the basic question of survival: Will the world's resources suffice to feed all those
extra billions? No sooner have we heard the arguments on
this than we find ourselves facing the next question: What
will be the quality of the life led by the inhabitants of an
overcrowded planet? In particular, what will be the effects
of overcrowding on the manifestations of aggression within
and between societies?

In former centuries, disease and early death exercised
so effective a form of population control that the vast
majority of mankind could not indulge in the luxury of
aspiring to a high standard of living. Simply to survive into
late adulthood, at the same level of subsistence as one's
forefathers, was good fortune enough. From the time of the
earliest prehistoric civilizations to the present day, in almost every human society, only the privileged elite were in
a position to cultivate their sensibilities and to expand the
boundaries of human experience and understanding. In
London, as recently as the beginning of the present century,
the very chances of survival through early infancy were
more than twice as high for the children of the rich as for
the children of the poor. Throughout the contemporary
world; survival has become generally attainable, for rich
and poor alike; and now, for the first time in the history of
mankind, education, self-awareness, and the aspiration for
a meaningful and satisfying life experience are being shared
by a majority of people.

Inevitably, once the killing diseases and the threat of
starvation have been averted, people become increasingly
aware of, and discontented with, minor forms of discomfort

* Dr. Carstairs is professor of psychological medicine at the University of
Edinburgh.

or unhappiness. One of the striking changes in morbidity in both highly developed and in developing countries during recent decades has been the apparent increase in neurosis and psychosomatic disorders. These functional illnesses—which some people would prefer to regard as manifestations of "problems of living" rather than of disease—have long been recognized among the privileged classes. Already in 1689, Thomas Sydenham declared that half of his non-fertile patients, that is, one-sixth of his total practice, were hysterical; and in 1733, George Cheyne (in his book entitled *The English Disease*) stated that a third of his patients were neurotic.

Both Sydenham and Cheyne were fashionable physicians, most of whose clientele was drawn from the wealthy minority of the English society of their day. Sydenham himself observed that hysteria was commoner among women of the leisured classes than among those who had to toil. It is only in the present day that the working classes have been in a position to enjoy the luxury of being neurotic; but recent surveys, both in Asia[1] and in Manhattan,[2] have shown that the rates for almost every form of mental illness are highest among the socioeconomically under-privileged sections of contemporary societies.

It must be emphasized that the very marked increase in the "visibility" of mental disorders in most countries of the world is partly due to the better control of infections and other serious physical illnesses. Neurosis is a byproduct of a raised level of expectation of the quality of life experience when these higher expectations are denied fulfillment. It can, at times, be manifested as what Charles Kingsley called "divine discontent," a spur toward the further enhancement of the standard of living—provided, of course, that steps can be taken to remedy the adverse environmental factors to which the symptoms have drawn our attention.

There are, however, many situations in which individuals feel themselves powerless to better their state: conspicuous instances can be found in the socially disorganized slum areas of great cities, especially in periods of very rapid growth such as that experienced by Chicago and Detroit in the early decades of this century, and by such cities as Tokyo, Calcutta, Rio de Janeiro, and other conurbations after the Second World War. Here we are confronted by this vital question: What will be the consequences, for mental health, of a continuing massive increase in human populations?

As yet, the science of human behavior is not sufficiently developed to be able to answer this question with precision, or even with confidence. Nevertheless it is possible to learn from studies of animals, both in their natural environment and under experimental conditions, and to note certain regularly occurring consequences of severe overcrowding: with due caution, one can infer some similar repercussions of overcrowding in man. There are also a number of direct observations, in human populations, on the interrelationships between overcrowding and certain indices of mental health, from which we can perdict with greater confidence the likely consequences of overcrowding on a still larger scale.

STUDIES OF ANIMAL BEHAVIOR

At first sight, it might seem that much could be learned from observations on species such as lemmings or voles, which are subject to periodic fluctuations of population size. There is still a good deal of controversy among naturalists as to whether these fluctuations are esesentially determined by rather gross environmental factors of food supply or infection or whether social interactions also play an important role. Films of lemmings taken during one of their mass migrations have shown that although scarcity of food may be one factor, the movement of the whole population takes on a cumulative momentum as the result of repeated, frenetic interactions, which have been described as showing a hysterical quality.

In recent years the work of ethologists has taught us a great deal about the interaction of innate, biological propensites and learning experiences in many animal species. At a relatively crude level, this can be demonstrated by a modification of the animal's adrenal size and activity. The adrenals play an essential role in an animal's response to stress, whether by fighting or by taking flight. There is a conspicuous difference between the size of the adrenals in wild rats and in rats which have been bred for generations in captivity, the latter having much smaller adrenal glands. When wild rats are caged, and allowed to breed, a diminution in adrenal size becomes apparent in a few generations.

In colonies in which there is a great deal of fighting, the mean size of the rats' adrenals increases by up to 30 percent—and this is true both of the aggressors and the victims. Observations in nature have shown marked diminution in adrenal size when rat populations are depleted. For example, the rat population in the sewers of Hamburg at one time became alarmingly large. A vigorous campaign of extermination succeeded literally in decimating their numbers. It was found that the size of the adrenals (in relation to total body size) significantly diminished after the reduction in the rat population. Similar findings were observed when numbers were reduced in an overcrowded herd of deer.

Adrenal activity is stimulated by social interaction, especially by the challenge of attack and the need for counterattack in self-defense. One interesting finding is that the quality of the stress response takes on a different character for the animal that is victorious in the contest. Such an animal can go from strength to strength, able to fight one battle after another; in the intervals of fighting, its sexual potency is also at a high level. In contrast, an animal which undergoes a series of defeats becomes debilitated, even although suffering no obvious physical injury, and is sexually less active. A biologist, Anthony Barnett, has shown that prolonged exposure to even moderate hostility can lead to weakness and death. He has epitomized this reaction as follows: "evidently the bodily response to humiliation resembles, in some ways, that to danger to life or limb."[3] Usually the loser in such contests is able to survive by escaping from the scene of battle and thereafter refraining from challenging its victor; but there are situations, both in the wild and in the captive state, where animals are unable to escape, and are repeatedly confronted by the threat of a contest in which they are doomed to defeat. There are well-authenticated observations, in rats, of the weaker animal's sudden death under such circumstances, and even careful postmortem examination has failed to show any organic trauma sufficient to account for these deaths.[4]

Another instance of the interaction of biological and social factors in the response to stress can be found in observations on the toxity of amphetamine drugs, whose action is similar to that of adrenalin, the secretion of the medulla of the adrenal gland. A relatively small dose of amphetamine will prove fatal to a rat that is confined in a cage with many other rats, whereas a rat that is kept in isolation can survive doses of amphetamine up to four times greater. It is presumed that the effect of the drug is greatly enhanced, in the former situation, by the numerous stressful interactions, with the other rats, each of which stimulates the output of more adrenalin until complete exhaustion supervenes.

These, of course, represent extremes of overstimulation. Many species of animals and birds have evolved self-protective behavior patterns to insure that such extremes will not occur. Typical of these behavior patterns is the "peck orders" or status hierarchy, by virtue of which a group of animals whose members meet each other regularly first fight each other, and then mutually agree to a rank order of ascendancy, after which the animal of inferior status invariably concedes in the face of a challenge from those above him in rank. More detailed studies have shown that status hierarchies can be either *absolute,* whereby every member of a group of animals invariably remains in the same position in relation to each of his fellows, or *relative,* in which under different circumstances of time or place, the individual's respective degrees of ascendancy over one other may change.[5] Absolute status hierarchies are most likely to be found where all the animals in a group share the same living space; they become most clearly defined when that space is a restricted one. Under such circumstances, Barnett has shown that adrenal size becomes inversely correlated with height in the social hierarchy.

Relative dominance is seen most clearly in animals that have individual territories. When on their home ground, they are often able to vanquish an intruder and compel him to retreat, whereas if they are challenged by the same individual on his home territory, they in turn will admit defeat. Many species of birds, and most mammals (including man), exhibit this kind of territorial behavior. Not only football teams, but all of us, tend to perform best on our home ground—mental as well as physical—and to resist anyone who ventures to challenge us there. Naturalists have recognized in territorial behavior, and in the varying degrees of dominance associated with the center and the periphery of the territory, a self-regulating mechanism that insures an optimal degree of dispersion of the species.[6]

When animals such as domestic cats, which customarily enjoy quite a wide range of movement, are crowded together in a limited space, there tends to emerge one particularly tyrannical "despot" who holds all the others in fear and also one or more whom Leyhausen terms "pariahs," at the bottom of the status hierarchy.[7] These unfortunate creatures, he observes, are "driven to frenzy and all kinds of neurotic behavior by continuous and pitiless attack by all the others." Although these "pariahs" bear the severest brunt, the whole community of cats held in such close confinement is seen to suffer. These cats "seldom relax, they never look at ease, and there is continuous hissing, growling and even fighting. Play stops altogether, and locomotion and exercise are reduced to a minimum."[8]

This clearly represents a pathological social situation, in which overcrowding and confinement conspire to accentuate disturbing confrontations between individuals. Another observer, studying the behavior of colonies of rats under different degrees of over-population, observed similar changes in their customary interrelationships. Where overcrowding was most marked, the enforced social interactions were seen to interfere with the satisfaction of quite basic biological needs such as feeding, nest building, and the care of their young. Normally mother rats whose nest is disturbed will carry their young, one by one, to a place of safety, but in overcrowded pens this behavior pattern was lost, and the rats' general maternal care became so faulty that in one experiment 80 percent and in another 96 percent of all the young died before reaching maturity. Among the males, some became ascendant over their fellows but others showed a number of disturbances of behavior, of which two patterns were particularly striking: some males appeared to opt out of sexual and social interaction altogether, sulking alone on the periphery of the group, while others became morbidly pensexual, mounting female rates, whether receptive or not, whenever they could do so without being attacked by one of the ascendant males. These hyperactive rats contravened many of the norms of behavior of their group, even becoming cannibal toward the young of their own kind.[9]

It has been maintained by some writers that the human

species is unique in its tendency to destroy its own kind; but this is not quite true. Colonies of rats will frequently attack, and even exterminate, single newcomers or groups of "alien" rats that are introduced into their midst. On the other hand, if several rats, previously reared in separate cages, are simultaneously introduced into a strange pen, they will spend several hours exploring the confines of the pen, and each other, without showing aggression; but after a relatively short interval any additional stranger introduced into this newly formed group will be liable to be attacked and killed.

It is, of course, a far cry from the behavior of rats and cats to that of humans; but observations on the behavior of higher primates have a more immediate relevance. Recent studies of apes and monkeys in their natural habitat have greatly modified earlier preconceptions about the frequency of both fighting and sexual behavior. These beliefs were much influenced by observations made by Zuckerman upon apes in zoos, which displayed almost incessant fighting and sexual competition;[10] but this has proved to be only a travesty of their conduct in their natural surroundings. Instead, it is the product of their being confined in overcrowded conditions without the possibility of escape. In the wild state, protective mechanisms operate to control the frequency of both the above types of behavior; but when groups of primates outgrow their territory, the frequency of quarreling and fighting increases.[11]

OBSERVATIONS ON HUMANS

It is perhaps significant that Leyhausen and Lorenz, the two naturalists who have devoted more attention than almost any others to the disruptive effects of overcrowding, themselves both underwent the painful experience of being closely confined in prisoner-of-war camps for several years. Their personal observations, which have been corroborated by other medical and psychiatric witnesses (e.g., Bettelheim, Cochrane, Gibbens),[12] were that when a group of men was penned up together in close quarters for many months on end, its members tended to become hyperirritable, and to find each other's small mannerisms positively intolerable.

These, too, like the observations on caged cats and rats,

were instances of extreme conditions; and yet one must realize that there are many impoverished groups in the world whose conditions of life today are scarcely better. In theory, of course, they can escape from their surroundings; but in practice the "culture of poverty" can induce a sense of despair of ever being able to escape.[13] One is tempted to draw an analogy between the rat that is subjected to a series of physical defeats, or the "pariahs" in an overcrowded colony of cats, and the members of problem families in our city slums who display a seeming inability to make a successful social adaptation. It appears that social institutions and transmitted value systems can create a sense of confinement no less demoralizing than the bars of a cage.

Many years ago, Farris and Dunham[14] drew attention to the ecological concentration of certain forms of mental illness in those parts of a large city where both overcrowding and social disorganization—or *anomie* as Durkheim[15] had earlier described it—were most marked. Subsequent research has challenged Dunham's specific contention that schizophrenia is generated by the conditions of life in a socially disorganized community; but many other studies have confirmed his finding that alcoholism, illegitimacy, divorce, delinquency, and numerous other forms of social pathology are most prevalent in such areas.

There remains, however, an interesting contrast in the social correlates of two particular manifestations of social pathology, namely, suicide and attempted suicide—at least, as they are observed in cities of the Western World. Suicide rates are highest in areas where many people live in a state of social isolation, bereft of the support of family, or of any other primary group. On the other hand, studies of attempted suicide have shown that the most important social correlate is overcrowding. Typically, the person who makes a nonfatal suicidal gesture has been harassed beyond endurance by recurrent friction within the domestic group, in cramped and overcrowded premises. Here, too, as in the instance of rats' dose resistance to amphetamine, one can see the mutual reinforcement of multiple factors. A majority of those who attempt suicide are relatively young men and women, who often have had a bad start in life with unstable or absent parent figures. These patients tend to experience great difficulty, in their turn, in forming

758

stable interpersonal relationships: they are often at the same time demanding and inconsiderate toward others, and yet are themselves emotionally immature and dependent. Their deficiencies prompt them to seek out partners from whom they hope to derive support, but all too often the partner whom they select is handicapped in much the same way; so far from meeting each other's dependency needs, these unfortunates only succeed in making each other's state even worse than before. Often, too, they turn to drink or drugs to allay their need for dependence, and this in turn further impoverishes their ability to form rewarding personal relationships.[16]

During recent years many countries have been obliged to take stock of increasing rates of alcoholism, crimes of violence, and attempted suicide. Sociological and social-psychiatric research has shown that there are clusters of disturbances that are found most commonly in overpopulated, underprivileged sectors of large cities; but several interacting factors, in addition to that of overcrowding, are believed to contribute to their appearance. In recent years mass outbreaks of violence have quickened attention to these phenomena. It is disquieting to be reminded that even in countries that have experienced an overall improvement in their standard of living during the last quarter century, an increasing number of people feel alienated from the goals, and the rewards, to which their fellow citizens aspire —and alienated so profoundly that they despair of ever being able to get back into the mainstream of humanity.

Alienation and despair are the product of extreme situations—such as, for example, were realized in the grotesque, doomed societies of the Nazi concentration camps. Many, if not most, of the inmates of such camps found themselves surrendering their customary standards of behavior and their values, becoming completely disoriented by the inhuman conditions under which they were forced to live.[17]

There have been crises in the course of human history when quite large sectors of mankind experienced this sense of alienation from participation in the life of their fellow countrymen. Sometimes after prolonged deprivation their discontents have exploded in outbreaks of revolution, as a result of which a new social order has been created; but at other times leaderless masses of the dispossessed have shown themselves only too ready to become the dupes of mentally unstable yet charismatic demagogues, who promished them a magical deliverance from their miseries. The historian Norman Cohn has shown how often in European history periods of social and economic disruption have resulted in the demoralization of large populations. Cohn has identified a number of social circumstances in which this is liable to occur. Conspicuous among these have been occasions in which long-settled means of production and traditional occupations have been rapidly superseded by new techniques, throwing many individuals out of work; circumstances in which different sectors of a population experience widely contrasting standards of living; and situations where traditional values are weakened, and customary authorities cease to fulfill their protective function. Common to all these circumstances is an all-pervading sense of uncertainty about the future.[18]

George Kennan has epitomized the consequences of such periods of uncertainty with his customary eloquence:

Whenever the authority of the past is too suddenly and too drastically underminded—whenever the past ceases to be the great and reliable reference book of human problems—whenever, above all; the experience of the father becomes irrelevant to the trials and searchings of the son—there the foundations of man's inner health and stability begin to crumble, insecurity and panic begin to take over, conduct becomes erratic and aggressive.[19]

Just how erratic and aggressive conduct can become in such situations is amply illustrated in Cohn's monograph. He shows that the rootless, uncertain populations who are the victims of too rapid social change tend to regress emotionally, and to clutch at magical solutions for their plight. Nor have leaders been lacking to offer them just such magical solutions, promising a millennium of effortless bliss just around the corner.

A characteristic of these millennial movements has been their tendency to begin on a note of generosity, brotherliness, and willingness to let all share equally in the plenty which is soon to be available. This was the case with the followers of Tanchelm, who inspired a vast following among the poor in Flanders in the early 12th century, and with those of Eudes de l'Etoile, who preached a millennium of universal riches to hordes of peasants in Brittany rendered landless by successive years of famine. Both of these

760

leaders were worshiped as divine during their short heydays.

Two hundred years later, the English "Peasants' Revolt" —fundamentally a rebellion against the feudal relic of villeinage, which restricted laborers' freedom to avail themselves of new forms of employment in trades and manufacturing—found a more down-to-earth leader in John Ball, who contrasted the "natural state of man," born equal and entitled to his fair share of the world's goods, with existing social inequalities. The peroration of one of his addresses went: "Good folk, things cannot go well in England nor ever shall until all things are in common and there is neither villein nor noble, but all of us are of one condition."

The most remarkable of all the European millennial movements was the 2-year reign (1534-36) of the Anabaptist sect in the German town of Münster. Members of this sect proclaimed a universal brotherhood, and held all their possessions in common; but like all their predecessors, they met with vigorous opposition from the established authorities, and this opposition, in every case, provoked counter aggression that was all the more extreme because it was fired with righteous indignation. The benign, ascetic Tanchelm surrounded himself with a ferocious bodyguard; Eudes was executed, threatening to return "on the third day" and wreak vengeance on the oppressors; John Ball soon began to advocate the extermination of all great lords, justices, and priests as a necessary prelude to the Kingdom of the Saints; and the Anabaptists of Münster found themselves tyrannized by a fanatical leader who personally and publicly executed anyone who questioned his "divine" authority.

In parentheses, it is interesting to observe a somewhat similar sequence of events during the past 5 years of student protest. In almost every case, these protests have occurred in vast, rapidly expanded campuses (Berkeley, Columbia, Paris, Rome, Tokyo, etc.) where students felt themselves alienated both personally from their teachers and ideologically from the aims of the university courses. Typically, student protest movements have started with generous, not to say utopian ideals and have taken an ugly turn only when they were confronted with measures of control that were not merely firm, but openly violent. When this happens,

761

the naive slogans of "Flower Power" are soon replaced by cries of "Kill the Pig."

One of Cohn's purposes, in reviewing earlier millennial cults, was to show the similarity between their origins, their magical expectations, and their decline into orgies of "highprincipled" killings and the corresponding sequence of events in Hitler's "thousand-year Reich." Similar outbreaks of unreason have occurred in recent times in less developed societies, typically in one of two social situations. The first occurs when a technologically undeveloped community is suddenly confronted with the material products of the industrialized West. This happened during both World Wars, and led to the outbreak of a series of Cargo Cults that bore a striking resemblance to the earlier European millennial movements, and that like them, began optimistically with promises of magical abundance, encountered the inevitable frustration of the hopes so aroused, and then frequently ended in bitterness and bloodshed.[20] The second situation, familiar to many of the newly liberated colonial countries, is that in which large numbers of the community have developed aspirations for a standard of living long before the economic and political institutions of their country have advanced to the point where these expectations could be fulfilled.

The common theme in all of these examples of the abrogation of commonsense, of contact with reality, and, in the face of frustrations, of the unleashing of extremes of violent and destructive behavior, has been the simultaneous arousal of extravagant aspirations together with the shock of realizing that these aspirations are not going to be. The mere juxtaposition of wealth and poverty is not sufficient by itself to excite a spirit of revolt. The stimulus to develop impossible expectations seems to come from a sense of inner insecurity and hopelessness, a total loss of confidence in one's own future. During the postwar era, this has been nowhere more apparent than in the ghettos of the great cities, both in the relatively rich, highly developed societies and in the hungry half of the world. The situation is aggravated when, as a result of uncontrolled population increase, standards of living actually begin to decline at the very time when, by marginal, vicarious participation in a "consumer culture," a people's material aspirations have been raised to new levels.

Today's underprivileged differ from those of previous generations in two respects: their actual poverty is much less severe, and their level of information about their better-off fellows is much greater, thanks to the mass media. As Dr. Sukarno put it, in a much-quoted speech:

> The motion picture industry has provided a window on the world, and the colonized nations have looked through that window and have seen the things of which they have been deprived. It is perhaps not generally realized that a refrigerator can be a revolutionary symbol—to a people who have no refrigerators. A motor car owned by a worker in one country can be a symbol of revolt to a people deprived of the necessities of life.

What he says of undeveloped societies applies with equal force to the impact of movies and television on the aspirations of the less privileged citizens of the technologically advanced countries.

In summary, it seems that overpopulation only aggravates the widespread threat to social stability presented by masses of our population who are basically unsure of their personal future, who have lost confidence in their chance of ever attaining a secure place in their community. It is imperative that we recognize the gravity of this threat because mankind today commands such destructive powers that we cannot afford to risk outbreaks of mass violence; and yet the lesson of history points to the threat of just such disasters. Unless the masses of our city poor can be persuaded that there is a future for them too in the Great Society, their morale is likely to crumble until vast human communities degenerate into the semblance of concentration camp inmates, if not even to that of Zuckerman's pathologically belligerent apes.

References

1. T. Y. Lin, "A Study of the Incidence of Mental Disorder in Chinese and Other Cultures," *Psychiatry*, vol. XVI (1953), pp. 313 ff.
2. L. Srole, T. S. Langer, S. T. Michael, M. K. Opler, and T. A. C. Rennie, *Mental Health in the Metropolis* (New York: McGraw-Hill, 1962).
3. S. A. Barnett, "The Biology of Aggression," *Lancet* (1964), p. 803.
4. *Ibid.*
5. P. Leyhausen, "The Communal Organization of Solitary Mammals," *Symposium of the Zoological Society (London)*, vol. XIV (1965), pp. 249 ff., and V. C. Wynne-Edwards, *Animal Dispersion in Relation to Social Behavior* (Edinburgh and London: Oliver & Boyd, 1962).
6. See Konrad Lorenz, *On Aggression* (New York: Harcourt, Brace & World, 1966), and Robert Ardrey, *The Territorial Imperative* (New York: Atheneum, 1961).

7. P. Leyhausen, "The Sane Community—a Density Problem? *Discovery*, vol. XXVI (Sept. 1965), pp. 27 ff.

8. *Ibid.*

9. J. B. Calhoun, "Population Density and Social Pathology," in L. J. Duhl, ed., *The Urban Condition* (New York: Basic Books, 1963), p. 33.

10. S. G. Zuckerman, *The Social Life of Monkeys and Apes* (London: Kegan Paul, 1932).

11. I. DeVore, *Primate Behaviour* (New York: Treubner King, 1965).

12. Bruno Bettelheim, "Individual and Mass Behavior in Extreme Situations," *Journal of Abnormal and Social Psychology*, vol. XXXVIII (1943), p. 417 ff.; A. L. Cochrane, "Notes on the Psychology of Prisoners of War," *British Medical Journal*, vol. I (1946), pp. 282 ff.; and T. C. N. Gibbens, *The Psychology and Psychopathology of Prisoners of War*, M.D. thesis, University of London, 1947.

13. Oscar Lewis, *Five Families: Mexican Case Studies in the Culture of Poverty* (New York: Basic Books, 1959).

14. R. E. L. Farris and H. W. Dunham, *Mental Disorders in Urban Areas* (Chicago: University of Chicago Press, 1939).

15. Emile Durkheim, *Le Suicide* (Paris: Ancienne Librairie Germer Bailliere, 1897).

16. W. I. N. and J. W. McCulloch, "Repeated Acts of Self-Poisoning and Self-Injury," *Proceedings of the Royal Society of Medicine*, vol. LIX (1966), pp. 89 ff.

17. L. Eitinger, *Concentration Camp Survivors in Norway and Israel* (London: Allen & Unwin, 1961).

18. Norman R. C. Cohn, *The Pursuit of the Millennium* (London: Secker & Warburg, 1957).

19. George Kennan, *Realities of American Foreign Policy* (Princeton: Princeton University Press, 1954).

20. Peter Worsley, *The Trumpet Shall Sound* (London: MacGibbon & Kee, 1957).

Chapter 22

DEFENSIVE CULTURAL ADAPTATION

By Bernard J. Siegel*

In this paper I explore the essential features of a class of societies whose members attempt to establish and preserve a cultural identity in the face of what they perceive to be threats to that identity from the environment. The paper considers groups under stress, but departs from the general theme of this symposium in that it deals with a

* Professor Siegel is professor of anthropology at Stanford University. Some of his extensive fieldwork and theoretical analysis of group adaptations to stress are summarized in his study, written with Alan R. Beals, of *Divisiveness and Social Conflict: An Anthropological Approach* (Stanford: Stanford University Press, 1966). Among his many articles are "Cultural Integration and High Anxiety Levels: Notes on a Psycho-Cultural Hypothesis" *Social Forces*, 1955, and "Conflict and Factionalist Dispute," *Journal of the Royal Anthropological Institute*, 1960.

strategy of coping with stress that is basically nonviolent in nature. Such groups are of interest in the present context because they demonstrate that violence is only one among several strategies of social response to environmental threat. Members of all the defensive societies with which I am familiar see their surrounding environment as hostile, and the people in it as prepared to engage at any time in destructive or depriving actions against them. Such groups have been difficult for the disinterested investigator to penetrate as an observer. Willing informants are few in number and are often subject to reprisal and disciplinary action; individuals in defensive societies who do not readily submit to authority figures are likely to lose their membership in the group and to be physically rejected.

This analysis is mainly paradigmatic, in that it is primarily concerned with specifying the structure of defensive adaptation, its elements, and their relationship. This is an inductive task, though its aim is to generate some casual explanations about a variety of questions. What dimensions of stress and prior conditions of the group are likely to have a defensive or some other outcome? Will groups that have adopted a defensive strategy in relation to the larger society have, because of their very nature, less likelihood of responding violently than those that have not? At present no definitive answers can be given to these kinds of questions, but it is possible to provide some informed speculation.[1]

For purposes of exemplification I have confined myself to certain groups in the United States that appear to exhibit this pattern. Investigations at Taos and Picuris Indian pueblos of eastern New Mexico first provided insights into the nature of the phenomenon; further confirmation was provided by studies of religious and ethnic enclaves like the Amish, Hutterites, and Mormons, and of the Black Muslims. The roster of societies for which the defensive paradigm is relevant includes many other historically unrelated groups: viz, Jews who lived, prior to World War II, in compact villages called "shtetls" in eastern Europe; certain villages of Japan and southeastern Asia; the Egyptian Copts; and village communities in the Alpine region of Europe.

THE STRUCTURE OF DEFENSIVENESS

Behavioral Controls and Training for Self-Restraint

Defensive groups have few and carefully controlled avenues for self-expression appropriate to the life situations usually encountered by their members. Rules of conduct tend to be very explicit, so that the individual must exercise great restraint over his own behavior, which in turn is closely supervised by an authoritative elite. The controls, therefore, are twofold, consisting in (1) the nurturance of self-discipline in the individual beginning very early (usually by the end of the second year), and (2) the allocation of authority or power at the broadest level to a small number of designated persons. The legitimation of political control is circular: it is derived from the imputed wisdom of the elite in interpreting cultural values; the values are, in turn, often elevated to sacred status, thus conferring additional authority upon the leaders.

One manifestation of control is the maintenance of a high level of anxiety, sometimes evidence in a low incidence of heavy drinking or the use of strong disapproval and swift application of sanctions against offending individuals. As Hallowell put it, we find—

a conscious strict control or even rejection of available anxiety-reducing patterns and concomitant elaboration of in-group symbols of identification. [. . . certain anxieties may be inculcated in individuals as part of the socialization process] in order to motivate them in the performance of patterns of behavior that are socially approved.[2]

In such groups there are many occasions for intensive interaction among all members in communal ceremonials and other collective enterprises. As part of their approved repertoire for coping with others, they also sanction various kinds of malevolent accusations—witchcraft or other forms of denunciation—that wax and wane in frequency of expression.

In the past we have loosely and commonly assumed that, in the absence of other outlets, both these types of institutionalized behaviors—i.e., intensive interaction and displacement—tended to give comfort to individuals, to relieve tensions or to dispel them temporarily. Actually there is no real evidence for this assertion. Stated in this way, the assumption is very difficult to prove or disprove. Are the real and supposed dangers of individuals removed, at least in part, by the comfort of common participation in group-centered activities? Is their tension (however we may propose to measure it) relieved by displacement of aggression upon others? To the extent that studies of authoritarianism and relevant psychoanalytic theory made sense to the student of behavior, he tended to accept such statements rather uncritically. The most we can say in the present context is that these behaviors are prominent and that they coexist with other structural features of defensiveness.

In the defensive group there thus appears to be a conscious attempt to maintain comparatively intense anxiety states among members by requiring constant exercise of control over behavior potentially destructive to the group in relation to external threats. Real and perceived threats to continued existence require continual emphasis upon and renewal of social cohesion; latent conflict or cleavage demands both internal and external controls. I would propose that, in comparison with nondefensive societies, brawling, overt domestic quarreling, and excesses in aggressive behaviors that disrupt ongoing activities or call attention to dissension within the group occur infrequently and endure briefly in defensive groups before they are suppressed. Although the evidence at present is meager, I would also hypothesize that the suicides that do occur are of the kind that Durkheim spoke of as "suicide altruists," for the reasons that he maintains.[3] For the individual, the gains of adaptive behavior are measured in a high degree of security (in the form of continual support and approval from all others, and his confident knowledge of norms). The corresponding losses are the comparatively great effort he must make in self-discipline as well as the submission he must always display over much of his adult life in the face of authoritative decisionmakers.

To provide examples, among pueblo Indians the early training for control of impulses, and particularly of direct forms of aggression, is almost proverbial. It is interesting to note the same emphasis among Black Muslims, in view of a popular image by nonmembers that portrays them as advocates of violence.[4] In the ideology of the movement, the black man is of vastly different metal from the white man and therefore must live in a way that is appropriate to that superiority, throwing off the vices taught his people by the malicious white man: tobacco, alcohol, gambling, gluttony, jealousy, father-absent families, several foods associated with the diet of the southern Negro, and the like. In other words, he must cast aside the entire stereotype of the "so-called Negro" and lead a new life of strict morality and devotion to the welfare and development of his people and of the institutions of the Nation of Islam. To remain a member in good standing, he must conform essentially to a puritanical moral code.

The temples of Islam carry out active recruiting programs in the black slums of a large number of American cities, but they try to be selective by retaining only those who are likely to respond positively to the rigid retraining process. The initial step seems to be the isolation of the individual from his former identity and his identification with a new role. Isolation from white men is particularly imperative in view of their corrupting influence. Ties with members of the non-Muslim Negro community obviously cannot be cut in all cases, nor is it always desirable that they should be. However, one's family and friends must recognize the change, or they too are liable to be cast aside, with however much regret. Training for submission to authority is continuous, and takes place in many domains of behavior simultaneously. Resocialization takes place over a long period of time, in the form of lessons. The aim is a transformation so sweeping that it affects every part of a man's life and of his self-conception, reinforced in every conceivable way.

Cultural Integration

A central characteristic of defensive adaptation is the presence of a few key values. This lends a keen sense of cultural integrity to the group, in the sense of being complete or whole. As commonly used, the term "cultural integration" refers essentially to the degree of interrelatedness, interdependence, or linkage to be found among the elements of a culture.[5] In turn, these linkages seem to reflect the operation of values or underlying principles common to more than one activity. A tightly integrated system is characterized by a strong centralization of values; that is, the tendency for broad sectors of custom to be related to a few key values.[6] Under these circumstances a person who might otherwise favor a given innovation will often discard the idea because he knows that substitution for one custom that he no longer values will mean the loss of others which he does value.[7]

A central value of all defensive groups appears to be subordination of the individual to the welfare of the group. This is reflected in the generalization of cooperative effort in many in-group activities, the settlement of disputes by knowledgeable authorities before they become unregulated, and the emphasis upon steady goal-oriented work habits.

Symbols and Identity

However varied the content of these values, they are reflected in supporting symbols. By means of these symbols a given aggregate of individuals develops an intensive sense of group identification. They state, in effect: "I am a Taos," "I am a shtetl member," and so forth, and this identification is supported by a few badges which members are emotionally reluctant to discard. The latter commonly include language and special colloquialisms (ordinary discourse among members is carried on in one language, another being employed in conversations with nonmembers). They may also include special customs of deference, punctilious observance of particular rituals, and, when encountered in the form of natural communities, selection of marriage partners from within the group and a particular territory.[8] Acceptance of and conformity to behavior consonant with these symbols is not open to discussion; alternative means of coping with social situations are either prevented from coming to the attention of the groups, or, if individuals learn about them and propose them for adoption, they are carefully screened.

Insofar as supporting symbols assume the significance we impute to them, one would expect as a corollary that identity problems that currently preoccupy so many students of personality development in our own society would be largely absent in groups with tightly integrated cultures. If such identity is originally weak, ambiguous, largely absent, or in a formative state, it will, under stress and as a group, become increasingly defensive, be invented and buttressed with available symbols from the past or present. In the process of emerging from the multimillion aggregate of American Negroes, the Black Muslims very deliberately developed a social identity by means of certain symbols to which they assigned special meanings. To gain and retain membership, for example, Black Muslims are expected to assume a Mohammedan name. They are exhorted to dress in a manner that will not betray lower-class origins and to eat certain foods and to avoid others. They, of course, attend distinctive temples and learn a ritual language associated with a special version of the Koran.[9]

Members of defensive societies tend to interact with nonmembers in conventional ways. When interrogated on issues they consider sensitive—and they are usually many and pervasive—members will respond with readymade answers which are meant to deceive. Potential innovations, as we have seen, are carefully screened by legitimate authorities. A special humor contains allusions deliberately confined to insiders. In general, social intercourse with nonmembers is of limited duration. Where enduring relations do occur (viz), between friends or godparents, between a patron or merchant and client or customer, they tend to be specific and established only with individuals who are known to be discrete and with whom there exists some implicit agreement to avoid all sensitive matters in conversation.[10]

Communication and Interaction Patterns

The net effect of such controlled intercourse and communication between members and nonmembers is to make the nonmember often want membership but to be kept at a distance, and to lead the member to reinforce emotionally the beliefs and behaviors which symbolize continuity of the group. To maintain this kind of solidarity requires continuous surveillance and some culturally available techniques that facilitate rapid communication and mobilization of public opinion. Most commonly these conditions are met by a dense or nucleated settlement pattern in which dwellings are located very close to, sometimes literally on top of, one another (as in pueblo societies and ghetto communities). Some numerically large and broadly dispersed groups that exhibit defensive structuring, like the Egyptian Copts, the Mormons, or the Black Muslims, have solved this problem by combining strong centralized authoritarian control at the top with the allocation of decisionmaking power in most daily affairs to highly autonomous neighborhood temples, church schools, and missions.[11] In the case of the latter, modern transport and communication techniques make possible continual links of the local groups to national leadership.

The Black Muslim group (the Nation of Islam) was founded in Detroit in the summer of 1930 by W. D. Fard Muhammad. At first, Fard simply went from house to house bringing people his message. As followers accumulated he secured a temple and instituted formal meetings. An organization was established to administer the cult both in ritual and in the recruitment of members. The group subsequently founded a parochial elementary and secondary school (the University of Islam); a minister, trained personally by the founder and assisted by junior ministers, was appointed to run the organization. In the early days all of these activities took place within a restricted district of Detroit. Headquarters were subsequently transferred to Chicago; the movement flourished and diffused to other cities where ministers, always subject to the overriding word of Elijah Muhammad, the present patriarch, were appointed to the local temples.

Perhaps because the central feature of any meeting is the sermon (or more precisely, the exhortation), there is a great deal of exchange preaching done between temples, and Elijah Muhammad himself travels all over the country to speak at gatherings. The establishment of a new tradition and the development of an orthodox commitment to it owe their success in large measure to mutually reinforcing communication networks: the acquaintance and interchange of ministers from diverse regions and the education of teachers on the school staffs at a single training center.[12]

Elites and Centralization of Authority

This pattern of shared understandings could not persist without the regular provision of strong centralized authorities for the group. Training individuals so that they will exert a considerable measure of control over their own behavior is characteristic of all defensive societies, but it does not work at all times. When cultural survival is thought to be at stake, the matter of regulation cannot be left exclusively to self-control. It is buttressed formally by a relatively small number of authoritarian powerholders. What is more, the legitimation of centralized authority stems from the urgent and apprehensive need for solutions to daily problems; the resource that confers power upon these offices is special knowledge. In most cases, therefore, the men who make decisions act in a sacred or quasi-sacred capacity. In some groups they may inherit their offices, but in all cases they must constantly validate their right to exercise the functions associated with them.

Thus the Catholic priests of Quebec villages and Coptic priests of Egypt, respectively, control ritual performances of the church and church-related education which, in each case, is primarily a manifestation of group autonomy.[13] In the case of Hutterites or Mormons, clergy are elected from among all male members in good standing. The priesthood or its equivalent is therefore very broadly based. The highest authority, however, is vested in a few individuals whose qualifications involve the ability to interpret the basic and traditional experiences and sacred texts of the group into living doctrine. The Hutterites sanctify their own history, using it as a sacred record for the interpretation of present problems and the presentation of appropriate solutions within the Hutterite tradition.[14] The Mormons similarly use the *Doctrine and Covenants,* which consists of instructions to the early Church and the establishment of precedents for church administration. Throughout the period of his leadership of the movement, Joseph Smith continued to receive divine guidance in times of difficulty, and the instructions given him at those times are regarded as valid for present difficulties as well. Mormon doctrine indeed awards the president of the church the power to receive additional revelation in order to supplement the recorded guidance of the past.[15]

A significant attribute of many defensive groups is the implementing role of women. It appears that in all such communities, at least, women provide a basis for cultural maintenance but are essentially ignorant of the symbolism that expresses the particular goals of the group in a particular way. They learn that certain symbolic behaviors or places are important to defend, but they may not know connotations that such behaviors, things, or places actually have in the ideology of the group. Being in this sense non-rationally committed to cultural values, they may seek, even more stringently and less discriminately than men, to prevent strangers from having access to knowledge about them. By the same token, males also tend to screen the kind of communication available to females within the group. Therefore, however much special knowledge of the outside world the former may acquire, traditional defensive attitudes will be transmitted anew to each generation by virtue of the important role of women in early cultural transmission and socialization.

EXTERNAL PRESSURES AND GROUP STRUCTURE

Groups develop the properties we outlined above in response to external pressures or stress that, at a certain point, are felt to be a threat to continued existence. The stresses most commonly identified in the anthropological literature are encounters with alien people who interfere with the conventional modes of utilization of the environment. Alien contact may render ambiguous or useless some of the customary rules for regulating human relations and satisfying emergent wants, or they may call into question the viability of the group's universal values, upon which its very continuity depends. To more narrowly defined acculturation studies we should add a variety of other environmental transformations: urbanization, industrialization, urban-rural interaction, and the like.

Taos and Picuris Pueblos: A Controlled Comparison

Defensive adaptation, then, is a response to environmental pressures and changes, and more particularly to certain dimensions or variables of these pressures. As a prototype of this interaction between group and environment, we consider briefly the experiences of Taos pueblo and compare them with the experiences of a close neighbor, the pueblo of Picuris. The two societies are especially valuable for our purpose because they share a long history

773

of settlement and tradition in the area out of a common past.[16]

Archeological evidence suggests that, prior to contact with agents of Western society, the ancestors of these peoples defended themselves against the enroachments of other Indian tribes that invaded their territories. In the past 400 years they engaged, first, in a number of hostile encounters with Spanish colonists and, later, in their relations with Anglos, had to compromise in many ways over land rights. When Coronado first visited them shortly after 1540, he estimated that they had roughly comparable populations. His estimate was around 3,000 inhabitants for each. Recent investigations at Picuris indicate this community (and Taos by implication) in fact had around 2,000 inhabitants. From his description and from more systematic investigation, we have every reason to believe that they shared a very similar social structure and culture. For reasons that are not entirely clear, both suffered dramatic population decreases at least through the middle of the 18th century, probably in part through the introduction of new diseases and in part through defections to the Spanish settlements. The Census for 1890 lists, in round numbers, 400 and 300 persons for Taos and Picuris, respectively. From that time onward there was a steady increase in the former and a slight reduction in the latter, both suffering from the influenzà epidemic after World War I. Today, however, Picuris has barely 100 persons, while Taos has over 1,200. As we shall see, these figures are closely related to corresponding differences in cultural vigor.

At this point—the turn of the century—environmental stresses on the two communities begin to diverge in what turned out to be important ways. Consider certain salient events at Taos during the periods of Mexican and Anglo political control: Boundaries were fixed (a process that has been in adjudication until very recently), thus stabilizing the ratio of people to resources among a traditionally agricultural people. A new community, part Spanish-American and increasingly Anglo in composition, was located only a mile from the Indian pueblo. Over the past 50 years it has attracted a variety of settlers and visitors, notably merchants, traders, teachers, builders, service persons, artists, and tourists. Pressure on the land was thus accompanied by the opening of new alternatives for employment—catering to the tourist trade, jobs as domestics, hotel aids and dancers, service station attendants and skilled workers.

This entire configuration of events was seen as a problem, or better perhaps as a set of problems. People continued to think of Taos citizenship as a good thing, but continuation of that entity is bound up with an agrarian adaptation, a supporting belief system about man's relation to nature, and related ceremonial activities. Increasing numbers of uncontrolled nonmembers in their midst, new jobs, and a conflicting set of rules regulating work habits may and do interfere unpredictably with pueblo expectations and demands. To render services and participate in activities of central concern to the village, one must leave work in which he is engaged elsewhere. Farming, by contrast, has traditionally been articulated with such demands. We can think of the new situation as a complication in patterns of communication. The settlement has become, as it were, encircled, and Taos leadership confronted with the problem of cultural survival. If we add (1) the presence of the United Pueblo Agency in Albuquerque and constantly changing, imperfectly understood policies toward Indians originating in Washington; and (2) modern transport that enables dissident individuals to leave the village for urban employment, often some distance away, the return to it in an indeterminant manner, we can see how complex the environment must now appear to the great majority of the group that is committed to continuity of its cultural system.[17]

During the same period many of the stresses observed at Taos have confronted Picurenses, but in a different way. Children attend Indian schools on and off the reservation (boarding school at Santa Fe) where the curriculum is established and teaching done by aliens. Picuris is a few miles removed from the main highway that passes hard by Taos and is within walking distance only to a Spanish-American village that provides no regular job opportunities. To opt for employment off the pueblo means residing in towns or cities, the closest of which is 24 miles away (Taos). Individuals who do so must rely almost exclusively upon secondary languages, English and Spanish, and forego many of the emotional gratifications associated with the use of the native language (especially participation in pueblo-centered activities like the ceremonial calendar and household rituals, which make use of intensive social interaction to which Picurenses are socialized very early in life).

Elsewhere I have summarized the contrasting nature of pressures and outcomes in the two communities as follows:

Perhaps the single most important factor that distinguishes the recent history of Picuris and Taos is the different impact of stress created by environmental changes. The proliferation of alternatives created in the immediate vicinity of Taos challenged the conventional power system, but in so doing strengthened it. The community as a whole began to take the shape of a nativistic movement. We might say that what happened in the process of this confrontation was the development of a keen sense of urgency in adapting to a perceived threat to cultural survival. In Picuris, by contrast, it is just this sense of urgency that is lacking. Being removed from the centers of development there is, so to speak, leisure in the contemplation of alternatives, perhaps too much leisure to confirm themselves in their beliefs. Disassociation from the pueblo, on the other hand, has seldom been a possible alternative except for those who have been incompletely socialized. The net result has been a classic example of pervasive anomie in the generation of young adult males (ages 16-38), partial integration in the next older generation (ages 40-58), and an integrated generation of elders (age 60).[18]

Dimensions of Perceived Stress

Examination of certain classes of historical events at Taos and Picuris will facilitate analysis of environmental pressures as people see them. From these cases perceived stress appears to vary according to its direction, intensity, complexity, ambiguity, control, and effect on group image. Until approximately the end of the 19th century, members of both groups might well have perceived the alteration of their environment by the intrusion of others in very similar ways on all of these dimensions. Clearly this stress-inducing intrusion was of long duration; each group had to contend increasingly with agents of Spanish and Anglo tradition for over 350 years. It was unambiguous (the "others" are clearly different and threatening), controlling over their actions, and depreciating to themselves, as was explicit in the colonizing, missionizing, and politically defining efforts of first one of the dominant groups and then the other. If we think of intensity in terms of frequency of interaction, their experiences probably differed little in this regard as well.

After 1900, however, some of these features began to vary in magnitude. Duration, control, and effect on group image remained roughly the same. The construction of a new road and motor transport, on the other hand, left Picuris relatively isolated but generated a very pronounced increase in rate of interaction between Taosenos and non-members. Not only were there many new occasions for rubbing shoulders at Taos—curious or interested outsiders and artists, new enterprises, amusements, and the like—but they confronted the pueblo dweller almost continuously in everyday life. Individuals and the group as a whole were faced with the problem of how to cope with these interactions. As one alternative, individuals might have been left free to make their own decisions at will: to remain traditionally occupied within the pueblo, communicating to a very limited degree with outsiders; to divide their time between both worlds; or physically to detach themselves from the group, either permanently by emigration or by leaving for indefinite periods and returning when emotionally or otherwise disposed to do so.

The strategy actually employed was to reinforce the value of group membership by selectively emphasizing traditional symbols. In the process Taosenos simplified the environmental context of their earlier life by redefining its complexity simply as threat, and they controlled the level of intensity of intercultural interaction by specifying the kinds, frequency, and content of relations that were permitted. The result was an affirmative defensive adaption that had revealed all the properties of this phenomenon described above.

At Picuris the aspects, but not the magnitudes, of environmental change were very similar to those at Taos. No such increase in stress intensity occurred; the environment to Picurenses remained very complex in terms of models and ambiguous concerning the messages they received. We observe, also, no such monolithic interpretation of such pressures. Some defined the situation as threat and emphasized a traditional solution; others, as new opportunities and new wants. An increasing majority, however, came to be confused by multiple choices of both valued goals and means of achieving them, to the point of immobilization of any effort and normlessness.

Interaction Between Group and Environment

It should be clear from this discussion that we must assume a continuing interaction between environmental pressures (as interpreted by an outside observer, or as perceived by members of some social entity) and the structure of groups in order to predict subsequent responses that the latter will make to environmental transformations.[19] Some previous tendency in the direction of centralized sociopolitical organization is probably necessary, in order to mobilize efforts of individuals to cope collectively with urgently felt needs for a more or less satisfying way of life in the face of forces that are perceived to be opposed to such an effort. The necessity for controlling the use of water in irrigation-based agriculture, it has been suggested, very possibly led to centralized community leadership among the eastern pueblos well before the Spanish contact period.[20] Another pattern sometimes occurs in a mass or aggregate of individuals with minimal organization structure. A social appeal to a felt need for value-oriented identity may attract a segment of such a population to a new, centralized structure. The Black Muslims are an outcome of such appeals among the northern urban Negroes of the United States.

By the same token, if the group-environment interaction process in the past had stabilized in a structure that was ill equipped to cope with new and traumatic perceived stress, we might predict an outcome other than defensive adaptation, no matter how closely the stress values approximated those described for Taos pueblo. I am not familiar personally with such a case from the annals of American history, but they are encountered in the anthropological literature.[21] I would hypothesize that a successful defensive reaction requires either a centralized prior structure or a loose one —viz, the earlier urban Negro ghetto community in its initial phase.

DISCUSSION AND IMPLICATIONS

Defensive Adaptation and Theories of Social Movements

The theory of defensive adaptation builds upon certain important lines of cultural theory and work on the problem of social movements. Several ethnic enclaves in the United States had their origins in social movements: the Mennonites, Amish, and Hutterites, for example, began as sectarian movements in Europe and the Mormons in America.

Smelser makes a distinction between a norm-oriented movement and a value-oriented movement.[22] The NAACP is an example of the former. In its attempt to advance desegregation in the United States, the NAACP is critical of certain practices in society but not of its fundamental democratic values. It proposes reforms as a more adequate realization of those values but does not advocate a far-reaching cultural transformation. A value-oriented movement, on the other hand, criticizes values; the Black Muslim movement is said to be value oriented and to advocate change at the core of society. "God is Black," their leaders assert, and thereby challenge the assumption that "God is White" with all that it connotes. In a very large sense, however, setting forth this dogma is simply a dramatic way of establishing a symbolic basis for identity and consensual commitment among individuals drawn from a distinctive but relatively unorganized social aggregate. Actually, in its efforts to socialize new members, the Black Muslims clearly stress central values of middle-class whites. The challenge to values of the larger society lies in the further assertion that the means by which this can be achieved is by complete segregation and new nationhood rather than by desegregation and increased meaningful interaction. The contrast with the NAACP in this respect is in means and not in goals. There is nevertheless a real difference in strategy; one is defensive, the other is not.[23]

Many defensive societies bear a close resemblance to a certain stage in the development of what Wallace, in a stimulating paper, has termed "revitalization movements," which are efforts to create a more satisfying culture from cumulative dissatisfactions.[24] Such movements emerge well along in the defensive process, after adherents have overcome hostility from the dominant community and a new cultural state, if suitably stress reducing, has become routinized and expressed through a new organization.

By far the most impressive scholarly contribution to the study of social movements is Aberle's analysis of the Peyote religion among the Navaho.[25] In this work Aberle has succeeded specifically in making an exhaustive and convincing evaluation of all the factors that differentiate those who are attracted and committed in varying degrees to the Peyote cult from those who are opposed to it. After examining all internal variables of Navaho society—viz, age, sex, education, livelihood, health, education, church membership, kin relations, participation in the tribal council, and degree of acculturation—he was forced to conclude that the only factor that was significantly associated with cult membership was the livestock reduction program initiated in 1933 by the national government, in an effort to control progressive erosion. This process he invites us to think of in terms of relative deprivation. Individuals who became members of the cult were not necessarily poorer than those who did not, but relative to others they lost a significantly greater amount of wealth.[26]

In a subsequent chapter[27] the author attempts to place the Peyote cult in the wider context of a theory of social movements that is full of useful insights. He arrives at some four types of such movements:

(1) Transformative movements that aim at total social-cultural change (comparable to Smelser's value-oriented movements and including millenarian movements and revolutions).

(2) Reformative movements that aim at a partial social-cultural change (comparable to Smelser's norm-oriented movements and including fluoridation movements, child-labor-law movements, and peasant rebellions).

(3) Redemptive movements that aim at a total change in individuals (the Peyote cult falls in this class, as would probably Jewish ghetto and shtetl communities, early Christianity, Mormonism, and the Black Muslims).

(4) Alternative movements that aim at a partial change in individuals (birth control movements).

He then proceeds to identify constant and variable features of each and to indicate the significance of relative deprivation, reference groups, and environmental contexts

780

in relation to choice of one or another type of movement. Aberle's observations are broad ranging and repay careful reading, although he makes no effort to construct an exhaustive theory of the phenomenon. By concentrating on process, this analysis understandably fails to indicate common structural characteristics of defensive adaptation that cut across several types of movements. Among the possible alternative reactions to status deprivation, however, the author does include a "defensive insistence on the rightness of its behavior in the face of known, or imagined, opposition." And, in discussing the context of social movements, he hypothesizes that ". . . transformative goals are most likely when a deprived group is segregated spatially or socially and when its involvement with the larger social order is either slight or decreasing or both" [as when confronted with a superior technology or physical enclosure].[28] He would, I suspect, put Taos pueblo in this category. One might as well or better argue, on the other hand, that Taos leadership has mobilized its efforts to prevent transformation or even redemption through changed behavior, by a process of involution or turning in upon itself.

In brief, theories of social movements share, as elements in their analysis, a number of behavioral and environmental characteristics with a paradigm of defensive adaptation. Not all instances of the latter, however, are subsets of the former. In particular, defensive adaptations never take the form of revolution by violent means.

Defensive Adaptation and Culture

Defensive coping in the first place is a response to stress and perceived threat to continuities of, or barriers to, a meaningful way of life. It is a strategy that occurs when protagonists have limited resources for direct and possibly violent confrontation with the source(s) of frustration. Nevertheless, there are many instances of aggressive collective confrontation in the face of limited resources. Activist and so-called militant groups in America today are cases in point. This suggests that it is necessary to take into account something more than either of these factors in order to predict a defensive outcome.

An understanding of defensive adaptation ultimately is derived from the single most fundamental attribute of culture. This can be stated simply: culture is (symbolic) communication. People who respond positively but defensively to perceived threat from whatever exogenous source—subjugation, exploitation, urbanization, industrialization, urban-rural interaction, and the like—must either have a tradition or, out of a felt need, succeed in creating one. In either case, sharing at least core values over the long haul requires the means for sustaining regular and frequent communication. Minority ethnic enclaves, whether composed of immigrant groups or small-scale societies that came to be surrounded by dominant others in the course of settlement in American history, meet this requirement. In addition to groups specifically mentioned in this essay, we should include the Spanish-Americans in the southwest and Mexican Americans in the west, Chinese, Italians, Irish, and so forth.

Not all of these groups perceived a danger to their cultural integrity, hence made a defensive adaptation. An interesting example of cognitive change in an altered social context is described in a sociology dissertation. The data for this study involved aspects of adjustment patterns of a small minority of Catholics in relation to a preponderantly Mormon majority (about 93 percent of the total) in a small Idaho city (total population about 8,000). The Catholic enclave, instead of losing elements of value identification in their relations with the Mormons, which they would according to a theory of social marginality, actually exhibited considerably more cohesion and support of communal values than did Mormons. In this situation the church authorities exercised greater control over the individual's behavior than was true in comparable urban parishes from which immigrants came. For example, the Irish Catholic element, comprising about 30 percent of the total within this group, revealed almost none of the traditional pattern of drinking, which in this community came to be severely frowned upon. Family-centered internalized control in other areas of overt behavior was similarly reinforced by the same external authorities. These conditions obtained despite amiable relations between Catholics and Mormons generally. Leaders of the Catholic enclave perceived danger of group extinction as a distinctive entity. They were also able to communicate the reality of this threat to members and to enforce latent control over individual behavior to emphasize collective goals.[29]

The Jews, with such a long historical tradition, are a special case. It would be possible and useful to investigate response patterns at various peak periods of stress in the trajectory of their experiences from classical to modern times. More directly relevant, perhaps, it would also be instructive to study comparatively the immigrant population of eastern European shtetl Jews in relation to second- and third-generation American-born Jews. Both orthodox Jewish and Mormon traditions stress the value of formal learning. In so doing they embrace a paradox within the context of the larger society; namely, the alienation of the young who are exposed to important conflicts between school and home and church by virtue of the content of what is learned and to what purpose. This paradox is only partly resolved by the establishment of parochial schools. It would be interesting to study Jewish university leadership roles in the current, seemingly anarchistic element of Students for a Democratic Society, and to compare this phenomenon with their goal-oriented activism of a generation ago (in Trotskyite and Stalinist movements) in relation to cultural commitment.

Shared value commitment need not restrict itself to societies in the conventional sense of the word. To pull together and to hold members in some kind of long-range organization with a sense of shared urgency, however, requires rapid communication that approximates face-to-face interaction. These are precisely the conditions that, in contemporary America, enable the creation of viable defensive groups, like the Black Muslims, from broadly distributed sectors of society.

In a personal communication, Dr. William S. Madsen, then engaged in a field study of Alcoholics Anonymous in the San Francisco Bay area, informed me that this group —and probably all Anonymous groups, like Heroins Anonymous and Gamblers Anonymous—pinpoints precisely the structural elements we have identified with defensive adaptations (including the stress values, derived in this instance from the perception of hostile norms of non-Alcoholics of the established society). Alcoholics Anonymous, of course, is not an enclave and does not recruit members from married group members. However, it does have rather explicit criteria for "citizenship" in the sense of minimal conformance with a set of standards of behavior. Nonconformists are rigidly excluded, leaving a residual group strongly committed to these standards and to the authoritative controls of a small elite.

People who participate in defensive organizations are, in a sociological sense, minorities in that they feel deprived in relation to dominant institutions. They exist at the sufferance of other who have the means, should they wish to employ them, to suppress completely their efforts at independent cultural identity. Dependency behavior and subordination of decisionmaking to powerful centralized leadership develops out of a necessity to cope rapidly with day-to-day situations with which the group may be confronted. So, too, training for impulse control has strategic value in these groups because they possess limited resources and in the long run cannot hope to succeed by violent means.[30] They might, of course, attempt to do so by coopting large numbers of the dominant society to their cause, but in this way they run the risk of losing or weakening their identity. The early Christians, themselves a defensive society, succeeded admirably in missionary efforts, but ultimately gave rise to a rash of schisms and sectarian movements. I would invite more knowledgeable students about the subject than I to speculate in this vein about the defensive nature of the trade-union movement at the time of its early florescence under Samuel Gompers, and perhaps even in the early phase of the CIO. Most of the violence associated with some strike activities in the 1930's was, after all, initiated by suppressive elements of the dominant society. The coopting of powerful members of the latter through the political process led to successful efforts at achieving the cultural goals of the labor movement—and in the end to its transformation and integration with the establishment. It is instructive to observe the conservative tendency of labor unionism today and the loss of the ideological persuasion that attended its earlier phases.

A final note. By inference, people who are organized defensively are less likely than members of weakly organized groups or persons who participate in temporary collectivities (viz. ad hoc confrontations) to engage in violence. This is so because they have come to share a sense of cultural purpose that, in the social context in which they

784

find themselves, can only be maintained by discipline and subordination of the individual to the larger entity. Crowds and assemblages are hard to discipline, given the nature of the communication process and unfiltered selection of participants. When defensive adaptation does occur, it always displays the same structure. Perhaps it is replicated in its essential features because for any group, category, or aggregate of people, it is the most economical and efficient means for coping with the problem of perceived severe stress applied over a long period of time.

Some of the remarks in this concluding section are more firmly wedded to the central analysis than others. I have engaged in a certain amount of speculation about selected problems of relevance to the nature of violence in America that clearly demand detailed, expert investigation. All of the comments, however, are shaped by a general paradigmatic theory of defensive adaptation.

References

1. Detailed historical analysis of the emergence of defensive societies—a history of the Mormons, of the Jews, at least from the 19th-century ghetto period through second-generation American Jewry, of Taos and other Indian pueblos, and of the Black Muslims—would provide some of the best evidence for the solution of these kinds of problems. Systematic comparisons of culturally related groups, which vary only with respect to specified dimensions of environmental changes, is another method of predicting alternative strategies of adaptation. For want of space both of these methods can be applied only in a limited way in this essay.
2. A. I. Hallowell, "The Social Psychology of Acculturation," in Ralph Linton, ed., *The Science of Man in the World Crisis* (New York: Columbia University Press, 1945). See also Bernard J. Siegal, "High Anxiety Levels and Cultural Integration: Notes on a Psychocultural Hypothesis," *Social Forces* (Oct. 1955).
3. Emile Durkheim, *Le Suicide* (Paris: Ancienne Librairie Germer Bailliere, 1897), ch. IV. See also the discussion of "institutional suicide" in Ruth Shonle Cavan, *Suicide* (Chicago: University of Chicago Press, 1927), pp. 69 ff.
4. Observations about the Black Muslims are derived primarily from two sources: C. Eric Lincoln, *The Black Muslims in America* (Boston: Beacon Press, 1961); and E. U. Essien-Udom, *Black Nationalism* (New York: Dell Press, 1962).
5. Or, as Ward Goodenough has expressed it, the "limiting effect [of each custom] on the forms that other customs can conveniently take." *Cooperation in Change* (New York: Russell Sage Foundation, 1963), p. 68. Hence, where there is a high degree of integration in this sense we would expect a continual scrutiny of inconsistencies and ambiguities among beliefs.
6. It is perhaps not accidental that the holistic approach to the concept of culture, an emphasis upon the functional interdependence of custom and belief, came early to dominate the thinking of anthropologists, as a consequence until recently of their almost exclusive concern with the study of small-scale, relatively isolated and discrete primitive societies. The communication network of defensive societies tends to approximate that of primitive isolated groups, and is indeed intended to foster isolation in the complex environments of the modern world.
7. Not all so-called tribal and peasant societies exhibit this reluctance to accept innovations and proliferate alternatives, a view once commonly assumed by Western advocates of technological innovation who encountered

so many negative experiences. Quite the contrary, as many postwar studies vividly reveal. This characterization, an artifact of oversimplified classification of human groups by many anthropologists, often masked their variability in this respect. The error was compounded by failing to consider as part of social theory the continuous interaction of group and environment. See, for example, Raymond Firth, *Elements of Social Organization* (London: Watts, 1951), p. 109.

8. The high degree of endogamy among orthodox Pueblo Indians, Jews, and Mormons is well documented. Among Black Muslims marriage with a white is emphatically prohibited. Less well known is the fact that, in comparison with blacks as a whole, marriage is strongly preferential within the group. When a member does marry a non-Muslim, great pressure is put on non-Muslim spouses to join the nation.

9. See Essien-Udom, *op. cit.*, p. 199.

10. To the investigator this wall of seclusion is both frustrating and challenging. The gates seldom open wide, and then for short intervals, always attended by vigilant gatekeepers—to use Kurt Lewin's graphic simile. This is why some of the best ethnographies are the products of members or former members who have become behavioral scientists and retain an entree into the group.

11. See Edward Wakin, *A Lonely Minority: The Modern Story of Egypt's Copts* (New York: Morrow, 1963), pp. 141 and 147 ff.; also Lincoln, *op. cit.*, pp. 15 ff. and 199. For many years the Copts had a strong central political organization. Its influence over the past few years had progressively weakened as they identified their own welfare in Egyptian colonial days with dominant European Christians. With the virtual elimination of other non-Moslem minority groups during the Nasser regime (Jews and non-Coptic Christian groups), they once more lived in a world in which they perceived the threat of being absorbed into the general population and of economic and social deprivation. It is interesting to note, as they recall with increasing alarm the belligerence of the Moslem Brotherhood and Egyptian nationalism, unmistakable evidence of increased Coptic nationalism.

12. Other dispersed defensive societies, like Mormons and shtetl Jews, similarly evolved mechanisms for frequent communication of active members both within and between communities.

13. Wakin, *ibid.*, Walter A. Riddle, "The Rise of Ecclesiastical Control in Quebec," doctoral dissertation, Faculty of Political Science, Columbia University, 1916, pp. 94 ff.; Everett Cherrington Hughes, *French Canada in Transition* (Chicago: University of Chicago Press, 1962), p. 9.

14. Lee Emerson Deets, "The Hutterites: A Study in Social Cohesion," doctoral dissertation, Faculty of Political Science, Columbia University, 1939, p. 17.

15. Thomas F. O'Dea, *The Mormons* (Chicago: University of Chicago Press, 1957), pp. 49, 130, and 143. See also Gaylon L. Caldwell, "Mormon Conceptions of Individual Rights and Political Organization," doctoral dissertation, Department of Political Science, Stanford University, 1952, p. 234. Both the Hutterites and Mormons initiate virtually all adolescent males into the Church's esoteric matters and responsibilities. From late adolescence on, they constitute a reservoir of potential members of the priesthood.

We do also find defensive societies in which the ultimate source of power is apparently not derived from a special religious knowledge. A Japanese sociologist informs us, for example, of a fishing hamlet in northeastern Honshu, so removed in modern times from communication with neighboring hamlets that it remains as isolated as one can possibly imagine under present conditions. This isolation, moreover, is preferred and controlled. Only a few households receive newspapers or magazines, or listen to a radio. This is in great contrast to the reading habits among Japanese as a whole. Eighty-five percent of men and 75 percent of women are natives of the hamlet. Local endogamy, in other words, is the role for all but a small percentage of members; the latter in turn select marriage partners from neighboring hamlets. The scope of life is so narrow that people rarely visit other hamlets that comprise the village, and they still continue an old practice of shopping as a community twice a year at the neighboring town.

Traditionally strong patriarchal control had long been exerted by family heads and by a village council consisting of older males, in conformance with Confucian values that defined desirable properties of family life.

These values provide the moral basis for action but cannot be said to constitute part of a religious system, in the sense of being codified in sacred literature, oral or written. In another sense, however, they might be thought of as belonging to the realm of the sacred, in that they necessitate acting out, with almost punctilious ritual, conformity to detail and a deeply felt reluctance to change. Today the custodians of this tradition suppress even more stringently on the part of the young any relaxation of the etiquette that symbolizes these authoritarian relations: the use of respectful language, seating customs at meals and during visits, the subservience of a man's wife to his mother, and the stern emphasis on hard work imposed upon the young. See Yoshio Saito, "On the Structural Analysis of a Fishing Village: The Case of Miyagi-Ken, Ojurugun, Onagawa-Machi," *Japanese Sociological Review*, vol. V (1955), pp. 24-26.

16. See, e.g., Fred Eggan, *Social Organization of the Western Pueblos* (Chicago: University of Chicago Press, 1950), pp. 291-324.

17. For a more detailed analysis of stress and social process in Taos pueblo, see Alan R. Beals and Bernard J. Siegel, *Divisiveness and Social Conflict: An Anthropological Approach* (Stanford: Stanford University Press, 1965), chs. 3 and 4.

18. Bernard J. Siegel, "Social Disorganization in Picuris Pueblo," *International Journal of Comparative Sociology*, vol. VI (1965), p. 205.

19. This point of view, and indeed most anthropological conceptions of society and culture, however inductively arrived at, is consistent with modern systems theory. In the interest of clarity, I have tried to avoid the introduction of unnecessary jargon. For an introduction to a systems outlook, the reader is referred to Walter Buckley, ed., *Modern Systems Research for the Behavioral Scientist* (Chicago: Aldine, 1968).

20. See Esther S. Goldfrank, "Irrigation Agriculture and Navaho Community Leadership: Case Material on Environment and Culture," *American Anthropologist*, XLVII (No. 2, 1945), pp. 262-277. Although she deals principally with the Navaho, Dr. Goldfrank considers also data relating to the pueblos.

21. See, for example, the excellent analysis of such a case among Yiryiront, a society of Australian Aboriginese, as recounted by Lauriston Sharp, "Steel Axes for Stone Age Australians," in E. H. Spicer, ed., *Human Problems in Technological Change* (New York: Russell Sage, 1952), pp. 69-90. The evidence that Sharp provides suggests, among other things, that sporadic stress encounters, however traumatic, will not lead to social change either in the direction of defensive structuring, other than disorganization, or in any other direction away from the status quo ante.

22. Neil J. Smelser, *Theory of Collective Behavior* (New York: The Free Press, 1963).

23. It is interesting in this regard to note the general detachment of American Indians from active involvement in and support of the civil rights movement. What the blacks are struggling for, they feel they already have and are not about to jeopardize their cultural vitality by participation in a larger incorporative organization.

24. A. F. C. Wallace, "Revitalization Movements," *American Anthropologist*, vol. LVIII (No. 2, 1956), pp. 264-281.

25. David F. Aberle, *The Peyote Religion Among the Navaho* (New York: Wenner-Gren Foundation for Anthropological Research, 1966).

26. This is a gross simplification of a much more sophisticated argument.

27. Aberle, *op. cit.*, ch. 19.

28. *Ibid.*, pp. 327, 330.

29. See Jack Homer Curtis, "Group Marginality and Adherence to Religious Doctrine in an American Community," doctoral dissertation, Department of Sociology, Stanford University, 1954.

30. If we were to inquire further, we would probably see that dispersed defensive associations tend to attract and to hold within the central core persons characterized by strong dependency needs, however varied their social and cultural backgrounds (substantial numbers of dissidents are sloughed off or removed in one way or another), and then to weld them into a novel organization.

CONCLUSION

I. THE COMMONALITY OF COLLECTIVE VIOLENCE IN THE WESTERN TRADITION

Future historians may marvel at the ostensible "rediscovery" of violence that has both fascinated and bemused contemporary observers. That the recent resurgence of collective nonmilitary violence in Western society is widely regarded as anomalous probably reflects both a cultural and a contemporary bias. We have tended to assume, perhaps unconsciously, that such violence was an uncivilized practice of more primitive societies that the civilized and affluent West had largely outgrown. Our historians have themselves been guilty of contributing to this popular illusion; while they have retained their fascination for military exploits, they have tended either to ignore the persistence of domestic turmoil except when it reached revolutionary proportions, or to minimize its significance by viewing it from the perspective of established authority. When viewed from the top down, violence was understandably regarded as an abnormal and undesirable breach of the public order.

On the contrary, Tilly concludes, "collective violence is normal."

Historically, collective violence has flowed regularly out of the central, political processes of western countries. Men seeking to seize, hold, or realign the levers of power have continually engaged in collective violence as part of their struggles. The oppressed have struck in the name of justice, the privileged in the name of order, those in between in the name of fear.

In Tilly's analysis, collective violence in the European experience was fundamentally transformed but not foredoomed by the processes of industrialization and urbanization. The old "primitive" forms of violence in feudal Europe—such as communal feuds and religious persecutions—were characterized by small scale, local scope, communal group participation, and inexplicit and unpolitical objectives. The subsequent evolution of the nation-state prompted such "reactionary" disturbances as food riots, Luddite destruction, tax revolts, and anticonscription rebellions. Although industrialization and urbanization muted such disorders by disrupting their cohesive communal base, the metropolitan society these forces forged gave rise to "modern" forms of protest—such as demonstrations and strikes—which involved relatively large and specialized associations with relatively well-defined and "forward-looking" objectives and which were explicitly organized for political or economic action.

Tilly's model suggests that modern collective protest, owing to its broader associational base, is more likely to occur on a large scale. But modern protest is less likely to become violent because the associational form gives the group a surer control over its own actions, and thus permits shows of force without concomitant damage or bloodshed. Moreover, the historic shift from communal to associational bases for collective protest brought into being a number of modern nonviolent mechanisms for the regulation of conflicts: the strike, the demonstration, the parliament, and the political campaign. Collective violence, then, historically belongs to political life, and changes in its form tell us that something important is happening to the political system itself.

What is happening to the political system in contemporary America? Preliminary to such an inquiry is the historical task of surveying the patterns of group violence that have accompanied the development of the United States. Brown has traced an overview of American collective violence, and his organizational categories of "negative" and "positive" violence in some ways parallel Tilly's analytical distinctions between reactionary disturbances, which center on rights once enjoyed but now threatened, and modern disturbances, which center on rights not yet enjoyed but now within reach. It might be more appropriate in this conclusion to discuss the American historical legacy of violence in relation to the contemporary relevance of the various categories Brown employed. Brown catalogued as "negative" forms of American violence that associated with feuds, lynching, political assassination, free-lance multiple murder, crime, ethnic and racial prejudice, and urban rioting. "Positive" forms were associated with the American Revolution and Civil War, agrarian uprisings, labor protests, vigilantism, Indian wars, and police violence.

Perhaps the historically violent episode that is least relevant to our contemporary concerns is the family feud.

The famous and colorful clan feuding seems to have been triggered by the Civil War in border areas where loyalties were sharply divided and where the large extended family of the 19th century provided both a focus for intense loyalties and a ready instrument of aggression. But this tradition has waned with the fading of the circumstances that conditioned its birth. It is arguable, however, that the brutalizing traditions associated with the Indian wars have left their callous imprint on our national character long after the estimated 850,000 American Indians had been ruthlessly reduced by 1950 to 400,000. Similarly, the violence associated with the American Revolution, the Civil War, and Reconstruction has surely reinforced the ancient notion that the ends justify the means, and clearly the defeat of the Confederacy and the failure of Reconstruction has convinced generations of white Southerners that Negro political participation and Federal efforts at reform are irrevocably linked with corruption and subversion.

Whether the long association with violence of agrarian uprisings and the labor movement has permanently faded with changing modern circumstances is fervently to be hoped, but by no means certain. Employer acceptance of unions during and after the New Deal suggests that that long and bloody conflict is largely behind us. But the stubborn persistence of rural poverty constitutes a latent invitation to a resurgence of latter-day populism.

Two other sordid American traditions that have largely waned but that recently have shown some signs of revival are vigilantism and lynching. Although vigilantism is associated in the popular mind with such frontier and rural practices as antirustler and antihorsethief popular "justice" in areas largely devoid of regular enforcement agencies, the largest local American vigilance committee was organized in San Francisco in 1856. If vigilantism is defined more broadly to include regional and even national movements as well as local organizations, then America's preeminent vigilante movement has been the Ku Klux Klan—or rather, the Ku Klux Klans, for there have essentially been three of them. The original Klan arose in the South in response to radical Reconstruction, and through terror and intimidation was instrumental in the "redemption" of the Southern state governments by white conservatives. The second Klan, by far the largest, was resurrected in Atlanta in 1915 and boomed nationally in the 1920's. Strong in the Midwest and Far West as well as the South, and making inroads even in the cities, the Klan of the 1920's—despite its traditional racist and xenophobic rhetoric—focused its chastisement less upon Negroes, Catholics, and Jews than upon local white Protestants who were adjudged guilty of violating smalltown America's Victorian moral code. The third Klan represented a proliferation of competing Klans in the South in response to the civil rights movement of the 1950's. Generally lacking the prestige and organizational strength of the earlier Klans, these groups engaged in a period of unrestrained terrorism in the rural and smalltown Black Belt South in the 1950's and early 1960's, but have belatedly been brought under greater control.

Lynching, vigilantism's supreme instrument of terror and summary "justice," has been widely practiced in America certainly since the Revolutionary era, when miscreant Tories were tarred and feathered, and worse. Although lynching is popularly associated with racial mob murder, this pattern is a relatively recent one, for prior to the late 19th century, white Americans perforce lynched one another—Negro slaves being far too valuable to squander at the stake. But lynching became predominantly racial from 1882 to 1903, when 1,985 Negroes were murdered in the tragic but successful effort of those years to forge a rigid system of biracial caste, most brutal and explicit in the South but generally reflective of national attitudes. Once the point—that this was a white man's country—was made, lynching gradually declined. Its recent resurgence in response to the civil rights movement is notorious, but it nowhere approximates its scale at the turn of the century.

The contemporary relevance of political assassination and freelance multiple murder needs no documentation to a nation that has so recently witnessed the murders of John and Robert Kennedy, Dr. Martin Luther King, and, on television, Lee Harvey Oswald—in addition to the chilling mass slaughtering sprees of Charles Whitman in Austin, Texas, and Richard Speck in Chicago. Historically, political assassination has become a recurrent feature of the political system only in the South during (the first) Reconstruction and in New Mexico Territory. Although four American Presidents have been assassinated since 1865, prominent politicians and civil servants occupying the myriad lesser levels of government have been largely immune. Whether the current spate of public murder is an endemic symptom of a new social malaise is a crucial question that history cannot yet answer, other than to observe that precedents in our past are minimal.

Similarly, historical precedents are few regarding massive student and antiwar protests. American students have historically succumbed to the annual spring throes of the panty-raid syndrome, but the current wave of campus confrontations is essentially an unprecedented phenomenon—as is the massive and prolonged opposition to the war in Vietnam. As Professor Brooks has observed, "unfortunately the past does not have much to tell us; we will have to make our own history along uncharted and frightening ways."

But the past has much to tell us about the rioting and crime that have gripped our cities. Urban mobs are as old as the city itself. Colonial seaports frequently were rocked for days by roving mobs—groups of unruly and often drunken men whose energies were shrewdly put to political purpose as Liberty Boys in the American Revolution. Indeed, our two principal instruments of physical control evolved directly in response to 19th-century urban turmoil. The professional city police system replaced the inadequate constabulary and watch-and-ward in response to the rioting of the 1840's and 1850's, largely in the Northeast. Similarly, the national guard was organized in order to control the labor violence—or more appropriately, the antilabor violence—of the 1880's and 1890's.

Probably all nations are given to a kind of historical amnesia or selective recollection that masks unpleasant traumas of the past. Certainly Americans since the Puritans have historically regarded themselves as a latter-day "Chosen People" sent on a holy errand to the wilderness, there to create a New Jerusalem. One beneficient side effect of our current turmoil may be to force a harder and more candid look at our past and at our behavior in comparison with other peoples and nations.

II. CONTEMPORARY AMERICAN VIOLENCE
IN HISTORICAL PERSPECTIVE

Our current eruption of violence must appear paradoxical to a generation of Americans who witnessed the
successful emergence from depression to unparalleled affluence of a nation they regarded as the world's moral leader
in defense of freedom. Only a decade ago America's historians were celebrating the emergence of a unique society,
sustained by a burgeoning prosperity and solidly grounded
on a broad political consensus.[1] We were told—and the
implications were reassuring—that our uniqueness was derived from at least half a dozen historical sources which,
mutually reinforcing one another, had joined to propel us
toward a manifestly benevolent destiny. We were a nation
of immigrants, culturally enriched by the variety of mankind. Sons of the frontier, our national character had grown
to reflect the democratic individualism and pragmatic ingenuity that had conquered the wilderness. Our new nation
was born in anticolonial revolution and in its crucible was
forged a democratic republic of unparalleled vitality and
longevity. Lacking a feudal past, our political spectrum was
so truncated about the consensual liberal center that, unlike
Europe, divisive radicalism of the left or right had found no
sizable constituency. Finally, we had both created and
survived the great transformation from agrarian frontier to
industrial metropolis, to become the richest nation of all
time.

It was a justly proud legacy, one which seemed to make
sense in the relatively tranquil 1950's. But with the 1960's
came shock and frustration. It was a decade against itself:
the students of affluence were marching in the streets;
middle-class matrons were besieging the Pentagon; and
Negro Americans were responding to victories in civil rights
and to their collectively unprecedented prosperity with a
paradoxical venting of outrage. In a fundamental sense,
history—the ancient human encounter with poverty, defeat and guilt as well as with affluence, victory, and innocence—had finally caught up with America. Or at least it
had caught up with white America.

Historical analysis of our national experience and character would suggest that the seeds of our contemporary
discontent were to a large extent deeply embedded in those

same ostensibly benevolent forces which contributed to our uniqueness. First, we are a nation of immigrants, but one in which the original dominant immigrant group, the so-called Anglo-Saxons, effectively preempted the crucial levers of economic and political power in government, commerce, and the professions. This elite group has tenaciously resisted the upward strivings of successive "ethnic" immigrant waves. The resultant competitive hierarchy of immigrants has always been highly conducive to violence, but this violence has taken different forms. The Anglo-Americans have used their access to the levers of power to maintain their dominance, using legal force surrounded by an aura of legitimacy for such ends as economic exploitation; the restriction of immigration by a national-origin quota system which clearly branded later immigrants as culturally undesirable; the confinement of the original Indian immigrants largely to barren reservations; and the restriction of blacks to a degraded caste. But the system was also conducive to violence among the latter groups themselves—when, for instance, Irish-Americans rioted against Afro-American "scabs." Given America's unprecedented ethnic pluralism, simply being born American conferred no automatic and equal citizenship in the eyes of the larger society. In the face of such reservations, ethnic minorities had constantly to affirm their Americanism through a kind of patriotic ritual which intensified the ethnic competition for status. As a fragment culture based on bourgeois-liberal values, as Hartz has observed, yet one populated by an unprecedented variety of immigrant stock, America's tightened consensus on what properly constituted "Americanism" prompted status rivalries among the ethnic minorities which, when combined with economic rivalries, invited severe and abiding conflict.

Most distinctive among the immigrant minorities was the Negro. The eternal exception in American history, Afro-Americans were among the first to arrive and the last to emerge. To them, America meant slavery, and manumission meant elevation to the caste of black pariah. Comer has seen in the psychological legacy of slavery and caste a psychically crippling Negro dependency and even self-hatred which is largely immune to mere economic advance. The contemporary black awareness of this tenacious legacy of racial shame is abundantly reflected in the radical rhetoric of black power and "Black-is-Beautiful," and goes far toward resolving the paradox of black rebellion against a backdrop of general—albeit uneven, as Davies suggests—economic improvement. Meier and Rudwick have charted the transformation of racial violence from white pogrom to black aggression—or, in the analysis of Janowitz, from "communal" to "commodity" rioting. While emphasizing that the transformation has led to violent black assault less against white persons than against white property, and while Janowitz speculates that the summer of 1968 may have been yet another turning point, we are reminded that history, even very recent history, is an imperfect guide to the future.

The second major formative historical experience was America's uniquely prolonged encounter with the frontier. While the frontier experience indubitably strengthened the mettle of the American character, it witnessed the brutal and brutalizing ousting of the Indians and the forceful incorporation of Mexican and other original inhabitants, as Frantz has so graphically portrayed. Further, it concomitantly created an environment in which, owing to the paucity of law enforcement agencies, a tradition of vigilante "justice" was legitimized. The longevity of the Ku Klux Klan and the vitality both of contemporary urban rioting and of the stiffening resistance to it owe much to this tradition. As Brown has observed, vigilantism has persisted as a socially malleable instrument long after the disappearance of the frontier environment that gave it birth, and it has proved quite congenial to an urban setting.

Similarly, the revolutionary doctrine that our Declaration of Independence proudly proclaims stands as a tempting model of legitimate violence to be emulated by contemporary groups such as militant Negroes and radical students who confront a system of both public and private government that they regard as contemptuous of their consent. Entranced by the resurgence of revolution in the underdeveloped world and of international university unrest, radical students and blacks naturally seize upon our historically sacrosanct doctrine of the inherent right of revolution and self-determination to justify their rebellion. That their analogies are fatefully problematical in no way dilutes the majesty of our own proud Declaration.

The fourth historic legacy, our consensual political philosophy of Lockean-Jeffersonian liberalism, was premised upon a pervasive fear of governmental power and has reinforced the tendency to define freedom negatively as freedom *from*. As a consequence, conservatives have been able paradoxically to invoke the doctrines of Jefferson in resistance to legislative reforms, and the Sumnerian imperative that "stateways cannot change folkways" has historically enjoyed a wide and not altogether unjustified allegiance in the public eye (witness the debacle of the first Reconstruction, and the dilemma of our contemporary second attempt). Its implicit corollary has been that forceful, and, if necessary, violent local and state resistance to unpopular federal stateways is a legitimate response; both Calhoun and Wallace could confidently repair to a strict construction of the same document invoked by Lincoln and the Warren court.

A fifth historic source both of our modern society and our current plight is our industrial revolution and the great internal migration from the countryside to the city. Yet the process occurred with such astonishing rapidity that it produced widespread socioeconomic dislocation in an environment in which the internal controls of the American social structure were loose and the external controls were weak. Urban historian Richard Wade has observed that—

The cities inherited no system of police control adequate to the numbers or to the rapid increase of the urban centers. The modern police force is the creation of the 20th century; the establishment of genuinely professional systems is historically a very recent thing. Throughout the 18th and 19th century, the force was small, untrained, poorly paid, and part of the political system. In case of any sizeable disorder, it was hopelessly inadequate; and rioters sometimes routed the constabulary in the first confrontation.[2]

Organized labor's protracted and bloody battles for recognition and power occurred during these years of minimal control and maximal social upheaval. The violence of workers' confrontations with their employers, Taft and Ross concluded, was partly the result of a lack of consensus on the legitimacy of workers' protests, partly the result of the lack of means of social control. Workers used force to press their grievances, employers organized violent resistance, and repeatedly state or federal troops had to be summoned to restore order.

The final distinctive characteristic—in many ways perhaps our most distinctive—has been our unmatched prosperity; we have been, in the words of David Potter, most characteristically a "people of plenty." Ranked celestially with life and liberty in the sacrosanct Lockean trilogy, property has generated a quest and prompted a devotion in the American character that has matched our devotion to equality and, in a fundamental sense, has transfomed it from the radical leveling of the European democratic tradition into a typically American insistence upon equality of opportunity. In an acquisitive society of individuals with unequal talents and groups with unequal advantages, this had resulted in an unequal distribution of the rapid accumulation of abundance that, especially since World World II, has promised widespread participation in the affluent society to a degree unprecedented in history. Central to the notion of "revolutions of rising expectations," and to Davies' J-curve hypothesis as well, is the assumption that unproved economic rewards can coincide with and often obscure a degree of relative deprivation that generates frustration and can prompt men toward violent protest despite measurable gains.

Our historical evolution, then, has given our national character a dual nature: we strive, paradoxically, for both liberty and equality, which can be and often in practice are quite contradictory goals. This is not to suggest that American society is grounded in a fatal contradiction. For all the conflict inherent in a simultaneous quest for liberty and equality, American history is replete with dramatic instances of the successful adjustment of "the system" to the demands of disparate protesting groups. An historical appraisal of these genuine achievements should give pause to contemporary Cassandras who bemoan in selfflagellation how hopelessly wretched we all are. These radically disillusioned social critics can find abundant evil in our historical legacy: centuries of Negro slavery, the cultural deracination and near extinction of the Indians, our initiation of atomic destruction—ad infinitum. Much as the contemporary literary Jeremiahs have, in Lynn's view, libeled the American character by extrapolating violence from its literary context, these social critics in their overcompensations have distorted the American experience in much the same fashion, although in an opposite direction, as have the more familiar superpatriotic celebrants of

797

American virtuosity. While a careful and honest historical appraisal should remind us that violence has been far more intrinsic to our past than we should like to think—Brooks reminds us, for example, that the New York Draft Riot of 1863 vastly exceeded the destruction of Watts—our assessment of the origins and dimensions of contemporary American violence must embrace the experience of other societies.

III. COMPARISONS OF PROTEST AND VIOLENCE

Whether the United States is now a "violent society" can be answered not in the abstract but only by comparison, either with the American past or with other nations. The historical evidence, above, suggests that we are somewhat more violent toward one another in this decade than we have been in most others, but probably less violent in total magnitude of civil strife than in the latter 19th century, when the turmoil of Reconstruction was followed by massive racial and labor violence. Even so, contemporary comparison with other nations, acts of collective violence by private citizens in the United States in the last 20 years have been extraordinarily numerous, and this is true also of peaceful demonstrations. In numbers of political assassinations, riots, politically relevant armed group attacks, and demonstrations the United States since 1948 has been among the half-dozen most tumultuous nations in the world.[3] When such events are evaluated in terms of their relative severity, however, the rank of the United States is somewhat lower. The Feierabends and Nesvold have used ranking scales to weigh the severity and numbers of such events during the years 1948 to 1965, rating peaceful demonstrations as having the least serious impact, civil wars the most serious impact on political systems. In a comparison that gives greatest weight to the frequency of violent events, the United States ranks 14th among 84 nations. In another comparison, based mainly on the severity of all manifestations of political instability, violent or not, the United States stands below the midpoint, 46th among 84 nations. In other words, the United States up to 1965 had much political violence by comparison with other nations but relative stability of its political institutions in spite of it. Paradoxically, we have been a turbulent people but a relatively stable republic.

Some more detailed comparisons are provided by a study of the characteristics of civil strife in 114 nations and colonies in the 1960's. The information on "civil strife" includes all reported acts of collective violence involving 100 or more people; organized private attacks on political targets, whatever the number of participants; and anti-government demonstrations involving 100 or more people. Three general kinds of civil strife are distinguished: (1) *Turmoil* is relatively spontaneous, partially organized or unorganized strife with substantial popular participation and limited objectives. (2) *Conspiracy* is intensively organized strife with limited participation but with terroristic or revolutionary objectives. (3) *Internal war* is intensively organized strife with widespread participation, always accompanied by extensive and intensive violence and usually directed at the overthrow of political regimes.

The comparisons of the strife study are proportional to population rather than absolute, on grounds that a demonstration by 10,000 of Portugal's 9 million citizens, for example, is more consequential for that nation than a demonstration by the same number of the United States' 200 million citizens is for ours. About 11 of every 1,000 Americans took part in civil strife, almost all of it turmoil, between mid-1963 and mid-1968, compared with an average of 7 per thousand in 17 other Western democracies during the 1961-65 period. Six of these 17 had higher rates of participation than the United States, including Belgium, France, and Italy. About 9,500 reported casualties resulted from American strife, most of them the result of police action. This is a rate of 48 per million population, compared with an average of 12 per million in other Western nations, but American casualties are almost certain to be overreported by comparison with casualties elsewhere. Strife was also of longer duration in the United States than in all but a handful of countries in the world. In total magnitude of strife, taking these three factors into account, the United States ranks first among the 17 Western democracies.

Despite its frequency, civil strife in the United States has taken much less disruptive forms than in many non-Western and some Western countries. More than a million citizens participated in 370 reported civil-rights demonstrations and marches in the 5-year period; almost all of them were peacefully organized and conducted. Of 170 reported antiwar demonstrations, which involved a total of about 700,000 people, the participants initiated violence in about 20. The most extensive violence occurred in 239 recorded hostile outbreaks by Negroes, which resulted in more than 8,000 casualties and 191 deaths. Yet the nation has experienced no internal wars since the Civil War and almost none of the chronic revolutionary conspiracy and terrorism that plague dozens of other nations. The most consequential conspiratorial violence has been white terrorism against blacks and civil-rights workers, which caused some 20 deaths between 1963 and 1968, and black terrorism against whites, mostly the police, which began in 1968.

Although about 220 Americans died in violent civil strife in the 5 years before mid-1968, the rate of 1.1 per million population was infinitesimal compared with the average of all nations of 238 deaths per million, and less than the European average of 2.4 million. These differences reflect the comparative evidence that, from a worldwide perspective, Americans have seldom organized for violence. Most demonstrators and rioters are protesting, not rebelling. If there were many serious revolutionaries in the United States, or effective revolutionary organizations, levels of violence would be much higher than they have been.

These comparisons afford little comfort when the tumult of the United States is contrasted with the relative domestic tranquillity of developed democratic nations like Sweden, Great Britain, and Australia, or with the comparable current tranquillity of nations as diverse as Yugoslavia, Turkey, Jamaica, or Malaysia. In total magnitude of strife, the United States ranks 24th among the 114 larger nations and colonies of the world. In magnitude of turmoil alone, it ranks sixth.

Though greater in magnitude, civil strife in the United States is about the same in kind as strife in other Western nations. The antigovernment demonstration and riot, violent clashes of political or ethnic groups, and student protests are pervasive forms of conflict in modern democracies. Some such public protest has occurred in every Western nation in the past decade. People in non-Western countries also resort to these limited forms of public protest, but they are much more likely to organize serious conspiratorial and revolutionary movements as well. Strife in the United States and other European countries is quite likely to mobilize members of both the working class and middle classes, but rarely members of the political establishment such as military officers, civil servants, and disaffected political leaders, who so often organize conspiracies and internal wars in non-European nations. Strife also is likely to occur within or on the periphery of the normal political process in Western nations, rather than being organized by clandestine revolutionary movements or cells of plotters. If some overt strife is an inevitable accompaniment of organized social existence, as all our comparative evidence suggests it is, it seems socially preferable that it take the form of open political protest, even violent protest, rather than concerted, intensively violent attempts to seize political power.

One evident characteristic of civil strife in the United States in recent years is the extent to which it is an outgrowth of ethnic tensions. Much of the civil protest and collective violence in the United States has been directly related to the nation's racial problems. Comparative studies show evidence of parallel though not identical situations in other developed, European, and democratic nations. The unsatisfied demands of regional, ethnic, and linguistic groups for greater rights and socioeconomic benefits are more common sources of civil strife in Western nations than in almost any other group of countries. These problems have persisted long after the resolution of fundamental questions about the nature of the state, the terms of political power and who should hold it, and economic development. It seems ironical that nations that have been missionaries of technology and political organization to the rest of the world apparently have failed to provide satisfactory conditions of life for all the groups within their midst.

IV. THE SOURCES OF VIOLENCE

Is man violent by nature or by circumstance? In the Hobbesian view, the inescapable legacy of human nature is a "life of man solitary, poor, nasty, brutish, and short." This ancient pessimistic view is given recent credence by the ethologists, whose study of animals in their natural habitats had led them to conclude that the aggressive drive in animals is innate, ranking with the instinctive trilogy of hunger, sex, and fear or flight.[4] But most psychologists and social scientists do not regard aggression as fundamentally spontaneous or instinctive, nor does the weight of their evidence support such a view. Rather they regard most aggression, including violence, as sometimes an emotional response to socially induced frustrations, and sometimes a dispassionate, learned response evoked by specific situations.[5] This assumption underlies almost all the studies in this volume: nature provides us only with the capacity for violence; it is social circumstance that determines whether and how we exercise that capacity.

Man's cultural diversity offers concrete evidence that this essentially optimistic view of human nature is justified. Man can through his intelligence so construct his cultural traditions and institutions as to minimize violence and encourage the realization of his humanistic goals. Cultural anthropologists have identified societies, such as four contiguous language groups in the remote Eastern Highlands of New Guinea, in which the rhythms of life were focused on a deadly and institutionally permanent game of rape and cannibalism. But they have also studied such gentle societies as those of the Arapesh of New Guinea, the Lepchas of Sikkim, and the pygmies of the Congo rain forest, cultures in which an appetite for aggression has been replaced by an "enormous gusto for concrete physical pleasures— eating, drinking, sex, and laughter." Revealingly, these gentle societies generally lack the cultural model of brave, aggressive masculinity, a pervasive model that seems so conducive to violence. Evidence that culture is a powerful if not omnipotent determinant of man's propensity for violence is the melancholy contemporary fact that Manhattan Island (population 1.7 million) has more murders per year than all of England and Wales (population 49 million). We need not resolve the interminable hen-and-egg debate over the primacy of nature versus nurture to conclude that man has the cultural capacity to minimize his recourse to violence.

One general approach to the explanation of the nature and extent of collective violence, supported by considerable evidence in this report, begins with the assumption that men's frustration over some of the material and social circumstances of their lives is a necessary precondition of group protest and collective violence. The more intense and widespread frustration-induced discontent is among a people, the more intense and widespread collective violence is likely to be. Several general attitudinal and social conditions determine the extent and form of consequent violence. People are most strongly disposed to act violently on their discontent if they believe that violence is justifiable and likely of success; they are likely to take violent political action to the extent that they regard their government as illegitimate and responsible for their frustrations. The extent, intensity, and organization of civil strife is finally determined by characteristics of the social system: the degree and consistency of social control, and the extent to which institutions afford peaceful alternatives to violent protest.[7]

If discontent is a root cause of violence within the political community, what kinds of conditions give rise to the widespread discontents that lead to collective violence? All societies generate some discontent because organized social life by its very nature frustrates all human beings, by inhibiting some of their natural impulses. Socialized inhibitions and outlets for such discontents are provided by every society, though their relative effectiveness is certainly an underlying factor in national differences in rates of aggressive crimes. Another fundamental factor may be the ecological one. Carstairs summarizes evidence that overcrowding of human populations may lead to aggressiveness. On the other hand, Tilly shows that high rates of immigration to French cities in the 18th and 19th centuries was, if anything, associated with civil peace rather than rising disorder. Lane also finds that increasing urbanization in 19th-century Massachusetts was accompanied by a decline in violent crime rates. Neither culture stress nor population concentrations per se seem to be consequential causes of upsurges in collective violence, though they probably contribute to the "background noise" of violence common to almost all cultures. Probably the most important cause of major increases in group violence is the widespread frustration of socially deprived expectations about the goods and conditions of life men believe theirs by right. These frustratable expectations relate not only to material well-being but to more intangible conditions such as security, status, freedom to manage one's own affairs, and satisfying personal relations with others. Men's rightful expectations have many sources, among them their past experience of gain or loss, ideologies of scarcity or abundance, and the condition of groups with which they identify. In any case, men feel satisfactions and frustrations with reference to what they think they ought to have, not according to some absolute standard.

New expectations and new frustrations are more likely to be generated in times of social change than social stasis. The quantitative comparisons of the Feierabends and Nesvold suggest, for example, that nations undergoing the most rapid socioeconomic change also are likely to experience the highest levels of collective violence. Large-scale socioeconomic change is ordinarily accompanied by changes in people's values, by institutional dislocations that affect people on top as much as people "on the way up," and even by the temporary breakdown of some social institutions. Rapid social change is thus likely to add to the discontents of many groups at the same time that it improves the conditions of some. In addition, it may contribute to the partial breakdown of systems of normative control, to the collapse of old institutions through which some groups were once able to satisfy their expectations, and to the creation of new organizations of the discontented. Under these conditions the motivational and institutional potential for collective violence is high.

Some specific patterns of social change are directly indicted as causes of collective violence. One is a pattern of rising expectations among people so situated that lack of opportunity or the obdurate resistance of others precludes their attainment of those expectations. American society is especially vulnerable to the frustration of disappointed expectations, for we have proclaimed ourselves the harbinger of a New Jerusalem and invited millions of destitute immigrants to our shores to partake of its fulfillment. "Progressive" demands by such groups that have felt themselves unjustifiably excluded from a fair share of the social, economic, and political privileges of the majority have repeatedly provided motivation and justification for group conflict in our past, as they have in the history of Western Europe. Demands of workers for economic recognition and political participation were pervasive and chronic sources of turmoil in the United States and Europe. The aspirations of the Irish, Italians, Slavs, and—far most conse-quentially—Negroes have also provided repeated occasion for violence in America. Demands for an end to discrimina-tory privilege have not been confined to minorities or ethnic strata either. The struggle for women's suffrage in the United States was not peaceful, and America has not heard the last of women's claims for effective socioeconomic equality with men. Although the current resurgence of protest by many groups testifies to the continued inequity in the distribution of rewards, it also reflects the self-sustain-ing nature of social adjustment in this most pluralistic of nations. The same process through which Americans have made successive accommodations to demands for equity encourages the regeneration of new demands.

Protective resistance to undesirable change has been a more common source of collective violence in America than "revolutions of rising expectations," however. For ex-ample, most ethnic and religious violence in American his-tory has been retaliatory violence by groups farther up the socioeconomic ladder who felt threatened by the prospect of the "new immigrant" and the Negro getting both "too big" and "too close." As Taft and Ross have demonstrated, most labor violence in American history was not a deliber-ate tactic of working class organization but a result of force-ful employer resistance to worker organization and de-mands. Companies repeatedly resorted to coercive and sometimes terroristic activities against union organizers and to violent strikebreaking tactics. The violence of em-ployers often provided both model and impetus to counter-violence by workers, leading in many situations to an esca-lating spiral of violent conflict to the point of military in-tervention or mutual exhaustion.

Aggressive vigilantism has been a recurrent response of middle- and working-class Americans to perceived threats by outsiders or lesser classes to their status, security, and cultural integrity. The most widely known manifestations have been the frontier tradition of citizens' enforcement of the law and Ku Klux Klan efforts to maintain class lines and the moral code by taking their version of the law into their own hands. Brown has traced the emergence of such vigilante groups as the "Regulators" of pre-Revolutionary South Carolina and the Bald Knobbers of the Missouri Ozarks in the late 1800's. There are many other manifestations of aggressive vigilantism as well; no regions and few historical eras have been free of it, including the present. A contemporary one is the sporadic harassment of "hippie" and "peacenik" settlements in rural and small-town America, and the neovigilante organizations of urban Americans, white and black, for "group defense" that often have aggressive overtones. There also is a vigilantism of a somewhat different sort, an aggressive and active suppression of deviancy within an otherwise-cohesive group. An historical example was the White Cap movement of the 1880's and 1890's, a spontaneous movement for the moral regulation of the poor whites and ne'er-do-wells of rural America. Such vigilantism also is apparent in the internecine strife of defensive black organizations, which have occasionally used violence to rid themselves of innovative "traitors" like Malcolm X.

Agrarian protests and uprisings have characterized both frontier and settled regions of the United States since before the Revolution. They have reflected both progressive and protective sentiments, including demands for land reform, defense against more powerful economic interests, and relief from onerous political restrictions. Among them have been Shays' Rebellion in Massachusetts, 1786-87; Fries' Rebellion in eastern Pennsylvania, 1799; some of the activities of the Grangers, Greenbackers, and Farmers' Alliance after the Civil War; and the "Green Corn Rebellion" of Oklahoma farmers during World War I.

Antiwar protest in American history also has a predominantly protective quality. The nation's 19th-century wars, especially the Civil War, led often to violent resistance to military conscription and the economic impositions of war. The 20th century has seen the development of a strong, indigenous strain of pacifism in the United States. The goals of those who have promoted the cause of peace, during both the First World War and the Vietnam war, have been protective in this sense: they adhere to a set of humanitarian values that are embodied in the basic social contract of American life, and see that contract threatened by those who regard force as the solution to American and foreign problems. The evidence of American history and comparative studies suggests no exact relationship between the occurrence of war and domestic protest against it, however. In the United States it appears to be the pervasive sense that a particular war and its demands are unjust or illegitimate that leads to protest and, occasionally, to violent resistance.

Davies identifies a third general pattern of change that is frequently associated with the outbreak of rebellion and revolution: the occurrence of a short period of sharp relative decline in socioeconomic or political conditions after a prolonged period of improving conditions. A period of steady progress generates expectations that progress will continue. If it does not continue, a pervasive sense of frustration develops which, if focused on the government, is likely to lead to widespread political violence. It is not only economic reversal in this pattern that leads to violence. People whose dignity, career expectations, or political ambitions are so frustrated are as likely to rebel as those whose pocketbooks are being emptied.

This specific pattern is identified in Davies' studies of socioeconomic and political changes affecting various groups before the outbreak of the French Revolution, the American Civil War, and the Nazi revolution. It may also be present in data on relative rates of white and Negro socioeconomic progress in the United States during the last several decades. From 1940 to 1952, nonwhite family income relative to educational attainment appears to have increased steadily and substantially in comparison with white income. In 1940 the average Negro with a high school education was likely to receive 55 percent of the earnings of a white worker with comparable education. This figure increased to 85 percent in 1952—but then declined to a low of 74 percent by 1962. These data call into question simplistic notions to the effect that unsatisfied expectations of black Americans increased to the point of violence simply because of "agitation," or because of unfulfilled promises. Rather it may have been real progress, judged by the firsthand experience of the 1940's and early 1950's, and probably also by reference to the rise of the black bourgeoisie, which generated expectations that were substantially frustrated by events of the late 1950's and early 1960's.

Discontent is only the initial condition of collective violence, which raises the question of the extent to which the actualization of violence is determined by popular attitudes and institutional patterns. A cross-national study by Gurr

807

was designed to provide preliminary answers to this question, by relating differences among nations in economic and political discontent, apparent justifications for violence, and institutional strength to differences in magnitudes and forms of civil strife. The results are that more than a third of the differences among contemporary nations in magnitudes of strife are accounted for by differences in the extent and intensity of their citizens' discontent, even though measured imprecisely. Attitudes about politics and violence are almost as important. Nations whose political systems have low legitimacy are likely to have extensive strife; nations with a violent past— and, by implication, popular attitudes that support violence—are likely to have a violent present, and future. Institutional patterns can meliorate or magnify these dispositions to violence. If physical controls are weak, and especially if they are inconsistent in application, strife is likely to be high. Similarly the weakness of conventional institutions, and the availability of material and organizational support for rebellion, lead to high levels of strife, particularly in its most intensive and violent forms.

The experience of the United States is consistent with this general pattern. For all our rhetoric, we have never been a very law-abiding nation, and illegal violence has sometimes been abundantly rewarded. Hence there have developed broad normative sanctions for the expression or acting out of discontent, somewhat limited inhibitions, and —owing to Jeffersonian liberalism's legacy of fear of central public authority—very circumscribed physical controls. Public sympathy has often been with the lawbreaker —sometimes with the nightrider who punished the transgressor of community mores, sometimes with the integrationists who refused to obey racial segregation laws. Lack of full respect for law and support for violence in one's own interest have both contributed to the justifications for private violence, justifications that in turn have helped make the United States historically and at present a tumultuous society.

On the other hand, the United States also has characteristics that in other countries appear to minimize intense revolutionary conspiracies and internal wars. Thus far in our history the American political system has maintained a relatively high degree of legitimacy in the eyes of most of its citizens. American political and economic institutions are generally strong. They are not pervasive enough to provide adequate opportunities for some regional and minority groups to satisfy their expectations, but sufficiently pervasive and egalitarian that the most ambitious and talented men—if not women—can pursue the "American dream" with some chance of success. These are conditions that minimize the prospects of revolutionary movements: a majoritarian consensus on the legitimacy of government, and provision of opportunity for men of talent who, if intensely alienated, might otherwise provide revolutionary cadres. But if such a system is open to the majority yet partly closed to a minority, or legitimate for the majority but illegitimate for a minority, the minority is likely to create chronic tumult even though it cannot organize effective revolutionary movements.

Some consequences of patterns of social control, legitimacy, and institutional development for the processes of collective violence are examined more fully below.

V. SOME CONSEQUENCES OF VIOLENCE

Does violence succeed? The inheritors of the doctrines of Frantz Fanon and "Ché" Guevara assert that if those who use it are sufficiently dedicated, revolution can always be accomplished. Many vehement advocates of civil order and strategists of counterinsurgency hold essentially the same faith: that sufficient use of public violence will deter private violence. This fundamental agreement of "left" and "right" on the effectiveness of force for modifying others' behavior is striking. But to what extent is it supported by theory and by historical evidence?

The two most fundamental human responses to the use of force are to flee or to fight. This assertion rests on rather good psychological and ethological evidence about human and animal aggression. Force threatens and angers men, especially if they believe it to be illegitimate or unjust. Threatened, they will defend themselves if they can, flee if they cannot. Angered, they have an innate disposition to retaliate in kind. Thus men who fear assault attempt to arm themselves, and two-thirds or more of white Americans think that black looters and arsonists should be shot. Governments facing violent protest often regard compromise as evidence of weakness and devote additional resources to counterforce. Yet if a government responds to the threat or use of violence with greater force, its effects in many circumstances are identical with the effects that dictated its actions: its opponents will if they can resort to greater force.

There are only two inherent limitations on such an escalating spiral of force and counterforce: the exhaustion of one side's resources for force, or the attainment by one of the capacity for genocidal victory. There are societal and psychological limitations as well, but they require tacit bonds between opponents: one's acceptance of the ultimate authority of the other, arbitration of the conflict by neutral authority, recognition of mutual interest that makes bargaining possible, or the perception that acquiescence to a powerful opponent will have less harmful consequences than resisting to certain death. In the absence of such bases for cooperation, regimes and their opponents are likely to engage in violent conflict to the limit of their respective abilities.[8]

To the extent that this argument is accurate, it suggests one kind of circumstance in which violence succeeds: that in which one group so overpowers its opponents that they have no choice short of death but to desist. When they do resist to the death, the result is a Carthaginian peace. History records many instances of successful uses of overpowering force. Not surprisingly, the list of successful governmental uses of force against opponents is much longer than the list of dissident successes against government, because most governments have much greater capacities for force, provided they keep the loyalty of their generals and soldiers. Some dissident successes discussed in this volume include the French, American, Nazi, and Cuban Revolutions. Some governmental successes include, in Britain, the suppression of the violent phases of the Luddite and Chartist movements in the 19th century; in Venezuela the Betancourt regime's elimination of revolutionary terrorism; in the United States the North's victory in the Civil War, and the quelling of riots and local rebellions, from the Whiskey Rebellion of 1794 to the ghetto riots of the 1960's.

Governmental uses of force are likely to be successful in quelling specific outbreaks of private violence except in those rare circumstances when the balance of force favors

810

its opponents, or the military defects. But the historical evidence also suggests that governmental violence often succeeds only in the short run. The government of Imperial Russia quelled the revolution of 1905, but in doing so intensified the hostilities of its opponents, who mounted a successful revolution 12 years later, after the government was weakened by a protracted and unsuccessful war. The North "won" the Civil War, but in its very triumph created hostilities that contributed to one of the greatest and most successful waves of vigilante violence in our history. The 17,000 Klansmen of the South today are neither peaceable nor content with the outcome of the "War of Northern Aggression."[9] State or federal troops have been dispatched to quell violent or near-violent labor conflict in more than 160 recorded instances in American history; they were immediately successful in almost every case yet did not significantly deter subsequent labor violence.

The long-range effectiveness of governmental force in maintaining civil peace seems to depend on three conditions identified by the papers in this volume: public belief that governmental use of force is legitimate, consistent use of that force; and remedial action for the grievances that give rise to private violence. The decline of violent working-class protest in 19th century England was predicated on an almost universal popular acceptance of the legitimacy of the government, accompanied by the development of an effective police system—whose popular acceptance was enhanced by its minimal reliance on violence—and by gradual resolution of working class grievances. The Cuban case was quite the opposite: the governmental response to private violence was terroristic, inconsistent public violence that alienated most Cubans from the Batista regime, with no significant attempts to reduce the grievances, mostly political, that gave rise to rebellion.

We have assumed that private violence is "successful" in those extreme cases in which a government capitulates in the face of the superiority of its opponents. This is not the only or necessarily the best criterion of "success," though. A better criterion is the extent to which the grievances that give rise to collective protest and violence are resolved. Even revolutionary victories do not necessarily lead to complete success in these terms. The American Revolution returned effective political control to the hands

811

of the colonists, but eventually led to an expansion of state and federal authority that diminished local autonomy to the point that new rebellions broke out in many frontier areas over essentially the same kinds of grievances that had caused the revolution. The Bolshevik revolution ended Russia's participation in World War I, which was perhaps the greatest immediate grievance of the Russian people, and in the long run brought great economic and social benefits; but the contingent costs of the subsequent civil war, famine, and totalitarian political control were enormous. The middle-class political discontents that fueled the Cuban revolutionary movement, far from being remedied, were intensified when the revolutionary leaders used their power to effect a basic socioeconomic reconstruction of society that favored themselves and the rural working classes.

If revolutionary victory is unlikely in the modern state, and uncertain of resolving the grievances that give rise to revolutionary movements, are there any circumstances in which less intensive private violence is successful? We said above that the legitimacy of governmental force is one of the determinants of its effectiveness. The same principle applies to private violence: It can succeed when it is widely regarded as legitimate. The vigilante movements of the American frontier had widespread public support as a means for establishing order in the absence of adequate law enforcement agencies, and were generally successful. The Ku Klux Klan of the Reconstruction era similarly had the sympathy of most white Southerners and was largely effective in reestablishing and maintaining the pre-war social and political status quo. The chronicles of American labor violence, however, suggest that violence was almost always ineffective for the workers involved. In a very few instances there was popular and state governmental support for the grievances of workers that had led to violent confrontations with employers, and in several of these cases state authority was used to impose solutions that favored the workers. But in the great majority of cases the public and officials did not accept the legitimacy of labor demands, and the more violent was conflict, the more disastrous were the consequences for the workers who took part. Union organizations involved in violent conflict seldom gained recognition, their supporters were harassed and often lost their jobs, and tens of thousands of workers and their families were forcibly deported from their homes and communities.

The same principle applies, with two qualifications, to peaceful public protest. If demonstrations are regarded as a legitimate way to express grievances, and if the grievances themselves are widely held to be justified, protest is likely to have positive effects. One of the qualifications is that if public opinion is neutral on an issue, protest demonstrations can have favorable effects. This appears to have been an initial consequence of the civil-rights demonstrations of the early 1960's in the North. If public opinion is negative, however, demonstrations are likely to exacerbate popular hostility. During World War I, for example, pacifist demonstrators were repeatedly attacked, beaten, and in some cases lynched, with widespread public approval and sometimes official sanction. Contemporary civil-rights demonstrations and activities in the South and in some northern cities have attracted similar responses.

The second qualification is that when violence occurs during protest activities, it is rather likely to alienate groups that are not fundamentally in sympathy with the protesters. We mentioned above the unfavorable consequences of labor violence for unions and their members, despite the fact that violence was more often initiated by employers than by workers. In the long run, federally enforced recognition and bargaining procedures were established, but this occurred only after labor violence had passed its climacteric, and moreover in circumstances in which no union leaders advocated violence. In England, comparably, basic political reforms were implemented not in direct response to Chartist protest, but long after its violent phase had passed.

The evidence supports one basic principle: Force and violence can be successful techniques of social control and persuasion when they have extensive popular support. If they do not, their advocacy and use are ultimately self-destructive, either as techniques of government or of opposition. The historical and contemporary evidence of the United States suggests that popular support tends to sanction violence in support of the status quo: the use of public violence to maintain public order, the use of private violence to maintain popular conceptions of social order when government cannot or will not. If these assertions are true—and not much evidence contradicts them—the prolonged use of force or violence to advance the interests of any segmental group may impede and quite possibly preclude reform. This conclusion should not be taken as an ethical judgement, despite its apparent correspondence with the "establishmentarian" viewpoint. It represents a fundamental trait of American and probably all mankind's character, one which is ignored by advocates of any political orientation at the risk of broken hopes, institutions, and lives.

To draw this conclusion is not to indict public force or all private violence as absolute social evils. In brief and obvious defense of public force, reforms cannot be made if order is wholly lacking, and reforms will not be made if those who have the means to make them feel their security constantly in jeopardy. And as for private violence, though it may bring out the worst in both its practitioners and its victims, it need not do so. Collective violence is after all a symptom of social malaise. It can be so regarded and the malaise treated as such, provided public-spirited men diagnose it correctly and have the will and means to work for a cure rather than to retaliate out of anger. Americans may be quick to self-righteous anger, but they also have retained some of the English genius for accommodation. Grudgingly and with much tumult, the dominant groups in American society have moved over enough to give the immigrant, the worker, the suffragette better—not the best—seats at the American feast of freedom and plenty. Many of them think the feast is bounteous enough for the dissatisfied students, the poor, the Indians, the blacks. Whether there is a place for the young militants who think the feast has gone rotten, no historical or comparative evidence we know of can answer, because absolute, revolutionary alienation from society has been very rare in the American past and no less rare in other pluralistic and abundant nations.

VI. SOME ALTERNATIVES TO VIOLENCE

Political leaders faced with outbreaks or threats of collective violence can respond in the two general ways that we discussed above: they can strengthen systems of forceful social control, or they can exert public effort and encourage private efforts to alleviate conditions leading to discontent. Primary reliance on force has indeterminate outcomes at best. If popularly supported, public force will contain specific outbreaks of private violence, but is unlikely to prevent their recurrence. At worst, public force will so alienate a people that terrorist and revolutionary movements will arise to challenge and ultimately overthrow the regime. The teaching of comparative studies is that governments must be cautious in their reliance on force to maintain order, and consistent in the exercise of the modicum of force they choose to use. These are policies that require both appropriate leadership and well-trained, highly disciplined, and loyal military and police forces.

The effort to eliminate the conditions that lead to collective violence may tax the resources of a society, but it poses less serious problems than increased resort to force. American labor violence has been mitigated in the past 25 years partly by growing prosperity, but more consequentially because employers now have almost universally recognized unions and will negotiate wage issues and other grievances with them rather that retaliate against them. The movement toward recognition and negotiation was strongly reinforced when workers in most occupations were guaranteed the right to organize and bargain collectively in the National Labor Relations Act of 1935. Taft and Ross judge the act to have been effective not just because it established procedures but because of the concerted effort to enforce them by the National Labor Relations Board and the willingness of both employers and unions to recognize the Board's authority. Their willingness may be a testimony also to their own and public dismay at the destructiveness of earlier conflicts. It is worth emphasizing that in this situation the long-range consequences of conciliatory response was a decrease not increase in violent conflict. In fact, violence was chronic so long as union recognition was denied. The outcome suggests the inadequacy of arguments that concessions necessarily breed greater violence.

The history of English working-class protest supports these interpretations. In the 19th century, when England was transformed by an industrial revolution in which a highly competitive, laissez faire market economy disrupted traditional employment patterns and led to sweatshop conditions for many urban workers, violent public protest then became chronic. Several conditions averted to what many Englishmen then feared as a threat of working-class revolt. One was economic growth itself, which led to a significant improvement in the standard of living of urban workers and to hopeful prospects shared by all classes. A second was the acceptance by upper-class political leaders of demands for political reform, and acceptance dictated by both principle and practicality that led to the enfranchisement and assimilation of the working classes into the English body politic. A third was a trend toward grudging toleration of, and ultimately the acceptance and encouragement, of working-class organization. Recognition of the right of workers to organize and bargain led to a flourishing not only of unions but of self-help organizations, cooperatives, and religious and educational groups, all of which together provided British workers with means to work toward the resolution of their discontents.

There were and are characteristics of English society that had no direct American parallels. Expectations of English workers were less high than those of ambitious immigrants to the United States. The English class structure, though more stratified and complex than the American, was generally accepted by all classes, seldom directly challenged. The laissez faire sentiments of British employers were tempered by an acceptance of civic responsibilities that developed more quickly than it did in the United States, and as one consequence English labor violence never reached the intensity that it did in the United States. Working-class demands for political reform were predicated on the common assumption that governments could be changed and the power of the state used to ameliorate the economic grievances of workers. Though the parallels are not exact, the English experience seems to suggest some general lessons for the contemporary United States: civil peace was established through a judicious, perhaps fortuitous, combination of governmental and political reform, and institutional development among the aggrieved classes of society.

Intensely discontented men are not will-less pawns in a game of social chess. They also have alternatives, of which violence is usually the last, the most desperate, and in most circumstances least likely of success. Peaceful protest, conducted publicly and through conventional political channels, is a traditional American option. As one of the world's most pluralistic societies, we have repeatedly albeit reluctantly accommodated ourselves to discontented groups using interest and pressure-group tactics within the political process as a means of leverage for change. But it also is an American characteristic to resist demonstrative demands, however legal and peaceful, if they seem to challenge our basic beliefs and personal positions. Public protest in the United States is a slow and unwieldy instrument of social change that sometimes inspires more obdurate resistance than favorable change.[10]

Another kind of group response to intense stresses and discontents is called "defensive adaptation" by Bernard Siegal. It is essentially an inward-turning, nonviolent response motivated by a desire to build and maintain a group's cultural integrity in the face of hostile pressures. The defensive group is characterized by centralization of authority; attempts to set the group apart by emphasizing symbols of group identity; and minimization of members' contacts with other groups. It is an especially common reaction among ethnic and religious groups whose members see their social environments as permanently hostile, depreciating, and powerful. Such adaptations are apparent, for example, among some Pueblo Indians, Black Muslims, and Amish, and many minority groups in other nations. This kind of defensive withdrawal may lead to violence when outside groups press too closely in on the defensive group, but it is typically a response that minimizes violent conflict. Although the defensive group provides its members some, essentially social and psychological, satisfactions, it seldom can provide them with substantial economic benefits or political means by which they can promote their causes vis-a-vis hostile external groups.

A third general kind of response is the development of discontented groups of positive, socially integrative means for the satisfaction of their members' unsatisfied expectations. This response has characterized most discontented groups throughout Western history. In England, social protest was institutionalized through the trade unions, cooperative societies, and other self-help activities. In continental Europe, the discontent of the urban workers and petit bourgeoisie led to the organization of fraternal societies, unions, and political parties, which provided some intrinsic satisfactions for their members and which could channel demands more or less effectively to employers and into the political system. In the United States the chronic local uprisings of the late-18th, the 19th, and the early-20th century—such as the Shay, Whiskey, Dorr, and Green Corn Rebellions—have been largely superseded by organized, conventional political manifestations of local and regional interests. Labor violence similarly declined in the United States and England once trade unions were organized and recognized.

The contemporary efforts of black Americans to develop effective community organizations, and their demands for greater control of community affairs, seem to be squarely in this tradition. So are demands of student protesters for greater participation in university affairs, attempts of white urban citizens to create new neighborhood organizations, and the impulse of middle-class Americans to move to the suburbs where they can exercise greater control over the local government.

The initial effects of the organization of functional and community groups for self-help may be increased conflict, especially if the economic and political establishments attempt to subvert their efforts. But if these new organizations receive public and private cooperation and sufficient resources to carry out their activities, the prospects for violence are likely to be reduced. The social costs of this kind of group response seem much less than those of public and private violence. The human benefits are likely to be far greater than those attained through private violence or defensive withdrawal.

VII. THE ADEQUACY OF PRESENT KNOWLEDGE

Do we know enough about the sources, processes, and consequences of collective violence, or about its forms and participants, its relations to social change, or its remedies and alternatives? The preceding conclusions may imply that we know a good deal. We do not. Many, perhaps most, of these conclusions are educated guesses or conjecture. This volume seems to be the first attempt to link the historical and comparative dimensions of research on the subject or group violence in America, and all we have proposed is a tentative, partial synthesis. To use an analogy, this volume is not an accurate atlas to well-mapped terrain; rather, it is equivalent to a 16th-century map of the New World, replete with sea serpents and expanses of terra incognita, its purported ranges and rivers based on reports of lone explorers.

Consider how new and little verified some of the information in this volume is. It includes the first general, empirically based commentary on the precise nature of violent protest over the long span of Western European history (by Charles Tilly). It includes the first comprehensive roster of American vigilante movements (by Richard Maxwell Brown) and the first general survey of American labor violence (by Philip Taft and Philip Ross). It reports, as an appendix, some results of the first attempt ever made to collect systematic data on the incidence and types of individual and collective political violence over a substantial period of American history (by Sheldon Levy). It reports the first crude effort to categorize and count the types, motives, and objectives of participants in collective violence in all nations, for the contemporary or any other era (by Ted Robert Gurr). It includes a pioneering analysis of defensive withdrawal, a common, nonviolent kind of group response to severe stress (by Bernard Siegal).

The conclusions offer other examples. We can speculate about, but do not know with any certainty, what the relative importance is among the historical forces that have contributed to our relatively high American levels of violence. We do not even know with any exactitude how high those levels were, or the details of their causation, variation, or resolution. We have speculated on the relative importance of discontent, attitudes about violence, and institutional patterns as causes of collective violence. These causal questions have been examined systematically in only a handful of comparative studies, and rarely at any depth in the historical dimension for the United States or any other society. Evidence hints that Americans are and have been more willing to take the law in their own hands, and to use violence, than citizens of many other Western societies But no one has done the survey and depth interview studies necessary to test this speculation or to identify the circumstances under which violence is thought to be justified. Nor have popular attitudes toward violence in most historical eras been thoroughly studied, though they could be either on the basis of what people did or what they wrote. We have speculated on the efficacy of public force in maintaining order and the uses of private violence in effecting change. Relatively few cases can be cited in support of the conclusions because few cases have been studied in this light; those few may be exceptional rather than typical, and only the examination of many cases representing different types of societies and situations can test the adequacy of our conclusions.

There are other uncharted regions. Something is known about the phases through which riots and some revolutions develop and decay. Not much is known about the processes of linked series of events, like the chronic labor violence or vigilante movements of the American past. What accounts for their establishment as a mode of action, and for their persistence or decline. Why, for instance, did the Ku Klux Klan of the 1920s collapse and disappear so suddenly, whereas rightist citizen groups in Europe evolved toward fascist regimes? Which groups took their cues from others, and how did they learn of others? Vigilante violence was often successful, and persisted; labor violence was seldom successful yet it too persisted; protest by suffragettes was successful and it ended. What accounts for such differences, both in outcome and duration? There are educated guesses, but no conclusions based on examination of many movements. Nor do we know much of the long-range consequences of violence. The farther removed we are in time from a major rebellion, revolution, or civil war, the less we know about its economic and social consequences. For riots and local uprisings we often know nothing of their aftermaths even a year later. Did the frontier rebellions of America leave any destructive and abiding traces in the attitudes or institutions or politics of the regions where they occurred? What has happened in the black ghettos wracked by riots between 1965 through 1968? Who is analyzing the consequences of different kinds of student tactics in the campus protests and rebellions of the last 4 years?

Alternatives to violence are little studied. More precisely,

820

the peaceful processes by which most social conflicts are resolved have been studied in great detail in many Western societies, but we know of very few studies that have compared groups under similar kinds of stress, or with similar kinds of demands, to determine the options open to them and the consequences of their choice of those alternatives. On this kind of knowledge a crucial policy issue depends: whether it is necessary for groups seeking reforms to resort to limited violence to dramatize their demands, despite the dangers of creating "backlash." Presumably the answers vary, depending on the society in which reforms are sought, the nature of the reforms, and the groups making and resisting them. And with regard to the backlash, does it necessarily occur, and if so among what people, when, and with what immediate and persisting consequences? What backlashes can be identified in American history, and in the histories of other Western societies? Backlashes almost certainly occur even when demands are made peacefully, but do they inhibit reform just as much as the backlash to violence? Then there are the critical questions about the resolution of violence. Probably foremost in the minds of most public and private officials who deal with public protest and violence is: What are the relative merits of concessions and coercion for maintaining an orderly and reasonably contented community? A case can be made for the desirability of either policy approach and any combination of them, by selective choice of examples. The careful study of comparable cases, historically and comparatively, needed for a judicious answer has scarcely been started.

One of our most optimistic conclusions is that we know enough to say what some of the important but unanswered questions about American violence are. The studies in this volume demonstrate that the procedures of historical and comparative research are adequate to the task of seeking further and more precise knowledge, though we lack enough men and women with the requisite training and skills, and adequate support, to do so in the near future. This report provides substantial insights into the causes and character of violence in America; we have yet to understand fully how civil peace is created and maintained in these circumstances. But at least we know that it is possible, for Americans and other people have done so before.

References

1. Exemplary of the "consensus school" of American historians are Daniel Boorstin, *The Genius of American Politics* (Chicago: University of Chicago Press, 1953); David Potter, *People of Plenty* (Chicago: University of Chicago Press, 1954); and Louis Hartz, *The Liberal Tradition in America* (New York: Harcourt, Brace & World, 1955). These scholars did not deny that the American past was replete with violence. Rather, they emphasized that America lacked the feudal past that had led to acute class animosity in Europe, that virtually all Americans shared the liberal ideology of Locke and Jefferson, and that Americans were highly pragmatic and did not take any ideology seriously enough to be fundamentally divided by it.

2. See Richard Wade, "Violence in the Cities: An Historical View," *Urban Violence* (Chicago: University of Chicago Press, 1969), pp. 7-26.

3. These absolute comparisons are from Michael Hudson, "Violence and Political Institutionalization in the United States: A Comparative Analysis," a working paper prepared for the National Commission on the Causes and Prevention of Violence, 1968.

4. See Konrad Lorenz, *On Aggression* (New York: Harcourt, Brace & World, 1966), and Robert Ardrey, *The Territorial Imperative* (New York: Dell, 1966).

5. See Leonard Berkowitz, *Aggression: A Social Psychological Analysis* (New York: McGraw-Hill, 1962), and Ashley Montagu, ed., *Man and Aggression* (New York: Oxford University Press, 1968).

6. See Geoffrey Gorer, "Man has No 'Killer' Instinct," *The New York Times Magazine*, Nov. 17, 1966.

7. "Frustration" interpretations of the impetus to collective violence are proposed by Davies, the Feierabends, and Nesvold, and, in somewhat different guises, by Comer and Carstairs. Gude considers some effects of legitimacy and force, Janowitz social control generally. Gurr's analysis deals with motivational, attitudinal, and institutional variables that lead to violence. Siegel examines the kinds of external stresses on a group and group attitudes that lead it to defensive institutional responses which minimize external violence.

8. This discussion is drawn from arguments and evidence in Ted Robert Gurr, *Why Men Rebel* (Princeton: Princeton University Press, in press), ch. 8. The survey datum is from Hazel Erskine, "The Polls: Demonstrations and Race Riots," *Public Opinion Quarterly* (Winter 1967-68), pp. 655-677.

9. On Klan membership in 1967, see U.S. Congress, House Un-American Activities Committee, *The Present-Day Ku Klux Klan Movement* (Washington, D.C.: Government Printing Office, 1967), p. 62.

10. Kenneth E. Boulding makes the same point in a discussion of the possible consequences of antiwar protest, in "Reflections on Protest," *Bulletin of the Atom Scientists*, vol. XXI (Oct. 1965), pp. 18-20.